Comparative Dravidian Linguistics

Comparative Dravidian Linguistics

Current Perspectives

BHADRIRAJU KRISHNAMURTI

WITH A FOREWORD BY
MURRAY B. EMENEAU

OXFORD
UNIVERSITY PRESS

OXFORD
UNIVERSITY PRESS

Great Clarendon Street, Oxford OX2 6DP

Oxford University Press is a department of the University of Oxford.
It furthers the University's objective of excellence in research, scholarship,
and education by publishing worldwide in

Oxford New York

Athens Auckland Bangkok Bogotá Buenos Aires Calcutta
Cape Town Chennai Dar es Salaam Delhi Florence Hong Kong Istanbul
Karachi Kuala Lumpur Madrid Melbourne Mexico City Mumbai
Nairobi Paris São Paulo Shanghai Singapore Taipei Tokyo Toronto Warsaw

with associated companies in Berlin Ibadan

Published in the United States
by Oxford University Press, Inc., New York

First published 2001

British Library Cataloguing in Publication Data
Data available

Library of Congress Cataloging in Publication Data
Data applied for

ISBN 0-19-824122-4

1 3 5 7 9 10 8 6 4 2

Typeset in Minion by Jayvee
Trivandrum, India
Printed in Great Britain
on acid-free paper by
T. J. International Ltd.
Padstow, Cornwall

To the memory of
G. J. Somayaji *(1900–1987)*
my teacher from 1945 to 1948
who introduced me to a comparative study
of the Dravidian languages
and Head of the Department of Telugu
where I served from 1949 to 1961
and
To the memory of
the Rev. Robert Caldwell *(1814–1891)*
whose pioneering work in comparative Dravidian philology
launched me into this field

Foreword

This volume of twenty-one chapters by Professor Bh. Krishnamurti joins the volumes of collected papers that have already usefully appeared in the field of Dravidian linguistics. Its title, *Comparative Dravidian Linguistics*, separates it cleanly from most earlier volumes, which generally were a mixture of descriptive linguistics, comparative linguistics, and even sociolinguistics. That is not to say, of course, that Bh. Krishnamurti in his scholarly career neglected all these (and other) linguistic interests. His volume on Konda or Kubi (1969) is a model of reported fieldwork.

This volume shows him a master of the neogrammarian method in several chapters. I single out Chapter 6 on the Brahui nasals, which is a model of what is to be achieved in treating a small body of data by accurate rule statement and analogy.

But new Dravidian (and other) material has forced scholars to consider some different methodology from that of the neogrammarians of the nineteenth century; Bh. Krishnamurti explores some important Dravidian material in that light (Chapters 9, 10, 20) and we hope a sound theory has been arrived at.

The volume will be immensely useful to scholars and students; many of the chapters come from highly inaccessible sources—and not only Indian, but European and American (one from Hawaii!) as well. My heartiest congratulations on its appearance.

M. B. Emeneau

Contents

Figures

Maps

Preface

The twenty papers reprinted in this volume were published during the period 1955–98, spanning forty-three years: Chapters 1 to 3 in the fifties, 4 to 7 in the sixties, 8 to 11 in the seventies, 12 to 15 in the eighties and 16 to 20 in the nineties. I have added a concluding chapter (Ch. 21) as an end of century evaluation of the major contribution to comparative Dravidian studies. My main interest has always been comparative linguistics, despite the fact that my interests extended into a number of other allied fields like dialectology, lexicography, second-language teaching, sociolinguistics, language planning, literacy, generative grammar, etc., in which I have published several studies during my long academic career. In addition to these, I was shouldering heavy teaching and administrative duties, mainly from 1962 to 1985, as Professor of Linguistics, Head of Department, Dean, Principal of Arts College, Member of the University Syndicate, etc., at Osmania University.

The second part of the century has seen a remarkable progress in comparative and historical studies of Indian languages, in the wake of the publication of Burrow and Emeneau's *A Dravidian Etymological Dictionary* (1961, revised 1984), closely followed by Turner's *A Comparative Dictionary of the Indo-Aryan Languages* (1966). I started my comparative study of Dravidian from the early fifties and collected cognates from over twenty different languages for about four years, all by myself. I was selected by the United States Educational Foundation in India for a Fulbright and Smith-Mundt fellowship in 1953 to pursue graduate studies in linguistics at the University of Pennsylvania during 1954–5. During that year my first paper (Ch. 1) was published in *Journal of the American Oriental Society.* Guided by eminent teachers in structural and historical linguistics and phonetics (Zellig Harris, Henry M. Hoenigswald, and Leigh Lisker), I completed my second M.A. during 1954–5. I attended the Linguistic Institute of the Linguistic Society of America at the University of Michigan, Ann Arbor, during the summer of 1955, where I was taught by William Moulton (morphology), Uriel Weinreich (language contact and borrowing), and Harry Hoijer (field-methods). I developed self-confidence and a good feel for the discipline after these courses and after meetings with many other luminaries in linguistics. The Rockefeller Foundation supported me for the summer courses and also for spending a year (1955–6) at the University of California, Berkeley, to work on my doctoral dissertation with M. B. Emeneau, whom I knew only through correspondence. I worked hard during that year, and after successfully completing a full load of courses for two semesters, I started writing my dissertation from May to August 1956. Emeneau, whom I have held as my true Guru since then, read the material on a daily basis and suggested improvements on the draft. I completed two long chapters and an etymological index of Telugu verbal bases, all in two volumes. I later moved to Pennsylvania to present my doctoral dissertation. After completing all the requirements for the award of a Ph.D., I returned to India in September 1956, after spending exactly two years in the USA. I was awarded the Ph.D. degree in 1957. I added two more chapters later and my *Telugu Verbal Bases: A Comparative and Descriptive Study* (*TVB*) was published by the University of California as UCPL 24 in 1961, a few months before the publication of *A Dravidian Etymological Dictionary*. *TVB* remained the main source of data and ideas for a structural analysis of the nominal and verbal stems of Proto-Dravidian and for a reliable account of comparative Dravidian phonology for nearly three decades until other books appeared (Emeneau 1970, Zvelebil 1970, Subrahmanyam 1983), drawing heavily on that pioneering effort. My *TVB* and Burrow and Emeneau's *A Dravidian Etymological Dictionary* opened a new era in comparative Dravidian studies. After the fifties, Burrow, accompanied by an anthropologist, Sudhibhushan Bhattacharya, concerned himself with fieldwork on new and old members of the Central Dravidian group (Parji, Kui, Kuvi, Pengo, Gadaba) and has not published much on problems of comparative phonology (except in a paper of 1968). Thus, in the latter part of the twentieth century, significant contributions to comparative phonology and to some aspects of morphology have come from fewer scholars, Emeneau, Krishnamurti, Subrahmanyam, and Kumaraswami Raja (one excellent paper and a small monograph). Sanford Steever, a young linguist who studied Tamil and linguistics at the University of Chicago, made several trips to India in the eighties and published several important papers on serial verbs, an interface between morphology and syntax of comparative Dravidian.

During the latter part of this century Dravidian studies have attracted scholars from different disciplines with varied interests. One dominant group consists of scholars—archeologists, historians, and linguists—who have a strong hunch that the undeciphered language of the Indus seals (Mohanjodaro and Harappa, 2500 BC) could be a form of Proto-Dravidian. Several Russian and Finnish scholars have been engaged in this effort. Some Japanese scholars noticed parallels between Dravidian (mainly they used Tamil) and Japanese. There have been growing adherents to the theory of the Nostratic macro-family which included Indo-European, Semitic, Altaic, Afro-Asian including Dravidian. In the seventies, there was an aggressive proposal on Elamite-Dravidian relationship. More and more scholars have started looking at the Dravidian languages from the perspective of their own interest, typological, historical, and comparative. However, I have not moved beyond the problems of hard-core historical-comparative linguistics concerning Dravidian.

How do these papers advance our knowledge of comparative and historical Dravidian in the second half of the twentieth century? With the exception of two survey papers (Ch. 5 and 14), the rest of the papers deal with some important problems of phonology and morphology/syntax of Dravidian. Ch. 1 deals with problems of Proto-Dravidian morphophonemics, defining the conditions for varying syllable-length in stems (verbal and nominal). It also seeks to explain how different languages happened to end up with 'favoured' syllable-types in stem formation, through contraction of disyllabic ones into monosyllabic, and trisyllabic into disyllabic through loss of a pre-suffixal high vowel. These are relevant to the whole family or to certain defined subgroups. When I published the paper I did not realize its far-reaching consequences. Ch. 2, already discussed in *TVB*, provides a neat solution to an unresolved problem in the southern languages (Tamil, Malayāḷam, Telugu, and Kannaḍa). Later on, I noticed that it had solved the problem of two subgroups (SD I and SD II; see Postscript of Ch. 2). Ch. 3 provided a comprehensive account of the reflexes of PD *ẓ in different Dravidian languages. Ch. 6 also solves a problem of comparative phonology in Brahui by showing that PD *n and *m split into *d/n* and *b/m* respectively, in definable environments. Ch. 7 analyses a Tamil text found in a 12th century literary work in Telugu to show that spoken Tamil had voiced stops in postnasal position and intervocalically, without exception; these facts are not suggested by traditional Tamil transcription which represented voiced and voiceless obstruents by the same set of symbols. Ch. 12 can be read with Ch. 2 since it extends the innovation of *i, *u > e, o [C-a to South-Central Dravidian languages. Ch. 11 shows a new sound change in pre-Parji and explains how this is carried into its synchronic morphology. Ch. 15 deals with extensive dialectal data from Gondi to show how a set of sound changes can produce disorder in morphology and how each dialect finds a new way of tackling the problem. Ch. 19 proposes a laryngeal phoneme *H for Proto-Dravidian with extensive supporting data, a thought which reached some kind of maturation after thirty-three years. I started working within the framework of lexical diffusion in the mid-seventies and Ch. 9, 10, and 20 deal with different Dravidian sound changes within that framework. It has been demonstrated that at least some sound changes are 'lexically diffused', and do not follow the neogrammarian path. Ch. 20 shows that a regular sound change does occur through the mechanism of lexical diffusion, which Labov (1994) doubted. These papers thus contribute to the theory of the nature of sound change, besides reformulating the changes more precisely. Ch. 13 proposes a new model of subgrouping within the framework of the theory of lexical diffusion. The major papers dealing with morphology (also naturally involving phonology) are Ch. 4, 8, 11, 15, 16, and 17. My discussion of the evolution of primary derivatives as originally tense-markers in Proto-Dravidian breaks new ground in our understanding of the formation of extended stems. It was published in 1997 and scholars have yet to study it thoroughly to evaluate its impact. These papers give insights into the nature of sound change, analogy (Ch. 4, 8), interplay between synchrony and diachrony (Ch. 11, 15, 17), and grammatical constraints on sound change (Ch. 4, 8, 15), besides solving several unresolved issues. In Ch. 18, which forms a survey of the patterns of sound change in Dravidian, I have observed that typologically motivated sound changes tend to be more regular than purely historical ones. Historical linguists need to study this proposal with reference to the other language groups. In several of my papers I have discussed the question of subgrouping of the Dravidian languages and come up with some revisions in my post-seventies' articles. Three survey articles (Ch. 5, 14, 21) critically evaluate the contributions to Dravidian studies from the beginning up to the end of the twentieth century.

I have not made any substantive changes in the texts of the original articles. I have added postscripts to some, critically reviewing the discussions and debates that followed their publication. I have slightly changed the original titles of three articles (Ch. 1, 16, 19). In Ch. 3, I have updated my analysis of the data from languages available since its first publication (1958). I have stated explicitly where I have revised my earlier views, particularly in the case of subgrouping. This collection of papers provides reliable data and plausible solutions to several outstanding problems in Dravidian phonology and morphology and launches this field into the next millennium.

It is now my honour and pleasure to thank the authorities of the Oxford University Press for accepting these papers for publication as a volume, particularly Mr John Davey, Consultant Editor, Linguistics, for actively pursuing the matter and for the interest he has evinced in seeing this project through. I am grateful to the two scholars, who refereed these papers for the Oxford University Press and made a strong recommendation for their publication (anonymous, but later known to me by their voluntary disclosure), W. Bright and R. E. Asher, whom I have always held in high esteem. I have taken upon myself the responsibility of bringing about uniformity in style, format, and transliteration with some occasional updating of data among the papers, published over a period of forty-five years. This task necessarily involved extensive corrections at the time of preparing the typescript for the press. In the process, I have missed many minor details and corrections. Dr Clive Tolley, the perceptive and careful copy-editor of this volume, has brought these to my attention. He richly deserves my thanks for his contribution in improving the quality and utility of this publication.

My Guru, M. B. Emeneau, has very kindly written a foreword to this collection, and I consider it a great blessing. My scholarship and achievements owe a great deal to his inspiring leadership in the field of Dravidian studies and to his unfailing good wishes.

Bh.K.

Hyderabad
15 June 1999

I was fortunate in receiving a Membership (Fellowship) in the School of Historical Studies of the Institute for Advanced Study, Princeton, during 1999–2000, to pursue my interests in study, research, and writing. Although I had submitted the press copy of the present volume to the Oxford University Press before I came to Princeton, I could attend to the other pre-publication phases efficiently during my stay here, because of the excellent facilities provided by the Institute. My grateful thanks are due to the authorities of the Institute for making this possible.

Bh.K.

Princeton
NJ 08540
USA
25 June 2000

Acknowledgements

Twenty of the articles appearing in this volume have been published either in professional journals or as chapters of books, including some Festschrifts. I gratefully acknowledge my indebtedness to the editors and publishers, and holders of copyright, for readily granting me permission to reprint the articles in this volume. I also express my gratitude to the co-authors in the case of two articles (Ch. 13 and 15) for permitting me to reprint the articles. Special acknowledgement must be made as follows:

1. 'The history of vowel-length in Telugu verbal bases', *Journal of the American Oriental Society*, 75 (1955), 237–52. Reprinted with prior intimation to the American Oriental Society.

2. 'Alternations *i/e* and *u/o* in South Dravidian', *Language*, 34 (1958), 458–68. Reprinted by permission of the Linguistic Society of America.

3. 'Proto-Dravidian *ẓ', *Indian Linguistics (Turner Jubilee Volume 1)*, 19 (1958), 259–93. Reprinted by permission of the Linguistic Society of India.

4. 'Dravidian personal pronouns', in Bh. Krishnamurti (ed.), *Studies in Indian Linguistics: Professor M. B. Emeneau Ṣaṣṭipūrti Volume*, 189–205. 1968: Poona & Annamalainagar: Centers of Advanced Study. Reprinted by permission of Annamalai University and the Linguistic Society of India.

5. 'Comparative Dravidian studies', in T. A. Sebeok (ed.), *Current Trends in Linguistics*, vol. 5 (South Asian Linguistics), 309–33. 1969: The Hague: Mouton & Co. Reprinted by permission of Mouton de Gruyter (Walter de Gruyter GmbH & Co.), Berlin.

6. 'Dravidian nasals in Brahui', in S. Agesthialingom and N. Kumaraswami Raja (eds.), *Seminar Papers on Dravidian Linguistics*, 65–74. 1969: Annamalainagar: Annamalai University, Department of Linguistics. Reprinted by permission of Annamalai University.

7. 'Some observations on the Tamil phonology of the 12th and 13th centuries', in R. E. Asher (ed.), *Proceedings of the II International Conference-Seminar of Tamil Studies*, 356–61. 1971: Madras: International Association of Tamil Research. Reprinted by permission of the International Association of Tamil Research, Madras.

8. 'Gender and number in Proto-Dravidian', *International Journal of Dravidian Linguistics*, 4 (1975), 328–50. Reprinted by permission of the Dravidian Linguistics Association of India, Tiruvananthapuram, India.

9. 'Sound Change: Shared innovation vs. diffusion', *Phonologica 1976*, 205–11. 1976: Wien: Akten der Dritten Internationalen Phonologie Tagung. Reprinted by permission of the Institut für Sprachwissenschaft der Universität Innsbruck, Austria.

10. 'Areal and lexical diffusion of sound change: Evidence from Dravidian', *Language*, 54 (1978), 1–20. Reprinted by permission of the Linguistic Society of America.

11. 'On diachronic and synchronic rules in phonology: A case from Parji', *Indian Linguistics*, 39 (1978), 252–76. Reprinted by permission of the Linguistic Society of India.

12. 'A vowel-lowering rule in Kui-Kuvi', in B. R. Caron et al. (eds.), *Proceedings of the Sixth Annual Meeting of the Berkeley Linguistic Society*, 495–506. 1980: Berkeley: University of California. Reprinted by permission of the Berkeley Linguistic Society.

13. (with Lincoln Moses and Douglas Danforth) 'Unchanged cognates as a criterion in linguistic subgrouping', *Language*, 59 (1983), 541–68. Reprinted by permission of the Linguistic Society of America.

14. 'An overview of comparative Dravidian studies since *Current Trends in Linguistics*, vol. 5 (1969)', in V. Z. Acson and R. L. Leed (eds.), *For Gordon Fairbanks*, 212–31. 1985: Honolulu: University of Hawaii Press. Reprinted by permission of the Director, Hawaii University Press.

15. (with G. U. Rao) 'A problem of reconstruction in Gondi: Interaction between phonological and morphological processes', *Osmania Papers in Linguistics*, 13 (1989), 1–21 (1987 volume). Reprinted by permission of the Head of the Department of Linguistics, Osmania University.

16. 'The emergence of the syllable types of stems (C)VCC(V) and (C)V̄C(V) in Indo-Aryan and Dravidian: Conspiracy or convergence?', in W. G. Boltz and M. C. Shapiro (eds.), *Studies in the Historical Phonology of Asian Languages* (Current Issues in Linguistic Theory, 77), 160–75. 1991: Amsterdam and Philadelphia: John Benjamins B. V. Reprinted by permission of John Benjamins Publishing Co., Amsterdam.

17. 'The origin and evolution of primary derivative suffixes in Dravidian', in H. H. Hock (ed.), *Historical, Indo-European and Lexicographical Studies (A Festschrift for Ladislav Zgusta on the Occasion of his 70th Birthday)*, 87–116. 1997: Berlin: Mouton de Gruyter. Reprinted by permission of Mouton de Gruyter (Walter de Gruyter GmbH & Co.), Berlin.

18. 'Patterns of sound change in Dravidian', in Rajendra Singh (ed.), *The Yearbook of South Asian Languages and Linguistics 1998*, 63–79. Reprinted with the permission of the Editor and the Publishers, Sage Publications India Pvt. Ltd., New Delhi.

19. 'Proto-Dravidian laryngeal **H* revisited', *PILC Journal of Dravidic Studies*, 7: 2 (1997), 145–65. Pondicherry: Pondicherry Institute of Linguistics and Culture. Reprinted by permission of the Director, Pondicherry Institute of Linguistics and Culture.

20. 'Regularity of sound change through lexical diffusion: A study of *s* > *h* > Ø in Gondi dialects', *Language Variation and Change*, 10 (1998), 193–220. Reprinted with the permission of Cambridge University Press.

Map 21.1 is adapted from that found on p. 374 of the *Oxford Encyclopedia of Linguistics* by permission of Oxford University Press.

A Note on Transliteration and Symbols

Transliteration

The citation forms from different languages are phonemic for all the literary languages, and for Toda, Kota, and Koḍagu of South Dravidian, Koṇḍa and Pengo of South-Central Dravidian, Kolami, Parji, Ollari, and Koṇḍekor Gadaba of Central Dravidian. For the rest of the languages, the forms are apparently written in a 'broad transcription' bordering on truly phonemic representation in some cases, e.g. Israel's Kuvi and Bray's Brahui. Some are not reliable, like the transliteration of different Gondi dialects described by various administrators and missionaries, Kuvi (F), (S), and Droese's Malto. In general, the plan of Burrow and Emeneau in copying the spellings as they occur in different sources when citing cognates in *DEDR* is followed, except for two important changes, (1) and (2); (3) to (10) explain the symbols which do not differ from the ones used in the *DEDR*.

(1) Long vowels marked with different diacritics in *DEDR* (copied as they were found in source materials) are normalized by the use of a macron over the vowel, e.g. *ā*, *ī*, *ū*, *ē*, *ō*.

(2) Retroflex consonants are indicated by a subdot: stops *ṭ*, *ḍ*, nasal *ṇ*, lateral *ḷ*, flap *ṛ*, sibilant *ṣ*, and frictionless continuant or approximant *ẓ*. This last one replaces a number of symbols used in the literature since Caldwell's time (1856), viz. *ṛ*, *ḷ̤*, *ḻ*, *ẓ*, *ṟ̤*; the last is the one used by *DEDR*. Old Tamil *āytam* ஃ is marked by *ḥ*. For the reconstructed stages of Proto-Dravidian or other proto-stages, I have used *w* to represent the bilabial semivowel consistently, and not *v*. I consider the Proto-Dravidian semivowel to be a bilabial. Similarly I have preferred *w* for Telugu instead of *v*. It must be noted that in no Dravidian language do [w] and [v] contrast.

(3) Alveolars are marked by a subscript bar where they are distinguished from dentals which do not carry any diacritic: dentals *t d n*, alveolars *ṯ ḏ ṉ*; in the literary languages of South India, alveolar [ḏ] is represented as a voiced alveolar trill, marked *ṟ*. Normally only *n* without a diacritic is used if dental-alveolar contrast is not present, as in Proto-Dravidian.

(4) The velar nasal is represented by two symbols: *ṅ* for the literary languages and Tuḷu, where it is conventionally used, and *ŋ* in the case of the other non-literary languages of South-Central and Central Dravidian; *ñ* is a palatal nasal.

(5) In the Nilgiri languages: *ï* = high back unrounded vowel, *ü* = high front rounded vowel, *ë* = mid central unrounded vowel, *ö* = mid central rounded vowel; Tuḷu *è* = [æ] higher low front unrounded vowel. In Toda *c* = [ts], *ẓ̧* = [dz], *č* = [tš], *ǰ* = [tž]; *θ* = voiceless dental fricative, *x* = voiceless velar fricative; *ł* and *ł̣* are voiceless laterals of alveolar and retroflex series, respectively; among the sibilants *s̱ ẕ* are alveolar, *š ž* are alveolo-palatal and *ṣ ẓ* are retroflex.

(6) ɂ marks a glottal stop in South-Central Dravidian; Gondi *-rr* is of uncertain phonetic value; it could be either a geminated flap or an alveolar trill [r̠] contrasting with flap [r]. Kuvi (S) *ẓ* = [ts], *ch* = [č]. We do not know how to pronounce Fitzgerald's word-initial *vw-*. In the Hill Maṛia dialect of Gondi *ɽ* represents a post-velar or uvular [ʀ] corresponding to South Dravidian [r̠]. In Koṇḍa the voiceless alveolar trill is transcribed *R*.

(7) Kuṛux and Brahui *x* = [x] voiceless velar fricative; Malto *q* = [q] voiceless uvular stop; the corresponding voiced sounds are written *g̱h* = [γ] and *ġ*, respectively. What is written as *n̰* in Malto by Droese appears to be a palatal nasal [ñ].

(8) The name of the language which used to be spelt Kuru<u>kh</u> has been changed here to the way it is pronounced, Kuṛux.

(9) Whenever a phonetic representation of a cited form is given within [ ], I have followed a combination of IPA symbols with established Roman types used in Indological publications. For instance, IPA uses a diacritic for dental stops and leaves alveolars unmarked, whereas in Dravidian a subscript bar is used for alveolars and the dentals are left unmarked because of the greater universality of dentals in South Asian languages.

(10) Sometimes verbs are given in the entries with their infinitive morphs, Ma. *-ka/-kka*, Tu. *-uni/-pini*, *-vuni/-puni*, Go. *-ānā*, Kui *-pa/-ba/-va*, Kuvi (F) *-ali*, (S) *-nai/ -inai*, Kuṛ. *-ānā*, Malto *-e*. While studying the comparative etyma these elements have to be eliminated. The form in parentheses cited after a verb root in any language is the past stem of the root, unless stated otherwise, e.g. Ta. *cel-* (*cen̠-r̠-*) 'to go'.

Symbols

-	Marks etymological or morphological break.
#	Marks the beginning or end of a word or any free form.
$	Marks syllable boundary.
*	Precedes a hypothetical form reconstructed for a proto-stage.
**	A form reconstructed on the basis of reconstructed forms (represents greater time-depth).
/ /	Enclose phonemic transcriptions.
[ ]	Enclose phonetic transcription.
// //	Enclose morphophonemic transcription.
/	What follows this marks the environment of the change preceding it.
[	Following environment of a given segment.
]	Preceding environment of a given segment.
+	Marks morpheme boundary.
B, D	A voiced stop.
C	A consonant.
L	A sonorant including nasals.

N	A nasal homorganic with a following stop.
P, T	A voiceless stop.
R	A liquid (trill, lateral, approximant).
V	A vowel; $\bar{V}$ = long vowel; $\breve{V}$= short vowel; $\breve{\bar{V}}$= long or short vowel.
X ~ Y	X alternates with Y, X varies with Y.
X < Y	X is historically derived from Y.
X > Y	X is historically replaced by Y (in Ch. 4, specifically phonemically).
X > Y/___Z	X is historically replaced by Y in the environment of a following Z.
X→Y	X becomes, or is replaced by, Y (descriptively).
X >> Y	X is morphemically replaced by Y.
X/Y	X or Y.

Abbreviations

Books

Abbreviations for journal titles are listed in the Bibliography.

B & B	T. Burrow and S. Bhattacharya (1953), *The Parji Language.*
CDIAL	*A Comparative Dictionary of the Indo-Aryan Languages* (see R. L. Turner in the Bibliography).
CVGD	*A Comparative Vocabulary of the Gondi Dialects*, T. Burrow and S. Bhattacharya (1960).
DED	*A Dravidian Etymological Dictionary*, T. Burrow and M. B. Emeneau (1961).
DEDR	*A Dravidian Etymological Dictionary*, T. Burrow and M. B. Emeneau. Revised edition (1984).
DEDS	*A Dravidian Etymological Dictionary—Supplement*, T. Burrow and M. B. Emeneau (1968).
DED(S)	*DED*, *DEN*, and *DEDS*.
DEN	*Dravidian Etymological Notes*, T. Burrow and M. B. Emeneau (1972).
LSI	*Linguistic Survey of India* (see G. A. Grierson in the Bibliography).
SII	*South Indian Inscriptions* (see s.v. in Bibliography).
TVB	*Telugu Verbal Bases* (see Bh. Krishnamurti 1961 in the Bibliography).

Caṅkam Texts and Literary Sources

Usages from literary texts are based on the citations in *Tamil Lexicon.* Caṅkam texts are from the second century BCE to the third century CE.

Aiṅk.	Aiṅkuṟunūṟu
Akan.	Akanāṉūṟu
Cilap.	Cilappatikāram
Ciṟup.	Ciṟupāṇāṟṟuppaṭai
Cīv.	Cīvakacintāmaṇi (10th century CE)
DNM	Deśīnāmamālā (Prakrit dictionary: see Banerjee (1931))
Kalit.	Kalittokai
Kṟḷ.	(Tiruk)kuṟaḷ
KT	Kuṟuntokai
Maṇi.	Maṇimēkalai
Maturai.	Maturaikkāñci

Naṉ.	Naṉṉūl (13th century CE)
Parip.	Paripāṭal
Patiṟ.	Patiṟṟuppattu
Perump.	Perumpāṇāṟṟuppaṭai
PN	Puṟanāṉūṟu
Tirikaṭu.	Tirikaṭukam
Tolk.	Tolkāppiyam (Tamil grammar: see Subrahmanya Sastri (1930))

Languages

A.	Assamese
Av.	Avestan
Aw.	Awadhi
B.	Bengali/Bangla
Bhoj.	Bhojpuri
Br.	Brahui
Brahm.	Brahmin caste dialect
CD	Central Dravidian
D	Dravidian
G.	Gujarati
Gad.	(Koṇḍekor Gadaba, field-notes of Krishnamurti, 1954); Bhaskara Rao, 1980
Go.	Gondi
GoA.	Gondi, Adilabad dialect
GoM.	Gondi, Maṛia dialect
H.	Hindi, Hindustani
Ha.	Halbi (Hindi dialect)
IA	Indo-Aryan
IE	Indo-European
K.	Kashmiri
Ko.	Kota
Koḍ.	Koḍagu
Kol.	Kolami
(E)	Emeneau 1955a (see Bibliography)
(SR)	Setumadhava Rao 1950 (see Bibliography)
Kon.	Konkaṇi
Ku.	Kumauni
Kui (BB)	Burrow and Bhattacharya 1961 (see Bibliography)
Kuṛ.	Kuṛux
Kuvi (BB)	Burrow and Bhattacharya 1960 (see Bibliography)
(F)	Fitzgerald 1913 (see Bibliography)
(S)	Schultze 1911 (see Bibliography)

L.	Lahnda
Ma.	Malayāḷam
Mar.	Marathi
Marw.	Marwari
MIA	Middle Indo-Aryan
Mth.	Maithili
ND	North Dravidian
Nep.	Nepalese
NIA	New Indo-Aryan
Nk.	Naiki / Naikṛi
(Ch.)	Naiki of Chanda
OIA	Old Indo-Aryan
Oll.	Ollari
Or.	Oriya
P	Proto-
P.	Panjabi
Pa.	Parji (dialects: N: Northern; NE: North-eastern; S: Southern)
PCD	Proto-Central Dravidian
PD	Proto-Dravidian
Pe.	Pengo
PIE	Proto-Indo-European
Pkt.	Prakrit
PSCD	Proto-South-Central Dravidian
PSD	Proto-South Dravidian
RV	Rig Vedic
S.	Sindhi
SCD	South-Central Dravidian
SD	South Dravidian
SD I	South Dravidian I (same as SD)
SD II	South Dravidian II (same as SCD)
Sinh.	Sinhala
Skt.	Sanskrit
Ta.	Tamil
Te.	Telugu
To.	Toda
Tu.	Tuḷu
WPah.	West Pahari

General

abl.	ablative
acc.	accusative

adj.	adjective
caus.	causative
cent.	century
class.	classical
conj.	conjunctive
cpd.	compound
dat.	dative
dial.	dialect(al)
dist.	distal
excl.	exclusive
fem.	feminine
fn.	footnote
gen.	genitive
hab.	habitual
hum.	human
id.	idem, having the same meaning
imper.	imperative
impf.	imperfect
incl.	inclusive
inf.	infinitive
inscr.	inscriptional
instr.	instrumental
intr.	intransitive
irreg.	irregular
loc.	locative, local (subdialectal)
lw.	loanword
M	Middle
masc.	masculine
Mdn.	Modern
n.	noun
neg.	negative
neut.	neuter
nom.	nominative
O	Old
obl.	oblique
pers.	person
pl.	plural
pp.	past participle
ppl.	participle
pres.	present
prox.	proximal
refl.	reflexive
retr.	retroflex

sg.	singular
tr.	transitive
v.	verb
var.	variant(s)
v.i.	verb intransitive
v.s.v.	vide sub verbo (see under the word)
v.t.	verb transitive

1

Alternations in Vowel Length in Telugu Verbal Bases: A Comparative Study

1. There are two grades of vowel length in Dravidian, viz., long and short,[1] which are distinctly phonemic.[2] In historical and phonetic discussions we can also speak of reduced and zero grades, but these are non-phonemic. The history of vowel length is one of the less discussed aspects of comparative Dravidian, though it is found to play an important role in etymology. I attempt to present here certain historical data concerning vowel length in Telugu with reference to the structure of verbal bases; but these conclusions are also applicable to other parts of the vocabulary, since the criteria governing vowel length are phonological rather than morphological.

2. Quantitative variations, occurring among the various Dravidian languages, have been explained in different ways; for instance, K. V. Subbaiya (1909: 160 ff.) explains the so-called aphaeresized forms in Telugu through accent shift, and vowel contraction, attended by metathesis.[3] This theory, with the other restatements that

I have not revised the text of this paper. I have only dropped the abbreviations (these are given at the beginning of the book), renumbered the sections and etymological groups, recast Appendix ii with cross-references to relevant entries in *DEDR*, added a short extension to footnote 19, and corrected typographical errors. In the early fifties, the Dravidian Gadaba was wrongly called Poya by Burrow and Bhattacharya which I followed. We later realized that its original name was Koṇḍēkōr Gadaba. Therefore, Poya was replaced by Gadaba. A postscript is added at the end of the original paper reviewing the discussion that has taken place on it and my own evaluation of the points raised.

[1] The transcription used in this paper is phonemic. /ẓ/ is a voiced retroflex fricative with a phonetic value nearer the American English /r/; /r/ is a post dental flap; /ṟ/ is a voiced alveolar trill; in Modern Telugu, there is no contrast between /r/ and /ṟ/; /ḷ/ is a strongly retroflexed voiced lateral; /Ṽ/ is of uncertain phonetic value in Old Telugu, but is a morphophonemic alternant of the pre-consonantal nasal closing the second syllable, e.g. *kalũgu* 'a hole', alternates with *kalungu*; *kalugu* 'to have, possess' (for more details, see §5 and fn. 9).

The material of this paper is based on the ancient dialects of the literary languages of Dravidian (viz. Ta. Ma. Te. and Ka.) as furnished by very valuable and authoritative dictionaries. The evidence of the non-literary languages is not very reliable in deciding problems of vowel length due to the absence of their earlier records on the one hand and due to a thorough decay of medial vowels on the other. The Kui evidence is to some extent useful in ascertaining the original grade of the radical syllables. I am grateful to M. B. Emeneau, Z. S. Harris, H. M. Hoenigswald, and L. Lisker for their valuable comments and suggestions.

[2] We can see this minimal contrast in a pair like Te. Ka. *paḍu* 'to fall', Ta. Ma. *paṭu* id.: Te. Ka. *pāḍu* 'to sing', Ta. Ma. *pāṭu* id.; Kol. Pa. *pāḍ-*; Kuṛ. Malto *pāṛ-*; GoM. *pār-*.

[3] Subbaiya gives a confusing set of definitions to explain this process in Telugu on pages 160, 161, 162, and 168. The examples he quotes frequently in this article are: Ta. *iralai* 'a deer', Te. *lēḍi* (a doubtful etymology); Ta. *ural* 'a mortar', Te. *rōlu*; Ta. *ivan*, Te. *wī̃ḍu* 'this man'; Ta. *avan* 'he', Te. *wā̃ḍu*; Ta. *iḷa*

he subsequently made, has held good for a long time. Recently, A. Master (1948: 341–2) objected to the various assumptions and hypothetical steps of K. V. Subbaiya to explain vowel-lengthening in Telugu and also doubted the existence of accent in Dravidian.[4] T. Burrow (1946a: 601), while incidentally explaining the shortening of radical vowels of the personal pronouns in oblique cases in Tamil, observes: 'It is a regular characteristic of early Dravidian that a long radical vowel is shortened when certain suffixes (presumably accented) are added. Thus, corresponding to nominatives *tām* "they themselves" and *nām* "we" (inclusive), the dative in Tamil is *tamakku, namakku* (original accentuation *tamákku, namákku*).' Burrow's hesitation at making a definite statement is evident by his placing the word 'accented' in parentheses. In the modern forms of these languages there is, however, stress of a phonetic but not of a phonemic nature. It is no doubt a fact that addition of suffixes reduces the length of the radical vowels in Dravidian but there is hardly any proof to show that they were accented. On the contrary, we notice that the suffixed vowel, which is responsible for this reduction, is itself dropped in a number of cases.

3. A study of a large amount of comparative vocabulary shows that this reduction of radical vowel length is more commonly associated with the derivative suffixes than the inflectional ones. The few cases of its occurrence with the inflectional suffixes include the examples of pronouns quoted by Burrow. One of the important conditions in the structure of these suffixes is that all of them have vowels as initials and most of them are short vowels. The rationale of this gradation phenomenon seems to lie in the admissible number and grouping of syllables in a stem morpheme rather than in a system of accentuation, for which we have no evidence. In short, metre and rhythm of a definable nature seem to control the vowel length in derived bases.[5] So far as Telugu verbal stems are concerned, it is possible to formulate certain principles governing this rhythmic syllable-patterning; but before proceeding to such an analysis, it is necessary to define the syllable-structure and the method of marking syllable-boundaries in Telugu.

4. Each syllable has a vowel as a necessary part of it. Any consonant or consonants which are not preceded by another vowel belong to the following vowel and form a single syllable with it. Single consonants occurring between two vowels always belong to the following vowel; but consonant groups are so divided that the last member of the group belongs to the following syllable and the remaining to the preceding; e.g. forms like *kūrcu* and *kruccu* contain two syllables each and are to be divided as *kūr|cu*, and *kruc|cu*, respectively.[6] We may now define the short and long

'tender', Te. *lē*-. He elaborated his theory in a subsequent restatement (Subbaiya 1923: 40), where he sought to explain the lengthening in Telugu purely on the basis of accent-shift.

4 This problem is discussed in some detail at the end of the present paper (see §§ 9.1–4).

5 Rhythm is defined as 'that property of a sequence of events in time, which produces on the mind of the observer the impression of proportion between the duration of the several events or groups of events of which the sequence is composed . . . Rhythm is a feature of such sequences as are recognizably proportioned to one another in duration.' (Sonnenschein 1925: 115, 119.)

6 'It is necessary to grasp the psychological fact that the initial consonant-sound or sounds of a

syllables: A short syllable is that which necessarily contains a short vowel and also includes any consonant(s) that belong to it in the preceding position. A long syllable is (a) one which contains a long vowel including any consonants that belong to it in the preceding and following positions; also (b) that which consists of a short vowel plus any following consonant that belongs to it. On this basis the above examples *kū|r|cu*, and *kruc|cu* are structurally similar.

5. Excluding a small class of bases consisting of two short syllables,[7] most of the Telugu verbal bases can be brought under two structural patterns: (a) Those consisting of three short syllables, e.g. *pa|ra|cu* 'to spread', *ma|ra|lu* 'to return'; this class also includes forms in which the middle syllable had originally a nasal (homorganic with the following suffix-consonant) as part of it, but which was lost from popular use in the pre-classical period;[8] (b) Those with two syllables, of which the first is long and the second short: *nāku* 'to lick', *nakku* 'to hide oneself', *kūrcu* 'to gather', *kruccu* 'to pierce, etc.', belong to this class. Even these two classes can be amalgamated, since in essence one long syllable is equivalent to two short syllables. There are however a few forms which have one long syllable in the initial position followed by two short syllables, but most of these forms have undergone such modifications as would fit them in one or other of the above two patterns and all these forms occur as free variants of each other in literature; e.g. Te. *nīlugu* 'to stretch one's body to full length': *nīlgu*/*nilugu*; *mālugu* 'to be put off (as a lamp), to perish': *mālgu*/*malugu* id.; *mūlugu* 'to groan': *mūlgu*/*mulugu* id. In trisyllabic forms in Telugu length in the medial and final syllables was not tolerated in a root-morpheme at some period in the formation of early Telugu and this tendency has led to many readjustments in certain historically derived patterns to make them suit one of the above two types; e.g. Te. *ārayu*/*arayu* 'to examine, seek, etc.' (< **ār-āy*); this form is made up of two independent bases *ār-* and *āy-*[9] and they are preserved as such in the sister languages, Ta. *ārāy* 'to examine', Ma. *ārāy*, Ka. *āray*, *ārayu*, *ārai*. The loss of the pre-consonantal nasal in trisyllabic bases is also to be attributed to this tendency, e.g. *kar-āgu* 'to be melted' (< *kar-angu*), *kal-āgu* 'to be disturbed' (< *kal-angu*).[10]

syllable (i.e. any sound or sounds which may precede the vowel-sound of the syllable) are negligible, so far as an effect upon the ear is concerned; the effective part of a syllable from the psychological point of view is its vowel-sound and any consonant-sound or sounds that may follow this vowel-sound within the syllable.' (Ibid. 124).

[7] Out of nearly 1100 verbal roots in Telugu, there are hardly some 10 belonging to this type (see §10).

[8] This is called in Telugu grammars *ardhānusvāramu* or *ara-sunna* (i.e. half-nasal), which is only a historical remnant of a lost nasal orthographically preserved. This preservation has helped the poets to revive its phonetic value when they need it for metrical exigencies and ignore it when not: even in the 9th and 10th century inscriptions written in poetry, we have the complete nasals being written without their phonetic value; if they were to be read as nasals, the metre would be disturbed (see *Epigraphia Indica* XV: 150). G. J. Somayaji (1947) has presented some useful historical data on this problem in the chapter *ardhānusvaratattvamu*.

[9] This etymology was given by Burrow (1946a: 612, fn. 1). Though this form has a special origin (in being a compound rather than a root + suffix), it has adjusted itself to the large class of forms in Telugu with the composition of a verbal root + the suffix *-ayu*, probably through analogy.

[10] The development described in §9.2 can also be ascribed to this tendency.

Before proceeding to examine the processes of shortening and lengthening of vowels in Telugu, it is necessary to justify our grounds for considering a given radical vowel as originally (in Proto-Dravidian) long or short. In some cases, especially in sequences of a V + *-y*, this is difficult to do, but in the majority of cases it can be done by comparison. It is now an agreed fact that Proto-Dravidian bases were all monosyllabic in structure. Therefore, it may be stated, as a general rule, that the grade represented by a form without suffixes can be considered as primary and the one represented by the form with suffixes as secondary in etymologically connected groups; for instance Te. *pāṟu* 'to run', beside *paṟacu* id.; Ta. Ma. Ka. *āẕ* 'to sink': Ta. *aẕuntu* 'to sink', v. i., *aẕuttu* 'to immerse'; Te. *mēyu* 'to graze': *mesawu* id.; Te. *tūṟu* 'to enter': *tuṟumu* 'to stuff in'; *nūṟu* 'to grind': *nuṟucu* 'to crush'. Sometimes, the etymologies are so divided that we may have to reconstruct two grades of length for Proto-Dravidian.[11]

Shortening of Long Vowels

6. A long radical vowel is shortened in the company of the following suffixes: *-ku*, *-gu*, *-cu*, *-tu*, *-du* when any of these is preceded by *a/ā or u/ū*; *-upu*, *-umu*, *-ayu*, *-iyu*, *-aru*, *-uru*, *-alu* and *-ulu*, etc.[12] Following are some typical examples (for more, see Appendix I):

1. *pal-uku* 'to say, speak'; Ta. *paṇi* 'to ask; to say'; Tu. *paṇpini* 'to say': Kui *plāpa* 'to enquire, ask; to say, address'; Br. *pān-* 'to say, speak' (PD **pāḷ-/pāṇ-*, suffix *-ukku*).

2. *cer-ugu*[13] 'to sift, winnow' (< **cēṟ-ugu/-uwu*): Ka. *kēṟu*; Ma. *cēṟuka*; Ko. *kēr-*, *kēry-*; Pa. Kol. Nk. *kēd-*; Gad. *kēy-*; Kuṛ *kẽs-*; Malto *kēs-*.

3. *paṟ-acu* 'to run, fly, flee'; Ta. *paṟa* 'to fly'; *paṟi* 'to escape, flow'; Ma. *paṟakka* 'to fly, flee'; Go. *parīt* - 'to fly'; Malto *parce* 'to run away': Te. Ta. Ma. Ka. *pāṟu* id.; Tu. *pāruni* id.

4. *giṟ-upu* 'to wink the eye as a signal': *gīṟu* id.; Ta. *kīṟu* 'to hint'.

[11] There are relatively few forms of suspicious vowel-grade in the root syllable, for instance, Te. *kanu* 'to see'; beside *kān-* in *kān-a-* inf. 'to see', *kān-a-ḍu* (neg. masc.), etc. *kān̄-cu* 'to see'; Ta. Ma. Ka. *kāṇ-* 'to see' (past stem *kaṇḍ-*), Br. *xan-* id.; > lw. Skt. *kāṇa-* 'blind in one eye', see (Burrow 1947b: 22). So also Te. *wan̄gu* 'to bend' (< **waṇ-gu*), *wān-cu* 'to bend', *wālu* id. with the etymologies from the sister languages point to a **wāḷ-/wāṇ*.

[12] In my reconstructions I have made no assumptions regarding the original form of these suffixes; all that I am concerned with here is to show that the radical syllable had originally a long vowel which was shortened when suffixes with an initial vowel were added. To that extent these reconstructions hold good. A study of the complete structure of the suffixes is a separate problem.

[13] Emeneau wondered whether *-r-* was not wrong here for *-ṟ-*. There are also a few more instances like *ūru* 'to ooze', for *ūṟu* even in the earliest literary records, which show that lack of contrast between these two phonemes was already present in the popular speech, which had often introduced confusion in writing (see Emeneau 1953a: 101).

5. *nuṟ-umu* 'to crush, powder; to thrash grain' (< **nuṟ-umbu* < **nūṟ-umpu*); Tu. *nuriyuni* 'to go to pieces'; *nuripuni* 'to powder'; Br. *nus-* id.: Te. Ta. Ma. Ka. *nūṟu* 'to grind, crush, etc.'; Go. *nōr-* id.

6. *nan-ayu* 'to blossom'; also *nan-ucu* id.; Ta. *naṉai* 'to flower'; Ka. *nane* id.: cf. Ta. *nāṉam* 'fragrant substance'; *nāṟu* 'to be fragrant'; Ma. Ka. *nāṟu* id., Tu. *nāduni* (*ṟ/n* alternation was found to be common in early Dravidian).[14]

7. *nul-iyu* 'to be twisted'; transitives: *nul-ucu*, *nul-upu*, and *nul-umu*; Ka. *nuli* 'to twist, wring'; Tu. *nuliyuni* 'to be broken': Ka. *nūl* 'to spin'; Tu. *nūpini* 'to twist'; Ta. Ma. *nūr* 'to spin'; Kui *nōlba* 'to twist'; Kuṛ. *nō̃ĕnā* id.

8. *wis-aru* 'to fan; to blow as wind', v.i. and v.t., v.t. 'to fling, throw'; Ta. *viciṟu* 'to fan, fling'; Ma. *visaruka* 'to fan, flutter the wings'; Ka. *bisuḍu* 'to fling': Te. *wīcu* id.; Ta. *vīcu*; Ma. *vīsu*, *vīju*, *vīyu*; Ka. *bīsu*; Tu. *bījuni*; Kui, *vīka*, *vīnja*.

9. *nim-uru* 'to stroke the body softly and caressingly' (also *niwuru*); Ka. *nivaru* id.: Ta. Ka. *nīvu* id.

10. *tar-alu* 'to start, proceed': cf. Te. *tāru* 'to approach'; v.t. *tārcu* 'to conduct'; Ta. Ma. *cār* 'to proceed, etc'.; Ka. *sār* id.; Tu. *sārluni* 'to proceed'; here, the Tuḷu form is specially interesting in that it seems to represent the original condition of the radical vowel-grade more nearly than the others.

7. It frequently happened in Early Telugu that the vowel preceding the occlusive suffixes, viz. *-ku/-nku*, *-gu/-ngu*, *-cu/-ncu*, *-du/-ndu*, etc., was lost in certain forms, after a long radical vowel was shortened. In such cases comparative evidence provides us a clue to the original grade of the root vowel. This loss of the medial vowel has led to three developments in Telugu.

7.1. Assimilation of the radical final consonant (usually a non-occlusive) with the suffix:

11. *cokku* 'to be intoxicated' (< **corku* < **coruku* < **cōr-ukku*), Ka. *sokku*, *sorku*, Tu. *corkuni*, Ma. *corukuka* 'to be stupefied', *corukkuka* 'to feel dizzy': Ta. *cōr* 'to languish, faint, etc.'; Ka. *sōr* id.; Kui *sōsa* 'to be intoxicated'.

12. *nikku* 'to stand erect, to be proud, etc'.; Ka. *niluku*, *niḷku*, *nikku* 'to strut; to rise up to': Ta. Ka. Ma. *nīḷ-* 'to grow long, to stretch oneself out'.

13. *kaggu* 'to become black (due to heat or smoke)', cf. *krāgu*, v.i. 'to burn'; Ta. Ka. *kari* 'to be charred, burnt'; Ma. *kariyuka*; Ka. *karaku*, *karku* 'black'; Tu. *karṅka* 'the state of being burnt'; Ka. *kargu* 'to turn black', Ta. *karuku* 'to be scorched', Go. *karw-* 'to burn': Ta. Ma. Ka. *kār* 'blackness'; Te. *kār* adj. id.; Kui *kāra* 'to be hot'; Kol. *kārī* 'black'.

[14] A few examples will suffice to show this correspondence: Te. *mānu* 'to heal, be cured'; Ta. *māṟu* 'to cure' v.i., *māṟṟu* 'to cure' v. t.; Kui, *māṟa* 'to be healed'; Te. *ūnu* 'to hold on to, lean on'; Ka. *ūṟu* 'to lean'; Te. *kanu* 'to bring forth'; Br. *xan* id.; Ka. *kaṟu* 'a calf'; Ta. *kaṉṟu* id. (< **kan-tu*), Ma. *kannu*; cf. Ma. *kaṟṟu* 'a baby, a calf'; Te. *cinuku* 'to sprinkle', n. 'a drop of rain'; Ma. *iṟuka* 'to drip, etc'.

14. *taggu* 'to become low, reduced'; Ka. *taggu, targu, taẓgu* id. (< **taẓugu* < **taẓunku*); Tu. *tagguni*: Ta. Ma. *tāẓ* 'to be lowered'; Ka. *tāẓ* n. 'being low'; Kui *tāli* adj. 'less, reduced in quantity'; Kuṛ. Malto *tār-* 'to fell a tree'.

15. *addu* 'to dip; to dye'; Ka. *aẓdu, addu* id.; Tu. *ard-* 'to bleach clothes'; Ta. *aẓuntu* 'to be immersed, etc.', *aẓuttu*, v.t.: Ta. Ka. *āẓ* 'to sink, etc.'; Ma, *āẓuka* id.

16. *biddu* 'to die'; Ka. *biddu, birdu, biẓdu*, pp. of *bīẓ* 'to fall': Tu. *būruni* id.; Ta. *vīẓ*, *viẓu* 'to fall'; Ma. *vīẓuka* id.

17. *ubbu* 'to swell, be puffed up, overflow'; cf. *uṟuwu* 'bigness, rise'; Ka. *ubbu, urbu* 'to swell, etc.'; cf. *uṟubu* 'rise, etc.'; Tu. *ubbuni* id.; Ta. *uṟuttu* 'to increase'; *uṟai* 'to swell'; n. 'greatness': Te. *ūṟu* 'to become fat or bloated, etc.'; Ta. *ūṟu* 'to increase, as flesh in a person'.

7.2. Metathesis in the last two members of the root syllables (probably to avoid the otherwise unsuitable sequences):

18. *mrokku, mroggu* 'to bend forward, kneel, etc.' (< **mẓo-kku/-ggu* < **moẓ-ku/gu* < **moẓ-u-ku/-gu* < **moẓ-u-nku* from **mōẓ* plus the suffix *-u-nku*); Ka. *moẓgu* 'to bend'; cf. *muẓgu* 'to fall, fall down' (< **moẓgu*), Go. *murs-* 'to stoop down'; Pa. *moṛk-* 'to bow': Kui *mrōnga* 'to crouch over'. The Proto-Dravidian root **mōẓ-* is the same as the one in Ta. Ma. *muẓam-* (< **moẓ-am*), Ka. *moẓ-a* 'a projecting joint'.

19. *braduku* 'to live, flourish', Mdn. Te. *batuku* (< **bar-duku* < **waẓ-u-du-nku/-du-kku* < **wāẓ-u-dunku/-dukku*); Ka. *barduku, barduṅku, baẓduṅku* 'to live': Ta. *vāẓ* 'to live, flourish, etc.'; Ma. *vāẓ-uka*; Ka. *bāẓ*.

20. *bruṅgu* 'to be immersed; to be hidden' (< **mẓungu* < **muẓ-ng* < **muẓ-u-ng-* < **muẓ-u-nk-*); Ka. *muẓuṅgu*; Tu. *murkuni*; Ta. Ma. *muẓuku*: Ta. *mūẓku, mūẓ* id.; Kuvi *mrūkh* id.; cf. Kuṛ. *bōr-* 'to immerse'; Pa. *būṛ-* 'to sink'.

21. *duwwu*[15] 'to comb' (< **ḍu-wwu* < **ẓu-wwu* < **uẓ-wu* < **ūẓ-uwu*); Ta. *uẓu* 'to arrange the hair with the fingers'; Pa. *uṛ-*, *uṛv-* 'to comb'; Gad. *uḍuv-* id.; Kuvi *ṛūss-* 'to dress (another's hair)', *rūcha* 'comb'; Kui *ṛūsa* 'to rub, scrape'.

7.3. Loss of the base final liquid when no metathesis takes place:

22. *ka-ngu* 'to fade, become dark, etc.' (< **kar-ng-* < **kar-ung-*); Tu. *karṅka* 'the state of being singed, blackness'; for other languages see *kaggu* above.

23. *po-ncu* 'to waylay, lie in wait' (< **por-nc-* < **por-unc-* < **pōr-uñc-*); Ka. *poncu* id. : Kui *pōrpa* 'to lie in wait'; Kuvi *pōrh (ali)*; cf. Ta. Ka. Ka. *pār* 'to wait for, etc.'.

24. *ce-ndu* 'to reach, get at, belong', *centa* 'proximity', adv. 'near' (< **cer-nd-/-nt-* < **cer-und-/-unt-* < **cēr-und-/-unt-*); SD and CD *cēr-/sēr-* 'to reach' (see Emeneau 1953a: 110–11).

[15] PD /ẓ/ develops to /ḍ/ in Telugu initially and intervocalically; *ḍ-* (< **ẓ*, **ṭ*) has again shifted to *d-* even in Old Telugu and very often we have both *ḍ-* and *d-* forms occurring side by side in early texts, as *ḍigu/digu* 'to descend'. The present form in the earlier stage occurs in a related meaning as *ḍūyu/dūyu* 'to scrape off, strip off' (< **ẓū-* < **ūẓ*).

25. *pa-mbu* 'to spread, increase' (< **par-mb-* < **par-umb-* < **pār-ump-*) (**pār-* underlies Te. *prā̃ku* 'to spread as a creeper'), Ta. *pampu* 'to be thick; to spread like vegetation, water, darkness, etc.'; *parampu* 'to spread (as water), etc.'; Tu. *parambuni* 'to spread'; Ka. Tu. *parbu* id.

7.4. In the above forms and similar ones, an analysis within the usage of Telugu yields only stems with short grade vowels, which should not be mistaken as representing the original due to the absence of any medial syllable. The pre-suffixal vowel must have been lost here, since otherwise there is no reason why a long radical vowel should be shortened. These instances also confirm our thesis that it was not the accentual influence of the affixed vowels that reduced the radical grade, but a tendency to adjust to a pattern of syllable grouping, inherent in these languages (see §**10**).

Lengthening of Short Vowels

8. Lengthening of the radical vowel occurs in Telugu mainly through the contraction of two successive syllables, of which the latter has *y* or *w* with the following vowel dropped. In other words we have short monosyllabic bases here with final *-y-* or *-w-*, followed by suffixes that begin with vowels. Most of these are liquid suffixes as against the plosive suffixes, i.e. a vowel + liquid (as *-al*, *-il*, *-ul*; *-ar*, *-ir*, *-ur*) as against a vowel + plosive or nasal-plosive group (as *-a-nku*, *-a-ncu*, *-u-ntu*, etc.).

8.1. Cases with the loss of a radical final *-y*:[16]

26. *ūr-cu* 'to breathe, respire, sigh' (< **uy-r-cu* < **uy-ir-cu*); Ta. Ma. *uyir* 'to breathe, etc.', Ta. *uy-* 'to live'; *uyirppu* 'respiration'; Te. *ūr-pu* id.: Ka. *usir* id. Tu. *usuru* 'breath'; Kuṛ. Malto *uj-* 'to breathe'; cf. Te. *ūr-ārcu* 'to console' (literally, 'to calm sighing').

27. *kū-lu* 'to fall down; to sink, drop, die'; Ka. *kūlu* id. (?lw. < Te.); Ta. *kūr* 'to bend'; Ma. *kūluka* 'to bend'; Kui *kūra* 'to fall down; to recline'; Kol. *kūl-* 'to drop'; all from **kuy-il/-ir* < **kus-ir*; cf. Ka. *kusi* 'to bend, be lowered, sink, etc.'; Tu. *kusuruni* 'to shrink'; Go. *kuss-* 'to fall, drop (as leaves)'.

28. *tū-lu* 'to shake, reel, stagger, etc.'; Tu. *tūluni* 'to totter, reel'; Ta. *tuy-al* 'to sway, swing, droop'; originally **cuy-al* (see Burrow 1947a: 142).

[16] As the examples show this is a very ancient change in South Dravidian which also extended to the other geographical groups: Ta. *peyar*, *pēr* 'name'; Ma. *piyar*, *peyar*, *pēr*; Ka. *pesar*; Tu. *pudar*; Koḍagu, *peda* (Tuttle 1930: §25); Te. *pēru*: Nk. *pēr*: Pa. Gad. *pidir*; Go. *parōl* (< **per-ōl*, < **pēr-ōl*). Gondi goes even a step further by adding one more suffix on the contracted form *pēr*. Kui has a doubtful etymology, i.e. *paḍa* (< **pala*); cf. Kuṛ. Malto *pinj-* 'to name'; Br. *pin-*. Sometimes the middle link may be altogether missing: Ka. *kesaṟu* 'mire', Ta. Ma. *cēṟu* (< **key-aṟu*); similarly Ta. *cey-*, Ka. *key-* 'a field', Te. *cēnu* (< **cey-m* < **cey-am*).

29. *kō-ru* 'to wish, desire'; Ta. *kōṟu, kōru* id.; Ma. *kōṟuka*; Ka. *kōṟu*; Tu. *kōruni* (< **koy-aṟ/-ar* < **kos-aṟ/-ar*); cf. Te. *kosaru* 'to desire' n. 'a desire' (Classical).

30. *sō-lu* 'to swoon, stagger, languish'; cf. Ka. *sōlu* 'to be defeated; to be overcome'; Ta. Ma. *tōl* id.; (< **coy-l-* < **coy-al*); cf. Ta. *toy-* 'to languish; to droop'; *toy-y-al* 'fainting; languishing'.

8.2. Cases with the loss of final *-w*:

31. *ū-yu* 'to spit' (< **uw-iyu*); cf. Te. *umiyu* id., Ta. *umi*; Ma. *umiyuka*: Ka. *ugi* id. (< **uwi*).

32. *cī-ku* 'to smack, suck', beside *cibuku* id. (< **ciw-uku* < **cip-ukku*); Ka. *cīpu, sīpu*; Ta. *cīppu*; Kuṛ. Malto *cīp-* id.; *cib-uku/ciw-uku* was from *cīp* + *ukku.*[17]

33. *pī-lu, pī-ru* 'to burst out' (< **piw-l-* < **piw-ul-*); cf. Te. *pig-ulu, piw-ulu* id. (this form is probably the metathetic counterpart of Ka. *piḷ-igu* 'to break, burst'); Ta. *piḷ* id.; Ma. *piḷ-aruka* id.; *piḷukka* 'to split'; Kui *plinga* v.i. id.; *plipka* (<*plik-p-*) v.t.; Pa. *pil-* 'to burst open'.

34. *tī-yu* 'to take out, pull out' (< **tiw-yu* < **tiw-iyu*), Te. *tiwiyu* id.; Ka. *tivi* id.

8.3. The cases of contraction where *w* is involved seem to be much later developments than the forms with *y*, since this variation is attested in the historic period unlike the latter. If we closely examine the examples given under shortening and lengthening in juxtaposition, we notice that they proceed in opposite directions. In the former case the prominence of the radical syllable is reduced and levelled to the size of the following syllables, whereas in the latter the syllables of both the base and the suffix contract together to make the radical syllable prominent. Consequently, **ūr-* (in *ūrcu*), *kūlu, tūlu, sōlu*, etc. appear as single morphemes, though they are structurally made up of two morphs each. It is even more interesting to note that some of such contracted morphemes are involved in the shortening process when suffixes are added to them. This can be exemplified by the form *cokku*, where the original base is **cōr-*; now we find that *cōr-* itself is a contraction of **coy-ar*, as is shown by Tamil *toy-* (< **coy-*) 'to languish'. This shows us how wide a barrier exists between *cokku* and **coy-* both in point of time as well as of structure: *cokku* < **corku* < **cor-ukku* < **cōr-ukku*, of which *cōr* < **coy-ar*. We can also test this cyclic development in a number of similar forms like *nūṟu, nūl, nīl*, etc., and this principle throws a flood of light on many a problem of etymology in Dravidian.[18]

[17] One could say that **cī-* is the original base here, while *-p* and *-k* are suffixes; but in Telugu the presence of the form *cibuku* 'to smack', tempts us towards this etymology; for similar cases, cf. Te. *ubusu* 'time, leisure'; *ūsu* id.

[18] I believe that an intensive investigation into this problem will eventually show that all such stems with an initial (radical) long vowel + a non-occlusive consonant can be etymologically resolved into two morphemes (as B1 + Ss2 or B2 + Sw2, see §10); a few more illustrations are given in the following:

(1) Te. *nūṟu* 'to powder, crush' (< **nuy-iṟ-* < **nus-iṟ*), cf. Te. Ka. *nusi* 'dust, powder': Te. *nūka* 'grits' (< **nuy-k-*), Ta. *nuccu* 'grits', also *noy*; Go. *nus-ī* 'flour weevil' (*-*ī* 'a fly'); Br. *nus-* 'to powder': Kuvi (S) *nui-* 'to mill'.

8.4. Radical vowels *i, u, e, o,* preceding *-y* that is followed by a vowel of non-derivational character, are invariably long in Telugu. In these cases, final *-y* has not contracted with the radical vowel to produce length as in the previous cases but occurs beside length.

35. *ī, īyu* 'to give' (< **iy-* < **ciy-/*siy-*), also *iccu* id. (< **iy-cc-* < **iy-tt-*); Ta. *ī*; Ka. *ī* (pp. *ittu*); Kui *sī-/jī-*; Kuvi *hī-*; Pa. Gad. *cī-*; Kol. *siy-*; Kuṛ. *ci-*; Malto, *ciy-*. [For Telugu *-cc* was the original past suffix here, not *-tt*.]

36. *mūyu* 'to shut, close etc.' (< **muy-* < **muc-/*mus-*); Ta. *mūyu*; Ta. Ka. Tu. *muccu* 'to close, cover'; Go. *muht-* 'to cover'; Kui *muspa* 'to cover'; Kuvi (S) *muh-* 'to bury'; Kuṛ. Malto *muc-* 'to close or shut up' Go. *muc-* 'to wrap round' Pa. Nk. *muy* Br. *must-* adj. 'closed'; cf. also Kuṛ. *musug-* 'to envelope'; Malto *musgr-* 'to be closed up'; *musg-* 'to pack up'.

37. *ēyu* 'to fling, throw, brandish (a weapon)'; Ka. *ēy-*, *ēsu* id. (pp. of *isu* [< **esu*] is *eccu*); Tu. *eyyuni, eyipuni*; Ta. *ey-*, *ē cu* id.; Ma. *eyyuka*; Go. *ēs-*; Pa. *ey-*; Gad. *ey-/ē -*; Kuṛ. *ecch-* 'to dash a liquid over'; Malto *ec-* 'to throw out'; cf. Kuṛ. *inj-* id.

38. *nēyu* 'to weave, plait'; (< **ney-* < **nec-/*nes-*); Ka. *ney, neyi, neyyu, nē, nēy-, nēyi, nēyu* id. pp. *nēdu, neyidu*; Tu. *neyuni, neyipini, nēpini, nēyuni*; Ta. *ney*; Ma. *neyka*, Kuvi *neh-/nēh-*; Kuṛ. *essnā* 'to weave, plait'; Malto *ese* id.; cf. Kui *ēspa* 'to spin'.

39. *cēyu* 'to do' (< **cey-* < **key-*); Ta. Ma. *cey-*; Ka. *key-, gey-*; Go. *kī-*; Kui *kiva, giva*; Kuvi *kī-*; Gad. *key-, kē -* (PD radical **ey-* > SCD *i-/ī-*).

40. *kōyu* 'to pluck, reap' (< **koy*), Ta. Ma. Ka. Tu. *koy-*; Kui *kōva*; Kol. *kōs-*; Pa. *koy-*; Gad. *koy-/kō -*; Kuṛ. *xoy-*, Malto *qoy-*.

8.5. An examination of a number of monosyllabic stems such as these in final *-y* shows that there was probably no contrast in Dravidian between short and long vowels (*i, u, e,* and *o*) before a *-y* in unbound root morphemes.[19] In other words, length was non-phonemic in sequences of V + *y* in radical syllables. Consequently we notice that some languages show a short vowel and some a long; even here, there does not seem to be any thorough regularity, since the same language may show both varieties, as Ka. *ney-/nēy-*; *noy/nōy-*, etc. But Telugu here is regular in representing the proto-condition by a long vowel only in all the forms concerned.

(2) Te. *nūlu* 'thread', *nulucu* 'to twist'; the form without the suffix *-l* is preserved in Tu. *nū(puni), nu(ppuni)* 'to twist'; cf. Kuṛ. *nõẽ-*.

(3) Ta. Ma. Ka. *nīḷ* 'to extend, become long' (< **niw-uḷ*); Tu. *nigacuni, nīcuni* v. i. 'to stretch out'; Ka. *niguḷ* 'to be extended'; Ka. *nimir* (< **niw-ir*), *nigur* (< **niw-ur*) id.; Pa. *nikip-/nikit-* 'to stretch out'; Ta. *nimir, nivar* id.; Ta. *niva* 'to rise, spread', Ma. *nika* id.; Te. *negayu*, Ka. *nege*; all these are traceable to the PD root **niw-* with the suffixes *-a, -ir, -ur, -uḷ*, etc.

[19] We can observe the situation in the individual languages as follows: In Tamil there is no contrast between short and long vowels (other than /a/) before *-y* in the radical syllables: *tuy* 'to enjoy by means of senses; to eat food' (no *tūy-*); *tēy* 'to rub away' (no *tey-*); *ney* 'weave', homonym n. 'oil' (no *nēy*); *puy* 'to be pulled out' (no *pūy*); *poy* 'to lie' (no *pōy*); *mūy* 'to cover' (no *muy*); *moy* 'to throng' (no *mōy*).

There is contrast between short and long /a/ before *y*: *kai* 'to be bitter', *kāy* 'to grow hot';

8.6. In sequences of a non-low vowel (*i*, *u*, *e*, or *o*) + *y* + an occlusive suffix (not preceded by a vowel), Telugu drops *-y* and lengthens the previous vowel. Sometimes *-y* is merely dropped without affecting the grade of the vowel.

41. *tūgu* 'to doze'; Ka. *tūgu*; Tu. *tūṅkuni*, *tūguni*; Ta. *tūṅka*; Ma. *tūṅṅuka*; Gad. *tuyng-* id. (all from **tuy-ng-/-nk-*); cf. Ta. Ma. *tuñcu* 'to sleep'; Kui *sunj-*; Kuvi *hūnjali*, GoM. *hunj-*; Seoni dial. *suncī* n. 'sleep', (*LSI* IV: 518) (< **cuy-nc-*; the ultimate root is **cuy-* as underlying Ta. *uyal/tuyal* 'to swing, reel', etc. (see Burrow 1947a: 142)).

42. *tōgu* 'to become wet; to sink, bathe' (< **toy-ṅg-*); Ka. *toy-*, *toyi*, *tō*, *tōy* 'become wet', etc.; Tu. *toipuni* 'to wash clothes'; Ta. *toy-* 'to be dipped'; *tōy* 'to bathe; to be soaked'; *toyali* 'washer-woman'; *toyyil* 'cultivated moist land'; Ma.

(diphthongal *-i*; *-y*); *tai* 'to sew', *tāy* 'mother'; *nai* 'to be crushed', *nāy* 'dog'; *pai* 'greenness', *pāy* 'to spring up'; *vai* 'to put', *vāy* 'mouth'. (In Dravidian *ai* = *ay*, see *Tolkāppiyam*, 58; the traditional transcription merely adheres to *ai*.)

There are, however, a few cases of contrast in length even after vowels other than /a/, but they can be explained on special grounds: *uy* 'to live', *ūy* 'to be overripe'; *ey* 'to shoot, *ēy* 'to be like, resemble'; *oy* 'to give', *ōy* 'to be reduced'; *koy* 'to pluck', *kōy* 'a vessel for taking toddy' (< Skt. *kōśa-*, *Tamil Lexicon*); *toy* 'to labour', *tōy* 'to be wet'; *pey* 'to pour down', *pēy* 'goblin' (cf. Kui *pēnu* 'god, spirit'); all these pairs are not Common Dravidian, for instance *ūy*, *ēy*, *ōy*, *kōy*, *toy* are not represented in the other languages in contrastive pairs. Since there is contrast in Tamil between a short vowel + *-y* and the corresponding long vowel, it is likely that in some of the forms with monosyllabic long vowels, *-y* could have been added through wrong division from non-sandhi junctures where it develops as a glide. Perhaps *ē-* and *pē-* might have added *-y* in sandhi in this way.

Again, certain vowel alternations have brought about the contrast: *cey* 'to do', *cēy* 'distance, length'; *cey-* is from **key*, while *cēy-* is probably an original alternant of *cā-* 'to spread', Te. Ka. Tu. *cācu* 'to stretch out the hands', etc. (*ā/ē-* alternation after *c-* is common in South Dravidian, cf. *cār/cēr* 'to approach'); similarly open and close vowels alternate in Dravidian before *-y* in the radical syllables, Ta. *uy/oy* 'to give', **miy-/*mey-* 'high, above' (Te. *mī-da*, Ta. *mē-l*; *ay-/ey-* as in **kay* 'hand', **key* 'to do'; Te. *wai-cu*, *wēyu* 'to throw'; Ta. *noy* 'grits', *nuccu* id.; *moy* 'to throng', *mūcu* id. (< **muy-c-*). SD *nūl-* 'twist', Kui *nōl* id. (< **noy-l*), SD *nūṟ-* 'to powder', Go. *nōr* (<**noy-r-*) id.; on the basis of this, we can explain contrast in Ta. *mey* 'body', *mēy* 'to graze' as follows: *mey* is probably *mai* since Telugu has *mēyi*, *mēnu*, and *mai-*; Ta. Ma. *mēni* id.; Kol. Nk. Pa. Gad. *mēn*, Go. *mēndur*; Kuṛ. *mẽd*; or else this form was originally *mē-* and the other one *mēy-/mēc-*. In some cases there is free variation in length, Ta. *cey* 'redness', also *cēy*; sometimes complementary distribution, as *veytu* 'that which is hot', beside *vē* 'to burn'.

The situation in Telugu is: *i*, *u*, *e*, and *o* are long before *-y*; there is no contrast with short vowels in this position; short and long vowels are in complementary distribution as *koyy-an/kōy-an* inf. 'to cut'; *weyy-an/wēy-an* 'to put, throw'; the forms with short vowels before doubling are rather innovations in later Telugu and very common in Modern Telugu. There is no such free variation after /a/, e.g. *kayya* 'a back-water stream'; *kāya* 'an unripe fruit'; therefore, short and long /a/ do not alternate in complementary environments as in the above cases. /-y/ is dropped before a consonant, *cēta* 'action', *cēyu* 'to do'; ultimately, we notice *cēy-/cē-* are in complementary distribution, so also *ceyy-/cēy-*. The situation is nearly similar in Kannaḍa (see Kittel 1903: §§48, 159, 162, 176, 187).

All these facts seem to prove that in Proto-Dravidian there was probably no contrast between long and short vowels before /y/ in radical syllables.

[Notwithstanding what I said above, it has been observed later that Proto-Dravidian long and short vowels do contrast before *-y*. Only Telugu has lost the contrast of length of non-low vowels before *-y* in root syllables; only long vowels occur here (see Postscript; Subrahmanyam 1970a). It must, however, be noted that most languages show free variation of non-low vowels before *-y* in the root syllables. Most of the languages lose *-y* regularly before an obstruent.]

tōyuka 'to dip, soak'; Br. _chōsh-_ 'to wash by rubbing'; cf. Te. _tōmu_ 'to wash by cleaning' (< *_tō-mb-_ < *_tōy-mp-_).

43. _pīku_ 'to pull out, weed out' (< *_piy-ṅk-_); Ka. _pīku_ id. (lw. < Te.); Ta. _piy_ 'to be put to rout; to pull out'; _pey-ar_ 'to uproot, displace' (< *_piy-ar_); Ma. _pēruka_ 'to be plucked' (< *_peyar_); Kuṛ. _pes-_ 'to pick out'; Go. _pehk-_ id. (_piy_ < *_pis-_).

44. _wēgu_ 'to be fried; to grieve, etc.' (< *_wey-ṅg-_); Ka. _bē_, _bēyu_, _beyyu_; Tu. _bēyuni_ 'to boil'; _besiyuni_ 'to be hot'; Ta. _vē-_ 'to burn, be boiled, be distressed'; Ma. _vēka_; Kui _vēva_ 'to be well cooked'; _vehpa_ 'to be hot'; Kuvi _veh-_ id.; Kol. _weiy-_ 'to burn'; Kuṛ. _bi_ 'to be cooked'; Malto _bice_ id.; Br. _bis-_ 'to bake' (< *_wey-_ < *_wec-_/*_wes-_).

45. _wīgu_ 'to become big, bloated; to be proud' (< *_wiy-ng-_); Ka. _bīgu_ 'to swell, etc.'; Ta. _vīṅku_ 'to increase, swell, etc.'; Ma. _vīṅṅuka_ id.; cf. Ta. _viy-am_ 'extensiveness'; _viy-al_ 'greatness, extension, abundance'; cf. Malto _bithge_ 'to expand' (< *_wicg-_), _bije_ 'to expand, widen' (_wiy-_ < *_wic-_/*_wis-_).

8.7. If we grant that length was non-phonemic in radical syllables before _-y_, then these examples do not attest any special case of lengthening in Telugu, but only show that Telugu adhered to long vowels in these sequences with the loss of _-y_. There are, however, a few cases where Telugu has lost the _-y_ with the preceding vowel being kept short: Te. _bonku_ 'to lie; a lie'; Ka. _boṅku_ id. (< *_poy-ṅk-_); Ta. _poy-_ 'to lie', _poykka_ 'falsely'; _pokkam_ 'falsehood' (< *_poy-kk-am_); Ma. _poy_ n. 'a lie', _pokkam_ 'falsehood'; cf. Tu. _pōka_, adj. 'mischievous'; Ka. _pusi_ 'to lie' (< *_posi_); GoM. _bus-_ 'to lie'. So also before geminates Telugu always has a short vowel: Te. _wemmu_ 'to be hot' (< *_wembu_ < *_wey-mp-_); Ta. _vempu_ id.; cf. Ta. _veytu_ 'that which is hot' (Akan.); 'heat' (Maturai.).

9. We now come to a special class of forms, in which the last two phonemes of the radical syllable are transposed with the vowel lengthened (or kept long) and followed by a consonantal suffix; corresponding to these the other literary Dravidian languages have sequences of short-syllabled bases + VC(C)-suffixes (as _-al_, _-ar_, _-anku_, etc.). It is convenient to present the material before discussing this phenomenon.

9.1. Examples with -V + a liquid or semivowel suffixes:

46. _krā-lu_ 'to move, shake'; Ka. _kaẓ-al_ 'to get loose, droop down'; Tu. _kariyuni_ 'to droop down'; Ta. _kaẓ-al_ 'to become loose; to run away'; Ma. _kaẓ-aluka_ id.; Go. _kar-ēng-_ 'to be shaken, swung'.

47. _wrā-lu_ 'to hang loose; to be tired, hang, bend, etc.'; Ka. _baẓ-al_ 'to droop, fade, become loose, dangle, slip'; Ta. _vaẓ-aṅku_ 'to swing one's body (as an elephant)'; _vaẓ-akku_ 'moving to and fro'.

48. _wrīlu_ 'to be separated; to go to pieces'; Ka. _viri_, _biri_ 'to break away, burst, separate'; Tu. _biriyuni_ id.; Ta. _viri_ id.; cf. _viriyal_ 'expanse'; Ma. _viriyuka_ 'to expand'; Te. _wiriyu_, _wirugu_ id.; Kui _vringa_, _vrīva_ 'to fall to pieces'; Kuvi _brīyali_ 'to topple over' (past stem, _brit-_); Pa. _virŋg-_ 'to be loosened'; Kuṛ. _bird-_ 'to break through'; cf. Br.

birring 'to separate out, distinguish, etc.'. It is to be noted here that the suffix **-l/*-il* appears only in Telugu.

49. *wrāyu* 'to write'; Ka. *bare, bari* id.; Tu. *barepini* id.; Ta. *varai, vari* id.; Ma. *varayuka* 'to draw a line', *variyuka* id.; Kui *vrīsa* 'to write, scratch'; Kuvi *brī-nai* 'to draw', GoM. *rās-* 'to write' (lw. < Te.).

50. *mrōyu* 'to sound (as musical instruments)'; cf. *mor-ayu* id.; Ka. *more* 'to hum, play a lute'; Ta. *mural* 'to make sound, sing'; Ma. *muraluka* 'to hum'; Kol. *muray-* 'to sound'.

9.2. Examples with suffixes consisting of -V + a stop, geminate, or a nasal+ stop:

51. *prā̃ku* 'to creep, crawl, spread'; Ka. *pare* 'to spread (as creepers or roots), etc.'; Tu. *parapuni* 'to flow, creep, crawl, etc.'; Ta. *para* 'to spread, extend etc.'; *parakku* 'to roam about'; Ma. *parakka* id.; Pa. *par-p-/par-t-* 'to spread'; Kuvi *prahpa* 'to spread out; to scatter over'; cf. Kui *pāspa* 'to spread a cover or cloth'; GoM. *parh-* 'to spread'.

52. *krā̃gu* 'to be burnt'; Ta. *karuku* 'to be scorched'; Tu. *karṅka* 'state of being burnt'; cf. Ta. Ma. Ka. *kari* 'to be scorched'; Kui. *kāra* 'to be hot'; (see §**7.1**: 13, §**7.3**: 22).

53. *mrēgu, mrēwu* 'to plaster, anoint' (in some dictionaries as *mrẽgu*); Ta. *meẓuku* 'to smear, varnish'; Ma. *meẓukuka* id.; cf. Kui *mrāṇḍa* 'to plaster'; Br. *mir-* id.

54. *mrõgu* 'to sound (as bells etc.)'; Ka. *moẓ-agu* id.; Ta. *muẓ-anku* 'to roar, thunder' v.i.; Ma. *muẓaṅṅuka* id.; cf. Kuṛ. *murr-* v.i. 'to thunder'.

55. *trōcu* 'to push out'; also *trōyu*; Kui *trōpa* 'to press forward with fingers' (past *trōte*); Ta. *tura* 'to drive away, expel'; Ma. *turattuka* id.; cf. Tu. *tor-* 'to kick'.

56. *prōcu* 'to nourish, protect'; Ka. *poṟu* 'to support' (pp. *pottu*); Pa. *porip-/porit-* id.; Ta. Tu. Ma. *pōṟṟu* 'to protect'; Ma. *poṟukka* 'to sustain'; Br. *porr-* 'to hatch'.

9.3. K. V. Subbaiya (1909: fn. 3), E. H. Tuttle (1930: §§27, 56), L. V. Ramaswami Aiyar (1931–2: 448 ff.) and M. B. Emeneau (1945: §8) argued that in forms of this type, accent had shifted from the first syllable to the second resulting in the lengthening of the accented vowel and the loss of the unaccented one; prior to this development the vowel of the second syllable was assimilated in quality to that of the first. A. Master (1948: 342), while disagreeing with this, proposes syncope and aphaeresis with compensation, which he calls proenthesis. He fails, however, to give an explanation for lengthening in certain forms as against others and his reconstructions for Telugu certainly do not predict this differentiation.[20] Without resorting to the vague

[20] For instance, he formulates a sequence like *a . . . a* > *ā* preceding a single consonant, and *a* preceding a double consonant. Now, are the single and double consonants originally there, conditioning the length of the preceding vowel, or does the preceding vowel also determine the length of the following consonant? He gives **parati* > Te. *pratti* 'cotton', **paẓata* > Te. *prāta* 'old'; why not *prāti* and *pratta*

theory of stress-displacement, it seems possible to explain length in these forms in two ways; firstly, that it results from contraction of two vowels across certain consonants (normally of a liquid or spirant type). In these contractions, it is always the quality of the root-vowel that prevails. We can therefore set up sequences that produce length, as *a-a* > *ā*; *i/e-a* > *ē*; *u/o-a* > *ō*;[21] the intervening consonants were *r*, *ṟ*, (*l*, *ḷ*), *ẓ* and this was presumably extended to a few other stops later on in a restricted number of forms.[22] A close analogy to this can be found in the Modern Tamil developments of *nēkku* < *eṉakku*; *nōkku* < *uṉakku*;[23] Te. *hāmu* < *ahamu* 'egotism'; *hāṅkāramu* < *ahaṅkāramu* 'pride, vanity'. In these forms there is no question of accent bringing about this change. It is the contraction of two vowels into one without affecting the quality of the radical vowel. Similarly *krālu* < *kaẓ-al*; *krā̃gu* < *kar-aṅ g-*; *mrēgu* < *meẓ-agu*; *mrō̃gu* < *moẓ-aṅg-*; *trōcu* < *tor-ac-*; *prōcu* < *poṟ-ac-*; *wrāyu* < **war-ay-*, *mrō yu* < *mor-ay-*. Secondly, cases like *mringu* 'to swallow' (< **miẓ-ng*); *krungu* (< **kuṟ-ng-*) 'to sink down', *trokku* (< **toẓ-kk-*) 'to tread upon', etc. can be explained by mere metathesis.[24] In other words the vowel of the second syllable in the pre-metathetic condition was probably of a reduced grade which was ultimately dropped. The unnatural sequence of the medial consonants created by this change could be avoided in one of two ways: either by metathesis of the radical syllable, or by the loss of the base final liquid or spirant (see §§**7.1–3**).

9.4. Another way of explaining length in the above cases in Telugu is by considering the Telugu radical syllables as preserving the Proto-Dravidian long-grade bases with weakened suffixes, while others show short-grade bases with strong-grade suffixes. Even here, we explain consonant-clusters as the result of metathesis to avoid undesirable sequences. Therefore, *krā-lu* < **kāẓ-l-* (*-l* weak-grade of *-al*, *-il*, *-ul*),

respectively? As a matter of fact, the latter form is *prā̃ta* going back to *prā-nta*, which according to Master should proceed from **paẓanta*; then like **karandu* > Te. *krandu* (340), it could be also *pranta*. He probably assumes that the length of the consonant is accidental, while the length of the preceding vowel is conditioned by it; again **awanṟu* becomes Te. *wāṇḍu*/*wāḍu*.

21 There was no contrast in early South Dravidian between a radical *i e*, on the one hand, and *u o* on the other, when followed in the next syllable by [*-a* in derivation. This state of affairs was represented by high vowels in the southern area (Ta. Ma.) and by the higher mid-vowels in the northern area. I am indebted to my teacher, Hoenigswald, for this suggestion. See Burrow (1940: 296) [also Ch. 2 of this book.]

22 Te. *l* (< **l*, **ḷ*) is not involved in the formation of clusters at the beginning of words; it occurs only in Kui-Kuvi. All **r*, **ṟ*, **ẓ* become *r* in Te. in clusters of this type.

23 R. P. Sethu Pillai (1937–8: 9).

24 Wherever there is length in the radical syllable in cases of this sort, which is not shared by the sister languages, we have to assume the existence of an /a/ vowel in the second syllable which was probably not weakened in the medial position as /i/ or /u/; where there is no length of the radical vowel, it is an indication that in the older form /u/ or sometimes /i/ existed in the second syllable, which was eventually weakened and dropped, leading to metathesis in the radical phonemes. The form *wrīlu* is a difficult case, which does not fit into this formula, unless we explain it as deriving from **wīr-l-* by metathesis; so also *krī*-below (< **kẓī-* < **kīẓ-*). [My later work showed that this was not really a problem; where the suffix vowel is identical with the root vowel, they contract to produce a long vowel; thus *wrīlu* is from *wir-il* (see Ch. 10, Appendix).]

wrī-lu < **wīr-l-*, *wrā-l-* < **wāẓ-l-*, *wrā-yu* < **wār-y-*, *mrō -yu* < **mōr-y-*; *prā̃-ku* < **pār-nk-*, *krā̃-gu* < **kār-ng-*, *mrē -gu* < **mēẓ-w-*; *trō -cu* < **tōr-cu*, *mrō̃-gu* < **mōẓ-ng-*, *prō -cu* < **pōṟ-cu*. In view of what we have shown in §6, the relationship between PD **kāẓ-*, **wīr-*, **wāẓ*, **pār-*, **kār-*, etc. and *kaẓ-al*, *wir-il*, *waẓ-al*, *par-a*, and *kar-i*, etc. is quite evident, i.e. the shortening in these forms is a later development due to suffixation.[25] I am personally in favour of this assumption, in which case, however, forms like Te. *reṇḍu* 'two' vs. Ta. *iraṇṭu*,[26] Te. *rē yi* 'night' vs. Ta. *irā*, have to be explained on a different level, probably by means of the former assumption. Then, we have to consider this as a special development that took place in a restricted region in Proto-Dravidian, which subsequently became a part of the Telugu-Kui area. [I do not subscribe to this alternative now.] We have a scattering of this tendency of metathesis resulting in initial consonant-clusters in Baḍaga and Toda in the south and in Brahui in the north.[27]

10. To sum up our observations in the form of formulae, let us assume for Dravidian five series of bases and two series of strong and weak suffixes.

10.1. Bases (abbreviated as B):

B1: A short vowel + *y* or *w*, as *noy-*, *oy-*, and *niw-*, etc.
(In some languages *-y* alternates with *-s-* in the medial position; also with *-g-* in a few cases.[28] Historically, *-y* is a weakening of an older *c/s* in some cases; there is also

[25] Most of the early writers on this complicated question of Telugu historical linguistics proceeded on the assumption that Tamil most closely represented the Proto-Dravidian vowel grade, while Telugu changed it by shifting the accent. A number of examples can be shown to the effect that Telugu has preserved the long vowels, while Ta. shortened these by suffixation. Examples: Te. *wāḍu* 'to use, make use of', Ta. *vaẓ-anku* 'to be in use'; *vaẓ-akku* 'usage (as of a word)', Ma. *vaẓi* 'usage'; cf. Ta. Ma. *vaẓi*, Ka. *baẓi* 'a way, path'; Te. *wānu* 'to make, fashion (pots)'; Ka. *bān* id.; Ta. *vaṉ-ai* 'to form, shape', *maṉ-ai* 'to make, fashion'; Ma. *manayuka* id.; Pa. *vāñ-* 'to make pots'; Malto *bānde* 'the way of doing'. Similarly, there is no reason why we should not derive Ta. Ma. *mar-am* 'tree'; Ka. Tu. *mar-a*; Go. *maṛ-ā*, Pa. *mer-i*, etc. from PD **mār-am*, on the basis of Te. *mrā-nu* (< **mār-n-* < **mār-m-*); *-m* weakened *-am*; it is curious that the form in Gad. is *mār-en* which is the nearest of all to the Proto-Dravidian form. Toda *mēṇ* (< **mār-m-*; Emeneau).

[26] Ta. *iraṇṭu* vs. Te. *reṇḍu* is a difficult case. According to our formulation it should be *rē ṇḍu/rēḍu*. Either homonymy with *ṟē ḍu* 'king' precluded this development or the vowel [a] in the second syllable was a weaker allophone of the phoneme /a/ with a higher mid-position nearing the neutral vowel ə; then **iranḍu* > **erənḍ u* > *reṇḍu* by metathesis.

[27] Toda *mẓā* 'cubit', also *mẓā gei* (Pope, see Marshall 1873: 258); Ka. *moẓa*; Ta. *muẓam*, etc. Toda *mẓā* 'rain', Ta. *maẓai*, To. *prea* 'big' (Metz), Ta. *peru*, etc. For Baḍaga, the *LSI*, IV: 403–4 gives a number of forms with metathesised /ẓ/, *hẓā* 'ruin', *hẓegi* 'saying', *yẓeddu* 'rising', *gẓattu* 'neck', etc. Br. *princh-* 'to squeeze'; cf. Ta. *piẓi* id.; more forms occur with *t-*, *trukk-* 'to pluck', Te. *truñcu*; Br. *trujj-* 'to choke', Te. *tuṟuku* 'to cram', etc.

Toda and Baḍaga are very badly recorded in the sources mentioned. Emeneau, who had done considerable fieldwork on these languages during 1935–8, tells me (in a private communication) that these items are wrong and that there are no reliable cases of metathesis resulting in consonant-clusters in the initial position in these languages.

[28] Cf. Ka. *usir* 'to breathe', Ta. *uyir*; Te. *nog-ulu* 'to be distressed' (< **noy-ul*); *pag-ulu* 'to be broken' (< **pay-ul*), cf. Ka. *pasu* 'to divide' (v.s.v. *payp-/payt-* in the etymological vocabulary of Burrow and Bhattacharya 1953). There are many more cases for *-g-* < *-y-* but these will suffice here.

probably an original base-final *-y* in Dravidian as in *koy* 'to cut', etc. This weakening had taken place in Proto-Dravidian itself and has, therefore, a wider representation.)

B2: A short vowel + *l*, *ḷ*, *r*, *ṟ*, *ẓ*, *s* (< *c*-); *ṇ*, *m*, and *n*, as *kal-*, *kiẓ*, *mar-*, *kuṟ(u)-*, *muẓ-*, *mes-*, *waṇ-*, *kum-*, *cin-*.[29]

B3: A long vowel, as *pā-*, *pū-*, *wī-*, *ē-*; *krā*, *prā*, etc.

B4: A long vowel + *l*, *ḷ*, *r*, *ṟ*, *ẓ*, *c/s*, *ṇ*, *m*, and *ṇ*, as *pāḷ*, *nūṟ-*, *ēc-*, *wāṇ-*, etc.

B5: A short vowel, as *no-*, *po-*, *ma-*, *and kro-*, *mro-*, etc.[30]

Consonants preceding the radical vowels are insignificant in the determination of syllable-structure. Except for B5, all the remaining types occur either as free or bound forms. B5 occur only as bound forms and have, therefore, a limited distribution.

10.2. Suffixes (S), strong suffixes (Ss), weak suffixes (Sw):

Ss1: *-ku*, *-nku*, *-kku*, *-cu*, *-ñcu*, *-ccu*; *-tu*, *-ntu*, *-ttu*; *-pu*, *-mpu*, *-ppu*; (also their voiced correspondents, *-gu*, *-ngu*, etc.); these preceded by *a* or *u* (*i* precedes rarely).[31]

Ss2: *-l*, *-ḷ*, *-r*, *-ṟ*, *-ẓ*, *-y/-s* (<**-c-*), *-m*, and *-n*, preceded by *a*, *i*, or *u*.

Sw1: Ss1 without the preceding vowel.

Sw2: Sw2 without the preceding vowel.

We now plot the various types of formations we obtain by the combination of the above bases and suffixes.

10.3. Primary Formations. B1, B2, B3, and B4 can occur independently. B1: Ta. *oy* 'to give', *koy* 'to pluck'; B2: Ta. *cel* 'to go', Ka. *sal* id.; Ta. *eṉ* 'to say'; B3: Te. *pō* 'to go', Ta. *pū* 'to flower'; B4: Ta. *tōl*, Ka. *sōl* 'to be defeated'. Tamil preserves a very few forms of the type B5 as *o* 'to be put together', *no* 'to pain', etc., but this structural type was probably going out of use in Proto-Dravidian itself by the time the descendants separated. There are a number of forms belonging to B2 that cannot occur by themselves but underlie secondary formations, which will be described below.

10.4. Secondary Formations I

Class 1. B1 + Ss1: *oc* + *anku* > *os-angu*, Te. *os-ãgu* 'to give', cf. Ta. *oy-* 'to give'.

[29] Te. *kal-ãgu* 'to be disturbed'; Ta. *kiḷ(ḷ)* 'to pinch'; Te. *mar-ãgu* 'to be addicted'; Ta. *kuṟ-ai* 'to diminish'; Ka. *muẓ-unku* 'to sink'; Te. *mes-avu* 'to graze'; Ta. *vaṇ-anku* 'to bend'; Te. *kum-ulu* 'to burn with grief'; Te. *cin-uku* 'to drizzle'.

There are some stems with a short vowel + a voiceless plosive as *k*, *c*, *t*, *p*, but these are not involved in the processes of shortening or lengthening of the radical vowel-grade under discussion.

[30] In a considerable number of cases this type is not primary since it is formed by the composition of B1 + a suffix (see fn. 17), but until this is proved in the majority of such constructions, it is convenient to consider this as a primary type, i.e. a single morpheme type, which also facilitates description.

[31] In Ta. Ma. Ka. Tu. short vowels *a*, *i*, or *u*, or the diphthong *ai* are equivalent, in effect, to this class of suffixes; for instances, cf. Te. *paracu* 'to spread', Ta. *par-a*; Te. *nuṟ-ucu* 'to thrash', Ka. *nuṟ-i*; Te. *wānu* 'to make (pots)', Ta. *maṉ-ai*.

Class 2. B1 + Ss2: *uc-ir* > Ta. *uy-ir* 'to breathe', Te. *us-uru* 'breath'; Ka. *us-ir* 'to breathe'; Kuṛ. Malto *uj-* id.

Class 3. B2 + Ss1: *kal-anku* > Ta. *kal-anku*, Te. *kal-angu*, *kal-ãgu* 'to be disturbed, etc.'

Class 4. B2 + Ss2: *mal-ar* > Ka. *malar* 'to return'; Te. *mar-alu* id.

Class 5. B3 + Sw1: *wī-cu* > Te. *wī-cu* 'to blow (as wind)', cf. *wīwana* 'fanning'.

Class 6. B3 + Sw2: *pā-r* > Te. *prā̃-ku* 'to spread' (< **pār-nk-*); cf. Ta. *pā* 'expanse'; (PN 233); **pā-y* > Ta. *pā-y* 'to leap, run, spread (as water), etc.'; **pā-ṟ-* > Ta. Te. Ka. *pāṟu* 'to run'.

Class 7. B4 + Sw1: *īẓ-cu* > Te. *īḍ-cu* 'to drag'; cf. Ta. *iẓ-i*, Ka, *iẓ-*, *iẓ-i*.

10.5. Secondary Formations II. Only the final types occur in Telugu; the remaining ones belong to pre-Telugu.

(1) B1 + Sw1 > B3 + Sw1: *toy-ngu* > *tō -ngu*, Te. *tō̃gu* 'to bathe'.
B1 + Sw1 > B5 + Sw1: *poy-nku* > *bo-nku* 'to lie', Ta. *poy* id.

(2) B1 + Sw2 > B3 + Sw2: *noy-l* > *nōl*, Ta. *nōl/nōṉ* 'to endure, suffer', PD **noy-* 'to be pained'.

(3) B2 + Sw1 > B5 + Sw1: *por-ndu* > *po-ndu*, Te. *pondu* 'to obtain'; Ka. *pordu; kuṟ-ngu* > *kru-ngu*, Te. *kru-ngu* 'to go down, sink'; (Mdn. Te. *ku-ngu* id.).

(4) B4 + Ss1 > B2 + Ss1: *nūṟ-ucu* > *nuṟ-ucu*, Te. *nuṟ-ucu* 'to crush'; *tūṟ-umpu* > *tuṟ-umpu*, Te. *tuṟ-umu*, Ka. *tuṟubu* 'to stuff in'.

(5) B4 + Sw1 > B3 + Sw1: *pār-nku* > *prā-nku*, Te. *prā̃ku* 'to spread' (Mdn. Te. *pā-ku*).

(6) B4 + Ss2 > B2 + Ss2: *tār-al* > *tar-al*, Te. *tar-alu* 'to go, proceed'.

(7) B4 + Sw2 > B3 + Sw2: *kāẓ-l* > *kẓā-l*, Te. *krālu* 'to shake'; Ka. *kaẓ-al.*
Numbers (3), (5), and (7) are developments peculiar to Telugu only.

10.6. Secondary Formations III

(1) B3-Sw1 + Ss1 > B2 + Ss1: *ē -c(u)-angu* > *ec-angu* Te. *es-āgu*, 'to increase'; cf. Te. *ē -cu* 'to increase'; *ē -pu* 'excess' (root **ē*).

(2) B3-Sw1 + Ss2 > B2 + Ss2: *wī-c(u) + ir* > *wis-ir*, Te. *wis-uru* 'to fan'; Ta. *vic-iṟi* 'a fan'.[32]

(3) B3-Sw2 + Ss1 > B4 + Ss1 > B2 + Ss1: *tū-ṟ-ukku* > *tūṟ-ukku* > *tuṟ-ukku*, Te. *tuṟ-ugu* 'to stuff in'; *tūṟu* 'to enter, pierce'; *tūpu* 'an arrow' (root **tū-*).

(4) B3-Sw2 + Ss2 > B4 + Ss2 > B2 + Ss2: *kō -ṟ + al* > *kōṟ-al* > *koṟ-al*, Te. *koṟ-alu* 'to wish', *kōru* id.

[32] Note that Old Telugu *sīwiri* 'fan', metathesized from **wīs-iri*, preserves the original long vowel.

10.7. Secondary Formations IV

(1) B4-Ss1 > B2-Ss1 > B2- Sw1 > B5-Sw1:

(a) *nīḷ-ukku* > *niḷ-ukku* > *niḷ-ku* > *ni-kku* 'to stand erect';
cō r-ukku > *cor-ukku* > *cor-ku* > *co-kku* 'be intoxicated'.

(b) *mūẓ-unku* > *muẓ-ungu* > *muẓ-ngu* > *mẓu-ngu*: cf. Te. *bru-ngu* 'to sink'.

(c) *pōr-uñcu* > *por-uñcu* > *por-ñcu* > *po-ñcu*: Te. *po-ñcu* 'to waylay'; Kui, *pōr-* id.

(d) *āẓ-uttu* > *aẓ-uttu* > *aẓ-tu*/*-du* > *a-ddu*: Te. Ka. *addu* 'to dip'; Ta. *aẓ-uttu* id., *āẓ* 'to sink'.

Items (b) and (c) are peculiar to Telugu; (d) is common to Telugu and Kannaḍa only, not to Tamil, Malayāḷam.

10.8. If we analyse the above final types into distributional categories, we observe that before

-Ss1	-Sw1
only B1- B2 - occur	B3- B4- B5-
-Ss2	**-Sw2**
B1- B2-	B3-

FIGURE 1.1. Distribution of bases and formative suffixes (typological-comparative)

It is evident from Fig. 1.1. that Ss1 and Ss2 occur in complementary distribution to Sw1 and Sw2. So also B1 and B2 are in complementary distribution to B3, B4, and B5. We further notice that before strong suffixes, B1 and B2 have historically replaced B4, B3-Sw1, and B3-Sw2; similarly before weak suffixes, B3 has replaced B1 and B4; B5 has replaced B1, B2, and B2-Sw1. We conclude from this that Early South Dravidian had seven widely represented norms of stem-suffix composition at the time of the separation of its descendants (see § **10.4**) and all other older types had adjusted themselves to these patterns (see Secondary Formations II and III; §§ **10.4–6**). The changes that these types had undergone were all prehistoric to South Dravidian since they were completed by the pre-separation period itself, i.e. in Proto-Dravidian or Early South Dravidian. We have, however, a few occasional survivals of this stage alternating with the regularly affected forms, for instance Ta. *nīẓ-al* 'shade', beside *niẓ-al*; Ka. *biẓ-il*/*bīẓ-il* 'a pendent root of a banyan tree,' cf. Ta. *vīẓ* 'to fall'; these are relatively few. The type B5-Sw1 was probably in a formative stage before the individual separation of South Dravidian commenced but subsequently developed fully in Kannaḍa and Telugu. The formations peculiar to Telugu and Kui with initial consonant clusters (see §**10.5**; Secondary Formations II: 3, 5, and 7; §**10.6**; IV: b) had their origin either in a restricted area in the Proto-Dravidian itself (see §**9**), or else developed after the separation of Telugu-Kui from the main colony; in either case they are prehistoric features belonging to the pre-Telugu-Kui period.

10.9. In final analysis, we notice that, in Telugu, the forms of the strong suffix class are all trisyllabic (three short syllables) and the forms of the weak suffix class are all disyllabic (initial long syllable + a short syllable). Of the primary formations (i.e. monosyllabic) occurring in Tamil and Kannaḍa, Telugu has preserved a few but most of them were modified to suit the Telugu pattern of one of the two above. Consequently B1 forms like **key* 'to do', **koy* 'to cut', have become *cēyu*, *kōyu*, etc.; in B2 the final consonant is doubled with the addition of an enunciative vowel: Ta. *kiḷ* 'to pinch', Te. *gillu*; Ta. *taḷ* 'to thrash', Te. *tannu* 'to beat' (< **taṇṇu*), Ta. *cel* 'to suit,' Te. *cellu*; B2 and B4: most of the bases of these types have taken a Sw1, as *īḍ-cu* 'to drag' (< **īẓ*), *tāl-cu* 'to wear' (< **tāḷ-*); in other cases a final vowel is appended, *kūlu*, *sōlu*, *tūlu*, etc. There are, of course, a few survivals of the monosyllabic type in certain paradigms, as *kan-* 'to see,' *kon-* 'to take', *tin-* 'to eat', *an-* 'to say', *win-* 'to hear', and *man-* 'to live', the past stems of which before the personal suffixes in Old Telugu are *kaṇṭ-*, *koṇṭ-*, *tiṇṭ-*, *aṇṭ-*, *wiṇṭ-*, and *maṇṭ-*, respectively. There are also a few others with two short syllables as *paḍu* 'to fall', *iḍu* 'to put', etc.

11. It is clear from the foregoing description that more than 98% of Telugu verbs were secondary formations on Proto-Dravidian or Common Dravidian stems, and that two main structural types of stem-suffix composition prevailed at the earliest known period in Telugu, to which the historically derived patterns had adjusted themselves. Changes in the length of the base and suffix-vowels are among the other means that led to this adjustment, such as metathesis, elision of consonants, contraction of syllables, and addition of enunciative vowels. The further changes that these verbal bases have undergone in Modern Telugu is a different problem and is not part of the present paper.

Appendix I

Examples for the shortening of a radical long vowel with the addition of suffixes beginning with a [-V:

57. *kun-uku* 'to doze, nod with sleep' (originally 'to bend'); Ka. *kuni*, *kun-ungu* 'to bend, contract oneself': Ta. *kuṉi* 'to bend, stoop'; Ma. *kuniyuka* id.: Ta. *kūṉu* 'to be bent down'; Ka. *kūn* id.; Ma. *kūnuka* 'to stoop'; Ta. *kūn*, Ka. Ma. *kūn* 'a bend, etc'; (> Skt. lw. *kūṇ* 'to contract, shrink'; Pkt. *kūṇ-* id., see Burrow 1948: 374).

58. *giṟ-uku* 'to scribble; to erase'; Ka. *kiṟuku* 'to scratch'; Ta. *kiṟukku* 'to scribble'; Ma. *kiṟukku* 'to erase, strike out'; Pa. *kirp-/kirt-* id.: Te. *gīṟu* 'to scrape, scratch'; Ka. *kīṟu, gīṟu* id.; Tu. *gīruni* 'scrape (a wound)'; *kīruni* 'to scratch'; Ta. Ma. *kīṟu* id.; Kui, *gīra* 'a line, mark'; Pa. *gīr*.

59. *cib-uku* 'to smack, such'; also *cīku* id. (< **cīp-ukku* < **cīp-ukku*): Ka. Ta. Kuṛ. Malto *cīp* id. (see §**8.2**).

60. *nem-aku* 'to search, seek; to grope' (< **niw- akku* < **nīw-akku*): Ta. Ka. *nīvu* 'to rub softly, to pass the hand gently over'; see *nim-uru* (§**6**: 9). (For a similar association of meaning cf. Te. *taḍawu* 'to rub softly, grope, search'.)

61. *il-ugu* 'to perish', also *īlgu, nīlgu, nilugu* id. (< **nīḷ-ugu*); Ka. *niḷku, niluku* 'to stretch oneself upwards': Ta. Ma. Ka. *nīḷ* 'to extend, stretch oneself out, etc'. (Burrow and Bhattacharya 1953 give Pa. *īl-* 'to fall off', as connected with Te. *īlugu*; even in that case we have shortening; Gad. *īl-* id.).

62. *es-ãgu* 'to shine, increase, etc.', *esakamu* 'splendour' (*es-angu* < **ēc-angu*); Ka. *ese* 'to shine, become manifest', *esaka* 'splendour, beauty': Te. *ē-cu* 'to increase, shine'; *ē-pu* n. 'splendour, excess, etc.'; the ultimate base is obviously *ē-/ey-* (compare *wīcu*: *wisaru*, where *wī-* is the ultimate root; see §**6**: 8), Ta. *eyta* 'abundantly'; *ē* 'abundance'.

63. *kaḍ-ugu* 'to wash (as hands, utensils, etc.)', also *kaḍ-uwu* in Old Telugu (< **kaẓ-ugu/-uwu*); Ka. *kaccu, karcu, kaẓcu* id. (< **kaẓ-ucu*); Ta. *kaẓuvu*; Ma. *kaẓuku-ka*: Ta. *kāẓ-avan* 'a washerman'.

64. *tuṟ-ugu* 'to stuff, cram' (< **tūṟ-ugu/-uwu*); Ka. *tuṟuku* id., *tuṟugu* 'to be thronged, packed'; Ta. *tuṟu* 'to be thick, closed, to cram'; Ma. *tuṟu-ka* 'to be stuffed', *tuṟuttuka* 'to force in, stuff'; Pa. *tutt-* 'to be blocked up'; Kuṛ. *turd-* 'to pass through any narrow aperture'; Malto *turg-e* 'to bury the ashes of the dead': Te. Ka. *tūṟu* 'to enter, penetrate'; cf. Ma. *tūruka* 'to be filled up (as a well)'; Kuṛ. *tūr-* 'to pierce through soft matter'.

65. *tor-ãgu* 'to flow, gush, drip' (< **tōr-angu*); Ka, *suri* 'to flow, pour out'; Koḍ. *tori* 'to pour out'; Ta. *cori, curai* id.; Ma. *coriyu-ka, curakka* id.; Ko. *corv-, cord-* '(of milk) to stream forth'; Toda *twar-, twarθ-* '(of milk) to gather in the udder; to flow': Ka. *sōr* 'to trickle, flow, leak, etc.'; Tu. *sōruni, tōruni* 'to ooze, leak; Ta. *cōr* id.; *tōr-* 'to pour'; Kuvi, *tṛōkhali* 'to fall'; Pa. *cōr-* 'to strain off water from boiled rice'; *cōr-* 'to trickle'; Gad. *cōr-* 'to pour'.

66. *tol-ãgu* 'to step aside; to vanish, recede' (< **tōl-angu* < **cōl-angu*); Ka. *tolagu, tolangu* 'to go away, depart, etc'; Ta. *tolai* 'to end, expire; to be defeated, lost'; v.t. 'to remove, destroy'; Ma. *tula-yuka* 'to end': Ta. Ma. *tōl* 'to be defeated'; Ka. *sōl*, Tu. *sōl, tōl* id. (see Burrow 1947a: 141).

67. *nil-ugu* 'to stretch (one's limbs); to strut; to die' (< **nīḷ-ugu)*; Ka. *niḷku, niluku* id.: Ta. Ma. Ka. *nīḷ-* 'to grow long' (see App. I: 61).

68. *per-ugu* 'to grow, become big'; Ta. Ka. *peruku* id.; Go. *pirr-* 'to grow'; Kol. *perg-*;

Kuṛ. *pard-* 'to grow in number; to thrive'; Br. *pir-* 'to swell': Ta. Ma. Ka. Te *pēr-* (adj.), 'big' (before vowels), and *peru* (before consonants).

69. *mes-ãgu, mes-awu* 'to eat'; Ta. *micai* 'to eat a meal'; *micaivu* 'food': Te. *mēyu* 'to graze'; Ka. *mē-*, *mēyu*; Tu. *mēpini*; Ta. Ma. *mēy*; Go. *mēī-*; Pa. Kol. *mēy-*; Nk. *mīy-*.

70. *sor-ãgu* 'to languish, faint'; Ka. *soragu* id.: Ka. *sōr*, Ta. *cōr* 'to languish' (v.s.v. *cokku*, §**7.1**: 11).

71. *oḍ-ucu* 'to defeat; bring under control': Te. *ōḍu* 'to be defeated; to run away'.

72. *nan-ucu* 'to blossom, flower' (same as for *nan-ayu*, see §**6**: 6).

73. *nul-ucu* 'to twist' (<* *nūl-ucu*, v.s.v. *nul-iyu*, §**6**: 7).

74. *par-acu* 'to spread' v.t.; Ka. *pari*, *pare*; Tu. *paraḍuni*; Ta. *para*; Ma. *parakka*; Kui *prahpa* 'to spread out earth, grain'; Kuvi (F) *press-* id.; GoM. *parh-* id.: Te. *prā̃ku* (< **para-ṅku*); v. s.v. *prā̃ku* §**9.2**: 51.

75. *nul-upu* 'to twist' (< **nūl-uppu*); v.s.v. *nuliyu* §**6**: 7.

76. *par-apu* 'to spread', v.s.v. *paracu* 74 above.

77. *paṟ-apu* 'to chase', caus. v. of *paṟ-acu* v.s.v. §**6**: 3.

78. *ciṟ-umu* 'to sprinkle, spill' (< **cāṟ-umu/umbu*): Ka. *sīṟu* 'to be sprinkled'; To. Baḍaga *sīr* 'spray'; Kui *sīrpa* 'to shake out, sprinkle'; cf. Go. (dial.) *jīriā* 'a fountain'. Is *cāṟu* from **ciw-iṟu*? Cf. Ta. *ciwiṟi* 'a kind of syringe, squirt'.

79. *tuṟ-umu* 'to stuff, cram' (< **tūṟ-umbu*); Ka. *tuṟubu* id.; v.s.v. *tuṟ-ugu*, 64.

80. *nul-umu* 'to twist', v.s.v. *nul-iyu*, §**6**: 7.

81. *ner-umu* 'to rub; to move on posteriors', (< **nēr-umbu*); Ma. *niraṅṅu* 'to creep, crawl; to drag along the ground': Kui, *nēra* 'to rub, scrape' Kuṛ. *nīṟ-* id.

82. *ar-ayu* 'to see, examine' (<**ār-āy-*): Ta. Ma. Ka. *ārāy* id. (see §5).

83. *col-ayu* 'to faint, swoon': Te. *sōlu* id.; v.s.v. §**8.1**: 30.

84. *uṟ-iyu* 'to ooze, leak': Te. *ūṟu* 'to ooze, well up'; v.s.v. *ubbu* §**7.1**: 17.

85. *er-iyu* 'to burn' v.i. (< **ēr-iyu*); Ta. *eri* 'to flame'; Ma. *eriyuka* 'to burn': Te *ērcu* v.t. 'to burn' (tr. of *eriyu*); Kui *ērpa* 'to kindle'; Go. *ērit-* 'to hurt'; Pa. *erip-/-it-* 'to burn the mouth'.

86. *jaḍ-iyu* 'to brandish, throw': Ma. *cāṭu-ka* 'to throw'.

87. *es-aru* 'to increase', also *ēsaru* (< **ē c-ar-*): Te. *ēcu* 'to increase'; v.s.v. *esãgu*, 62.

88. *kam-aṟu* 'to be signed, burnt' (< **klāw-aṟu*); Ka. *kamaru* id.; Ta. *kamaṟu* 'to be excessively heated': Ka. Tu. *kāvu* 'heat, glow'.

89. *kam-alu*, v.s.v. *kam-aṟu*, 88.

90. *waḍ-alu* 'to wither (as a flower, etc.)' (< **wāḍ-al-*); Ka. *baḍa* 'weakness'; Tu. *baḍa* 'lean, thin': Te. *wāḍu* 'to wither'; Ka. *bāḍu*; Ta. Ma. *vāṭu*; Kui *vāra* 'to be tired'.

Appendix II

TABLE 1.1. *Etymologies cited with alternations in vowel-length and their reconstructions*

[This table replaces the one in Appendix ii of the original paper. I have added *DEDR* entries in column 1 and modified the reconstructions in some cases in column 2; columns 3 and 5 remain the same. Column 4 has the new serial numbers of etymologies cited in the paper. Where two entries occur in column 1, they represent differences between my original groupings of etyma and what *DEDR* considers appropriate. I questioned the entries that I consider doubtful.]

DEDR	PSD/PD reconstruction	OTe. base	No. in article	Mdn. Te. forms
285	*āẓ/*aẓ-V-	addu	15	addu
377	*ārāy (< *ār-āc-)	ar-ayu	82	—
		ār-ayu	§5	—
548	*īḷ/*iḷ-V-	il-ugu	61	—
418	*ciy-/*cī-	i-ccu, īyu	35	icc-, iyy-~iww-
645	*uy-(<*uc-)	ū-rcu	26	—
761	*ūṯ-/*uṯ-V-	uṟ-iyu	84	uriyu
666	*ūr-/*ur-V-	ubbu	17	ubbu
578, 636	*ū-y- (*uw-iy-)	ūyu, umiyu	31	ūs-/ūy-
811	*ēr/*er-V-	er-iyu	85	ēr-uc- (tr. only)
778, 870	*ē-c-/*ec-V-	esā-gu	62	—
777, 870	*ē-c-/*ec-V-	es-aru	87	—
805	*ey (< *ec-)	ēyu	37	ēs-/ēy-~eyy-
946, 1041	*ōṭ-/*oṭ-V-	oḍ-ucu	71	—
1278	*kā-r-/*kar-V-	kaggu	13	kaggu
1278	*kā-r-/*kar-V-	ka-ngu	22	—
1369	*kāẓ-/*kaẓ-V-	kaḍ-ugu	63	kaḍugu
1230	*kā-w-/*kaw-V-	kam-aṟu	88	kamuru
1230, 1458	*kā-w-/*kaw-V-	kam-alu	89	kamulu
1902, ?1927	*kū-n-/*kun-V-	kun-uku	57	kunuku, n.
1907, 1636	*kū-l (< *kuy-il-/*kuc-il)	kū-lu	27	kūlu
2119	*koy	kōyu	40	kōs-/kōy-~koyy-
2232	*kō-r-/-ṯ- (< *koy-Vr-/Vṯ- < *koc-Vr-/-Vṯ-)	kō-ru	29	kosaru, kōru-kon- refl.
1278, 1292	*kā-r-/*kar-V-	krā̃-gu	52	—
1349	*kāẓ-/*kaẓ-V-	krā-lu	46	—
1623	*kī-ṯ-/*kiṯ-V-	giṟ-uku	58	gīku, gīru
1623	*kī-ṯ-/*kiṯ-V-	giṟ-upu	4	girupu, gilupu
2621	*cīp-/*cip-V-	cib-uku	32, 59	—
2640	*cīṯ-/*ciṯ-V-	ci-ṟ-umu	78	—
2621	*cīp-/*cip-V-	cī-ku	32	cīku
2812	*cēr-/*cer-V-	ce-ndu	24	cendu
2019	*kēṯ-/*keṯ-V-	cer-ugu	2	cerugu
1957	*key-	cēyu	39	cēs-/cēy-~ceyy-
2853	*cōr-/*cor-V- (*coy-Vr)	co-kku	11	sokku

DEDR	PSD/PD reconstruction	OTe. base	No. in article	Mdn. Te. forms
2884, ?3558	*cō-l-/*col-V- (*coy-Vl)	col-ayu	83	solayu
2297	*cāṭ-/*caṭ-V-	jaḍ-iyu	86	jaḍus-/daḍus-
3178	*tāẓ-/*taẓ-V-	ta-ggu	14	taggu
2460	*tār- (< *cār-)	tar-alu	10	tar(u)lu
3407	*tiw-iy-	tīy-/tiw-iy-	34	tīs-/tīy-~tiyy-
3367	*tūṯ-/*tuṯ-V-	tuṟ-ugu	64	dūru
3367	*tūṯ-/*tuṯ-V-	tuṟ-umu	79	turumu
3376	*tuy-nk- < *cuy-nk-	tū̃-gu	41	tūgu
3376	*tuy-il < *cuy-il	tū-lu	28	tūlu
2883	*tōr-/*tor-V- (< *cō-r-)	tor-āgu	65	—
3519, 3558	*tōl-/*tol-V- (?< *cōl)	tol-āgu	66	tolugu
3555	*tōy-nk-	tō̃-gu	42	—
3340	*tōr-/*tor-V-	trō-cu	55	tōs-/tōy-~toyy-
689	*ūẓ-/*uẓ-V-	du-wwu	21	duwwu
3631, ?2918	*nān-/*nan-V-	nan-ayu	6	—
3662, 3692	*nīḷ/*niḷ-V- (< *niw-uḷ)	ni-kku	12	nikku
3691	*nīw-/*niw-V	niw-uru/ nim-uru	9	nimuru
548, 3662	*(n)īḷ-/*(n)iḷ-V-	nīl-ugu/nil-	61	nīl-ugu
3728	*nū-ṯ-/*nuṯ-V	nuṟ-umu	5	nurumu
3726	*nūl-/*nul-V-	nul-iyu	7	—
3726, ?3717	*nūl/*nul-V-, *nuḷ-	nul-ucu	73	nuluc-
3726, ?3717	*nūl/*nul-V-, *nuḷ-	nul-upu	75	nulupu
3726, ?3717	*nūl/*nul-V-, *nuḷ-	nul-umu	80	nulumu
?3691	*nīw-/*niw-V-	nem-aku	60	nemaku (dial.)
3749, ?2927	*nēr-/*ner-V-	ner-umu	81	nerumu
3745	*ney- (< *nec-)	nēyu	38	nēs-/nēy~neyy-
3972	*pār-/*par-V-	pa-mbu	25	—
3949	*pār-/*par-V-	par-acu	74	paruc-
3949	*pār-/*par-V-	par-apu	76	parupu
4020	*pāṯ-/*paṯ-V-	paṟ-acu	3	pāru
3887	*pāḷ-, *pāṇ-/*paḷ-V, *paṇ-V-	pal-uku	1	paluku
4171, 4212	*piy-nkk-	pī̃-ku	43	pīku
4129, ?4171	*piy-ul, *pig-ul	pī-lu	33	pīlu, pigulu
4411	*pē-/*per-V-	per-ugu	68	perugu
4596	*pōr-/*por-V-ncc-	po-ncu	23	poncu
3949	*pār-/*para-V-	prā̃-ku	51	pāku
4283	*pōr-/*por-V-	prō-cu	56	—
5430	*wīẓ-*wiẓ-V-nt-	bi-ddu	16	—
4459	*poy-nkk- (< *poc-)	bo-nku	§17	bonku
5372	*wāẓ-/*waẓ-V-	bra-d-uku	19	batuku
4975	*mūẓ-/*muẓ-V-	bru-ngu	20	—
4915	*mūy- (*muc-)	mūyu	36	mūs-/mūy-~muyy-

DEDR	PSD/PD reconstruction	OTe. base	No. in article	Mdn. Te. forms
5093	*mēy	mēyu	69	mēs-/mēy-~meyy
5082	*mēẓ-/*meẓ-V-	mrē-gu	53	—
4990, 5123	*mōẓ-/*noẓ-unk(k)-	mro-kku, mroggu	18	mokku, moggu
4989	*mūẓ-/*muẓ-ank-	mrō̃-gu	54	mōgu
4973	*mūr-/*mur-V-	mrō-yu	50	—
5222	*wāṭ-/*waṭ-V-	waḍ-alu	90	waḍulu
5450	*wī-c-/*wic-V-	wis-aru	8	wisuru
5448	*wiy-nk-/-nkk-	wī̃-gu	45	(wirra) wīgu
5517	*wē-/*wey- (< *wec-), *wey-nk-	wẽ̄-gu	44	wēgu
5263	*war-ay	wrā-yu	49	rās-/rāy-
5293, ?5369	*waẓ-al	wrā-lu	47	wālu
5411	*wir-il	wrī-lu	48	—
2853, ?2687	*cōr-/*cor-V-	sorā-gu	70	sorugu
2884	*cō-l-/*coy-al	sō-lu	30	sōlu

Postscript

P 1. This was my first paper to be published in a professional journal. It has been the most frequently cited one in subsequent Dravidian studies. *A Dravidian Etymological Dictionary* (1961) by Burrow and Emeneau came much later. Cognates from the dictionaries of different Dravidian languages were collected by me for six years (in India) for my doctoral dissertation *Telugu Verbal Bases: A Comparative and Descriptive Study* which was completed in 1956 at the University of California, Berkeley, under the supervision of M. B. Emeneau. It was published (with two additional chapters) also in the same year as the *DED* (Krishnamurti 1961). Therefore, the etymologies given in this paper may not agree entirely with the groupings of *DED* (1961) or *DEDR* (1984). However, the rules need not be revised because of minor differences in a few specific cases.

P 2. Although this paper deals comparatively with verbal bases, the rules framed here have a wide-ranging application in other grammatical categories also and in different languages (§1). The conclusions made in this paper have been covered in my *TVB* (§§1.288–300). Stated in precise terms, the rules are:

Rule 1. (C)$\bar{V}$C→(C)VC-/#___+V(Ø/C/CC/CCCV) [Proto-Dravidian]. A long vowel in a root syllable becomes a short vowel when followed by a derivative (or formative) suffix beginning with a vowel. In Proto-Dravidian (C)$\bar{V}_1$C and (C) V_1C contrast when no vowel derivative follows. But only (C)V_1C is found in the environment ___+V_2. Therefore, the above rule belongs to Proto-Dravidian through internal reconstruction. The form with a long vowel is the older one which is shortened when followed by a formative -V, which may be optionally followed by extended suffixes or a zero. Evidence of the operation of this rule is seen in almost all the Dravidian languages. Since I was working on a comparative study of Telugu verbal bases, I showed examples from my data (§§**6–10**, Appendices I, II).

Rule 2. $V_2 > Ø / (C)V_1C_1$___$+C_2C_3(u)$. [V_2 = *u* or *i*; C_1 = a liquid or resonant: *r, l, ẓ*; C_2 = a homorganic nasal (N), when C_3 = an obstruent (P), or C_2C_3 = geminate obstruents (PP) obstruents]

The derivative vowel, *i* or *u*, after the change according to Rule 1, may be lost later before extended suffixes, viz. -NP(P)/-P(P). The lost vowel is attested in some of the languages or its prior occurrence is inferred from the fact that the underlying root had a long vowel. This development (loss of the medial vowel) represents an isogloss which covers the languages of South Dravidian I (other than Tamil and Malayāḷam, i.e. Kannaḍa, Tuḷu, etc., some members of South-Dravidian II or South-Central Dravidian (Telugu, Gondi, etc.), and of Central Dravidian (Parji, Kolami, etc.). A consequence of this was to change trisyllabic bases to disyllabic, (a) through regressive assimilation in some languages of South Dravidian I and II (Kannaḍa, Tuḷu, Telugu), e.g. Te. *taggu*, Ka. *taggu, targu, taẓgu* (< **taẓ-ug-* < **taẓ-u-ng-*) 'to become low', Ta. Ma. *tāẓ* 'to be lowered'; or (b) through metathesis (South-Central Dravidian: Telugu, Kui, Kuvi, etc.), e.g. Te. *brungu* 'to sink', Kuvi *mrūkh-*; Ka. *muẓungu*, Tu. *murk-uni*, Ta. *mūẓ, mūẓku*, Pa. *būṛ* 'to sink' (§§**7.1–2**); and (c) through loss of the root-final resonant and retention of the suffixal nasal + obstruent cluster, e.g. *ce-ndu* 'to belong' (< **cer-nd-* < **cer-u-nd-* < **cēr-u-nt-*). This last one is confined to Telugu (see §**7.3**) only.

Rule 3. $(C)V_1S\text{-}V_2\text{-} > (C)\bar{V}_1\text{-}/\#$___$+L/+NP, +PP$. [$V_1$ = any short vowel /i e a o u/; S = any semivowel /y w/, or a semivowel-like consonant, i.e. a laryngeal /H/ or an intervocalic /g/ which was phonetically [ɣ]; V_2 = *a, i, u*; L = a semivowel, liquid or resonant: *y, w, r, ṟ, l, ẓ*; N = nasal, P = obstruent].

For example Te. *ūr-cu* < **uy-i-r-cc-*; Te. *tū̃-gu* < **tuy-ng-* 'to doze' (see §§**8.0–2, 6**). The change involved is compensatory lengthening of the root vowel converting disyllabic and trisyllabic bases into monosyllabic and disyllabic, respectively. In Telugu, PD *V*y* and *V̄*y* always give V̄*y* (where V = [–low]; in Modern Telugu V̄*y* ~ V*yy*) through length neutralization: PD **koy* 'to cut': **mēy* 'to graze' > Te. *kōyu, mēyu* (§**8.4**; also see Subrahmanyam 1970a).

Rule 4. $(C_1)V_1C_2\text{-}V_2\text{-}L/\text{-}CC\text{-} > (C_1)C_2\bar{V}_1\text{-}L\text{-}/\text{-}CC\text{-}$. [$V_2$ = -*a* and C_2 = *r, ṟ*, or *ẓ*; L = semivowel, liquid, or resonant, CC = NP or PP].

Metathesis with vowel contraction takes place in South-Central Dravidian languages, e.g. Te. *wrā-lu* (< **waẓ-a-l*) 'hang loose', *krā̃gu* (< **kar-a-ng-*) 'be burnt' (§**9**). Adequate examples with comparative data are given for all the above rules.

Finally, I constructed a typological model with five types of bases (B1 to B5) and two series of suffixes (S), strong (Ss1, Ss2) and weak (Sw1, Sw2). In terms of the patterns generated by combining the bases with the suffixes, I showed how different historical changes took place to yield the final types in so far as the Telugu data were concerned (§§**10.1–8**). I described all these changes briefly in *TVB* (§§1.121–59, 1.173–85, 1.288–90). More than anything, this paper helped me to gain insights into the structure of roots and formative suffixes in Proto-Dravidian. I was able to formulate clearly the principles underlying the structure of roots and derivative suffixes (phonotactic rules) in Proto-Dravidian in *TVB* for the first time (§4.3; pp. 237–8). These observations have since become standard knowledge about Dravidian.

P 3. Rule 1 which belongs to the morphophonemics of Proto-Dravidian has been widely discussed. Another rule which was mentioned in *TVB* (§1.91) but elaborated by Emeneau (1970a: 101–3) reads:

Rule 5. (C)VPP → (C)VP-/#___+V. When a vowel derivative follows, a root which ends in a double consonant changes it into a single consonant. In terms of syllable structure, like Rule 1, a heavy syllable falls together with a light syllable when a derivative/formative vowel is added across the etymological boundary. Rules 1 and 5, which are complementary morphophonemic rules within Proto-Dravidian, can be collapsed as:

Rule 6. $(C)\bar{V}_1C$/ $(C)V_1CC \rightarrow (C)V_1C$/#___$+V_2$. Prosodically, $\bar{V}_1$ and V_1C have the same weight which became V_1 when another syllable was added, e.g. **cupp+ar* > **cuw-ar* 'salt'. The only problem with Rule 5 (as I explained in *TVB* §1.91), is the difficulty of getting evidence of a contrast between P and PP when they form the end of roots (nominal or verbal). Any root with a final obstruent doubles it, if it is also a free form (word), followed by an enunciative *-u*, e.g. **kaṭ-* 'to build' is represented as *kaṭṭu* in the four literary languages. When this is followed by a formative suffix vowel it is always **kaṭ*-V. Geminates which arise from assimilation (see Rule 2 above) are not weakened when followed by a formative vowel.

P 4. Many scholars have discussed these Proto-Dravidian morphophonemic rules (Zvelebil 1967, 1970b, Emeneau 1970a, Sambasiva Rao 1973, 1977, Krishnamurti 1961, 1976a, Subrahmanyam 1975, 1977c, Gopinathan Nair 1979, among others). Zvelebil (1967), while calling Rules 1 and 5 Krishnamurti's and Emeneau's Rules added a third one, Zvelebil's Rule, viz.

Rule 7. $(C)\bar{V}C$- ~ (C)VCC-. This is not a derivational rule like the others. I have discussed the status of this in another paper (see Ch. 16 of this book). Emeneau (1970b: 28–31) while elaborating on Rule 1 claimed that it occurred mainly in the case of verbs but was also found in certain nouns, numerals, and adjectives. Sambasiva Rao (1973) claimed that the reduction of syllable length in Rule 6 and the alternation in Rule 7 operate only when the basic and derived forms belong to the same grammatical category (verbs, nouns, etc.). If, by such an addition, verbs are derived from nouns or nouns are derived from verbs, the expected shortening of the syllable does not occur (Sambasiva Rao 1973: 222–3). The so-called Zvelebil's Rule should not have been combined with the other two, because it reflects a development mainly in South Dravidian in which PD *(C)V̄CC- ([CC = PP] preserved in Tamil and Malayāḷam) merged with (C)V̄C- (in the other languages) thereby establishing a complementary pattern with (C)VCC-, e.g. Te. *pāḍu* 'sing', *pāṭa* 'song', *paṭṭu* 'silk': Ta. Ma. *pāṭu* 'sing': *pāṭṭu* 'song', *paṭṭu* 'silk'. Sambasiva Rao (1973: 228) takes forms of this kind as an exception to Zvelebil's Rule because, here, a noun is derived from a verb! In my review (1976a: 146–8) of Zvelebil (1970b), I have shown why the above alternation cannot be considered a Proto-Dravidian rule:

> Therefore, the alternation proposed by Zvelebil is limited only to PD root morphemes, illustrated by such cases as Ta. *cūṟu/cuṟṟu* 'to revolve' (*DED* 2238), Ta. *mēṭu/meṭṭu* 'mound' (*DED* 4151), but in such cases only one type is widely distributed in the family as **cuṯṯ-* and **meṭṭ-* making the other type idiosyncratic to one or two languages. This makes it doubtful if we can reconstruct the alternation (C)V̄C-~(C)VCC- to PD at all. If enough evidence could be shown from different languages supporting *-g-*, *-ḍ-*, *-s-*, *(-ṟ-)*, *-d-*, *-w-* after long vowels alternating with *-kk-*, *-ṭṭ-*, *-cc-*, *(ṯṯ-)*, *-tt-*, *-pp-* after short vowels respectively in etymologically related primary root morphemes, one could set up Zvelebil's formula as a morpheme structure rule in PD. What Zvelebil has noticed is the condition in various languages after the operation of the rule PP→P/(C)V̄___#, which eliminated contrast between (C)V̄PP and (C)VPP as illustrated by me for Telugu. (Krishnamurti 1976a: 147–8)

Subrahmanyam (1975, 1977c) questioned the assumptions of Sambasiva Rao (1977) and a controversy raged between them. Their discussions are summarized in Gopinathan Nair (1979). Sambasiva Rao showed several examples of the rules not applying to nouns derived from verbs (235–40), e.g. *kār* 'be pungent': *kār-am* 'pungency' (236; only Tamil has the verb form with a long vowel [*DEDR* 1466], which could be even a back formation from the noun). He could not show clear cases of verbs derived from nouns followed by derivative vowels. In this paper I have shown clearly that prosodic criteria in syllable patterning explain the various changes illustrated, and therefore the rules are clearly phonological and not conditioned by grammatical criteria. The so-called derivative vowels involved in Rules 1 and 5 belong to a deeper chronological layer (i.e. Proto-Dravidian itself) and do not carry any discernible semantic content. These vowels, viz. *a, i, u*, were inserted presumably to avoid unnatural phonological sequences (and to preserve the identity of the root) when verb roots with long syllables were followed by tense-voice suffixes of the shape L, NP, PP, NPP, e.g. **mūẓ-nk-/mūẓ-nkk-* 'to sink' (v.i and v.t) > **muẓ-u-nk-*, **muẓ-u-nkk-* [*DEDR* 4993]. They are like epenthetic vowels, which functioned as phonological facilitators and not true derivational morphs. Derivative suffixes like *-am* in *kār-am* 'pungency' or *-ai* in *kaṭṭ-ai* 'bund' are synchronic noun formatives in the languages of South Dravidian and do not represent the same chronological layer of Proto-Dravidian. A counter example to Sambasiva Rao's claim is Ta. *kān* 'jungle', *kān-am* 'woodland', *kān-al* 'forest, grove' [*DEDR* 1418]; why is there no vowel-shortening here, although a noun is derived from another noun? The reason is that synchronic noun-forming morphs (which are added to existing free forms to derive other free forms) behave differently from primary derivatives of Proto-Dravidian, e.g. Te. *kōru* 'to wish': *kōr-ika* 'a wish' (*-ika* < **-ikkai*), Ta. *kūṭu*, Te. Ka. *kūḍu* v.i. 'to join': Ta. *kūṭ-al*, Ka. *kūḍ-al* 'confluence of two rivers', Te. *kūḍ-al-i* 'junction' [*DEDR* 1882]. Subrahmanyam advances the following arguments (1975, 1977c) against Sambasiva Rao's hypothesis: (a) The so-called Zvelebil's Rule cannot be clubbed with the other two, which are clearly derivational. (b) In many cases Proto-Dravidian has the same base as a noun, verb, or adjective, e.g. **pōr* 'to fight', n. 'a fight': **por-u* 'to fight' [*DEDR* 4540], **wittu* 'to sow', n. 'seed': **wit-ay* v. 'to sow', n. 'seed' [5401]. In some cases roots are identified only on structural and etymological grounds, e.g. **kākk-ay* n. 'crow', **yān-ay* 'elephant'. Then, how does one decide whether the short vowel forms **por-u* 'to fight', and **wit-ay* 'to sow' are derived from the verb stems and not the noun stems? Rao's contention that since the root syllable is reduced in length, the original form must be a verb is clearly circular. On semantic grounds the nouns seem to be more basic in the above cases. (c) Rao's verbs derived from original nouns are doubtful cases and Subrahmanyam has given reasons why they are so (1977c: 230–2). (d) Subrahmanyam says that the rule governing length-reduction works widely in verbs, numerals, and adjectives, but not in nouns (1975: 4–6). The disyllabic nouns that are derived from verbs are never affected by this process, while trisyllabic nouns like the following *are* affected by it: Ta. *kaḷa-avu* 'theft' (against *kaḷḷ-am* 'theft', *DED* 1156)' (1975: 11). (e) He further suggests that if Rao's hypothesis was correct it should also operate when inflectional suffixes followed the roots since the form class did not change in the case of inflection (1975: 12–13). This is not maintainable, because derivational processes and inflectional processes behave differently in their phonological effect on the root to which they are affixed.

Neither of these scholars looked at whether synchronically relevant noun formatives in the southern literary languages such as *-ay*, *-am*, *-al*, *-i* were the ones that caused these exceptions. In the final analysis, Sambasiva Rao has not established anything new. Rules 1 and 5 are purely phonological in terms of maintaining equal syllable weight within each member of the same form class; the vowels *-a*, *-i*, *-u* are added to heavy-syllabled roots as stem-formatives at a distant past within Proto-Dravidian. Note that the short vowel which is added acts as a stem-formative before consonantal suffixes within the same form class, e.g. *īr-* 'two' (before a vowel), *ir-u* (before a consonant), *ciṟ* [V ~ *ciṟ-u* [C adj. 'small'. The change is purely phonological within the same form class. The question of change of the grammatical category with the addition of a such formatives does not arise, unlike in the case of suffixes which are clearly marked as derivational morphemes (Sanskrit *krit* and *taddhita* type) within a synchronic framework. The former suffixes do not affect the syllable quantity of the root. Note that denominal suffixes (those that are added to verbs to derive nouns) like *-am*, *-ay*, *-al*, *-i*, etc. are added to free forms of bases, e.g. Ta. *tappu* (< **tap-*) 'to err': *tapp-al* 'fault', *tapp-aṟ-ai* 'lie', *tapp-itam* 'blunder', but not in *taw-a-ṟu* 'to slip'. The contrastive *-a-ṟu* here is not a synchronic deverbal suffix

[*DEDR* 3071]; similarly, *-am* and *-a-wu* are not to be treated as the same type of derivative suffixes in *kaḻḻ-am* (*-am* synchronically productive, more recent) and *kaḷ-a-wu* (*-a-wu* comparatively identifiable, much older). Another good case showing the derivation of a verb (and also a noun) with a shortened syllable from an older noun is provided by **kēḷ* n. 'relations, kindred': **keḷ-ay* v. 'to multiply', n. 'kindred'. Ta. *kēḷ* n., *kiḷ-ai* v. and n. [*DEDR* 208].

2

Alternations *i/e* and *u/o* in South Dravidian

1. With the help of the work so far done in comparative Dravidian studies, it is possible to reconstruct the following phonemes for Proto-Dravidian:[1]

Consonants

p	t	ṯ	ṭ	c	k
m	n		ṇ	ñ	
		l	ḷ		
		r	ẓ		
w				y	

Vowels[2]

i		u
e		o
	a	

Since all short vowels contrast with long vowels, we set up a phoneme of length, marked /¯/. All consonants except those of the alveolar and the retroflex series occur initially, and every consonant except **ñ* occurs finally in a word. A non-morphemic (the so-called enunciative) /u/ occurs regularly after a final stop and optionally after a final sonorant (any consonant that is not a stop).

1.1. The Proto-Dravidian root morphemes are all monosyllables, open or closed, of the following types: (C)V̆, (C)V̄; (C)V̆C, (C)V̄C. Forms representing all these types

This paper represents a small part of the research done during the year 1955–6 at the University of California, Berkeley, under a fellowship from the Rockefeller Foundation. The paper was originally presented at a Seminar in Historical Linguistics in the fall of 1955, and has since been improved. I am indebted to M. B. Emeneau for his suggestions and comments, and for his kindness in placing his personal library on Dravidian at my disposal. I am also grateful to William Jacobsen for a number of useful comments during the preparation of this paper in its original form.

[1] [-ṟ-] in all the South Dravidian languages is a reflex of PD **ṯ* in intervocalic position. A voiced alveolar trill originally, it subsequently fell together with the alveolar flap *r* in all the South Dravidian languages except Toda, where *r* and *ṟ* still contrast (information from Emeneau). *ẓ* is a voiced retroflex spirant in Old Tamil (also in some dialects of Modern Tamil), Old Malayāḷam, Old Kannaḍa, and also probably in Old Telugu (inscriptional). A tilde in Telugu is the symbol used here for the traditional *ardhānusvāra*, which, in classical Telugu, was phonemically zero after long vowels, and after short vowels a nasal phone homorganic with the following stop and freely alternating with zero.

[2] The diphthongs *ai̯* and *au̯* are not treated as unit phonemes here, since they can be structurally interpreted as **ay* and **aw* in Proto-Dravidian. **y* and **w* pattern with the other sonorants, such as *n*, *l*, *r*. For instance, the Common Dravidian word for 'hand', written *kai̯* in the literary languages, can be phonemicized for Proto-Dravidian as **kay*, patterning with the other CVC bases, e.g. **koy* 'to cut, reap', **cal* 'to go'.

occur either free, or bound to a sequence of derivative suffixes, e.g. **kal* 'stone', **kalanku* 'to be disturbed (as water)'. A derivative suffix is (a) one of the vowels *i, a, u* (often short, rarely long); (b) one of the following consonants or consonant groups: *p, mp, pp; t, nt, tt; ṯ, nṯ, ṯṯ; ṭ, ṇṭ, ṭṭ; c, ñc, cc; k, nk, kk; m, n, ṇ; ḷ, r; ẓ; y, w*; or (c) more frequently, a combination of (a) and (b) in the order V + C or V + CC.

1.2. In disyllabic and trisyllabic forms of $(C_1)V_1C_2$-V_2 or its extended types[3] in Proto-Dravidian, the etymological boundary[4] occurs between C_2 and V_2; whatever precedes this is the root element and whatever follows is a part of the derivative suffix. V_1 stands for any one of the five short vowel phonemes, V_2 for any one of the phonemes *i, a,* or *u*. C_2 can be any Proto-Dravidian consonant except **ñ*.

2. In contrast to Proto-Dravidian, the situation in the older stages of the literary languages of South Dravidian is as follows.

When V_2 (i.e. the derivative vowel) is **i* or **u* or zero, all four languages (Tamil, Malayāḷam, Telugu, and Kannaḍa) preserve the Proto-Dravidian **i*, **e*, **u*, **o* in the position of V_1 (i.e. the radical vowel); but when V_2 is an **a*-vowel,[5] Ta. and Ma. show *i* and *u* (but not *e* and *o*), and Te. and Ka. show *e* and *o* (but not *i* and *u*) for V_1. This situation may be presented in a diagram:

TABLE 2.1. *Reflexes of root-vowels in the literary languages*[6]

<table>
<tr><th>Environment:
Proto-Dravidian</th><th>*C-i], C-u], C-Ø]
Tamil-Malayāḷam</th><th>*C-a]</th><th>*C-i], C-u], C-Ø]
Telugu and Kannaḍa</th><th>*C-a]</th></tr>
<tr><td>*i</td><td>i</td><td rowspan="2">} i</td><td>i</td><td rowspan="2">} e</td></tr>
<tr><td>*e</td><td>e</td><td>e</td></tr>
<tr><td>*u</td><td>u</td><td rowspan="2">} u</td><td>u</td><td rowspan="2">} o</td></tr>
<tr><td>*o</td><td>o</td><td>o</td></tr>
<tr><td>(*a</td><td>a</td><td>a</td><td>a</td><td>a)</td></tr>
</table>

Examples:

1. **iṭ-i* > Ta. *iṭ-i* 'to break, crumble'; Ma. *iṭ-ika*; Ka. *iḍ-i*; Te. *iḍ-iyu*.
2. **iṭ-u* > Ta. *iṭ-u* 'to put, give'; Ma. *iṭ-uka*; Ka. *iḍ-u*; Te. *iḍ-u*.
3. **teḷ-i* > Ta. *teḷ-i* 'to become clear; to know'; Ma. *teḷ-iyuka*; Ka. *tiḷ-i* (< **teḷ-i*, see §6); Te. *tel-iyu* 'to know; to be known; to become clear'.

[3] Extended types are forms where the suffix is longer than simple V, e.g. PD **kil-ay* 'to cry'; **kal-anku* 'to be disturbed, as water'.

[4] Throughout this paper, the etymological boundary is marked by a hyphen, so as to show the root and the derivative suffix elements separately in each language and thus to facilitate comparison and reconstruction. The hyphen has no phonemic value.

[5] PSD **-a* = *-a* in Tamil, Malayāḷam, Kannaḍa, and Telugu; **-ay* = *-ai* in Tamil, *-a/-ay* in Telugu, *-e, -a/-ay* in Malayāḷam, *-e* in Kannaḍa and Tuḷu.

[6] In the discussion that follows, I use a single square bracket [to mark off a following environment.

4. *keṭ-u > Ta. keṭ-u 'to perish, decay'; Ma. keṭ-uka; Ka. keḍ-u/kiḍ-u; Te. ceḍ-u.

5. As opposed to these: (a) ? *iṇ-a/*eṇ-a > Ta. iṇ-ay v.i. 'to agree; to unite'; Ma. iṇ-ayuka; Ka. eṇ-e 'equality'; Te. en-ayu v.i. 'to agree, suit'; (b) similarly, ? *piṇ-a/*peṇ-a > Ta. piṇ-ay v.i. 'to entwine', v.t. 'to join, link'; Ma. piṇ-ayuka id.; Ka. peṇ-e 'to intertwine, etc.' (final -e < *-ay); Te. pen-ayu id.

6. *pul-i > Ta. Ma. Te. Ka. pul-i 'tiger'.

7. *koḷ > Ta. Ma. koḷ/koṇ- 'to grasp, seize, etc.'; Te. konu 'to hold, take'; Ka. koḷ/koṇ- id.

8. ? *cuṯ-a/*coṯ-a- > Ta. cuṟ-a, cuṟ-ā, cuṟ-āvu 'a shark'; Ma. cuṟ-ā, tuṟ-āvu; Ka. coṟ-a; Te. coṟ-a, soṟ-a.

2.1. It is clear from the foregoing that before a derivative *-a, both PD *i and *e turn up as i in Tamil and Malayāḷam, and as e in Telugu and Kannaḍa; similarly, PD *u *o > Ta. Ma. u, Te. Ka. o. Therefore, given for these languages only a set of forms in which an a-vowel begins the derivative suffix, one cannot be certain whether the original vowel is *i or *e, *u or *o. There are two possible interpretations for this situation. One is that, in this environment, PD *i *u fell together with *e *o in Telugu and Kannaḍa, and *e *o fell together with *i *u in Tamil and Malayāḷam. Since these phonemic mergers move in opposite directions, one has to assume that they took place independently in each set of languages:

IN THE ENVIRONMENT [C-a

Ta. & Ma.		Te. & Ka.	
i	u	*i	*u
↑	↑	↓	↓
*e	*o	e	o

It is, however, an extreme accident that two simultaneous shifts yielding the same result (i.e. loss or neutralization of contrast between each set of two vowels) should have taken place in neighbouring languages independently. If we consider this a development immediately following the Proto-Dravidian stage, we imply a strong language boundary which ties up Telugu and Kannaḍa as a subgroup, as opposed to Tamil and Malayāḷam; but there is no other isogloss to support the assumption. On the contrary, Telugu is closer to its northern neighbours in phonology than to its southern and south-western ones.

2.2. A more plausible explanation is this. Since all four languages have one feature in common, namely loss of contrast between i, e on the one hand and u, o on the other, this should have taken place at a period common to all of them, say in Proto-South Dravidian. In other words, it was in Proto-South Dravidian itself that the convergence of the four Proto-Dravidian vowel qualities into two took place. Let us assume for the time being that we do not know the qualities of these two vowels, i.e. whether they were i-u-like or e-o-like. Then we may symbolize the resultant qualities of this merger as X and Y;[7] PD *i *e [-a > PSD *X [-a; PD *u *o [-a > PSD *Y [-a. In our records of Tamil and Malayāḷam, X = *i*, and Y = *u*; but in Telugu and Kannaḍa, X = *e* and Y = *o*. If we have some means of knowing whether X and Y were *i-u*-like or *e-o*-like after the merger in Proto-South Dravidian, we can easily attribute a later shift to one group or the other within South Dravidian. This interpretation differs from the earlier one in assuming three stages instead of two, viz. Proto-Dravidian, Proto-South Dravidian, and South Dravidian; the shift is stated to have taken place in only one direction at a time. Instead of setting up two simultaneous and independent mergers—in Tamil and Malayāḷam, and in Telugu and Kannaḍa respectively—we are actually setting up only one shift in Proto-South Dravidian, with a later change in the divided South Dravidian which brought about the juxtaposition in developments. Two problems remain. (a) How can one discover the Proto-Dravidian vowel qualities? (b) In what direction did the merger take place in Proto-South Dravidian, **i *u* > **e *o*, or the reverse?

3. Most earlier writers on this problem took it for granted that the Tamil-Malayāḷam vowels represented the Proto-Dravidian qualities, and attributed all later shifts to Telugu and Kannaḍa (Caldwell 1913: 136–7, Grierson 1906: 288, Subbaiya 1909: 160 ff., Sreekanthaiya 1935: 769–80). Burrow (1940) was the first to propose internal reconstruction within South Dravidian itself. Since all the languages in question preserve the Proto-Dravidian vowel qualities when the derivative suffix begins with a consonant, *i*, *u*, or zero, he suggested that we compare forms having a derivational *-a* 'with kindred words in which the radical i/e and u/o are not followed by a or ai'. Obviously, the radical vowel occurring in closed syllables or in forms with a following derivative *-i* or *-u* represents the Proto-Dravidian quality, e.g. Ta. *oṭ-i* 'to break' *uṭ-ai* id. (< **oṭ-ay*).

The principle is therefore to discover, for each doubtful set of forms in South Dravidian, reliable etymologies where an *a*-vowel does not occur at the beginning of the derivative suffix (i.e. V_2), when the radical vowel (V_1) is short. Three broad environments can be set for this purpose: (a) where there is a short radical vowel in closed syllables, i.e. the type (C)VC, followed either by a consonantal suffix or by zero; (b) where there is a long radical vowel in closed or open syllables, irrespective of the quality of the vowel beginning the derivative suffix (a Dravidian heavy base, i.e. (C)V̄C, usually alternates with the corresponding light base (C)V̆C when a vowel derivative follows (Krishnamurti 1955: 247–8); generally, all South Dravidian languages preserve the qualities of the Proto-Dravidian long vowels); and (c) where there is a short radical vowel in open syllables, and the derivative suffix begins with *-i* or *-u*.

Sometimes the evidence of the non-literary languages of Central Dravidian and North Dravidian is useful in tracing the quality of the Proto-Dravidian radical

[7] If we follow the Prague School, *X and *Y are descriptively archiphonemes, with *X representing **i/e* and *Y representing **u/o*. It is arbitrary whether these archiphonemes are written **i *u* or **e *o*. It does matter historically, however, whether *X and *Y represent **i *u* or **e *o*, since our choice indicates the direction of the phonetic change that resulted in the loss of phonemic contrast. See Hoenigswald (1946: 40), §4a.

vowel, though it does not help us to trace the qualities of the derivative vowels, since in most cases these are lost. Many divergences from the Proto-Dravidian system appear in these languages even in radical vowels, so that one cannot set up regular phonemic correspondences to explain all the material. But if two or more geographically distant or historically less proximate members of the family agree with one set of South Dravidian (Tamil-Malayāḷam or Telugu-Kannaḍa) in showing the same vowel quality, that quality can be taken as Proto-Dravidian.

In a few cases, the evidence of Gondi is useful in this way. When there is *i*/*e* alternation among the South Dravidian languages, the Proto-Dravidian quality can be decided by comparison with Gondi, where, in the dialect described by Trench, PD **i* > *i*, but **e* > *a*. In the Adilabad dialect, as reported by Burrow and Bhattacharya, PD **e* is preserved.

4. With the help of the principles stated, we can usually reconstruct the Proto-Dravidian vowel qualities. There are of course residual forms for which reconstruction of the original vocalism is impossible for lack of related forms in the required environments. This section lists examples of the reconstruction of Proto-Dravidian vowel qualities.

4.1. Forms with a short radical vowel in closed syllables are used to reconstruct the Proto-Dravidian vowel qualities in the following examples.

9. **kil/*kin*: Ta. *cil-a* 'some, a few'; Ma. *cil-a* id.: Ka. *kel-a* 'some, several'; Tu. *kel-a*, *kel-avu* id. :: Ta. *ciṉ-mai* 'smallness, fewness' (Tolk.).

10. **cin/*cil*: Ta. *tiṉ-avu* 'itching'; Ma. *cin-aṅkuka* 'to be touchy', *-akkuka* 'to scratch': Ka. *ten-asu* 'itch' :: Ta. *tiṉ/tiṉṉu* 'to cause irritating sensation on skin' (cf. also Ta. *cuṉ-ai*, Ma. *cun-ekka* 'to itch'; Ma. *cin-ikka* 'to be touchy'; Te. *jil-a* 'itch'; Kui *sili sili āva* 'to touch'; Kur. *cilgā* 'itching', Malto *cilge* id.).

11. **cen*: Ta. *ciṉ-ai* 'to form, arise' (Kṟḷ.), 'to bud'; n. 'branch of a tree' (PN); Ma. *cin-a* 'branching out (as an ear of corn)'; *cin-ekka* 'to branch out; to sprout (of rice)': Ka. *ten-e* 'a spike, an ear of corn' :: Te. *ennu* (loss of **c-*) 'an ear of corn'; Go. *san* 'a head of Juar'; GoA. *sen* 'head of rice'; Pa. *cen* id.; Kol. (Kinwaṭ) *sen* id., Nk. *sen* id.; cf. Kui *tema* 'an ear of corn, a head of paddy'.

12. **tup*: Ta. *tuv-ar* 'coral, red colour; red ochre; to be red': Ka. *tog-aru* id.; Te. *tov-aru*, *tog-aru* id. :: Ta. *tuppu* 'red coral (Cīv.); red, redness'; cf. Kui *ṭōperi* adj. 'red'; ?*tūgu* 'bloody, blood'.

13. **poc/*poẓ*: Ta. *puẓ-ai* 'a tube, pipe'; *puẓ-al* 'a drain'; Ma. *puẓ-a* 'a river': Ka. *poẓ-e* 'a river' :: Ka. *pocca* 'river, stream' (*c*/*ẓ* alternation is common in Dravidian).

4.2. In the following examples, long vowels in monosyllabic bases, alternating with the corresponding short vowels in open syllables, attest the Proto-Dravidian vowel qualities. In some cases, long radical vowels are not shortened even when a vowel suffix follows.

14. **kīẓ*: **kiẓ*-V-: Ta. *kiẓ-aṅku* 'esculent or bulbous root (as potato), *Dioscorea*

aculeata'; Ma. *kiẓ-aṅṅu* id.: Ka. *geṇ-asu, geẓ-asu,* Te. *gen-asu, gen-usu* (lw. < Ka.), Tu. *ker-eŋgu* 'sweet potato'. All these forms are derived from the base **kīẓ* 'below': Kuṛ. *kītā, kiyyantā* adj. 'lowermost'; *kiyyā* 'beneath; below, down'. The words meaning 'lowland, east' also belong here, cf. Ta. Ma. *kiẓ-akku,* Ka. *keḷ-agu,* etc.

15. **ēṯ* : **eṯ*-V-: Ta. *iṟ-ai* 'to go beyond, excel', n. 'height, eminence; king, husband, superior'; *iṟ-aivaṉ* 'god; king'; Ma. *iṟ-ān* 'Sire (used in answering princes)': Ka. *eṟ-e* 'master'; *eṟ-ati* 'mistress'; Te. *ṟēḍu* (< **eṯ-anṯu*) :: Ta. Ma. Ka. *ēṟu* 'to ascend, rise, increase'; Tu. *ēruni* id.; Br. *hē-f* (*-f* is causative) 'to raise'.

16. **nūẓ*: *nuẓ*-V-: Ta. *nuẓ-ai* 'to creep through a narrow passage; to pass, insert; a narrow way'; Ma. *nuẓ-ayuka* 'to creep in': Ka. *noẓ-e* id. :: Tu. *nūruni* 'to creep in'; *nurumpe* 'a hole'; Ta. *nūẓ-il* 'hole, opening'; *nuẓ-untu* 'to crawl, creep'; Malto *nurgr-* 'to move onward, to slide'.

17. **cōn*: **con*-V-: Ta. *cuṉ-ai* 'a mountain pool or spring' (Kalit.); *cuṉ-aivu* 'rocky water'; Ma. *cun-ekka* 'to ooze out' :: Ka. *sōne* 'light continued rain, drizzle'; Te. *sōna* 'a stream, drizzle'.

4.3. In the following, the quality of the Proto-Dravidian vowel is attested by its occurrence in open radical syllables, before derivative suffixes with initial *i* or *u*.

18. **iṭ-*: Ta. Ma. *iṭ-aṟu* 'to stumble, trip down'; *iṭ-ar* 'hindrance; trouble'; Ma. *iṭ-antu* 'to walk with difficulty'; *iṭ-ampuka* 'to stumble, knock against'; *iṭ-ayuka* 'to hit against': Ka. *eḍ-aṟu, eḍ-avu, eḍ-apu* 'to stumble, trip'; *eḍ-aru* 'strait, obstacle'; Tu. *eḍ-aṅkuni* 'to hit, kick'; Te. *eḍ-aru* 'obstacle, trouble' :: Ta. *iṭ-u* 'to hit against'; *iṭ-i* id.; Kui *iska* 'to collide'; Malto *irp-* 'to tumble'; *iṛmb-* 'to collide'; Te. *ḍī konu* id.

19. **veṯ-*: Ta. *viṟ-a* 'to fear' (Tolk.); *viṟ-appu,* n. 'fear'; Ma. *viṟ-a* 'tremor': Ka. *beṟ-agu* 'alarm, amazement'; Tu. *ber-aguni* 'to be astonished'; *ber-agu* 'amazement'; Te. *veṟ-acu* 'to fear'; *veṟ-ãgu* 'surprise' :: Ta. *veṟ-i,* n. 'fear' (Tolk.); Go. *varī-* 'to fear'; *varre* 'fear' (dial.); Kui *brā* 'confused, amazed' (< **vrā* < **veṯ-a-*)'; cf. *bree inba* 'to be afraid'.

20. **nur-*: Ta. *nur-ai* 'foam, froth'; Ma. *nur-a* id.: Ka. *nor-e* id.; Tu. *nur-e/nor-e* id. :: Te. *nur-ũgu, -uvu* id.

21. **por-*: Ta. *pur-ai* 'cataract (on eye)': Ka. *por-e, hor-e* 'a fold, layer'; Te. *por-a* 'cataract; layer, flake, peel of skin'; *por-aṭa* 'a page' :: Ta. *por-ukku* 'flake, skin; thin layer that peels off; bark of tree' (Cīv.).

4.4. The non-literary languages are used in the following to identify the Proto-Dravidian vowel qualities.

22. **ir-*: Ta. *ir-a* 'to beg alms, solicit' (Kṟḷ.); Ma. *ir-akkuka* id.; *ir-appu* n. 'begging': Ka. *er-e* 'to beg, ask, solicit'; *er-avu, er-aval* 'an object of desire, a thing borrowed'; Tu. *er-avu* 'the act of lending or borrowing anything'; Te. *er-avu* 'a thing borrowed' :: Kui *rīṛa* 'a sum borrowed' (< **ir-aṯ-*); Malto *irgr-* 'to borrow, take a loan'.

23. **teṯ-*: Ta. *tiṟ-a* 'to open (as a door)': Ka. *teṟ-e* id.; Tu. *ter-apu* 'space'; Te.

teṟ-acu 'to open' :: Go. *tarī-* 'to open (of a door)' (Go. *a-* < **e-*); Kui *trēppa* 'to lay out' (< **teṯ-a-*).

24. **pul*/**pun-*: Ta. *pul-am* 'knowledge, learning, wisdom' (Kṟḷ.); *pul-aṉ* id. (Tolk.); Ma. *pul-am* 'perception by senses': Ka. *pol-a* 'an object of direction; sight' :: Pa. *pun-*, *pund-*, *putt-* 'to know'; Go. *pund-* id. (< **punṯ-*); Kui *pumba* id.; cf. Tu. *pinpini* 'to know, understand, comprehend'.

25. **pok-*: Ta. *puk-ai* 'smoke'; Ma. *puk-a* id.: Ka. *pog-e*, *hog-e*; Tu. *pug-e*; Te. *pog-a* id. :: Pa. Kol. Nk. *pog* 'smoke'; GoA. *poya.*

5. The second problem is to determine the phonemic status of *X and *Y in Proto-South Dravidian, i.e. the vowel qualities that resulted from the merger of Proto-Dravidian **i* **e* and **u* **o* respectively. There is now a plausible explanation. In all the South Dravidian languages, the root and suffix vowels commonly contract with the loss of a medial *-*k*- [g], *-*y*- (< *-*y*- or *-*c*-), or *-*w*- (< *-*w*- or *-*k*-). These contractions yield a series of long vowels:

TABLE 2.2. *Unumlauted and umlauted vowels in syllable contraction*

I.	(a)	*iC-	[i/u	>	ī-	(c) *eC- [i/u/a > ē-
	(b)	*iC-	[a	>	ē-	
II.	(a)	*uC-	[i/u	>	ū-	(c) *oC- [i/u/a > ō-
	(b)	*uC-	[a	>	ō-	

Proto-Dravidian **e* and **o* do not change in quality, in contracted forms, but are simply lengthened. Proto-Dravidian **i* and **u*, on the other hand, preserve their quality in contractions only when they are not originally followed by -*a*; in the sequences **i*C- [*a* and **u*C- [*a*, they behave in the same manner as original **e* and **o* to produce *ē*- and *ō*-. In the environment [C-*a*, then, all the South Dravidian languages show *ē* and *ō*, regardless of the Proto-Dravidian quality.

5.1. The following examples illustrate these formulas.

26. **tiy-a-* > *tē*-: Ta. *tīy-am* 'sweetness'; Te. *tīy-amu*/*tiyy-amu* id.; *tiyya*, adj. 'sweet'; Ka. *sī* 'sweetness'; *siyy-ane* 'sweetly': Ta. *tē-m* (< **tiy-am*) 'sweetness, honey, bee'; *tē-ṉ* 'honey'; Ma. *tē-n* id.; Ka. *tē-nu*/*jē-nu*; Kota *tē-n*; Te. *tē-ne* :: Pa. *tī-ni* 'bee'; Pa., Oll. *tī-n* 'honey'; Gad. *tīnu*; Kuṛ. *tī-nī* 'bee' (< **tiy-m*/**tiy-am*).

27. **mik-a-* > *mē*-: Ta. *mik-u* 'to excel, surpass'; *mik-ai* 'to increase'; n. 'abundance' (Kṟḷ.); 'greatness, excellence'; *mik-al* 'abundance, greatness'; *mik-a* 'abundantly'; Ma. *mik-akka* 'to exceed, increase, etc.'; *mik-avu* 'eminence'; Ka. *mig-ilu* 'to exceed'; Tu. *mig-iluni* 'to excel, surpass'; *mikk-uni* 'id.': Te. *mig-ulu* 'to exceed'; *mikk-ili* 'much': Ta. *mē-* (< **mik-a-*) 'excellence'; *mē-l*, *mē-l-imai* id.; Ma. *mē*

'over'; *mē-nma* 'excellence'; Ka. *mē* 'that which is above'; *mē-m, mē-l* id.; Tu. *mē-lu* id.; Te. *mē-lu* 'above' (in *mēlkanu* 'to wake up'); *mē-li* 'excellent'; *mē-lmi* 'excellence'. The ultimate base is **miy-/*mī-*.

28. **kec-a->*key-a->*kē-*: Ka. *kes-u, kēsu, kēs-a, kes-avu* '*Arum colocasia*': Ta. *cē-mpu, -mpai*; Ma. *cē-mpu, -mpa*; Tu. *tē-vu, cē-vu*; Te. *cē-ma* (< **kē-mp-* < **key-amp-*).

29. **tew-i-> tē-*: Ta. *tev-iḷ* 'to become filled'; *-iṭṭu* 'be cloyed'; n. 'loathing of food from satiation'; Ma. *tik-aṭṭuka* 'to become full to the throat'; *tek-iṭṭu* 'belching': Ma. *tē-ṭṭuka* 'to belch, ruminate'; Ta. *tē-kku* (< **tew-Vkku*; V = *i, u, a*); Ma. *tē-kku*; Ka. *tē-ṅku, -gu*; Tu. *tē-guni*; Te. *tē-ncu/-cu* (< PD **tew-*); cf. Kui *tēpk-* (< **tē k-p-*) 'to vomit'.

30. **kuw-a-> kō-*: Ta. *kuv-aṭu* 'a hill, mountain; top of a hill'; Ma. *kuv-aṭu* id.; Tu. *kubālu* 'a pinnacle'; Kui *kupṛe* 'a hillock, lower hill' :: Ta. *kō-ṭu* 'peak of a hill; horn'; Ka. *kō-ḍu* id.; Tu. *kō-ḍu* 'a horn'. All these are derived from **kuw-a-* < **kup-a-*; cf. Ta. *kuv-i* 'to be piled conically, etc.' Go. *kōr*, Pa. *kōḍ*, Kui *kōju* 'horn' are probably loanwords from Proto-South Dravidian in the shape **kōṭ-* (< PD **kuw-aṭ-*). [Actually, PSCD **ṯ* < PD **ṭ* is now an established change.]

31. **cuw-a- > *cō-*: Ta. *cuv-al* 'the upper part of the shoulder': Kui *suk-oṛi* 'shoulder blade'; *suk-oli* id.; Br. *cug̱h-* 'the nape of the neck': Ta. *tō-ḷ* id.; Ka. *tō-ḷ/tō-ḷu* 'the arm'; Tu. *tō-ḷu* id.

32. **puk-a->*pō-*: Ta. *puk-avu, -al* 'entering' (Aiṅk.) : Ta. *puk-u* 'to reach, enter; to go, proceed', v.t. 'to cause to enter' (Tolk.); Ma. *puk-uka* 'to enter' :: Ta. *pō* (< **puk-a-*) 'to go, proceed'; Ma. *pōka* id.; Ka. *pōgu* id.; Tu. *pōpini* id.; Te. *pōvu, pō-* id.

33. **tok-a->*tō-*: Ta. Ma. *tuk-al* 'skin'; Ka. *tog-alu*, Tu. *tug-alu*, Te. *tov-alu* id.: Te. *tokka* 'peel of fruit, body, etc.'; Kuṛ. *cokkā* 'the skin or shell of fruits, etc.' :: Ta. Ma. Ka. *tō-l* 'skin'; Te. *tō-lu* id. The stem also occurs in the same form in Parji, Ollari, Kolami, Naiki, Gondi, and Kuvi, probably borrowed from the neighbouring Telugu (see Emeneau 1955a: Vocab. No. 3137).

5.2. Examples can also be given of the contrasting developments, where PD **i* and **u* in contraction have preserved their quality in Proto-South Dravidian when not followed by *-a* in the next syllable.

34. **niw-u->*nī-*: Te. *niw-uṟu* 'ashes': Ta. Ma. Ka. Te. *nī-ṟu*, Go. *nī-r* id.

35. **nik-u-/-i>*nī-*: Ka. *nig-uḷ* 'to stand erect'; *nig-ur* 'to be stretched forth, be extended; to lengthen out, spread, rise, etc.'; Tu. *nigacuni* id.; Te. *nig-uḍu* 'to extend, stretch, spread; to become erect'; Ma. *niv-iruka* 'to rise, stand erect': Ta. *nī-ḷ* (< **nik-uḷ*) 'to grow long'; Ka. *nī-ḷ*, Te. *nī-lugu* id.; Ta. Ma. *nī-ṭu* 'to grow long'; Kui *ḍrīnj* (< **nṛī-* < **niṭ-i-*).

36. **uy-i- > *ū-*: Ta. *uy-ir* 'to breathe hard'; *uy-irppu* 'sighing'; Ma. *uy-ir*, n. 'breath'; Ka. *us-ir* 'to breathe'; Tu. *usuru* 'breath'; *usu* 'a deep sigh'; Kuṛ. *ujj-*, Malto *uj-* 'to live' : Te. *ūrcu* 'to breathe, sigh' (Classical).

5.3. The foregoing examples indicate that before a derivative *-a* in Proto-South-Dravidian, contrast between Proto-Dravidian **i* and **e* was neutralized in the direction of **e* and contrast between **u* and **o* was neutralized in the direction of **o*; in this environment, before the contractions took place, Proto-Dravidian **i* and **u* fell together in Proto-South Dravidian with **e* and **o* respectively. Since most of these contractions are common to all the South Dravidian languages, their formation must be attributed to a common period before their separation, viz. to Proto-South Dravidian. From this analysis, it follows that the phonemic status of *X and *Y is **e* and **o*. Within South Dravidian, Telugu and Kannaḍa preserved these qualities, while Tamil (and Malayāḷam) shifted them at a later stage to **i* and **u*. A number of survivals of this merger stage, however, survive in Old Tamil literature (i.e. *e-* [*a*- and *o-* [*a*), which probably point to a dialect in Old Tamil where the later shift did not occur. Examples:

37. Ta. *cey-al* 'action, acquisition' (Kalit.): *cey* 'to do' (< **key*).

38. Ta. *cel-avu* 'going, passing' (Tolk.); Te. Ka. *sel-avu* 'leave, permission': Ta. Ma. *cel* 'to go' (< **cal/*cel*).

39. Ta. *ceṟ-al* 'anger, open hatred' (PN); *ceṟ-u* 'to be angry at' (Parip.); n. 'anger' (Tirikaṭu.).

40. Ta. *teṟ-al* 'heat' (Parip.); 'ruining' (PN): *teṟ-u* 'to burn, scorch' (Kṟḷ.); 'to destroy' (Kalit.); n. 'anger, burning'; Pa. *ted-*, *tett-* 'to be fierce (of sun's heat)'.

41. Ta. *peṭ-ai* 'female of birds' (Tolk.); *peṭṭ-ai* id. (Tolk.); cf. *peṇ-ṭu* 'woman'; *peṇ* 'female of animals, woman' (Kṟḷ.).

42. Ta. *pey-al* 'showering' (Kṟḷ.), 'rain' (Kṟḷ.): Ta. *pey* 'to rain, fall as dew' (Kṟḷ.); 'to pour down' (Kalit.); Ma. *peyyuka* id.

43. Ta. *koḷ-ai* n. 'hold, determination' (Kalit.): *koḷ* 'to hold'.

44. Ta. *kol-ai* 'killing, murder' (Maṇi.); Ma. *kul-a* id.; Ka. *kol-e*, Te. *kol-a* id.; Ta. *kol*, Ta. Ma. *kollu* 'to kill'.

45. Ta. *toṭ-ar* 'to follow in succession' (Patiṟ.); 'to be linked', n. 'chain' (PN); *toṭ-ai* 'fastening, tying' (Kalit.): *toṭ-u* 'to be connected; to fasten' (PN).

46. Ta. *toṭ-aṅku* 'to begin' (Aiṅk.); *tuṭ-aṅku* id. (later form); Ma. *-tuṭaṅṅuka* id.; Ka. *toḍ-āgu*, Te. *toḍ-āgu*; Malto *toṛg-* 'to be in readiness for action': Ta. *toṭ-u* 'to begin, etc.'

47. Ta. *tok-ai* 'assembly, association' (Tolk.); 'flock, bunch, etc.': *tok-u* 'to assemble, collect' (Maṇi.); 'to add, total' (Tolk.); *tok-uti* 'assembly, company' (Tolk.).

48. Ta. *noṭ-ai* 'price, selling' (Patiṟ.): *noṭ-u* 'to sell' (PN).

49. Ta. *poṟ-ai* 'small hillock, burden, load' (Kalit.): *poṟ-u* 'to bear'; Kol. *pode* 'top, high up' (see Emeneau 1955a: Vocab. No. 701).

5.4. Though these examples point to a development in Old Tamil not normally expected (*e*C[*-a* and *o*C[*-a* instead of *i*C[*-a* and *u*C[*-a*), their radical vowels, *e* and *o*, may represent the Proto-Dravidian qualities rather than the Proto-South Dravidian, e.g. *noṭ-ai* 'price', *noṭ-u*. Since *u* occurs in the derivative syllable, the radical vowel represents the quality of the Proto-Dravidian vowel phoneme in that position. In view of the following case, however, this explanation is not tenable.

50. Ta. Ma. *pey-ar*, *pē-r*, (later) *piy-ar* 'name'; Ka. *pes-aru*; Tu. *pud-aru* (< **pid-ar-*; *i* > *u* after *p*); Te. *pē-ru*; Kol. Nk. *pē-r* (lw. < Te.); Pa. Oll. Gad. *pid-ir*; Kuṛ. Malto *pinj-* 'to name'; Br. *pin* 'a name'.

In this set of cognates, Tuḷu, Parji, Ollari, Gadaba, Kuṛux, Malto, and Brahui furnish evidence for a Proto-Dravidian **i*-form, probably **pinc-* > **picc-*, whence Ka. *pes-ar* by the weakening of **cc* between vowels, a common Dravidian development; cf. also Tu. *pud-ar* (*-d-* < **-t-* < **-c-*). OTa. *pey-ar* does not, therefore, represent the Proto-Dravidian vowel quality in the root syllable, but rather the Proto-South Dravidian, viz. **e*, into which the Proto-Dravidian **i* merged in the environment [*-a*. We can therefore safely conclude that *e* [*-a* and *o* [*-a* in Old Tamil are survivals of the Proto-South Dravidian stage which were left unaffected by the secondary shift that changed all **e* [*-a* and **o* [*-a* of Proto-South Dravidian to *i* [*-a* and *u* [*-a*.

5.5. The phonemic identification of *X and *Y as **e* and **o* has an important consequence: it fixes a relative chronology for the metathesized forms in pre-Telugu (Master 1948: 342 ff., Ramaswami Aiyar 1931–2: 448 ff.). We can now say with certainty that metathesis in the phonemes of the radical syllables took place in pre-Telugu when there was only one set of vowels, **e* and **o*, for PD **i* **e* and **u* **o* respectively, before *a* in the next syllable. Consequently the metathesized forms always show long *ē* and *ō* in contractions after metathesis. Examples:

51. PD *iC-a-* > PSD *eC-a-* > Te. *Cē-*: Te. *rē*, *rēyi* 'night'; Ta. *ir-ā*; Ma. *ir-avu*: Ta. *ir-uḷ* 'darkness'; Te. *ir-ulu* id.; Ma. *ir-u* 'to be black'; Kol. *cir-um* 'very dark' (see Emeneau 1955a: Vocab. Nos. 3025, 3051).

52. PD *eC-a-* > PSD *eC-a-* > Te. *Cē-*: Te. *lē-*, *lẽta* 'soft, tender, young'; Ta. *iḷ-am* 'tender, young' (in compounds); *iḷ-ai* 'youth'; Ma. *iḷ-akka* 'to be tender': Ka. *eḷ-a* 'tenderness, weakness' :: Ta. *eḷ-i* 'to become feeble'; *eḷ-imai*, *eḷ-umai* 'weakness' (Tolk.).

53. PD *uC-a-* > PSD *oC-a-* > Te. *Cō-*: Te. *rō-lu* 'mortar'; Ta. Ma. *ur-al*; Ka. *or-al*, *or-alu*; Tu. *or-alu*. All contain the common Dravidian base **ur-* 'to rub, crush, grind'; cf. Ta. *ur-iñcu/-iñu* 'to wear away by rubbing'; Kui *rūsa* 'to crush, grind'.

54. PD *oC-a-* > PSD *oC-a-* > Te. *Cō-*: Te. *ṟō-lu* 'to lament, cry': *oṟ-alu* id.; Ka. *oṟ-alu*, *-aḷu*, *-lu* 'to scream' :: Kuvi *oṛp-* 'to grieve, sorrow'; *oṛh-* 'to groan'; Kui *oṛpa* 'to pine for'; cf. Ta. *oṟ-u* 'to afflict, rebuke'.

The first set shows that metathesis and vowel contraction in pre-Telugu must have taken place after the loss of initial PD **c-*, a development which to some extent affected all the South Dravidian languages (Burrow 1947a: 132–47). Since the phonemic merger discussed in this paper occurs only in the South Dravidian languages, all of which also show the development of an alternation between **c* and zero, we have two parallel isoglosses which unite the South Dravidian languages as against the Central and North Dravidian languages.

6. In Classical Kannaḍa, another phonetic shift occurred independently, by which Early Kannaḍa radical *e* and *o* fell together with *i* and *u* respectively when followed in the next syllable by *i* or *u*. (Sreekanthaiya 1935: 783–97, Burrow 1940: 296–7, Gai 1946: 5–6.) This shift is dated to the 8th century AD Examples:

55. *id-ir* 'opposite' < **ed-ir*: Te. *ed-iri* 'opponent'; *ed-uru* 'opposite': Ta. *et-ir* id.; *sur-i* 'to pour down' (< **cor-i*): Ta. *cor-i* id., Te. *tor-ãgu* id.; *pur-i* 'to fry' (< **por-i*): Ta. *por-i*, Te. *por-ãṭu* id.

7. As stated earlier, the developments described in this paper belong only to the ancient stages of the South Dravidian languages, accessible to us through literary records. The situation in the modern vernaculars is altogether different. In present-day Tamil and Malayāḷam, all instances of the older *i*- and *u*- [C-*a* tend to be pronounced as *e* and *o*, as in Telugu and Kannaḍa, e.g. OTa. *il-ai* > Mdn.Ta. *el-ai*; similarly, *iṭ-am* > *eḍ-am*; *ciṟ-ai* > *cer-ai*; *uṭ-al* > *oḍ-al*; *kur-aṅku* > *kor-aṅgu*.[8] On the other hand, in Modern Kannaḍa and Telugu, *i*[C-*a* and *u*[C-*a* are common, e.g. Te. *mid-aṭa* 'a grasshopper', *uḍ-ata* 'squirrel' (< OTe. *miḍuta*, *uḍuta*), Ka. *tig-aṭu* 'rind', *nil-avu* 'standing', *huḷ-a* 'a worm'. In most of the Telugu and Kannaḍa cases, it is the derivative vowels that have undergone modification through vowel harmony, not the radical vowels.

Postscript

P 1. This paper also has been widely cited in Dravidian literature. Burrow (1940: 295–6) observed that only *i u* occurred before [*a* in Tamil-Malayāḷam and *e o* in Telugu-Kannaḍa, and that this meant that there was neutralization between high and mid vowels, which he called 'confusion'. He further says: 'Since this confusion is common to all the languages concerned, we may assume in all probability that it had already taken place in the parent language itself.' He did not specify what he meant by the parent language, Proto-Dravidian or Proto-South Dravidian. However, this insight was definitely remarkable. But the next sentence, 'Whether in this case the parent language showed *i* and *u* or *e* and *o*, it is not possible to say and is of no great importance' (296) is not correct. It was certainly important to determine which set of vowels merged with which.

I have shown in this paper that the sound change involved three stages. The Proto-Dravidian stage when all the five vowels occurred unchanged in the root

[8] For Modern Tamil, see Sethu Pillai (1937–8: 6–8). For Kannaḍa, see Sreekanthaiya (1935: 780–1, 797–8).

syllable (C)V_1C, irrespective of the quality of -V_2 in the following syllable. Only *i*, *u*, *a* occurred as -V_2. The next was the Proto-South Dravidian stage, in which high vowels in the root syllable (-V_1) merged with mid-vowels, when followed by *-a* as -V_2 in the following syllable. This phenomenon is now widely referred to as 'Dravidian umlaut'. At some point after this change, there was a third stage, viz. Tamil-Malayāḷam changed these mid-vowels to high vowels at a very early period. I gave arguments to prove that the sound change took place only in one direction each time and it was the high vowels that merged with mid-vowels (and not vice versa) before a low vowel in the next syllable in Proto-South Dravidian. Proto-Dravidian vowel-qualities can be found to remain unchanged before high vowels or when no vowel follows (when the root is also a free form). Both Sreekanthaiya (1935) and Burrow (1940) identified these environments and I was able to make a more definitive statement of the diagnostic environments needed to reconstruct the Proto-Dravidian vowel qualities.

P 2. Like his predecessors Burrow dealt with this phenomenon only in the four literary languages, contrasting Tamil-Malayāḷam with Telugu-Kannaḍa within 'South Dravidian'. My subsequent researches showed that Telugu is a close sister of Gondi-Koṇḍa-Kui-Kuvi and not of Kannaḍa which is a member of South Dravidian. My classifying Telugu with the Central group in *TVB* (Ch. IV) has since received acceptance from the other Dravidian scholars. In that case it poses a problem for this paper. How was it that Telugu and Kannaḍa which belonged to different subgroups shared the sound change of shifting the Proto-Dravidian high vowels to mid-vowels in an identical environment? In the 1970s I found a solution to the problem. The merger that I posited for Proto-South Dravidian should include not only the group of languages consisting of Tamil-Malayāḷam-Koḍagu-Toda-Kota-(Tuḷu)-Kannaḍa, etc. but also the group consisting of Telugu-Gondi-Koṇḍa-Kui-Kuvi-Pengo-Manḍa. I called the first subgroup South Dravidian I and the second South Dravidian II or South-Central Dravidian. I noticed other shared innovations between these two subgroups. Chapter 15 in this volume provides evidence for this claim. My rule thus remains vindicated as a change at an undivided stage of these two subgroups, viz. Proto-South Dravidian. Linguistic data from the other South Dravidian languages discussed in the papers on Kota, Koḍagu, and Toda by Emeneau (1969a, 1970b, 1979) show that they have *e*, *o* before [*-a*. A number of sound changes affecting the quality of radical vowels in these languages are explainable in terms of the Proto-South Dravidian vowel qualities inherited by them. This fact provides an independent validation of the rules that I formulated, although I did not realize it at the time of writing this article. I was also uncomfortable with Telugu sharing a sound change with Kannaḍa with which it did not constitute a subgroup, as I pointed out in my paper. Subrahmanyam (1983: 210) wrongly says that the sound change in Telugu was independent of the other South Dravidian languages, 'at a later stage due to areal contact'. But it goes beyond Telugu to all members of South Dravidian I and II, but not to the other subgroups. Areal influence should also have included Parji, Kolami, Naiki, and Gadaba (Central Dravidian) which are surrounded by South Dravidian II languages.

P 3. Only Tuḷu shows both sets, *i/u*C-*a* (similar to the dissimilation change in Early Tamil) and *e/o*C-*a*, the Proto-South Dravidian sound change, dialectally. The former occurs in North Common dialect (Nc) and the latter in all other dialects, viz. South Brahmin (Sb), South Common (Sc), and North Brahmin (Nb). It appears that mid > high in the environment C-*a* in Nc looks like an independent innovation within Tuḷu, unrelated to the early Tamil sound change; e.g. *nel-a* (Sb, Sc, Nb): *nil-a* (Nc) 'floor'; *pos-attï* (Sb, Sc), *pos-atï* (Nb) : *pus-atï* (Nc) 'new' (Kekunnaya 1994: 42). Koraga, a tribal language spoken in the Tuḷu area also shows both the developments, e.g. *or-e, ur-e* 'deer' in different dialects (Bhat 1971, see comparative dialect vocabulary). The following two etymologies show the operation of this change in different subgroups:

56. PD **koṭ-ay* > PSD **koṭ-ay* 'umbrella': (a) SD I **koṭ-ay* > Ta. *kuṭ-ai*, Ma. *kuṭ-a*; (retention in) Ko. *keṛ* (< **keṛ-e* < **koḍ-e* < **koḍ-ay*), To. *kwaṛ-* (< **koṛ-* with loss of derivative vowel), Koḍ. *koḍ-e*, Tu. *koḍ-ɛ*; (b) SD II **koṭ*-V- > Te. *goḍ-(u)gu* id. [*DEDR* 1663].

57. PD **iḷ-a-* > PSD **eḷ-a-* 'tender, young': (a) SD I **eḷ-a-* > Ta. *iḷ-a*, Ma. *iḷ-a*; (retention in) Ko. To. *eḷ*, Koḍ. *ëḷe-ë*, Ka. *eḷ-a*, *eḷ-e*, Tu. *eḷ-atï*, *eḷ-e*; (b) SD II **eḷ-a-* > Te. *el-a*, *lē*-, Go. *ley-or* 'young man', Kui-Kuvi *la-a-* 'young' (< **le-e-*); (c) CD **iḷ-a-* > Pa. *il-ed* 'young man', Oll. *il-e* 'bride' [*DEDR* 513]. North Dravidian also has **i* forms.

Kamatchinathan (1972) illustrates the lowering of Classical *i u* to *e o* in colloquial Tamil, accompanied by rounding (*miḷ-aku* > *meḷaku* > *moḷ-avu* 'pepper') after bilabial consonants, or dissimilatory unrounding in some cases (*puṟā* > *poṟā* > *peṟā* 'dove'), and other kindred developments. He notes that Laccadive Malayāḷam still preserves the state of the high vowels of the Tamil Classical stage (1972: 166).

The rules treated in this paper need no modification in view of recent writings on comparative Dravidian phonology (Emeneau 1970a, Subrahmanyam 1983, Zvelebil 1970b, 1990a).

3

Proto-Dravidian *ẓ

0.0. Applying the usual procedures of comparison and reconstruction to Dravidian, we can set up on definite grounds the following phonemes for Proto-Dravidian:[1]

Consonants						Vowels		
p	t	ṯ	ṭ	c	k	i		u
m	n		ṇ	ñ		e		o
		l	ḷ				a	
		r	ẓ					
w				y				

0.1. Since long vowels contrast with the corresponding short vowels in all the Dravidian languages, a phoneme of length marked /¯/ can be set up for Proto-Dravidian. No consonant of the alveolar or the retroflex series, i.e. /ṯ l r ṭ ṇ ḷ ẓ/ begins a word in Proto-Dravidian. The Proto-Dravidian radical elements are all monosyllables and of the following types: 1. (C)V̌C; 2. (C)V̌(C = consonant; V̌ = vowel, long or short; the initial consonant may or may not occur). These root types may occur free, or bound to a series of derivative suffixes of the following types:-(V)CC/-(V)C. Suffixes beginning with a vowel occur after consonant-final roots (type 1); suffixes beginning with a consonant usually occur after vowel-final roots (type 2). Consonant-final bases with a long radical vowel, i.e. (C)V̄C (Krishnamurti 1955: 240–2), alternate with the corresponding short-vowelled bases when suffixes beginning with a vowel follow, e.g. **kīẓ* 'below, underneath': **kiẓ-anku* 'root' (a hyphen is used to distinguish the root syllables from the suffixes in reconstructed forms).

0.2. PD *ẓ as stated earlier does not occur initially in a word. It occurs either as

[1] The symbol ẓ is introduced in this paper for Proto-Dravidian in preference to ṛ, ḻ, r̤, etc., since it is not used for any other phoneme either in Proto-Dravidian or in the Dravidian languages, and the subscript dot fits it nicely into the retroflex series of consonants, all of which have the same diacritic.

For a complete bibliography of Dravidian Dictionaries and Vocabularies, see Emeneau (1955a: xiii–xiv), to which should be added the following: Burrow and Bhattacharya (1953); Bhattacharya (1957).

My sources for Toda and Kota are the unpublished verb-indexes of these languages kindly supplied to me by Emeneau. Further, I have liberally used his comparative vocabulary of Kolami for various items not recorded elsewhere. The transcription is fairly phonemic for OTa., OMa., Ko., To., Te., Ka., Kol., Pa., and Gad.; for the rest, what we have here is a sort of *broad transcription.*

the root-final consonant or the suffix-final consonant, e.g. *_īẓ_ 'to pull'; *_pak-aẓ_ 'to praise'. Forms in which both the root and suffix finals occur as _ẓ_ in succession are however rare. Since derivative suffixes are generally variables, we may not always find as consistent a set of reflexes for *_ẓ_ occurring in the suffix syllables as for *_ẓ_ in the root syllables; for the latter a regular line of developments can be traced.

0.3. Judging from its developments in the different Dravidian languages and from the phonetic description of its reflexes in languages where it is phonemically preserved, and also from the evidence of loanwords between early Dravidian and Indo-Aryan, *_ẓ_ appears to be the most characteristic of the Proto-Dravidian phonemes with a peculiar phonetic value. *_ẓ_ is phonemically preserved in Old Tamil ழ, Old Malayāḷam ഴ, Old Kannaḍa ೞ, and Old Telugu ఴ, certain caste and regional dialects of Modern Tamil and Malayāḷam in South Dravidian, and Parji _ṛ_ in Central Dravidian. Tolkāppiyam (_c._ 1st century AD) describes _ẓ_ (ழ) as a retroflex fricative, occupying a place between the hard series and the soft series (_iṭai-y-eẓuttu_). Naṉṉūl (13th century) says that _ẓ_ is produced by slightly scraping on the middle of the hard palate with the tip of the tongue.[2] J. R. Firth describes the phonetic value of _ẓ_ in Modern Tamil as follows: 'a frictionless continuant having an obscure unrounded back quality, "ẓ" is made by drawing back the whole tongue and spreading the blade laterally, making it thick, short and blunt, so to speak, so that it approaches the middle of the hard palate. The result is a very retracted liquid sort of r-sound.' (Firth 1934: Appendix xvi) The early Tamil loanwords from Sanskrit have a _ẓ_ substituted for _ṣ_, e.g. _cēẓam_ < _śeṣa_ 'remainder'; _nāẓi_ < _nāḍi_ (a measure of time).[3] Kēśirāja, a Kannaḍa grammarian of AD 1260 says that _ẓ_ is produced by pronouncing _ḍ_ with greater pressure (_Śabdamaṇidarpaṇa, sūtra_ 19) (Kittel 1920). It is also mentioned that Sanskrit _ṭ_ and _ṭh_ become _ẓ_ in Old Kannaḍa loanwords (ibid. 20). Dravidian intervocalic _ṭ, ḍ_ also develop to _ẓ_ in Old Kannaḍa itself in consonantal sandhi before stops, e.g. _nōẓpam_ (< _nōḍu_ + _pam_; PSD *_nōṭ_- 'to see'). From the above data, we can assume that the reflex of *_ẓ_ in the older stages of the literary languages was a kind of retroflex fricative. Burrow has not described the phonetic value of his symbol _ṛ_ in Parji, which is the regular correspondent of *_ẓ_.

0.4. Caldwell (1956: 161–2) says that this peculiar Dravidian sound _ṛ_ (*_ẓ_) interchanges with five different sounds in the various Dravidian languages, viz. _ṇ ḷ ḍ r_ and _y_. Subbaiya (1909: 209–10) describes its distribution in each of the South Dravidian languages and Gondi. But many of his etymologies are incorrect and have therefore led him to set up wrong correspondences; for instance, PD *_ẓ_ > Te. _r, y,_ and _ḷ_ in the intervocalic position is not correct. The other writers on this problem are A. F. Thiagaraju (1933: 75–88) and L. V. Ramaswami Aiyar (1935) of whom the latter has attempted to cover fairly much the entire area of Dravidian but with little success in establishing a consistent line of distribution of *_ẓ_, even among the literary languages. An attempt is made in this paper to show rather precisely the regular

[2] _Naṉ._ 83 (ed. Dandapāṇi Desikar, 1957). [3] Anavaratavinayakam Pillai 1919: 32–4.

reflexes of *ẓ in each of the Dravidian languages and to present etymologies, posing certain problems in reconstruction. A diagnostic list of forty etymological items is given as an appendix to the article to avoid repetition of cognates under each language treated. Except Toda, Kota, and Koḍagu, for which adequate material is not available, the conclusions are based on a thorough examination of the individual languages and can therefore be applied with fair regularity even to etymologies not included in the test list.

1. Kannaḍa

1.1. *ẓ is preserved phonemically in Old Kannaḍa till about the middle of the 10th century, marked in the inscriptions by the symbol ೞ (ẓ) (Narasimhia 1941: 161–2, Gai 1946: 16–7). Later, it has developed (a) to ḷ (frequently) and ṇ (infrequently) in the prevocalic and word-final positions, and (b) to *r* before stops (i.e. in the preconsonantal position). Both these developments are in complementary distribution and therefore structurally constitute a single development.

1.2. Out of the thirty-one Kannaḍa etyma occurring in the test list, corresponding to PD *ẓ, eighteen have *ẓ/ḷ*, three have *ẓ/ṇ*, and three more have *ṇ* without any corresponding *ẓ*-forms—all in environment (a);[4] in environment (b), three cases show *ẓ/r/Ø* (Ø = assimilation to the following consonant), two show *r/Ø* without any **ẓ*-alternants, and one has *ẓ/Ø* without any evidence for the intermediary *r*-stage,[5] e.g.

(1) *ẓ/ḷ* (< **ẓ*):

iẓi/iḷi 'to descend' (1); *eẓe/eḷe* 'to pull' (2); *uẓu/uḷu* 'to plough' (3); *ēẓu/ēḷu* 'seven' (9); *aẓu/aḷu* 'to weep' (10); *kaẓal/kaḷal* 'to slip off' (11); *kaẓi/kaḷi* '(time) to pass, etc'. (12); *kīẓ/kīḷ* 'being low' (16); *koẓavi/koḷavi* 'a blow-pipe' (17); *koẓe/koḷe* 'to be rotten' (18); *kōẓi/kōḷi* 'fowl' (23); *tāẓ/tāḷi* 'palmyra tree' (26); *neẓal/neḷal* 'shade,

[4] The alternation of *ḷ/ṇ* is an interesting phenomenon in Kannaḍa which has not been worked out. Narasimhia and Gai only mention *ẓ* > *ḷ* and *r* in complementary environments; however, there are quite a few cases in which Ka. has doublets in *ṇ* for forms in *ḷ* derived from PD **ḷ* as well as **ẓ*. Sometimes, only *ṇ* forms occur for etyma with **ẓ* under the same conditions as *ḷ* < **ẓ* (see §1.2(2); examples for *ṇ/ḷ* < **ẓ*: *tuḷi/tuṇi* 'to tread, trample' (< **toẓ-i*); *noṇa/noḷa* 'a fly' (< **nuẓ-a*); *moṇa/moḷa* 'cubit, projecting joint' (< **moẓ-a-*). It is likely that there has been a local Kannaḍa dialect since the period of Old Kannaḍa where *ṇ* must have occurred either as a free variant of *ḷ* (< **ḷ*, **ẓ*) or as its substitute, from which it spread to the other areas through literature. A number of 11th century inscriptions from Bellary, Hadagalli, Hospet areas show *ṇ* variants corresponding to the *ḷ* forms elsewhere, e.g. *noṇamba*: *noḷamba*, *hoysaṇa*: *hoysaḷa*, etc. This situation may suggest that the *ṇ* dialect has been somewhere in the north or north-east of Karṇātaka (I am indebted to B. Ramachandra Rao for the inscriptional material).

[5] It should be remembered that it is only by the strength of tradition that *ẓ*- forms have been preserved in literary texts. In other words, wherever *ẓ* occurred in the post-tenth century texts, it is not as though *ẓ* was phonemically distinct from *ẓ/ṇ* or *r* with which it gradually fell together. In the alternations presented here as *ẓ/ḷ*, *ẓ/ṇ*, and *ẓ/r*, *ẓ* is a grapheme representing a single phoneme in Old Kannaḍa or pre-Kannaḍa, but later, certain distributions of three phonemes, *ḷ*, *ṇ*, and *r*.

shadow' (28); *paẓa, haẓa/ haḷa* 'old' (30a), *pāẓ, hāẓu/ hāḷu* 'ruin, devastation' (30b); *piẓi, hiḷ/ hiḷi* 'to squeeze out' (32); *puẓu, huẓu/ huḷu* 'worm' (33); *pēẓ, hēẓ/ hēḷu* 'to speak' (35); *poẓal, hoẓal/ hoḷalu* 'town' (36).

(2) *ẓ/ ṇ* (< **ẓ*):

gaẓe/ gaṇe 'bamboo pole, etc.' (13); *pūẓu, hūẓu/hūṇu* (alternatively *hūḷu*) 'to be buried' (34); *muẓuṅgu/ muṇuṅgu* 'to dive' (39b).

(3) **ẓ/ ṇ* (< **ẓ*): in the following, the *ẓ* alternants are not attested:

koṇasu 'young of wild beasts' (21); *taṇal* 'to glow' (25); *paṇ, paṇṇu, haṇṇu* 'fruit' (29).

(4) *ẓ/ r/* Ø (< **ẓ*):

taẓgu/ targu/ taggu 'to become low' (27); *poẓtu/ portu, pottu/ hottu* 'sun, time' (37); *kaẓcu* (inscr.)/ *karcu/ kaccu* 'to wash' (15).

(5) **ẓ/ r/* Ø (< **ẓ*); *ẓ*-alternants are not attested for the following:

**koẓvu/ korvu, korbu/ kobbu* 'to be fat', n. 'fat' (19); **uẓdu/ urdu/ uddu* 'black gram' (4).

(6) *ẓ/* r/* Ø (< **ẓ*):

kaẓte/ karte/ katte* 'ass' (14).

1.3. PD **ẓ* which fell together with *r* in Kannaḍa during the 10th century was gradually being assimilated to the following stop-suffix about a century later. We come across cases of complete assimilation of *r* (< **ẓ*) to the following stop as early as AD 1029 (see *kāl-gacci* 'having washed the feet', *SII*, vol. xi–i, No. 65, line 46; Gadag Tq., Dharwar Dt.),[6] i.e. exactly a century after the first occurrence of *r* < *ẓ* was recorded in AD 930 (Narasimhia, 1941: 61, 72 ff.). About the same time we also come across forms like *gadde* (< *gaẓde*), *eppattu* (< **eẓpattu*), etc. in the inscriptions. In the century that followed, the change seems to have extended fairly much to the whole of the Kannaḍa area causing confusion in the orthodox literary tradition. The missing links in the assimilation chain of the above sample forms indicate how the tradition has failed in some cases to restore the archaic spelling after the linguistic change was completed.

1.4. The following forms may be considered loanwords in Kannaḍa since they do not conform to the regular developments:

(1) *neraḷ, nirelu* 'shade' (28), beside the regular *neḷal* id. cf. Tu. *nirelï*.

(2) *koḍa* 'youth', beside the regular *koṇasu*, see (21); Te. *koḍuku* 'son' (< *'youth, young person'), *kōḍe* 'young male of cattle', *kōḍalu* 'daughter-in-law' (22).

The first of these is apparently a loanword from Tuḷu, in which the regular development is *r* < **ẓ*. The second item is a problem since Telugu, from which this could

[6] Information from B. Ramachandra Rao.

be a borrowing, does not have *koḍa-*. It was probably taken into Kannaḍa in the shape **kōḍa-* (as occurring in Te. *kōḍalu*, etc.), and later the radical long vowel might have been shortened under the influence of the regular Kannaḍa form *koṇasu.*

2. Koḍagu

2.1. The material of Cole as well as that of Emeneau agrees in showing regularly *ḷ* for PD **ẓ*-, e.g.

ïḷi 'to descend' (1); *ūḷ* 'to cultivate' (2); *kūḷu* 'rice', Ta. Ma. Ka. *kūẓ* 'porridge', Te. *kūḍu; nëḷa* 'shade' (28); *pāḷu* 'waste land' (30b); *puḷu* 'worm' (33); *pōḷu* (Cole) 'daytime', *bodi* (Emeneau) (37); *bāḷu* 'to live', Ta. Ma. *vāẓ*, Ka. *bāḷ*; *moḷa* 'cubit', Ta; *muẓam* id., see §17 (4).

2.2. The following items show assimilation of *ẓ* to the following suffix stop:

kate 'ass' (14); *bodi* (Emeneau) (37).

We need to know whether these two forms are loanwords from Kannaḍa.

3. Telugu

3.1. **ẓ* was preserved in inscriptional Telugu represented by the phoneme symbolized ఴ (*ẓ*) till the middle of the 9th century AD. It subsequently fell together with *ḍ* and *r* in complementary environments as follows:

3.2. **ẓ* > *ḍ*:

(a) Intervocalically, (b) finally (before a non-morphemic *u*), and (c) in closed syllables before stops. Examples: (a) *kaḍacu* '(time) to pass' (12); *gaḍa* 'shaft of bamboo, etc; stick' (13); *gāḍida* 'ass' (14); *kaḍugu* 'to wash' (15); *kōḍalu* 'daughter-in-law' (22); *kōḍi* 'fowl' (23); *tāḍi* 'palm tree' (26); *nīḍa* 'shade, etc.' (28); *piḍucu* 'to squeeze' (32). (b) *ēḍu* 'seven' (9); *kīḍu* 'low, inferior' (16); *kōḍu* 'to sift, winnow' (20); *cūḍ-* 'to see' (24); *pāḍu* 'desolation' (30b); *pūḍu* 'to be buried' (34). (c) *īḍcu* 'to drag, pull' (2); *ūḍcu* 'to remove, sweep' (8); *ēḍcu* 'to weep' (10); *kīḍpaḍu*/*kīḍwaḍu* 'to fall low in circumstances' (16); these forms have also doublets in old literature with intervocalic -*ḍ*- as follows: *īḍucu, ūḍucu, ēḍucu, kīḍupaḍu*, etc.

3.3. After the separation of Central Dravidian from the main colony of Proto-Dravidian, Telugu and Kui developed initial alveolar and retroflex consonants (not admissible in Proto-Dravidian) through metathesis, attended, in some cases, by contraction of root and suffix vowels.[7] This resulted in the position of **ẓ* also being

[7] This development in Te. and Kui (also to some extent in Tu. and Go.) has been discussed at length by many writers: Subbaiya (1909: 160–2); Tuttle (1930: §§ 27, 56); Emeneau (1945: 191, §8; 1953a: §§10, 26, 27); Ramaswami Aiyar (1931–2: 448 ff.); Master (1948: 340–64); Krishnamurti (1955: 245–6).

shifted to the word-initial position in the early Telugu period itself (i.e. Telugu of the early inscriptions, 5th to 9th centuries). In this position, *ẓ developed to *ḍ*-. As far as Telugu is concerned we can sum up this development in formulas as follows:

	PD		Pre-Te.		Early Te. (inscr.)		Classical Te.
(a)	*V*ẓ*-*u*C-	>	(*V*ẓ*-C-)	>	*ẓ*V-CC-	>	*ḍV-CC-*
(b)	**i*/*eẓ-a-*	>	(**ẓe-a-*)	>	*ẓē-*	>	*ḍē-*
	**u*/*oẓ-a-*	>	(**ẓo-a-*)	>	*ẓō-*	>	*ḍō-*
	**aẓ-a-*	>	(**ẓa-a-*)	>	*ẓā*	>	*ḍā-*

For example *ḍiggu* 'to descend' (1) **iẓ-ik*/*-iw* > (**iẓ-g-*) > *ẓi-gg-* > *ḍi-ggu*; *ḍĕ̄ku* 'to crawl, as an infant'; Ma. *iẓayuka* id. **iẓ-ank-* > (**ẓe-ank-*) > *ẓē-nk-* > *ḍē-nku*/*ḍĕ̄-ku*

3.4. This initial *ḍ*- developed a tendency to change to *d*-, even by the 11th century AD, i.e. the beginning of the literary period in Telugu. Both *ḍ*- and *d*- forms occur freely in the early classics; *d*- forms preponderate in later Telugu works (14th and 15th centuries). The change is almost complete in modern Telugu, the only survival being *ḍebbhay* 'seventy' (classical: *ḍebbadi* < *ẓebbadi* < **eẓ-padi* < **eẓu-pat-*, see 9).

The Parji-Kolami subgroup, which does not share the development of metathesis of Telugu-Kui, also shows a number of items with initial *ḍ*- arising out of PD *-*ẓ*. These forms are obviously loanwords from an early Telugu dialect in which *ḍ*- (< **ẓ*) had not yet developed to *d*-. It is interesting to note that a *ḍ*- can be recovered with the evidence of these languages for certain classical Telugu items, which occur only with an initial *d*-, and without doublets in *ḍ*, e.g. *dukki* 'tillage' (3), *duppi* 'antelope' (5); *duwwu*$_1$ 'to comb' (6); *duwwu*$_2$ 'tiger' (7).

3.5. **ẓ* > *r*: Under the conditions described above for metathesis and vowel contraction, a Proto-Dravidian sequence with an initial consonant and root-final *ẓ* develops into an initial cluster in early Telugu with **ẓ* (< **ẓ*) as the second member. In such cases **ẓ* (pre-Classical Te. **ẓ*) has merged with /*r*/ in Classical Telugu. This *r* (i.e. part of C*r*- sequences) is progressively lost in later Telugu. The changed formulas may be stated as follows:

(1) Metathesis following the loss of post-radical vowel *u*:

PD		Pre-Te.		Early Te. (inscr.)		Classical Te.
*C^1V^1*ẓ*-*u*C^2-	>	(C^1V^1*ẓ*-C^2-)	>	C^1*ẓ*V^1-C^2C^2-	>	C^1*r*V^1-C^2C^2-
**koẓ-uw-*	>	(**koẓ-w-*)	>	**kẓo-ww-*	>	*kro-ww(u)*

For other forms of this type, see *krinda* 'below' (16); *kruḷḷu* 'to rot' (18); *kro-*, *krotta* 'new, tender' (21); *trampi* 'embers' (25); *pruccu* 'to be worm-eaten', *pruvvu* 'a worm' (33); *proddu* 'sun' (37); *mruggu* 'to ripen' (38); *bruṅgu* 'to sink' (39).

(2) Metathesis with vowel contraction:

PD		Pre-Te.		Early Te. (inscr.)		Classical Te.
**Ci*/*eẓ-a-*	>	(**Cẓe-a-*)	>	*Cẓē-*	>	*Crē-*
**Cu*/*oẓ-a-*	>	(**Cẓo-a-*)	>	*Cẓō-*	>	*Crō-*
Caẓ-a-	>	(**Cẓa-a-*)	>	*Cẓā-*	>	*Crā-*
kuẓ-aw	>	(**kẓo-aw*)	>	*kẓō-w*	>	*krō-wi*

For other examples, see *prā-*, *prā̃ta* adj. 'old' (30a); *prēgulu* 'intestines' (31); *prēlu* 'to chat, prate' (35); *prōlu* 'town; a division of district; suffix to place-names' (36); *mrēgu* 'to smear, anoint' (40).

3.6. In Telugu there are a few forms with a **ẓ* assimilated to the following stop as in Kannaḍa. These are either loanwords from Kannaḍa after the process of assimilation was completed there, i.e. post-10th century, or formed at a period common to Telugu and Kannaḍa. It is more likely that these are original formations in Kannaḍa alone since Telugu does not preserve a single case with the unassimilated sequence -*r*C-(< **ẓ*C) which is very common in Middle Kannaḍa (§**1.3**). On the other hand, the normal development in Telugu in such cases would be metathesis of the type (1) described above (§ **3.5**): e.g.

uddulu 'black gram' (4); *taggu* 'to be lowered, humbled' (27). A few others not occurring in the Appendix are as follows: *tottu* 'slave'; Te. *addu* 'to immerse'; Ka. *aẓdu, ardu, addu* 'to sink, dye'; Ta. Ma. *aẓuttu* 'to sink'; Te. *akkara* 'desire, love'; Ka. *akkaṟu, aẓkaṟu* id.; *aẓuku* 'to love, like'; Ta. *aẓuku* id.; Te. *eccarika* 'waking up; warning'; *eccarincu* 'to wake up'; Ka. *eccaṟ, eẓcaṟ* 'to be awake, be cautious'; Ta. Ma. Ka. *eẓu* 'to rise, etc.'; PSD **eẓu-* 'to wake up, rise'.

3.7. The Telugu development of metathesis of **ẓ* in contrast to the Kannaḍa development of its assimilation to the following stop can be seen in the following sets: Te. *krowwu* 'fat': Ka. *korbu, kobbu* (19); Te. *proddu* 'sun': Ka. *poẓtu, portu, pottu, hottu* (37); Te. *braduku* 'to live'; Ka. *barduṅku, barduku.*

3.8. While the regular development of **ẓ* is to -*ḍ*- in Telugu in the intervocalic position, there are, however, a few forms which run contrary to this development by showing -*n*-, -*ṇ*-, and -*ḷ*-. There are probably ten or so of this type which can be explained on special grounds. The -*n*-/-*ṇ*- and -*ḷ*-forms are apparently loanwords from the neighbouring Kannaḍa, in which -*ḷ*/-*ṇ* < **ẓ* is the rule, e.g.

1. *āṇi* 'circular shape (of pearls etc.)'; Ka. *āṇi, āẓi* 'roundedness'; Ta. Ma. *āẓi* id.
2. *āḷwār*, Ka. *āḷvār*, Mdn. Ta. *āḷvār*, OTa., OKa. *āẓvār* 'a Vaiṣṇavite mendicant'.
3. *genusu* 'sweet potato'; Ka. *geṇasu, geḷasu*; Tu. *kereṅgu, kireṅgu*; Ta. *kiẓaṅku* 'root'; Ma. *kiẓaṅṅu* id.; Kol. *kirre* 'root' (16).
4. *cōḷa* 'name of a dynasty', beside the regular *cōḍa*; Ka. *cōḷa*, Ta. Ma. *cōẓa.*

5. *gōla* 'howling, lamenting, wailing', beside the normal form *gōḍu* id.; Ka. *gōẓ* id.; Ma. *kōẓa* 'violence'; Tu. *gōlu id.*
6. *tāḷamu* 'bolt, latch'; Ta. Ma. Ka. *tāẓ*, Ka. *tāẓu* id.
7. *punugu* 'civet': Ka. Tu. *puṇugu*, Ta. Ma. *puẓuku* (Mdn. Ta. *puṉuku).*
8. *pokkili* 'naval', Ka. *hokkuẓu*, Ta. *pokkuḷ* (Jaffna dial.); *koppūẓ* (Parip.).

4. Tamil and Malayāḷam

4.1. PD **ẓ* is maintained in Old and Middle Tamil and Old Malayāḷam. In Modern Tamil also it is preserved in certain regional and class dialects. Caldwell (1956: 144) states that in the southern districts of the Tamil country, it is pronounced by the mass of the people as *ḷ*, and in Madras and the neighbourhood in the speech of 'the vulgar, *ṛ* (= *ẓ*) has become *y* or a silent letter'. Thiagaraju (1933: 76) mentions the area of *ẓ* as the North Tamil Division, i.e, the districts of Madras, Chengleput, N. Arcot, S. Arcot, Salem, and Coimbatore; it is pronounced as *ḷ* in the South Tamil Division, i.e. Trichinopoly, Tanjore, Putukkottai, Madura, Ramnad, and Tinnavelley. The Brahmin dialect from whatever part of the country still preserves the *ẓ*- pronunciation.

4.2. Ramaswami Aiyar (1935: 141) quotes a case of secondary *ẓ* in Tamil from *ḷ* in an 11th century inscription, *kēẓvippaṭi*, instead of *kēḷvippaṭi*: cf, *kēḷ* 'to hear'.

4.3. Old Indo-Aryan consonants of the retroflex series, i.e. *ṭ*, *ḍ*, and *ṣ*, are replaced by *ẓ* in loanwords found in Old and Middle Tamil and Malayāḷam (see fn. 3):

Ta. *uẓai* 'dawn' < Skt. *uṣas*; Ta. Ma. *nāẓi* 'a measure of time' < Skt. *nāḍī*-; Ma. *puruẓa* 'a male' < Skt. *puruṣa*-; Ma. *kiriẓi* 'work, labour' < Skt. *kṛṣi*-.

In these and similar cases, *ẓ* is a secondary development in Tamil-Malayāḷam during the historic period but not from a common South Dravidian source of borrowing from Old Indo-Aryan. Actually, there is no evidence of OIA *ṣ* > **ẓ* having merged with PD **ẓ* in Common South Dravidian, i.e. Proto-South Dravidian.

4.4. Before plosives and nasals, *ẓ* tends to be dropped in colloquial Tamil with the preceding vowel being lengthened, *koẓandai* 'child' > *kōndai*; *pōẓdu* 'sun, time' > *pōdu* (Sethu Pillai 1937–8: 22).

4.5. Our main source for reconstruction of the PD **ẓ* is the materials of Old Tamil and Old Malayāḷam. However, there are quite a few Proto-Dravidian forms with **ẓ* for which Tamil Malayāḷam lack correspondences; see items 8, 22, 24, 26, 31, and 35. A PD **ẓ* is reconstructed in these cases on the basis of the regularity of correspondences in the rest of the languages. In item 34, Malayāḷam and not Tamil shows *ẓ* (< **ẓ*).

4.6. An alternation of *ẓ* with *c*/*y* of a greater time depth occurs in a number of Tamil and Malayāḷam forms. This problem is discussed in §17.

4.7. A few forms with *ẓ* in Malayāḷam have peculiar variants noted in the dictionary of Gundert which call for attention:

1. *ẓ, ṣ* / *k*: *ēẓaṇi, ēṣaṇi*/*ēkaṇi* 'backbiting, talebearing'; Ta. *ēccu* 'to rail at' (§17).
2. *ẓ*/*v*: *uẓiyuka*/*uviyuka* 'to spit'; *kaẓuṅṅu*: *kavuṅṅu* 'a boa of the thickness of an areca nut tree yielding an inferior fat'; *cuẓa*: *cuva* 'taste, flavour'.
3. *ẓ*/*y*: *pēẓatti*/*pēyatti* 'a variety of fig tree'; *maẓakkuka*/*mayakkuka* 'to beat, wash clothes'.
4. *ẓ*/Ø: *tiẓiṅṅuka*/*tiṅṅuka* 'to be thronged, crowded'.

Though phonemically reliable, the available material for Kota and Toda is inadequate and therefore the conclusions for these languages have to be *ad hoc*.

5. Kota

5.1. Out of the fifteen items for Kota included in this paper, corresponding to PD **ẓ*:

(1) Seven have *ṛ* (retroflex flap):

ag- (*aṛt-*) 'to weep' (10); *ug-* (*uṛt-*) 'to plough' (3); *kaṛt* 'ass' (14); *kaṛt-* 'to wash' (15); *paṛv-* (*paṛd-*) 'to become ripe' (30a); *piṛc-* 'to clench the hand' (32a); *peṛc-* 'to talk irrelevantly' (35).

(2) Three have *ḷ*:

koḷv- (*koḷd-*) 'to putrefy'; *kaḷd* 'ass' (abusive, beside *kaṛt*, 14); *moḷm* 'cubit' (§17d)

(3) Two have *y*:

kayt- 'to wash' (beside *kaṛt-*, see above); *kod-* (*koyd-*) 'to winnow' (20).

(4) One indicates an older assimilation of **ẓ* to the following consonant:

tag 'to withdraw from a fight' (< Ka. *taggu, targu, taẓgu*, 27)

(5) One has *r*:

nerl 'shade' (< Ka. *neraḷu*, lw. from Tu. §1.4.).

(6) One has lost the reflex of **ẓ* with lengthening of the preceding vowel:
pū 'worm' (33).

Of the above examples, *ag-*, *ug-* are also from older assimilated forms, i.e. **agg-* (< **aẓ-g-*) and *ugg-* (< **uẓ-g-*); note that *ṛ*, the reflex of *ẓ*, occurs in the past stems of these forms. Eliminating the *ḷ* forms and those with assimilation as probable loanwords from Kannaḍa (§1.1), we can conclude that the regular development in Kota for PD **ẓ* is *ṛ*.

6. Toda

6.1. The Toda material is as complex as it is inadequate. There are over nine developments for **ẓ* in the available material, none of which is statistically predominant:[8]

1. *š*—4: *ušt* 'to take off clothes' (8); *pošf-* 'to ripen' (29); *möšk* 'to smear cowdung on floor' (40); *pïšt* 'time' (37).
2. *y*—2 *katy* (probably metathesis of *kayt*) 'ass' (14); *tōy* 'to be lowered' (27).
3. *ṣ*—2: *īṣf-* 'to drag, pull' (2); *uṣf-* 'to plough' (3).
4. Loss—2: *puf* 'worm' (33); *pum* 'fruit' (29).
5. Assimilation—1: *tog* 'to be humbled' (27).
6. Loss with vowel-lengthening—2: *ïx-* 'to descend' (1); *nēs̱* 'shade' (28).
7. *ṛ*—1: *oṛ-* (*oṛy-*) 'to weep' (10).
8. *ḷ*—1: *kwaḷp* 'fat' (19).
9. *ḍ*—1: *kwaḍ* 'to rot' (18).

Ruling out (2) and (7) as probable borrowings from Kota, and (5) and (8) as borrowings from Kannaḍa, we are left with (1) (3) (4) (6) and (9) as the normal developments in Toda, perhaps originally distributed in complementary environments.

7. Tuḷu

7.1. Tuḷu contains a great deal of dialect mixture representing different castes and regions. In the common or the non-Brahmin dialect, *r* is the regular reflex of PD **ẓ*. In the Brahmin dialect, which is strongly influenced by Kannaḍa, *ḷ* (< **ẓ*) is the rule though *r* also occurs in many cases,[9] e.g.

(1) *r*/*ḷ* in different caste dialects:

Common dialect	Brahmin dialect
arpini (Männer 1886) 'to weep'	*aḷpuṇa* (16)
iripuṇi 'be reduced, come down'	*iḷipuṇa* (18)
kuripuṇi 'to rot'	*kuḷipuṇa* (18)

[8] After sending this paper to the press, I have seen an article by Emeneau (1958b: 15–16) in which he has dealt with the developments of PD **ẓ* in Toda (§ 62). He gives 33 etymological sets pointing to reconstructions in PD **ẓ* for which Toda has the following reflexes arranged according to their statistical priority: *w* (7), Loss (6), *š* (4), *ṛ* (4), *ḷ* (4), *ḍ* (3), *ṣ* (2), *y* (2), *ḷ* (1).

[9] The Tuḷu items of the Brahmin dialect included here are those elicited from B. Ramachandra Rao, who is a native Tuḷu speaker and a Brahmin. He is also familiar with the variants of the common dialect or the non-Brahmin dialect; the infinitive suffix is *-uni*, *-puni*/*-pini* in Männer, but Ramachandra Rao always uses a retroflex consonant in the suffix, the difference between the non-Brahmin and Brahmin dialect forms being that of the final vowel of the infinitive. *ï* = unrounded high back vowel; *è* = open ɛ or æ.

kōri 'fowl'	*kōḷi* (23)
tāri 'palm tree'	*tāḷi* (26)
nirelï 'shade'	*niḷelï* (28)
puḷñcuṇi 'to squeeze'	*puḷñcuṇa* (32)
puri 'worm'	*puḷi* (33)
murkuṇi / *murṅguṇi* } 'to sink'	*muḷïkuṇa* (39)

(2) *r* (< *ẓ) in the common as well as the Brahmin dialects:

kare 'picottah pole, bamboo pole, etc.'	*kare* (13)
urdu 'black gram'	*urdu* (4)
parndï 'fruit'	*parndï* (29)
portu 'sun'	*portu* (37)

(3) *ḷ* (< *ẓ) in both the dialects:

ēḷï 'seven'	*ēḷï* (9)
kiḷï 'below, beneath'	*kīḷï* (16)
koḷvè 'water pipe'	*koḷavè* (17)
koḷalï 'flute'	*koḷalï* (17)
hāḷï 'desolation'	*hāḷï* (30b)

It may be concluded that *r* (< *ẓ) is the regular Tuḷu development and the *ḷ*-forms may all be loanwords from Kannaḍa; or, the isogloss of Ka. *ḷ* (< *ẓ) may have cut through a contiguous Tuḷu area which was predominantly populated by Brahmins; from this area the *ḷ*-forms could have been diffused to the other parts of the country even across the *r*-dialect.

7.2. There are a few forms with *-ḍ* in Tuḷu noted in Männer's dictionary, which is the normal development in Telugu:

kīḍï 'inferior' (16); *koḍi* 'a sprout'; *koḍipuṇa* 'to sprout' (21); *kōḍè* 'a young, inexperienced man' (cf. 19, 21); *paḍili* 'barren, uncultivated, desolate' (30b).

Probably, these forms represent another local dialect in the Tuḷu area which is yet to be traced.

8. Kui-Kuvi

8.1. The Kui-Kuvi subgroup is the north-eastern neighbour of Telugu and shares with it the development of metathesis in the root phonemes, when the second syllable happens to contain a liquid sonorant (*r, *ṯ [-ṟ-], *l, *ḷ, or *ẓ). In such cases as well as in others, PD *ẓ is represented by Kui *ṛ* a retroflex flap according to the description of Winfield (1928: 3). Correspondingly, Kuvi has *r* in the dialect treated by Fitzgerald and *l* in that of Schulze.

8.2. Out of the nineteen Kui items of definite cognation occurring in the appended list, thirteen show *ṛ* as follows:

ṛīva (*ṛīt-*) 'to weep, cry' (10); *ṛūva* 'to plough' (3); *ṛūsa* 'to scrape up' (7); *gṛāsa* 'to cross' (12); *kṛohpa* 'to winnow' (20); *koṛgi* 'newly sprouted' (21); *kōṛa* 'first shoot' (21); *kṛōga* 'fat' (19); *pṛāḍi* 'old' (30a, b); *piṛu*, *pṛiu* 'worm' (33); *pṛihpa* 'to squeeze out' (32); *pṛēnu* 'bone' (31); *bṛuḍga* 'to sink' (39).

8.3. In three or four forms, *ẓ has developed to *r*, but all of them can be interpreted as representing a different dialect of Kui, which is probably closer to Kuvi, e.g.

krōga 'fat' (< **koẓaw*, 19); *krōḍu* 'a tube' (< **kuẓal*, 17); *bārti* 'longevity' (< **wāẓt-*), Te. *brāti* 'prosperity', Ta. *vāẓcci* 'living', Ka. *bāẓti* id. (< **wāẓ-*).

For the first of the above items, the Gunupur dialect has a retroflex flap instead of *r*, i.e. *kṛōga*.[10] It is therefore likely that *ṛ*- variants could be discovered for the rest of the forms also in some other Kui dialects.

8.4. There is, to a restricted extent, in Kui a development similar to that of Telugu, i.e. *ẓ > *ḍ*/*d* when occurring word initially through metathesis, e.g.

ḍripa (*ḍri-t-*) 'to drag' (< **ẓri-*, < **iẓ-ir-*) (2); *dīva* (*dī-t-*) 'to fall down from, to descend' (1).

The last form is specially interesting in that it shows the shift of *d*- < *ḍ*-, operating in Classical and Middle Telugu. Since the above two items with initial *ḍ*-/*d*- do not have exact parallels in Telugu which may warrant any borrowing, they may be taken as independent developments in a dialect of Kui whose boundaries probably overlapped with the dialect mainly treated by Winfield.

8.5. The remaining Kui items have *h* (*kahpa* 'to wash', 15) and *j* (*koju* 'fowl', 23), corresponding to SD *ẓ*. However, they presuppose some other phoneme than *ẓ in each case in the proto-language, i.e. *h* (< **s* < **c*), *j* (< **ḏ* < **ṯ*). A discussion of these items is made elsewhere (see §§**17**, **18**).

8.6. The available Kuvi cognates are not many, but among the items included here, the percentage of regularity is fairly high. PD *ẓ develops to *r*/*l* in different Kuvi dialects.

Fitzgerald:	Schulze:
rui- 'to plough'	*lū* (3)
rūca 'comb'	*lūẓa* (*ẓ* = *ts*) (7)
rī- 'to weep'	*li*- (10)
grānc- 'to cross over'	*glā*- 'to pass, transgress' (12)
kōrss- 'to winnow'	*kloh*- id (20)
prīyūli 'worm'	*pliyuli* (33)

For 1 and 2 in the Appendix, we notice that both the dialects have *r*.

During a brief field-trip to the Araku Valley (71 miles north-west of Visakhapatnam), the present writer came across a dialect of Kuvi near Araku, which has *ṛ*

[10] Information from Burrow who recently did fieldwork in this area.

(retroflex flap) for PD *ẓ. The material is however scanty but it contains three diagnostic items as follows:[11]

koṛas- 'to winnow' (20); *ṛū-* 'to plough' (3); *pṛiyuli* (pl. *pṛika*) 'worm' (33).

8.7. It may be concluded from a comparison of Kui and Kuvi material that *ṛ* had originally been the regular reflex of PD *ẓ in the whole area of Kui-Kuvi and that the merger of this with *r* or *l* started later mainly in the present Kuvi area, gradually creeping across its borders into the present Kui also.

9. Gondi

9.1. Gondi is a cover term for a group of divergent dialects. Many of the Gondi dialects have *-ṛ* regularly for *ẓ, e.g. *uṛ-* 'to plough' (3); *āṛ-* 'to weep' (10); *uṛp-* 'to clean a threshing floor' (8); *ēṛung* 'seven' (9); *kaṛēng-* 'to be swung'; *koṛs-* 'to sprout' (21); *koṛving* 'fat' (19); *koṛiāṛ* (Williamson) 'daughter-in-law' (22); *puṛī* 'worm'; *puṛit-* 'to be worm-eaten' (33); *muṛ-* 'to ripen' (38); *muṛung-*, GoM. *muṛand-* 'to dive, sink' (39); *sūṛ* 'to see' (24).

9.2. Relatively fewer items occur with *r* instead of *ṛ* in Trench's Gondi, e.g. *sūr-* 'to expect' (24); *tarīt-* 'to be hot (as sun)' (25); *pīr* 'to squeeze' (32); *koriāṛ* 'daughter-in-law' (22). This is again a case of dialect mixture since some of the other Gondi dialects show *ṛ* in the corresponding forms (see Appendix, especially 22, 24, 32).

9.3. The Adilabad and Maṛia dialects have an initial *ḍ-* for PD *ẓ in a few early Telugu loanwords, e.g. GoM. *ḍig-* to descend: OTe. *ḍigu* (1); *ḍū* (pl. *ḍūwal*) tiger: MTe. *duwwu* (6); GoA. *ḍuppal* a spotted deer: Mdn. Te. *duppi* (5).

After eliminating the marginal cases of dialect mixture, the regular Gondi development for PD *ẓ would be *ṛ*.

10. Parji

10.1. PD *ẓ is preserved as a separate phoneme in this language as distinct from *ṭ*, *ḍ*, and *r*. The Parji language of Burrow and Bhattacharya contains thirty two etyma in which PD *ẓ is regularly represented by *ṛ*. Since *ẓ is represented by no other phoneme than *ṛ* in this language, the regularity of correspondence is one hundred per cent. Of course, we need to eliminate the early Telugu loanwords, occurring with initial *ḍ-* (§3.4), viz. *ḍukki* 'tillage': Te. *dukki* (3), *ḍū* (pl. *ḍūgal*) 'tiger': MTe. *duwwu* (6). Twenty etyma with *ṛ* (< *ẓ) have been included in the Appendix, see 1, 2, 3, 7, 8, 10, 13, 16, 19, 21, 24, 25, 26, 28, 30a, b, 31, 32, 33, 38, 39.

[11] From the official report submitted to the Andhra University, Waltair, by G. B. Kelley and myself on a linguistic investigation of the Araku area.

10.2. The rest of the items in Parji with *ṛ* < **ẓ* are as follows:

uṛñi/*nuṛñi* 'mosquito'; *kāṛ* 'a grain'; *kuṛub* 'pit'; *kuṛayp-* 'to heap up', *kūṛer-* 'to assemble', *gumṛi* '*Gumelina arborea*'; *pōṛ-* 'to split, cleave'; *muṛd-* 'to lie flat on the face', *muṛdil* 'prone', *moṛk-* 'to salute respectfully'; *uṛ-* 'to spit'; *taṛung* 'liver' (< PCD **taẓ-unk-*); ?*nūṛ* to wear; *vīṛ* to sell (< PCD **wīẓ-*).

10.3. Though PD **ẓ* = Pa. *ṛ*, Pa. *ṛ* is not always from PD **ẓ*. In other words, Pa. *ṛ* is a pool of more than one source, for instance NIA *r*/*ṛ* = Pa. *ṛ*, e.g. Pa. *kuṛta* 'coat, shirt'; *guṛ* 'jaggery', etc. In a few marginal cases PD **ṭ* and **r* occur as *ṛ*, though the regular correspondences in Pa. are *ḍ* and *r* respectively, e.g. *gaṛdit* 'hornet' (Ma. *kaṭannal*, Te. *kaḍūduru*, etc.); *naṛub* 'middle' (Te. *naḍumu*); *goṛonga* 'crane', cf. Tu. *korṅgï*, Te. *koṅga*.

11. Ollari

11.1. The Ollari language is a recently recorded member of the Dravidian family and is closely allied to Parji and Gadaba of the Parji-Kolami subgroup in Central Dravidian. Bhattacharya's Ollari vocabulary of about seven hundred items contains twelve etyma with *ṛ* traceable to proto-forms with **ẓ*. In the sample tested, the percentage of regularity is as high as in the case of Parji. Seven out of the twelve *ṛ*-items occur in the Appendix. The remaining five are as follows: *kuṛap* 'to heap up' (Pa. *kuṛayp*); *kuṛup* 'well' (Pa. *kuṛub* 'pit'); *toṛon* 'brother' (Ta. *tōẓaṉ* 'companion'; Kui *tōṛenju*, Kol. Nk. *tōren*); *nevuṛ* 'saliva' (see Emeneau 1955a: Vocab.); *vīṛ* 'to sell' (ibid. 1042).

12. Gadaba

12.1. The Gadaba language spoken in about twelve tribal villages around Sālūr in the Srīkākuḷam Taluq (north-east of Andhra) has no published account about it except the fieldnotes of the author which contain about a thousand vocabulary items and texts. Out of this material, fifteen etyma traceable to forms with **ẓ* have been discovered. Thirteen among these occur in the Appendix. The regular correspondence in this language for PD **ẓ* is *ḍ* in all positions, e.g.

āḍ- 'to weep' (10); *iḍg-* 'to descend' (1); *uḍuv-* 'to dress hair' (7); *ūḍ-* 'to plough' (3); *kaḍcil* (pl.) 'fuel, dried sticks' (13); *kiḍin* 'below' (16); *kuḍuŋ* 'be rotten at bottom, as a fixed pole' (18); *koḍkuṭ* 'fat' (19); *koḍc-*/*koḍus-* 'to sprout' (21); *ḍuppi* (lw. < OTe., 5); *cūḍ-* 'to see' (24); *paḍiŋ-* 'to ripen, become ready for harvest' (29); *puḍut* 'insect' (33).

12.2. *tōṇḍud* 'sister', *tōṇḍōṇḍ* 'brother' have *-ṇḍ-* for PD **ẓ* unlike Pa. Oll. *ṛ*, Kol. and Nk. *r* which do not show the pre-consonantal nasal. The reconstructed form should therefore be **tōẓ-nt-* (> **tōṇ-ṭ-*), as in many other similar cases in

Central Dravidian (see §19). The last form is *vīḍ-* 'to sell' (Pa. Oll. *vīṛ-*, Kol. Nk. *vīr-*, see Emeneau 1955a: Vocab. 1042).

13. Kolami and Naiki

13.1. Out of the thirty two Kolami etyma in the consolidated vocabulary of Emeneau (1955a) traceable to proto-forms with *ẓ, the common reflex is *r* for *ẓ occurring in ten forms as follows:

ar 'to weep' (10); *ur* 'to harrow' (3); *urunde* 'black gram' (4); *koral* 'younger brother's wife' (22); *koru* 'fat' (19); *tari* 'to burn' (25); *purre* 'worm' (33); those not included in the Appendix, *kumre* '*Gumelina arborea*' (Emeneau 1955a: Vocab. 3078); *tōren* younger brother (ibid. 944); *vīr* 'to sell' (ibid. 1042).

13.2. Some nine out of the rest are loanwords from early as well as later Telugu and therefore do not conform to the regular development:

bat 'to live' (Mdn. Te. *batuku*, OTe. *braduku*, OKa. *barduku*); *dig-* 'to descend', Te. *digu* (see 1); *ḍol-* 'to be felled' (OTe. *ḍollu* < **ẓo-l* < **oẓ-l-*; cf. Ta. Ma. *uẓal* 'to dangle'); *gāḍdi* 'ass' (OTe. *gāḍda*, Old and Mdn. Te. *gāḍida*, 14); *mēg-* 'purify with cowdung solution' (OTe. *mrēgu*, 40); *poddu* 'sun' (Mdn. Te. *poddu*, OTe. *proddu*, 37) *duva* 'pather'. (MTe. *duwwu*, 6); *miŋeŋ* 'to swallow' (Mdn. Te. *miṅgu*, OTe. *mringu*; cf. Ma. *miẓuṅṅu*, Ta. *viẓuṅku* id.); *muḍsū* 'knee' (Mdn. Te. *muḍuku*, *muḍusu*, Ta. *muẓam*, Ma. *muẓi* joint).

13.3. *nīṇḍa* 'shade,' *panḍ* 'to become ripe,' *pīnḍ* 'to squeeze' have an original *ẓ assimilated to the following nasal-stop suffix (see §19). We are still left with a few more anomalous forms, i.e. *kovve* (Emeneau puts it with PD **koẓ-uw*, see his Vocab. 422; Appendix 21); *maguḍ* 'to vomit' (ibid. 480); *muḍ-* 'to talk' (ibid. 548); *nōlaŋg-* 'to crawl' (ibid. 603). In the last of these *l* is a reflex of *ḷ alternating in Proto-Dravidian itself with *ẓ (see §17 b); etymologies for the remaining three are not thoroughly convincing, on the basis of irregularity in form in *kovvu* and *muḍ-* and the meaning in *maguḍ-*.

14. Kuṛux and Malto

14.1. Unfortunately, not many cognates are available in these two languages for *ẓ forms of South Dravidian. It is therefore not possible to make definite conclusions. However, the predominant reflex seems to be *c*/*s* (rarely *y*) after all vowels, and more frequently after the high vowels, *i* and *u*, e.g.

Kuṛ. *īc-* 'to pull out'; Malto *ic-* 'to take off' (2); Kuṛ. *uy-* (*uss-*) 'to plough' (3); Kuṛ. *khajj-* 'to cleanse the head with clay', Malto *kaj-* 'to wash, as clothes' (15); Kuṛ. *kīta*, *kiyyā*, *kiyyantā* 'below' (16); Kuṛ. *xos-* 'to decay, rot', cf. Malto *gojnār-* 'to be or become dirty' (18); Kuṛ. *paccā* 'old', *pacc-* 'to grow old', Malto *pac-* 'to become old', *pacge* 'old' (30a); Kuṛ. *pocgō* 'worm', *pocc-* 'to be rotten', Malto *pocru* 'worm' (33).

14.2. A few items seem to have *r* for **ẓ*:

Kuṛ. *ur-* 'to rub off the leaves, etc. by passing the hand along' (8); Kuṛ. *xōr-* 'to sprout, flourish', Malto *qōroc-* id. (21) (?< IA); Kuṛ. *tār-* 'to fell, cut off', Malto *tār-* id. (27); Kuṛ. *perperer-* 'to prate' (35; probably onomatopoeic).

14.3. Malto has *ṛ* in one case and *l* in another for **ẓ*:

peṛq- 'to talk, speak' (35); *pilq-* 'to squeeze' (32a).

We can dismiss the first three items of §**14.2**, and the first of §**14.3**, on account of their doubtful cognation. It may therefore be concluded that *c* or *s* (*y*) is the usual reflex of **ẓ* in these two languages.

15. Brahui

15.1. Brahui has seven definite cognates for South Dravidian forms with **ẓ*, out of which (1) five show *r*/*rr*, (2) one shows *ḻẖ* (voiceless l?), and (3) one drops the reflex (?) of **ẓ* lengthening the preceding vowel:

(1) *xarr-* (*xarr-ā-*) 'to proceed on foot' (12); *xarr-* (*xarr-is-*) 'to sprout' (21); *kēragẖ* (alternants: *kē*, *kī-*, *ki-* 'below') 'bottom' (16); *princh-* 'to squeeze out' (32, a; lw.?< Baluchi); *mir-* 'to plaster' (40).

(2) *piḻẖ-* 'to squeeze' (32, a); cf. Malto *pilq-* id.

(3) *pū* 'worm' (33).

The normal development is, therefore, *r* < **ẓ*.

16. The foregoing conclusions may be summed up in a tabular form. In the quantitative presentation in Table 3.1 only the regular developments have been taken into consideration. The percentage of regularity of a given reflex for each language is computed in relation to the total number of cognates available in that language out of the forty reconstructed forms in the appended test list.

17. An examination of a number of etymological groups yields two or more related reconstructions each for Proto-Dravidian, in which **ẓ* itself stands in alternation with some other phoneme, viz. **c*, **ḷ* ,**ṯ*, and **r*, of which the **ẓ*/**c* (> *y*) alternation is the commonest, e.g.

(1) **ẓ*: **c*
  (a) PSD **īẓ*: PCD and PND *īc-* (2)
  (b) PSD **eẓ*-V-, *ec*-V-: PCD *ēc-*

Ta. *iẓai* 'utter, say' (Tolk.); *icai* 'to sound' (Tolk.); 'to play, as a lute; to indicate;' n. 'sound word, praise' (Kṟḷ.); *iyampu* 'to sound' (PN); tr. 'to praise, speak'; Ma. *iyampuka* id.; Kui *ēsa* 'to sing; to say, tell'.

TABLE 3.1. *Reflexes of Proto-Dravidian *ẓ (based on 40 selected etymologies)*

	OTa.	Ma.	To.	Ko.	Koḍ.	Ka.	Tu.	Te.	Go.	Kui	Kuvi	Kol.	Pa.	Oll.	Gad.	Kuṛ.	Malto	Br.
Development with count	ẓ 35	ẓ 30	š 4	ṟ 7	ḷ 6	{ ẓ/ḷ 18	r/l 9	{ ḍ 18 (+3)	ṟ 11	ṟ 13	r/l 6	r 7	ṟ 20	ṟ 7	ḍ 13	c/s 5	c/j 4	r 5
	c 1	c 1	y 2	ḷ 3	Ø̂ 2	ẓ/r/Ø̂ 3	r 3	r 16	r 3 (+2)	r 2 (+1)	r 2	d 2	ḍ 2			r 4	r 2	l̲h̲ 1
			ṣ 2	y 2		*ẓ/r/Ø̂ 2	ḷ 5	Ø̂ 3	ḍ 3	ḍ 1	ṟ (2)	ḍ 1				j 1	l 1	Ø̄ 1
			Ø 2	Ø̂ 1		ẓ/*r/Ø̂ 1	ḍ (4)	d 3 (+1)		d 1		Ø 1				y 1 (+1)	r 1	
			Ø̂ 1	Ø̄ 1		ẓ/ṇ 3				h 1		Ø̂ 1						
			Ø̄ 2	r 1		*ẓ/ṇ 3				j 1								
			ṟ 1			c 1												
			ḷ 1			r (1)												
			ḍ 1			ḍ (1)												
Total no. of cognates	36	31	16	15	8	31	17	40	17	19	8	12	22	7	13	11	8	7
Statistically predominant reflexes and their count	ẓ 35	ẓ 30	š 4	ṟ 7	ḷ 6	ẓ/ḷ 18 ẓ/r/Ø̂ 6	r 12	ḍ 18 r 16	r 11	r 13	r/l 6	r 7	ṟ 20	ṟ 7	ḍ 13	c/s 5	c/j 4	r 5
Percentage of regularity (to nearest integer)	97	97	25	47	75	77 (58+19)	71	85 (45+40)	64	68	75	58	91	100	100	45	50	71

Ø Complete loss   Ø̂ Loss through assimilation   Ø̄ Loss with lengthening of preceding vowel

/ Indicates that alternative developments occur either in different dialects (class or regional), or different periods of the history of the language in question.

{ Developments enclosed with this mark occur in complementary distribution and therefore count as a single development.

() Numbers enclosed in parentheses refer to alternative developments already included in the count of more regular (or older) developments.

(c) PSD *oẓ: *ōy

Ta. *uẓa* 'to suffer' (Maṇi.); *uẓappu* 'suffering' (Tolk.); 'effort, exertion'; Ma. *uẓakka* 'to be wearied, despair': Ta. *ōy* 'to be diminished, be reduced' (Tolk.); 'to become weary, tired, weak'; *uyavu, uyal, uyakkam* 'distress, suffering'.

(d) PSD *eẓ-ay: PCD *ēc-

Ta. *iẓai* 'to be reeled (as yarn); to spin'; n. 'yarn; single twisted thread' (Naṉ.); Ma. *iẓa*, n. id.; Ka. *eẓe* 'thread': Kui *ēspa* (*ēs-t-*) 'to spin thread, spinning'.

(e) PSD *kāẓ/ kaẓ-uw: PCD and PND *kac-* (15)
(f) PSD, PCD, *kūẓ/kōẓ: PSD, PND *koc-* (18)
(g) PSD *kōẓ/koẓ-V: PSD, PCD *koc-* (20)
(h) PD *piẓ-: *pic-* (32)
(i) PSD *piẓ-: PCD *pic-/*piy-

Ta. *piẓai* 'to be emancipated from sins and births; to escape; to live, subsist'; n. 'escape, life'; Ma. *piẓekka* 'to slip through, to support life'; *piẓeppu* 'livelihood': Tu. *pīṅkuni* (< *piy-nk*) 'to escape'; Go. *piss-* 'to be saved; to live, earn one's living'; Kui *pihpa* 'to release'; Kuvi (F) *piss-* 'to forsake', (S) *pih-nai* 'to release'.

(j) PSD *poẓ-: *poc-

Ta. *puẓai* 'tube, pipe'; *puẓal* 'drain'; Ma. *puẓa* 'river, drain', Ka. *poẓe* 'river': Ka. *pocce* 'stream, river'.

(k) PD *māẓ/*maẓ-V-: *māc/*māy-

Ta. *maẓuṅku* 'to be dim'; *maẓuku* id.; *maẓai* 'a cloud'; Ma. *maẓuku* 'to grow dim'; cf. Kui *mārga* 'to hide': Ta. *mācu* 'stain, defect' (Kṟl); 'darkness'; *māy* 'become lustreless'; *mā* 'blackness' (Cilap.); Ma. *māccu* 'dirt'; *māyuka* 'to grow dim'; Tu. *māsuni* id.; Te. *māyu* 'to be hidden', 'become dirty'; *masugu* 'cloudiness'; *masi* 'black dust; ink'; Kui *māsi* 'filth'; Kuvi (F) *maci* 'dirty', *māsk-* 'to mask'; Malto *mask-* 'to vanish (of person)'; forms with *y* (< *c*) also occur in many languages.

(2) *ẓ: *l/ṇ (l /ṇ alternation is common in Proto-Dravidian)

PD *mūẓ/*muẓ-V-: *mūḷ/mūṇ , mūḷ-V-/mūṇ-V- 'to sink, immerse' (39, a, b).

(3) *ẓ: ṭ

PSD *kōẓ-i: PCD *kōṭ* 'fowl' (23)

(4) *ẓ: *r: *Ø

PSD *mūr/murV-: PCD *mūr/mur-V-: PND *mū-* 'cubit'.

Ta. Ma. *muẓam* 'cubit' (from Ta. *muẓam-* 'joint', cf. Ta. Ma. *muẓaṅ-kāl* 'knee'; *muẓaṅ-kai* 'elbow, measured for cubit'); Ko. *moḷm* id.; To. *magoy* id.; Ka. *moẓakey* 'elbow'; *moḷa, moṇa* id.; 'joint'; Koḍ. *moḷa* 'cubit'; *moḷa-kay*; 'elbow'; Tu. *mora*, *mura, moḷa* id.; *moraṅgè, muraṅgé* (< **muẓam-kay-*) id.; OTe. *mrŏkālu* 'knee': Te. *mūra* 'cubit', Kui *miru, mriu* id.; Pa. Kol. *mūra* id.: Kuṛ. *mū-kā* 'knee, elbow'; Malto *mū-ke, muki* 'cubit' (see Emeneau 1955a: Vocab. 562).

18. Two interpretations are possible to explain alternative developments in the reconstructed stage itself. Studying the eleven cases under §17(1) with **ẓ*/**c* alternation, one can say that in pre-Dravidian (older stage of Proto-Dravidian), there was a phoneme different from either **ẓ* or **c* and that it fell together with **ẓ* in one area and **c* in another area in Proto-Dravidian. If this solution were to be adopted we should expect **ẓ*/**c* alternation to supply us isoglosses binding mutually exclusive areas. This is possible in the case of sets (a), (d), (e), (i) which provide isoglosses separating South Dravidian as the *ẓ*-area and Central and North Dravidian as the *c*-area. Problems arise when we consider sets (b), (c), (f), (g), and (j) which indicate overlapping of the *ẓ*- and *c*-zones. Even this could be reasonably explained through the phenomenon of dialect mixture, since we do not know precisely the dialect composition in Proto-Dravidian. It may therefore be correct to assume that the languages we now group as South, Central, and North Dravidian on a linguistic basis were after all not so very far apart in the Proto-Dravidian stage and therefore dialect mixture is as much permissible at the Proto-Dravidian stage as it is during the historic period of any modern Dravidian language. Sets (h) and (k) indicate **ẓ*/**c* in the whole family and therefore cannot be explained on the same grounds as the rest of the cases above, unless we say that the dialect mixture was so great as to spread to almost every part of the Proto-Dravidian area.

18.1. For §17 (3) and (4) we get clean isoglosses separating South Dravidian as the *ẓ*-zone and Central Dravidian as the **ṯ*- and *r*-zones respectively.

18.2. Are we therefore to set up three phonemes in pre-Dravidian, one phoneme to explain **ẓ*/**c* (in 11 sets), another to explain *ẓ*/**ṯ* (1 set) and still another to explain **ẓ*/**r* (1 set) in Proto-Dravidian? If we do, say, set up **X, **Y, **Z in pre-Dravidian, of which **X fell together with **ẓ*/**c*, **Y with **ẓ*/**ṯ* and **Z with **ẓ*/**r* in Proto-Dravidian, we should expect these alternations to present themselves in quite a few sets in the modern Dravidian languages rather than in one or two. As far as **ẓ*/**c* is concerned, there is a considerable number of sets of cognates which show the development; not all of them have been included here. We are therefore justified in setting up an **X in pre-Dravidian to explain **ẓ*/**c* in Proto-Dravidian. But evidence for **ẓ*/**ṯ* and **ẓ*/**r* is too small to warrant the positing of two different phonemes in pre-Dravidian.

18.3. An alternative explanation is as follows: It was stated earlier (§**0.1**) that the Dravidian roots can be resolved into two proto-types (C)V̆̄C-, and (C)V̆̄-, with which derivative suffixes beginning with vowels or consonants may occur. The criterion to separate the roots from the suffixes is that roots are constant elements in relation to the derivative suffixes which are variable elements and are limited in number; the procedure to follow is comparing related forms in the same language;

Ta. *tiri, tiruku, tiruntu, tirumpu*; *tirai* ('curtain'), *tiruḷ*, etc. indicating some specialized idea of 'moving' or 'revolving' yield, on comparison, a root **tir-* and a series of suffixes, *-i, -uku, -untu, -umpu, -ai, -uḷ*, etc. which occur with similar other roots of the (C)VC type, e.g. **am-* 'to make', *am-ai, am-ar*, etc. On the comparative level, we notice that the phonemes occurring as part of the root syllables fall into systematic series of correspondences making it possible to reconstruct the proto-system. On the other hand the phonemes of the suffix syllables do not fall into such a single-line correspondence system.

18.4. With the background of these remarks, if we study the forms of the (C)V̆̄C type in the Dravidian languages of which the final appears a variable in relation to (C)V̆̄-, we can conclude that the final -C is a derivative suffix on the level of inner derivation, e.g. (34).

**pūẓ*: Ma. *pūẓu* 'to be buried'; Ka. *pūḷ*, Te. *pūḍu* id.; Kol. *pur-* 'to be filled up'. **pūnt-/pūtt-*: Ma. *pūntuka* 'to sink in the ground'; *pūttuka* 'to bury'; Kuṛ. *putt-* 'to set (of sun)'.

There is no question that the two reconstructions **pūẓ*: **pūnt*/**pūtt-* are related. We can explain the variables in these forms as derivatives with greater time depth behind them, in which case **pū-* is the root in Proto-Dravidian and **-ẓ*, **-nt*/**-tt* are different suffixes.

18.5. Extending the same principle to **mūẓ-*: **mūḷ-*/**mūṇ-* 'to sink' (39a, b), **kōẓ-*/**kōṯ-* 'fowl' (23), and **mūẓ -*/**mūr-* 'cubit', we can separate the final phonemes, which vary, as originally derivative suffixes at the pre-Dravidian stage. Since the suffix phonemes do not yield to single-line reconstruction as do the root phonemes, the question of accounting for the alternations **ẓ*/**ḷ*, **ẓ*/**ṯ*, and **ẓ*/*r* as part of the reconstructed system is irrelevant.

19. Proto-Dravidian **ẓ* is optionally assimilated to the following nasal-stop suffixes in a few cases in Central and Northern Dravidian. This development gives a clear isogloss separating South from Central Dravidian. It may be noted that Tuḷu and Telugu occupy a midway position between Central and South Dravidian, e.g.

1. **piẓ-* 'to squeeze': Ta. Ma. Ko. Tu. Te. Kui, Pa. Go. Br. (32); **piz-(u)nt* (> **piṇ-ṭ*): Tu. *purñc-, pīṇṭ-*, Te. *piṇḍu*; Kol. Nk. *pīnḍ-* id.
2. **paẓ-*V- 'fruit, to ripen': Ta. Ma. To. Ko. Ka. Pa. Oll. Gad. (29); *paẓ(u)nt-* (> **paṇ-ṭ-*): Tu. *parndï* 'fruit'; Te. Kuvi *paṇḍu*; Go. *panḍ-* 'to ripen'; Pa. Kol. *panḍ-*; Kuṛ. *pān- (panj-)* 'to ripen'.
3. **nīẓ-al* 'shade': Ta. Ma. To. Ka. Tu. Te. Go. Pa. (28); **nīẓ-nt*: Kol. Nk. *nīnḍa* id.

20. The terms South, Central and North Dravidian have been used throughout this paper without a definition of their common linguistic features or their boundaries. It will be irrelevant in this paper to go into a discussion of this problem.

Appendix I

1. PD **iẓ-*, **iẓ-i*, **iẓ-ik/-uk*

Ta. *iẓi* 'to descend, dismount, fall, be lowered'; tr. 'to lower'; *iẓiccu, iẓittu* 'to lower'; Ma. *iẓika* 'to descend'; *iẓikka* 'to lower'; To. *īx-* 'to descend'; *īk-* tr.; Ka. *iẓi* 'to descend, become less'; *iẓiku* 'to lower'; Koḍ. *iḷi-* v.i., *iḷip-* tr.; Tu. *iriyuni* 'to fall, drop'; Te. *ḍiggu/ḍigu, digg/digu* 'to descend, etc.', *ḍincu/dincu* tr.; Kui *dīva* (*dī-t-*) 'to fall, etc.', Kuvi *rī-* 'to fall'; (S) *rē-* id.; GoM. *ḍig-* 'to descend'; (Nandgaon dial.) *ḍīk-t-* 'felled' (*LSI* IV: 522); Pa. *iṛ-*, *iṛv-* 'to descend'; Oll. *iṛg-*, Gad. *iḍg-* id.; Kol. (SR) *ḍig-*, (Kinwaṭ dial.) *ḍigg-*, (E) *dig-* id.; Nk. *ḍigg-* id. (Kui GoM. Kol. Nk. forms are loanwords from early Telugu) [*DEDR* 502].

2. PD **īẓ/*iẓ-V-*

Ta. *iẓu* 'to draw, pull'; Ma. *iẓekka* id.; *iẓukka* 'to draw, pull (of clothes)'; Ko. *iḷv-* (*iḷt-*) 'to drag on ground'; To. *īṣf-* (*īṣt-*) id.; Ka. *īẓ*, *iẓ* 'to pull, drag'; *eẓe, eḷe* id.; Te. *īḍcu* id.; Kui *ḍripa* (*ḍri-t-*) 'to drag away, abduct'; Kuvi (F) *rej-*, (S) *ren-* (*rett-*) 'to drag, pull'; Kuṛ. *īc-* 'to draw out, pull out with friction'; *īs-* id.; Malto *ic-* 'to take off'; *icgr-* 'to come off' [*DEDR* 504].

3. PD **ūẓ-/*uẓ-u*, **uẓ-uk-*

Ta. *uẓu* 'to plough, dig up'; Ma. *uẓuka*; Ko. *ug-* (**ugg-* < **uẓ-g-*), past *uṛt-*; To. *uṣf-* (*uṣt-*) id.; Ka. *uẓu, uḷu* (*uẓt-*, *utt-*) id.; *uẓke, uḷuke, ukke* 'ploughing'; Koḍ. *ūḷ* id.; Tu. *ura* 'ploughing'; *ūḍuni* 'to plough' (?*ḍ*); Te. *dukki* 'tillage' (< **ḍukki*); Kui *ṛūva* (*ṛū-t-*) 'to plough'; Kuvi (F) *ruiyali*, (S) *lū-* id.; Koṇḍa *ṛū-*; Go. *uṛ-* 'to plough'; Pa. *ūṛ-* 'to plough', *ḍukki* 'tillage' (lw. < Te.); Oll. *uṛ-*; Gad. *ūḍ-*; Kol. (E) *ur-* 'to harrow'; (SR) *ūrr-* id.; Nk. *ur-* id.; Kuṛ. *uy-* (*uss-*) id.; Malto *ur-* 'to turn up the soil (as pigs do)' [*DEDR* 688].

4. PD **uẓ-unt-*

Ta. *uẓuntu* 'black gram' (Aiṅk.); Ma. *uẓunnu*; Ka. *urdu, uddu* id.; Tu. *urdu*; Te. *uddulu*; Kol. (Kinwaṭ dial.) *urunde*; Nk. *urndaḷ*; Pkt. (DNM.) *uḍida* [*DEDR* 690].

5. PD **uẓ-*, **uẓ-ay*, **uẓ-upp-*

Ta. *uẓai* 'deer'; Tu. *ure* 'deer'; Pa. *uṛup* 'spotted deer'; Gad. *ḍuppi* id.; Te. *duppi* id. (< **ḍuppi*); GoA. *ḍuppal* id.; Kol. (Kinwaṭ dial.) *ḍuppi* (Go. Kol. and Gad. forms are loanwords from early Telugu) [*DEDR* 694].

6. PD **uẓ-uw-*

Ta. *uẓuvai* 'tiger' (Cīv.); Te. *duwwu* id. (Classical); GoM. *ḍū*, pl. *ḍūval*, (dial.) *duvāl*; Pa. *ḍū*, pl. *ḍuval* id.; Kol. *duva* 'panther', (Kinwaṭ dial.) *ḍū*, pl. *ḍūgul* id. (Go. Pa. and Kol. forms are loanwords from early Telugu) [*DEDR* 692].

7. PD **ūẓ-/*uẓ-V-*, **uẓ-aw-*

Ta. *uẓu* (fut. *uẓu-v-*) 'to arrange or adjust (as the hair with fingers)' (Cīv.); Te. *duwwu* 'to comb hair' (< **ḍuwwu*); *ḍūyu/ḍuyyu* 'to strip off leaves etc. of a twig by hand; to draw out a sword'; Go. *uṛ-*, Koṇḍa *ḍūs-* 'to comb'; Kui *ṛūsa* 'to rub, scrape'; Kuvi (F) *rūss-* 'to dress (another's hair)'; *rūca* 'comb'; (S) *lūca* id.; Pa. *uṛ-*, *uṛv-* 'to comb'; Gad. *uḍuv-* id. [*DEDR* 689].

8. PD **ūẓ-*

To. *uṡt-* 'to take off, clothes, ring, etc.'; Te. *ūḍcu* 'to take off clothes, etc.; to pull off (feathers of a bird); to clean floor by sweeping'; Go. *uṛp-* 'to clean a threshing floor'; Pa. *ūṛcip-* (*ūṛcit-*) 'to heap up, put together'; Kuṛ. *ur-* 'to rub off the leaves, etc. by passing the hand along' [*DEDR* 695].

9. PSD, PCD **ēẓ-/*eẓ-u-*

Ta. *ēẓu* (adj. *eẓu-*) 'seven'; Ma. *ēẓu*, *eẓu* id.; Ko. *ēye*, To. *öw*; Ka. *ēẓu/ēẓu*, *ēẓu/ēḷu*; Tu. *ēḷï*, *eḷï*, Te. *ēḍu*, *ḍe-* (< **ẓe-* < **eẓ-*); Go. *ēṛuṅg-* id. (ibid.) [*DEDR* 910].

10. PD **yāẓ-/*yaẓ-V-* (?**y*)

Ta. *aẓu* 'to weep, cry' (Kṟḷ); *aẓivu* 'distress'; Ma. *aẓuka* 'to weep, cry'; Ko. *ag-* (*aṛt-*) id.; To. *oṛ-* (*oṛy-*) id.; Ka. *aẓu/aḷu* (*aẓt-/aḷt-*) id.; *aẓa/aḷa* 'weeping'; Tu. *arpini* 'to weep'; *aẓïpuṇa* id.; Te. *ēḍcu* id.; Kui *ṛī-* (*ṛī-t-*), Kuvi (F) *rī-*, (S) *lī- id.*; Go. *āṛ-*; Pa. Oll. *aṛ-*; Gad. *āḍ-*; Kol. (SR) *arr*, (E) *ar-*; Nk. *ar-* [*DEDR* 282].

11. PD **kaẓ-al*

Ta. *kaẓal* 'to run away, get loose'; Ma. *kaẓaluka* 'to slip'; Ka. *kaẓal* 'to slip off, get loose'; Te. *krālu* 'to move, shake; wave as a banner'; Go. *kaṛēng-/kasēng-* 'to be shaken, swung'; Kui *kṛeŋga* 'to be shaken' [*DEDR* 349].

12. PD **kaẓ-*

Ta. *kaẓi* 'to pass (as time); to walk, proceed; to expire, die'; tr. 'to pass through'; Ma. Ka. *kaẓi* 'to go or be removed very far; to pass away;' Tu. *kariyuni* 'to pass time' (Brahm. *kaḷepuṇa*); Te. *kaḍacu* id.; Kui *gṛāsa*, *gṛāpa* 'to cross over'; Kuvi (F) *grānc-*, (S) *glā-* (*glā-t-*) 'to transgress; to pass'; Br. *xarr-* 'to proceed on foot' [*DEDR* 1356].

13. PD **kāẓ/*kaẓ-V-*

Ta. *kāẓ* 'oar; iron rod; firewood; rafter; post to which a cow is tied'; *kaẓai* 'spiny bamboo; pole used for propelling boats; shaft of a bamboo'; *kaẓi* 'rod, cudgel, staff, stick'; Ma. *kāẓ* 'stalk'; *kaẓa* 'bamboo pole'; *kaẓal* 'shaft, pole, piece of sugar cane'; Ka. *gaẓe*, *gaṇe* 'bamboo rod; pole; churning stick'; Tu. *kare/gare* 'oar; long stick'; Te. *gaḍa* 'pole shaft, etc.'; Pa. *kaṛpa* 'thin stick'; *kaṛcil* 'wood'; Oll. *kaṛme* 'big stick', *kaṛsil* 'fuel'; Gad. *kaḍcil* 'fuel, etc.'; cf. Malto *kaḍe* 'a stem'; Kuṛ. *kaṛka* 'thin stick' [*DEDR* 1370; items from Kuṛux and Malto are not given].

14. PD **kāẓ/*kaẓ-ut*

Ta. *kaẓutai* 'ass'; Ma. *kaẓuta*; Ko. *kaṛt*, *kaḷd*; To. *katy*; Ka. *kaẓte*, *katte*; Koḍ. *katte*; Tu. *katte*; Te. *gāḍida/gāḍda*; Kol. *gāḍdi*; Nk. *gāṛdi* [*DEDR* 1364].

15. PD **kāẓ/*kaẓ-V-*, **kac-*

Ta. *kaẓuvu* 'to wash' (Kṟḷ); *kāẓiyaṉ* 'a washerman'; Ma. *kaẓukuka* 'to wash'; Ko. *kaṛt-/kayt-* id.; Ka. *kaẓcu* (inscr.), *karcu*, *kaccu* id.; Te. *kaḍugu*, *kaḍuwu* 'to wash, cleanse with water; to scrub; to bathe, lave'; Kui *kahpa (kah-t-)* 'to wash the face, plaster, anoint'; Kuṛ. *xajj-* 'to cleanse head with clay'; Malto *kaj-* 'to wash as clothes' [*DEDR* 1369].

16. PD **kīẓ*/**kīẓ*-V-

Ta. *kīẓ* 'bottom, beneath; below; inferiority; low caste'; Ma. *kiẓu* 'below'; *kīẓ, kīẓ* 'place below'; Ka. *kīẓ* 'being low, meanness'; *kīẓ* 'below, beneath'; *kiẓgu* 'to be low'; Tu. *kiri* 'mean, inferior'; *kirīdī* 'low, mean'; *kīḷi, kīḍi* 'inferior, low'; Te. *kīḍu* 'low, mean'; *kīḍpaḍu* 'to fall low in circumstances'; *krinda* 'below'; Pa. *kiṛin* 'below'; Gad. *kiḍin* 'below'; Kol. *kirre* 'roots'; cf. Ta. *kiẓaṅku*, etc.; Kuṛ. *kiyyā* 'beneath', *kiyyantā*, adj. 'below, bottom'; Br. *kēragh̠-* 'bottom, below'; *kē-*, *kī-* id. [*DEDR* 1619].

17. PD **kuẓ-al*, **kuẓ-awi*, **kuẓ-a-*

Ta. *kuẓal* 'flute, pipe'; *kuẓāy* 'any tube-shaped thing'; *kuẓi* 'to be hollowed out; a pit'; Ma. *kuẓal* 'tube, flute'; *kuẓi* 'a hollow'; Ka. *koẓal* 'hollow tube, flute'; *koẓavi* 'blow pipe'; Tu. *koẓavè* id.; Te. *krōwi, krōlu* 'tube, pipe, syringe'; Kui. *krōḍu* id. [*DEDR* 1818].

18. PD **kūẓ*/**kuẓ*-V-, **kuc-* **koc-*

Ta. *kuẓai* 'to become soft; to become spoiled' (Kṛḷ); Ma. *kuẓayuka* id.; *kūẓ* 'rotten'; *kūẓa* 'rottenness'; Ko. *koḷv-* (*koḷd-*) 'flesh putrifies and falls'; To. *kwaḍ-* 'to rot'; Ka. *koẓe* 'to become rotten; to grieve'; *koẓaku* 'being worn out'; Tu. *kuriyuni, kuripuni* 'to decay, rot'; (Brahm. *kuẓipuṇa*); *kure* 'filth'; Te. *kruḷḷu* 'to decay' Kuvi (S) *glōng-* 'to become mellow (of meat)'; Gad. *kuḍuṅ-* 'to be shaky in ground (as a pole rotten at bottom)'; Kuṛ. *xoss-* 'to decay, rot'; cf. Malto *gojnār-* 'to be or become dirty'; cf. Ma. *kuyimpu, kuśumpal* 'mustiness, decay' [*DEDR* 1822].

19. PD **koẓ-u*, **koẓ-uw*/**koẓ-aw*

Ta. *koẓu* 'to grow fat'; n. 'fat'; *koẓuppu* id.; Ma. *koẓu* 'fat, thick'; *koẓuppu*, n. 'fatness'; To. *köw, kwaḷp* 'fat'; Tu. *komma* 'fat' (< **kor-m-*); Ka. *korvu, korbu, kobbu* v., n. 'fat'; *korcu* 'to brag'; Te. *krowwu* 'to be proud, arrogant'; n. 'fat'; Kui *krōga* (dial. *kṛōga*) n. 'fat'; Kuvi (F) *korova* id.; GoA. *koṛvinj* 'fat'; Koṇḍa *koṛvu* 'fat'; Pa. *koṛ/koṛv-* 'to be fat'; Gad. *koḍkuṭ*, Kol. Nk. *koru* 'fat' [*DEDR* 2146].

20. PD **kōẓ-*/**koẓ-V-*, **koc-*

Ta. *koẓi* 'to sift in a winnowing fan; to criticize'; *koẓippu* 'sifting'; Ma. *koẓikka* 'to winnow, sift'; Ko. *kod-* (*koyd-*) id.; To. *kwïc-* (*kwïč-*) id.; Te. *kōḍu* 'to winnow'; Kui *kṛohpa* (*kṛoh-t-*) id.; Kuvi (F) *kōrss-* (*kōrst-*); (S) *kloh'-* id.; Go. *kōss-* 'to sift in a *sūpa*'; Koṇḍa *koṛs-* 'to winnow' cf. Ka. *koccu* 'to shake flour in a small fan to separate impurities' [*DEDR* 2144].

21. PD **kōẓ*/**koẓ*-V-

Ta. *kōẓ* 'thriving, luxuriant, rich' (Akan.); *koẓu* 'to prosper, flourish'; *koẓuntu* 'tender twig, shoot, sprout'; *kuẓa* 'young, tender' (Tolk.); Ma. *koẓunnu* 'tender twig, young shoot'; Ka. *koḍa* 'tenderness'; *koṇasu* 'young of wild beasts'; Tu. *korè* 'weak, small'; *koḍipuni* 'to bud, germinate'; *koḍi* 'a sprout'; Te. *krotta* 'new, fresh'; *kro-* id.

in compounds; *koḍuku* 'son (< *young person)'; Kui *kōṛu* 'a bud, sprout'; adj. 'new'; *koṛgi* 'newly sprouted'; *koṛgari* 'new shoot'; Go. *koṛs-* 'to sprout'; Pa. *koṛ* 'very young'; *kaṛc-* 'to sprout'; *koṛuŋg* 'new shoots'; Gad. *koḍus-* 'to sprout'; Kuṛ. *xōr-* id.; Malto *qōroc-* id.; Br. *xarr-* id. [*DEDR* 2149].

22. PCD **kōẓ-āḷ*

Go. (Williamson) *koṛiāṛ* 'daughter-in-law'; Te. *kōḍalu* 'daughter-in-law'; Pa. *koṛol* 'bride'; Kol. *koral* 'younger brother's wife'; Nk. *koraḷ* 'daughter-in-law'; Oll. *koṛāl* 'son's wife, younger brother's wife'; cf. Ta. *kōẓai* 'bashful person' [*DEDR* 2149].

(Items 19, 21, 22 are probably etymologically related, belonging to three meaning groups).

23. PSD **kōẓ-i* / PCD **kōṯ-*

Ta. *kōẓi* 'fowl'; Ma. *kōẓi*; Ka. *kōẓi*, *kōḷi*; Tu. *kōri* (Brahm. *kōḷi*); Te. *kōḍi*; Kui *koju*, pl. *koska*; Kuvi (F) *koiyū* 'fowl', pl. *kōska*; Go. Pa. *korr*; Oll. Gad. *korr*; Kol. (E) *kor*; pl. *koḍl* 'hen'; Nk. *kor*, pl. *koḍl* [*DEDR* 2248].

24. PCD **cū-ẓ-* / PSD **cū-ṭ*; PD **cū-* + **ṭ* or **ẓ* (suffixes)

Ta. *cūẓ* 'to deliberate, consider'; Te. *cūḍ-* 'to see', allomorph of *cūcu*; Kui *sūṛa* 'to see'; *sūṭa* 'to point with the finger'; GoA. *sūr* id.; GoM. *huṛ-* id.; (Trench) *sūr* 'to expect'; Koṇḍa *suṛ-*; Pa. *cūṛ* 'to see'; Oll. *sūṛ* id.; Gad. *cūḍ-* id.; cf. Ta. *cuṭṭu* 'to point out, show'; Ma. *cūṇṭu* 'to point out'; Ka. Te. *cūpu* 'sight, appearance'; *sūṭi* 'aim'; Ka. *suṭṭu* 'to show'; Tu. *sū-/tū-* 'to see' [*DEDR* 2735].

25. PD **taẓ-*, **taẓ-al*

Ta. *taẓal* 'to glow, be very hot, burn'; Ka. *taṇalu* 'glowing coals'; Te. *trampi* (< **taẓ-ump-*) 'burning coals'; Go. *taṛmī* 'glowing pieces of wood-ash'; *tarī-t-* 'to be hot (of sun)'; Pa. *taṛ-/taṛv-* 'to be hot'; Kol. (E) *tari-* '(fire) burns'; (SR) *tarīy-* id.; Nk. *tar-* 'to catch fire'; *tarp-* tr. [*DEDR* 3115].

26. PD **tāẓ*/**tāẓi*

Ma. *tāḷi* '*Corypha umbraculifera*'; Ka. *tāẓ*, *tāẓu*, *tāḷi* 'the palmyra tree'; Tu. *tāri* id., (Brahm. *tāḷi*); Te. *tāḍi*, *tāḍu* id.; Go. *tāṛ*, *tāṛi*, Koṇḍa *tāṛ maran* id. Pa. *tāṛ* 'toddy palm' [*DEDR* 3180].

27. PD **tāẓ*/ **taẓ-unk*, *-ukk*

Ta. *tāẓ* (*tāẓ-nt-*) 'to fall, be lowered; to decline, sink; to bow down'; (*tāẓ-tt-)* tr. 'to depress, lower'; Ma. *tāẓuka* 'to sink, come down, bow, subside'; *tāẓttuka* 'to lower'; To. *tōy-* (*tōs-*) 'to be lowered'; *tog-* 'to be humbled'; Ko. *tag-* 'to draw back from a fight'; Ka. *taẓ* 'being low'; *taggu* (< *targu*, < *taẓgu)* 'to become low; to stoop, decline'; Tu. *tagguni* 'to be humble, incline, lean,' *tāruṇè* 'to sink down'; Te. *taggu* 'to be lowered, become reduced; to shrink; to decrease, etc.'; cf. Kuvi (F) *taleni* 'below'; Kuṛ. *tarkā*, adj. 'quiet, calm'; Kuṛ. Malto *tār-* 'to fell, cut off'; Br. *daṛ-* 'to get down, descend'; *tamm-* 'to fall, lie down'; Kuṛ. *tamm-* '(of fever) to cease' [*DEDR* 3178].

28. PD **nīẓ*, **niẓ-al*, **nīẓ-nt-*

Ta. *nīẓal*, *niẓal* 'shade, shadow, reflection, lustre'; Ma. *niẓal* 'shadow'; To. nēs̱; Ko. *nerl*; Ka. *neẓaḷ*, *neralu*, *neḷalu*, *neḷḷ u* 'shade, shadow, shelter, reflection'; Koḍ. *nëḷa* id.; Tu. *nirelï*, *ireli* id.; Te. *nīḍa* 'shade, shadow, reflection, protection'; (Rājpāḷayam dial.) *nīṇḍa* id.; Go. (dial.) *nīṛā* 'shadow'; Pa. *nīṛa*; Oll. *nikiṛ*; Gad. *nīṛa*; Kol. (E) *nīṇḍa*; Nk. *nīnḍa* [*DEDR* 3679].

29. PD **paẓ-V-*, PCD **paẓ-nt-* (> **paṇ-t-*), **paẓ-nc-*, **paẓ-nk-*

Ta. *paẓu*, *paẓuṉu* 'to ripen'; *paẓam* 'ripe fruit' (Tolk.); Ma. *paẓukka* 'to grow ripe, suppurate'; *paẓam* 'ripe fruit'; To. *pošf-* (*pošt-*) 'to ripen'; *pum* 'fruit'; Ko. *paṛv-* (*paṛd-*) 'become ripe'; *paṇ* 'fruit'; Ka. *paṇ*, *paṇṇu*, *haṇṇu* 'a ripe fruit'; CD: Tu. *parndï* 'ripe fruit'; *parnduni* 'to ripen, mature'; Te. *paṇḍu* 'to ripen'; n. 'ripe fruit'; Kuvi (S) *paṇḍu* 'ripe fruit'; Go. *panḍ-* 'to ripen'; Pa. *paṛñ-* (< **paẓ-nc-*) 'to ripen'; *paṇḍ-* '(plant) matures'; Oll. *paṛŋg-* id.; Gad. *paḍiŋg-* id.; Kol. *paṇḍ-* 'to become ripe'; Kuṛ. *pā̃n-* (*pañj-*) 'to ripen; (boil) festers'; Malto *pān-* 'to ripen'; *pāntr-* 'to ripen; to teach manners' [*DEDR* 4004].

30a. PD **paẓ-a-*, **paẓ-u-*

Ta. *paẓa*, *paẓutta* 'old'; *paẓacu*, n. 'that is old by time'; Ma. *paẓa*, *paẓutta* 'old'; *paẓacu*, n. 'that is old by time'; Ma. *paẓa* 'old'; *paẓakka* 'to grow old'; *paẓukka* id.; Ka. *paẓa* 'old, worn out'; *haẓa*, *haẓa* id.; Tu. *parkī* 'old; worn out'; Te. *prā-*, *prā̃ta* 'old, worn out'; Kui, *pṛāḍi* id.; Kuvi *pṛā?i* id.; Go. *paṛna* 'old' Koṇḍa *paṛay;* Kuṛ. *paccā* 'old'; Malto *pac-* 'to become old'; *pacge* 'old' [*DEDR* 3999].

30b. PD **pāẓ/*paẓ-*V-.

Ta. *pāẓ* 'desolation, ruin, damage; waste; barren land' (PN); *pāẓi* id.; Ma. *pāẓ* id.; Ka. *pāẓ*, *hāẓu*, *hāḷu*, 'ruin desolation'; Tu. *hāẓi* 'ruin, destruction'; *paḍilï* 'barren'; Te. *pāḍu* 'desolation, damage'; adj. 'desolate, devastated'; Pa. *paṛeya* adj. 'waste' (or soil, etc.).
(Items 30a and 30b are etymologically related.) [*DEDR* 4110].

31. PCD **piẓ-aw/-uw*, *piẓ-ak/ank*

Te. *prēgu/prēwu* 'intestine'; Kui *pṛēnu*, pl. *pṛēka* 'bone, kernel'; Pa. *piṛul/piṛuvul* 'intestines'; cf. Oll. *puṛug* 'stomach, intestine, belly', Gad. *puḍug* 'stomach' [*DEDR* 4193].

32. PD **piẓ-*V-*/*pic-*V-; PCD **piẓ-nt* (> *piṇ-ṭ-*)

(a) Ta. *piẓi* (*piẓi-nt-*) 'to squeeze'; Ma. *piẓiyuka* 'to wring out'; Ko. *piṛc-* 'to clench (hand)'; Ka. *piẓi* 'to squeeze out'; Tu. *purecuni* id.; Te. *piḍucu* 'to squeeze, wring, press out'; Kui *pṛihpa* (*pṛiht-*) 'to squeeze out'; Pa. *pīṛi* 'press'; *ney pīṛi* 'oil press'; Go. *pīr* 'to squeeze, wring, milk'; Koṇḍa *piṛs-* 'to squeeze' Malto *pilq-* 'to squeeze,' Br. *pil̠h̠-*, *princh-* id. [*DEDR* 4183].

(b) Ta. *picai* 'to squeeze; to rub, apply on skin' (Parip.) *picakku* 'to squeeze between fingers'; Ko. *pick-* id.; *picg-* 'to be soft; to be squeezed'; Ka. *pisuku*, *pisuṅku*, *hisaku* 'to squeeze'; Tu. *piskuni*, *pīsuni* id.; Te. *pisuku*; Kuvi (S) *pic-* 'to wring'; Go. *pick-* 'to knead flour'; Pa. *pīc-* 'to grind' (> Skt. *picc-* 'to squeeze': see

Burrow 1945: 109–110, which is more likely to be from PD **pic-* rather than from **pirc-* as Burrow assumed) [*DEDR* 4135].

(c) Tu. *purñcuni* 'to squeeze'; Te. *piṇḍu* 'to squeeze, press out (as juice)'; Tu. *pīṇṭuni* 'to wring'; Kol. (E) *pīnḍ*, Nk. *pīnḍ* 'to squeeze' [*DEDR* 4183].

33. PD **puẓ-V-*

Ta. *puẓu* 'worm'; v. 'to breed worms, be rotten'; Ma. *puẓu*, 'worm, maggot'; *puẓukka* 'to putrefy, rot'; To. *puf* 'worm'; Ko. *pū* id.; Ka. *puẓu, huẓu, huḷu* id.; *puẓi, huẓi, huḷi* 'to be eaten by worms'; *purcu* 'ruin'; Koḍ. *puḷu* 'worm'; Tu. *puri* 'worm'; *purkuni, purṅguni* 'to rot'; Te. *pruwwu* 'worm'; *purwu/purugu* id.; *pruccu* 'to be eaten by worms'; Kui *pṛiu, piṛu* (pl. *pṛīka, piṛka*) 'worm'; Kuvi (F) *prīyūli* (pl. *prīka*) 'worm'; (S) *pliguli* 'insect'; Go. *puṛī* 'worm, insect'; *puṛī-t-* 'to breed worms (of a foul wound)'; Koṇḍa *piṛvu* 'worm'; Pa. *puṛut* (pl. *puṛtil*) 'a worm'; Gad. *puḍut* (*puḍtul*); id.; Kol. Nk. *purre* id.; Kur. *pocgō* 'worm, caterpillar,' *pocc-* 'to be rotten'; Malto *pocru* 'worm'; Br. *pū* 'worm' [*DEDR* 4312].

34. PD **pūẓ* (< **pū-ẓ-*)

Ma. *pūẓuka* 'to be buried'; *pūntuka* 'to sink in ground', *pūttuka* 'to bury'; Ka. *pūẓ, pūẓu, hūẓu, hūḷu, hūṇu* 'to wrap in, bury'; Tu. Te. *pūḍu* 'to be buried', *pūḍ* (*u*) *cu* 'to bury'; Kol. (E) *pur* '(hole) to be filled up'; Nk. *purp-* 'to bury'; cf. Kuṛ. *putt-* 'to set (of sun only)'. **-ẓ, *-nt/*-tt* are different derivative suffixes, see esp. Ma. Kuṛ [*DEDR* 4376].

35. PD **pēẓ/*peẓ-V-*

(a) Ka. *pēẓ, pēẓu, hēẓu, hēḷu* 'to speak, tell:' *pēẓika* n. 'talk'; Ko. *peṛc-* 'to talk irrelevantly'; Te. *prēlu* 'to prate, prattle'; Malto *peṛq-* 'to talk, speak', Kuṛ. *per-perer-* 'to prate'.

(b) Ta. *pēcu* 'to speak, roar, abuse'; Ma. *pēcuka* 'to speak, chatter (as birds)'; *pēccu* 'speech'; Ko. *pēc* 'to talk to oneself' [*DEDR* 4430].

36. PSD **poẓ-al/-il*

Ta. *poẓil* 'park; division of a country' (Perump.); Ma. *poẓil* 'watered ground; sandy shore'; Ka. *poẓal, hoẓal, hoḷalu* (> *oḷal, ōḷ*) 'a dwelling place, a town'; Te. *pẓōlu* (inscr., 9th cent.); *prōlu* (> *pōlu, -wōlu*) id.; a suffix added to a number of place-names, e.g. *gollaprōlu, niḍudawōlu*, etc. [*DEDR* 4555, 4558].

37. PD **pōẓ, *pōẓ-t/*poẓ-utu*

Ta. *poẓutu, pōẓtu* 'time, sun'; Ma. *poẓutu* id.; *pōḷ* 'time'; Ko. *poṛt* 'time, sun'; To. *pïšt* (dial. *pošt*) 'time, luck'; Ka. *poẓtu, portu, pottu, hottu* 'time, sun'; Koḍ. *bodï* (dial. *bëdi*) 'heat of sun'; Tu. *portu* 'time, daylight, sun'; Te. *proddu* (> *poddu* id.); *appuḍu* 'then, that time' (*ā+*poẓu*); Go. *appōṛ* 'then'; Kol. *poḍ*, Nk. *podd* 'sun' [*DEDR* 4559].

38. PD **mūẓ/*muẓ-uk-*

Ta. *mūẓ* 'to be mature' (Patir.); Ma. *muẓukka* 'to grow ripe, mature'; cf. *mūkka* 'to ripen'; Te. *mruggu* (> *muggu*) 'to ripen (off the tree)'; Go. *mūṛ* 'to ripen (of a boil), etc.'; Pa. *mur-* 'to ripen after being plucked' [*DEDR* 5046].

39a. PD **muẓ*, **mūẓ -unk-*/**muẓ-ukk-* (**mū+ẓ*)

Ta. *mūẓku* 'to plunge, be hidden' (Cir̲up.); *muẓuku* 'to be immersed'; Ma. *muẓukuka* 'to sink'; Ka. *muẓuṅgu, muẓgu, muẓucu* 'to dive'; Tu. *murkuni* 'to sink, immerse'; Te. *bruṅgu* 'to be immersed, be hidden'; Kui. *bṛuḍga* 'to sink completely in'; Kuvi *mrūkh-* 'to drop into'; Go. *muṛung-* 'to be drowned'; GoM. *muṛand-* 'to sink'; Pa. *būṛ* 'to sink'; cf. Kur. *bōr* 'to immerse' [*DEDR* 4993].

39b. PD **mū-ḷ/mū-ṇ*

Ka. *muṇugu, muṇigu* 'to sink under water'; Tu. *muḷuguni, muṇuguni* 'to sink'; Te. *munūgu, muṇūgu*; Ta. Ma. *muṅku* 'to sink' (< **muṇ-k-*); Pa. Gad. *mulg-* 'to dive', Kuṛ. *mulux-* 'to sink, disappear'; Malto *mulg* 'to dip in'. (This series in comparison with the above indicates that in PD itself, **ẓ* and **ḷ*/**ṇ* were different derivative suffixes added to the root **mū-*) [*DEDR* 4993].

40. PD **meẓ-*, **meẓ-uk-*

Ta. *meẓuku* 'to cleanse floor with cowdung water; smear body with sandal paste'; Ma. *meẓukuka* 'to anoint'; To. *mös̆k* 'smear cowdung on floor'; Te. *mrēgu, mrēwu* 'to smear'; Go. *maṛhutt-* 'to paint cattle for the Pola festival'; Br. *mir-* 'to plaster'; cf. Kui *mrānḍa* 'to plaster, smear over'; Malto *mānḍr-* 'to apply something to one's own body' [*DEDR* 5082].

Postscript

P 1. When this paper was published in 1958, it superseded all earlier studies (Caldwell 1913, Subbaiya 1909, Thiagaraju 1933, Ramaswami Aiyar 1935) on the problem of identifying the reflexes of the most characteristic of Dravidian phonemes, viz. **ẓ* in different Dravidian languages. Adequate numbers of cognates were not available for Toda, Kota, and Koḍagu of South Dravidian until the publication of *DED* in 1961. In the revised *DEDR* of 1984, a few items from the other Nilgiri languages have been included, such as Iruḷa, Kur̲umba, and Baḍaga. Also published wordlists of some of these languages are now available. I have at the moment with me vocabularies of Iruḷa, Jēnu Kur̲umba, and Shōlega (Zvelebil 1979, 1988, 1990b). Also a short description of Koraga (Bhat 1971) is available. These languages do not add any new insights into the developments of **ẓ* and we are also not sure of their status in relation to the neighbouring major languages, Tamil and Kannaḍa within South Dravidian. In South-Central Dravidian, lexical items from different dialects of Gondi (Burrow and Bhattacharya 1960), descriptive accounts of Koṇḍa (Krishnamurti 1969b), Pengo (Burrow and Bhattacharya 1970), and Kuvi (Israel 1979) were published between the sixties and eighties. Only Gondi (to the extent available), Kui, and Kuvi were covered in the article in 1958. In the Central Dravidian group, I cited some items for Konḍekor Gadaba from my fieldnotes. A monograph on Koṇḍekor Gadaba (Bhaskararao 1975) is now available. I am treating Gadaba as a separate language and not as a co-dialect of Ollari. I will draw on these additional lexical sources in the postscript to make the study up to date. Burrow (1968a) questioned my identifying *c* and *s* as the normal reflexes of PD **ẓ* in Kuṛux-Malto of North Dravidian. Emeneau (1971b, 1980b) discussed at length the developments of PD **ẓ* in Koḍagu and Brahui. I have to take into account their suggestions and discussion. The text of my paper remains the same except that I have dropped the family tree diagram on p. 285 of the original article. The developments of PD **ẓ* do not provide any isoglosses along genetic lines and the diagram is actually dated. There are other articles in this volume which will discuss the question of subgrouping of the Dravidian languages in detail.

P 2. South Dravidian. The description of the developments in the literary languages—Tamil, Malayāḷam, Telugu, and Kannaḍa was adequate. The Toda developments for PD **ẓ* were published by Emeneau (1958b) which I saw after this paper had gone to the press. I included his conclusion in fn. 8. The developments of Toda, Kota, and Koḍagu were mentioned by Emeneau (1970a: 98–9) as follows—Toda: *ḍ*, *ṛ*, *š*, *ṣ*, *w*, *y*, Ø; Kota: *ḷ*, *ṛ*, *g*, *y*, Ø (conditions not stated); Koḍagu: *-ḷ-*, Ø[C. These compare favourably with what I discussed in §§ **2, 5, 6**.
[Note: The number preceding a reconstruction is the entry no. of *DED(R)*; reference is also made to entry nos. in the Appendix to the article.]

Toda

Subrahmanyam (1983: 428–38) tried to give the conditions of different developments in some cases:

(1) Toda has 9 instances of *-ḍ* < **ẓ* in verbs of pre-Toda $(C_1)V_1C_2$-V_2- type in which C_2 was **ẓ* and V_2 was **-i*, **-u*, or **-ay*, e.g. 851a. PSD or pre-Ta. **eẓ-u* (past *eẓ-u-nt-)* 'to rise' > To. *öḍ-* (*öḍ-θ-*), 1356 PSD **kaẓ-i* (*kaẓ-i-nt-*) 'time to pass' > To. *koḍ-y-* (*koḍ-s-*), 1822 PSD **koẓ-ay* (> Ta. *kuẓ-ay*: *kuẓ-ay-nt-*): 'to rot' > To. *kwaḍ-* (*kwaḍ-θ-*), 2698 pre-Ta. **cuẓ-i-* (*-nt-*, *-tt-*) 'to circle' > To. *tuḍy-* (*tuḍ-s-*, *tuḍ-c-*). After the loss of V_2, **ẓ* occurs in pre-consonantal position in verb inflection where it develops to *ḍ*.

(2) In 5 instances **ẓ* > *-ṛ* > *-ṛ* in Toda, e.g. 282 PSD **yāẓ*: **yaẓ*-V- > pre-Ta. **aẓ-u-* (*aẓu-t*) > To. *oṛ-* (*oṛ-y-*) 'to cry, weep'. Subrahmanyam (1983: 432–3) says the conditions separating the replacement of *ẓ* by *ḍ* from those by *ṛ* are not clear. But the verb stems here are generally of (C)VCC type, e.g. 1012 pre-Ta. *oẓ-u-kk-* > *wïṛk-* 'to embroider', 851a. PSD **eṭ-u-* (*eṭ-u-pp-*, *eṭ-u-tt)* > *öṛf-* (*öṛ-θ-*) 'to carry', etc. incorporating an erstwhile tense suffix.

(3) In noun stems the final vowel is lost and *-ẓ* becomes *-w*, 4749 SD **maẓ-ay* 'rain': To. *maw*, 4318 pre-SD **poẓ-a-* > Ma. *puẓa*: To. *pāw* 'river'.

(4) There are several cases in which *ẓ* merged with *r* in pre-consonantal position, and this *r* developed to *š* or *ṣ*; this is usually followed by an obstruent, *t* or *k* in

nouns or by *f* (< non-past **w*; past with *t*) in verbs, e.g. 4004 pre-Ta. *paẓ-u-* (fut. *paẓ-u-w-*, past *paẓu-tt-*) > *pošf- (poš-t-)* 'to ripen', 4749 pre-Ta. *maẓ-u*, pre-Toda-Kota **maẓ-u-ttu* > To. *mošt* 'axe', Ko. *maṛt-*.

(5) When *-*ẓ* occurs in the root-final position (#___*ẓ*.), or when -V_2 is lost followed by extended suffixes in the underlying form, *-*ẓ* is often lost with compensatory lengthening of V_1, e.g. 1619 PSD **kīẓ* > To. *kī* 'low, below', 3679 PSD **neẓ-al* > To. *nēs̱* 'shade', 4993 PSD **muẓ-u-nk-* v.i., **muẓ-u-nkk-* v.t. 'to sink, drown.' > To. *mūx-*, *mūk-* (*mūx-y-*, *mūk-y-*) 'to sink, to drown'.

(6) In a few cases PSD *ẓ* becomes To. *y* in verbs of (C)V̄C-type, e.g. 3178 PSD **tāẓ*- > To. *tōy* (*tōs-*) 'to be lowered.'

The conditions for the emergence of different reflexes are not entirely clear. Emeneau in a forthcoming paper ('Some Toda developments of Proto-Dravidian **r̤*') deals mainly with PD *-*ẓ* > To. -*w* in a considerable number of cases. It is difficult to explain the difference in vowel length between To. *maw* 'rain' (: Ta. *maẓai*) and *pāw* 'old' (: Ta. *paẓai*). At least one clear rule emerges: Following high vowels *-*ẓ* is lost in the word-final position.

Kota

(1) With the loss of -V_2, root final *-*ẓ* of PSD or pre-Kota becomes *ṛ* before a consonant in derivation or inflection, e.g. 817 pre-Ko. *eẓ-u-* (*eẓ-u-v-*, *eẓ-u-nt-*) > Ko. *eṛ-v-* (*eṛ-d-*) '(smoke) rises up', 4559 PSD **poẓ-u-tt-* > Ko. *poṛ-t-* 'sun, time'. There are 15 cases of this type.

(2) Root final *-*ẓ* becomes Ø; it becomes -*y* before a pre-Kota front vowel *i*, or *e* (< *-*ay*) as (-V_2) which was later lost in disyllabic stems, e.g. 1619 PSD **kīẓ* > To. *kī* 'below', 2248 **kōẓ-i* > Ko. *kōy* 'fowl', 4753 pre-Ta. *maẓ-ay* > pre-Kota **may-e*, Ko. *may* 'rain'. These items are mostly free forms, nouns or adjectives of disyllabic type. Subrahmanyam (1983: 429–30) gives 12 for -*y* and 2 for zero.

(3) In 7 cases pre-Kota *-*ẓ* was assimilated to a following voiced stop, mostly a velar, e.g. 282 PSD **aẓ-u-nk-*, **aẓ-u-tt* > Ko. *ag-* (*aṛt-*) 'to cry', 688 PSD **uẓ-u-w-/-k-*, **uẓ-u-tt-* > Ko. *ug-* (*uṛ-t-*) 'to plough'.

(4) In a few cases, the root vowel is compensatorily lengthened, 4993 PSD **muẓ-u-nk-*, **muẓ-u-nkk-* > Ko. *mūg-* (*mūg-y-*) 'to submerge oneself', *mūk-* (*mūk-y-*) 'to submerge'.

(5) In nouns ending in -*u*, *-*ẓ* is dropped and the root vowel is compensatorily lengthened, e.g. 4312 PSD **puẓ-u* > Ko. *pū* 'worm'.

(6) In 3 cases of the type *(C)V_1*ẓ*-V_2*l* in pre-Kota, *ẓ* becomes *r* with the loss of the following vowel (V_2), 1818 PSD *koẓ-al* > Ko. *kor-l* 'tube', 3679 PSD *neẓ-al* > Ko. *ner-l* 'shade'.

(7) In over a dozen items Ko. has *ḷ* corresponding to *-*ẓ*, about which Subrahmanyam (1983: 432) says, 'they are all loans', e.g. 2698 PSD **cuẓ-i* > Ko. *cuḷy* 'whirlpool', 5372 PSD **wāẓ* > Ko. *vāḷ* '(woman) lives with husband.'

Koḍagu

Emeneau (1971b, repr. 1994: 203–8) discussed thoroughly the developments of PD *ẓ in Koḍagu and was able to state the phonological conditions precisely:

Rule 1. PSD *ẓ > ḷ/ V___V. Intervocalically, PSD *-ẓ becomes *-ḷ*, e.g. 338 pre-Ta. **āẓ-am* > *āḷ-a* 'depth', 1511 *koẓ-al* > *koḷ-a* 'flute' (note loss of final liquid), 853 pre-Ta. **eẓ-u-tu* > *ëḷ-ï-du* 'to write', 426 PSD *iẓ-i* > *ïḷ-i* 'to descend'. These include both nouns and verbs. Emeneau cites 24 examples.

Rule 2a. PSD *-ẓ > -y~-yy/(C)a___+ i; **b.** pre-Koḍ. *i > Ø/___#. Disyllabic forms of the type *(C)*aẓ-i* change *ẓ to *y*, and later, the final vowel is lost, e.g. 1136 pre-Ta. **kaẓ-i* (*-v-*, *-nt-*) v.i., (*-pp-*, *-tt-*) v.t > *kay* (*-p-*, *-c-*) 'to undo (knot)'. There are 4 clear cases of this kind.

Rule 3. *-ẓ > Koḍ. Ø/___+C (a) In 7 stems of (C)V̄ẓ- ~ (C)Vẓ-V(C)-type, *-ḷ* occurs finally alternating in paradigms with zero from short-syllabled alternants in which a consonant follows *ẓ (with V_2 lost) in derivation or inflection, e.g. 427 PSD **ūẓ-*: **uẓ-u* > Koḍ. *ūḷ-*, *ūḷï* (imper.), *up-* (future), *ut-* (past) 'to plough'. (b) *ẓ is lost before a consonant in inflection or derivation; also *ẓ* + *d* > *dd.* 1154 pre-Koḍ. **kaẓ-u-tt* > Koḍ. *kat* 'wash', 3540 PSD **puẓ-u-nkk*, pre-Koḍ. **puẓ-u-kk-* > *puk-* to boil', 4096 PSD **muẓ-u-nk* > *muŋŋ-* 'to dive' (cf. Malāyaḷam has *muẓuṅṅu* id.). Emeneau cites 21 instances under this class.

4. 3 items show loss with compensatory lengthening of the radical vowel, e.g. 593 Pre-Koḍ. **uẓu-kk-* > Koḍ. *ūk-* 'to comb'.

Iruḷa

Zvelebil (1979) gives a glossary of 626 lexical items for Iruḷa. The following developments are noted for *ẓ in 7 items:

(1) (a) Loss in the root-final position with loss of the following -V_2, e.g. 282 pre-Ta. **āẓ*: *aẓ-u* > *ë-* (*ëg-*, *ëd-*; *-g* non-past, *-d* past stem suffixes) 'to cry'; 1369 **kaẓ-u-* > *kë-* (*këg-*, *këd-*) 'to wash'; 1619 **kīẓ*: *kiẓ-*V- > *kë̄e*, *kūge* (dial.) 'down, below'.
(b) Loss with compensatory lengthening of the root-vowel as in other Nilgiri languages, e.g. 4312 PSD **puẓ-u-* > *pū* 'worm'.

(2) In two cases *ẓ becomes *y* before *-i*, which is not lost in nouns, e.g. 1818 **kuẓ-i* > *kuy-i*, *kuyy-i*, *guyy-i* 'pit', 5295 PSD **waẓ-i* > *vay* (*vayk-*, *vayt-*) 'to wipe clean, scrape'.

(3) In three cases an intervocalic *ḷ* occurs corresponding to older *ẓ, e.g. 853 pre-Ta. *eẓuttu* > *eḷuttu* 'letter', 1364 pre-Ta. *kaẓutay* > *kaḷude*, *kë̄ḷude* 'donkey', 4949 PSD *muẓ*-V- 'joint' > *muḷi* 'knee' (cf. Ta. *muḷ-i* id). It appears that these three are loanwords from modern Tamil.

Other Nilgiri Languages/Dialects

Kapp's (1987) data show two developments for PD **ẓ* in Ālu Kuṟumba: (a) intervocalically *ḷ* , e.g. 616 **kīẓ > cī̈ḷï* 'pus': Ta. *cīẓ* id., 1606 **ēẓ > ē̈ḷu* 'seven': Ta. *ēẓu* id., 4146 **piẓay > pё̈ḷe* 'to live': Ta. *piẓai* id.; (b) loss and compensatory lengthening of the preceding vowel, if it was short, e.g. 504 **īẓ/*iẓ-V > ī̈ (ī̈p-, ī̈t-)* 'to pull': Ta. *īẓ/iẓu* id., 1619 **kīẓ/ V- > kī̈e* 'the place below': Ta. *kīẓ/kiẓ-a-* id., 5430 **wīẓ/wiẓ-V- > bī̈- (bī̈v-, bidd-)* 'to fall': Ka. *bīẓ, bīḷ, Ta. vīẓ, viẓu* 'to fall'. The *ḷ*-forms and *b- < *w-* are developments normal to Kannaḍa or some Kannaḍoid dialect.

Baḍaga also has different realizations: (a) **-ẓ* merged with *-ḷ (< *-ḷ)* in pre-Baḍaga as in Kannaḍa. It could be that Baḍaga was a dialect of Kannaḍa at that stage. Later, this *ḷ* became Ø in Baḍaga; (b) after such loss, when two syllables contracted, either vowel-sequences were created, or compensatory lengthening took place, or a *-y-* was inserted instead, as a hiatus preventer to form a new syllable (Pilot-Raichoor 1997: 138), e.g. 1822 **koẓay* > Ka. and pre-Baḍaga *koḷe* > Baḍaga *koe* 'dirt', 698 **uḷ* > Ka. and pre-Baḍaga *oḷage* > Baḍaga *ōge* 'inside', 4753 **maẓay* > Ka. and pre-Baḍaga *maḷe* > Baḍaga *mē* 'rain', 1356 **kaẓi* > Ka. and pre-Baḍaga *kaḷe, kaḷi* > Baḍaga *kai/kayyi* 'to spend (time, money)'. The conditions governing different developments are not clear yet. The retroflex vowels that Emeneau referred to in his 1939 article are no longer heard in Baḍaga (see Emeneau 1992: vii–viii). He recorded *ē̈u* (<* *ēẓ*) 'seven', which is recorded now as *iu/iyyu* (Hockings and Pilot-Raichoor 1992).

Zvelebil's word lists of Jēnu Kuṟumba (1988) and of Shōlega (1990b) are not adequate to declare them as separate languages. (a) Jēnu Kuṟumba shows intervocalic *ḷ* and loss through assimilation in *uḷu* 'worm' (Ka. *huḷu, puḷu, puẓu*; 4312), *katte* 'ass' (Ka. *katte, karte, kaẓte < *kaẓ-u-tt-*; 1364), *koḷalu* 'oboe' (Ka. *koḷalu, koẓ-al* 'tube, flute'; 1818). (b) Shōlega also has *ḷ* for **ẓ* intervocalically: *aḷa, aḷeya* 'old' (Ka. *haḷa, paḷa, paẓa* 'old'; 3999), *kī̈ḷe* postposition 'under' < **kīẓ*; 1619), *guḷi* 'pit' (Ka. *guḷi < *kuẓ-i*; 1818), *bāḷi* 'plantain' (Ka. *bāḷe < *wāẓ-ay*; 5373). In both these dialects the developments are Kannaḍa-like. They share Kannaḍa *h < *p*, and *b- < *w*. It is impossible to go beyond this point.

Koraga

Bhat (1971) briefly described three dialects of Koraga spoken by basket-making tribes in South Canara District surrounded by Tuḷu. Two dialects (Onṭi, Tappu) have *r* for **ẓ* just like Tuḷu; one dialect (Mudu) spoken by Kannaḍa bilinguals has *ḷ* forms like Kannaḍa, e.g. 5430 PSD **wīẓ- > būru, būḷu* 'to fall' (cf. Tu. *būruni*, Ka. *bīḷ, bīẓ*), 5373 SD; **wāẓ-ay > bāre, bāḷe* 'plantain' (cf. Tu. *bārè, bāḷè*). Bhat's data has 15 items requiring the reconstruction of pre-Koraga **ẓ*.

P 3. South-Central Dravidian. The following items from Koṇḍa, Pengo, and Manḍa show that all South-Central Dravidian languages with the exception of

Telugu represent *ẓ by ṛ. In certain Gondi dialects ṛ later merged with *r*. Burrow and Bhattacharya (1963: 234) have recorded ṛ for Kuvi and they think that the recordings of Fitzgerald and Schultze were inaccurate in representing PD *ẓ by *r* and *l*, respectively. Another recent source for Kuvi is Israel (1979).

TABLE 3.2. *Correspondences for PD *ẓ in Koṇḍa, Kuvi, Pengo, and Manḍa of SCD*

DED(R)	PSCD reconstruction	Gondi	Koṇḍa	Kuvi	Pengo	Manḍa
688	*ūẓ/*uẓ-V- 'to plough'	uṛ-, ur-	ṛū-	ṛū-	ṛū	ṛū-
282	*yāẓ/*yaẓ-V- 'to cry, weep'	āṛ-, aṛ-, ar-	aṛ-ba-	ṛi-	aṛ-	ṛī-
1356	*kaẓi 'to pass time, to spend, to discard'	—	kaṛ-s-‡	gṛah-‡	kṛac-‡	gṛah-‡
1818	*kūẓ-/kuẓ-V- 'to form pit, hollow'	koṛi 'ditch'	kuṛŋi- 'to form pits'	gṛayu 'hole'	kṛoy 'pit'	kṛay 'pit'
2146	*kōẓ/koẓ-V- 'to flourish, gow fat'	koṛvinj n. 'fat'	koṛvu n.	koṛva	kṛō- 'to be fat'	kuṛva- n.
2149	*koẓi-āḷ 'daughter-in-law'	koṛiyāṛ	koṛya, koṛesi	kuṛia, kuṛiya	koṛiya gāṛ	kuṛiya gāṛ
2735	*cūẓ- 'to see'	sūṛ-, sūr, suṛ-, huṛ-	suṛ-	—	huṛ-	huṛ-
3679	*nīẓ/*niẓ-V- 'shade'	nīṛa n.	nīṛa n. nīṛga	ṛīa	ṛīga	ṛīge
3999	*paẓ-V- 'old'	paṛna 'old'	paṛay, pṛāy (dial.)	pṛāʔi, pṇaʔayi	pṛān	pṛānca
4312	*puẓ-V- 'worm, insect'	puṛi/ puri, n., puṛīt- v.	piṛvu n., piṛku, pl.	pṛiyul n.	pṛī pl.— pṛiku	

‡ With meaning change 'to defecate, excrete', cf. Ta. *kaẓicc-al* 'diarrhoea', *kaẓical* 'that which is rejected'.

It is now fairly certain that ṛ corresponds to PSCD *ẓ in five of the six languages. *DED(R)* has not abandoned the forms given by Fitzgerald and Schultze which I have discussed in the paper. They supplemented these with items from the field-notes of Burrow and Bhattacharya (1963) to which I added Israel (1979). These forms show ṛ like the other sister languages.

P 4. Central Dravidian. Burrow (1968a: 62) mentioned that in Naiki of Chanda, *ẓ (a) changes to *y*, (b) is dropped before a consonant, or (c) dropped with compensatory lengthening of the preceding vowel; e.g. 689 **uẓ-u* > Nk. *ū* 'to comb', 3120 **taẓ-u-ng* 'liver' > Nk. *taŋg*; 3727 **ūẓ-* 'to wear' > Nk. *ū-/ūy-* (*ūṭṭ-*). Burrow further noticed that PD **ḷ* is also treated alike in this language (63). This means that **ẓ* fell together with **ḷ* and that developed into Naiki *y* and zero. Parji and Ollari show *ṛ* and Gadaba has *ḍ* and Kolami *r* (see §§ **10–13**).

P 5. North Dravidian. Burrow (1968a), followed by Pfeiffer (1972), proposed different reflexes for Kuṛux-Malto. He says that **ẓ* is generally lost in 9 items in these two languages, it has *-s-/ -ss-* in 5, *-c-/ -cc-* in 3, *-y-* in 2, *-ṛ-* in 4, etc. (66–7), e.g. pre-Kuṛux-Malto 4990 **muẓ-a-kkāl* > Kuṛ. *mū-kā*, Malto *mū-ke* 'knee'; examples for *s* and *c* are given in the article (§§ 14–15) which he presumes represent suffixes before which PD **ẓ* could have been lost; the examples show one-to-one correspondence of **ẓ* to *c* so clearly that it is not necessary to posit palatal suffixes, followed by loss of **ẓ* before these. The palatal suffixes in verbs like Te. *īḍ-cu* 'to drag' (see Appendix 1) and *pru-ccu* (Appendix 33) are traced to pre-Telugu past participial stems in *-cci-* which incorporated into the base (*TVB* 162–3). That these forms provided a model for Kuṛux-Malto is somewhat far-fetched. Burrow agrees to the other reflexes, *y*, *ṛ*, *r*/*rr*, and *l* (68). We notice loss in many languages and it could have occurred in Kuṛux-Malto also, beside the reflexes treated in my article. Pfeiffer (1972: 156–7) has given 2 cases for *-y-/-yy*, 19 for -Ø, 3 for *-ṛ-*, 3 for *-r-/-rr-*. There are 3 instances of *-j-/-jj-* in which it is possible that PND *-ẓ* was assimilated to a palatal which was voiced by contact with it, viz. 851 **eẓ-uc-* > Kuṛ. *ej-* 'rouse from sleep', 1012 **oẓ-uc-* > Kuṛ. *ōj-*, Malto *ōj-* 'to spin', 1369 **kaẓ-uc* > Kuṛ. *xajj-* 'to cleanse head with clay', Malto *kaj-* 'to wash'. But Kuṛ.-Malto *c* does not show either voicing, or the lengthening of the root-vowel. Therefore, in 504 **īẓ-* > Kuṛ. *īc-*, Malto *ic-* 'to pull', 3999 **paẓ-*V- > Kuṛ. *paccā* 'old', Malto *pac-* 'to become old', 4312 **puẓ-u-w* > Kuṛ. *pocgō* 'worm', Malto *pocru* 'worm' (note that Kuṛ. *-g* corresponds to **-w*), I maintain that PND **ẓ* = Kur.-Malto *c*/*s* is a viable correspondence.

Burrow's thrust of argument in his 1968 article was to show that my choice of the symbol *ẓ*, as opposed to *r̤*, was not justified by Kuṛux-Malto data. Actually I did not make any phonetic assumption that PD **ẓ* was a voiced sibilant, despite the fact that I cited Old Tamil borrowings from Sanskrit in which intervocalic **ṣ* was replaced by **ẓ*. Toda does have *ṣ* and *š* as reflexes of PD **ẓ*. The only criterion that I stated was that the symbol *ẓ* would make better sense as a retroflex continuant rather than the host of other symbols like *ḷ̤*, *l̤*, *r̤* which would not make it look like a retroflex. The symbol *ṛ* which several authors have used for **ẓ* is also not suitable since it is used in Dravidian subgroups for a retroflex flap. This symbol **ẓ* has come to stay and is now widely used in Dravidian studies.

Emeneau (1971b, 1980b) treats the Brahui reflexes of PD **ẓ* in great detail. Besides endorsing my treatment in this article, he adds two more developments (1971b: 208–10): (a) **ẓ* > *ṛ* in 3 items: 4160 **pēẓ*/**pēṇ* > Br. *pēṛ-* 'to roll round', 4183b **wīẓ* 'to milk' > Br. *bīṛ-*, 3168 **tāẓ*/ *taẓ-*V- 'to get down' > Br. *daṛ-*; (b) **ẓ* > *ḍ* in 1 item: 4193 **piẓ-*V- 'intestines' > Br. *piḍ* 'belly, stomach'. He has given in all 4 items recording the loss or assimilation of *ẓ in Brahui (2 in addition to mine). In his 1980a paper Emeneau discussed three items showing PND *ẓ = Brahui lateral _l_, _l̠h̠_, e.g. 4616 *_maẓ_-V- > Br. _mal̠h̠_- 'son', 4312 *_puẓ-u_ > Br. _pū_ (with loss and vowel-lengthening); there is also _pul-makkī_ 'tape worm', in which _pul_ can be taken to derive from *_puẓ-u_, 4183 PD *_piẓ-i_ > Br. _pil̠h̠_ which I have already treated. It is still not possible to discover the phonological conditioning of different developments in Brahui.

P 6. Conclusion. In the original paper (in the pre-_DED_ days) I took only 40 typical etymological sets requiring PD *ẓ and treated the developments in individual languages of the whole family; therefore, I could not look at the entire language data of a few languages as was done by Burrow for Kuṛux-Malto or Emeneau for Toda, Koḍagu, and Brahui.

It is important to note that PD *ẓ, by its peculiar articulatory position and effort, has merged with almost every possible sound in the coronal region, obstruent, sonorant, affricate, fricative, and glide, viz. _r_, _l_, _ḷ_, _ṛ_, _s_, _c_, _š_, _ṣ_, _ḍ_, _y_, beside merging with zero in several languages across the board. Only Toda shows _w_ (< *ẓ). The developments do not provide clear isoglosses, typically marking subgroups. The only one we could perhaps mention is *ẓ > _ṛ_ in a South-Central Dravidian subgroup. It is an isogloss rather than a marker of a subgroup. A similar isogloss also binds Parji and Ollari within Central Dravidian. From its varied developments within individual languages, it appears that the phoneme *ẓ was retained until recent times and later merged with different phonemes, perhaps because of its typological oddity in the broader Indian linguistic area.

4

Dravidian Personal Pronouns

1. The etymologies for the pronouns of the first person singular and plural given in *A Dravidian Etymological Dictionary* by Burrow and Emeneau under the entries 4234, 4231, and 3019 fall into five phonological groups of alternating stems in the nominative and oblique as follows:[1]

TABLE 4.1. *The first person pronouns in nominative and oblique cases*

GROUP I: First person singular 'I' (*DED* 4234)	Nominative	Oblique
Ta.	yāṉ	en-
Ma.	—	en-
To.	ōn	en-
Ko.	ān	en-, e-
Koḍ.	—	en-
Ka.	āN[2]	en-
Tu. (dial.)	yānï, ēnï	en-
Te.	ēnu	—
Go. (dial.)	anā, annā, ana	—
Kui	ānu	—
Pe.	ān(eŋ)	—
Kol.	ān	an-
Nk.	ān	an-
Pa.	ān	an-
Oll.	ān	an-
Gad.	ān	an-
Kuṛ	ēn	eŋg-
Malto	ēn	eŋg-
Br.	ī	(?) kan-

[1] The lists of cognates by *DED* have been supplemented with additional items for Gondi, Kui, Kuvi, and Naiki from the following recent publications: Burrow and Bhattacharya (1960, 1961, 1963) and Bhattacharya (1961). The Koṇḍa material is taken from my work, *Koṇḍa or Kūbi, a Dravidian Language* (1969c). Additional items for the literary languages have been drawn from different published and unpublished sources. T. Burrow has kindly supplied me with the relevant items for Pengo and B. Ramachandra Rao for Tuḷu.

[2] In Kannaḍa, morphophonemic //N, M// are phonemically /m/ finally, but /n/ and /m/ respectively in gemination. Intervocalically N = /n/, M = /m/ or /v/. Apparently PD *n fell together with *m in early

Group II

	Nominative	Oblique
Ta.	nāṉ (> mdn. nā:)	—
Ma.	ñān (dial. nān)[3]	—
Koḍ.	nānï, nā	nan-, nā-
Ka.	nāN	nan-
Te.	nēnu ; nānu (mdn. regional substandard)	nan-, nā-
Go. (dial.)	na(n)nă, nan	nā-
Koṇḍa	nān	nā-
Kui (BB)	nānu	nan-, nā-
Kuvi	nānū (F), nānu (S)	nā
Pe.	—	naŋg-, nā

Group III: First person plural 'we' (exclusive, unless otherwise specified) (*DED* 4231)

	Nominative	Oblique
Ta.	yām; yāṅ-kaḷ[4]	em-
Ma.	—	eṅ-ṅaḷ-
To.	em	em-
	om (incl.)	om- (incl.)
Ko.	ām	em-; am- (incl.)
Koḍ.	eŋ-ga	eŋ-ga-
Ka.	āM	em-
Tu. (dial.)	yaṅ-kuḷï, eṅ-kuḷï	yaṅ-kuḷe-, eṅ-kuḷe-
Te.	ēmu	—
Go.	amm-ăṭ, amm-oṭ, amm-ok	—
Kui	āmu	—
Pe.	āp(eŋ)	—
Kol.	ām	am-
Nk.	ām	am-
Pa.	ām	am-
Oll.	ām	am-
Gad.	ām	am-
Kuṛ.	ēm	em-
Malto	ēm	em-

Kannaḍa or pre-Kannaḍa in the utterance final position, but the contrast is preserved elsewhere, see Ramachandra Rao (1964: §§ 2.7, 8.4.4).

[3] Chandrasekhar (1953: 88–9) quotes one instance of Ma. *nāṉ* in a 10th century inscription and suggests, in agreement with Ramaswami Aiyar, that '*ñān* may have been a west coast archaism'. In old and modern Malayāḷam *ñān* is the standard form of the 1st pers. sg.; only *ñān* (but not *nān*) occurs in *Rāmacaritam*, the earliest literary work in Malayāḷam (*c.* 12th century AD); see George (1956: 159).

[4] 'The double plurals *nāṅkaḷ* and *yāṅkaḷ* are found as early as the Cīvakacintāmaṇi period', Subbaiya (1923: 1).

Group IV

	Nominative	Oblique
Ta.	nāṅ-kaḷ	—
Ma.	ñāṅ-ṅaḷ	ñaṅ-ṅaḷ-
Koḍ.	naŋ-ga	naŋ-ga-
Te.	nēmu, mēmu	mamm-, mā-
Go. (dial.)	mamm-ăṭ, mā-ṭ, mām-aṭ, mamm-oṭ, mamo, mar-aṭ, mamma, mām	mā-
Koṇḍa	māp	mā-
Kui (BB)	māmu	mā-
Kuvi	māmbū (F), māmbu (S) mārrō (F), māro (S)	mā-
Pe.	—	maŋg-, mā-

Group V: First person plural 'we' (inclusive unless otherwise specified) (*DED* 3019)

	Nominative	Oblique
Ta.	nām	nam(m)-
Ma.	nām	nam(m)-
Ka.	nāM (nām, nāvu)	nam(m)-
Tu.	nama	nama-
Te.	manamu	mana- (? < nam-a-)
[Go.	namoṭ (excl.)	mā-]
Kol.	nēnḍ	nēnḍ-
Nk.	nēnḍ/nēm	nēnḍ-
Kuṛ	nām	nam-, naŋ-g-
Malto	nām	nam-
[Br.	nan (incl. and excl.)	nan-]

2. A dash implies that a formally related stem is missing in the nominative or in the oblique as the case may be. Thus in Group I, Malayāḷam and Koḍagu have the oblique forms *en-* but lack a formally related **ān* or **ēn*, this gap being filled by *ñān* in Malayāḷam and *nānï* in Koḍagu (see Group II), which are apparently not formally related to the oblique *en-*. So also the formally related oblique stems are absent for Telugu, Kui, Gondi, and Pengo in Group I.

3. Reconstruction of the proto-forms for each of the groups is beset with several problems of phonology and morphology:

Phonological Problems:

(1) The quantitative and qualitative variations between the radical vowels in the nominative and those in the oblique (rows): *ā/a, ē/e, ā/e* in Groups I and III; similarly, *ā/a, ā/ā*, and *ē/ā* in Groups II, IV, and V;

(2) Consonantal alternations (columns and rows): *y-/Ø-* in Groups I and III, *ñ-/n-* in Group II, and *ñ-/n-/m-* in Group IV, and *n-/m-* in Group V.

Morphological Problems:

(1) The occurrence of two plurals, one inclusive and one exclusive, and also the co-existence of two singulars, one with a nasal *ñ-* or *n-* and one without it or with *y-* (Tamil);

(2) Singular: plural opposition represented by *-n*: *-m* on the one hand (Groups I, II, III, IV, V), and by *-ṅ*: *-ṅ-kaḷ* (< *-m-kaḷ*), *-ṅ-ṅ-al* (< *-ṅ-gaḷ*), *-(m)m-ăṭ/-oṭ*, *-r*, *-ok*, *-ṇḍ*, *-p*, on the other (Groups III, IV, and V);

(3) The replacement of *n*-forms by *m*-forms in a subgroup of Central Dravidian (Groups IV and V);

(4) The different types of oblique formation, e.g. Ka. *nān/nan-* vs. Koṇḍa *nān/nā-* (Group II, etc.).

4. Groups I and III are closely related phonologically. Earlier writers who have proposed either **ēn/***en-* or **ān/***an-* for Proto-Dravidian have ignored the fact that, generally, PD **ā-/***a-* = *ā-/a-* and PD **ē-/***e-* = *ē-/e-* in all Dravidian languages.[5] A correspondence in which *ă* and *ĕ* alternate widely looks to a *different* reconstruction from either **ă* or **ĕ*, and in most such cases it is an alternation conditioned by a preceding palatal consonant, **y*, **ñ*, or *c*.
Study the following examples:

1. PD **āṯu*: Ta. *āṟu*, Ma. *āṟu-ka*, Ko. *ār*, To. *ōṟ* (< **āṟ*), Ka. *āṟu*, Tu. *āṟ-uni*, *āj-uni*, Te. *āṟu*, Kol., Nk. *ār*, Pa. *ēd-* (< **āṟ*), Go. *ār-*, Kui *āja* (intr.), *āspa* (tr.) 'to be cooled; to get dried; to be extinguished (as lamp), etc.' (*DED* 346).

2. PD **ēẓ*: Ta. *ēẓ(u)/eẓu-*, Ma. *ēẓ(u)/eẓu-*, Ko. *ēy*, Ka. *ēẓ(u)*, *ēḷ*, *ēḷ(u)-*, Tu. *ēḷï*, Te. *ēḍu*, Kol. *ēṟ*, *eḍ-*, Go. *ēṛung*, *ērung* 'seven' (*DED* 772).

3. PD ? **yāṯu/***yēṯu*: Ta. *yāṟu* (> *āṟu*) 'river', Ma. *āṟu* 'id.': Te. *ēṟu* 'river, stream', Go. *ēr-*, Kui *ēsu*, Kuvi *ēju*, Koṇḍa *ēṟu* 'water' (*DED* 4233).

A Proto-Dravidian **ă* or **ĕ* therefore does not represent a correspondence in which *ā/ē* alternate. As shown by the etyma in 3 above, where there is an alternation of *ā/ē*, Old Tamil has *yā* (> *ā-* in Middle and Modern Tamil). Burrow has systematically discussed this problem and posited **i̯ā-/* or *ii̯ā-/* for Proto-Dravidian which develops to *yā-* (> *ā-*) in Tamil, *ā* in some languages, and *ē* in others with some overlap (Burrow 1946a). Though we cannot be certain about the phonetics of the reconstructed phonemes, we can certainly admit that a palatal *y-* preceding the vowel is responsible for the alternation in the following vowel, as it is true in the case

[5] For the views of earlier scholars in favour of **ēn/***en-* see Chandrasekhar 1953: 88–9, fn. 2. Goda Varma (1941–2); Zvelebil reconstructs **ān: an-* for PD (1962: §5–9). Subbaiya considers **ǣ-* = (*yǣ-*) as the Proto-Dravidian vowel in the 1st pers. sg. and pl. forms (1923: 12–18).

of **ñ* and **c* also. I proposed earlier **yĀn* (nom.)/ **yĀn-* (obl.), in which *Ă represents a neutralization of contrast between **ă* and **ĕ* after **y* (*TVB* § 4.88). This is clearly borne out by the absence of any evidence leading to a reconstruction of **yā-* contrasting with **yē-*. This archiphoneme *Ā was implemented in South Dravidian as an *a*-quality vowel when long and as an *e*-quality vowel when short. In Central Dravidian (other than Telugu) it was identified as *ā/a*, i.e. **yĀn/*yĀn-* > *ān/an-*, and in Kuṛux-Malto as *ē/e*, i.e. **yĀn/yAn-* > *ēn/en-*, regularly. Except in Old Tamil, the loss of *y* (or its elimination as a contrasting unit in word-initial position) is prehistoric to most of the other languages. Even Old Tamil has *en-* in the oblique form [yen] < **yAn*, for the reason that *e-/ye-* never contrasted. Gondi has shortened the vowel in *annā* in the nominative owing to shift of stress to the second syllable (the form having become disyllabic); To. *ō* presupposes an older **ā*, while Br. *ī* < **ē* is noticed elsewhere also, though less frequently than *ē-* < **ē-*, e.g. *xīsun*: Kuṛ. *xēso* (Emeneau 1962d: §§ 2.16–18).

From the foregoing discussion we conclude that PD **yĀn/*yAn-* in the singular and **yĀm/*yAm-* in the plural account for all the forms in Groups I and III. Consequent on the loss of **y-*, the archiphoneme *Ā/*A (with and without length) is represented differently in different languages with a fair degree of consistency. In all cases in which Old Tamil has *yā-*, this correspondence does not work as regularly as in the case of pronouns (Burrow 1946a: 599–600). **-n* represents singular and **-m* represents plural, and **yĀ-* can be segmented as the first person root.

5. Ma. *ñān/en-* presupposes an original regular pair **ān/en-* of which **ān* was replaced by *ñān* even before Malayāḷam separated from Tamil by about the 10th century (morphological replacement); so also Koḍagu *nānï/en-* presupposes **ān/en-* or **ēn/en-*. The alternation *nā-/nē-* in Groups II, IV, and V can be explained similarly in terms of an original **ñĀn* (preserved only in Malayāḷam), again with *Ā representing a neutralization of **ā/*ē*. The reasons for the emergence of **ñān* beside **yān* in the first person singular aside, **ñ* > *n* is an established development, whereas the reverse change of **n-* > *ñ-* is unattested. Malayāḷam preserves PD *ñ-* in a larger number of cases than Tamil; in Tamil *ñ-* > *n-* dates to the earliest known period (Burrow 1946a: 608–16). (Hereafter *Ă is transcribed as **ă*.)

Except in standard Telugu, Kolami, and Naiki (see Group V), the **ā* of PD *ñā-* is realized as *ā* in most languages. The wide representation of the forms beginning with a nasal consonant *ñ-/n-* is a consequence of retention of a Proto-Dravidian feature and is not to be considered an innovation in the post-Proto-Dravidian period.

In Malayāḷam and Koḍagu the *ñ-/n-* forms have completely replaced *ān*, as can be surmised from the survival of *en-* in the oblique. Ta. *nāṉ* beside *yāṉ*, Ka. *nān* beside *ān*, Te. *nēnu/nānu* beside *ēnu*, Gondi *nan(n)ă* beside *an(n)ă*, Kui *nānu* beside *ānu*, and Te. Go. Kui-Kuvi-Koṇḍa *nā*-forms in the oblique all point to the antiquity of the *n*-forms. Stronger evidence for the necessity of reconstructing forms with an initial nasal consonant proceeds from Groups IV and V.

6. The existence of two plurals, one exclusive and one inclusive, is certainly a Proto-Dravidian feature (Burrow 1946a: 596–7)[6], represented by distinct sets: **yām*/**yam* 'we (exclusive)' (Group III), **ñām*/**ñam*- 'we (inclusive)' (Groups IV and V). *DED* 3019 implies a reconstruction **nām* for the inclusive plural, in which case Old Telugu *nēmu*, Nk. *nēm*, and Kol. Nk. *nēṇḍ* with an *ē* vowel in the radical syllable remain unexplained. This should lead us to reconstruct **ñām*/**ñam*- 'we (inclusive)' for Group V to which are traceable Ta. Ma. Ka. Kuṟ. Malto *nām*/*nam*-, Tu. *nama*, Te. *(ma)namu*, Nk. *nēm*; OTe. *nēmu*, Go. (dial.) *nam-oṭ*, Kui (BB) *nāmu* are also derived from **ñām*- although they have a difference in meaning, i.e. 'we (exclusive)'.

7. It is now possible to establish an original morphophonemic connection between **yām*/*yam*- 'we (exclusive)' and **ñām*/**ñam*- 'we (inclusive)'. A clue is supplied by a relic Caṅkam usage of Early Tamil in the set *yāy* 'my mother': *ñāy* 'your mother' < **n-yāy*, where **n*- has been interpreted as a bound allomorph of the second person root **nī*- (**nī-n* sg., **nī-m*, pl.; see §**14** below) (Bloch 1954: 80–1).[7] Old Tamil, which reflects the Proto-Dravidian syllable structure, does not admit of initial consonant clusters. Also note Ta. *ñāya*- < Skt. *nyāya*- 'justice', where *ñ*- < *ny*- is clearly attested. As a parallel to this case, we can reasonably assume that Proto-Dravidian /*ñām/ 'we (inclusive)' is a phonemic representation of a morphological complex, morphophonemically //*n-yām// 'you and we (exclusive)' = 'we (inclusive)'.

The existence of two plural forms **yām* and **ñām* corresponding to one singular form **yān* apparently led to a defective paradigm even though the two plurals had different lexical meanings. Another singular form **ñān* was therefore analogically created to match the plural **ñām* even though it could not be distinguished from **yān* grammatically or semantically. The foregoing discussion may be summarized in the following formula for Proto-Dravidian.

1st person sg.		1st person pl.
yān*/yan*-		**yām*/*yam*-
		↓
ñān*/ñan*-	←	**ñām*/*ñam*- (< //*n-yām/*n-yam-//)

The fact that many languages of South and Central Dravidian have derivatives of **ñān*- for the first person singular. should lead us to reconstruct it for Proto-Dravidian.

8. The above proportional pattern for Proto-Dravidian, though formally complete and symmetrical, is functionally defective inasmuch as the functional

[6] Burrow, however, reconstructs **nām* for Proto-Dravidian.

[7] P. Meile in an outline of a lecture reported in *Bulletin de la Société de Linguistique de Paris* 46.1. xiii (1950), quotes *ñāy* in Kalit. 107, 26, and says with regard to *n*- 'il joue le rôle d'un radical'.

The analysis of *yāy* 'mother or my mother' as *y-āy* is due to an attempt to analyse it on parallel lines as *ñāy*. Note that Koṇḍa *yāya*, Go. *yāyāl* 'mother' do not include possessive meaning.

(semantic and/or grammatical) difference between the two plurals **yām*: **ñām* is not paralleled by a functional difference between the two singulars **yān*: **ñān*. As a consequence, several typological readjustments are possible in languages which have inherited this proto-system, as follows:

(1) The two sets **yān*/**yan-* and **ñān*/**ñan-* can continue as the characteristics of different social or regional dialects, but in identical function until one set is overlaid by the other which may eventually emerge as the sole standard set.

This situation is clearly reflected in many languages. Ta. *nāṉ*, Ka. *nān*, and Te. *nēnu* (~ *nānu*) (< **ñān*) appear in written literatures later than the derivatives of **yān*/**yan-*.[8] They must have been in popular (or even substandard) use for a long time as rivals of the forms traceable to **yān*/**yan-* before they entered literature. Gondi *annā*: *nannā*, Kui *ānu*: *nānu* still remain as regional variants. Increased density of communication among the speakers of various social and regional dialects would again bring the two sets into rivalry.

(2) A functional (grammatical or semantic) distinction could develop between **yān*/**yan-* and **ñān*/**ñan-* to justify their formal difference; if this happened, it would also preserve the semantic distinction between **yām* and *ñām* intact.

Apparently a situation, whereby the derivatives of **yān* and **ñān* could be assigned contrastive functions, has not developed in any Dravidian language.

(3) The sets **yān*/**yan-* and **ñān*/**ñan-* could both continue if they developed grammatical complementation. No language supplies evidence even for the operation of this phenomenon.

(4) If (2) and (3) failed, then the absence of functional contrast between **yān* and **ñān* would tend to weaken and eventually obscure the functional distinction between **yām* and **ñām*, thus making one of them just as superfluous as one of the singular forms: a consequence of this would be the elimination of one pair of singular–plural from the system, i.e. either **yān*: **yām* or **ñān*: **ñām*; or the loss might affect one member in each pair resulting in a phonologically unrelated but functionally complete pair of singular: plural, i.e. **yān*: **ñām* or **ñān*: **yām*. Factors favouring the retention of one member of the pair against the other are its relative frequency, popularity, social prestige, etc. The operation of this principle is amply illustrated by most of the Dravidian languages.

In Toda and Kota of South Dravidian, and in Parji, Ollari, and Gadaba of Central Dravidian, the derivatives of **ñān*: **ñām* have been completely dropped; and with them

[8] In Tamil '*nāṉ* appears for the first time in literature of the eighth or ninth century', 'The mention of *nām* (the plural of *nāṉ*) in the Tolkāppiyam and the late appearance of *nāṉ* as singular in the eighth or ninth century literature and later—make us conclude that even *nāṉ* was current in popular speech long before it became literary' (Subbaiya 1923: 11). *Ān* 'I' occurs in Kannaḍa inscriptions from the 7th century onwards, and both *ān* and *nān* occur in inscriptions and literature from the 10th century (AD 942), see Gai (1946: 66). In Pampa Bhārata (AD 942), *nāN* occurs five times as opposed to a large number of occurrences of *āN* (Ramachandra Rao 1964: §3.8). In Telugu, Nannaya's Mahābhāratamu (AD 1062) has four clear cases of *nēnu* as opposed to innumerable occurrences of *ēnu*, but the oblique of both is *nan-*, *nā* (*Nannaya padaprayōgakōśamu* [*A Concordance of Nannaya*], see Ramakrishna Rau and Venkatavadhani 1960).

should have also originally disappeared the difference between the 'exclusive' and 'inclusive' plurals (see Groups I and III; in II, IV, V these languages are not represented).

In Kannaḍa *āN/aN-*: *āM/aM-* were progressively replaced by *nāN/naN-*: *nāM/naM-* with the latter assuming also the semantic role of *āM/aM-*. In Koḍagu both sets still remain in a defective pattern; singular: *nā(nï)/nan-* (< **ñān*/**ñan-*), *nānï/en-* (< **ñān*/**yan-*); plural: *eŋ-ga, naŋ-ga* (< **yām-*, **ñām-* + **-kaḷ*); *DED* cites both the plural forms as 'exclusive', and we do not know how the variants are distributed. It appears that *nānï/nan-* (sg.): *naŋga/naŋga-* (pl.) is the most complete pair and has better chances of superseding the defective pair traceable to **ñān*/**yan-*: **yām*/**yam-*.

The relevant data from Telugu, Gondi, Kui, Kuvi, Koṇḍa, and Pengo need special treatment owing to an additional complication of the emergence of stems with initial *m-* (see §§**9–10**). In these languages also, the fact that the distinction between exclusive and inclusive was originally disturbed could be shown by the co-existence of dialect variants derived from **yām* and **ñām* undistinguished as to function; e.g. OTe. *ēmu, nēmu* 'we (exclusive)', Go. *am-oṭ, nam-oṭ* id. Kui *āmu, nāmu* id. (< **yām*, **ñām*). Subsequent independent innovations had restored the inclusive plural; Te. *manamu*, Go. *aplō* (< ? Munda or Marathi), Kui *āju*, Pengo *ās/āh*, and Koṇḍa *māṭ*, which are not traceable to **ñām*.

Brahui also illustrates this phenomenon by *ī* (sg.): *nan* (pl.) (< **yān*: *ñām*) a formally unrelated pair; again here, the inclusive: exclusive distinction in the plural is necessarily eliminated, *nan* signalling both the meanings.

(5) If (4) had failed, i.e. if the functional contrast between the exclusive and inclusive plurals is too strongly established in the system to be shaken by the lack of some similar contrast in **yān*: **ñān*, then the former would remain, and one of the singular forms might drop out. This would lead to a restoration of the situation similar to that present in the proto-language to start with. Then, only one singular **yān* or **ñān*, but both the plurals **yām* and **ñām* would survive.

This principle is illustrated by Kuṛux and Malto; *ēn/en-* (sg.): *ēm/em-* (pl. exclusive), *nām/nam-* (pl. inclusive). Here the innovation is the loss of a derivative of **ñān*. Tuḷu, Kolami, and Naiki also bear testimony to the loss of one of the rival singular forms:

	'I'	'We (exclusive)'	'We (inclusive)'
Tu.	*yānï, ēnï/en-*	*yaṅ-kuḷe/eṅ-kuḷe-*	*nama*
Kol.	*ān/an-*	*ām/am-*	*nēnḍ*
Nk.	*ān/an-*	*ām/am-*	*nēnḍ, nēm*

It is also possible that in Kolami *nēnḍ* was a later innovation after losing the inherited inclusive plural form *nēm* originally.

(6) Free forms are more easily susceptible to morphological replacement through analogical levelling or otherwise than bound forms. In the case of personal pronouns in Dravidian, the nominative forms are free, whereas the oblique stems occur bound in morphological or syntactic constructions (Emeneau 1953b).

Morphological replacement may affect formally related sets of nominative/oblique (**yān*/**yan-*: **yām-yam-*; *ñān*/*ñan-*: **ñām*/*ñām-*), in such a way that the nominative of one set may be replaced by the nominative of another set; the consequent replacement possibilities are:

(a)	*ñān*/**yan-*	replacing	**yān*/**yan-*
(b)	*yān*/*ñan-*	replacing	**ñān*/**ñan-*
(c)	*ñām*/**yam-*	replacing	**yām*/**yam-*
(d)	*yām*/**ñam-*	replacing	**ñām*/**ñam-*

In such formally discrepant sets, the oblique stem serves as a basis for the identification of the replaced nominative. Examples for (a) are Ta. *nāṉ*/*en-*, Ma. *ñān*/*en-*, Koḍ. *nānï*/*en-* in which *(*y*)*ān* or *ēn* (< **yān*) in the nominative was replaced by a form traceable to **ñān*. Examples for (b) occur in Central Dravidian: Te. *ēnu*, *nēnu*/*nan-*, *nā*, Go. *annā*, *nannā*/*nā-*, Kui *ānu*, *nānu*/*nan-*, *nā-*. In terms of our formulation, the formally discrepant (unpaired) nominatives, Te. *ēnu*, Go. *annā*, and Kui *ānu* spread dialectally replacing the paired nominatives.[9] Examples for (c) are available in Tamil and Malayāḷam, in which the derivatives of **yām* are replaced by those of *ñām* in the nominatives (Group III and IV): Ta. *nāṅ-kaḷ*/*em-* (see §**8** below for an explanation of *-kaḷ*), replacing *ām*/*em-*, Ma. *ñāṅ-ṅaḷ*/*eṅ-ṅaḷ*, *ñaṅ-ṅaḷ*. Examples for (d) occur again in Telugu, etc. in Central Dravidian (see §9).

(7) In case of any or all of the possibilities (4) to (6) operating, analogical levelling might affect the alternating members of nominative/oblique with formally matched or unmatched stems, thus bringing about a formal similarity or obliterating a formal distinction between the members of the set.

In Toda, sg. *ōn*/*en-*, pl. *em*/*em-* (instead of **ōm*/*em-*) shows that the inherited oblique *em-* replaced the inherited nominative **ōm*. Similarly, it appears that Br. *nan* 'we (exclusive-inclusive)' with a short vowel is an oblique stem which serves both as nominative and oblique. In Modern Tamil, *naṅga(ḷ)*/*naṅgaḷ-*, Ma. *ñāṅṅaḷ*/*ñaṅṅaḷ*, Koḍ. *naŋga*/*naŋga-*, *eŋga*/*eŋga-*, Tu. *eṅkuḷï*/*eṅkuḷe-* 'we (exclusive)', Kol. Nk. *nēnḍ*/*nēnḍ-* 'we (inclusive)' all show the replacement of obliques by innovated nominative stems. Tu. *nama*/*nama-* 'we (inclusive)' with shortened *-a-* in the nominative, points to the analogical extension of the oblique stem to the nominative, replacing an expected **nēm* or **nām*.

(8) An overriding typological principle seems to be that whenever an inherited contrast requiring retention (determinable by linguistic or non-linguistic factors) is threatened by a linguistic change, it either resists such change, or, if it fails to do so, another change (morphological or phonological) will be innovated to restore it.

This phenomenon is amply illustrated by the Dravidian languages in their treatment of exclusive/inclusive plurals.

[9] In view of the facts stated in fn. 8, it is theoretically possible that the discrepant nominatives are retentions of regular sets traceable to **yān*/**an-* in which the oblique surrendered to replacement by the oblique of the alternative pair **ñān*/**ñān-*, which fact also favoured the later replacement of a derivative of **yān* by that of its rival **ñān*.

	'I'	'We (exclusive)'	'We (inclusive)'
Ta.	*nāṉ*(<< *yāṉ*)	*nāṅ-kaḷ* (<< *yām*, *yāṅ-kaḷ*)	*nām* (< **ñām*)
Ma.	*ñān* (<< **ān*)	*ñāṅ-ṅal* (<< **ām*-, *eṅ-ṅaḷ*)	*nām* (< *ñām*)

In Tamil *nām* (< **ñām*) dates to the earliest period in literature, and *nāṉ* (<< *yāṉ*) makes its appearance in literature from the 8th century AD. Analogical levelling was completed when *nāṅ-kaḷ*, derived apparently from inclusive **ñām* with the addition of -*kaḷ* to distinguish it from *nām* 'we (inclusive)' was innovated to take over the erstwhile variants *yām*, *yāṅkaḷ*. This replacement was accelerated by the fact that the semantic distinction between *yām* 'we (exclusive)' and *nām* 'we (inclusive)' was being weakened by the promiscuous use of *yām* in both meanings (Subbaiya 1923: 3, 19 ff., Burrow 1946 a: 597, fn. 9, Zvelebil 1962: 67). Modern Tamil has [nā̃:] 'I', *naŋga/naŋgaḷ*- 'we (exclusive)', *nāma*~ *namba/namma*-~ *nambaḷ*- 'we (inclusive)' (in the last set -*mb* < -*m* by an intrusive -*b*).

Toda and Kota, which have lost the derivatives of PD **ñān*: **ñām* and thereby also the exclusive–inclusive contrast, restored it by a phonological innovation:

Ko. *ām* 'we'/obl. *em*- (exclusive), *am*- (inclusive);
To. *em/em*- 'we (exclusive)'; *om/om*- 'we (inclusive)'.

A subgroup of Central Dravidian comprising Telugu, Gondi, Kui, Kuvi, Koṇḍa, and Pengo, which have progressively replaced the set < **yām*/**yam*- by the set < **ñām*/**ñam*-, had apparently lost the exclusive–inclusive distinction, which they later restored through independent innovations by bringing new inclusive forms into existence, Te. *manamu*, Go. *aplō*, Kui *āju*, Pe. *ās/āh*, Koṇḍa *māṭ* (see §11).[10]

[10] One of the typological pressures for the restoration of exclusive–inclusive distinction might have proceeded from the prevalence of parallel distinction in finite verbs which include personal suffixes bearing concord with pronominal words in the subject position. With the exception of Malayāḷam, which lost pronominal reference in finite verbs around the 9th century AD or so, all other languages which had or still have exclusive–inclusive contrast in pronouns (either inherited without loss or inherited, lost, and restored) possess a parallel contrast in verbs. A similar situation obtaining in Proto-Dravidian could have been primarily responsible for the innovation of an inclusive pronoun **ñām* to fill a gap in the subject-verb concord pattern.

Personal pronoun		Personal suffix in verbs	
		excl.	incl.
OTa.	*yām*	*-em*, *-ēm*	*-am*, *-ām*
	nām		*-am*, *-ām*
OKa.	*ām* (excl.)	*-em*, *-evu*	
	ām (incl.)		
	or		
	nām (incl.)		*-am*
Ko.	*ām* (excl. & incl.)	*-ēm*	*-ōm*
To.	*em*	*-em*	
	om (incl.)		*-um* (< *-am*)
OTe.	*ēmu*, *mēmu* (excl.)	*-mu*	
	manamu (incl.)		*-amu*
Go.	*ammaṭ*	*-ām/-ōm*	

9. A real difficulty lies with Telugu, Gondi, Kui, Kuvi, Koṇḍa, and Pengo which possess forms beginning with *m*- mostly in the first person plural nominative and entirely in the oblique (Group IV).

The Proto-Dravidian relation between the nominative and the oblique stems seems to lie basically in the alternation between long and short radical vowels, i.e. nominative/oblique = (C)V̄C/(C)V̆C-. This is attested clearly by Groups I and III reconstructable to PD **yān*/**yan*- and **yām*/**yam*-. But in a subgroup of Central Dravidian consisting of Telugu, Gondi, Kui, Kuvi, Pengo, and Koṇḍa, there was a shared innovation whereby a different relation developed between the nominative and oblique stems, viz. (C)V̄C/(C)V̄-, beside the regular type (C)V̄C/(C)V̆C- (*TVB* §4.48, fn. 7). This explains *nā*- (< **ñān*), which uniformly obtains as the oblique in all these languages, as opposed to the nominative *nān* or *nēn*. A consequence of this innovation in this subgroup should have resulted in an absence of the singular–plural distinction because in the proto-forms **ñān*: **ñām* it is the final consonants -*n*: -*m* that carry this contrast.

It appears that this mode of oblique formation necessarily led to another innovation by which the singular–plural opposition was shifted to the initial position by substituting *m*- for *n*- in the plural, thus restoring the original contrast (see §8 (8) above).

PCD	Proto-Te.-Kui-Go.
sg. **ñān*/**ñan*-	*nān*~*nēn*/(*nan*-), *nā*-
pl. **ñām*/**ñam*-	*nām*~*nēm*/(*nam*-), **nā*->>/*mā*-

10. The next step in the chain of adjustments as a consequence of the above change seems to be an analogical levelling of the nominative stems by replacing an initial *n*- by *m*- even though the singular–plural opposition remained unaffected there (§8 (7)). Notice the following:

	'I'	'We (exclusive)'
Te.	*ēnu*; *nēnu*/—; *nan*-, *nā*-	*ēmu*; *nēmu*, *mēmu*/—; *mamm*-, *mā*-
Kui	*ānu*; *nānu*/—; *nā*-	*āmu*; *māmu*/—; *mā*-
Kuvi	—; *nānu*/—; *nā*	—; *māmbu*, *māro*/—; *mā*
Koṇḍa	—; *nān*/—; *nā*-	—; *māp*/—; *mā*-
Go.	*an*(*n*)*ă*; *nan*(*n*)*ă*/—; *nā*-	*ammoṭ*; *namoṭ*, *mammoṭ*/—; *mā*-
Pe.	*ān*(*eŋ*);—/—;*naŋg*-, *nā*-	*āp*(*eŋ*);—/—; *maŋg*-, *mā*-

The following points support the hypothesis that the nominatives have been analogically restructured on the basis of the oblique stems in the first person plural through sound substitution and not sound change:

	Personal pronoun	Personal suffix in verbs	
		excl.	incl.
	aplō		-*aṭ*
Kui	*āmu*, *māmu* (excl.)	-*amu*	
	āju (incl.)		-*asu*
Kuṛ.	*ēm*	-*am*	
	nām		*at*

(1) Old and literary Telugu has *ēmu* and *nēmu* traceable to PD **yām* and **ñām* respectively. The alternation of *ē-/ā-* in *mēmu/mamm-, mā-* cannot be explained as being induced by the preceding *m-*; therefore it reflects an original alternation *nēm* (< *ñām*)/*nā-*, *nam-* of which *nā* >> *mā-* (see explanation above). A proportional pattern like *nēnu*: *nā* :: ?: *mā* would be expected to lead to *mēmu* as the nominative of the first person plural, which still bore ample resemblance to the basic forms *ēmu* and *nēmu*.

(2) The coexistence of phonologically discrepant and non-discrepant pairs like Te. *ēmu*: *mā* beside *mēmu*: *mā*, Kui *āmu*: *mā-* beside *nāmu*: *mā*, Go. *nammaṭ*, *ammaṭ*/*mā-*, beside *mammaṭ*: *mā-* all point to the stability of the oblique forms as against variations in nominative stems. This situation also points to the relatively high antiquity of the oblique stem *mā-* as opposed to the nominative stems.

11. It is clear from the above discussion that the progressive regularization of **ñān*: **ñām* at the expense of **yān*: *yām* in this subgroup of Central Dravidian had necessarily led to the obliteration of the exclusive–inclusive distinction, which most of the languages sought to restore through independent innovation.

The Telugu inclusive plural *manamu* is comparatively unique and can be explained in either of two ways: (a) The original nominative/oblique pair was *nām*/*nama-*, of which the oblique developed into *mana-* through metathesis, and the nominative was then reformed as *mana-mu* by the addition of the plural *-mu*. (b) *manamu* is a contamination of **māmu* 'we (exclusive)' and **nām* (< PD **ñām* 'we (inclusive)'. The first alternative sounds more plausible inasmuch as the oblique, being bound in its occurrence, may be assumed to be older and more stable, which was responsible for remodelling the nominative form.

Go. *aplō* (?< Munda or Marathi *aple* 'of you') is definitely a recent innovation; Kui *āju* 'we (inclusive)' looks to PD **āṯu* or **ānṯu* (*ṯ* = [ḏ/ṟ]) but no etymologies are available to support this. Koṇḍa *mā-p* 'we (exclusive)' vs. *mā-ṭ* 'we (inclusive)' is again a later distinction introduced by replacing *-m* of **mām* by two morphs *-p* and *-ṭ*. We do not know the origin of *-p* in Koṇḍa and Pengo as a plural morph,[11] while *-ṭ* seems to be an innovation shared by Koṇḍa with Gondi and is related in some manner to the second person plural suffix used in verbs in the negative imperative (prohibitive); cf. Koṇḍa *son-m-a* 'don't go!' (2nd sg.), *son-m-aṭ* 'don't go!' (2nd pl.).[12]

Kol. Nk. *nēnḍ* 'we (inclusive)' seems to be based on **ñām* but for the final cluster *nḍ*, not explicable in the present state of our knowledge. The fact that Naiki, which is more closely allied to Kolami than to any other language, preserves a form *nēm* shows that *nēnḍ* was a recent innovation which replaced an earlier *nēm* in Kolami also.

[11] For the possibility of a 'structural borrowing' from the neighbouring Munda languages, cf. Santālī *ām-pā*, Muṇḍārī *ā-pē*, Korwa *a-pe*, Kūrkū *ā-pē*, Khaṛiā *am-pe*, Juang (dial.) *ā-pere*—'you (pl.)' (*LSI* IV: 240–2).

[12] Note the more extensive use of *-ṭ/-āṭ/-oṭ* as a plural morph in Gondi in the 1st pers. pl. *amm-aṭ*., etc. and the 2nd pers. pl. *imm-aṭ*. In finite verbs a personal suffix-*īṭ* occurs when the subject is 2nd pers. pl. *immaṭ*; the hortative verbs also have a final *-aṭ*, e.g. *tittaṭ* 'we (both) ate'; neg. imp. 2nd sg. *-mā*, pl. *-māṭ*: Trench (1919: 11 ff.).

It is therefore clear from the foregoing discussion that in this subgroup of Central Dravidian, the exclusive–inclusive contrast was more a restoration through independent morphological innovation in each language than retention.

12. The accretion of another plural morph on a stem which is already a plural seems to be an areal feature involving Tamil, Malayāḷam, Koḍagu, Tuḷu, Telugu, Gondi, Pengo, and Koṇḍa, because it cuts across the genetic subgrouping. Kuṛux and Malto remain uninfluenced by this areal 'drift', though in respect of inherited features, they go more with South Dravidian than with the Telugu-Gondi-Kui-Kuvi-Koṇḍa-Pengo subgroup of Central Dravidian.

13. Summary. Proto-Dravidian had **yān* 'I', **yām* 'we (exclusive)', and **ñām* 'we (inclusive)'; *ñām* is morphophonemically traceable to **n-yām* 'you and we', of which *n-* was a bound allomorph of PD **nīn*/*nīm* 'you' (sg./pl.); *ñām* gave rise to another singular form **ñān* 'I' on the analogy of **yān*: **yām*. The *ā* vowel following **y-* or **ñ-* is an archiphoneme representing a neutralization of contrast between *ā* and *ē*. Consequently the vowel is variously represented either as *ā* or *ē*.

The oblique stems of pronouns occurred with a shortened vowel, **yan-*, **yam-*, **ñan-*, **ñam-* respectively, again with **a* representing **a*/**e*. The absence of functional contrast between **yān*: **ñān* to match that of **yām*: **ñām* has led to many typological readjustments in all the Dravidian languages which have inherited the formally symmetrical but functionally defective Proto-Dravidian system (§**8**).

The derivatives of **ñān*: **ñām* have progressively replaced the derivatives of **yān*: **yām*, mainly in the nominative forms of South Dravidian (see Group II) and in both the nominative and oblique forms in the Telugu-Gondi-Kui-Kuvi-Koṇḍa-Pengo subgroup of Central Dravidian. Telugu, Gondi, Pengo, and Kui also preserve the derivatives of **yān*: **yām* even though in the oblique only the derivatives **ñān*/**ñām* occur.

Tuḷu in South Dravidian, Kolami and Naiki in Central Dravidian, and Kuṛux and Malto in North Dravidian still preserve the Proto-Dravidian phonological and semantic contrasts between the singular and the plural by dropping one of the rival variants in the singular.

When Ta. *nāṉ* and Ma. *ñān* (< PSD **ñān*) replaced the earlier *yāṉ* (< PSD **yān*), there apparently arose a discrepant set as follows:

	'I'	'We (exclusive)'	'We (inclusive)'
Ta.	*nāṉ* (<< *yāṉ*)	*(y)ām*	*nām* (< **ñām*)
Ma.	*ñān* (<< *ān*)	**ām*	**ñām*/*nām* (< **ñam*)

The plural exclusive was therefore ousted by an extension of the distribution of the *ñ-*/*n-* base through a morphological innovation of addition of *-kaḷ* (plural morph) to distinguish the exclusive plural from the inclusive plural, i.e. Ta. *nāṅkaḷ*, Ma. *ñāṅṅaḷ* 'we (exclusive)': Ta. Ma. *nām* 'we (inclusive)'. This was apparently motivated by the presence of **yāṅkal* in Old Tamil or even in pre-Tamil as a variant of **yām*. This explains the doublet for 'we (exclusive)' in Koḍ. *eŋga*, *naŋga*, and Tu.

eṅkuḷï. Kota and Toda, having lost the derivatives of **ñām/ñam-*, have restored the exclusive–inclusive contrast by exploiting the alternation of *am/em* (< **yām*) for a grammatical or semantic purpose. In Central Dravidian the Parji-Kolami subgroup (also including Ollari, Gadaba, and Naiki) has faithfully preserved the derivatives of **yān/*yan-*, and only Kolami and Naiki show any evidence of an original derivative of *ñām* (> Nk. *nēm*, Kol. Nk. *nēnḍ*).

In the other subgroup of Central Dravidian consisting of Telugu, Gondi, Kui, Kuvi, Koṇḍa, and Pengo, a chain of innovations had taken place. An original nominative/oblique relationship by a stem variation of the type $(C)_1\bar{V}_2C_3/(C)_1\breve{V}_2C_3$- was replaced by the type $(C)_1\bar{V}_2C_3/(C)_1\bar{V}_2$-. This necessarily led to the obliteration of the singular–plural contrast in the oblique because it was the final consonants *-n*: *-m* which signalled this difference. The contrast was restored by substituting *m-* for *n-* in the plural oblique: *mā-* << *nā-*. The plural nominative stems were further analogically reformed by substituting *m-* for *n-* on the basis of the oblique to form a parallel set with the singular form. The replacement of the derivatives of **yām* by those of **ñām* in this group has obliterated the exclusive–inclusive distinction, which each language has innovated in an independent manner.

14. The etymologies for the second person singular and plural given under entries 3051 and 3055 of *DED* fall into three phonological groups, as follows:

TABLE 4.2. *The second person pronouns in nominative and oblique cases*

GROUP I: Second person singular 'thou' (*DED* 3051)

	Nominative	Oblique
Ta.	nī	niṉ(ṉ)-
Ma.	nī	nin(n)-
To.	nī	nin-
Ko.	nī	nin-
Koḍ	nīnï, nī	nin-, nī-
Ka.	nīN	nin(n)-
Tu.	ī	nin-, in-
Te.	nīwu, īwu	nin-, nī-
Go.	—	nī-
Koṇḍa	nīnu	niŋ-, nī-
Kui	īnu (W)	nī-
	nīnu (BB)	nin-, nī,
Kuvi	nīnū (F), nīnu (S)	nī-
Pe.	īn(eŋ)	niŋg-, nī-
Kol.	nīv	in-
Nk.	nīv, īv	in-
Pa.	īn	in-
Oll.	īn	in-
Gad.	īn	in(n)-
Kuṛ.	nīn	niŋg-

Malto	nīn	niŋg-
Br.	nī	nē-, n-

GROUP IIA: Second person plural 'you' (*DED* 3055)

	Nominative	Oblique
Ta.	nīm, nīṅ-kaḷ, nīr, nīyir	—
Ma.	niṅ-ṅaḷ	niṅ-ṅaḷ-
To.	nïm	nim-
Ko.	nīm	nim-
Koḍ.	niŋ-ga	niŋ-ga-
Ka.	nīM (nīm, nīvu), nīṅ-gaḷ	nim(m)-
Tu. (dial.)	nī-kuḷï, in-kuḷu, īru	ni-kuḷe-, in-kuḷe-, īre-
Te.	īru	—
Go. (dial.)	nim-aṭ, nim-eṭ; im-eṭ, imm-aṭ, imm-āṭ	—
Kui	nīm (BB)	nim-
Pe.	īp(eŋ)	—
Kol.	nīr	im-
Nk.	nīr	im-
Pa.	īm	im-
Oll.	īm	im-
Gad.	īm	imm-
Kuṛ.	nīm	nim-
Malto.	nīm	nim-

GROUP IIB

	Nominative	Oblique
Ta. (Old)	—	num-; (Mdn.) um-, uṅ-kaḷ
Br.	num	num-

GROUP IIC: Second person singular 'thou' (*DED* 3051)

	Nominative	Oblique
Go. (dial.)	nimā, nim(m)a, nim-aṭ, nim-eṭ; ima, immā, imm-aṭ, imm-āṭ, im-eṭ	nī-

GROUP III

	Nominative	Oblique
Te.	mīru	mimm-, mī
Go.	mim-eṭ, mīṭ	mī-
Koṇḍa	mīru	miŋ-, mī-
Kui	mīmu (BB)	mī
Kuvi	mīmbū (F), mīmbu(S)	mī-
Pe.	—	miŋg-, mī-

15. All the forms of Group I are explicable through PD **nīn*/**nin-* 'thou'. In South Dravidian, Tamil, Malayāḷam, Kota, Toda, Koḍagu, and Tuḷu have lost the final *-n* of the nominative, but have preserved it in the oblique stems. All the other languages generally preserve the final *-n* of the nominative. Pre-Telugu *nīnu* (cf. obl. *nin-*) suffered a replacement of the final syllable *-nu* by *-wu*. The nominative forms of Kolami and Naiki, *nīvu*, apparently borrowed from Telugu, had replaced an original **īn* (cf. oblique *in-*). A shared innovation in the (Tuḷu)- Parji-Kolami-Naiki-Ollari-Gadaba subgroup of Central Dravidian is the loss of the PD *n-* in both the nominative and the oblique. A similar loss of initial *n-* took place independently in Tuḷu and in a literary dialect of Telugu (as shown by one of the variants, *īwu* < *īn-*), Kui, and Pengo.

The singular form in the various Gondi dialects has the root *im-* or *nim-* (Group IIC) which, on a comparative basis, ought to be a plural stem. Since the plural is distinguished by the addition of other plural morphs *-ăṭ*, *-eṭ*, the inherited plural stem had replaced the inherited singular.

The nominative/oblique relationship of Proto-Dravidian of the type $^*(C)_1\bar{V}_2C_3/(C)_1\breve{V}_2C_3$- was partially replaced by the type $C_1\bar{V}_2C_3/C_1\bar{V}_2$- as a shared innovation in Telugu, Gondi, Kui, Kuvi, Koṇḍa, and Pengo, all of which uniformly have *nī-* as morphologically free oblique stem as opposed to morphologically bound **nin-* in the accusative and dative cases, cf. Te. *nin-nu* 'thou (acc.)', Koṇḍa *ni-ŋi* (< **nin-gi*) (acc. dat.). Even Koḍagu shows a similar development. Kuṛ. Malto *niŋg-* 'you' (nom.) (< **nin-g-*) was originally a dative stem normalized as the oblique.

16. Forms under Group II look to PD **nīm*/*nim-* 'you (pl.)'. The South Dravidian languages innovated double plurals by adding a plural suffix **-kaḷ* to plural stems. This innovation, shared by Tamil, Malayāḷam, Koḍagu, and Kannaḍa, may well go back to a Proto-South-Dravidian stage, except that Toda and Kota do not share it. It is also possible that it took place in pre-Tamil after Toda and Kota had separated. Tu. *ni-kuḷï*, and Ka. *nīṅ-gaḷ* could also reflect a typological or areal borrowing from Tamil.

As in the case of the singular form, the Kolami-Naiki-Parji-Ollari-Gadaba subgroup of Central Dravidian has lost the initial *n-* both in the nominative and oblique as a shared innovation, i.e. PD **nīm*/**nim-* > **īm*/**im-*. Kolami and Naiki *nīr*/*im-* presupposes an earlier set **īm*/*im-* of which the nominative was replaced by **nīr*, possibly a borrowing from pre-Telugu, judging from what had happened in the singular (see §15). OTe. *ī-ru*, Go. (dial.) *imm-*, and Kui *ī-ru* reflect the loss of an initial *n-* (as also in the singular of Te. *īwu* 'thou') and the replacement of plural *-m* by a synonymous morph *-r* occurring as the personal plural suffix of demonstrative nouns. Gondi innovated an extended form by adding a plural morph *-aṭ*/*-eṭ* on the inherited plural stem *nīm-*, *nim(m-)*, *im(m)-* (loss of initial *n-*), which it construed as singular, and by which it ousted the inherited singular **nīn*/**nin-* ~ *in-*.

As in the case of the first personal forms, Kuṛux and Malto retain the

Proto-Dravidian contrasts faithfully and have remained unaffected by areal influences from or innovations in South or Central Dravidian.

Group IIB has forms which cannot be directly related to **nīm*/**nim*-; the normal oblique in Tamil should be **nim*- but it is actually *num*- or *um*- in Old Tamil, and *uṅ-kaḷ* in Middle and Modern Tamil. It was suggested that pre-Tamil *nim*- > *num*- in which *i* > *u* under the influence of the following bilabial nasal -*m* (Bloch 1954: 32); the fact that Brahui also has *num*- could possibly be evoked to set up this change for Proto-Dravidian, as exclusive retentions between Tamil and Brahui are rare.

17. Group III represents a subgroup of Central Dravidian which behaves differently in the formation of the oblique. The oblique *mī*- common to all these languages can be explained on the same grounds as the first plural oblique *mā*- (§9), i.e. that it is a morphological replacement of *nī*- (< **nīm*) by *mī*- in order to distinguish it from the singular oblique *nī*- (< **nīn*). The plural oblique *mī*- thus formed the model for the nominative stems to be reformed analogically in terms of the proportion *nīnu*: *nī*- :: *mīmu* (<< *nīm*-): *mī*. Consequently Gondi has *mim-eṭ*, beside the original *nim-eṭ*, *nim-aṭ*, *im-eṭ*, *imm-aṭ*, still preserved in certain dialects. Telugu, Kuvi (BB), and Koṇḍa, *mī-ru* (<< **nī-ru* << **nī-m*) beside Kui *ī-ru*, (BB) *mīmu*, Kuvi (S) *mīmu* (< *nīm*-) show the extension of the oblique *m*- to the nominative forms by replacing an original *n*-.

The replacement of plural -*m* by -*r* belonging mainly to demonstrative pronouns and nouns denoting the human group occurs in both South Dravidian and Central Dravidian: Ta. *nī-r*, *nī-yir*, Tu. *ī-ru*, Te. *ī-ru*, Kol. Nk. *nī-r*, Kui *ī-ru*, Kuvi (BB) *mī-ru*, and Koṇḍa *mī-ru*. Since the languages involved are geographically, but not genetically, contiguous, we have to consider this an areal feature, and not a feature ascribable to Proto-Dravidian. Kuṛux and Malto, which remain unaffected either by the innovations or by the areal features of South Dravidian or Central Dravidian, do not show this morph replacement.

18. Summary. The second person singular and plural forms in Proto-Dravidian are **nīn*/**nin*- and **nīm*/**nim*- respectively. With the exception of the Telugu-Gondi-Kui-Kuvi-Koṇḍa subgroup of Central Dravidian, all other languages bear testimony to these reconstructions mainly by their oblique stems. In each subgroup these forms have been modified by several phonological and morphological innovations.

Phonological innovations: (a) Loss of initial *n*- regularly in a sub-group of Central Dravidian involving mainly Parji, Ollari, and Gadaba. Independently, however, Tamil, Tuḷu, Telugu, Gondi, Pengo, and Kui also dialectally lose an initial *n*-. (b) *-*n* > -Ø in the nominative in South Dravidian. (c) Tamil oblique *num*- < *nim*- presumably by a conditioned sound change.

Morphological innovations: (a) Addition of a plural suffix on a stem that is already plural, perhaps as an honorific singular, gave rise to several extended stems in many languages: SD **nīm-kaḷ* and the addition of -*ăṭ*, -*eṭ* in Gondi. (b) Replacement of the plural morph *-m* by *-r*, extending the distribution of the latter. This is an areal tendency involving both South Dravidian and Central Dravidian. (c) The replacement of nominative/oblique relationship of the type $C_1\bar{V}_2C_3/C_1\breve{V}_2C_3$- by the type $C_1\bar{V}_2C_3/C_1\bar{V}_2$- in the Telugu-Gondi-Kui-Kuvi-Koṇḍa-Pengo subgroup of Central Dravidian was an innovation which would have resulted in a merger of the plural oblique *nī* (< *nīm*) with the singular oblique *nī-* (< *nīn*). A further morphological innovation of *nī-* (< *nīm*) >> *mī-* restored the original contrast of singular and plural, but in the initial position instead of in the final.

Postscript

P 1. This was a difficult paper on a difficult problem. Earlier, K. V. Subbaiya (1923) dealt with it thoroughly, although his reconstructions were questionable (Burrow 1946a: 597–8). M. Collins in his remarks on Subbaiya's monograph claimed that initial *n-* of *nām* 'we (inclusive)' was tacked on to the singular forms *ān*/*ēn* 'I', thus creating doublets like Ta. *nāṉ* beside *yāṉ*, Te. *nēnu* beside *ēnu*, etc. Burrow (1946a: 598) endorsed this view. Since the *n-* forms were widely distributed in many languages which would fall into South Dravidian, viz. Tamil, Malayāḷam, Toda, Kota, Kannaḍa, Tuḷu, Koḍagu, and also in the subgroup that we earlier considered a branch of Central Dravidian, viz. Telugu, Gondi, Koṇḍa, Kui, Kuvi, and Pengo, I thought such restructuring must be a shared innovation at a common stage, if any, of all those languages. There are no *n-* forms for 'I' in the 'other branch' of Central Dravidian, viz. Kolami, Naiki, Parji, Ollari, and Koṇḍekor Gadaba, nor in North Dravidian, viz. Kuṛux, Malto, and Brahui. But it was not possible in our thinking for there to have been a common stage for the two groups of languages that developed the doublets.

I reconstructed **ñām* as the inclusive plural in Proto-Dravidian, deriving it as a morphological complex from **ni-yām* 'you and we', on the basis of relic forms in Ancient Tamil *yāy* 'my mother' (< *y-āy*), *ñāy* (**ni-āy*) 'your mother', and *tāy* (*t-āy*) 'his/her mother' (Meenakshisundaran 1968: 226). Taking the hint from Collins, I reconstructed a back-formed **ñān* out of **ñām* and proposed that *nā-*/*nē-* alternation both in the first person singular and in the plural inclusive in some of the languages can be explained only in terms of a PD **ñ-*. Burrow (1946a) had not thought of PD **ñām-* because he did not know the Kolami *nēṇḍ*, Naiki *nēm* 'we (inclusive)' at that time. He reconstructed **nām* as it was represented in many languages including Kuṛux and Malto. Actually in his 1946 article he treated the alternation of *ā*/*ē* after **ñ-* which merged with *n-* in all languages except Tamil and Malayāḷam. He asserted, 'Since an alternation *nā-*/*nē-* is due in these cases to the fact that the nasal was originally palatal in these cases, it is reasonable to assume that a form *ñā-* is represented in cases where we find an alternation *nā-*/*nē-* even if no such *ñā-* form is found in Tamil or Malayāḷam' (1946a: 604). He gave two examples for such reconstruction, but did not include *nā-/nē-* alternation in the personal pronouns in the singular and plural.

P 2. The morphological aspects of the problem are even more interesting. Burrow argued for different first person plurals in the inclusive and exclusive as being a feature of the 'parent language' (1946a: 576–7). However, he had not noticed that the loss or blurring of the difference in the meanings of 'inclusive' and 'exclusive' occurred exactly in those languages which developed doublets in the singular from **yān* and **ñān* corresponding to the two plurals **yām* 'we (exclusive)' and **ñām* 'we (inclusive)'. Since the formal difference in the singular forms does not match the formal and functional (semantic) difference in the plural forms, I thought of a number of possible changes to follow such a formally symmetrical but functionally defective pattern in the descendant languages. I could explain the entire data in terms of these typological possibilities (see §§7, 8).

P 3. There is one important revision that I have made. The inclusive plural **ñām* was already present in Proto-Dravidian. But the innovation of a singular based on this form (as a back-formation) was also attributed to Proto-Dravidian in the article (§7). My later study showed that in fact the Telugu-Kui group (South Dravidian II) was not a subgroup of Central Dravidian, but went better with the Tamil-Kannaḍa subgroup (South Dravidian I). I therefore called the two subgroups South Dravidian I and South Dravidian II, the latter also called South-Central Dravidian. These both had a common stage Proto-South Dravidian (see Fig. 21.1). In my postscript to Chapter 2, I demonstrated that vocalic umlaut (PD **i* **u* > PSD **e* **o*/___ C+*a*) was shared by both South Dravidian I and South Dravidian II, but not by Central Dravidian. The derivatives of **ñān* are noticed only in South Dravidian I and South Dravidian II. Therefore, it was at the common stage of these two subgroups, i.e. Proto-South Dravidian that the innovation of **ñān* took place; the exclusive–inclusive difference was blurred exactly in those languages which had developed doublets in *n-* for the first singular and plural. Central Dravidian and North Dravidian languages show the inherited three-way distinction, with forms derived from **yān* 1st sg., **yām* 1st pl. (excl.), and **ñām* 1st pl. (incl.). I posited the loss of the derivatives of **ñān* in these languages as an innovation reverting to *status quo ante* because, at that time, I reconstructed **ñān* for Proto-Dravidian. I later realized that it would be methodologically simpler to set up **ñān* for Proto-South Dravidian rather than for Proto-Dravidian. This means that §8 (5) has to be dropped from the paper. I have not done so here, or made other consequential revisions elsewhere in the original paper, for the sake of the readers who need to understand the progressive stages in my thinking and to judge if I have taken the right steps or not. Everything falls into place now and the theoretical model that I have proposed in my paper (including the above revision) explains best all the anomalous developments in the phonology and morphology of the Dravidian personal pronouns. This was the internal test which would prove that my method was correct.

P 4. Now I will briefly survey the views expressed by other Dravidianists on these problems both before and after the publication of this article. Subbaiya's reconstruction of the vowel for the first person as **ǣ-* was rejected by Burrow (1946a: 598) and I supported the latter's view (see fn. 5 of my article). I explained the alternation of *ā* and *ē* after **y* as being due to neutralization of two phonemes *ă̄*/*ĕ̄* after palatal **y* and **ñ*, and occasionally after **c-*. Even Tamil had *ē* corresponding to **yā* at an earlier stage, e.g. OTa. *yātu* > *ētu* 'which one?' (Meenakshisundaran 1968: 228). It is not strictly correct to reconstruct **yā* either for Proto-South Dravidian or for Proto-Dravidian; therefore, I posited **yĀ̆*, in which **Ā̆* represented a neutralization between *ă̄* and *ĕ̄* in Proto-Dravidian (§ 4). While treating Proto-Dravidian **y-* and **ñ-*, Burrow pointed out that in Old Tamil **yām* was occasionally used for 'we (inclusive)' also. Later on *yām-kaḷ* was created to mean 'we (exclusive)' (see fn. 4 of my article). At some later date *nām-kaḷ* derived from *nām* 'we (inclusive)' came to be used for 'we (exclusive)' replacing Early Tamil *yām* both in Tamil and Malayāḷam (Burrow 1946a: 597; see § 13 of my article). Surprisingly Burrow did not discuss how Ma. *ñān* happened to have *ñ-* corresponding to *n-* in Middle Tamil and many other languages. He did point out that Malayāḷam preserved **ñ-* even in cases in which Tamil had lost it (1946a: 606). He has also not touched upon the initial consonant in Ma. **ñāṅṅaḷ* (< **ñām* + *kaḷ*) corresponding to Ta. *nāṅ-kaḷ*. While endorsing M. Collins' remarks that *nān* was created analogically from *nām*, Burrow says, 'Just as *yāṉ* of the singular corresponds to *yām* (excl.) of the plural, so a form *nāṉ* is created by analogy corresponding to the plural *nām* (incl.)' (1946a: 598). Apparently he was referring here to the *n-* forms in Tamil and all other languages that have them. He further says,

> Whereas in the plural of the first person two forms with different meanings are to be postulated for the parent language, in the first person singular only one form—that represented in Tamil by *yāṉ*—is to be regarded as original. This is clear because the forms beginning with *n-* only appear in comparatively modern times. (1946a: 597)

He cites *n-* forms in Kannaḍa, Telugu, Kui, and Kuvi also. He did not say anywhere that these *n-* forms had developed independently in each language, which would be a rare coincidence and therefore absurd. Alternatively, the *n-* forms should emerge from a shared innovation, in which case their surfacing in literature much later could be easily explained on sociolinguistic grounds. Their later use in literature should not be used as an argument against their common origin at the undivided stage of Proto-South Dravidian. Also the oblique forms in South Dravidian II begin only with *n-* and *m-* and, being bound forms, are much older than the ones derived from **yān*, **yām* (> *ān*/*ēn*, *ām*/*ēm*) which occur only in the nominative case, as free forms in South Dravidian II. Another problem was the oblique forms derived from **mā-* in South Dravidian II. Burrow explained this

> as a result of aphaeresis of the initial vowel: thus corresponding to Ta. dative *emakku* 'to us' we have Te. *mākun* (< **emakun*), Kui *māngi*, Go. *mākun*. From these forms *m-* is extended to the nominative: thus modern Telugu *mēmu* for older *ēmu*, Kuvi *māmbu* beside Kui *āmu*,

Go. *mammaṭ* beside *ammaṭ*. Telugu goes further and prefixes it to the inclusive *nām*/*nam*- as well, thus producing the disyllabic *manamu* (1946a: 597, fn. 4).

The difficulty with this supposition is that the so-called aphaeresis (now better known as metathesis) occurred in South Dravidian II in stems of the canonical type $(C_1)V_1C_2\text{-}V_2$- where C_2 is an apical consonant, viz. *ṟ, *ḍ, *r, *l, *ḷ, *ẓ (*TVB* 51–68, Krishnamurti 1978a) and not a nasal (only Kuvi has a few instances of ṇ), never a bilabial nasal. There are two sporadic cases where non-apicals are involved as C_2 (**at*-V- 'she/it', **aw-anṯ*- 'he' in the third person pronouns, also in the proximal and interrogative forms) but only in Telugu and Koṇḍa. There is no item involving a nasal as C_2 in the whole subgroup. This would then be the only example of its kind for all these languages. It cannot be accepted for that reason. I have found a more plausible explanation for the origin of *mā*- in the plural in South Dravidian II (see §9).

P 5. Zvelebil (1962) can be passed over in silence since he revised his reconstructions later (1990a: 24–5). Unfortunately, he reconstructed **ān* 'I', **ām* 'we', **nām* 'we (inclusive)' and realized later that they would not account for changes in the vowel qualities. In his book (1990a: 24–47) he has changed some of the reconstructions but did not address other questions like the loss and restoration of exclusive–inclusive plural distinction in the languages that have *n*-doublets, the origin of Ma. *ñ*- forms, and the origin of *m*- obliques in South-Central Dravidian, etc.

Subrahmanyam (1970b) generally followed Burrow and has to be rejected for the same reasons. He proposed something that Burrow did not. He derives SD I *n*-forms as back-formations from **nām* and those of Telugu-Kui, etc. (South Dravidian II) as arising from metathesis of **en-a*. Thus SD I and SD II *n*- forms for 'I' have different genetic histories, Ta. *nān* deriving from **nām* but Kui *nān* from **en-a*-. This dichotomy is totally unnecessary as well as surprising since the resulting forms are the same in genetically related languages. Like Burrow, Subrahmanyam has no satisfactory explanation for Malayāḷam *ñ*- forms, *ñān*, *ñāṅṅaḷ* (< **ñām+kaḷ*), except to say that they are secondary replacements of *y* by *ñ*. The front vowel *ē* in Kol. *nēnḍ* and Nk. *nēm* 'we (inclusive)' beside Te. *nēmu* is not explained properly. Subrahmanyam has also not addressed the question of why new forms for the first person inclusive had to be created in a number of languages which had lost the original semantic contrast.

Another innovation shared by South Dravidian I (Tamil-Kannaḍa) and South Dravidian II (Telugu-Manḍa) is the creation of an alternative plural of the second person, by the addition of the third person human plural suffix -V*r* on the root **nī* in the place of -*m* (pl.): cf. Ta. *nīr*, *nīyir*, Tu. *īru*, Te. *īru*, *mīru (<< *nīr-)*, Koṇḍa *mīru*, Kui *īru*, Kuvi (BB) *mīru*. In Central Dravidian Kolami-Naiki have *nīr*/ *im*-, but Parji, Ollari, Gadaba *īm*/*im*-. This means that the nominative form was borrowed by Kolami-Naiki from pre-literary Telugu before *nīr*- was morphologically replaced by *mīru* (see §17). The bound oblique *im*- vouchsafes the original (replaced) nominative **īm* as is found in the other members of Central Dravidian.

The pre-Telugu **nīr* also rules out Subrahmanyam's assumption of *m*-initial plural forms by metathesis (from something like **im-i-*) in South-Central Dravidian. In the original paper I called the *r*-feature an areal tendency (§17), although I mentioned the point about the Kolami-Naiki forms being borrowings from early or pre-Telugu. It would now seem better to treat this feature as a shared innovation by South Dravidian and South-Central Dravidian. The Kolami-Naiki nominative forms in *nīr* are very valuable, since they record what could have been the pre-Telugu second plural forms. There are many such borrowings from early Telugu in Kolami and Naiki, such as a number of *ḍ*-initial words which changed to *d*- even from the earliest literary period (11th century AD) in Telugu but were retained unchanged in Kolami-Naiki, e.g. OTe. *ḍiggu-/ḍigu-* (> *digu*) 'to descend', Kol. (Kinwaṭ) *ḍigg-*, Nk. *ḍigg-*, Nk. (Ch.) *ḍig-*; the inherited forms of Central Dravidian occur in Pa. *iṛ v-*, Oll. *iṛg-*, Gad. *iḍg-* from PD **iẓ-i* [*DEDR* 502].

P 6. Emeneau (1991) has discussed at length the Brahui oblique of first person singular *kan-* which cannot be derived from PD **yan-*. He takes the pre-Brahui form to be **an-* and suggests that *k-* could have been added to it by wrong analysis, when the inflected oblique occurred after plural noun stems ending in *-k* or verbs ending in an inflexional *-k* (present-future, negative, imperative, etc.). This is perhaps the most plausible explanation in the present state of our knowledge. Andronov (1975a) does not take our knowledge of pronouns any farther and his reconstructions are suspect, because he derives *nām* < *ñām* < *yām* for which there is no evidence (17–18). He derives Ma. *ñān* from **yān* as a hypercorrect form! He has no explanation for the vowel alternation in *nēnu/ nānu/ nan-* in Telugu and for Kol. Nk. *nēm/ nēnḍ* in the first person inclusive plural, as opposed to *nām* in others. Like Burrow and Subrahmanyam he derives the *nā-* and *mā-* forms in South-Central Dravidian from metathesis of **an-a-*, and **am-a-*. The reasons why these reconstructions are wrong have already been given in § **P 5**.

P 7. Conclusion. I consider this paper as a breakthrough in comparative morphology of Dravidian. Because of its difficult theoretical framework and difficult reading, some people have looked for simpler ways out but they have not analysed all the problems involved and therefore have not raised the right kinds of questions. The revision that I have proposed here in **P 3** must be taken into account and also the fact that **ñān* was innovated analogically from the proportional pattern *yān*: *yām* :: ? : *ñām* at the undivided stage of South Dravidian I and South Dravidian II, i.e. Proto-South Dravidian. The validity of the reconstruction of * *ñām* is supported by sound comparative method and is independent of its suggested (presumably speculative) pre-Dravidian origin from ***n-yām*.

I have not discussed one other pronoun, viz. the reflexive PD **tān*/**tan-* 'self' since it does not involve any serious problem in reconstruction in any language or subgroup. Br. *tēn* has an aberrant shift of *ā* > *ē* which Emeneau (1991: 8) thinks proceeded from the influence of pre-Br. *ē* in the first person ***ēn*, before it became *ī*.

The only question still unexplained is the vowel-length variation between the nominative and oblique forms in each set. The oblique stems have a short vowel, whether they are followed by a consonant or a vowel. I have reconstructed a laryngeal **H* within these stems to account for irregular vowel-length, ***yaHn*, ***yaH-m*, etc. There is a rule that **H* lengthens the preceding vowel in a free form and is lost before a consonant in a bound form (Krishnamurti 1997c: 157; see Ch. 19). There is no other way one can explain the length variation (see Ch. 1). Would a laryngeal explain Br. *k-* in *kan-* from **aHn-* with **aH-* > **Ha-* > **ka-*? It is tempting, since there is one other example: Br. *kun-ing* 'to eat, drink' < **Huṇ-* (< PD ***uHṇ*; see Krishnamurti 1997c: 154). *DEDR* 600 connects it to the traditional **uṇ* 'to eat, drink'. Emeneau (1991: 2) explains Br. *k-* as resulting from a contamination with Sindhi *khāiṇu* 'to eat'.

5

Comparative Dravidian Studies

1. Introduction

1.1 The Dravidian family consists of around 22 languages spoken by about 110 million people in South Asia. In terms of population figures (in millions), they may be listed in the following order:[1] Telugu (37.67 m.), Tamil (30.56 m.), Kannaḍa (17.42 m.), Malayāḷam (17.02 m.), Gondi (1.5 m.), Kuṛux or Oraon (1.14 m.), Tuḷu (940,000), Kui (510,000), Brahui (300,000), Kuvi or Khond (190,000), Kōya

[1] Except for Parji and Ollari, the following population figures are based on the 1961 Census, cf. *Census of India 1961* vol. 1, Part IIC(ii), *Language tables* (Calcutta, 1965). [The figures are rounded slightly. See Ch. 21, App. I for up-to-date figures.] The figures given for many of the non-literary languages look highly suspicious, compared with the 1951 Census, particularly for Kui, Kuvi (represented by the name Khond or Kondh), Naiki, Parji, Kuṛux, and Malto, recording an erratic rise or fall in each case.

	1951		1961
Kui	206,509		512,161
Kuvi (Kondh/Khond)	280,561	Khond/Kondh	168,027
		Naikadi	1,494
Naikpodi	268,921	Naiki-Kolami	8
		Naikpodi	46
Parji	19,847		109,401
Kuṛux	644,042		1,142,511
Malto	23,857		88,676
Gadaba	54,454		40,194

There is apparently a mix-up in classifying Kui and Kuvi mother tongue speakers in the 1961 Census, while 83,914 Parji speakers (included in the figures above) returned from Orissa are likely to belong to either Kui or Kuvi, since 'poroja' (< Skt. *prajā* 'people') is a common Oriya term for 'tribals'. The number of Parji speakers returned for Madhya Pradesh is 24,718 which looks nearer the truth regarding Parji. We still do not know how to sort out the Naiki varieties. Though there is little scope for confusion with Kuṛux and Malto, it is hard to decide which Census figures are right, those of 1951 or 1961. The Gadaba figures in both the 1951 and 1961 Census include both Dravidian Gadabas, and Munda Gadabas. The Dravidian Gadabas, who call themselves Koṇḍekor Gadaba, live in the Srikakulam District of Andhra Pradesh. The population breakdown of Gadabas for Andhra Pradesh in the 1961 Census is 8,401 which is more likely to be the approximate figure of the speakers of Koṇḍēkōr Gadaba. I have therefore only taken this figure as valid.

The population figure for Ollari, which is not listed in the 1951 and 1961 Census, is taken from the 1931 Census. I have considered Ollari and Gadaba as different languages (departing from the view of Emeneau and Burrow) since the question has not been decided on the basis of comparison of the phonology and syntax of the two. Material on Manḍa, which Burrow and Bhattacharya have recently discovered as a separate language, has not yet been published and the name also does not figure in the 1961 Language Census. 'Pengu' (Burrow and Bhattacharya record it as 'Pengo') is returned by 1,254 speakers according to the 1961 Census, but publication of Burrow and Bhattacharya's material on this language is still awaited.

(140,000), Malto (90,000), Koḍagu (80,000), Kolami (50,000), Parji (20,000), Koṇḍa or Kūbi (13,000), Gadaba (8000), Naiki (1500), Pengo (1300), Kota (900), Ollari (800), and Toda (800). With the exception of Brahui, which is spoken in Baluchistan in Pakistan, the rest of the languages are spoken in the Republic of India, mainly concentrated in the south, central, and eastern parts [see Map 21.1]. Only the four major languages, viz. Tamil, Malayāḷam, Kannaḍa, and Telugu, which have independent scripts and literary histories dating from the early pre-Christian era to the 11th century AD, have been recognized in the VIII Schedule to the Constitution of India. These languages constitute respectively the basis for the demarcation of the four linguistic States of South India, viz. Madras (now Tamil Nadu), Kerala, Mysore (now Karnaṭaka), and Andhra Pradesh. The rest of the Dravidian languages have no orthographies of their own and, with the exception of Tuḷu and Koḍagu, they are generally classified as 'tribal languages'.

2. Bibliographical Sources

2.1. *The Linguistic Survey of India*, vol. IV, gives exhaustive bibliographies of works of the 19th century at the end of the grammatical sketches of the languages described—'Tamiḻ, Malayāḷam, Kannaḍa, Telugu, Kūi, Gōṇḍī, Kuruk͟h, Mālto, and Brāhūī'. Burrow and Emeneau's *A Dravidian Etymological Dictionary* gives a list of bilingual dictionaries of the Dravidian languages which they used as the sources for cognates.

2.2. The first attempt to collect most of the relevant titles to build a systematic bibliography for Dravidian was made by M. Andronov in a recent article, 'Materials for a bibliography of Dravidian linguistics' (1964a). This consists of a list of 629 titles of articles and books followed by two appendixes: (i) Book reviews: 50 titles, and (ii) Dictionaries: 67 titles. Andronov incorporates in his listing most of the significant works on comparative Dravidian as well as those bearing on the description of individual languages, from the beginning until about 1962. However, he missed many reviews and several of the articles by L. V. Ramaswami Aiyar and E. H. Tuttle on comparative problems. His listing of dictionaries and grammars fails to include some important works published in the native languages, and page references for articles are not given throughout. M. Israel (1966) published a supplement to Andronov's bibliography, in which he listed 102 new titles of mostly journal articles and a few books. He has spotted about 30 articles by Ramaswami Aiyar which Andronov missed. Israel follows Andronov's format except that he also gives page references of journal articles. Most recently, Stephen E. Montgomery (1968) has published 'Supplemental materials for a bibliography of Dravidian linguistics' in which he adds 17 books, 103 journal articles, 73 reviews, and 2 dictionaries to Andronov's bibliography. Montgomery's listing also includes unpublished M.A. and Ph.D. dissertations on Dravidian languages submitted to universities in the

USA. Israel and Montgomery independently prepared these supplements and submitted them for publication at about the same time. Consequently, there are 25 items which overlap in the two lists. An addendum of 15 titles has been appended to Montgomery's article by the editor of the *Ṣaṣṭipūrti* volume (Krishnamurti (ed.) 1968a) in order to bring the bibliography up to date. These three bibliographies have a fairly complete coverage and constitute a good starting point for a more extensive and annotated bibliography for Dravidian, taking into account also works published in the vernacular languages. Excluding reviews, for the present, we have a consolidated list of 928 titles (Andronov 696 + Montgomery 135 + Israel 97 excluding items duplicated), of which about 200 titles directly deal with problems bearing on comparative Dravidian. Of these, 73 titles have been published after 1947 and the remaining before.[2]

2.3. A topical breakdown of the contributions published since 1947 yields the following classification:

		Articles	*Books*
1.	General surveys, etc.	5	1
2.	Bibliographies	3	
3.	Comparative and historical grammars (or, materials for . . .)	1	9
4.	Comparative phonology	11	
5.	Comparative morphology	8	
6.	Etymological studies	6	2
7.	Language contact (lexical and structural borrowing between Dravidian and Indo-Aryan)	11	1
8.	Subgrouping and lexico-statistics	3	
9.	Interrelationship between Dravidian and the language families outside India	10	2
		58	**15**

3. Before 1947

3.1. As early as 1816, Francis Whyte Ellis of the Indian Civil Service introduced the notion of comparative Dravidian philology when he asserted in his *Dissertation on the Telugu language*[3] that 'the high and low Tamil, the Telugu, grammatical and

[2] In order to do justice to 'current trends', I have strictly confined my treatment to contributions which explicitly deal with problems of comparative Dravidian and I have kept out of consideration even valuable descriptive works on individual languages though they certainly throw light on our understanding of comparative problems.

[3] Published as 'Note to the Introduction' of A. D. Campbell, *A Grammar of the Teloogoo Language* 1–32 (Madras, 1816); reprinted with an editorial note by N. Venkata Rao in *Annals of Oriental Research of the University of Madras* 12: 1–35 (Madras 1954–5).

vulgar, Carnataca or Cannadi, ancient and modern, Malayala or Malayalam . . . and the Tuluva' are the members 'constituting the family of languages which may be appropriately called the dialects of Southern India'; 'Codagu' he considered 'a local dialect of the same derivation'. Speaking about Malto, he says, 'the language of the Mountaineers of Rajmahal abounds in terms common to the Tamil and Telugu'. His purpose was to show that Tamil, Telugu, and Kannaḍa 'form a distinct family of languages', with which 'the Sanscrit has, in later times, especially, intermixed, but with which it has no radical connexion'. He produced considerable illustrative material, mainly lexical and some grammatical, from Telugu, Kannaḍa, and Tamil in support of his thesis. However, it was the publication of Robert Caldwell's *Comparative Grammar of the Dravidian or South Indian Family of Languages* in 1856[4] which marked a real breakthrough in Comparative Dravidian studies. Caldwell enumerated only twelve Dravidian languages[5] and, as the title of his work suggests, he mainly drew upon the literary languages of the south with greater attention paid to Tamil which he had studied for over thirty-seven years by the time he brought out a second edition of this work in 1875. With inadequate sources and with the comparative method still in its infancy, Caldwell could not have done better. He succeeded in showing family likeness among the Dravidian languages in phonology and morphology and in disproving the Sanskrit origin of the Dravidian languages, a view strongly advocated by many oriental as well as western scholars before and even after him. He also attempted to demonstrate a possible affinity between Dravidian and the so-called 'Scythian' languages ('a common designation of all those languages of Asia and Europe which do not belong to the Indo-European or Semitic families', *LSI* IV: 282).

Caldwell's *Comparative Grammar*, instead of stimulating research, was followed by a long spell of inaction in this field for about half a century. It apparently failed to engage the attention of vernacular experts who strongly believed in Sanskrit as being the source of all Indian languages.[6] Secondly, the English language had not spread among native language scholars well enough to awaken them to the far-reaching consequences of Caldwell's work. Western scholars (missionaries and administrative officials) exposed to the study of both the literary and non-literary languages in India concerned themselves mainly with the preparation of grammars and bilingual dictionaries for individual languages.[7]

[4] 2nd rev. edn London, 1875; 3rd edn revised by the Rev. J. L. Wyatt and T. Ramakrishna Pillai, London, 1913; 3rd edn reprinted twice by the University of Madras, 1956, 1961.

[5] Tamil, Malayāḷam, Telugu, Canarese (Kannaḍa), Tuḷu, Kudagu or Coorg (Koḍagu), Tuda, (Toda), Kota, Goṇḍ (Gondi), Khond or Ku (Kui), Orāon (Kuṛux or Orāōn), Rajmahāl (Malto). The modern spellings are given in parentheses. Caldwell also adds a note on Brahui in the Appendix to his 2nd edn (see 3rd edn repr. in 1956: 633–5).

[6] A typical example of this is M. Seshagiri Sastri, *Notes on Aryan and Dravidian Philology* (Madras, 1884) which, at some length, compares Tamil and Telugu with Sanskrit, Greek, and Latin. This work, however, contains useful comparative information for Indo-European philology.

[7] For the major South Dravidian languages, see particularly C. P. Brown (1852), H. Gundert (1872), F. Kittel (1894), A. Männer (1886). Grammatical sketches and vocabularies on Koḍagu, Tuḷu, Gondi, Kui, Kuṛux, Malto, and Brahui appeared during the later half of the 19th century.

3.2. During the later part of the nineteenth century, Caldwell, Gundert, and Kittel undertook investigations into the Dravidian borrowings in Sanskrit.[8] Summarizing the results of these studies, Kittel submitted a classified list of 420 Sanskrit items with Dravidian etymologies in the preface to his *A Kannaḍa-English Dictionary*, pp. xvii–xliii (Mangalore, 1893) and also set forth the principles for identification of Dravidian loanwords in Sanskrit. Julien Vinson published many articles in *République Française*, *Revue de Linguistique*, *Revue scientifique*, and *Journal Asiatique* during 1873–1919, which covered general surveys of the Dravidian languages and a few problems of comparative phonology and morphology. He also dealt with word-parallels between Dravidian and Basque in one article.[9]

The publication of the *LSI*, vol. IV (Calcutta, 1906), on 'Muṇḍā and Dravidian languages' brought new material to light and stimulated fresh interest in comparative Dravidian studies. The survey was a pioneering effort of great significance, but it suffered from many shortcomings, the most significant of which was the exclusion of the political divisions of south India from the scope of the survey.[10] Several of the central Dravidian languages which recently came to light were either not noticed or left out in the unsurveyed area, or wrongly included under Gondi or Kui as their dialects.

3.3. The period 1900–47 was characterized by considerable activity in comparative Dravidian studies mainly channelled in four directions: (a) discovering cognates and phonetic correspondences and attempting to reconstruct Proto-Dravidian forms; (b) a systematic inquiry into the question of contact between Sanskrit and Dravidian; (c) speculation on the question of affinity between Dravidian and the other language families outside South Asia; (d) study of the unexplored non-literary languages with a view to gaining better understanding of comparative problems. Among the Indian scholars K. V. Subbaiya and L. V. Ramaswami Aiyar emerged as the two outstanding contributors to comparative Dravidian studies, while J. Vinson, J. Bloch, and P. Meile of France, A. Master and T. Burrow of England, E. H. Tuttle and M. B. Emeneau of the United States were the most prominent names among the western scholars who devoted themselves to Dravidian studies during this period.

3.4. K. V. Subbaiya (1909–11) planned a comparative grammar of Dravidian in a series of articles but gave up the attempt after publishing three of them in *Indian Antiquary*. He succeeded in formulating certain correspondences and problems in comparative phonology more precisely than Caldwell had done and also attempted reconstruction of 'primitive Dravidian' forms. Following Caldwell he considered

[8] H. Gundert, 'Die dravidischen Elemente in Sanskrit' (1869: 517–30), Robert Caldwell III (1956: 565–87).

[9] 'Le mot *dien* en basque et dans les langues dravidiennes', *Revue de linguistique* 13 (1879). This has not been accessible to me.

[10] The Madras Presidency, the princely States of Mysore, Travancore and Cochin, Coorg, and the Nizam's Dominions. (*LSI* I: 1.25 [1927]).

Tamil forms as representing Proto-Dravidian in most cases; one such reconstruction disproved by recent researches was for the correspondence Ta. Ma. *i*-, *u*- = Te. Ka. *e*-, *o*- in the environment [C*a*, of which the Tamil-Malayāḷam vowels were considered by Subbaiya as preservations of the 'primitive Dravidian' qualities. Subbaiya's statements on phonological correspondences, which Caldwell barely noticed, include, among others, *k*-/*c*-, *p*-/*h*-, *ā*/*ē*, metathesis and vowel contraction in Telugu and some other Central Dravidian languages. Subbaiya's monograph (1923) on the first person pronouns is yet another piece of evidence of his thoroughness in collecting relevant data, though his conclusions generally proved to be wrong; for instance: (a) his derivation of Ma. *ñān* and Ta. *nāṉ* 'I' from an ultimate *ǣn* through an intermediary **ǣ̃n*; (b) his assertion that Proto-Dravidian did not have exclusive and inclusive plurals in the first person; (c) his hypothesis of accent shift from the first syllable to the second in the Central Dravidian languages. By and large, he seems to have basically picked up Caldwell's notions (some of which were presented on the observation of limited data) and tried to put forth more data in support of his hypotheses. Collins' remarks on *Dravidic Studies II* and *III* given as appendixes to the series are full of critical insights.

3.5. The most prolific and indefatigable among the contributors to Dravidian studies during the first half of the 20th century was L. V. Ramaswami Aiyar. A very good scholar in Tamil and Malayāḷam, he had first-hand knowledge of Tuḷu, and had access to primary sources in Telugu and Kannaḍa. Being a Professor of English in the Maharaja's College, Ernakulam, he was also exposed to trends in Indo-European philology. With this background, he meticulously studied the available grammars and vocabularies of both the literary and non-literary languages and published over a hundred papers and books on Dravidian during the period 1925–50. His papers brought to light a large mass of useful information from the grammatical and literary works of the major Dravidian languages, not otherwise accessible to many western scholars. Though his pioneering work was in Malayāḷam and Tuḷu linguistics, he published many papers on problems of comparative phonology, morphology, and word-studies. In my opinion the most significant of his papers are 'Dravidic sandhi' (1934–8), 'Apheresis and sound displacement in Dravidian' (1932), and 'The history of the Tamil-Malayalam alveolar plosive', (1937: reprints pp. 1–32, 1–51). He regularly contributed articles to *Educational Review* (Madras) during the period 1925–36, which, among others, included a series on a comparative study of the verb in Old Tamil, Tuḷu, Kui, Kuṛux, Gondi, and Brahui. His studies cover almost all aspects of comparative Dravidian, even though his contribution to comparative morphology was not very impressive.

Jules Bloch's *magnum opus* on Dravidian, *Structure grammaticale des langues dravidiennes* (1946), supplements Caldwell's grammar by filling many of the lacunae from the better known non-literary languages (particularly Kui, Gondi, Kuṛux, Malto, and Brahui), of which only fragmentary information was available to Caldwell. Bloch skips phonology and confines himself to a comparative study of the morphological classes with special reference to data from the non-literary languages. Several insightful remarks can be found in this work particularly in his chapters on the noun and the verb, though Bloch does not attempt morphological reconstruction. S. K. Chatterji (1926: 170–8) and J. Bloch (1934: 321–31) pointed out the presence of many Dravidian structural features in Indo-Aryan in phonology and morphology, positing a possible Dravidian substratum in Middle and New Indo-Aryan in support of a hypothesis, adumbrated earlier by Caldwell (1956: 52–61), Stevenson, and Hodgson. Emeneau gave a more systematic expression to similar ideas in developing his 'linguistic area' hypothesis (see §**4.5**). Pierre Meile's 'Sur la sifflante en dravidien' (1943–5) presents a thorough interpretation of the loss of PD **c* in South Dravidian, and in this he anticipated some of the conclusions of Burrow's independent treatment of this problem in his 'Dravidian studies VI' (1947).

During the period 1919–38, E. H. Tuttle of the United States published several short articles on Dravidian problems; his earlier researches were summarized in his *Dravidian Developments* (1930). Though sometimes extremely fantastic in his reconstructions of clusters like **sN*-, **stl*- for Proto-Dravidian, he could be credited with some original ideas on the question of subgrouping and on scattered problems of comparative phonology and morphology. His greatest handicap was the lack of a first-hand knowledge of any one of the Dravidian languages.

3.6. Though Burrow and Emeneau independently started their study of Dravidian in the mid-thirties, their individual contributions represent a more modern, systematic, and rigorous approach to comparative Dravidian. During the period 1938–48 Burrow published a series of articles in *BSO(A)S* (vols. 9–12), which systematically dealt with many problems of comparative phonology. His lucid and definitive statements on the developments of PD **k*, **c*, **y*, and **ñ*, the question of voiced stops in Dravidian, and the alternations *i/e* and *u/o* in South Dravidian, constitute the beginning of a true comparative phonology for Dravidian.[11] His interest in Sanskrit led him to an inquiry into its lexical borrowings from Dravidian. Continuing the work of Gundert and Kittel, he illustrated many Dravidian loanwords from the time of the Rigveda and throughout the history of Sanskrit.[12] In 'Dravidian studies IV' (1944), he has dealt with the problem of a possible affinity between Dravidian and Uralian, examining the etymologies of words for body parts.

Emeneau, who began his career as a Sanskritist, an anthropologist, and a linguist (being a pupil of Edgerton, Sturtevant, and Sapir) evinced keen interest in Dravidian about the same time as Burrow, and spent three years (1935–8) in India studying four non-literary languages—Toda, Kota, Koḍagu of South India, and Kolami of Central India. Before 1947 most of his publications in the Dravidian field dealt with descriptive and anthropological aspects of the languages of the Nilgiri tribes. His

[11] 'Dravidian studies I' (1938), 'Dravidian studies II' (1940), 'Dravidian studies III' (1943), 'Dravidian studies V' (1946).

[12] 'Some Dravidian words in Sanskrit' (1946, 1947).

first full-fledged paper on comparative Dravidian, 'The Dravidian verbs "come" and "give"', which already showed his intense interest in comparative Dravidian studies, appeared in 1945.

4. After 1947

4.1. During the period 1947–66, most of the significant contributions to comparative Dravidian studies have been made by Emeneau and Burrow. Of the others devoted to Dravidian studies, particular mention may be made of S. Bhattacharya, Bh. Krishnamurti, T. P. Meenakshisundaran, and P. S. Subrahmanyam of India, K. Zvelebil of Czechoslovakia, M. Andronov and Yu. Glazov of the USSR, and W. Bright of the USA. It is convenient to deal with trends in comparative Dravidian studies during the past two decades under the following headings: (a) Phonology, (b) Morphology, (c) Etymological studies, (d) Language contact, (e) Subgrouping, (f) Affinity between Dravidian and the language families outside South Asia.

4.2. Phonology. Burrow's 'Dravidian studies VI' (1947) discusses the problem of loss of PD **c-* in South Dravidian. He also gives a number of instances in which a PD **c* is not lost in South Dravidian. It still remains a problem whether we need to set up two types of **c* or one for Proto-Dravidian on the basis of comparative evidence, i.e. PD $*c_1$- > SD Ø-; PD $*c_2$- > SD *c-/s-*. But no member of the Central Dravidian subgroups, which preserve **c*, bears independent testimony to the existence of two types of **c* by showing contrastive developments. Secondly, in a number of instances, doublets occur in South Dravidian itself with and without **c*. On the whole it appears, when we look at the different dialects of Gondi showing all the stages of *s-* > *h-* > Ø-, that this is a change still in progress, moving from the southern to the central region. A similar change, *s-* > *h-*, is also attested in Sinhalese from the second century AD.[13] On the basis of a proper name *Satiya puto* (= *Satiya putra*) in an Aśokan Inscription (3rd century BC), which later occurs in Puṟanāṉūru as *Atiya māṉ* (*māṉ* < **makaṉ* 'son' corresponding to Skt. *putra-*), Burrow dates the change **c* > Ø to a period intermediate between the 3rd century BC and 'the time of the earliest Tamil classics'. Since *c-* < **k-* in the environment of front vowels was not affected by *c-* > Ø-, the latter change must have taken place before the beginning of palatalization in South Dravidian, which was also shown to have taken place prior to the early Caṅkam age in Tamil. He therefore attributes the changes **c* > Ø and **k-* > *c-* to the early pre-Christian era with the latter change operating after the completion of the former. Burrow also notes a number of instances of the alternation of *c-/t-* in Dravidian, contrasting with the above two developments.

[13] Also see P. B. F. Wijeratne (1945: 592–3). The author shows how *s* > *h* has been in operation in Sinhala from the earliest time, in Old Sinhala *h* > Ø in some cases. In modern times 'forms with *s* and *h* exist side by side', but this latter *h* of Mdn. Sinhala does not disappear (ibid. 593).

Emeneau (1953a) shows by extensive illustration that Toda represents PD **c-* by *t-*, and PD **k-* remains Toda *k-* before front vowels unlike Tamil which palatalizes it. In a recent paper Burrow (1968a) affirms that PD **ẓ (r̤)* is represented by zero in Kuṛux and Malto and not by *-c-/-s-* as understood before. In their recent descriptions of Parji, Kui, and Kuvi, Burrow and Bhattacharya discuss the reflexes of Proto-Dravidian phonemes in these languages, particularly those of **c*, **ẓ (r̤)*, **ṯ (ṟ)*, and **ḷ*.[14]

Emeneau (1961a) has recently noticed a new correspondence in which Kuṛux, Malto, and Brahui have *k-* (rarely *x-*) followed by back high vowels *u* and *ū*, when South and Central Dravidian have *c-/s-* (< **c-*), alternating with *t-*. The groups he quotes are summarized in the following reconstructions:

SD and CD	ND
**cuṭ-*	**kuṭ-* 'to burn, to be hot'
**cum-*	**kum-* 'to carry, support'
**cur-*	**kur-* 'to whirl, curl'
**cur-* (perhaps related to the above)	**kur-* 'to shrink, shrivel up'
**cer-/*cur-/*cor-*	**ker-* 'to insert'
**cal-/*cel-*	**kel-* (> Br. *kal* 'water spring')
**cēr-/*cār-*	**kēr-* 'near'
**cāy/cĕ̄y-*	**key-* 'to die'

His conclusion is that PD **c-* is velarized in North Dravidian when followed by high back vowels, *u* and *ū*. The only counter-examples are the onomatopoeic ones, PD **cuṯ-V-* 'to sniff up' and **cūmp-* 'to suck'. He also discusses the possibility of PD **c* > ND *k-* before *e/ē* to explain the remaining cases.

E. Annamalai (1968) collects many common Dravidian etyma from *DED* with **kĭ̄*, **kĕ̄* involved in onomatopoeic expressions, in which **k-* > *c-* does not occur in Tamil, Malayāḷam, and Telugu as expected.

In his *Brahui and Dravidian Comparative Grammar* Emeneau traces Brahui vowels to Proto-Dravidian sources (1962d: 7–20). He has further discovered that, in the initial syllable of a word, *e* and *ē* do not contrast in Brahui, perhaps under the typological influence of the surrounding Indo-Aryan and Indo-Iranian languages. He observes that the Proto-Dravidian mid-vowels **e *o* are either raised to *i u* or lowered to *a* in most cases in Brahui; also PD **o* > Br. *ō*. The conditioning factors of these varied developments are still not known, though one can see that the changes were working towards a typological goal of gradual elimination of contrast between *e* and *ē*, and *o* and *ō* induced by the surrounding Indo-Aryan and Iranian languages under conditions of extensive bilingualism. The other vowels generally retain the Proto-Dravidian qualities.

Krishnamurti's *Telugu Verbal Bases* (1961) has a wider coverage than the title suggests. He presents a comparative phonology for Dravidian (6–132), keeping Telugu

[14] Burrow and Bhattacharya (1953: 1–8); 'Some notes on the Kui dialect as spoken by the Kuṭṭia Kandhs of north-east Koraput' (1961); 'Notes on Kuvi with a short vocabulary' (1962).

as the centre of attention. Some of the problems treated originally under phonology include the question of voiced stops in Dravidian, the development of initial consonant clusters and *ḍ-*, *r-*, *ṟ-*, *ḷ-* through metathesis and vowel contraction in Telugu and other Central Dravidian languages (§§1.121–59) and several developments resulting from the loss of vowels in unaccented syllables (§§1.180 ff., 2.9–21). Earlier, Krishnamurti (1958a) dealt with the problem of merger of PD **i-* **u-* with **e-* **o-* in Proto-South Dravidian in the environment [C-*a*. In another article (1955) he has systematically treated the alternation of long and short vowels in Dravidian and observed that *(C)V̄C fell together with *(C)VC- when followed by a -V in the next syllable. In cognates having the syllable types (C)V̄C and (C)VC-V-, the (C)V̄C type was shown to be older. In another paper (Krishnamurti: 1958b) he has extensively discussed the reflexes of PD **ẓ* in each of the Dravidian languages.[15]

4.3. **Morphology.** Compared to the progress made in the area of comparative phonology, work done in comparative morphology is frustratingly meagre and slow.

L. V. Ramaswami Aiyar (1947) adds a footnote to Emeneau's article 'The Dravidian verbs "come" and "give"' supporting, with the authority of traditional grammatical works and modern usage, Emeneau's statement on the distribution of the irregular Tamil verbs *va-* 'to come (to 1st or 2nd person)', *ta-* 'give (to 1st or 2nd person)'. He says that 'Malayāḷam still preserves the Tolkāppiyam usage; . . . *taru* and *varu* are used with the first and second persons and *koṭu* and *cel* invariably with the third person'.

In his paper on 'Dravidian kinship terms' (1953b), Emeneau discusses an interesting morphosyntactic phenomenon in Dravidian, which he calls 'inalienable possession'. Constructions of certain kinship terms involve a pronominal base in the plural denoting literally 'our', 'your', 'their', etc. used attributively to a following kinship stem 'brother, sister, father', etc., both constituting a morphological complex, like Ta. *eṅkai* 'my sister' (from *em-* 'our', *kai* 'sister'), etc. He illustrates this phenomenon in Tamil, Kota, Gondi, Kolami, Kuvi, and Kuṛux, and justifiably sets up 'inalienable possession' of kinship terms as a Proto-Dravidian trait. In Kolami, however, it is found to be a syntactic feature. We can add to the list also Telugu and Koṇḍa which also invariably use plural possessives *mā-*, *mī-* as attributes to terms denoting (near) kinsmen, 'father, mother, brother, sister', etc. But here the construction is clearly syntactic; e.g. Te. *mā anna*, Koṇḍa *mā anasi* 'my (lit. our) elder brother', Te. *mā amma*, Koṇḍa *mā yāya* 'my (lit. our) mother'.

[15] Burrow and Emeneau prefer to transcribe this as **r̤* (perhaps a voiced retroflex frictionless continuant) on the grounds that it has never been a sibilant. My reasons for using **ẓ* instead of **r̤* are mainly typographical, because it is decidedly a retroflex consonant, and all retroflexes are indicated by a subscript dot. Secondly Skt. *ṣ* (retroflex voiceless sibilant) is replaced by *ẓ* in Early Tamil borrowings in the intervocalic position. The sound in question is definitely unlike a trill or an affricate in any of the languages in which it still obtains. Though the choice of *ẓ* or *r̤* to represent this Proto-Dravidian sound is arbitrary, I thought it would make more sense to use a symbol which looks like a member of the retroflex series.

In another article, of 1957, Emeneau speaks of the role of analogy in sound substitution in the forms of numerals for one to three in Dravidian. Kota *eyḏ* 'two' had *ḏ* instead of the expected -*ḍ* from PD **ir-aṇṭ-*, on the analogy of the final consonant in *oḏ* 'one' (< **on-ṯ*), and *mūnḏ* (< **mū-nṯ*) 'three'. This article is of particular importance in accounting for the irregular phonological developments presented by numerals in some of the Dravidian languages. He wonders if numerals should be considered 'non-cultural' items as Swadesh claimed, and shows several instances of borrowing the so-called basic numerals one and two from one language to another in Dravidian. Comparatively this article is significant inasmuch as Emeneau reconstructs the protoforms for most of the numerals from one to ten. A more recent contribution by Emeneau (1961a) seeks to explain comparatively the demonstrative pronouns (? adjectives) in Brahui, *dā* (proximate), *ō* (intermediate), and *ē* (remote). Emeneau traces Br. *ō* to PD **u-/*ū* (intermediate between **i/*ī* 'this' and **a/*ā* 'that'), and Br. *ē* to either PD **a/*ā* or to PD **ē* (because of Kui having both *a* and *e* for different degrees of 'remoteness' from the speaker). Br. *dā-* is matched with Malto *ná* [*nā-*] 'that one (here)', because PD **n-* = Malto *n-*, Br. *d-*. Emeneau also identifies the existence of PD **ī* (proximate) in a declinable enclitic pronoun -*ī*. The only difficulty in accepting Emeneau's equation Malto *ná* = Br. *dā-* is that Brahui seems to have a conditioned split of PD **n-* > *d-* before the Proto-Dravidian front vowels **ĭ̄* and **ĕ̄* (**e* = Br. *a*), and *n-* elsewhere.[16] The exceptions are few and etymologically doubtful. The reconstruction of **e* as a fourth demonstrative purely on the basis of Kui and Brahui evidence is also questionable, for there are still unexplained aberrations in vocalism in most of the non-literary languages. I would recall my suggestion of reconstructing a laryngeal (or *h-* type of sound) in the demonstrative and interrogative series for Proto-Dravidian, viz., **iH-*, **uH-*, **aH-*, **ya/eH-*, in which the laryngeal element presumably holds a clue for the unexpected vocalism in Kui, Kuvi (also the unexpected *h-* here), and Brahui (see Krishnamurti 1963). Note that in low class Telugu of Telaṅgāṇā, *gĭ̄*, *gă̄* are the counterparts of *ī*, *ā* of the other dialects. A parallel development of **H* to *g* occurs in colloquial Tamil, e.g. OTa. *eHku* 'steel', Modern Ta. *eggï* 'id.'.

In his Brahui and Dravidian Comparative Grammar, Chapter III (pp. 21–45), Emeneau traces comparatively the history of a class of ten verb stems in Brahui with final *n/r-* alternation. The *n/nn-* allomorphs occur before the infinitive suffix -*ing*, and the *r/rr-* allomorphs occur before present non-finite -*isa* and probable future -*ō* (+ personal suffixes), and the imperative second singular {Ø∞ a∞e}. There are further details not mentioned here. The stem alternants are (a) *hunn-/hur-* 'look', (b) *tōn-/tōr* 'hold', (c) *pān-/pār-* 'say', (d) *kann-/kar-* 'do', (e) *dann-/dar-* 'cut', (f) *tin-/tir-* 'give', (g) *ha-tin-/ha-tir-* 'bring', (h) *bann-/bar-* 'come', (i) *mann-/mar-* 'become', (j) *ann-/ar-* 'be'. Of these (a) *hunn-/hur-*, (i) *mann-/mar-*, and

[16] I have discussed this development in my forthcoming paper 'Dravidian nasals in Brahui'. Br. *dā* 'this' looks so strikingly similar to Pashto *dā* 'this' that it seems much simpler to consider it a straight borrowing from Pashto (see Shafeev 1964: 34–5).

(j) *ann-/ar-* are traced to PD **un-/uṯ- ~ ṟ-* and **man-/maṯ- ~ ṟ-*, and **an/āṉ- ~ ṟ-* (*r-*?) respectively, with *n/r-* alternation of Brahui proceeding from a similar alternation of **n*/**ṯ* ~ **ṟ* in Proto-Dravidian. The *n*-allomorphs of (b) (e) (f) (g) and (h) have been considered analogical formations, because the *r*-allomorphs are accountable comparatively and not the *n*-allomorphs. Similarly the *r*-allomorph *pār-* of (c) *pān-/pār-* is analogical, since *pān-* is traceable to PD **pāṇ /paṇ*-V-. In set (d) one of the allomorphs is *kē-*, traceable to PD **key* 'do', but the remaining allomorphs *kar-/kann-* are traceable to Sindhi and Lahnda (Indo-Aryan) *kar-* and Baluchi (Iranian) *kan-*. This chapter eminently illustrates the parallel roles of analogy and borrowing in bringing about regularization in the paradigms even of basic verbs such as 'come', 'eat', 'do'.

In a recent publication, Kamil Zvelebil (1964: 21–32), while presenting a tagmemic description of the language of a 6th century Tamil prose inscription found in the village of Paḷḷaṉkōvil in the Tanjore district, attempts reconstruction of the proto-forms of eighty-eight Tamil roots segmented from the text of the inscription.

Emeneau's paper 'The South Dravidian languages' read at the Kuala Lumpur Tamil Conference (1966) aims at a thorough comparison of past-tense formation as the basis for a genetic subgrouping of the South Dravidian languages, Tamil, Malayāḷam, Kannaḍa, Koḍagu, Toda, and Kota [see Emeneau 1967a]. Emeneau's article on noun formatives [Emeneau 1966] **-kuḷi*/**-kuṇi*, **-tal-ay*, and *-uḷ* in South Dravidian is a contribution to derivational morphology, which calls for a great deal of work with more extensive coverage.

Krishnamurti's *Telugu Verbal Bases*, Chapter II, deals with several aspects of derivational morphology of Dravidian, which include, among others, a morphophonemic analysis of the root and formative elements in Proto-Dravidian, a description of syllable adjustments that have taken place in different languages consequent on loss of unaccented vowels of the root and suffix morphemes. The possibility of some formative suffixes having an original grammatical function has been suggested (§§ 2.38, 84 ff.).

In a recent article on 'Dravidian personal pronouns' (Krishnamurti 1968b), he has made an attempt to explain certain phonological and morphological problems in reconstructing the proto-forms of words meaning 'I, we (exclusive), we (inclusive), you (sg.), you (pl.)'. For the first person he reconstructs for Proto-Dravidian, sg. **yān/(y)ēn* 'I', pl. **yām/(y)ēm* (exclusive), **ñām/ñēm* (inclusive). **ā*/ **ē* do not contrast after **y* or **ñ* on well-attested evidence. PD **ñām* is further interpreted as a phonemic representation of morphophonemic **n-yām* 'you and we (exclusive)', = 'we (inclusive)', in which *n-* is a bound allomorph of the second person pronominal root **nī-n* 'you' (sg.), **nī-m* 'you' (pl.). Another singular form **ñān* was formed from **ñām*, on the analogy of **yām*: **yān*. The Proto-Dravidian sets **yān*: **yām*: : **ñām* were formally symmetrical but functionally defective, because **yān* and **ñān* do not have a functional distinction parallel to their formally related pair in the plural, **yām*: **ñām*. This anomalous 'system' in Proto-Dravidian triggered several readjustments in the subgroups and languages that inherited it. In terms of such theoretical possibilities, all the comparative data have been examined and accounted for.

P. S. Subrahmanyam (1964) draws on comparative evidence to explain the Parji past-stem formative *-ñ* (e.g. *ko-ñ-* from *koy-* 'reap') as arising from an older *-nd-* (< **-nt-*) palatalized to *-ñj-*, after palatal vowels or semivowels. The Parji stem-formative *-k-m-* in the present tense is equated with the non-past complex *-kk-um* of a class of Old Tamil finite verbs, e.g. Pa. *kāk-m-en* (root *kā-p-/kā-t-* 'to wait for'): Ta. *kā-kk-um* (root *kā-* 'id.'), and Subrahmanyam reconstructs **-kk-um-* for Proto Dravidian, a feature which South Dravidian and Parji of Central Dravidian inherited and retained. Another article by the same author (1965) shows parallels between Tamil and Kui in employing overt oppositions in the derivative suffixes in the formation of intransitive and transitive stems.

4.4. **Etymological studies.** A basic tool for intensive comparative work on any language family is a dictionary of cognates based on a rigorously worked out system of phonological correspondences. A new era in comparative Dravidian began in 1961 with the publication of Burrow and Emeneau's monumental work, *A Dravidian Etymological Dictionary.* This fulfils the greatest need in the field felt by every serious student of comparative Dravidian since Caldwell and it has already given a thrust to research in Dravidian, judging from the fact that there has hardly been an article or publication since 1961 which has not liberally drawn on the materials collected and organized in this work. The dictionary has 4,572 numbered entries (pp. 1–385), followed by word indexes for individual languages (pp. 387–574), an index of English meanings (pp. 585–604), and an index of flora (pp. 605–9).

Since it is the first work of its kind, the authors have deliberately refrained from giving reconstructions for each group of etyma constituting an entry. However, they have covertly suggested such reconstructions by the very manner they have arranged the entries, which follows the order of Proto-Dravidian phonemes with the Tamil alphabetical order imposed on it. Certain etymological groupings are tentative and need further discussion and elucidation, but a large number of them stand. A supplement was issued by the authors in 1962 (Emeneau and Burrow 1962) which consists of 336 entries, each representing a group of words identified as common Dravidian borrowings from Indo-Aryan. Strictly speaking, this is a complement rather than a supplement, for its scope is grouping non-native cognates which need to be identified and eliminated in an etymological dictionary. A second supplement has been projected and is to be published shortly, which will contain additional groupings and corrections detected and listed since the publication of the work in 1961. One of the significant features of this dictionary has been its broad coverage of languages, materials on some of which have been brought to light for the first time; the vocabularies of Toda, Kota, and Koḍagu from Emeneau's unpublished field notes were first published in the dictionary. The field trips of Burrow and Bhattacharya in Central India in 1950–1, 1957–8, and again in 1964–5 and in 1966 have enriched the dictionary, in making available new and additional lexical material from Parji, Kolami, Ollari, Gadaba, Naiki, Gondi, Kui, Pengo, and Manḍa. The last two have been discovered since the publication of the dictionary in 1961, and the forthcoming second supplement includes cognates from these two.

A work in comparative Dravidian lexicography was published by the University of Madras in 1959 (Sethu Pillai 1959). This is planned broadly on the lines of Carl D. Buck's *A Dictionary of Selected Synonyms in the Principal Indo-European Languages* (Chicago, 1949), and confines its sources to the major languages of South India, viz., Tamil, Malayāḷam, Kannaḍa, Telugu, and Tuḷu. There are 2,000 entries semantically classified under 22 sections, such as heavenly bodies, cardinal points, mountains, sea, etc. This is not thoroughly a comparative dictionary in the sense we understand it, since synonyms which are not cognates have also been cited in many places, and the editors have not paid much attention to phonetic correspondences in their selection of 'cognates'. Krishnamurti (1961, Part II: 277–503) has a large etymological index comprising 1,236 primary verbal bases in Old and Modern Telugu with reconstructions.

In the wake of the publication of *DED*, Emeneau has discovered new correspondences between Brahui and the other Dravidian languages, which he set forth in a recent article (1962c). Burrow and Bhattacharya's descriptive accounts of Parji, Kui, Kuvi, Gadaba, and Gondi include etymological vocabularies (the ones published since 1961 have references to *DED* entries);[17] so does Bhattacharya's work on 'Naiki of Chanda' (1961).[18]

4.5. Language contact. Burrow's 'Dravidian studies VII' (1948) includes a further list of 315 items from Sanskrit which he traces to Dravidian sources. Chapter VIII of *The Sanskrit Language* (London, 1955) deals with the 'non-Aryan influence on Sanskrit' (pp. 373–88) and summarizes his earlier researches on Dravidian loans in Sanskrit with a long list of borrowed items and etymologies from Dravidian. In his 'Linguistic prehistory of India' (1954), Emeneau examines the current hypotheses of Aryan and Dravidian contacts based on archeological and linguistic evidence, and submits a list of thirteen early Sanskrit loanwords from Dravidian with copious etymological notes.

Another field in which Emeneau has done considerable research during the past decade is the 'linguistic area' hypothesis. Though this work is seemingly outside the scope of comparative Dravidian, it has far-reaching consequences for our understanding of the prehistory of Dravidian and helps in sorting out genetic phenomena from areal or diffusional ones. His first elaborate formulation of the hypothesis occurs in the paper 'India as a linguistic area' (1956), in which he speaks of several parallel phonological and morphological features between Dravidian on the one hand and Indo-Aryan (and also Munda) on the other; e.g. the use of retroflex consonants, distinction between the dental and palatal affricates *t͜s d͜z* and *t͜š d͜ž*, the

[17] See fn. 14; also by the same authors 'A comparative vocabulary of the Gondi dialects' (1960), 'Gadaba supplement' (1962).

[18] Bhattacharya 1961.

addition of the same set of case morphemes both to the singular and plural oblique stems, the use of verbal participles as heads of subordinate clauses in sentence construction, transformation of verbs into verbal adjectives followed by noun heads, extensive use of echo words, and the use of quantifiers or classifiers. He defines a 'linguistic area' as 'an area which includes languages belonging to more than one family but showing traits in common which are found not to belong to the other members of (at least) one of the families'. In a subsequent paper (Emeneau 1962a) he explains this phenomenon as a consequence of structural borrowing through extensive bilingualism.

In a further article, Emeneau (1964a) shows how bilingualism of the Dravidian Brahuis in Iranian Baluchi, a neighbouring prestige language, led to several structural changes in the Brahui system in the direction of Baluchi, viz. (a) the elimination of distinctions between *e/ē*, and *o/ō*; (b) borrowing an aspectual suffix *-a* identifiable with the general Iranian 'aorist' prefix *a-*; (c) the use of a subordinating conjunction *ki* as in Hindi-Urdu and Baluchi; (d) loss of the Dravidian gender system. M. Andronov (1964b) recently discussed the whole problem of similarity between New Indo-Aryan and Dravidian in a broader perspective. He thinks that the crucial period in the transformation of Indo-Aryan was 'the transition from the Apabhraṃśa stage to New Indo-Aryan'. At this stage 'the quantitative accumulation of isolated new structural elements ended in a qualitative change of the whole structure'. He assumes that Proto-Dravidian had already disintegrated into several languages and subgroups even by the time of the first contact between the speakers of Dravidian and Indo-Aryan. The development of nasalized vowels, diphthongs, and aspirates in some of the Dravidian languages is traced to the typological influence of New Indo-Aryan. A feature of modern Dravidian morphology is the gradual replacement of the 'synthetic negative forms' of the verb by 'special negative words' as in Indo-Aryan. In syntax he calls attention to the development of compound and complex sentences in Dravidian. Andronov thinks that there is a possibility of both Dravidian and Indo-Aryan in India drawing closer together to form a new family of languages with their native bases completely obscured by borrowed phenomena. He thinks that the 'genetic' conception of language is not 'primordial or perpetual' and linguistic relationships are basically 'historic', not 'naturalistic'.

The most recent contribution on areal typology involving many Dravidian languages is William Bright's 'Dravidian metaphony' (1966). The lowering of the short high vowels *i-*, *u-* to *e-*, *o-* when followed by a low vowel *-a* in the next syllable is characteristic of Proto-South Dravidian, and is represented in all South Dravidian languages, Tamil, Malayāḷam, Kannaḍa, Toda, Kota, Koḍagu, Tuḷu, and Telugu. Bright observes this phenomenon of 'metaphony' operating in some of the Middle and Modern Indo-Aryan and also the Munda languages of eastern India—extending from Assam to Ceylon—which he calls a 'linguistic area' in the sense in which Emeneau has used the term.

While it has been amply demonstrated that Dravidian and Indo-Aryan share many structural features both in phonology and grammar, the mechanism through which the transmission of such features from one family to another takes place is still not clear. It is true that extensive bilingualism or multilingualism has been invoked as the main factor at work. It is generally accepted that language contact in the initial stages leads to lexical borrowing—with an assimilatory (*tadbhava*) phase preceding the appropriation (*tatsama*) phase. Transmission of phonological structural features can thus be a direct consequence of lexical borrowing. Transfer of morphological and syntactic features is expected to follow at a more advanced stage of language contact, necessarily presupposing extensive lexical borrowing. The implication of this assumption is that a situation in which a given language or family of languages displays large-scale structural borrowing from a neighbouring language or family of languages without extensive lexical borrowing should lead us to question the validity of the above hypothesis. This is relevant in the contact situation between Dravidian and Indo-Aryan. It is the Dravidian languages (particularly South Dravidian) which show evidence of extensive lexical borrowing but only a few traits of structural borrowing from Indo-Aryan. On the contrary, Indo-Aryan (particularly Middle and Modern) shows large-scale structural borrowing from Dravidian, but very little lexical borrowing. How can we reconcile these conflicting facts in order to work them into the framework of a bilingual situation?[19]

4.6. Subgrouping. Scattered observations on the question of subgrouping of the Dravidian languages occur in the earlier writings of L. V. Ramaswami Aiyar and E. H. Tuttle. Thus, the former discusses common features among South Dravidian in a series of articles, 'Some parallelisms and divergences in South Indian Dravidian' (*Educational Review*, Madras, December 1938; January, February, March 1939). Another such paper which implies South Dravidian subgrouping is 'Semantic divergences in Indo-Aryan loanwords in South Dravidian', *Journal of Oriental*

[19] That Middle Indo-Aryan and New Indo-Aryan have been built on a Dravidian substratum seems to be the only answer. The fact that the invading Aryans could never have outnumbered the natives, even though they politically controlled the latter, is a valid inference. We may formulate the situation as follows: If the speakers of L_1 (mother tongue) are constrained to accept L_2 (second language) as their 'lingua franca', then an L_3 will develop with the lexicon of L_2 and with a mixture of the dominant structural features of L_1 and L_2. L_1 = Dravidian languages, L_2 = varieties of Sanskrit, L_3 = Middle Indic. This is also true of modern Indian varieties of English (L_3), which have English (L_2) lexicon but a large number of structural features of Indian languages (L_1). Here, of course, the situation is different since the native languages have not been abandoned. But what is interesting to note is that Indian languages have freely borrowed words from English but no structural features; transfer of only structural features excluding the lexicon is evident when Indians speak English as a second language.

The hypothesis that most of the present New Indo-Aryan speakers should have been originally Dravidians and also presumably Kolarians (Munda speakers) was suggested long ago (see Caldwell, 1956: 52–61). Quoting Hodgson, Caldwell says 'that the North-Indian vernaculars had been derived from Sanskrit, not so much by the natural process of corruption and disintegration as through the overmastering, remoulding power of the non-Sanskritic elements contained in them' (53); Emeneau says that 'a Dravidian substratum is easily accessible in its [Indo-Aryan's] dozen or more living languages, and in that a Proto-Dravidian can be worked out, given enough scholars interested in the matter' (1954: 285); also Chatterji, 'Dravidian philology' (1957), see particularly 212–13 in which he speaks of a non-Aryan substratum of Aryan.

Research, 8: 252–66, 9: 64–77 (Madras, 1937–8). In his discussion of correspondences, however, Ramaswami Aiyar speaks of South Dravidian and North Dravidian but no specific mention of Central Dravidian as a subgroup occurs. He considers Telugu to be a member of South Dravidian though he observes, for instance, that 'the Telugu masculine singular ending *-ṇḍ* (inscriptional *-ńd́ = nṟ*) beside *-n* of other southern speeches, has relatives only in Kui *-nj*, Kōlamī *-nd* and Bhili *-nd* of Central India' ('Dravidian nominal inflexions', *Educational Review*, Madras, September 1936). Tuttle speaks of 'stress-displacement' as a common characteristic of early Telugu, Gondi, and Kui (*Dravidian Developments* [1930] §27); elsewhere, he speaks of Gondi, Kui, and Tuḷu forming a 'group' (ibid. §32). Burrow speaks of loss of **c/s* as a shared feature of South Dravidian. No explicit discussion on subgrouping within Dravidian occurred until recently. The discovery of Parji as a separate language and of the other allied languages, Ollari and Gadaba, during the last fifteen years or so has made it possible to speak of subgrouping in Dravidian. In the preface to *The Parji Language* (1953), Burrow and Bhattacharya have tentatively stated that the nearest relations of Parji are Ollari and Poya (wrong name for our Koṇḍēkōr Gadaba). 'These three have again in turn a special connection with Kolāmī and Naiki'. They also speak of 'many signs of special connection between Gondi-Koṇḍa and Kui-Kuwi' (p. xi).

Emeneau (1955a) devotes a full chapter (Ch. X, 141–71) to the 'Comparative position of Kolami'. His discussion based on phonology, grammar, and lexicon supports Burrow and Bhattacharya's closer subgrouping of Kolami-Naiki and Parji-Ollari-(Gadaba). Gondi joins these at a higher node and Telugu, Kui, and Kuvi at a still higher one.

For a long time Telugu was considered a member of the South Dravidian group. Krishnamurti (*TVB*, Ch. IV 'The place of Telugu in the Dravidian family', 236–74) amply demonstrated that Telugu 'is an off-shoot of the Central Dravidian branch of Proto-Dravidian with very intimate genetic relationship with the Kui-Kuvi-Koṇḍa subgroup'. The features it shares with South Dravidian are said to arise from its 'intimate geographical contact with the members of South Dravidian from a very remote past'.

Discussion about Kuṛux, Malto, and Brahui as a North Dravidian group occurs in 'The position of Brahui in the Dravidian family' in Emeneau (1962c: 62–70). In phonology, **w- > b-*, **k- > x-* before all vowels except *i ī*, and **c- > k-* before *u ū*, are said to be shared innovations in North Dravidian. The use of *-k* as past morpheme in certain subclasses of verbs, and the use of *o/ō* as 'probable future' are outstanding morphological innovations of this subgroup. As Emeneau finally remarks 'A more refined statement of the position of North Dravidian will have to await more detailed treatment of Brahui and of Kurukẖ and Malto as well' (70).

Emeneau's paper 'The South Dravidian languages' (MS 1965b, publ. 1967a) seeks to set up subgroups within South Dravidian on the basis of the past-stem formation. The first split in South Dravidian occurs between Kannaḍa and the rest. A subsequent branching opposes Koḍagu with Tamil-Malayāḷam, Toda and Kota.

A further branching separates Tamil from Toda-Kota. An offshoot of Tamil is Malayāḷam and an offshoot of Kannaḍa is Baḍaga. Except Kannaḍa, all other languages of South Dravidian share the feature of forming past stems by the addition of **i*, **tt*, and **nt* (the last two Emeneau phonemicizes as **t* and **nd*). They also share a feature of intransitive–transitive opposition in a large number of stems indicated by the alternation of **-nt*/**-tt* [= **-nd*, **-t*]. The Tamil-Malayāḷam feature of palatalization **k-* > *c-* is not shared by Toda, Kota, and Koḍagu, and on the evidence of relative chronology of **k-* > *c-* in Tamil (dated approximately to a period between the 3rd and 1st centuries BC), Emeneau posits the split of the Toda-Kota subgroup from pre-Tamil to a time prior to the 3rd century BC. Contrary to earlier suppositions, Emeneau now clearly shows that Koḍagu does not belong to the Kannaḍa subgroup, but is more closely related to the rest. Its actual location in the complex of Tamil-Malayāḷam-Toda-Kota does not clearly emerge from Emeneau's discussion. Emeneau's evidence that Toda-Kota, on the one hand, and Kannaḍa, on the other, do not have parallels to past stems of Class VII verbs of Tamil (e.g. *naṭa* 'to walk', past: *naṭa-nt-*, future: *naṭa-pp-*), a feature which Koḍagu also shares with Malayāḷam, shows that it belongs to a lower node than that of Toda and Kota which have apparently lost this Proto-South Dravidian feature. But Emeneau's diagram on page 13 assumes an earlier split opposing Koḍagu with Tamil, Malayāḷam, Kota, and Toda. The family tree diagrams of the three branches of Dravidian may be tentatively represented as in Fig. 5.1 on the basis of the latest knowledge in the field.[20]

4.7. **Affiliation.** One of the most widely discussed problems of Dravidian from Caldwell's days has been the question of the relationship of the Dravidian family with languages outside India. A theory which has been barely kept alive for well over a century now is the Dravidian affinity with Ural-Altaic, subsumed under the so-called 'Scythian' or 'Turanian' family of the 19th century. Caldwell gave a full-scale treatment to this theory in his *Comparative Grammar*, and stated that the Dravidian languages 'bear a special relationship to a particular family included in that group, the Ugro-Finnish' (1956: 65). Burrow in his 'Dravidian studies IV' (1944) gives a brief history of this theory with bibliographical references up to that date, and supports it with seventy-two etymologies of words denoting body parts in Dravidian and Uralian. He said that this article was 'a first instalment of evidence supporting the theory of Dravidian-Uralian relationship. . . . details of phonology and other questions that arise are reserved for future contributions to this series' (331).

During the period under review, three important papers have appeared in support of this theory by two Altaic scholars, Karl Bouda (1953, 1956) and Karl H. Menges (1964). The last article reviews the whole history of the theory and seeks to show parallels in phonology and morphology between Dravidian and Uralian. The representation of PD **c* as *c* or *s* in different Dravidian languages is said to have parallels in Altaic. His discussion centres around the correspondence PD **ṯ* [*ṟ*] =

[20] [In Ch. 8 and subsequent papers, it will be noticed that I have changed this position. I have given arguments for revising the subgrouping.]

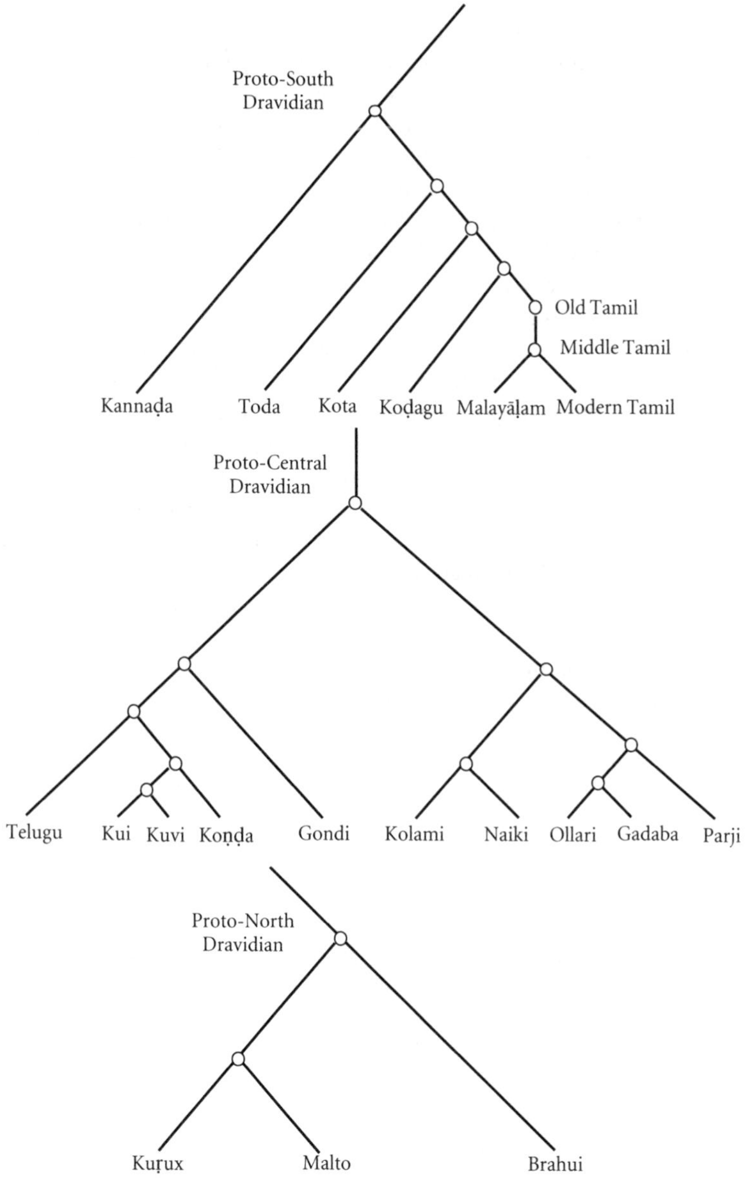

FIGURE 5.1. Family tree of the Dravidian languages (pre-revised)

Kui *j/s*, regarding which Burrow (1944: 346) suggested earlier that PD **ṯ* [-*ṟ*-] developed out of an original **s* or **z*, similar to the process called 'rhotacism' in Indo-European. This equation is not supported by the comparative method applied to Dravidian. The discovery of Koṇḍa which is more closely related to Kui than to any other language of Central Dravidian shows that it still preserves a single PD **ṯ* as *ṟ* in most positions and changes it to *R* before voiceless stops; PD **ṯṯ* = Koṇḍa *R*; Koṇḍa *ṟ* = Kui *j*, and *R* = *s*. The developments of other Central Dravidian languages are also explainable in terms of PD **ṯ* and **ṯṯ*. The series of changes that this phoneme has undergone (except in Malayāḷam and Jaffna Tamil) seems to have been prompted by a typological pressure exerted by the Indo-Aryan five-point stop system, whereby PD **p t ṯ ṭ c k* (with six distinctive points of articulatory positions) has progressively become a five-point system with the alveolar merging with a dental, a retroflex, or a palatal stop (sibilant). The redistribution of /*ṯ*/ as a calculated change towards a typological goal of eliminating it from the system was presumably necessitated by the distinctive features of voice and aspiration having developed contrastive roles only for **p* **t* **ṭ* **c* **k*, through loanwords from Indo-Aryan, leaving *ṯ* defective.

Menges further calls our attention to the paucity of forms with *l* and *r* initially in Dravidian and in Altaic. The idiosyncratic development of Ka. *p*- > *h*- is said to have parallels in Altaic. Altaic Mongolian, Tungus -*h*, Tungus *p* > *f*-, *x*-, *h*-, Ø- (76). It is relevant to ask here what validity one can attach, in discussions of genetic relationship, to parallel sound changes in two geographically removed languages or language groups. *s*- > *h*- occurred in Greek as well as in Dravidian, but what does this prove? If change of one sound into another takes place owing to a shift either in manner or in point of articulation by gradual steps, many unrelated languages in the world can be shown to have parallel sound-shifts—which fact may be of interest perhaps in a discussion on language universals, but is of little use in deciding the question of 'affinity'. For instance, *p*- > *h*- is definitely datable to the 10th century and is restricted to Kannaḍa only. It is certain that a parallel change in Mongolian and Tungus says nothing about the relationship between Dravidian and Altaic. Until a valid theory is constructed which interprets genetic relationship in terms of such prehistoric (?) areal correspondences, the hypothesis of affinity between Dravidian and Ural-Altaic can be taken as still unproven. At the same time, it must be admitted that there is a fairly large amount of morphological and lexical evidence to show that there are good chances of some original relationship having existed between these two families.

M. Andronov (1961) cites some morphological evidence in support of this hypothesis. The formation of the past stems by -*t*-, -*tt*-, the future by *-*k* or *-*p*, the plural formation by **ḷ* or **k* are shown to have parallels in Finno-Ugrian. He also quotes a Russian ethnographer S. P. Tolstov, who proposes prehistoric ties between Finno-Ugrians and Dravidians in the second millennium BC.

The works of Lahovary (see the Bibliography)[21]—seeking to establish a relation-

[21] Only the most recent work in English has been accessible to me (1963).

ship between Dravidian and the languages of the peri-Mediterranean families and Basque—may be characterized as a colossal adventure in 'time' and 'space'. I shall only quote here what L. Zgusta and K. Zvelebil said, reviewing his *La Diffusion*: 'some degree of first-hand knowledge is absolutely necessary for a work based on comparison of different elements. If one does not possess at least some knowledge of the things compared, the comparison may be absolutely grotesque' (*AO* 29 (1961), 127–30; p. 130).

Attempts to trace genetic connections between Dravidian on the one hand and other languages such as Caucasian, Korean, Egyptian, or Sumerian on the other may be passed over in silence, since the methods and materials used in their support have been unimpressive.

5. Problems and Prospects

5.1. When compared to the work done on other language families like Indo-European and Semitic, progress made in comparative Dravidian studies is still meagre. The quality of comparative work necessarily depends on the adequacy and quality of the descriptive work on individual languages constituting the family. Much progress has been registered in this area since 1947 owing to several favourable circumstances, such as exposure of the younger generation of Indian scholars to modern linguistic thought and the encouragement given to research on Indian languages by Universities, State Governments, and the University Grants Commission. Many unpublished M.Litt. and Ph.D. dissertations are now available in the South Indian universities which include descriptive grammars of early classics, historical grammars of inscriptions, and loanword studies between Dravidian and Indo-Aryan.

Although the number is small, there are experts outside India dedicated to the study of Dravidian languages. The contribution of Kamil Zvelebil of Czechoslovakia to Tamil linguistics during the past fifteen years has been phenomenal. Many Russian scholars like M. Andronov, Yu. Glazov, and Z. N. Petruniceva have displayed first hand knowledge of the literary languages of the South in their publications. During the past decade, in the USA, there have been several young linguists interested in the study of Dravidian languages such as Leigh Lisker, William Bright, G. B. Kelley, W. McCormack, Andrée Sjoberg, Stephen Montgomery, Dan Matson.

5.2. Though considerable knowledge has been acquired in the area of comparative phonology of Dravidian, correspondences have been clearly worked out only for the phonemes of the root morphemes. We still need good accounts of comparative phonology for Central Dravidian and North Dravidian. Beyond what has been reviewed in this chapter, very little comparative work has been done on the inflectional and derivational morphology of Dravidian since Jules Bloch. Dialect dictionaries and dictionaries prepared on historical principles are desiderata for the literary languages. Modern descriptions of the Central and North Dravidian languages, particularly for the different dialects of Gondi, Kuvi, Gadaba, and Malto are badly needed to provide the quality of materials available for the other literary and non-literary languages. Even languages like Kui and Kuṛux have several dialects calling for separate descriptions.

Historical grammars of the literary languages are still a desideratum. At least a good historical grammar of Tamil is now available (Meenakshisundaran 1965). Historical grammars for the languages of the early inscriptions are available for Telugu, Kannaḍa, Tamil, and Malayāḷam, but we need several such grammars to cover all the available inscriptions, for the language of the inscriptions reflects the popular stream of speech which, in the major Dravidian languages, has all along been different from the literary language.

6

Dravidian Nasals in Brahui

1. There are at least six definite etymological groups supporting the correspondence Brahui *d-*: other languages *n-* (< PD **n-*) as follows:

1. PD **neyttV̄r*/**nettVr* 'blood'. Ta. *neyttōr*; Ka. *nettar(u)*; Tu. *netterï*; Te. *netturu*; Go. *nettur*, *netur*; Kui *nederi* [balance word with *raka* 'blood' (which is Oriya)]; Kuvi (F) *netori*; Koṇḍa *netir*; Kol. *netur*; Nk. *nettur*; Pa. *netir*; Gad. *nettūr*: Br. *ditar* (*DED* 3106).

2. PD **nēr-*: **ner-*V*-nal* 'yesterday'. Ta. *neruṉal*, *neruṉai*, *neṉṉal* 'yesterday': Br. *daro* (*DED* 3109).

3. PD. **nēr*: **ner-*V- 'to cut off'. Ta. *nēr* 'to cut off, sever'; Ka. *nēr* id. (*DED* 3127): Br. *dann-* (pres. *dē-*, imp. *da-*, *dar*, *darak*, past *darē*) 'to cut (of a knife), blight, usurp, carry off' (*DEDS* 3127).

4. PD **nēr* 'sun, time'. Ta. *nēram* 'time, season, opportunity'; Ma. *nēram* 'sun, day, light, time, season, hour, turn'; Koḍ. *nēra* 'sun, time'; Tu. *nērḍè* id. (*DED* 3128; cf. 2371): Br. *dē* 'sun, sunshine, day, time' (*DEDS* 3128).

5. PD **nīr* 'water'. Ta. *nīr* 'water, sea, moisture'; Ma. *nīr* id.; Ko. *nīr* 'water, semen'; To. *nīr* 'water'; Ka. *nīr*; Koḍ. *nīri*; Tu. *nīri*; Te. *nīru*; Kol. Nk. *īr* 'water'; Pa. Gad. *nīr* id.; Kui *nīru* 'juice, sap, essence': Br. *dīr* 'water, juice, sap' (*DED* 3057).

6. PND **nēr* 'who'. Kuṛ. *nē* 'who'; Malto *nēre(h)*, *nēri(th)*, *nērer* 'who, which man/woman/men, etc.': Br. *dēr*, *dē* 'who' (sg. and pl.) (*DED* 4228).

Of these, the identification of Group 5 Br. *dīr* vs. other languages *nīr* first occurs in Caldwell (1913: 634), and that of Groups 1, 4, 5, and 6 occurs in the etymological comments on Brahui vocabulary given by Bray himself (1934, v.s.vv.). However, Bray suggested a wrong grouping of Ka. *nēsaṟ(u)* 'sun' with Ta. Ma. *nēram*, under Br. *dē* 'sun, time' (Group 4). Burrow and Emeneau had earlier preferred the grouping of Br. *dē* 'sun, time' with Ta. *ñāyiṟu*, Ka. *nēsaṟu* (*DED* 2371). They have recently accepted my suggestion that Br. *dē* goes better with *DED* 3138 **nēr* than with 2371 **ācaṯ-* and this revision appears in the recent supplement to *DED* (*DEDS* 3128).

2. In a recent article, Emeneau (1962c: 60-1) has discussed his identification of the etymology Ta. Ka. *nēr* 'to cut off' with Br. *dann-*, *dē- dar*, *dēr-* and reconstructed PD. **nēr-*/**ner-*V- to account for the correspondence. PD **e* > Br. *a-* is an established correspondence which Emeneau has amply illustrated elsewhere (1962d: 10).

He has also discussed the etymological grouping of Br. *darō* 'yesterday' with Ta. *nēṟṟu, neruṉai*, etc. in *DED* 3109 (Emeneau 1961b: 4). He included two series of etyma under this etymology reconstructing to **nēr* and **nēṯ* [= nēṟ], presumably on the assumption that the final *-ṟ* and **-ṯ* could be treated as derivatives with **nē* as the ultimate root (1961b: 4).

7a. PD **nēṯ* 'day'. Ta. *nēṟṟu* 'recently'; Ko. *nēr* (obl. *nēṯ-*) 'yesterday'; *minēr* 'any day before yesterday'; To. *ïnēṟ* 'yesterday'; *mu-nēṟ* 'day before yesterday' (*DED* 3109).

7b. **nēr*: *ner*-V- 'yesterday' or 'day'. Ta. *neruṉal, neruṉai, neṉṉal* 'yesterday'; Ma. *innalē* 'yesterday' (here, the first element is not cognate with Ta. *neru-*); Ka. *ninne* 'yesterday'; Te. *ninna* (here, the final syllables Ka. *-ne*, Te. *-na*, seem to be cognate with Ta. *-nai* in *neruṉai* rather than with *-nal*); G. *ninnē* (obl. *ninnēṯ*). In some languages **nāḷ* 'day' underlies the second element of such compounds (*DED* 3025); also cf. 4119 (b) Ta. *muṉ-ṉāḷ* 'yesterday'; Te. *monna* 'day-before-yesterday' (<**mun-nay*).

There are two doubtful etymologies which have been proposed for the correspondence Br. *d-*: other languages *n-*. One of these, frequently cited with a question mark, is impossible and is therefore rejected here (Emeneau 1961b: 4), viz.

PD **nā*, **nāl-ku/nān-ku* 'tongue'. Ta. Ma. *nā, nāvu, nākku* 'tongue'; Ko. *nālg, nāv*; To. *nōf*; Ka. *nālage, nālige*; Koḍ. *nāvu*; Tu. *nālayi* (*nālāyi*); Te. *nāl(i)ka, nāl(u)ka*; Kol. Nk. *nālka*; Pa. *nevāḍ*; Oll. *nāŋ*; Gad. *nāngu*; Koṇḍa *nālka*: Br. *dūī* 'tongue' (*DED* 3009).

Another one, which Emeneau (1961b: 4–5) recently proposed with a certain amount of hesitation is the grouping of Br. *dā* 'this' (proximate demonstrative) with Malto *nā* 'that one here', which is an extended form of the further demonstrative which is 'generally employed when the party referred to is present'. It would appear simple and less cumbersome to consider Br. *dā/dād* 'this' as a straight loanword from the neighbouring Pashto, which has *dā* 'this' (Shafeev 1964: 34–5).

The six definite etymologies listed above thus establish Br. *d-* as a reflex of PD **n-*. While discussing the etymologies involving this correspondence, Emeneau (1962c: 61) says that 'these are in unexplained contrast with six instances of **n-* > Br. *n-*'. He mentioned this difficulty even earlier (1961b: 5): 'this correspondence is not entirely cleared up, since there are a number of clear instances in which PD **n-* is represented in Brahui by *n-* (*DED* entries 2980, 3019, 3051, 3055, 3064, 3089). We cannot go further at the moment.' This is precisely the problem that I attempt to clear up in this paper.

3. The following groups support the derivation **n-* > Br. *n-*. (All of these have been included in *DED*.)

8. PD **nar-/*ar-* 'to fear; to be terrified'. Ta. *aral, aruḷ* 'to be terrified'; n. 'fear'; Ka. *araḷ* 'terror'; Tu. *naraṅguni* 'to hesitate'; *naraguri* 'sheepish man'; Te. *aragali* 'hesi-

tation'; Kol. *ari* 'fear'; *arp-* 'to terrify'; Nk. *ari* 'fear'; Pa. Oll. Gad. *nar* 'fear'; Malto *arkar-* 'to be terrified': Br. *narring* 'to flee, run away' (*DED* 2980).

9. PD **ñām* (less likely **nām*) 'we (inclusive)'. Ta. *nām/namm-*; Ka. *nāvu-* (*nam-*); Tu. *nama* 'we (inclusive)'; Te. *nēmu* 'we (exclusive)', *mana-mu* (< **nama-*) 'we (inclusive)'; Nk. *nēm* 'we (inclusive)'; Go. *namoṭ* 'we (exclusive)'; Kuṛ.-Malto *nām* (*nam-*) 'we (inclusive)': Br. *nan* 'we' (no inclusive–exclusive difference) (*DED* 2980; for discussion, see Krishnamurti 1968b).

10. PD **nīn/nin-* ~ **īn/*in-* 'you (sg.)'. Ta. *nī* (*ninn-*); Ma. *nī* (*nin-*); Ka. *nīnu* (*ninn-*); Tu. *ī* (*nin-*); Te. *nīvu* (*nin-*before acc.); Pa. Oll. Gad. *īn* (*in-*); Kol. Nk. (obl.) *in-*; Go. *nimā, immā*; Kui *īnu* (*nī-*), Kuvi *nīnu* (*nī-*); Koṇḍa *nīnu* (*nī-*); Kuṛ Malto *nīn* (*ning-*): Br. *nī* (obl. *nē-*, *n-*; enclitic gen., dat., acc. *-ne*) (*DED* 3051; Krishnamurti 1968b: 202–5).

11. PD **nīm/*nim-* ~ **num-* 'you (pl.)'. Ta. *nīm* (*num-*); most other languages of SD and ND have *nīm* (*nim-*); Pa. Gad. Oll. *īm* (*im-*): Br. *num* (obl. *num-*) 'you (pl.)'.

12. PD **nunk-* 'to swallow'. Ta. *nuṅku* 'to swallow'; Ko. *nuŋg-* 'to gulp down'; To. *nug* id.; Ka. *nuṅgu* id; Tu. *niṅguni* 'to swallow'; Kuṛ. *nunux-*id.; Malto *nungh̠-* id.: Br. *nugh̠ushing* 'to swallow, devour' (*DED* 3064; cf. also 3062).

13. PD **nūṯ*: **nuṯ-*V- 'to crush, pulverize'. Ta. Ma. *nūṟu, nuṟukku* 'to crush, grind'; Ka. *nūṟu, nuṟi, nuṟuku* id.; Tu. *nuripuni* 'to powder'; Te. *nūṟu* 'to grind'; *nūrcu, nuṟucu* 'to thrash'; Go. *nōr-* 'to grind': Br. *nusing* 'to crush, grind'; *nusxal* 'hand-mill' (*xal* 'stone'); *nut* 'flour' (*DED* 3089).

14. PD **naḷ* ~ **nāḷ/*naṉ* ~ **nāṉ* 'night'. Ta. *naḷ* 'night'; Kol. *āle*; Nk. *āḷe* id.; Pa. *nendu-nal* 'midnight'; Koṇḍa *nāṟa*; Kui *nāḍangi* id. (*DED* 2997, 2985). Alternatively, **nal/*al.* Ta. Ma. *al* 'night, darkness'; Ta. *nallam* 'blackness, darkness'; Te. *nalla, nalupu* 'blackness' (*DED* 199, 2990): Br. *nan* 'night'.

A close look at the reconstructions of all the groups 1 to 14 (excepting 10) would show clearly that the development **n-* > Br. *d-* is in complementation with **n-* > Br. *n-*; the former occurs before the reconstructed front vowels **ĭ*, **ĕ* and the latter before the non-front vowels **ă*, **ŭ*, **ŏ*. In other words, these developments represent a split of the Proto-Dravidian phoneme **n-* into *d-* and *n-* in complementary environments in Brahui. This conclusion also implies that **e-* > *a-* in Brahui should antedate **n-* > *d-* (see Groups 2 and 3). It will be noticed that the Brahui items with *n-* followed by a front vowel are all later borrowings from the neighbouring Indic and Iranian languages.

4. There are 20 entries listed with *nĕ* and 32 with *nĭ* in Bray's *Etymological Vocabulary* (1934). With the exception of the variants of the second person singular pronoun constituting 4 entries, viz. *nē* (dative-accusative of *nī*), *nē* (oblique base of *nī*), *-ne* 'thee, of thee' (enclitic form of the pronoun of the second person genitive, dative, and accusative); *nī* 'thou', all the remaining 48 entries have been identified by Bray himself as loanwords from Persian, Arabic, Baluchi, etc. Therefore, the only

exception to the above formulation of *n- > Br. *n-/d-* is the second person singular pronoun *nī* which needs satisfactory explanation.
There are three possible explanations:

(1) That *nī* 'thou' being a very basic item might have resisted sound change.

(2) A more plausible explanation would be that *nī*, which presumably became **dī* by the sound change, could have been restored analogically owing to the preponderance of the *n-* forms. Study the following paradigm (Bray 1909: 77):

The Second Person

	Sg. 'thou'	Pl. 'you'
nom.	*nī*	*num*
gen.	*n-ā*	*num-ā*
dat.-acc.	*n-ē*	*num-e*
abl.	*n-ē-ān*	*num-e-ān*
instr.	*n-ē-aṭ*	*num-e-aṭ*
conj.	*n-ē-to*	*num-to*
loc.	*n-ē-ṭī*	*num-ē-ṭī*
	n-ē-āi	*num-e-āi*

Under the analogical influence of *nā* and *num-* the nominative *dī* would have been restored to its original shape *nī* after sequences with *n-* before front vowels were introduced in Brahui through borrowing. Here the principle is that a morph may regain its original phonemic form through analogy after the alternation in which it is involved has ceased to be automatic owing to later sound shifts or borrowing (see Hoenigswald 1960: 108–9). It is also doubtful if *-ē* which is an inflectional morpheme in *n-ē* (Bray 1909: 77) would have the same effect as radical *ē* traceable to a Proto-Dravidian front vowel, which we hold responsible for the development **n-* > *d-*. The inflectional increment in the singular forms is *ē* instead of *e* because of lack of contrast between *e/ē* in word-initial syllables (Emeneau 1962d: 7). Note also that Pashto has *di-* as a weak pronoun in the second person singular (Shafeev 1964: 33).

(3) A third proposal posits a non-front vowel in Proto-Dravidian for the second person singular and plural owing to the peculiar alternation of *i/u* in **nim-/*num-*. This alternation is usually explained as having arisen from the rounding of *i* to *u* before a bilabial in Proto-Dravidian itself. Since such a change is not common in cases even with the same environments, this alternative requires further investigation before we can set up a new vowel phoneme in Proto-Dravidian.

At the moment (1) and (2) seem to be the best possibilities. In any case, the formulation of a phonemic split in Brahui seems fairly certain judging from the way the etymologies are distributed. One residual form cannot be taken to disprove a sound change establishable on the basis of preponderantly positive data.

5. Only two of the Dravidian nasals are preserved in word-initial position in Brahui: **n* and **m*. As with the other Dravidian languages, PD **ñ-* > Br. *n-*, e.g. **ñām* > Br. *nan* 'we'. It would be interesting to see if a similar phonemic split could be

discerned in the case of PD **m* also. There seems to be alluring evidence in support of the hypothesis, viz. PD **m* [front vowel > Br. *b*-, **m* [non-front vowel > Br. *m*-.

The *DED* has 18 Brahui entries with initial *b*- for which there are Dravidian etymologies as follows:

b [*a*	3	(*DED* 4311, 4317, 4548)
b [*ā*	4	(*DED* 4503, 4355, 4385, 4540)
b [*ē*	3	(*DED* 3627, 4179, 4552, 4569, 4552, 4565)
b [*i*	6	(*DED* 4419/4457, 4449, 4472, 4503, 4540, 4564)
b [*ī*	1	(*DED* 3440)
b [*u*	1	(*DED* 4503)

Of these, all instances of *ba*- are derivable from **wa*-; *bā*- is traceable to **wā* in two cases (*DED* 4355, 4385); in one case, i.e. Br. *bāsing* (*ing*) 'to become hot', *bās* is traceable to **wēc*- (*DED* 4540), involving **ē* > *ā*; Br. *bāṭagh̲* 'summit, top' along with *biṭ*, *buṭ* 'mound, hillock' is compared with Ta. *viṭam* 'mountain', Ko. *beṭ*, Ka. *beṭṭa beṭṭu* 'big hill', Koḍ. *beṭṭa*, Tu. *beṭṭu* (*DED* 4503). There is here a cross-reference in *DED* to 4151, i.e. **mēṭ*/**meṭṭ*- > Br. *bāṭagh̲*, *biṭ* with *ē* > *ā*; *e* > *i* and *m* > *b* before a front vowel. This first grouping is more likely since it is exactly parallel to Br. *bāsing*, *bising* (*DED* 4540) < PD **wēc*-/*wec*-V-. Of the three instances of Br. *b* [*ē*, one seems certainly derivable from PD **mēy*: Ta. *mēy*, 'to graze, etc': Br. *bei* (= *beī*) 'grass fit for grazing' (*DED* 4170). *DED* gives cross-references here to 4552 Ta. *vēy* and to 4569 Ta. *vai*, etc. Of these alternatives, the basic meaning of Ta. *vēy* (*DED* 4552), etc. seems to be 'to cover, thatch' and indirectly refers to 'thatch grass' (occurring only in Kui). No language seems to denote the notion of 'grazing' under this entry. *DED* 4569 Ta. *vai* 'grass, straw of paddy' is possible but again no language implies the notion of 'grazing'. The remaining cases with Br. *bē*- are derivable from **wē*-. The ones with *bi*- are all traceable to PD **wi*- or **we*-.

Br. *bil*: Ta. *vil* 'bow' (4479); Br. *bining* 'to bear': Ta. *vin̲ā* 'to ask, listen' (4472); Br. *birring* 'to separate, pick out': Ta. *vēr̲u* (4564); Br. *bising* 'to bake': Ta. *vey*- 'be hot' (4540); Br. *biṭing* 'to throw': Ta. *viṭu* 'to leave' (4419) or *viẓu* 'fall', etc. (4457); Br. *biṛing* 'milk': Kuṛ. *bīn*-, Kui *vṛīs*- id. (3440); Br. *biṭ*, *buṭ*: Ta. *viṭam* 'mountain' (4503) (see discussion above).

Br. *biṭ*- v.t. 'to throw, throw down, let drop, shed'. v.i. 'to come down, descend' seems to go equally well with *DED* 3974(a)—Ka. *miḍi* 'to leap, jump', *mīṭu* 'jumping'; Te. *miṭṭu* 'to leap'; Kol. *miṭ* ; Nk. *muṭṭ*- 'to leap, jump'.

There is another precious etymology unfortunately missing in *DED* which supports the correspondance Ta. *mē*-: Br. *bē* - (< **mē*), viz. *DED* 4173: Ta. *mē* 'excellence', *mēl* 'above'; Ma. *mē* 'over'; Ka. *mē* 'that which is above'; Br. *bē* 'over, on'. Bray (1934, s.v.) suggests that to the same root belong *bēṭ* 'on', *bāṭagh̲* 'summit', etc.

6. The foregoing discussion suggests a strong parallel between **n* > Br. *n*-/*d*- and **m* > Br. *b*-/*m*-. There are nearly 25 instances cited in the *DED* for Brahui preserving **m-* before non-front vowels. There are only two instances of *m-* followed by a front vowel, viz. Br. *milī* 'marrow': Ta. *mūḷai* 'brain' (*DED* 4146); Br. *miring*: Ta. *meẓuku* (*DED* 4169). The first of these is not a clear case since most languages point to PD **muḷ-V-* with a non-front vowel following *m-*. In that case we can posit assimilatory change **u- > i-* in Brahui after **-ai* > Br. *ī* and after *m* [front vowel > *b-* was completed. Br. *miring* 'plaster' is the only solid exception, but even here the vowel is not uniformly **e* in the other Dravidian languages.

It is not within the scope of this paper to discuss the developments of Dravidian nasals in non-initial positions.

(Participants in the discussion following the seminar presentation of the first version of this paper: N. Kumaraswami Raja, A. Kamatchinathan, and K. Balasubramanian.)

7

Some Observations on Tamil Phonology of the 12th and 13th Centuries

1. Owing to the limitations of Tamil orthography, it has not so far been possible to say, in clear terms, when intervocalic and post-nasal stops became voiced in Tamil. An analysis of a Tamil text occurring in a Telugu literary work of the 12th century now provides conclusive evidence on this question. This evidence confirms the conclusions reached earlier on comparative grounds that intervocalic and post-nasal stops were completely voiced in Tamil (subphonemically, of course) even by the time of the branching off of Malayāḷam from Tamil, i.e. about the 10th century. A few other significant observations on spoken Tamil of the 12th and 13th centuries can also be made on the basis of this text.

2. The following Tamil passage occurs in *Paṇḍitarādhyacaritra*, a Telugu literary work of the 12th century[1] written by Pālkuriki Sōmanātha:

Arulu giriti yenne yaranē pirāne
ciri-giri-nilayanē civane yāṃḍavane
aṃgamāṟuṃ dāne yāy iruṃḍavane
maṃgayar pāṃganē mallik(a)-ārjunane
yān unakk aḍiyanēn akhila-nāyakane
yēnam illālāne yillav illavane
aṟu-vattu-mūvarukk ātma-nāyakane
maṟu-nālum ariyāda mallik(a)-ārjunane
ālāla-gaṃḍane yādi-yaṭravane
cūliyē mallik(a)-ārjunane yannavane
yella yillādāne yeṃgum uḷḷavane
colla vallādāne mallikārjunane
ārum miḍat tirunīṟum uḷḷavane
yēr-ērum īcane yella-mallayane
vēdiyaru tudikkum ādiyē civane
cōdiyē mallikārjunane yannavane

[1] There is dispute among scholars regarding the exact date of the author and his works. The difference ranges from the late 12th century to the middle of the 13th century (see Ārudra, *Samagr-āṃdhra-sāhityaṃ*, vol. 2: 219).

The passage is an exact transliteration of the text in Telugu script. It presents few spelling problems; [ṃ] is the Telugu *anuswāra*, a morphophoneme used as a cover symbol for all the nasals before homorganic stops. The text is composed in the Dwipada metre[2] and describes how the Tamil devotees climbing the hills of Śrīśailam (the hill-abode of Lord Śiva)[3] used to worship Lord Mallikārjuna (the one as white as jasmine, Lord Śiva).

I do not know if the epithets have been taken from any Śivaite work in Tamil. Most of the passage is a collection of epithets of Tamil and Sanskrit origin in praise of Lord Śiva, ending with the vocative particle -ē. Though there are several unintelligible words and constructions, it appears that Sōmanātha quoted the forms as he heard them but did not take them from any written work, as is evident from the phonetics of the passage. There are few text variations in the printed sources of the passage and the metrical requirements do not seem to have led to any serious distortion or obscuring of the linguistic forms; one positive case is the shortening of the vocative -ē at the end of stanzas (see note 2). Most of the deviations from Tamil orthography may therefore be taken to represent the way Tamil was spoken at the time of Sōmanātha (12th–13th centuries).

3. Interpretation of the passage. Ch. Radhakrishna Sarma (hereafter Ch. R.; pp. 38–43) with the help of M. Rajamanikkam, Reader in Tamil, University of Madras, and M. Shanmugam Pillai, attempted an interpretation of this passage.[4] I have also consulted two of my colleagues in the Tamil Department at Osmania University, K. Cingaram and Singaravelu, who offered alternative suggestions for the interpretation of some of the constructions. Each of the constructions in the passage may be translated into English as follows:

Line 1: *arulu giriti yenne* (not intelligible); Ch. R. suggests *aruludi eṉṉai* 'bless me' but this makes the stanza short of two morae; could it be *aruludi giriyaṉē*

[2] *Dwipada* is a native Telugu metre with couplets (two stanzas). Each stanza consists of three *Indragaṇas* followed by one *Sūryagaṇa*. An Indragaṇa is a foot of three or four syllables, the total weight of which should be four to five morae. A light syllable has one mora (L) and a heavy syllable has two morae (H). The Indragaṇas are thus LLLL, LLLH, HLL, HLH, HHL, LLHL (HLLL is not allowed); a Sūryagaṇa has two or three syllables, the total weight of which is three morae, i.e. HL or LLL (LH is not allowed). Line 5 divided into gaṇas is as follows:
yā-nu-nak-: HLH = 5 morae (Indragaṇa)
ka-ḍi-ya-nē-: LLLH = 5 morae (Indragaṇa)
na-khi-la-nā: LLLH = 5 morae (Indragaṇa)
ya-ka-ne: LLL (Sūryagaṇa)
The *yati* is agreement between the consonant + vowel of the first syllable of the line (here *yā*) and the consonant + vowel in the first syllable of the third gaṇa (here *na*; *-n* belongs to another word, so the agreement is between *yā* and *a-*; and *y* being a semivowel has a Ø consonantal value). *Prāsa* is agreement in the consonant of the second syllable of a pair of lines. In 5 and 6 the *prāsa* is the consonant *n* beginning the second syllable.

[3] Śrīśailam temple is located in the Eastern Ghats in the Kurnool District of Andhra Pradesh.

[4] I am indebted to Ch. Radhakrishna Sarma for making the relevant parts of his M. Litt. thesis available to me for my study. The observations on the historical phonology of the language are all my own.

'bless (me), the mountain-dweller'? *giriyaṉ* is, I am told, grammatically possible. It is tempting to keep *enne* as a spoken equivalent of *eṉṉai;* *(y)aranē* 'Hara'; Ch. R. interprets the form as *aṟaṉē* 'thou, the righteous'; *pirān-ē* 'the great one!'

Line 2: *ciri-giri-nilayan-ē* 'O resident of Śrīśailam, *civan-e* 'O Śiva!' *(y)āṃḍavan-e* 'O Master!'

Line 3: *aṃgamāṟuṃ dāne . . . avane* (meaning not clear) 'You are the one with the six angas (?) being yourself!'

Line 4: *maṃgayar pāṃgan-ē* 'O one having a lady as a part of the body (Skt. *ardhanārīśvāra*)'; Ch. R. suggests correction as *mangayōrpāgaṉ-e* which seems needless.

Line 5: *yān unakk aḍiyanēn* 'I am thy servant'. *akhilanāyakan-e* 'O supreme Lord'.

Line 6: *(y)ēnam illālān-e.* Ch. R. does not give the translation of this construction; it is likely that it is a wrong form of *ēṉam illādāṉ-ē* 'O one without (even) a vessel (= begging bowl!)'. *(y)illav illavane.* Ch. R. suggests alternative reading *illam illiyaṉ-ē* 'O one without an abode' which sounds plausible. The alteration *-m-/-v-* is evidenced in Tamil and the other Dravidian languages in the intervocalic position.

Line 7: *aṟuvattu . . . nāyakan-e* 'O Master of the souls of the sixty-three nāyanārs'.

Line 8: *maṟu . . . mallik(a)-ārjunan-e* 'Mallik(a)-ārjuna, the one not known by the four vedas.' Ch. R. suggests this by reading *maṟu-nālum* as *maṟai nālum* 'the four Vedas'.

Line 9: *ālāla-gaṇḍan* is derived from Skt. *hālāhala-kaṇṭha-* 'the one who locked poison in his throat, the poison-throated one'. *(y)ādi-yaṭravan-e* = *ātiyaṟṟavaṉ-ē* 'the one without a beginning/birth'.

Line 10: *cūliy-ē* 'O Śūli (one who carries the trident)'. *yannavane* = *eṉṉavaṉ-ē* 'O my Lord'.

Line 11: *(y)ella yillādāne* = *ellai illādāṉ-ē* 'O limitless one!' *(y)eṃgum uḷḷavane* 'the omnipresent one'.

Line 12: *colla vallādān-e* 'O indescribable one'.

Line 13: *āṟum miḍat tirunīṟum uḷḷavane.* The first part is not clear. Ch. R. drops *miḍat* and interprets the rest as 'the God who has the River Ganga and the holy ashes'; *miḍattu* can be taken to represent *miḍaṟṟu* obl. of *miḍaṟu* 'neck'; in speech, *miḍattu* × *tirunīṟum* > *miḍattirunīṟum* by haplology?

Line 14: *(y)ēr-ērum īcan-e* 'O one who rides the bull'. *(y)ella-mallayan-e* 'Mallayya, who shines brilliantly' (Ch. R.).

Line 15: *vēdiyar(u) tudikkum ādiy-ē* 'O first God worshipped by the Brahmins'.

Line 16: *cōdiyē* 'O, the Light!' (< Skt. *jyōti-*).

4. The importance of the passage lies in the light it throws on spoken Tamil of the 12th and 13th centuries. It is clear that the language does not so much represent the contemporary written form of Tamil as its spoken form. Since it is the earliest

available record of Tamil speech in a sister language, the data can be utilized to make a few significant remarks on the phonetics of the Middle Tamil writing system.

4.1. Stop Consonants. All stop consonants occur regularly voiced in the intervocalic and post-nasal positions, without exception in the native vocabulary and mostly in the loanwords also:

ciri-giri (2), *aṃgam* (3), *maṃgayar pāṃgan* (4), *eṃgum* (11), *aḍiyanēn* (5), *iruṃḍavan* (3), *āṟuṃ dān-e* (3), *ariyāda* (8), *ālāla-gaṃḍan* (9), *illādān* (11), *vallādān* (12), *miḍatt-* (13), *vēdiyar* (15), *tudikkum* (15), *ādiyē* (15), *cōdiyē* (16).

Intervocalic *-c-* occurs, in one instance, as [c], i.e. *ī-cane* (14).

In the case of definite Sanskrit compounds, which Sōmanātha had no difficulty in identifying, he preferred to retain the Sanskrit spellings, although we would expect voiced counterparts of *-k-* in (*akhila*) *nāyakane* (5, 7) and *mallik-ārjunan* (8, 12). Intervocalic **ṯ-* occurs clearly as a voiced trill being written by the Telugu counterpart - ఱ - (voiced alveolar trill).

4.1.1. Chatterji (1956: 20–8) wrote a few years ago that voicing of intervocalic stops developed only during the Middle Tamil period, which according to his classification, is AD 1350–1800 (23). We see that such a stand cannot be maintained any more. Lenis pronunciation of intervocalic single stops as a phonetic feature could be reconstructed even to Proto-South Dravidian if not to Proto-Dravidian (*TVB* 29–33). Meenakshisundaran (1965: 128–32) considers this phonetic tendency to be evident in Tamil only from the 9th century onwards, and he thinks that there was a long period of free variation between voiced and voiceless stops after the 9th century. He also says that 'the voicing of the plosives after nasals was probably more frequent' (1965: 132). It appears that the conservatism in the writing tradition is responsible for variant spellings of voiced and voiceless stops, which cannot be taken to reflect free variation in speech. If the data should be interpreted historically, voicing of intervocalic and post-nasal single stops became an accomplished fact at the phonetic level even in Proto-South Dravidian. Consequently in Malayāḷam, Old Tamil NP > NB > NN (sequences of nasal + voiceless stop progressively assimilated to nasal + voiced stop and then to nasal + nasal), e.g. *ṅk* > *ṅg* > *ṅṅ*, even by the 10th century (*TVB* 33, §1.78).

Skt. *-s-*, *-ś-* > Middle Tamil *-c-* as noticed in Rajakēcari (11th century; see Meenakshisundaran 1965: 130) and *īcan* (see above), whereas PSD *-c-* [-s-] as well as borrowed Skt. and Pkt. *-s-* became [-y-] or Ø long before then. Initially /c/ occurs consistently as [c] even though it would have been possible for Sōmanātha to represent it by [s] or [ś] in Telugu writing if he heard it so; e.g. *ciri-giri* (2), *cūli* (10), *colla* (12), *civan* (15), *cōdi* (16). Here, *c-* occurs consistently both in loans from Sanskrit and Prakrit and in the native items. I wonder if the Modern Tamil pronunciation of [ś] for /c/ started after the 13th century. Also note that Malayāḷam, an offshoot of Middle Tamil (the West-coast dialect), still has only a stop realization for /c/ initially.

4.1.2. The inscriptional Tamil of the sixth century possesses voiced stops only in tatsama-loans marked in grantha, e.g. *vajranandi, bhūmi, paradatti, narabhayan* (Zvelebil 1964: 64). A Sanskrit initial *s-* remains as such and is not represented as *c-*. In contrast to this state of affairs, we notice uniform voicing of stops in intervocalic and post-nasal position in the native element of Tamil as an accomplished fact by the 12th century.

The sequence *ṟṟ* was articulated as [ṭr] as evidenced in the Telugu transcription *ādiyaṭravan* (= Ta. *ātiyaṟṟavaṉ*) and confirmed by the modern reading tradition. Early Tamil **ṟṟ* could be granted at least two variant articulations *ṯṯ* and *ṯṟ*; the former became *tt*/*ṭṭ* in different dialects whereas *ṯr* > *ṭr* only in the reading tradition. Perhaps the second must have all along been a spoken standard pronunciation of this sequence by the literates.

There are several examples of voiceless geminate stops still being recognized as such: *aṟu-vattu-mūvurakk* (7), *unakk(u) aḍiyanēn* (5), *tudikkum* (15), *miḍatt-* (13), unlike in later and modern Tamil in which *-kk-* > *-k-* whereby the original opposition of single vs. double is resolved as voiced vs. voiceless opposition, at least in the case of stops. The two *n*'s, dental and alveolar, were not distinguished in speech, hence they do not find a place in the Telugu system of writing. This may also be due to the fact that Telugu has a symbol (న) only for one nasal in the dental-alveolar region.

4.2. The following consonantal segments and clusters can be isolated from the text:

p	t		c	ṭ	k			tm
	d		j	ḍ	g	kk	ṅg	ṭr
							ṇḍ	rj
						tt	nd	
m		n		ṇ		nn		
		rṟ				mm		
		l		ḷ		ḷḷ		
v				y				

In the case of vowels, it is striking that all occurrences of front vowels (after pause) have the onglide *y-*, e.g.: (*y*)*ēnam* (6) (*y*)*illa* (6), (*y*)*eṃgum* (11), (*y*)*ella* (*y*)*illādān* (11), (*y*)*ella-* (14), (*y*)*ēr-ērum* (14).

The occurrence of *y-* before *aranē* (1), *āṃḍavane* (2), *āyi* (3), *ādi* (9) is perhaps inserted by the Telugu scribes following a Telugu sandhi rule.[5] It is also interesting to note the lowering of the position of /e/ after /y/; ye > yE/yɛ transcribed as *ya-* in Telugu *yannavan* (10, 16) for *eṉṉavaṉ*. Old Tamil word final *-ai* became *e* = [ɛ] even by the 13th century, *enne* (1) for < *eṉṉai*. In one unaccented position *-ai* is noted as

[5] When there is hiatus (absence of sandhi) between two vowels, a *y* is added before the second vowel (Bālavyākaraṇamu, Sandhiparicchēdamu, sūtramu 3).

-u-, i.e. *maṟu-nālum* (8), but there is a text variant *maranālum* (Ch. R.) in which older *-ai* > *-a*. The *kuṟṟiyalukaram* (short u) is replaced by *-u* in one case, perhaps for want of a symbol in Telugu; *vēdiyaru tudikkum* (15).

4.3. The vocalic segments occurring in the passage may be charted as follows:

i	ī			u	ū
e	ē			o	ō
		a	ā		

Note that no diphthong is recorded in the text. One possible exception might be *yellayillādāne* (11), but even here *ella* < *ellai*, with the following *y-* inserted by a Telugu sandhi rule (see above).

8

Gender and Number in Proto-Dravidian

0. A language has grammatical gender if the nominal stems of that language are classifiable in their morphology/syntax partly on the basis of binary semantic oppositions like animate: inanimate, human: non-human, male: female (with animate and/or human categories), etc. At least, it is noticed that, in languages with grammatical gender, stems denoting male-human always belong to the masculine gender. Languages differ in their degree of grammatico-semantic correlation in the classification of nominal and pronominal stems.

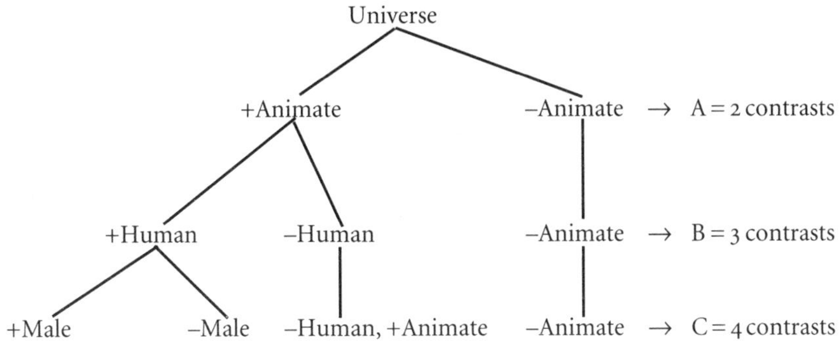

A= +Animate vs. –Animate; B= +Human vs. –Human Animate and –Animate; C= +Human Male vs. –Male Human. (i.e. female), –Human Animate and –Animate[1]

FIGURE 8.1. Semantic correlates of gender systems

In terms of the above tree model, we may say that gender systems have their genesis in the left branching of the universe in the process of naming; languages which

[1] Languages falling under A have a primary contrast of animate and inanimate as in the Bantu languages of Africa and Algonquian languages of North America. A three-way contrast is possible in languages of B and C (e.g. Indo-European), viz. masculine, feminine, and neuter with a lot of overlap in the non-male-human categories between form and meaning. Languages of B and C with a two-way gender system (viz. masc.–fem. or masc.–neut.) as in Hindi, for instance, show an even greater degree of overlap between form and meaning. Normally derivational processes derive the marked ones (indicated with minus features) from the unmarked, i.e. inanimate from animate, feminine from masculine. Fig. 8.1 mainly reflects the oppositions present in the Dravidian gender subtypes.

are right-branching with [–Animate] as the primary basis of classification possess classifier systems rather than gender (Krishnamurti 1967).

1. Dravidian languages have grammatical gender with a very high degree of correlation between the semantic and syntactic behaviour of nominal stems.

Dravidian gender distinction appears in noun stems (basic or derived), third person (demonstrative) pronouns, finite verbs, and nominal predicates. The demonstrative pronouns which can substitute for nouns can be taken as the best basis of gender distinction in Dravidian.[2] Gender and number are interrelated categories in Dravidian and they have to be dealt with together as a single system.

There are six maximum semantic and formal contrasts represented in Dravidian gender. Only one Dravidian language, viz. Pengo, has all the six differences. The following chart shows for each language the third person pronouns and their respective semantic ranges (data mainly drawn from Shanmugam 1971; 1–29, and *DED(S)*).

TABLE 8.1. *Semantic and formal contrasts in the 3rd person pronouns (remote) in different Dravidian languages*

	1 'he' (hum.)	2 'she' (hum.)	3 'it' (non-hum.)	4 'they' (hum. male)	5 'they' (hum. female)	6 'they' (non-hum.)

A. SOUTH DRAVIDIAN (SD I)

PD	**awan̠t̠u*	**awaḷ*	**atu*	**awar*	—	**away*
1. Ta.	*avann̠*	*avaḷ*	*atu*	*avar*		*avai*
(Kāṇ.)	*aveⁿ*	*ava*	*adu*	*avru*		*adu*
(Eruk.)			*adu*			*ay*
2. Ma.	*avan*	*avaḷ*	*atu*	*avar*		*avai*
3. To.		*aθ*				*aθām*
4. Ko.	*avn*	*avḷ*	*ad*	*avr*		*ad*
5. Iruḷa	*avɛ*	*ava*	*adu*	*avru*		*ave*
6. Koḍ.	*avën*	*ava*	*adï*	*ayŋga*		*adï*
7. Ka.	*avaM*, *avanu*	*avaḷ*	*adu*	*avaru*		*avu*
(Gow., S. Hav.)	*ãvã*		*adi*			*avu*
(Hāl.)	*avənu*	*avəḷu*	*adu*	*averu*		
8. Tu.	*āye*	*āḷï*	*avu*	*ākuḷu*		*aykuḷu*
				ārï		*avu*

[2] In Dravidian it is more often the meaning than the form of a nominal stem that determines its gender. Replaceability by one of the demonstrative pronouns is a testable syntactic criterion. The primacy

B. South-Central Dravidian (SD II)

9. Te.	*wāṇḍu*	*adi*		*wāru*		*awi*
10. Go.	*ōr*	*ad*		*ōṛ/ōṛk*	*av*	
(Koya)	*ōṇḍ*	*addu*		*ōr*	*avvu*	
11. Koṇḍa	*vāṉṟu*	*adi*		*vār*	*avi*	
12. Kui	*a?anju*	*?āri*		*āru*	*āvi*	
13. Kuvi	*āasi*	*ādi*		*āri*	*āti*	
14. Pe.	*avan*	*adel*	*adi*	*avar*	*avek*	*avaŋ*

C. Central Dravidian

15. Kol.	*am/amd*	*ad*		*avr*	*adav*	
16. Nk.	*avnd*	*ad*		*avr*	*adav*	
17. Pa.	*ōd/ōḍ*	*ad*		*ōr*	*av*	
18. Oll.	*ōṇḍ*	*ad*		*ōr*	*av*	
19. Gad.	*ōṇḍ*	*ad*		*ōr*	*av*	

D. North Dravidian

20. Kuṛ.	*ās*	*ād*		*ār/abṛar*		*abṛā*
21. Malto[3]	*āh*	*āth*		*ār*		*āth*
22. Br.	*ōd*			*ōfk*		

The following abbreviations are used for social (caste) dialects: Kāṇ. = Kāṇikkāra; Eruk. = Erukala; Gowḍa = Gowḍa; S. Havyaka; Hāl. = Hālakki.

Each row has cells and each cell represents a semantic space occupied by one form. If there is only one form occupying the space of two or three cells, its meaning also correspondingly expands to include those meanings. Thus in Telugu and the other South-Central Dravidian languages *adi* (corresponding to PD **atu*) means 'she, it' because it occupies the semantic space of 'she' (human female) and that of 'it' (non-human animate and inanimate).

2. The following generalized types and subtypes of distribution can be set up from Table 8.1 (contrasts in form are in bold).

of pronouns in gender distinction is also seen in their being copied in the finite verbs as a characteristic of subject-verb agreement and in the pronominalization of abstract nouns and adjectives by the addition of pronominal suffixes (cf. §§ **15**, **16**).

[3] Malto has iterative forms *āw āwer* 'those persons' and *āw āwe* 'those things' 'when the pronoun points back to objects or circumstances previously mentioned or understood, and is then, for the sake of signifying a plurality of objects, doubled' (Droese 1884: 31–2). These forms are reminiscent of PD **awar* and **away*.

TABLE 8.2. *Major types and subtypes in gender-number distinction*

		Singular			Plural			
I	(a)	1	2	3	4	5	6	Ta. Ma. Iruḷa, Ka. Tu.
	(b)	1	2	3	4	5	3	Ta. (Kāṇ.), Ko., Koḍ.
	(c)	1	2	3	4	5	6	Ka. (Gow., S. Hav.)
	(d)	1	2	3	4	5	6	Ka. (Hāl.)
	(e)	1	2	3	4	5	6	To. Ta. (Eruk.), Br.
II	(a)	1	2	3	4	5	6	Go., Koya, Kui, Kuvi, Koṇḍa; Pa., Kol., Nk., Oll., Gad.
	(b)	1	2	3	4	5	6	Pe.
III		1	2	3	4	5	6	Te., Kuṛ., Malto

3. The above Tables (8.1 and 8.2) show that the formal contrasts range from two to six. Erukala (Ta. dialect), Toda, and Brahui have only number but no gender. It is interesting to note that in all these it is the 'neuter' forms (Erukala *atu*, To. *aθ*, Br. *ōd*) both in the singular and the plural that have extended their semantic ranges with the loss of 'human' pronouns. Thus, To. *aθ* 'he, she, it': *aθām* 'they (men, women, others)'.

These developments have to be treated as independent typological changes in the respective languages which do not represent the dominant patterns. On the other hand, Pengo, unlike any of its near sisters, Kui, Kuvi, and Koṇḍa, has all the six contrasts—*avan/avanj-* 'he', *adel* 'she', *adi* 'it'; *avar* 'they (men)', *avek* 'they (women)', *avaŋ* 'they (non-human)'. Here the forms *adel* 'she' and *avek* 'they (women)' are innovations derived from *ad-* and *av-* by the addition of *-el* (< *āḷ*) and *-ek* (female plural suffix). The female human nouns have a plural suffix *-k* as opposed to *-ṅ* added to non-human nouns, e.g. *gaṛce-k* 'girls': *kōḍi-ŋ* 'cows'.[4] Finite verbs show only a five-way contrast in their pronominal agreement (singular man: others; plural men: women: others). Here the pronominal suffix *-at* agrees with both *adel* 'she' and *adi* 'it' pointing to the primacy of the *ad* form (Burrow and Bhattacharya 1970: 24–32, 63).

4. Within South Dravidian we notice three other minor patterns (formal contrasts are in bold).

[4] The specialization of the *-k* suffix (or more accurately the absence of *-ŋ*) as the plural marker of female human nouns (mainly kinship items) as opposed to non-human appears in the other languages of the Gondi-Manḍa subgroup. Kui *-ska*: sg. *angi* 'younger sister', pl. *angi-ska* (Winfield 1928: 14), Go. *-hk*: sg. *sēlar* 'younger sister' pl. *sēlā-hk* (Trench 1919: 36), Koṇḍa *si-k*: sg. *bīb-si* 'elder sister': pl. *bīb-sik*. Pengo has apparently extended this derivational mechanism into the demonstrative system and innovated a new grammatical category both in the singular and in the plural. Kui *-sk* and Go. *-hk* are traceable to morphemes *si-k* (Krishnamurti 1969c: §§ 4.7.17; Subrahmanyam 1969b: § 3.5).

TABLE 8.3. *Subtypes in gender and number within South Dravidian*

	Singular			Plural			
(a)	1	2	3	4	5	3	Ta (Kāṇ), Ko., Koḍ.
(b)	1	2	3	4	5	6	Ka. (Gow., S. Hav.)
(c)	1	2	3	4	5	6	Ka. (Hāl.)

The above are atypical of the South Dravidian literary languages. In (a) the singular non-human pronoun has replaced the plural, whereby the number distinction in the non-human category is neutralized. This reflects an analogical projection from the nominal system where the neuter plural suffix **kaḷ* is infrequently used in South Dravidian (Subrahmanyam 1969b, §31). Subtype (b) shows only a three-way contrast by eliminating female human in the singular and by dropping the human category in the plural (see §7 below). The semantic ranges of *adi* and *avu* are therefore extended respectively to mean 'she, it' and 'they (men, women, and others)'. Subtype (c) is even more puzzling because the human noun *averu* is used for the non-human category also. In the process of category collapsing, we normally expect as well as find the non-human or neuter as the unmarked one which takes over the function of 'human' and not vice versa. These dialect varieties show independent developments in the direction of simplifying the systems found in the standard varieties. Simplification has taken place in the typologically expected direction in all these languages except Hālakki Kannaḍa. An extreme process of such simplification totally eliminating gender is noticed in Erukala, Toda, and Brahui.

5. Elimination of the above exceptional cases leaves us with three dominant types of gender-number distinction in Dravidian as follows:

TABLE 8.4. *Major types of gender-number distinction*

	Singular			Plural			
I	1	2	3	4	5	6	Ta., Ma., Iruḷa, (standard) Ka., Tu.
II	1	2	3	4	5	6	Go., Koya, Koṇḍa, Kui, Kuvi, Manḍa; Pa., Kol., Nk., Oll., Gad.
III	1	2	3	4	5	6	Te., Kuṛ., Malto

Type II is the most widely distributed. Type III is similar to Type II in the singular and Type I in the plural. Notice, in the plural, there are only two formal contrasts traceable to PD **awar* and **away*. The difference lies only in their meaning ranges: Types I and III **awar* 'they (men and women)': **away* 'they (non-persons)'. Type II **awar* 'they (men, [men and women in mixed groups])': **away* 'they (others)'. In the singular also there is difference in the semantic range of **atu* between Type I, on the one hand, and Types II and III, on the other. Types II and III, **atu* 'she, it'; Type I 'it' (non-human animate and all inanimate), because there is a separate form **awaḷ* for 'she'.

6. The question is which of these types represents the Proto-Dravidian system. Bloch (1954: 5–7) and Krishnamurti (1961: §4. 30) argued in favour of Type II as representing the proto-situation since it is symmetrical and can constitute a logical starting point for the derivation of Types I and III. Emeneau hesitatingly (1955a: §10.17) and Subrahmanyam with certainty (1969b: §6), but basing the arguments on Emeneau's, thought that Type III represents the proto-system, since it occurs in widely divergent languages like Kuṛux-Malto and Telugu. Burrow and Bhattacharya (1953: §12) consider the South Dravidian system (Type I) with its three-way distinction in the singular as representing the proto-system. In this paper, I advance arguments in favour of Type II being the retention of the Proto-Dravidian system and account for Types I and III as innovations.

7. There were only two formal contrasts in the plural which corresponded to two parallel contrasts in the singular in Proto-Dravidian. The creation of **awaḷ* in Proto-South Dravidian is an innovation which therefore restricted the meaning **atu* to only the non-human group.[5] All Dravidian languages have derivative stems denoting female human by the addition of the suffix *-āḷ*. This goes back to Proto-Dravidian, in view of **mak-aḷ* 'daughter' as opposed to **mak-an̠ṯu* 'son' (*DED(S)* 3768).

Ta. *makaḷ*, Ma. *mōḷ*, Ko. *mōḷ*, Ka. *magaḷ*, Koḍ. *mōva* (loss of *ḷ*), Tu. *magaḷu*; Go. *miyāṛ*, *miyāl̄ī*, Koṇḍa *gālu/gāṛu*, Pe. *gāṛ*, Manḍa *gāṛ/-m-gāṛ*, Pa. *māl*, Ga. *māl* 'daughter'; ? Br. *maḻẖ* 'son'.

The extension of this derivational process to the demonstrative system would yield **awaḷ*, **iwaḷ*, and **yāwaḷ*. The lexical (derivational) distinction of the female human in the singular is noticed in all Dravidian languages with the addition of several derivative suffixes (Shanmugam 1971: 115–23).[6] If Burrow and Bhattacharya were correct in assuming Type I in the singular as representing Proto-Dravidian then we should say that the Telugu-Kui subgroup and Kuṛux-Malto subgroup independently lost **awaḷ* and extended the semantic range of **atu* to include female human. Burrow and Bhattacharya's point would have been proved if any language, even fortuitously, extended the meaning of **awan̠ṯu* ('man') to include female human also, since the semantic gap created by the loss of **awaḷ* could be filled by extending the

[5] Emeneau had pointed this out as early as 1955a (§ 10.17).

[6] It is unfortunate that Shanmugam often confuses male and masculine, female and feminine (semantic and grammatical nomenclature).

distribution of either **awanṯu* or **atu*. Since this had not happened it would be more plausible to posit an innovation in South Dravidian than posit a uniform innovation in three unrelated subgroups, Telugu-Manḍa, Kolami-Parji, Kuṛux-Malto.[7] Most scholars now agree that a binary contrast as **awanṯu*: **atu* in the singular represents Proto-Dravidian and South Dravidian innovated **awaḷ* (Emeneau 1955a: § 10.17, Krishnamurti 1961: § 4.30, Subrahmanyam 1969b: § 6.) The Kannaḍa dialects—Gowḍa and Havyaka—have only the derivatives of **awanṯu* and **atu* which could as well be relics of the pre-South Dravidian pattern. We must, however, admit that **awaḷ* should be a common innovation in the major languages of South Dravidian and therefore goes back to the Proto-South Dravidian stage.

8. Once the ground is cleared of the singular category, the Proto-Dravidian reconstructions stand as follows:

Singular		Plural
**awanṯu* 'he', **atu* 'she, it'	:	**awar* '?', **away* '?'

Now the only question to be resolved is the distribution (meaning) of **awar* and **away* in Proto-Dravidian. The only argument cautiously advanced by Emeneau (supported by Subrahmanyam 1969: §§ 6, 9 and endorsed by Shanmugam 1970: 123) is that Type III represented by such unrelated languages as Telugu and Kuṛux-Malto should be a retention of the Proto-Dravidian system. This is, of course, a sound general principle if it could be proved on other grounds that the concerned feature is definitely a retention and not a typologically (but not genetically) motivated innovation. By simply applying this as a rule of thumb, we would have to say that the system represented by Toda and Brahui, for instance, is proto (i.e. only number distinction without gender), since they represent genetically remote subgroups. We have ruled out this possibility by showing that it is an independent innovation, typologically motivated (a process of simplification) and not genetically shared. No decisive evidence has been shown to rule out a similar possibility in the case of defining the meaning of **awar* in Types I and III.

There are two possible interpretations, viz. (a) Proto-Dravidian had **awar* 'they (human)' and **away* 'they (non-human)' as found in Types I and III. In that case Kui-Manḍa and Kolami-Parji subgroups innovated a distributional (i.e. meaning) shift which led to these forms being redefined as **awar* 'men' **away* 'all others' (women, animals, and inanimate); (b) PD **awar* meant 'men' and **away* 'all others' as in Type II and the other languages (South Dravidian, Telugu, Kuṛux-Malto) extended the meaning of **awar* 'they (men)' to 'they (men and women, or human)' and restricted the meaning of **away* 'they (non-men)' to 'they (non-human)'. In terms of Hoenigswald's diagrams (1960: 27–47), these alternatives can be presented as follows:

[7] I use the following abbreviations for subgroups: Telugu-Manḍa = Telugu, Gondi, Kui, Kuvi, Koṇḍa, Pengo, and Manḍa; Gondi-Manḍa = all languages in Telugu-Manḍa except Telugu; Kui-Manḍa = Kui, Koṇḍa, Pengo, and Manḍa; Kolami-Parji = Kolami, Naiki, Parji, Ollari, and Gadaba; Kuṛux-Malto = Kuṛux and Malto.

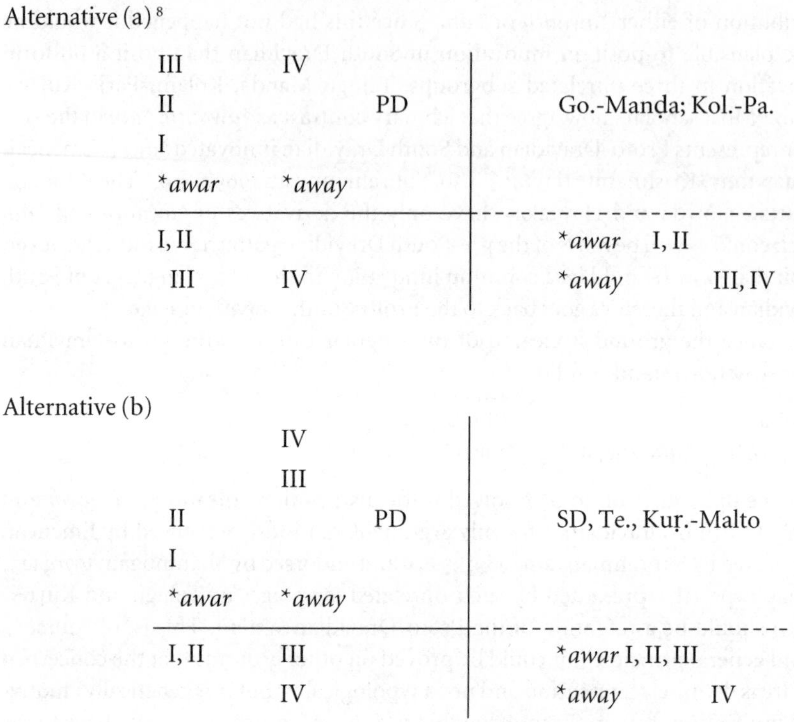
Alternative (a)[8]
III
IV
II
PD
Go.-Manḍa; Kol.-Pa.
I
*awar
*away
I, II
*awar I, II
III
IV
*away
III, IV
Alternative (b)
IV
III
II
PD
SD, Te., Kuṛ.-Malto
I
*awar
*away
I, II
III
*awar I, II, III
IV
*away
IV

Roman numerals represent syntactic/semantic environments: I = the environment in which the reflex of **awar* occurring as subject of a sentence is interpreted as 'men'; II = 'men and women'; III = 'women'; IV = 'non-human'.

FIGURE 8.2. Two possibilities of semantic split in the third person plural

As a 'natural' semantic shift alternative (a) is much less motivated than alternative (b). It would be hard to conceive of contexts in which the meaning of **awar* 'human' would be split so as to align the female human with the non-human and inanimate categories. On the contrary, linguistic contexts where reference has to be made to combined groups of men and women would be more normal, which would lead to the semantic shift **awar* 'men' > **awar* 'men and women' > **awar* 'women'. It is, therefore, likely that Type II represented the proto-situation and South Dravidian, Telugu, and Kuṛux-Malto gradually expanded the distribution of **awar* to embrace all groups of human (mixed or exclusive, irrespective of sex) restricting **away* to non-human. This change is sociolinguistically and typologically motivated and is not a shared innovation.

9. Subrahmanyam (loc. cit.) says that the 'Central Dravidian' languages other

[8] Evidence for the use of the reflexes of PD **awar* in the sense of 'men and women' (mixed groups) in Gondi-Manḍa and Kolami-Parji languages is given in §12 below.

than Telugu (Gondi-Maṇḍa, Kolami-Parji subgroups) restricted the meaning of **awar* 'they (human)' to 'they (men)' and aligned female human with the neuter category on the analogy of the singular where we have **awanṯu* 'man': **atu* 'other' (female human, non-human animate, and inanimate). If he agrees that in the singular man vs. others is primary, then why is it not primary also in the plural? This gives us a more symmetrical proto-system. There is no such universal rule that the more irregular should be more archaic or proto.

10. Just as the innovation of **awaḷ* 'she' in South Dravidian has restricted the meaning of **atu* to 'non-human', no separate form for female human was innovated in the Gondi-Maṇḍa and Kolami-Parji subgroups to restrict the meaning of **awar* to 'men' only. In the absence of a third formal contrast being innovated, such meaning shift is possible only if the contexts require the extension or restriction of the meanings of either **awar* or **away*.

It can be shown that the semantic structure of PD **awar* and **away* as represented by Type II is more complex than that of the forms in Types I and III. Languages belonging to Types I and III have simplified the system as follows.[9]

	Type II			**Types I and III**	
(a)	**awar*	**away*	→	*awar*	**away*
	$\begin{bmatrix}+\text{human}\\ +\text{male}\end{bmatrix}$	$\left(\begin{bmatrix}+\text{hum}\\ -\text{male}\end{bmatrix} \begin{bmatrix}+\text{anim}\\ -\text{hum}\end{bmatrix} [-\text{anim}]\right)$		$[+\text{hum}]$	$\begin{bmatrix}\pm\text{anim}\\ -\text{hum}\end{bmatrix}$

	Types I and III			**Type II**	
(b)	**awar*	**away*	→	*awar*	**away*
	$[+\text{hum}]$	$\begin{bmatrix}\pm\text{anim}\\ -\text{hum}\end{bmatrix}$	→	$\begin{bmatrix}+\text{hum}\\ +\text{male}\end{bmatrix}$	$\left(\begin{bmatrix}+\text{hum}\\ -\text{male}\end{bmatrix} \begin{bmatrix}+\text{anim}\\ -\text{hum}\end{bmatrix} [-\text{anim}]\right)$

FIGURE 8.3. Semantic simplification of gender-number in innovative languages

[9] In semantic specification, I have eliminated the features [+pronoun, +plural] since they are common to all the forms in question.

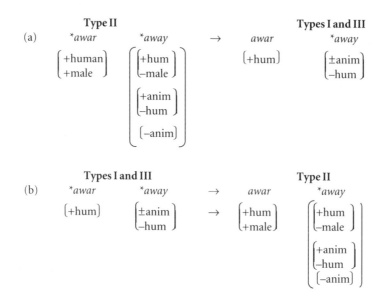

Alternative (a) represents a category simplification (progression from complex to simpler semantic and syntactic choices) which is therefore a change rather than retention. This is similar to what happened in Toda and Brahui in which the gender system was totally eliminated.

	Pre-Toda			**Toda**
**awan*	**awaḷ*	**atu*	→	*aθ*
[–pl, +hum, +male]	[–pl, +hum, –male]	[–pl, –hum]		[–pl]

FIGURE 8.4. Semantic simplification of gender-number in Toda

Therefore, in terms of semantic feature specification it could be said that the Proto-Dravidian gender-number system as represented by Type II is more complex than the derived systems (Types I and III).

11. Normally plural stems denote the meaning of the singular stems plus the notion of plurality where there are parallel formal contrasts between the singular and the plural. Thus, the singular forms **awanṯu* 'man', **atu* 'others', have corresponding plural forms **awar*, **away*. It is therefore normal to expect **awar* not to include any substantial change in the meaning of **awanṯu* except for the addition of plurality. This gives us a normal and symmetric pattern for Proto-Dravidian both in form and in meaning.

Singular	Plural
**awanṯu* 'he' (that man)	**awar* 'they' (men)
**atu* 'she, it' (the one other than man)	**away* 'they' (other than men)

This would then be a starting point from which Type I is produced by splitting the distribution of **atu* when **awaḷ* 'she' was innovated. A shift in the plural came about (Types II and III) with the extension of the meaning of **awar* 'men' to 'men and women' and 'women' as a consequence of changes in the social context of the use of language.

12. Gondi-Manḍa and Kolami-Parji subgroups use their finite verbs of the masculine plural both to represent 'they (men)' as well as 'they (men and women)'. When it is necessary to use a verb as the predicate of a co-ordinate subject denoting men and women, only the masculine plural form is used, e.g. Koṇḍa:

vār vātar 'they (men) came'; *avi vāte* 'they (women) came'; *avi vār vātar* 'they (women) and they (men) came'; but not **avi vār vāte.*

Here, the verb agreement is with the masculine plural which means that a finite verb like *vātar* could occur as predicate in two environments, viz. when 'men' and 'men/women' is the subject. Subrahmanyam (1971: 417–19) cites similar finite verbs from

Gondi, Parji, and Kolami. The Parji example *ōr verrar* 'they (brothers and their wives) came' is revealing since *ōr*, a demonstrative pronoun, refers to a mixed group of 'men and women'. So also in Koṇḍa there are a few contexts where both the demonstrative plural and the finite verb refer to mixed groups of 'men and women', e.g.

vāru maRar (8.447) 'they (brothers, sisters-in-law) stayed' (Krishnamurti 1969c: 138); *variŋ uṇḍeŋ kūktan* (8.459) 'he called them (men and women) to eat' (ibid. 138); *uṭar tiRar, ḍēvad sōta bastar, nālgi ayli koṛok, nālˀer moga koṛor* (8.465) '(They) ate and drank, came out into the verandah—the four women and the four men' (ibid. 139).

These examples provide the correct historical link in the semantic shift of the derivatives of **awar* from 'men' to 'men and women'. The innovation of South Dravidian, Telugu, and Kuṛux-Malto provides the last link in the semantic chain, i.e. using **awar* for the exclusive group of women which is absent in the Gondi-Manḍa and Kolami-Parji subgroups.

13. We have until now believed that Telugu-Gondi-Koṇḍa-Kui-Kuvi-Pengo-Manḍa and Kolami-Naiki-Parji-Gadaba-Ollari are the sub-branches of the Central Dravidian main branch. This was the position I had held even until 1965. However, my recent researches point to a closer affinity between the Telugu-Manḍa subgroup and South Dravidian (Kannaḍa-Tamil), which leaves the Kolami-Parji subgroup as the only branch of Central Dravidian.[10] Our preconceptions about subgrouping have led us to establish certain features as innovations binding the languages of the Central Dravidian group, and one of these is the gender system. Now we notice that the Telugu-Manḍa subgroup and the Kolami-Parji subgroup preserve the Proto-Dravidian gender system and since they are not related except at the level of Proto-Dravidian this is not a shared innovation but a retention.

It was the same aprioriness about Central Dravidian that led scholars to believe that **awan* 'he' was Proto-Dravidian as represented in South Dravidian whereas **awanṯu* whose reflexes occur in Telugu-Manḍa and Kolami-Parji is said to be an

[10] Substantial evidence for this revision comes from phonology and morphology which it is not possible to go into in any detail in this paper. PD **c-/s-* > **h-* > Ø- operates in SD as well as in the Te. -Manḍa group. PD **i* **u* are lowered to **e* **o* before **a* in both the groups e.g. **cup*: **cuwar* 'salt' : Go. *sovar, hovar, ovar*, Koṇḍa *sōru*, Kui *sāru*, Kuvi *hāru*, Kuvi *hāru*, Pe. *hōr*, Manḍa *jār* id. [*DED(S)* 2201]. This subgroup shares with SD **u* > **o-* before *-a* and *s-* > *h-* > Ø. Its own innovations include *ova* > *ō* > *ā*; *s-* > *j-*. In the formation of transitive stems from intransitives by changing stem-final (intr.) -NP > (tr.) (N) PP, the Konda-Kui-Kuvi-Pengo-Manḍa sub-group retains the PD trait as well as SD. The clinching evidence comes from a study of the personal pronouns. It was at the undivided stage of these two sub-branches (SD and Te.-Manḍa) that **ñān* was innovated as a doublet of **yān* 'I'. Only these languages represent an *ṉ*-form beside the derivatives of **yān*. As a consequence of this the distinction between the two 1st pers. plurals (incl.: excl.) became disturbed only in these languages. This revision represents my present thinking as opposed to my earlier postulation of **ñān* at the PD stage itself (Krishnamurti 1968: 194 ff.). I would now refer to two SD branches : SD I = Ta., Ma., To., Ko., Koḍ., and Ka.; SD II = Te., Go., Koṇḍa, Kui, Kuvi, Pe., and Manḍa; CD then consists of Pa., Kol., Nk., Oll. and Gad.

innovation (Emeneau 1955a: §10.15, Subrahmanyam 1969b: §5). However, I have always thought **awanṯu* 'he' to be the Proto-Dravidian form and **awan* an innovation in South Dravidian by the loss of final *ṯ* (*TVB* § 4.44, Burrow and Bhattacharya 1970: §68). The following arguments favour **awanṯu* as Proto-Dravidian.

(1) Loss of a final consonant is a more normal process than addition.

(2) The oblique stem in all languages reconstructs to **awan-* (Emeneau 1955a: §10.15).

	Nominative	Oblique
SD	**awan*	*awan-*
Te.-Manḍa	**awanṯu*	*awan-*
Kol.-Pa.	**awanṯu*	*awan-*

In South Dravidian either the final consonant is lost or the nominative might have been restructured on the analogy of the oblique as suggested by Burrow and Bhattacharya (1970: §68, 35–6). In Koṇḍa finite verbs agreeing with the masculine singular subject end in *-an*, e.g. *vānṟu kitan* 'he did'. But when this clause is followed by a vowel (interrogative *a* or co-ordinate *e*) the verb form has *ṟ* following *n*:

vānṟu kitanṟ-a? 'Did he do (it)?' *vānṟu kitanṟ-e soRan* 'He did (it) and went.'

These examples show that the underlying forms had **kitanṟ-*, of which the final *ṟ* was lost in the utterance-final position. A similar situation is noticed in Pengo where the third person demonstrative pronoun is *avan* in the nominative but in oblique when followed by a vowel it is *avanj-* (< *awanṯ-*) (Burrow and Bhattacharya 1970: §68).

(3) Within South Dravidian Kannaḍa has relic forms which attest to an original nominative *-*t* in plural formation of certain masculine nouns and pronouns: (sg.) *avan* 'he', (pl.) *avandir* 'they', *ivan* 'this man': *ivandir*, *magan* 'son': *magandir* 'sons'. The historical and etymological analysis of these forms should be *avand-ir*, *ivand-ir*, and *magand-ir* with *-ir* as human plural added to the stems derivable from **awanṯ*, **iwanṯ*, and **makanṯ*, although traditional grammarians have treated *-dir* as plural (Ramachandra Rao 1972: 54). Some of the Modern Kannaḍa dialects have generalized *-ndər* and *-ndru* as the plural suffix after kinship terms (Kushalappa Gowda 1968: 218).

The above arguments prove beyond doubt that **awanṯu* was Proto-Dravidian with the loss of *ṯ* in South Dravidian as an innovation.

Once it is known that Telugu-Manḍa and Kolami-Parji do not constitute the Central Dravidian branch, the foregoing account establishes that the gender-number system as shown in Gondi-Manḍa, and Kolami-Parji is a retention in them and not an innovation.

14. In languages which employ -V*r* as human suffix its use for denoting the exclusive group of women is rare, being the last link in the evolution of its meaning. For instance: *-ru* occurs in Old Telugu only with a small class of noun stems denoting male human. e.g. (sg.) *mallūḍu* 'wrestler': (pl.) *malluru*; (sg.) *bālūḍu*, (pl.)

bāluru 'boys'; it also occurs in indefinite demonstrative plural like *pekkuru* 'many persons'. There is a single case where *-ru* occurs with a stem denoting a female human exclusively, *āṇḍ-ru* 'women' derived from PD **āḷ*. This also shows that the innovation is not thorough-going in all the languages concerned. In this respect the Telugu case is not different from that of Gondi-Manḍa.

The reflexes of PD **-ka*, **-ḷ*, and **-kaḷ* (which were originally limited to the non-masculine nouns) extended to the masculine (human) nouns—threatening the replacement of -V*r*. As a consequence, most of the literary languages as well as some non-literary languages have confined the use of -V*r* to the polite singular in the third person. Thus Te. *wāru* 'he' (polite) as opposed to *wāḷḷu* (< *wāṇḍ-* 'he', *-ḷu* 'they' human). Tuḷu also uses *ārï* 'he' (polite) and *ākuḷu* 'they' (human). (For a similar usage in Tamil, Malayāḷam, and Kannaḍa see Shanmugam 1971: 128–9).

15. In synchronic as well as diachronic treatment of languages, the pronominal system is much more basic and primary than pronominal agreement in the finite verbs and predicative nouns. The choice of pronominal suffixes in finite verbs proceeds from the choice of the subject noun phrase of a sentence (which is replaceable by a pronoun), and not vice versa. Secondly the pronominal (gender-number-person) contrasts found in finite verbs or predicative nouns are either of the same number or fewer than pronouns that govern them as subjects of sentences and not vice versa. In Dravidian also there are languages which have more contrasts in subject pronouns than the pronominal suffixes in the finite verbs; on the contrary, there is no language which has more pronominal reference contrast in the finite verbs than the number of pronouns that govern them in the subject position.[11] Since 'agreement' between the subject and the verb in gender, number, and person is a redundant system, we notice the process of simplification affecting the verb system first. Consequently, there is no one-to-one relationship between the number of pronouns used as subjects and their corresponding reference in the finite verbs. This diachronic process is well attested by the Dravidian languages.

16. Out of the six possible contrasts in the demonstrative pronouns in Dravidian, only Pengo has all six; it has only five contrasts in pronominal reference in finite verbs.

TABLE 8.5a. *Pronominal suffixes in finite verbs in Pengo*

	Subject pronouns		Finite verbs	
	Singular	Plural	Singular	Plural
Pengo	1 2 3	4 5 6	1 [2 3]	4 5 6

Numbers are used as before to represent semantic ranges 1 = 'he' (man), 2 = 'she' (woman), 3 = 'it' (non-person), 4 = 'they' (men), 5 = 'they' (women), 6 = 'they' (non-persons); Ø = absence of a category (unexpected/uninherited); –(minus) = loss of a category; [ ] enclose the semantic range represented by a formal contrast. Formal contrasts corresponding to

[11] Shanmugam (1971: 10–11) gives a comparative chart of the number of contrasts between demonstrative pronouns and pronominal reference in finite verbs. He cites the case of Kasaba (?) finite verbs.

semantic ranges are underlined. Both the pronominal words as well as the corresponding pronominal suffixes in verbs are indicated by numbers, defined above. (Data drawn from Subrahmanyam 1971: 401–2; Shanmugam 1971: 1–29)

The rest of the languages show a maximum of five formal contrasts. Simplification of categories in the verbs seems more typologically motivated then genetically. Therefore we notice patterns of category neutralization within the languages of a subgroup, among the dialects of a language, between two stages of the same language, and even different types of finite verbs of the same language.

In South Dravidian I (Kannaḍa-Tamil subgroup) the innovation of the feminine singular is found both in the pronominal system and in the predicates. However, in the finite verbs, different languages simplify pronominal reference in different ways.

Standard Tamil (Old and Modern), Old Malayāḷam, Iruḷa, Standard Kannaḍa, and Tuḷu have all five contrasts both in the subjects and in the predicates:

TABLE 8.5b. *Pronominal suffixes in finite verbs in South Dravidian I (major languages)*

Subject pronouns		Finite verbs	
Singular	Plural	Singular	Plural
1 2 3	[4 0] 6	1 2 3	[4 0] 6

The Kāṇikkāra dialect of Tamil, Modern Malāyaḷam, Erukala (Tamil dial.), Koḍagu, and Toda have lost gender-number distinction in the verb system either by a total loss of personal suffixes (as in Modern Malayāḷam) or by extending the distribution of the non-human suffix (3) (as in Toda and Koḍagu). They nonetheless retain pronominal contrasts in the subject position to varying degrees.

TABLE 8.5c. *Pronominal suffixes in finite verbs in South Dravidian I (minor languages)*

	Subject pronouns		Finite verbs	
	Singular	Plural	Singular	Plural
Ta. (dial. Kāṇ)	1 2 3	[4 0] 6	– – –	– 0 –
Erukala	[– – 3]	[– 0 6]	– – –	– 0 –
Mdn. Ma.	1 2 3	[4 0] 6	– – –	– 0 –
To.	[– – 3]	[– 0 6]	[– – 3	– 0 –]
Koḍ.	1 2 3	[4 0] 3	[– – 3	– 0 –]

Kota which is more closely related to Toda than any other member of South

According to this there is only one neut. sg. form in demonstrative pronouns but both singular and plural reference in finite verbs. However he quotes only a four-way contrast in verbs on p. 8. Masc. sg. and fem. sg. are represented alike *ujjixā* 'he rules' 'she rules'. More information is needed before this can be taken as an exception.

Dravidian has four contrasts in pronouns as well as in the verbs with extension of the neuter (non-human) singular to the plural also.

TABLE 8.5d. *Pronominal suffixes in finite verbs in Kota*

Subject pronouns		Finite verbs	
Singular	Plural	Singular	Plural
1 2 3	[4 0] 3	1 2 3	[4 0] 3

In some of the modern Kannaḍa dialects also we notice category reduction. Gowda Kannaḍa has three subject pronouns 1, 3, and 6, but only number distinction in the plural. This means that the gender-distinction is totally lost in the finite verbs, but among the subject pronouns gender is lost in the plural but not in the singular. In the Southern Havyaka dialect of Kannaḍa, there are three parallel contrasts both in subjects and in finite verbs.

TABLE 8.5e. *Pronominal suffixes in finite verbs in Kannaḍa dialects*

	Subject pronouns		Finite verbs	
	Singular	Plural	Singular	Plural
Ka. (Gowd. dial.)	1 [–3]	[–0 6]	[– –3]	[– – 6]
(S. Hav.)	1 [–3]	[–0 6]	4 [–3]	[– 0, 6]

In South Dravidian II, i.e. Gondi, Koṇḍa, Kui, Kuvi, Pengo, and Manḍa (Telugu excepted) and in Central Dravidian (Kolami, Naiki, Parji, Ollari, and Gadaba) which represent the Proto-Dravidian system, there are four contrasts both in the subject pronominal system and in the finite verbs. There is not a single case of neutralization or overlap in agreement:

TABLE 8.5f. *Pronominal suffixes in South Dravidian II*

Subject pronouns		Finite verbs	
Singular	Plural	Singular	Plural
1 [0 3]	4 [0 6]	1 [0 3]	4 [0 6]

When it was a question of referring to mixed groups of 'men and women', 4 (men) semantically covered 5 also; otherwise 5 goes with 6.

Though Telugu and Kuṛux and Malto agree with the above in their subject pronominal system they part company in their pronominal reference system in verbs. Kuṛux and Malto have lost non-human plural reference in verbs by extending the semantic range of the singular form. This simplification occurred in the verbs in both Kuṛux and Malto, but it extended into the subject pronouns only in Malto.

TABLE 8.5g. *Pronominal suffixes in finite verbs in Telugu, Kuṛux-Malto*

	Subject pronouns		Finite verbs	
	Singular	Plural	Singular	Plural
Te.	1 [o 3]	[4 o] 6	1 [o 3]	[4 o] 6
Kuṛ.	1 [o 3]	[4 o] 6	1 [o 3]	[4 o] 3
Malto	1 [o 3]	[4 o] 3	1 [o 3]	[4 o] 3

Finally, we come to Brahui which has lost all semantic traces of gender both in the subject pronouns and in the verbs. Emeneau has argued that this is due to the influence of Baluchi or Persian (1965a: 59, 71).[12]

TABLE 8.5h. *Pronominal suffixes in finite verbs in Brahui*

Subject pronouns		Finite verbs	
Singular	Plural	Singular	Plural
[– o 3]	[– o 6]	[– o 3]	[– o 6]

17. From a study of the subject-verb concord of the pronominal system in Dravidian, we notice that the languages which have retained the Proto-Dravidian system of contrasts in the subject position have retained all the contrasts in the finite verbs also. It is only in the subgroups or languages which have innovated either a

[12] In Brahui the non-personal pronouns *ō-d* 'he, she, it' and *ō-fk* 'they' have totally replaced the masculine pronouns (*-d* < **at-*; *-f* < **aw-*; *-k* is nominal plural and *ō* demonstrative base). However, all the four Dravidian gender contrasts *in form* are available in the Brahui data although their meaning is neutralized. The indefinite pronouns have suffixes *-as, -a, -ar, -ad, -ar*—all in free variation, e. g. *ēkh-adar, ēkh-*ar, *ēkh-*a, *ēkh-*as 'that much'. The interrogative is *arā* 'which one?' (anim. or inanim.). The personal suffixes in finite verbs preserve the formal differences of Dravidian gender (Bray 1909: §§142–5, 149, 222–4) though the semantic distinction is lost.

	3rd person	
	Singular	Plural
Present indefinite	*e* / *ē*	*ir* / *ēr*
Present future	*ik*	*ira*
Probable future	*oe*	*or*
Past conditional	*as*	*ur*
Past	*ār*	*ur*
Imperfect	*āra*	*ura*
Pluperfect	*as* / *ur*	*as* / *ur*

These illustrate a semantic loss of gender distinction under the structural influence of Baluchi which led to free variation of forms. The fact that traces of PD formal contrasts of gender are still preserved as *-d, -f*: V*s*, V*r* (< **at-*, **aw-*: **anṯ*: **ar*) without analogical levelling in form shows that Brahui sustained such loss only in recent times (after it had separated from Kuṛ. and Malto). On formal grounds there is evidence that Brahui originally had a four-way contrast of gender-number as in the other two ND languages.

feminine category in the singular or a human category in the plural that the process of simplification is widely prevalent. The process affects verbs more than the subject pronouns, plural category more than the singular, number category more often than gender. If this is any evidence it only shows that, once the process of change and deviation from the proto-system begins it leads to a chain reaction of changes resulting in a simpler system than the ancestral type. We can take this as additional evidence for Type II representing Proto-Dravidian.

18. Summary. Three dominant types of gender-number distinction have been identified, of which the one represented by the languages of the subgroups South Dravidian II (Gondi, Koṇḍa, Kui, Kuvi, Pengo, and Manḍa) and Central Dravidian (Kolami, Naiki, Parji, Ollari, and Gadaba) is argued to be the retention of the Proto-Dravidian type with four contrasts in demonstrative pronouns and in pronominal reference in finite verbs. The reconstructed forms are:

Singular	Plural
**awanṯu* 'he'	**awar* 'they (men), (men and women)'
**atu* 'she, it'	**away* 'they (women and non-human)'

The other major types and subtypes have been shown as resulting from innovations, of which at least one is genetically traceable, i.e. **awaḷ* in South Dravidian I. The rest of the innovations constitute typologically motivated changes resulting in fewer contrasts and simpler systems.

In this paper I have not made any attempt to explain the various phonological changes or innovations which have affected the forms of different languages since no controversial issues are involved there.

19. From a synchronic and diachronic study of gender-number in Dravidian the following general observations can be made:

(1) Category neutralization in agreement takes place in verbs before it spreads into the subject pronominal system.

(2) Neutralization takes place either (a) by loss of pronominal suffixes or (b) by extending the distribution of one of the unmarked category markers (i.e. non-human or neuter **atu*).

(3) Reduction of gender-number categories tends to be more typologically than genetically motivated and therefore does not serve always as a strong basis for sub-grouping.

(4) The number of gender-number contrasts in governed positions is never larger than it is in the governing positions.

(5) Category simplification (neutralization) takes place more often in governed positions than in the governing positions.

(6) The male-human category does not overlap either formally or semantically with the other exclusive categories. The overlap is always found in non-male-human categories.

(7) In the process of simplification of categories, there are cases of suspension of

(a) both number and gender (Malayāḷam etc. in verbs); or (b) suspension of gender but retention of number (Kannaḍa dialects Gowḍa and South Havyaka in verbs; Toda and Brahui in pronouns) but no language has retained gender alone while totally suspending number.[13]

(8) In gender-number reconstruction the contrastive evidence of subject pronouns is more basic and primary than agreement features in verbs.

(9) In the process of simplification (neutralization) it is more often the unmarked categories (singular in number, non-masculine in gender) that extend their ranges of usage than the marked ones. Thus non-masculine **atu* (sg.) replaces **away* (pl.), non-masculine **atu* and **away* replace masculine *awanṯu* and *awar* respectively and not vice versa. (exception Hālakki dialect of Kannaḍa).

(10) Concord contrasts cannot be taken as the basis of reconstructing the gender-number system of Proto-Dravidian or any one of its subgroups.

Postscript

P 1. Since this paper was published in 1975, there has not been much discussion on the arguments advanced here proposing the masculine and non-masculine in singular and plural, attested by South-Central Dravidian and Central Dravidian languages, as the type representing Proto-Dravidian gender. It would be useful to quote the relevant passages from Emeneau (1955a: §10.17, 148–9):

> Type (1) is found in the Southern bloc and nowhere else. Type (2) is found in the area that, if not undivided, yet is nearly continuous; Go. and Kol.-Pa. are contiguous, and Kui is not too far removed. Type (3) has the greatest gap, that between Te. and Kuṛ. is wider than between Go. and Kui. As between types (2) and (3) there is a slight dip toward priority of (3). Perhaps the skewness of (3), as mentioned above, is to be added as makeweight.
>
> We end the discussion with a probability, though not certainty, that the Te. and Kuṛ.-Malt. type of gender is that of PD.

On p. 149 (fn. 5), Emeneau refers to Jules Bloch who says that type (2) is '"l'état le plus ancien"; he has hardly argued it'. The three types that Emeneau has set up correspond to the three major types that I have mentioned in Table 8.2. In my *TVB* (§4.30, 255–7), I set up two major types with two subtypes under Type I.

Type I: A two-way distinction in the singular as well as in the plural with two subtypes as follows:

(a) male person sg. : non-male person sg. (i.e. female person and non-person)
male person pl. : non-male person pl. (female persons, animals, and inanimate objects)

[13] This observation is supported by two grammatical universals formulated by Greenberg (1963: 95): '*Universal* 36. If a language has the category of gender, it always has the category of number.' '*Universal* 37. A language never has more gender categories in non-singular number than in the singular'.

(b) male person sg. : non-male person sg.
person pl. (male and female persons) : non-person pl. (animals and inanmates)

Type II: A three-way distinction in the singular and a two-way distinction in the plural, viz.
male person sg. : female sg. : non-person sg.
person pl. : non-person pl.

All Central and North Dravidian languages including Telugu belong to type I and the South Dravidian languages to type II.

Emeneau has also rejected the possibility of Type II representing Proto-Dravidian. The contention is between Type I (a) and I (b) which is obscured by my collapsing them into one type on the basis of a 'two-way distinction in the singular and plural'.

P 2. This paper marked a turning point in my rethinking on the subgrouping of the Dravidian languages. From then on I have found more and more evidence to separate the Telugu-Manḍa subgroup from Kolami-Parji and have found evidence for the former being a sub-branch of Proto-South Dravidian. I started calling the Tamil-Toda subgroup South-Dravidian I and the Telugu-Manḍa subgroup South-Dravidian II (also called South-Central Dravidian sometimes to distinguish it geographically). In view of this revision, what was considered an innovation in all the so-called Central Dravidian languages is now reinterpreted as a shared retention of the Proto-Dravidian system of gender-number distinction in two independent subgroups. Steever and Zvelebil have adopted this reclassification. Emeneau has not expressed an opinion on this, one way or the other. Subrahmanyam sticks to the earlier stand that Central Dravidian languages comprise both the Telugu-Manḍa and Kolami-Parji subgroups. Andronov also follows the same, although his reconstruction of Proto-Dravidian features in phonology and morphology is generally flawed in methodology.

What is to be understood is that the innovation in Telugu, on the one hand, and Kuṛux-Malto, on the other, is very subtle, viz. the last shift in the meaning chain i. 'men' > ii. 'men and women' > iii. 'women'. This is a very natural and non-unique semantic shift. All Dravidian languages have taken the first two steps including the members of South-Central Dravidian and Central Dravidian. South Dravidian has taken the final step also. Telugu being contiguous with the literary languages has added this final link in meaning-shift in the plural. A similar shift must have independently occurred in Kuṛux-Malto, perhaps under the influence of surrounding Indo-Aryan languages (e.g. Hindi *ve* 'they' [people or non-people]). In the Proto-Dravidian system, an exclusive group of 'men' was denoted by **awar* and an exclusive group of 'women' by **away*. While the above semantic shift is very natural and unmarked, the derivation of the type representing Central Dravidian and South-Central Dravidian from the assumed proto-state, involving a meaning shift from '*persons' > 'men' and '*non-persons' > 'women', is highly unnatural and marked.

P 3. Subrahmanyam (1976a) tried to counter my position without adding any new arguments to his 1969b article. He insists that South-Central Dravidian and Central Dravidian languages innovated the semantic shift as stated above on the analogy of the singular **atu* 'she, it'. But he fails to show a proportional analogy of the unlikely type: **awanṯu* *'he, she': **atu* 'she, it' :: **awar* 'men, women': **away* 'women, others [animate beings, and things]'. What analogical influence can the singular exert, since there is no semantic overlap in the singular in the case of 'female person' between the 'human' and 'non-human' categories? The semantic shift affecting the 'female person' in the plural has nothing to do with analogy. Also for Subrahmanyam, Telugu-Manḍa and Kolami-Parji still belong to Central Dravidian and the prevalent gender system is a shared innovation. He forgot that it was I that proposed Telugu to be a member of the erstwhile Central Dravidian in *TVB* (Ch. 4) and I have changed that position with adequate reasoning.

P 4. Andronov (1977a) discusses the Proto-Dravidian gender briefly. He apparently takes the South Dravidian system of three-way distinction in the singular and the two-way distinction in the plural as representing Proto-Dravidian in agreement with Burrow and Bhattacharya (1953: §12). Andronov's reconstructions look, by and large, as if they are based on Old Tamil and not on comparative method. Surprisingly he considers (fn. on p. 105) the personal and demonstrative pronouns lexical and only the verb-suffixes grammatical! The anaphoric use of pronouns, particularly the demonstrative pronouns in the third person, is an aspect of syntax of the Dravidian languages and is definitely grammatical. Another view of his which is not acceptable is his proposal that the exclusive–inclusive distinction in the first person plural is not Proto-Dravidian (101). He further says, 'the problem of the origin and development of gender can only be solved on the basis of determining the original type of the grammatical gender in the verb, as the lexico-grammatical gender in nouns is a mere reflection of the purely grammatical gender in verbs' (107). The agreement markers are secondary to subject nouns and pronouns (see §**19** of this article). He says that the non-masculine suffix *-*tu* (related to **atu*) first replaced *-*aḷ* (of **awaḷ*) in all subgroups, and then it was added to the masculine suffix *-*an* to produce *-*anṯu* (related to **awanṯu*) in South-Central, Central, and North Dravidian. The final morph in **awanṯu* is perhaps **-*tu* but there is no justification for considering it the neuter *-*tu* (with which it is homophonous) at the level of meaning in any of the Dravidian languages (109). We can safely ignore these ingenious explanations since they are not based on the comparative method.

P 5. Zvelebil (1990a: 19–20) repeats what Emeneau proposed in 1955 without any further discussion of all the issues involved. Nikita Gurov (1991), a Russian Indologist, endorses the reconstruction of the third person pronouns in the present article and creates a hierarchical list of semantic features to account for the pronominal system in Proto-Dravidian including the personal pronouns (Ch. 4). He distinguishes the masculine vs. non-masculine in terms of the feature [+/–Socially Active]. He argues that in primitive societies,

> there are functions (economic and religious), from which all females are debarred, and on the contrary, there are functions which must be performed by all members of human

collectively, or even exclusively by women. The traces of such practice still can be found in the social and religious life of the Dravidian tribes of Central and South India, e.g. the Raj-Gonds of Adilabad (see Fürer-Haimendorf 1979: 408–9, 440–42, 458–9, . . .) . . . It must be added that the final variant of Bh. Krishnamurti's model of the Proto-Dravidian system of gender and number implicitly suggests such an interpretation. (24, fn. 4)

P 6. An abridged version of this paper on gender and number in Proto-Dravidian occurs in a recent article of mine (Krishnamurti 1997a) published in French. An English version of this is expected to be published in the Festschrift for George Cardona (in press).

9

Sound Change: Shared Innovation vs. Diffusion

0. This paper is intended to be a contribution to the theory of lexical gradualness of sound change on which several important studies have appeared recently (Wang 1969, 1974, Chen and Wang 1975, Chen 1972, Chen und Hsieh 1971).[1] It further proposes, on quantitative grounds, criteria for distinguishing a shared innovation from the phenomena of diffusion and drift.

1. Consonant clusters and apical (alveolar and retroflex) consonants do not occur word-initially in Proto-Dravidian.This situation is reflected in the native element of all languages except those of the South-Central subgroup, viz. Telugu, Gondi, Koṇḍa, Kui, Kuvi, Pengo, and Manḍa. These languages are geographically continuous and are spoken in the contiguous states of Andhra Pradesh, Madhya Pradesh, and Orissa. The languages of this subgroup have many cognates which show word-initial apicals as well as consonant clusters with an apical as the second member. The phonological processes underlying these changes can be represented by the following generalized rules.

C_1 = [–syllabic]: all consonants admissible in word-initial position in Proto-South Central Dravidian, viz. /p t c k b d j g m n w/.

V_1 = [+V, –long]: any Proto-South Central Dravidian short vowel which occurs in the root syllable, viz. /i e a o u/.

$\bar{V}_1 = V_1$ which is [+long].

L = [+C, +apical, –nasal]: alveolar and retroflex non-nasal consonants which occur only non-initially in Proto-Dravidian, viz. /t̲ r l ṭ ẓ ḷ/; in Proto-South Central Dravidian /t̲/ → [r̲]/[d̲], the alveolar stop is realized either as a trill or as a voiced stop; so also the retroflex stop /ṭ/ is [ṛ]/[ḍ](=voiced flap or stop).[2]

[1] This is a condensed version of a paper representing part of the research I conducted during my fellowship year 1975–6 at the Center for Advanced Study in the Behavioral Sciences, Stanford. Grateful acknowledgement is due to the Center for facilitating my research during that year. I thank Douglas Danforth for writing a program for computerizing the comparative Dravidian data and his wife Catherine Danforth for typing the data into the computer. I have had many useful discussions with M. B. Emeneau, William S-Y Wang, Ilse Lehiste, and R. M. W. Dixon and benefited from their suggestions.

[2] I have found it efficient in Dravidian to distinguish alveolar and retroflex consonants as [+apical] and dentals and palatals as [–apical]. PD *t *t̲ *ṭ *c can therefore be treated as a natural class. For a detailed discussion of this problem, see Krishnamurti 1978b: fn. 4 [Ch. 11 of the present work, fn. 2].

$\breve{V}_2$ = [+V, –long, + {+high, +low}]: non-mid short vowels /i u a/ which are the only ones that occur in this position.

- = etymological boundary that separates the root from the formative suffix.

X = any consonant, obstruent or sonorant, or a nasal plus stop combination.

Rule 1' a. $V_1L\text{-}V_2X > L\bar{V}_1\text{-}X$
Conditions: $V_2 = V_1$, or V_2 is [+low] when V_1 is [–high, –low]

b. $V_1L\text{-}V_2X > LV_1\text{-}X(X)$
Conditions: V_2 is [+high] and $V_2 \neq V_1$; X is optionally geminated when it stands for a single consonant.

Note that a and b are complementary developments and are therefore treated as a single rule.

Rule 1". This is exactly the same as Rule 1' except that a C_1 precedes V_1. Rule 1' produces initial apicals and Rule 1" word-initial consonant clusters with apicals as second members. Rules 1' and 1" can be collapsed as

Rule 1 a. $(C_1)V_1L\text{-}V_2X > (C_1)L\bar{V}_1\text{-}X$
b. $(C_1)V_1L\text{-}V_2X > (C_1)LV_1\text{-}X(X)$

Both these rules occur in all the seven languages of this subgroup but not with the same degree of generality. These processes have been called metathesis with vowel contraction (contraction of V_1 and V_2 into $\bar{V}_1$) in a. but simple metathesis following loss of V_2 in b. (TVB §§1.121–59). There is also evidence to show that Rule 1' operated first and subsequently was generalized by involving syllables with initial consonants also. Supporting evidence for this observation comes from the following facts: All languages have Rule 1' as formulated above. But Rule 1" does not occur in that form in all the languages. For instance, in Telugu and Koṇḍa in Rule 1" L = *ṯ*, *r*, *ẓ* (only phonetic resonants and non-laterals) and C_1 excludes the anterior nasal /n/; in Telugu *ṯ*[ṟ] and *ẓ* merge with *r* in CL clusters; in Gondi Rule 1' occurs, but there are no instances of initial consonant clusters derived by Rule 1". However, in certain Gondi dialects, a few lexical items bear testimony to the operation of both Rules 1" and 2. It appears that Rule 1' is the older and Rule 1" a later extension of Rule 1' which led to the collapsing of these two as Rule 1 operating in its most generalized form in Kui-Kuvi-Pengo-Manḍa. Rule 1" is diachronically followed by Rule 2, with which it has a feeding relationship:

Rule 2. CLV-X > **a.** CV-X (Telugu)
b. LV-X (all other languages)

The consonant clusters formed by Rule 1" are simplified by this rule. In Telugu it is the apical which is lost whereas in the others the simplification is by loss of the first member. Rule 2 also establishes a common stage for six of the languages of this subgroup after Telugu had split off. The following examples illustrate Rules 1', 1", and 2.

1. PSCD **ūẓ*/**uẓ-u* 'to plough': OTe. *ḍukki* 'ploughing' (Mdn. Te. *dukki*); Go. *uṛ-*;

Koṇḍa *ṛū*; Kui *ṛū*; Kuvi *ṛū-*, *rū-*, *lū-*; Pe. *ṛū-* [*DED(S)*529]. Rule 1' applies in all but Gondi.

2. PSCD **carac*/**tarac* 'snake': OTe. *trācu*, Mdn. Te. *tācu* 'cobra'; Go. *tarāsh*, *taras*; Koṇḍa *saras*, (dial.) *srāsu*; Kui *srās*, *srācu*; Kuvi *rācu*, Pe. *rāc*; Manḍa *trehe* id. [*DED(S)* 1949]. Rule 1" applies in all but Go.; Rule 2 in Telugu, Kuvi, and Pengo.

2. The phenomenon explicated by Rule 1 is called 'apical displacement'. The *Dravidian Etymological Dictionary* (1961) and its supplements (1968, 1972) have been scanned for etymologies which require an apical consonant in the reconstructed root syllables of the type *(C)VL-. There are 644 entries involving 6,896 lexical items fulfilling this qualification in the South-Central subgroup.[3] Only cognates from six languages—Gondi, Koṇḍa, Kui, Kuvi, Pengo, and Manḍa—have been taken into account. The entire data were fed into a PDP 10 computer. In subsequent stages, 75 entries which do not have cognates in at least two of the six languages have been dropped. Also 241 entries which do not fulfil the structural conditions as stated in Rules 1 and 2 have been eliminated. Finally 328 entries qualified for consideration; out of this total, in 262 entries, some language or other shows the operation of one or more of the Rules 1', 1", and 2. The formal relations between the lexical input and output to Rules 1', 1", and 2 are stated as pattern correspondences between the proto-language and each of the six descendant languages as follows (> = corresponds to or becomes; *r* = retention; *c* = change):

	Proto		Derived	
ia.	*LV	>	LV	(*r* of *c* in Proto)
ib.	*CLV	>	CLV	(*r* of *c* in Proto)
iia.	*VL	>	VL	(*r*)
iib.	*VL	>	LV	(*c*)
iiia.	*CVL	>	CVL	(*r*)
iiib.	*CVL	>	CLV	(*c*)
iv.	{CLV / *CLV}	>	LV	(*c*)

Patterns ia and ib suggest that 'apical displacement' is reconstructable to the proto-stage itself, implying that none of the languages registers cognates of VL or CVL type. Patterns iia and iiia suggest absence of change and iib and iiib presence of

[3] Each entry has a minimum of one lexical item for each of the languages represented in the data, including Proto. For most of the entries, however, many variants are listed which fall broadly into two classes: (a) grammatical, i.e. plural stems in the case of nouns, past and non-past stems in the case of verbs; (b) dialectal, i.e. items from multiple sources identified by the initials of authors and/or from different places identified by abbreviations of place-names.

Unless otherwise stated, all lexical items for a given language under a given entry count as one item in the tables, since they all possess a single cognate root morph.

change (operation of Rules 1' and 1"). A subset of the output of ib and iiib is the input to iv which represents the simplification rule (i.e. Rule 2). The computer has scanned through the lexical items under each entry and language and printed a + symbol if the correspondence is present. The following tables show the results of computer-aided analysis of the data.

TABLE 9.1. *Number of entries showing apical displacement*

	Proto			Derived	Gondi	Koṇḍa	Kui	Kuvi	Pengo	Manḍa
ia.	*LV:	24	>	LV	10	5	14	18	11	8
ib.	*CLV:	28	>	CLV	0	0	19	11	15	10
iib.	*VL:	53	>	LV	16	18	30	23	14	9
iiib.	*CVL:	223	>	CLV	0	3	98	59	32	28
iv.	{CLV :(32) / *CLV :(28)}		>	LV	7	12	8	26	25	17
Total items with change:					33	38	169	137	97	72
Total entries (328) and cognates:					211	178	235	223	155	110
% of entries affected by change:					16%	21%	72%	61%	63%	65%

All languages show evidence of having shared Rule 1' as implied by patterns ia and iib. Although there is no evidence of CLV in contemporary dialects of Gondi, it is clear from pattern iv that Rule 1" must have operated on a few lexical items in this language which then became the input to Rule 2. This is a good case of an earlier sound change being stopped from spreading because a subsequent sound change demolishes the structures created by it (Wang 1969). This also shows that, in such a situation, the feeding order emerges as the marked one. Rule 1" creates word-initial consonant clusters whereas Rule 2 simplifies such clusters. Koṇḍa has the operation of Rule 1" in some regional dialects (Krishnamurti 1969c: 21); but all dialects show evidence of the operation of Rule 2 presupposing the earlier operation of Rule 1". Kui-Kuvi-Pengo-Manḍa show extensive application of Rules 1' and 1". Rule 2 is widely spread in Kuvi, Pengo, and Manḍa but less so in the other languages. Several entries have both changed and unchanged lexical items associated with the four patterns (see Table 9.2):

TABLE 9.2. *Number of entries with lexical free variation*

	Pattern	Gondi	Koṇḍa	Kui	Kuvi	Pengo	Manḍa
ii.	VL/LV	4	2	4	1	1	0
iii.	CVL/CLV	0	2	19	23	3	2
iv.	CVL/LV	6	3	2	0	1	0
	CVL/CLV/LV	—	—	—	1	—	—

These figures show that Rule 1', 1", and 2 are still operative in the individual languages although they are no longer mutually intelligible. Table 9.3 shows how many entries with apical displacement are shared by combinations of two to six languages and how many entries attest the operation of the rules in single languages.

TABLE 9.3. *Number of shared and unshared cognates with change*

Language combinations	ia.	ib.	iib.	iiib.	iv.	Total
six	0	0	1	0	2	**3**
five	3	0	2	1	1	**7**
four	2	1	9	12	5	**29**
three	7	5	7	8	5	**32**
two	10	16	12	36	12	**86**
one	0	6	13	70	16	**105**
Total entries	**22**	**28**	**44**	**127**	**41**	**262**

The number of entries shared is in inverse proportion to the number of languages sharing them. This kind of distribution of cognates-with-change indicates that the rules of apical displacement had a long history, dating from the undivided stage of these six languages into the modern period. Among the two-language combinations Kui-Kuvi share 41/86 entries (47.7%), and Pengo-Manḍa 14 entries (16.3%); among the four-language combinations Kui-Kuvi-Pengo-Manḍa share 18/29 entries (62%), and among the five-language combinations Koṇḍa-Kui-Kuvi-Pengo-Manḍa have three out of seven shared entries (41%). These figures attest to the continued life of Rules 1 and 2 through successive branchings of this subgroup as (Go. (Koṇḍa (Kui-Kuvi) (Pengo-Manḍa))). Judging from historical evidence of Telugu 'apical displacement' is found even in the pre-Telugu period dating to over two millennia ago. It appears that only a small segment of the lexicon was affected by Rule 1' followed by Rule 1" at a common stage of these languages; these are followed by Rule 2. Since the simplification rule differentiates Telugu from the rest of the languages of the subgroup it is reasonable to think that Rule 2b started at a common stage of these six languages in a restricted environment and was progressively generalized at subsequent points of branching.

For instance, *nL- > L- in all languages [*DED(S)* 3046, 3076, 3141, 3113]; $\begin{Bmatrix} \text{w} \\ \text{s} \end{Bmatrix}$ L- > L- in all but Kui [*S*861, *S*878, *S*472, 1986, 2160, 4459, 1986a];
C [–continuant] > Ø / # ___ C [+apical, + obstruent]
in Kuvi, Pengo, and Manḍa [943, 1090, 2667, 3897].

3. Both apical displacement and cluster simplification are found in all languages of this subgroup, but each language has followed a different lexical schedule for the implementation of the rules. However, the small number of cognates shared by all or most of the languages show that the rules go back to a common stage of development of the six languages. In terms of this study I propose that a shared innovation is a shared rule in shared cognates; lexical and areal diffusion results from a shared rule spreading through successive splits of a language subgroup into individual languages. This phenomenon is characteristically found when a given phonological rule (or process) is found in one or more related languages but not necessarily in cognates. A shared rule in unshared native elements is caused through the phenomenon of diffusion. The manner in which a sound change is lexically distributed therefore provides the basis for distinguishing a shared innovation from diffusion. There is, however, a chance of cognates being affected by a shared rule at a post-split stage. Since this is a rare coincidence, the percentage of such items is always bound to be very small. In traditional comparative method a shared innovation is always understood as a shared phonological process without reference to the lexicon that it affects. This has necessarily led to difficulties in separating shared innovation from areal and lexical diffusion.

4. Sapir's 'drift' (1949: 172) is a kind of pre-existing design in the 'pre-dialectic' stage of a language family producing structurally similar results even after centuries of split and separation of its members. Robin Lakoff (1972) calls this a 'meta-condition' on change which is outside the individual synchronic rules of grammar or even language universals. Examined in this light what happened in South-Central Dravidian seems to be part of an overall 'pre-dialectic' drift in the Dravidian family presumably to maintain (C)VC structure of the root syllable while favouring even distribution for apicals on a par with non-apicals and also the gradual elimination of the alveolar stop from the six-stop system. It is interesting to note that the members of the Southern subgroup, viz. Tamil, Malayāḷam, Iruḷa, Kannaḍa, and Tuḷu have a latent tendency or a restricted rule to drop word-initial short vowels preceding apical consonants, thereby permitting alveolar and retroflex consonants to occur word-initially. Again, this change has affected only some and not all of the lexical items which fulfil the structural conditions.

Discussion: Lehiste wondered if 'apical' would be the apropriate term for alveolars and retroflexes, since dentals could also be called apicals. Krishnamurti said that in Dravidian dentals are laminals and alveolars and retroflexes are apicals. Chomsky and Halle (1968: 312) point out that in a language in which both dentals and alveolars are distinctive, only one set is apical while the other is laminal. The feature [±apical] groups *t ṯ ṭ c* as a natural class in Dravidian which is supported by the sound pattern of the Dravidian languages. Panagl asked if verbs are among the first to be affected by sound change rather than the other stem classes. Krishnamurti said that the ten lexical items which show change in six/five languages are part of the basic vocabulary involving both verbs and nouns meaning 'two, month/moon, mango, open, enter, dig, sacrifice, pile up, burn, scatter'.

10

Areal and Lexical Diffusion of Sound Change: Evidence from Dravidian

o. 'Apical displacement' is the name given to a set of sound changes in the Dravidian family, whereby alveolar and retroflex consonants which occur as C_j in Proto-Dravidian stems of the type *$(C_i)VC_j$-V . . . shift their position to produce structures of the type *$(C_i)C_jV$- . . . in a well-defined subgroup of languages, viz. Telugu, Gondi, Koṇḍa, Kui, Kuvi, Pengo, and Manḍa. With the help of a computer analysis of relevant etymologies, it has been shown that apical displacement affected less than a dozen items at a common stage of the above subgroup. The rules gradually spread to the rest of the lexicon over the following two millennia, and the change is still in progress in some languages of this subgroup. It has been demonstrated that, of the items which fulfil the structural conditions of the change, 72% are covered by it in Kui; about 63% in Kuvi, Pengo, and Manḍa; but only about 20% in Gondi and Koṇḍa. A chronological layering of lexical items is established in terms of particular combinations of languages which share the cognates-with-change. Areal diffusion is characterized as the gradual lexical spread of an inherited rule—as opposed to the traditional notion of shared innovation, which is marked by shared rules in shared innovative cognates. A large class of exceptions to sound change at any given point of time can arise when the change has not yet affected the entire eligible lexicon.

There are at least seven interdependent variables associated with any sound change: (a) time, (b) space, (c) speakers and hearers, (d) replaced and replacing sounds or sound sequences, (e) structural (phonological and grammatical) conditions for replacement, (f) social factors governing replacement, and (g) lexical items that fulfil the structural and social conditions of replacement. Traditional historical linguistics has considered variables (a), (b), (d), and (e) as central to the study of sound change, while (c), (f), and (g) have been assumed as generally

This paper represents part of the research I conducted during my fellowship year 1975–6 at the Center for Advanced Study in the Behavioral Sciences, Stanford. Grateful acknowledgment is made to the Center for facilitating my research during that year. My thanks go to Douglas Danforth for writing a program for computerizing the comparative Dravidian data, and to Catherine Danforth for typing the data into the computer. I have had many useful discussions with M. B. Emeneau and William S-Y. Wang, and have benefited from their suggestions. An earlier version of this paper was presented at the Third International Phonology Meeting held in Vienna, September 1–4, 1976. Ilse Lehiste, R. M. W. Dixon, and Matthew Chen have read the article and made several useful comments, which I gratefully acknowledge.

invariant factors. Thus the 'regularity' hypothesis implied that, at a given time and place, all lexical items that fulfilled the structural conditions of a sound change would undergo such change in the speech of all speakers in all social settings. Analogy and borrowing were generally invoked to explain exceptions to sound change. Similarly, the 'gradualness' hypothesis has been studied in terms of the same four variables: temporal, spatial, phonetic, and structural (linguistic context).[1] However, recent studies in sociolinguistics, acoustic phonetics, and historical linguistics have sharpened our understanding of the twin concepts of regularity and gradualness of sound change along social, perceptual, and lexical dimensions.

Labov's formulation of variable rules (1972b), governed by such factors as age, attitude, and social status of speakers, not only captures minute transitions between the end-points of a sound change, but also accounts for the causation of certain linguistic changes. Another significant study is that of Chen and Wang 1975 (see also Chen and Hsieh 1971, Chen 1972, Wang 1969, 1974), showing the lexical gradualness of sound change in a computerized study of 68,000 lexical entries from twenty-one major Chinese dialects. They show how the homonyms of Middle Chinese have split into phonologically distinct pairs in different modern dialects, with the process gradually spreading from fewer lexical items to more (1975: 260–1). Although the notion of gradual lexical spread of a sound change is not altogether novel, as is acknowledged by Chen and Wang (275), it has not been tested with data from different language families. This paper provides quantitative evidence in support of the hypothesis, with data from the Dravidian languages illustrating a set of atypical sound changes in one of the subgroups. It also demonstrates how a shared innovation, as now conceived in the standard theory of historical linguistics, can be distinguished from the phenomenon of diffusion, if we observe the mode of areal and lexical spread of an inherited phonological rule. An attempt is also made to examine Sapir's notion of 'drift' (1921: 155) *vis-à-vis* the areal and lexical diffusion of a sound change in genetically related and geographically contiguous languages.

Apical Displacement in Dravidian

1.1. The twenty-three Dravidian languages spoken in the subcontinent of South Asia are classified into four subgroups of closely related languages: (1) Southern (SD I): Tamil, Malayāḷam, Iruḷa, Koḍagu, Toda, Kota, Kannaḍa, Tuḷu; (2) South-Central (SD II): Telugu, Gondi, Koṇḍa (Kūbi), Kui, Kuvi, Pengo, Manḍa; (3) Central: Kolami, Naiki, Parji, Ollari, Gadaba; and (4) Northern: Kuṛux, Malto, Brahui. Whether Subgroup 2 is genetically closer to Subgroup 1 or to Subgroup 3 is a disputed point, irrelevant to our immediate interest. We are here concerned with a set of sound changes which are considered a definite innovation shared by the languages of Subgroup 2.

[1] For a critical review of current and traditional views on sound change, see Chen (1972: 457–68).

Consonant clusters and apical (alveolar and retroflex) consonants do not occur word-initially in Proto-Dravidian.[2] This situation is reflected in the native element of all the languages except those of Subgroup 2. The languages of this subgroup share many cognates with word-initial apicals, as well as consonant clusters with apicals as second members. Thus, corresponding to root syllables of the types VL and CVL (where L = apical) in the other languages, these languages have LV or CLV in a large number of items. A subsequent sound change has simplified CL clusters to C or L under statable conditions. The actual phonological processes involved in these shifts are not the subject-matter of this paper, nor are the phonetic and perceptual bases of these processes, since they are not relevant to the pattern of areal and lexical spread.

Two proposals have so far been made to explain the phenomenon of sound change:[3] (a) shift of prominence or stress from the root vowel to the following non-root vowel, resulting in the eventual loss of the weakened root vowel, i.e. *(C)VL-V- > (C)ØL-V-; (b) metathesis of VL followed by contraction of root and non-root vowels, i.e. *(C)VL-V- > *(C)LV-V- > (C)LV̄-, shifting the etymological boundary in both instances to the post-vocalic position. Without going into which of these proposals might be correct, I would designate the phenomenon by the neutral name 'apical displacement', in terms of what happened rather than how it came about.

1.2. The Proto-Dravidian apical consonants involved in the displacement are *ṯ [r̠/d] (alveolar stop), *ṭ [ḍ] (retroflex stop), *l *ḷ (alveolar and retroflex laterals), *r (alveolar flap), *ẓ (retroflex fricative), and occasionally *ṇ (retroflex nasal).[4] Not all

---

[2] I propose the following distinctive-feature matrix to define the sixteen PD consonantal phonemes:

	p	t	ṯ	ṭ	c	k	m	n	ṇ	ñ	l	ḷ	r	ẓ	w	y
syllabic	−	−	−	−	−	−	−	−	−	−	−	−	−	−	−	−
consonantal	+	+	+	+	+	+	+	+	+	+	+	+	+	+	−	−
sonorant	−	−	−	−	−	−	+	+	+	+	+	+	+	+	+	+
continuant	−	−	−	−	−	−	−	−	−	−	+	+	+	+	+	+
anterior	+	+	+	−	−	−	+	+	−	−	+	−	+	−	+	−
coronal	−	+	+	+	+	−	−	+	+	+	+	+	+	+		
apical		−	+	+	−			−	+	−	+	+	+	+		
nasal							+	+	+	+	−	−	−	−		
lateral											+	+	−	−		

The feature [± apical] subclassifies coronals, and sets off alveolars and retroflexes as a subclass against dentals and palatals. In terms of the above matrix, most of the phonological processes in Dravidian can be described with great economy and simplicity. The unconditioned merger of *ṯ with the reflexes of *t, *ṭ, and *c can be shown to involve change in one or two features; similarly, unconditioned mergers (ḷ > l, ṇ > n, ẓ > ḷ/r), found in many Dravidian languages, can be described as involving a change in one or two features each.

[3] See here the Appendix I below.

[4] Nasals are not generally involved in apical displacement. There is only one case involving *n in Old Telugu: *an-* 'say', *an-aN* 'to say' (inf.); Kuvi shows four instances of initial clusters with ṇ (<*ṇ) as the second member (see *DED(S)* S785, 3643, 3994, 3999). In certain rare and sporadic items, consonants other than apicals are involved in the shift of position, viz. **umuḷ* > *mūḷ* 'to urinate' (Koṇḍa, Kui, Kuvi, Pengo, Manḍa), [*DEDS* 553]; **magaḷ* > **mgāḷ* > *gāḷ* 'daughter' (Koṇḍa, Pengo, Manḍa), [*DEDS* 3768].

There are arguments in favour of considering *n as a dental word-initially and as an alveolar non-initially (Krishnamurti 1961: 128, fn. 53; Shanmugam 1972: 83). For one thing, it explains why *n, which

the seven languages of the subgroup implement the displacement rules in the same manner and to the same extent, and not all lexical items which fulfil the structural conditions are covered by the sound changes in any language. Telugu has word-initial *l* (< **l*, **ḷ*), *r* (<**r*, **ṯ*), and *ḍ* (<**ṭ*, **ẓ*), but only *r* (<**r*, **ṯ*, **ẓ*) as second member in initial consonant clusters; a dental nasal is never involved as the first member of a cluster, and a lateral or a retroflex stop (**ṭ*) is never the second member. Gondi has word-initial *r* (< **r*, **ṯ*), *l* (< **l*, **ḷ*), and *ḍ* (< **ṭ*, **ẓ*); it has no consonant clusters, but there are a few cases of LV, implying an earlier stage *CLV. Koṇḍa has word-initial *ḍ r l ṛ ṟ*, traceable to PD **ṭ *r *l/ḷ *ẓ/ḷ *ṯ* respectively; it has consonant clusters only dialectally, involving *r ṛ ṟ* (< **r *ẓ/ḷ *ṯ*) as second members. Kui, Kuvi, Pengo, and Manḍa have word-initial *ḍ r ṛ l*; in addition, *r ṛ* occur as second members of clusters in all these languages. Kui and Kuvi also have *l* (< **l*, **ḷ*) as the second member. In all these languages, *ṛ* is from **ẓ* or **ḷ*, and word-initial **ṯ* develops to *j*. This is only a very general statement of correspondences in relevant environments.

Table 10.1 presents the reflexes of *L in the languages of Subgroup 2 in the two relevant environments: (1) #___ (word-initial), and (2) #C___V . . . (following a word-initial consonant). Dialectal and diachronic variants are enclosed in curly braces; the phonetic representations of the Proto-Dravidian phonemes are enclosed in square brackets.

TABLE 10.1. *Correspondences of Proto-Dravidian apicals in South-Central Dravidian*

PD		Telugu	Gondi	Koṇḍa	Kui	Kuvi	Pengo	Manḍa
*ṯ [r/ḏ]	(1)	{ṟ, r}	r	ṟ	{j, d}	{j, d}	j	{j, d}
	(2)	r	—	ṟ	r	r	r	{r, j}
*ṭ [ḍ]	(1)	{ḍ, d}	{ḍ, d}	ḍ	ḍ	{ḍ, d}	ḍ	ḍ
	(2)	—	—	—	{ṛ, r}	{ṇ/{g, m}___, r/C___}	ṛ	—
*r	(1)	r	{r, ṛ}	r	r	r	r	r
	(2)	r	—	r	r	{r, ṛ}	r	r

can occur initially, is not a member of the class of consonants involved in displacement. Phonetically, we may say that only non-initial liquids and resonants have participated in the changes; **ṯ* and **ṛ* are phonetically trill [ṟ] and flap [ṛ], respectively.

PD		Telugu	Gondi	Koṇḍa	Kui	Kuvi	Pengo	Maṇḍa
*ẓ	(1)	ḍ	{ḍ, r}	ṛ	ṛ	{ṛ, r, l}	ṛ	ṛ
	(2)	r	—	ṛ	ṛ	{ṛ, r, l}	r	r
*l	(1)	l	l	l	l	l	l	l
	(2)	—	—	—	{r/m___, l}	{r/t___, l}	l	l
*ḷ	(1)	l	{r, l}	{ṛ, l}	l	l	ṛ	ṛ
	(2)	—	—	—	l	{ṛ, r, l}	ṛ	ṛ
*ṇ	(1)	—	—	—	—	—	—	—
	(2)	—	—	—	—	{ṛ, ṇ} /m___	—	—

The changes underlying apical displacement go back at least two millennia, judging from the inscriptional and literary evidence in Telugu. It will be shown below that the changes are still in progress in some of the languages and dialects of this subgroup. The following etymological groups illustrate the sound changes, and the number preceding each group refers to the entry in *DED(S)*:

592. PD **ūẓ/*uẓ-u* 'to plough': OTe. *ḍukki* 'ploughing' (Mdn. Te. *dukki*); Go. *uṛ-*; Koṇḍa *ṛū-*; Kui *ṛū*; Kuvi *ṛū-*, *rū-*, *lū-*; Pe. *ṛū-*.

1949. PD **carac/*tarac* 'snake': OTe. *trācu*, Mdn. Te. *tācu* 'cobra'; Go. *tarāsh*, *taras*; Koṇḍa *saras*, (dial.) *srāsu*; Kui *srās*, *srācu*; Kuvi *rācu*; Pe. *rāc*; Maṇḍa *trehe*.

I have treated the rules of apical displacement earlier (*TVB* 51–68) in so far as Telugu is concerned. At that time data from Pengo and Maṇḍa were not available. The publication of *DED*(*S*) now makes it possible to look at the problem afresh, and also to estimate the lexical spread of apical displacement in this subgroup. In the quantitative study below, Telugu is excluded, since it is unequally placed in relation to the other languages of the subgroup because of its long recorded history and wealth of vocabulary.

The Quantitative Study

2.1. For the other six languages and their dialects of Subgroup 2 (viz. Gondi, Koṇḍa, Kui, Kuvi, Pengo, and Manḍa), a total of 644 entries,[5] involving 6,896 lexical items drawn from *DED*(*S*), have been fed into a PDP 10 computer. Entries have been selected so as to fulfil the following conditions:

(1) Each group of cognates under an entry requires an apical consonant (labelled L) as C_2 in the reconstructed root syllable of the form $*(C_1)\breve{\bar{V}}C_2$, i.e. *VL, *V̄L, *CVL, *CV̄L. A reconstructed apical consonant may occur singly or in combination with other segments as follows (phonetic representations are given in brackets; see fn. 4 above regarding the status of the nasals):

> Alveolar: **t̠* [d̠/r̠], **n*, **l*, **r*; **nt̠* [nd̠/nr̠], **t̠t̠* [t̠t̠/R] ([R] = voiceless trill)
> Retroflex: **ṭ* [ḍ], **ṇ*, **ḷ*, **ẓ*; **ṇṭ* [ṇḍ], **t̠ t̠*[ṭṭ/ṭ]

(2) Each entry should have cognates in at least two of the six languages; consequently, 75 entries which occur in only one language have been dropped from initial analysis. They are distributed as follows: Gondi 46, Koṇḍa 4, Kui 21, Kuvi 3, Pengo 1. Several of these forms also attest apical displacement, and they have been utilized as a separate group in this study (see Table 10.7, below). The remaining 569 entries (6,459 lexical items) have cognates in two or more languages of the subgroup.

Reconstructions for the entries have also been computerized, as another language designated 'Proto'. These reconstructions are of the four types *VL, *CVL, *LV, *CLV; the last two represent entries which provide no clues as to the Proto-Dravidian types *VL, *CVL, but are listed under apicals and consonant clusters in the reconstruction-based alphabetization adopted by *DED(S)*. All reconstructions, therefore, do not belong to a common stage of Gondi-Koṇḍa-Kui-Kuvi-Pengo-Manḍa. The time depth of a reconstruction is naturally correlated with the number of languages that have reliable cognates under a given entry. Thus 3113 **nelanj* 'moon, month', reconstructed for all six languages, reflects a greater time depth than *S*819 **mṛāṇ* 'a kind of rat', based on cognates found only in Pengo and

[5] Each entry has a minimum of one lexical item for each of the languages represented in the data, including the reconstructed proto-language. For most of the entries, however, many variants are listed, which fall broadly into two classes: (a) grammatical, i.e. plural stems in the case of nouns, past and non-past stems in the case of verbs; (b) dialectal, i.e. items from multiple sources, identified by the initials of the authors, and/or from different places, identified by abbreviations of place-names. The true picture of dialect classification, either regionally or socially, is not known; nor is it implied by the sigilla of *DED(S)*. There is approximately 5% duplication of lexical items in the data, caused by different sources citing the same form. One of the aims of computerizing the data is to make some observations on the dialect distribution of the six languages studied. For this reason, repeated items keyed to different authors and/or localities have not been dropped from the data. Some of the grammatical or regional variants will show the change in question, while others will not.

Unless otherwise stated, all lexical items for a given language, under a given entry, count as one item in the tables, since they all possess a single cognate morph.

Manḍa.[6] 'Proto', therefore, refers to different stages of development of these six languages of Subgroup 2.

2.2. When compared with the syllable structure of the Proto forms, apical displacement in the six derived languages involves the following relations:

(1) If the root syllable in Proto is of the form $*V_1L\text{-}V_2$, it may be represented as LV_1 or LV_2 in the derived language. Alternatively, the proto-syllable remains unchanged.

(2) If the proto-syllable is $*CV_1L\text{-}V_2$, it may be represented as $CL\breve{\bar{V}}_1$ or $CL\breve{\bar{V}}_2$ in the derived language, or it may remain unchanged.

(3) Under certain conditions, CLV_1/CLV_2 are retained in some languages, whereas others simplify them to LV_1/LV_2 by dropping C. ($*V_1L$ and $*CV_1L$ are invariably root syllables; V_2 is part of the stem formative.)

(4) Comparative data may only allow us to reconstruct $*LV_1/*LV_2$ or $*CLV_1/*CLV_2$, without providing any clue as to the form of the root syllable before apical displacement took place. These must be considered retentions of a change that took place at a common stage of the languages concerned.

In the above patterns, the quality of the root vowel (V_1) is generally reconstructable for each etymological group; but that of the formative vowel (V_2) is uncertain, since it was either lost or modified in most of the Dravidian languages. Only in some cases is it possible to reconstruct V_2 on the basis of the evidence in the literary languages.[7] Consequently, in the patterns formulated for computer identification, the position of L in relation to a vowel is indicated, but the etymological status of the vowel is not specified as V_1 or V_2. Thus a formula of the type $*VL > LV$ can refer to either $*V_1L > LV_1$ (metathesis) or $V_1L\text{-}(V_2) > LV_2$ (loss of the root vowel); similarly, $*CVL > CLV$ may represent either $*CV_1L > CLV_1$ (metathesis) or $*CV_1L\text{-}V_2 > CLV_2$ (loss of the root vowel).

The number of reconstructions and the number of cognates available in each of the languages are as follows (all dialectal and grammatical variants given in *DED(S)* for a given language under an entry count as one cognate; see fn. 5 above):

Proto	Gondi	Koṇḍa	Kui	Kuvi	Pengo	Manḍa
569	376	331	373	380	288	197

The differences in these figures are caused in varying degrees by absence of cognates and by lack of exhaustive coverage of the vocabulary in the sources available to the authors of *DED(S)*—and, to a negligible extent, by non-detection of cognates. The

[6] Pengo and Manḍa *ṛ* is from either **ẓ* or **ḷ* in the environment #C___. In the absence of decisive cognates from any other language, the reconstruction has *ṛ* only in **mṛāṇ*, representing a common stage of Pengo-Manḍa.

[7] There are only a few instances where one can be certain that the lengthened vowel is V_2 and not V_1, e.g. 3901 **maṯinṯu* [maṟinṟu] 'son': Go. *marrī*; Koṇḍa *maṟin(ṟ)*-; Kui *mṟīenju* (sg.), *mṟīka* (pl.); Kuvi (F) *miresi, mṟīesi*; Pe. *mazi*; Manḍa *tā-mji* 'his son' (*-mji* < **-mṟi* < **maṟi*). Kui-Kuvi-Manḍa forms look to **mṟī* from **maṟi*, by loss of the root vowel. Kuvi *miresi* is disturbing, since it suggests **miṟi* < **maṟi* (see Appendix I).

Gondi vocabulary is rather extensive (Burrow and Bhattacharya 1960), covering many of the regional dialects and more than a score of sources; the vocabulary for Maṇḍa is scanty, and the number of cognates would have been greater if the language had been more thoroughly surveyed.

2.3. Answers to the following questions are sought in the computer analysis:

2.3.1. What is the size of the lexicon that fulfils the structural conditions for apical displacement in each of the six languages studied?

2.3.2. How many and which items are affected in each language by the sound changes that produce apical displacement? The four relationships listed in §**2.2** have been structured into the following formulas, so that the computer will identify them and print out a '+' symbol if the pattern is present for a given entry (> = becomes; *r* = retention; *c* = change):

(1) (a) *LV > LV (*r* of *c* at the proto-stage)
    (b) *CLV > CLV (*r* of *c* at the proto-stage)
(2) (a) *VL > VL (*r*)
    (b) *VL > LV (*c*)
(3) (a) *CVL > CVL (*r*)
    (b) *CVL > CLV (*c*)
(4) $\left\{\begin{array}{l} \text{CLV} \\ \text{*CLV} \end{array}\right\}$ > LV (*c*; simplification of CLV either attested or reconstructed)

Patterns 1(a–b) suggest that apical displacement is reconstructable to the proto-stage itself; Pattern 4 suggests that CVL became *CLV followed by loss of C in some of the languages, although *CLV may not be attested in any of them.

2.3.3. How many and which items attesting the change are shared by two or more languages? How many items register the change or retention in only one language?

The hypothesis is that a change is shared by two or more languages to the extent that cognates affected by the change are also shared. If two or more languages show the innovation in a large number of items, of which only a small percentage is shared, then it is assumed that the inherited change has spread in each language to the rest of the lexicon, by diffusion, after its separation from the sister languages.

2.3.4. In terms of the number of shared cognates-with-change, how closely are the languages related to each other?

2.4. After a preliminary analysis of all the 569 entries in terms of the patterns set forth in §**2.3.2** above, the reconstructions of entries that failed to generate change in any of the six languages were examined, to see if there are any structural conditions that disqualify them from apical displacement. It emerged that items with the following properties are not involved in change in any of the six languages:

(1) Stems which are also free forms traceable to Proto *(C)VL or *(C)V̄L without any derivative suffix following them:

1238. **kāl* 'leg': Go. *kāl*, Koṇḍa *kāl*, Kui *kāḍu*, Kuvi *kāl*, Pe. *kāl*, Maṇḍa *kāl*.

3288. **pal* 'tooth': Go. *pal* (pl. *palk*), Koṇḍa *pal* (pl. *palku*), Kui *paḍu* (pl. *paṭka*), Kuvi *pallu* (pl. *palka*), Maṇḍa *pal*.

(2) All stems with an alveolar nasal (**n*) as L, regardless of what follows; also stems with root-final **ṇ* followed by a homorganic stop (see fn. 4 above):

3326. **panḏi* 'pig': Go. *paddi*, Koṇḍa *panṟi*, Kui *paji*, Kuvi *pajji*, Pe.-Maṇḍa *panji*.

2670. **tin* (past **tinḏ-*, **tiṯṯ-*) 'to eat': Go. *tind* (*titt-*), Koṇḍa *tin* (*tiR-*), Kui *tin* (*tis-*), Kuvi *tinj* (*tic-*), Pe. *tin-* (*tic-*), Maṇḍa *tin-* (*tic-*).

(3) All stems traceable to *(C)V̄̆L, where L is an alveolar or retroflex stop, followed by a voiceless stop:

3012. **nāḏ* (pl. **nāṯk-*, obl. **nāṯṯ-*) 'village': Go. *nār* (pl. *nāhk*), Koṇḍa *nāṟu* (obl. *nāṭ-*), Kui *nāju* (pl. *nāska*), Pe. *nāz* (*nāsku*), Maṇḍa *nāy* (obl. *nāṭ*).

3136. **noḍ*/**noḏ* 'to wash': Go. *norr*, Koṇḍa *noṟ-* (*noRt-*), Kui *nog-* (*nogd-*), Kuvi *nor-*, Pe. *noz* (*nost-*), Maṇḍa *nuy*.

(4) All stems traceable to forms with a geminate following the root vowel, i.e. *(C)V̄̆LL, regardless of the inflectional or derivational origin of the LL:

961. **kaṭṭ-* 'bank of river': Go. *kaṭṭā* 'dam'; *kaṭ* 'bank of a river'; Koṇḍa *gatụ* (pl. *gaṭku*) 'bund, bank'; Kui *kāṭ-* 'fasten, fix'; Kuvi (Sunkara meṭṭa dial.) *gaṭṭu* (pl. *gaṭku*) 'bund of field'; Pe. *kaṭa*.

3566. **puṭṭi* 'anthill': Go. *putti*, Koṇḍa *puRi*, Kui *pusi*, Kuvi *pucci*, Pe. *puci*.

2670a. **tin* (**tiṯṯ-*): see above.

3115. **nelli* 'emblic myrobalan (*Phylanthus emblica*)': Go. *nelli*, *nalli*; Koṇḍa *neli*; Kui *neli*, *neḍi*; Kuvi *lelli*.

(5) Nominal stems (free forms) of the type (C)V̄L- followed by a short vowel:

S278. **kūli* 'paddy': Koṇḍa *kūli*, Kui *kūḍi*, Pe. *kūli*, Maṇḍa *kūli*.

S385. **sāri* 'bread, cake': Go. *sāri*, *sāṟi*, *hāri*, *āri*; Kuvi *hēra*, *hē'ra*; Pe. *hāri*; Maṇḍa *hāri*.

There are in all 241 entries that fall under the above five types, and are thus disqualified for analysis. Table 10.2 shows the number of entries which fulfil the structural conditions for apical displacement, after we eliminate single-language entries and the disqualified ones.

TABLE 10.2. *Number of proto-forms with cognates*

	Proto	Gondi	Koṇḍa	Kui	Kuvi	Pengo	Manḍa
Total entries	644	422	335	394	384	289	197
Single language entries	−75	−46	−4	−21	−3	−1	−0
	569	376	331	373	381	288	197
Not qualified (see §**2.4**)	−241	−165	−153	−138	−158	−133	−87
Qualified	**328**	**211**	**178**	**235**	**223**	**155**	**110**

It has been noted that the entries of the last row in Table 10.2 require reconstructions of the following two types: (a) *(C)VL- followed by a vowel or an extended suffix, -VC, -VCC; (b) *(C)V̄L- followed by a stop suffix (here L is not a voiceless alveolar or retroflex stop). The suffixes following the root syllable are mostly derivational, but occasionally inflectional (cf. Appendix I below).

Table 10.3 gives the number of items that have undergone change in terms of the formulas set up in §**2.3.2**, and the percentage of the lexicon subject to this change.

TABLE 10.3. *Number of entries showing apical displacement*

	Proto	CHANGE	Gondi	Koṇḍa	Kui	Kuvi	Pengo	Manḍa
(1a)	*LV : 24	*LV > LV	10	5	14	18	11	8
(1b)	*CLV : 28	*CLV > CLV	0	0	19	11	15	10
(2)	*VL : 53	*VL > LV	16	18	30	23	14	9
(3)	*CVL : 223	*CVL > CLV	0	3	98	59	32	28
(4)	CLV : (32) *CLV : (28)	{CLV, *CLV} > LV	7	12	8	26	25	17
			33	38	169	137	97	72
Total no. of qualified entries	328		**211**	**178**	**235**	**223**	**155**	**110**
% of entries affected by change			16%	21%	72%	61%	63%	65%
% of entries not affected by change			84%	79%	28%	39%	37%	35%

Note that Pattern 4 represents subsets of 1b and 3, because the rules implied by the latter patterns are in a feeding relation to the rule implied by Pattern 4. By the same token, the simplification rule implied by Pattern 4 must be chronologically later than the rule producing clusters implied by Patterns 1b and 3. The figures in Tables 10.2 and 10.3 are plotted in Fig. 10.1.

Under Patterns 2, 3, and 4 shown in Table 10.3, there are several entries registering both the presence and absence of change. Most of these represent dialect variation within each language. The number of entries involved in such variation (a subset of the figures given in Table 10.3) is shown in Table 10.4.

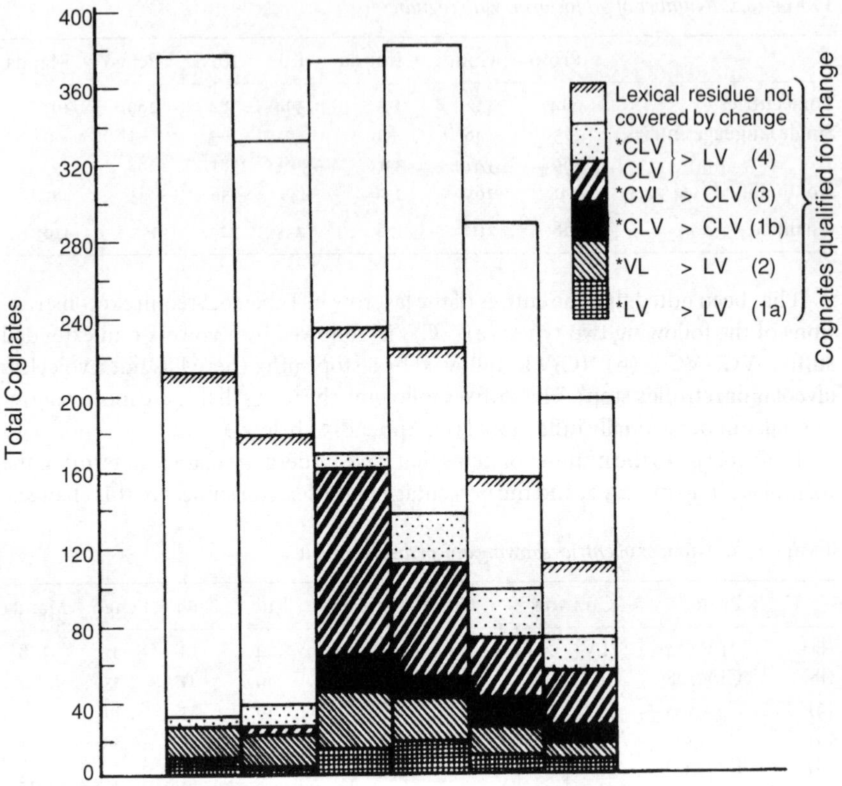

FIGURE 10.1. Lexical distribution of apical displacement

TABLE 10.4. *Number of items with lexical free variation*

	PATTERN	Gondi	Koṇḍa	Kui	Kuvi	Pengo	Manḍa
(2)	VL/LV	4	2	4	1	1	0
(3)	CVL/CLV	0	2	19	23	3	2
(4)	CVL/LV	6	3	2	0	1	0
	CVL/CLV/LV	—	—	—	1	—	—

2.5. From a study of the tables and Fig. 10.1, the following observations can be made:

(1) The languages most affected by the rules of apical displacement are Kui-Kuvi-Pengo-Manḍa; the ones least affected are Gondi and Koṇḍa. Nearly three-fourths of the Kui lexicon is affected by change, as opposed to two-thirds of Kuvi-Pengo-Manḍa, and less than one-fourth of Gondi and Koṇḍa.

(2) All the languages show evidence of the rule implied by the pattern *VL > LV. None of the modern Gondi dialects shows CLV in any lexical item, and in Koṇḍa CLV is found only dialectally. However, both Gondi and Koṇḍa had a stage of *CVL > CLV, as evidenced by *CVL/CLV > LV in a small segment of the lexicon. It appears that the simplification rule, which undoes the effects of the rule generating initial clusters, must have prevented the lexical spread of the cluster-forming rule in Gondi and Koṇḍa dialects.

(3) The lexical space covered by Pattern 4 has historically passed through the stage implied by Patterns 1b and 3. This means that all the languages have implemented all the rules, but with different degrees of lexical spread.

(4) The pattern of free variation (presumably representing subdialectal variation) suggests that the rules are still operative in the individual languages, although the languages are no longer mutually intelligible.

2.6. The next step is to see to what extent apical displacement is shared by two or more languages under each pattern, and to what extent it is operative in each language separately. Table 10.5 shows the number of items-with-change occurring in one to six languages.

TABLE 10.5. *Number of shared and unshared cognates-with-change*

Language combinations	(1a) *LV > LV	(1b) *CLV > CLV	(2) *VL > LV	(3) *CVL > CLV	(4) CLV/*CLV > LV	TOTAL
six	0	0	1	0	2	3
five	3	0	2	1	1	7
four	2	1	9	12	5	29
three	7	5	7	8	5	32
two	10	16	12	36	12	86
one	0	6	13	70	16	105
Total entries	22	28	44	127	41	262

Table 10.5 shows only the number of items affected by change shared by some or all of the six languages studied here.[8] The table does not take into account cognates unaffected by change. For instance, for the seven entries shared by three languages under Pattern 2 (*VL > LV) some or all of the remaining languages may have cognates showing VL rather than LV.

The following observations can be made from a study of the etymologies which underlie the figures in Table 10.5:

(1) At the undivided stage of the six languages, only a small percentage of the total lexicon is affected by the sound changes that produced apical displacement.

[8] The specific languages involved in combinations of five, four, three, etc., as well as the entry numbers of the items in *DED(S)*, are included in a Supplement which could not be printed here because of space limitations. Interested scholars may obtain these details from me.

Only ten items are involved in change in combinations of all the five or six languages, whereas there are 105 items that have undergone change in single languages (see Table 10.6, below). Reconstructions of the ten items are as follows.

(a) *LV > LV (three items):

*S*837. **rēv* 'dig' (Go.-Kui-Kuvi-Pe.-Manḍa). No other language has cognates.

*S*833. **rōnj* (intr.), **rō cc* (tr.) 'pile up' (Go.-Koṇḍa-Kui-Pe.-Manḍa). No cognates available from other languages.

*S*846. **lāk* 'to sacrifice' (Go.-Kui-Kuvi-Pe.-Manḍa). PD **aḷakk-*.

(b) *VL > LV (three items):

401. **ĭ̄r*/*(*e*)*raṇḍ* 'two' (Go.); **rī*/**rĭ̄ṇḍ* (Koṇḍa-Kui-Kuvi-Pe.-Manḍa).

258. **ḷōnj* (intr.), **ḷōcc* (tr.) 'to scatter, bail out' (Go.-Koṇḍa-Kui-Kuvi-Pe.).

565. **rū* 'to burn' (Koṇḍa-Kui-Kuvi-Pe.-Manḍa). PD **ūr*/**uru*.

(c) *CVL > CLV (one item):

*S*677. **pẓī* 'unripe mango' (Koṇḍa-Kui-Kuvi-Pe.-Manḍa); Koṇḍa also has *piṛika* in the southern dialect. PD **piẓikkāy*.

(d) *CVL > $\left\{\begin{matrix}\text{CLV}\\ \text{*CLV}\end{matrix}\right\}$ > LV (three items):

2667. **ṟē* 'to open' (Kui-Kuvi-Pe.-Manḍa); Go. *terr-*, *ter-* in most dialects, Koi (dial.) *reh-*; Koṇḍa *teṟe-*, *ṟe-*, PD **teṯ-a* [*teṟ-a-].

3113. **leñ j* 'moon, month' (< **nlē nj* < **nelanj*) (Kui-Kuvi-Pe.-Manḍa); Gondi *nelenj*, *lēnj*; Koṇḍa *nela* (pl. *neleŋ*), dial. *lēnzu*. PD **nil-a*/**nel-a*.

3076. **ṛug* (intr.), **ṛukk* (tr.) 'enter, crouch' (Koṇḍa-Kui-Kuvi-Pe.-Manḍa) (<**nẓug*<**nuẓ-g*). PD **nuẓunk-*/**nuẓunkk-*.

The basic nature of most of these items ('two, moon, sacrifice, burn, open, enter' etc.) suggests that they represent inherited sound change and not borrowing. It also seems plausible that *VL > LV is an older rule, since none of the languages has the VL variant, even dialectally, for all three items under (1a). But it is certain that all three processes implied by Patterns (1)–(4) are inherited from the common stage, though they are lexically restricted. *CL > L, historically the last rule, at first affected only certain clusters (where *C = **n* and *L = **ṯ* [*ṟ]), and later spread to others.[9]

[9] The rules for *CL > L are as follows:
(1) *n* > Ø / #___ (all languages; e.g. 3046, 3076, 3141, 3113).
(2) $\left\{\begin{matrix} w \\ s \end{matrix}\right\}$ > Ø / #___ $\left\{\begin{matrix} r \\ l \\ ḷ \\ ẓ \end{matrix}\right\}$ (all but Kui; e.g. *S*861, *S*878, *S*472, 1986, 2160, 4459, 1968a).
(3) [–continuant] > Ø / #___ [-sonorant, +apical] (Kuvi, Pengo, Manḍa; e.g. 943, 1090, 2667, 3897).
The examples of the last rule involve the loss of *g*, *t*, *p*, *m* before *ṟ* (< **ṯ*) and *ṛ* (< **ṭ*).

(2) The sound changes that led to apical displacement must have gradually spread, lexically and geographically, over the centuries. To judge from the number of items in the last row, the changes are still in progress in individual languages.

(3) The number of items involved in change is in inverse proportion to the number of languages sharing the change. A possible interpretation of this situation is that the few innovative cognates shared by all five or six languages belong to the earliest chronological stratum (around the early Christian era), and the largest number found in the last row of Table 10.5 to the most recent or even contemporary period. Such an inverse ratio can then be taken to represent the time dimension of the areal and lexical diffusion of a sound change, although the actual time depth can be known only from recorded or reconstructed historical facts.

(4) The number of cognates-with-change shared by particular combinations of languages clearly reflects the hierarchical relations of the six languages (see Fig. 10.3 below). Among the two-language combinations, Kui-Kuvi share 41 items (i.e. 41/86 = 47.7%) and Pengo-Manḍa 14 items (i.e. 14/86 = 16.3%); among the four-language combinations, Kui-Kuvi-Pengo-Manḍa share 18 items (i.e. 18/29 = 62%); among the five-language combinations, Koṇḍa-Kui-Kuvi-Pengo-Manḍa have three shared items (i.e. 3/7 = 43%). Despite Hoenigswald's criticism of quantitative studies on language subclassification as 'acts of desperation' (1966: 8), there is no sure way of distinguishing an authentic 'shared innovation' from the areal diffusion of an inherited rule except by looking at the sharing pattern of the number of lexical items affected by the rule. This study shows that a shared innovation (say, a phonological rule) is relevant in subgrouping only to the extent it is also shared lexically by the languages in question.

A language-wise breakdown of the items in the last row of Table 10.5 is shown in Table 10.6. (Since all entries are shared by at least two languages, the implication is that at least one other language has an unchanged cognate for each item that is affected by change. However, Kui CLV corresponds to LV in some other languages.)

TABLE 10.6. *Number of items showing change in individual languages*

		Gondi	Koṇḍa	Kui	Kuvi	Pengo	Manḍa	TOTAL
(1a)	*LV > LV	0	0	0	0	0	0	**0**
(1b)	*CLV > CLV	0	0	6	0	0	0	**6**
(2)	*VL > LV	2	1	6	3	1	0	**13**
(3)	*CVL > CLV	0	1	48	13	5	3	**70**
(4)	{CLV, *CLV} > LV	1	4	0	5	4	2	**16**
	TOTAL	**3**	**6**	**60**	**21**	**10**	**5**	**105**

The 75 entries which have been dropped from the initial computer analysis because they lack cognates in at least one other language of the subgroup (see § **2.1**, point 2) also contain 25 entries which register change under one of the four major patterns (see Table 10.7). Even here, Kui claims the largest share of items-with-change.

TABLE 10.7. *Single-language items (without cognates) showing change*

	Gondi	Koṇḍa	Kui	Kuvi	Pengo	Manḍa	TOTAL
(1a) *LV > LV	—	—	—	—	—	—	0
(1b) *CLV > CLV	—	—	1	—	—	—	1
(2) *VL > LV	3	1	4	—	—	—	8
(3) *CVL > CLV	—	1	12	2	—	—	15
(4) {CLV / *CLV} > LV	1	—	—	—	—	—	—
TOTAL	4	2	17	2	0	0	25

From Tables 10.2–7, it is clear that the process underlying the pattern *CVL > CLV is still active in Kui-Kuvi, while the simplification process implied by *CLV > LV is independently active in Koṇḍa-Kuvi-Pengo-Manḍa. Nearly half the total number of Kui entries sharing CLV are idiosyncratic to that language.

2.7. The number of items that each language shares with all its sister languages is shown in Table 10.8. These figures represent the total number of innovative cognates shared under the four patterns considered. For the six languages we get 15 (i.e. $6 \times (6–1)/2$) pairs.

TABLE 10.8. *Number of shared cognates-with-change*

	Gondi	Koṇḍa	Kui	Kuvi	Pengo	Manḍa
Gondi						
Koṇḍa	16					
Kui	18	18				
Kuvi	22	20	88			
Pengo	11	19	48	49		
Manḍa	10	9	40	42	57	

The above figures represent 'proximity measures' between pairs of languages within this subgroup. If we apply the 'multidimensional scaling' proposed by Shepard (1962), the computer produces a precise monotonic configuration of the distance between the languages, as shown in Fig 10.2. The principle is that the languages most closely related have the smallest distance between them.[10]

[10] Douglas Danforth kindly provided the following note on the computer programming of these data (updated in January 1974): '<SUBSYS>MDS6 is a modified version of MDS5M, written by Joseph B. Kruskal of Bell Telephone Laboratories, Murray Hill, New Jersey. The main documentation for this multidimensional scaling program is available from Campus Computing Center, Pine Hall, Stanford University, Stanford, CA 94305. Three main aspects of the program have been modified from the version

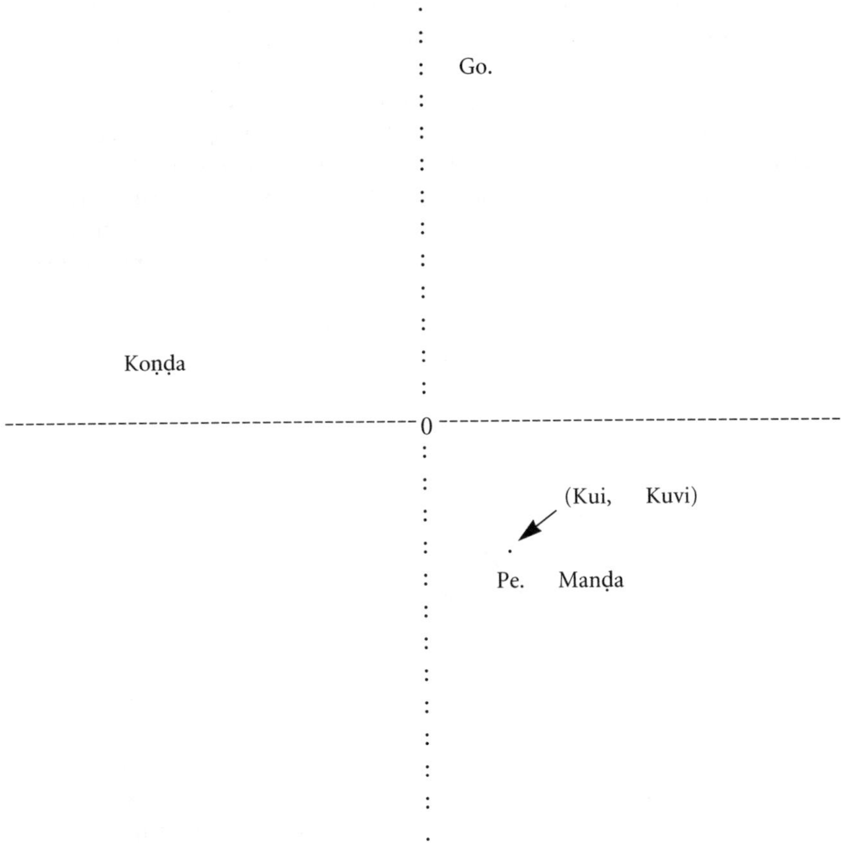

FIGURE 10.2. Shepard diagram showing the relative distance among the six languages in terms of shared cognates-with-change

There are at least two variables not controlled in the Shepard diagram. First, there is no consideration of the degree of sharing of cognates-with-change in relation to the total number of cognates available for any two languages. If this were controlled, Kui and Kuvi would be separated slightly, not represented as a single entity. Second, cognates-with-change between a pair of languages may represent either common inheritance or application of an inherited rule to cognates-without-change—which would, in effect, produce items that look like inherited

that I implemented on the 360: (1) As is to be expected, the input-output is somewhat different. Basically, for (only) the first data deck in the input stream, the program asks a few questions of the user, and then runs essentially in (compute-bound) batch mode. (2) The default options in MDS6 are, for most users, much more reasonable than in the 360 version. (3) Using an arrangement the details of which will be supplied on request, a set of data will automatically be rescaled using 41 different initial configurations, after which the user keeps the file having the minimal stress value, and deletes the rest. Note that the stress value in Fig. 10.2 is zero, which is printed at the centre of the figure.

cognates-with-change (see discussion in §3). The genetic and areal aspects of spread of a sound change are collapsed in the notion of proximity in the Shepard diagram. We still do not have a procedure for evaluating the function of physical contiguity in the maintenance of an inherited sound change in related but distinct languages. Thus the Shepard diagram, which translates multiple relationships into degrees of distance, may reflect greater depth than the traditional tree diagram, which lays a heavy premium on the notion of shared innovation. Such a tree diagram, based on our knowledge of the relationships among these languages, is shown in Fig. 10.3 (no data on the grammatical structure of Manḍa are available).

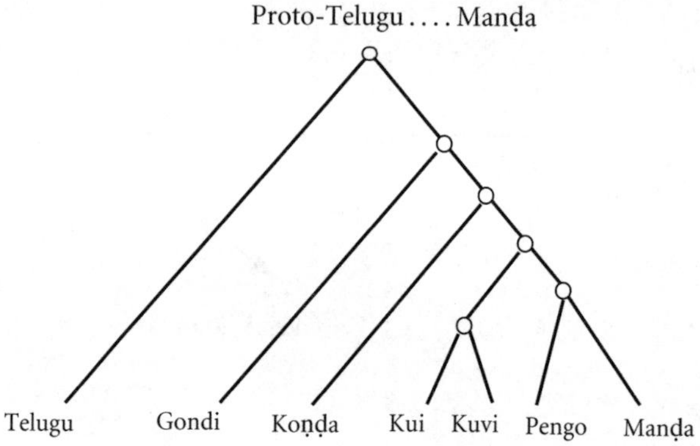

FIGURE 10.3. Family tree diagram of Subgroup 2 languages

It is interesting to see how closely the Shepard diagram reflects the genetic relationships combined with aspects of areal diffusion. It is possible to construct a tree diagram on the basis of Fig. 10.3 reflecting hierarchical relations: Kui-Kuvi is the closest cluster, which combines with Pengo-Manḍa, then with Koṇḍa, and finally with Gondi. In a tree diagram, only the configuration of nodes matters, not the length of branches and sub-branches (Hoenigswald 1966: 3, fn. 8). For this reason it cannot reflect the chronological distance between any two languages as accurately as does the Shepard diagram, based on multidimensional scaling. In the absence of adequate data, the position of Manḍa relative to Kui-Kuvi and Pengo is not certain. However, it is clear that Kui-Kuvi-Pengo-Manḍa constitute a definite subgroup within the South-Central branch. There is substantial independent evidence in support of the other hierarchical relations represented in Fig. 10.3.

Conclusions

3.1. Two languages (L_1 and L_2) may share a pair of cognate morphs (m_1 and m_2) which show the operation of an identical phonological rule (R_1), because of one of the following circumstances:

(1) L_1 and L_2 have inherited m_1 and m_2 from a common ancestor *L, in which *m developed from *n by the operation of R_1.

(2) L_1 and L_2 have inherited R_1 from *L in other inherited morphs-with-change, and have independently applied the rule to n_1 and n_2 (derived from *n) to produce m_1 and m_2.

(3) Only L_1 has inherited m_1 from *L (perhaps shared by the other sister languages L_3, L_4 etc.); but because of cultural need and geographical contact with L_1, L_2 has borrowed m_1 as m_2.

(4) Both L_1 and L_2 have independently developed an identical rule R_1, and have applied it to inherited morphs n_1 and n_2 to produce m_1 and m_2.

The comparative method assumes position (1) as the basis of reconstruction. It has no way of distinguishing the consequences of (1) from those of (2). Typically, however, the consequences of (1) and (2) will remain different except for rare cases of coincidence, since the inherited rule is not likely to follow the same lexical schedule for its implementation in sister languages. Proposal (3) is a classical case of dialect or language borrowing; we can resort to this as an explanation only when it is supported by known external history of the dialects or languages concerned, or when the loanword phonology is distinctly different from that of the native element. Position (4) is possible insofar as certain 'natural' phonological processes are concerned, such as loss of word-final consonants, vowel harmony, palatalization of velars before front vowels, nasalization of vowels before nasals etc. (Schane 1972, Ohala 1974).

The data in this paper suggest that the results of (1) and (2) can usually be distinguished by looking at the manner in which a sound change is lexically distributed. To the extent that cognate morphs registering a sound change are shared, the sound change is also shared from a common ancestral stage. A phonological rule thus inherited in a small segment of the lexicon can continue to operate for centuries, even after the split of the ancestral speech community into subgroups and finally into independent languages. Only the phenomenon of lexical diffusion of the apical displacement rules can explain the type of lexical distribution found in Tables 10.4–7. The 12 entries showing *CVL > CLV under the four-language combination (see Table 10.5) are shared by Kui-Kuvi-Pengo-Manḍa. Under two-language combinations, this pattern is shared in cognates in 24 entries by Kui-Kuvi and in 4 entries by Pengo-Manḍa. This circumstance, combined with the lexical free variation of change in certain items in individual languages (see Table 10.4), shows that we are dealing here with a change-in-process which has been running its course from the Proto-South Dravidian stage through successive splits into the modern languages of Subgroup 2. The sound changes have slowed down in Gondi and Koṇḍa, but are still going strong in the rest of the subgroup, engulfing more and more lexical items which fulfil the structural conditions.

3.2. While the theory of lexical diffusion of sound change has firm empirical foundations, there are still some major questions to be answered. What kind of lexical items become the early victims of a sound change? Other structural conditions for the implementation of a sound change being equal, is there anything in the semantic domain of certain lexical items, or in their frequency, that makes them more vulnerable to change than others? What determines the momentum of a sound change in its lexical diffusion? How can the results of this theory be utilized in genetic subgrouping?[11]

The Dravidian data presented here seem to show that the lexical items registering the earliest traces of apical displacement refer to concepts fundamental to the communication and culture of the tribal groups, viz. 'two, moon/month, sacrifice, open, enter' etc. (see § **2.6**). The momentum of a rule seems to be intimately associated with the generalization of its structural conditions. Kui-Kuvi-Pengo-Manḍa have generalized the apical displacement rules to include all possible segments in the structure of the root syllables which have undergone the change. The collapsing of *VL > LV and *CVL > CLV gives the following general rule for these four languages:[12]

$$
\begin{array}{lllll}
\text{(C)} & \text{V} & \text{L} & & \text{V} \\
\left(\begin{bmatrix}\text{+segment}\\ \text{–syllabic}\end{bmatrix}\right) & \begin{bmatrix}\text{+syllabic}\\ \text{–long}\end{bmatrix} & \begin{bmatrix}\text{–syllabic}\\ \text{+apical}\\ \text{–nasal}\end{bmatrix} & \# & [\text{+syllabic}] \\
(1) & 2 & 3 & 4 & 5 \quad \rightarrow \\
\text{(C)} & \text{L} & \text{V} & \# & \\
(1) & 3 & \underset{[\text{+long}]}{2} & 4 & \varnothing
\end{array}
$$

Here 1 = [–syllabic], viz. all consonants (including the semivowel **w*) which occur word-initially,[13] namely **p*(*b*), **t*(*d*), **c*(*j*), **k*(*g*), **m*, **n*, **w*; and 3 = all alveolar and retroflex consonants other than nasals, viz. **ṯ* [ḏ/ṟ], **ṭ* [ḍ], **l*, **ḷ*, **r*, **ẓ*. Kuvi has further generalized this rule by including nasals, i.e. **n* and **ṇ*. The rest of

[11] Wang has now drawn my attention to Hsieh 1973, who deals with subgrouping by using the number of innovative cognates shared by pairs of languages within a subgroup. Hsieh's conclusion coincides with what I have independently observed from the Dravidian data. For instance, he says: 'The more phonological forms two or more dialects share with respect to a commonly initiated but independently executed sound change, the longer they must have developed together, and hence the more closely related they are' (88).

Hsieh operates with the notions of 'primary' and 'secondary' groups of dialects, setting up 'a certain number of shared items as a criterion of closeness' (81). The primary group is enlarged when the criterion of shared items is reduced, and it has fewer members when the criterion of shared items is increased. The 'conclusive primary groups' coincide with the traditional Mandarin and Wu groups of twenty Jiang-su dialects studied by Hsieh with respect to the split of Middle Chinese tone 1. It is not possible to summarize his method here, but it fails to interpret the figures in establishing clear hierarchical relations. The case with the Dravidian data is clearer, as shown by the interpretation of the figures in Table 10.5.

[12] This is only one of the two rules, presented for illustration (see § 1.1 above, and Appendix I below).

[13] Voicing of obstruents is not distinctive in Proto-Dravidian; but for the proto-stage of the six languages considered here, there are a few cases which require us to reconstruct voiced initial stops.

the languages apply only restricted variants of the rule (see § 1.2). To quote Chen (1972: 474–5) 'As the phonological innovation gradually spreads across the lexicon, ... there comes a point when the minor rule gathers momentum and begins to serve as a basis for extrapolation. At this critical cross-over point, the minor rule becomes a major rule, and we would expect diffusion to be much more rapid.' But how is this critical cross-over point determined differently in different languages?

3.3. Is the Dravidian phenomenon a case of what Sapir called 'drift'? By implication, Sapir imputed drift to inherited 'tendencies' when he said:

> The momentum of the more fundamental, the pre-dialectic, drift is often such that languages long disconnected will pass through the same or strikingly similar phases. In many such cases it is perfectly clear that there could have been no dialectic interinfluencing. (1921: 172)
>
> ... Modern Irish, English, Italian, Greek, Russian, Armenian, Persian, and Bengali are but end-points in the present of drifts that converge at a meeting point in the dim past. (153)

Sapir's concept of drift is much more complex than these remarks imply. It is a pre-existing design, as it were, in language, governing the direction of its change as a whole. Lakoff (1972) identifies drift as a 'metacondition on change', which is outside the individual synchronic rules of grammar or even language universals; but she fails to show how such a metacondition enters a group of dialects or languages.

If there were a drift underlying the apical displacement rules, it presumably had the function of maintaining the CVC structure of the root syllable while at the same time giving apical consonants an even distribution with the other consonants by promoting them to the word-initial position. This is also interpretable, then, as 'typological pressure' operating within a group of sister languages which are also 'areal neighbours' (Hoenigswald 1966: 11). It is interesting, however, to point out here that many languages of Subgroup 1 (viz. Tamil, Malayāḷam, Iruḷa, Kannaḍa, and Tuḷu—but not Toda or Kota) have a tendency or a restricted rule to drop word-initial short vowels preceding apical consonants, thereby permitting alveolar and retroflex consonants to occur word-initially. Again, this change has affected only some of the lexical items which fulfil the structural conditions.[14]

[14] Ramaswami Aiyar (1931–2) has discussed this problem at some length; and so has Andronov 1975b, insofar as Tamil is concerned. From the word-indexes in *DED(S)*, I have collected the following numbers of items for the languages of Subgroup 1, in the native element, which have an initial apical consonant resulting from the loss of a preceding short vowel:

Language	Vowel lost	No. of items	Word-initial apicals
Tamil	*i*	3	*r*, *ṟ*
Malayāḷam	*i*	6	*r*, *ṟ*, *l*
Koḍagu	*i*, *e*	3	*r*, *ṟ*
Kannaḍa	*a*, *e*	6	*r*, *ṟ*, *l*
Tuḷu	all short vowels	25	all apicals (except nasals)
Iruḷa	all short vowels	22	all apicals (except nasals)

Data for Iruḷa were obtained from R. Perialwar, a research scholar at Annamalai University. This language, considered to be a dialect or an offshoot of Tamil, has lexically extended the phenomenon and also generalized the rules, as has Tuḷu.

3.4. In this paper I have attempted to show that the rules of apical displacement can be traced to a common stage of Subgroup 2 of the Dravidian languages, including Telugu. At that stage, only a few lexical items were affected by change. The rules inherited through the shared items became further generalized and continued to operate through successive splits of the subgroup into independent languages, affecting more and more lexical items. The profile of lexical distribution of the sound changes given in Table 10.5 reflects the time depth of the changes; it also reflects the subclassification of these languages, which is corroborated by other shared features not discussed in this paper.

The areal diffusion of a sound change is interpreted here as the lexical spread of an inherited rule in genetically and geographically contiguous languages. The Dravidian data and analysis support the hypothesis that sound change spreads lexically, and that one group of exceptions to sound change represents items which are not yet affected by change at a given point of time.

Appendix I
Historical background of apical displacement

In partial revision of my earlier proposal that metathesis and vowel contraction caused apical displacement in Subgroup 2 (Krishnamurti 1955, §19; 1961: 51–68), I now believe that both metathesis and the location of stress, in terms of syllable weight, operated in complementary environments to produce the sound changes in question. A possible scenario of developments would be as follows:

STAGE I: When PD root syllables of the (C)V̆̄C type were followed by inflectional morphemes of types -C, -CC, or -CCC, a short vowel (*i*, *u*, *a*) was inserted as a stem formative between the root and the inflection. When followed by a stem-formative vowel, *(C)V̄C merged with *(C)VC (Krishnamurti 1955). The form of the inflected stem was *(C)VC-VC (-VCC, -VCCC). For instance, in the case of verbs, some of the reconstructed inflections are *k, *nk, *p, *mp (non-past intransitive), *kk, *nkk, *pp, *mpp (non-past transitive), *t, *nt (past intransitive), *tt, *ntt (past transitive). The inflected stems of a root like *kuẓ would then be *kuẓ -a/i/u -nk/nkk etc., with the syllable division *(C)V$CVC . . . (Krishnamurti 1955: §4.5).

STAGE II: The second syllable, being heavy (i.e. CVC as opposed to light CV), carried stress only when V_1 and V_2 were of the same quality or when V_2 was [+low]. The sequences of V_1 and V_2 were:

$(C)V_1C\text{-}V_2 \ldots$	
i	i
u	u
a	a
i/e	a
u/o	a

When the consonant between V_1 and V_2 was R (a liquid, a phonetic continuant ([r̲] ← /*t̲/), or a flap (*r* < **ẓ*, **ṭ*, **l*)), V_1 tended to become weaker in articulation, being closely followed by more prominent V_2 across a lighter consonant. This led to the lengthening of V_2 and the loss of V_1, producing initial apicals and consonant clusters, followed by a long vowel which was identical with V_1 in quality. There is evidence that, before this happened, **e$a* and **o$a* also became **e$e* and **o$o*, respectively. Consequently **moẓ-ang* > **moẓ-ong* > *mẓōng-* 'to roar'. At some point between Stage I and Stage II, the inflectional morphemes were evolving as mere stem formatives, losing their grammatical significance; this is clear from the fact that **nk*/**nkk*, **mp*/**mpp*, **nt*/**ntt* retained their voice distinction, but lost the tense meaning. Consequently, voice became a derivational category, and new tense morphemes were added to disyllabic and trisyllabic stems which carried contrast in transitivity. [See Ch. 17 of this volume for a fuller treatment of this problem.]

Where V_1 and V_2 were not identical in quality, V_2 tended to be weakened and lost, bringing the root-final consonant R into contact with the suffix consonant, e.g. **miẓ-u-ng* > **miẓ-ng* 'swallow'. The vowel sequences were:

$*(C)V_1C\text{-}V_2 \ldots$	
i	u
e	u/i
a	u/i
u	i
o	u/i

Presumably, **i* merged with **u* in V_2 position. The loss of **u* in the second syllable is a much older tendency, found in all four subgroups of the Dravidian family. Therefore, it appears that vowel lengthening operated only in the environments which preserved V_2.

Stage III: The outputs of Stage II with patterns like (C)VL-C . . . were subjected to assimilation in Subgroup 1, but to metathesis in Subgroup 2. The function of metathesis was to preserve the root syllable from threatened assimilation of the final consonant. Therefore *(C)VL-C . . . > (C)LV-C . . ., e.g. **miẓ-ng* > **mẓi-ng(u)* > Te. *mringu* 'to swallow'.

Stage IV: During this stage, the consonant clusters formed through the earlier processes were again simplified by loss of R in Telugu (see *TVB* §1.145) and loss of C in the other languages of Subgroup 2. The rules of apical displacement must have started at least two thousand years ago, and are still going on in some of the languages of this subgroup, particularly in Kui. This scenario is supported by historical and comparative data which cannot be presented here. Illustrative etymologies given in §1.2 and §2.6 of this paper may be examined in the light of the above remarks. (For an insightful study of the historical relationship between syllable-weight, stress, and vowel duration, see Hyman 1975: 19–35.)

11

On Diachronic and Synchronic Rules in Phonology: A Case from Parji

0. Three historical changes which occurred during the pre-Parji and historical Parji stages are discussed, viz. vowel-raising before pre-Parji alveolar consonants (*a* > *e*), deretroflexion (*ḷ*, *ṇ* > *l*, *n*), and alveolar stop merger (**ṯ* > *ṭ*/*t*, **ḏ* > *ḍ*/*d*) in different dialects. A chronological sequencing of these three sound changes accounts for the forms which have so far been considered historically irregular or deviant. Some of these rules are still found operative in the synchronic grammar of Parji: for instance stem-final *a* alternates with *e* before the plural suffix *-l*. The verb forms of the three dialects, Southern, North-eastern and North-western, described by Burrow and Bhattacharaya, differ in their phonological make-up. Most of these differences have been explained as arising from synchronic and diachronic interaction of the above rules.

1. Parji is a Central Dravidian language spoken by a small tribal people numbering about 25,000 in the forests and hills south of Jagdalpur in the Bastar district of Madhya Pradesh, bordering on Orissa and Andhra Pradesh.[1] T. Burrow and S. Bhattacharya, who discovered the language as an independent member of the Dravidian family, also published a description of it (1953) consisting of phonology, morphology, some texts, and an etymological vocabulary. They have also suggested that its nearest relations are Ollari and Pōya (since corrected as Ollari Gadaba and Salur Gadaba) with 'a special connection with Kōlāmī and Naikī' (xi). That these languages constitute a subgroup within central Dravidian has been adequately demonstrated by subsequent writings (Emeneau 1955a: 141–63; *TVB* 236–69; Subrahmanyam 1969a-i).[2] We are here concerned with a problem of Parji phonology

This paper represents part of the research I conducted at the Center for Advanced Study in the Behavioral Sciences. Stanford, California, during 1975–6, as a Resident Fellow. I express my indebtedness to the authorities of the Center for awarding me a Fellowship and for providing all facilities for my research. Irene Bickenbach deserves thanks for typing the paper neatly. I have benefited from the comments of M. B. Emeneau and Paul Kiparsky; however, they do not agree with me on all the points discussed in the paper. I alone am responsible for any errors in the interpretation of data.

[1] The 1961 Census report (Vol. 1. Part 2. C(ii)) puts Parji speakers at 109,401 as compared to the 19,847 of the 1951 Census. The number of Parji speakers returned for Madhya Pradesh, where it is mainly spoken, is 24,718. This latter figure appears to be correct. It also compares favourably with the figure 12,363 returned in the 1981 Census. (B & B 8; also Krishnamurti 1969a: 309. fn. 1).

[2] In all published literature on Dravidian subgrouping, Central Dravidian is said to consist of two branches: (a) Telugu, Gondi, Kui, Kuvi, Koṇḍa, Pengo, and Manḍa; (b) Kolami, Naikṛi, Naiki

(diachronic and synchronic) and examination of some general issues in the propagation of a sound change.

In their brief account of the historical phonology of Parji, Burrow and Bhattacharya (1953: 1) refer to a vocalic sound change in this language as follows: 'A special feature of Parji is the tendency to turn Dravidian *a*, *ā* into *e*, *ē*. The change may also appear in loanwords from Halbi, but only apparently in the case of the short vowel. Although frequent, this development is by no means universal, and words are also abundant in which *a*, *ā* are preserved.' Emeneau (1970a: 8, 10) states that corresponding to PD **a* and *ā*, Parji 'sometimes' has *e* and *ē* respectively. Zvelebil (1970b: 41) echoes the same uncertainty when he says, 'it is not quite clear when . . . Pa. has *e* and when *a* for PD **a*.' He lists *ē*, *ā* as the reflexes of PD **ā* (44). Although the problem seems to be one of historical interest, it will be shown that it has application in the synchronic phonology of the language as well.

1.1. A closer scrutiny of the Parji material with the help of the *Dravidian Etymological Dictionary* (1961) and its two Supplements (*DED(S)* 1968 and *DEN* 1972) has revealed that this seemingly irregular pattern is a consequence of the interaction of three ordered rules which operated in pre-Parji or early Parji.

Parji has five stops with voice contrast / k c ṭ t p g j ḍ d b /; four nasals / ŋ ñ n m /, two liquids / r l /, two semivowels / y v /, a retroflex flap / ṛ /, and two fricatives / s h / (the last infrequent). There are five vowels with length contrast / a i u e o ā ī ū ē ō /.[3]

The vocalic shift took place before alveolar consonants of the pre-Parji stage, which included a separate stop series, viz *ṯ* and *ḏ*, as formulated below.

Rule 1. Vowel-raising (in pre-Parji)[4]

V [+low] > [–low, –high, –back]/#(C)___C [+anterior, + apical]

A low vowel (*ă*) is changed to a mid-front vowel (*ĕ*) when followed by an alveolar

(Chanda), Parji, Ollari, and Gadaba. Here I am using Central Dravidian to refer only to the Kolami-Parji subgroup. I now consider the Telugu-Manḍa subgroup a branch of South Dravidian which I call South Dravidian II (South Dravidian=South Dravidian I). Some of the arguments in favour of this revision are given in Krishnamurti 1975a: 347, fn. 10, and 1976a.

[3] B & B (§9 (2)) transcribe short and long nasalized vowels mainly before the voiced dental stop, but they treat nasalization as a phonetic phenomenon. All such items can be synchronically represented as vowel + nasal sequences: /ñ/and/ŋ/ also can be represented as /nj/ and /ng/ respectively.

[4] In pre-Parji as in Modern Malayāḷam, Toda, Kota, and Iruḷa, there was a three-way contrast in the stop series produced by raising the tongue tip or blade (coronal), viz. *t* (dental), *ṯ* (alveolar), and *ṭ* (retroflex). Chomsky and Halle (1968: 312 ff) propose the feature [±distributed] to distinguish *t*, *ṯ*, *ṭ* in combination with [±anterior] and [±coronal]. The feature is based on 'length of constriction along the direction of air flow', or 'the length of the zone of contact' (312). The strong empirical basis they have put forth for this feature is that dental and alveolar consonants do not both have apical articulations in any language. Diffloth (1976) and Schiffman (1976) have examined in detail the inadequacies of the Chomsky–Halle feature-matrix for explaining some very common phonological processes in Dravidian, but they have not proposed any alternative feature.

I find it more efficient to use the feature [±apical] as a substitute for [±distributed] insofar as Dravidian languages are concerned. In Dravidian, the dental consonants are articulated with the blade of the tongue and alveolars with the apex; it is the retroflexed apex that is involved in the articulation of consonant, viz. *ṯ [ḏ], *ṯṯ, *nṯ [nḏ], *n, *r, *l. Since Parji merges ḏ with *d*/*ḍ* and ṯṯ with *tt*/*ṭṭ* in different dialects, it is clear that PD *ṯ remained intact in all environments (single, geminate, and postnasal) in pre-Parji (Emeneau 1955a: 151–2). The above rule apparently operated before the merger took place.

Examples for Rule 1 (only cognates from Ollari, Gadaba, Kolami, Naikṛi, and Naiki (Chanda)) are cited along with one or two diagnostic forms from other subgroups. Numbers refer to entries in *DED(S)*. Pre-Parji reconstructions are given which reflect voicing contrasts in obstruents not present in Proto-Dravidian.[5]

1.1.1. Before *ḏ, *nḏ, *ṯṯ (items involved 5 + 5 + 2):

1. **āḏ-*(346): Pa. *ēd-*, (NE) *ēḍ* 'to cool, cool off'; Kol. *ār-* 'to become dry', *ārp-* 'to dry up, heal' (tr.): Ta. *āṟu* id.

2. **panḏi* (4364): Pa. *pend*, (NE) *penḍ*; Oll. *panḍ*, Gad. *panḍu*: Ta. *panṟi*, Koṇḍa *panṟi* id.

3. **vaṯṯ-* (4355): Pa. *vett-*, (NE) *veṭṭ-* 'to wither'; *vetip-* 'to dry' (tr.); Kol. *vat-*(*vatt-*) 'to parch grain'; Oll. *vaṭ*(*ṭ-*) 'to dry up': Ta. *vaṟṟu* 'to go dry'.

We can contrast the above with the following items in which pre-Parji *a*, *ā* have not changed when followed by dental or retroflex obstruents:

4. **katt-* (1015): Pa. *katt-* 'to cut, slaughter'; Oll. *kat-*; Kol. *katk-* 'strike down (man), break down (tree)'.

retroflex consonants. In terms of this feature the six-way contrast of the obstruents in Proto-Dravidian and in the languages that preserve it can be represented as follows:

	p	*t*	*ṯ*	*ṭ*	*c*	*k*
Anterior	+	+	+	–	–	–
Coronal	–	+	+	+	+	–
Apical		–	+	+	–	

In view of the fact that [±apical] subclassifies all coronal consonants, the feature [±coronal] can be eliminated as redundant in specifying these segments. It can be used mainly to group labials and velars [–coronal] as a natural class. In the above representations *t ṯ ṭ c* emerge as a natural class specified by the presence or absence of apicality in the front or non-front part of the oral tract. Non-apicals are laminals. The following phonological processes in Dravidian are captured more naturally by the above matrix: (a) The unconditional merger of *ṯ with dentals or retroflexes in most of the languages, because it is the most highly marked segment: *ṯ* → *t* is [+apical] > [–apical]; *ṯ* → *ṭ* [+anterior] > [–anterior], each change requiring a change in only one feature. (b) Dental stops assimilate to the next alveolar or retroflex nasals or laterals *l* + *t* → *ṯ*, *ḷ* + *t* → *ṭ*, *t* → *ṯ*/*n* + ___, *t* → *ṭ*/*ṇ* + ___; (c) -*ṯ* > -*c* (also *ḏ* > *j*) in Tuḷu, Kui, Kuvi, Pengo, and Manḍa [+anterior, +apical] > [–anterior, –apical, +strident]. (d) *t* → *c* after front vowels; both being [–apical] require change only in the feature [+anterior] → [–anterior]: (e) *c* → *s*/___+*t* in Telugu requires [–continuant] → [+continuant]; (f) *ṯ* → *ṟ* → *r* requires mainly a change in the feature [±sonorant] because *ṯ* and *r* are both apical. Although Chomsky and Halle claim to have other uses for [±distributed] in distinguishing bilabials from labiovelars and hard from soft dentals, it was invented mainly to subclassify the coronal obstruents.

[5] *DED* (xxiv) treats Ollari and Koṇḍēkōr Gadaba as two dialects of Ollari, marked Gad. (Oll.) & Gad. (S). Similarly Naiki of Chanda is now considered a separate language, whereas Naikṛi, given in *DED* as Naiki, is said to be a dialect of Kolami (Bhattacharya 1961: 86). Since this matter has never been dealt with conclusively by anybody, I have in this paper cited all as independent languages. We still lack clear criteria to distinguish a dialect from a language.

5. **kaṭṭ-* (961): Pa. *kaṭṭ-* 'to tie, bind; to build'; Oll. *kaṭ-*, Gad. *kaṭṭ-*, Kol. *kaṭ-*, Nk. *kaṭṭ-*, Nk (Ch.) *kaṭ-*.

Also notice that *e* and *ē* preceding a pre-Parji *ḏ*, *nḏ*, *ṯṯ* remain unchanged:

6. **keḏ* (1648): Pa. *kedp-* (*kedt-*) 'to shut (door)', Kol. *get-* (*gett-*) 'to close door firmly': Ta. *ceṟi-*(*-pp-*, *-tt-*) 'to close, shut', *ceṟu* (*ceṟṟ-*) 'to hinder, prevent.'

7. **kēḏ* (1679): Pa. *kēd*, (NE) *kēḍ-* 'to winnow'; Oll. Gad. *kēy*; Kol. Nk. *kēd-*; Nk. (Ch.) *kēd-* id.

1.1.2 Before **n*, **r*, **l* (items involved 2 + 16 + 17):

8. **man-* (*manḏ-*, **maṯṯ-*) 'to be, become' (3914): Pa. *men* (*mend-*, *mett-*) 'to be; to stay'; Oll. *man-*; Nk. (Ch.) *man-* id.: cf. Te. *manu* 'to stay, live'.

9. **var* (**varnd-*) 'to come' (4311): Pa. *ver-* (*veñ-*) 'to come'; Oll. *var* (*vadd-*), Gad. *vār* (*vadd-*), Kol. Nk. *var* (*vatt-*), Nk. (Ch.) *var-*(*vat-*). Cf. Ta. *varu* (*vant-*, *vā-*).

10. **pāl* 'milk' (3370): Pa. *pēl*; Oll-. Gad., Kol., Nk. (Ch.) *pāl*.

The phonetic motivation for the vowel shift seems to be that the raised position of the tongue in the front part of the oral tract in the articulation of the alveolar consonants results also in the raising of the low vowel to mid-position anticipatorily.[6]

1.2. Some time after the Vowel-raising Rule had ceased to operate, pre-Parji retroflex continuants became deretroflexed. i.e., *ḷ*, *ṇ* > *l*, *n* in all contrasting positions (finally and intervocalically).[7]

Rule 2. Deretroflexion

C [–anterior, +apical, {+nasal, +lateral}] > [+anterior]/#(C) V___ $\left\{\begin{matrix}\#\\ V\end{matrix}\right\}$

Retroflex [–anterior, +apical] nasal and lateral became alveolar [+anterior, +apical]. The Vowel-raising Rule does not operate in the case of *l*, *n* < **ḷ*, **ṇ*. If Rule 2 had preceded Rule 1 in point of time, it would have been in a feeding relation to Rule 1. But, as it happened, Rule 2 now is in a counter-feeding relation to Rule 1.

11. **kaḷ*-V- 'threshing floor' (1160): Pa. *kali* 'threshing floor', Oll. *kalin*, Kol. *kalave*; Nk. (Ch.) *kalay* id.

12. **māḷ* 'daughter' (3768; PD **mak-aḷ*): Pa. *māl*, Oll. *māl* id.

13. **kan* 'eye' (973): Pa. *kan*, Oll. *kaṇ*, Gad. *kanu*, Kol. *kan*, Nk. *kan* id. cf. also the

[6] Coronal consonants are [–low] and [–high] just like the mid-vowels, although these features are considered redundant. The Parji sound change would receive explanatory adequacy only in terms of these redundant features (Chomsky and Halle 1968: § 4.2.1; p. 307).

[7] Retroflex **ḷ*, **ṇ* are deretroflexed to *l*, *n* in all but the SD I languages. This apparently has happened as an areal drift within each subgroup and language separately, but producing the same overall result. In SD II languages, **ḷ* > *ṛ*/*l*; for a discussion of this trend, see *TVB* §§ 4.14–17. In internal sandhi we still have traces of the underlying contrast between *ḷ*: *l*, *ṇ*: *n* in most of the languages. Cf. the past stems of **uṇ* vs. **tin*, **koḷ* vs. **nil* in *DED(S)* respectively.

verb forms Pa. *kanḍp-* (*kanḍt-*) 'look for, seek', Oll. *kanḍp-* id. Kol. *kanḍt-* 'to appear' are traceable to PCD **kaṇḍ-* the past stem of **kăṇ-* 'to see'.

1.3. Burrow and Bhattacharya (1953 §7; 4–5) refer to the different treatments given to the Proto-Dravidian alveolar stop in different Parji dialects. The North-western and Southern dialects have *d, nd, t*(*t*) for PD **ṯ* **nṯ*, **ṯṯ* (pre-Parji *d̲*, *nd̲*, *t̲t̲*) but the North-eastern dialect has *ḍ, nḍ, ṭ*(*ṭ*), correspondingly. The earlier two rules apply to all dialects. Therefore, the Dialect Split Rule formulated below must have occurred during recent times within the Parji language. In other words, Rules 1 and 2 operated at a time when the three dialects were still united and Rule 3 after there arose a split between the North-west and South on the one hand and North-east on the other.

Rule 3. Dialect Split

$$\text{C [+anterior, +apical, −sonorant]} \rightarrow \left\{\begin{matrix}\text{[−apical] NW \& S} \\ \text{[−anterior] NE}\end{matrix}\right\} / (\text{C})\breve{\text{V}}\_\_$$

Converted into segments, Rule 3 reads:

$$\begin{bmatrix}\underline{\text{d}} \\ \text{n}\underline{\text{d}} \\ \underline{\text{tt}}\end{bmatrix} \rightarrow \textbf{a.} \begin{bmatrix}\text{d} \\ \text{nd} \\ \text{tt}\end{bmatrix} \text{(NW \& S)}$$

$$\rightarrow \textbf{b.} \begin{bmatrix}\text{ḍ} \\ \text{nḍ} \\ \text{ṭṭ}\end{bmatrix} \text{(NE)}$$

For examples, see under **1.1.1** above. Notice that all three dialects show the shift of *ă* > *ĕ* irrespective of the developments of the alveolar consonants.

2. Exceptions:

(1) One clear set of exceptions represents demonstrative and personal pronouns, one numeral and one interjectional word. This is an excellent case of grammatical constraint on the spread of a sound change.

14. **an-* (1): Pa. *ana, ani* 'there', cf. Kol. *anaŋ* 'in that way'. (Pe. *ani* 'over there', Go. *anī* 'then', Kui *āne* 'that direction', Kuṛ. *annū, ānū*, 'by that way', Malto *ani* 'then'; Ta. *aṉṟu* 'then'; *an-* 'such and such', etc).

15. **(y)ār* (4228): Pa. *āra, āro* (adj.) 'what'; *āre* 'where', *āroḍ* 'whither': *ēd*, (NE) *ēd* 'who' (obl. *ēr*); *ēri* anybody; Oll. *ēynḍ* 'who' (masc. sg.), *ēyr* 'who' (pl.); *ered* 'which'; Gad. *eyir* 'who'; Kol. *er* 'who' (masc. pl.); Nk. *ēn* 'who' (sg.), *ēr* (pl.); Nk. (Ch.) *ēn* (obl. *ēr-*) 'who' (masc.), *ēd* 'which' (fem.-neut.). In Parji, the *ē-* forms are normal, derivable from pre-Parji (or Proto-Parji-Ollari-Gadaba) **eyand̲*, **eyar*; but the *ā-* forms are unique in form as well as in function; *ār-* which looks like a masculine plural form occurs as the interrogative base. We have to look into the neighbouring Munda languages to see if there is anything like that there.

16. **ān* (obl. *an-*) 'I' (4234): Pa. *ān* (*an-*); Oll., Gad., Kol., Nk., Nk. (Ch.) *ān* (*an-*) id.

17. **tān* (*tan-*) 'oneself' (2612): Pa. *tān-*(*tan-*), Oll. *tān* (*tan-*), Kol. *tān* (*tan-*).

18. The third person demonstrative masculine singular pronoun in Pa. is *ōd*, (NE) *ōḍ* (obl. *ōn-*) 'he, that man' and the plural *ōr* 'they, these men' which are derived from Proto-Parji-Ollari-Gadaba **ōnḏ* < **awanḏ*, with the contraction of **awa-* to *ō-*. This is a shared innovation of the three languages which antedates the Vowel-raising Rule of pre-Parji, cf. Oll., Gad. *ōnḍ* (sg.), *ōr* (pl.); Kolami and Naiki have different forms: Kol. *amd* (sg.), *avr* (pl.), Nk. *avnd*, *avr* (< PCD **awanḏ*, **awar*). The third person masculine suffixes in finite verbs follow the Vowel-raising Rule *-ed* (sg.), *-er* (pl.) < **-anḏ*, **-ar*.

19. **al*-V- (*S*35): Pa. *ale* exclamatory vocative (cf. Ka. *ale* interjection in calling a woman; Pe. Kuvi Koṇḍa *ale* term of affection, interjection). It is possible that this has spread by diffusion from the other language group of Central India, viz. Kui-Koṇḍa, etc.

20. *nāl*-V- (3024): Pa. *nāluk* 'four', the adjective is *nel-*(< **nal-*); Kol. Nk. *nāliŋ* id. SD **nāl-nk*/*nāl-nkk-*.

(2) A second set of exceptions (numbering 13) is native items which have *r* or *rr* and not the expected *d*/*ḍ* corresponding to pre-Parji **ḏ*. Most of these do not have cognates in Parji's closest relatives, Ollari and Gadaba. At least several look like possible borrowings from the neighbouring Dravidian languages, viz. Gondi or Telugu where **ṯ* > **r(r)* is a normal development. Presumably, when these items were first introduced into Parji they had an **ṟ* (contrasting with **r* and **ḏ*) which failed to produce the same effect on the preceding vowel as the alveolar consonants.

(3) A third subset (16 items) has doubtful etymologies, including wrong recording in one case (*DED* 1952), metathesis of *vl* to *lv* that puts *l* after the low vowel (Pa. *cavl*, (S) *calv-* [1927], *gavla*, *galva* 'jaw' [1124]) in two cases, and one clear case of reborrowing from Indo-Aryan, possibly Oriya, i.e. Pa. *alac* 'illness' [200]. Some of the others which do not share cognates in this Central Dravidian subgroup are suspected borrowings from Gondi or Telugu.

Clearly identified Indo-Aryan loanwords have been excluded from consideration, e.g. *jāl* 'net' cf. Oriya *jāla* 'net, snare' (*CDIAL* 5213). Also excluded here are several items with IA *ca-*, *sa-* which show *e* in Parji owing to the influence of the preceding palatal or sibilant irrespective of the following consonant; e.g., Pa. *cet* 'truth' (Skt. *satya*), *cecān* 'hawk' (Ha. *chacān*).

(4) This leaves us a final set of six items where a Parji low vowel *ă* is followed by **r* or **n*, only two of which have clear cognates in Ollari and Gadaba also. These six, along with a few others which could be reclassified into this set from (3) above, can be called true exceptions. They do not exceed a dozen all told, as compared with 47 cases where the sound change operates regularly. True exceptions represent the part of the lexicon not covered by the sound change before it ceased to operate.[8]

[8] Chen and Wang (1975) have advanced persuasive arguments in favour of the lexical diffusion of sound change. Also see Wang (1969) for competing changes as a cause of residue. Notice that Rules 2 and

However, there is no exception where a low vowel is followed by *d*/*ḍ* (< **(n)ḏ*). There are also no clear cases where Rule 1 has operated in the environment of *l*, *n* < **ḷ*, **ṇ*.

3. A rule that looks like the converse of Rule 1 is evidenced by three items:

Rule 4.
V [–low, –high, –back] → [+low]/#(C)___C [–syllabic, +sonorant, –nasal]

A mid-front vowel (*e*, *ē*) becomes a low vowel before liquids: *l* [–nasal, +lateral] and *r* [–nasal, –lateral].

21. **vēr* ((4554): Pa. *vār* (pl. *vār-kul*) 'root'; Oll. Gad. Kol. Nk. *vēr* id.

22. **merp-* (4163): Pa. *marp-* (*mart-*) 'to lighten'; *med-* 'to flash' (tiger's eye, etc.); Gad. *mers-* 'lightning', Kolami, Naiki. *merp-* 'to lighten, glitter'; cf. Te. *merupu* 'lightning'; OTe. *meṟayu*. Kannaḍa, Telugu, Parji point to PD **ṯ*; notice Parji has *med-* (< **meḏ-*) which is not affected by Rule 4. This suggests that there was a variant *mer-* (< **meṟ-*) in which the vowel is lowered.

23. **per-*V (3621): Pa. *parṭub*, (S) *parup* 'cream'; Nk. *perag*, *perg*, Kol. *pereg* 'curds'; cf. Te. *perugu* 'curds'; *pēru* 'to curdle'; Kannaḍa and Toda give evidence for *ṟ* < **-ṯ-*. Kolami and Naiki forms look like Telugu borrowings, whereas the Parji form has a meaning not attested in any other language.

24. In another case (*S*813), Pa. *melk-* 'to lighten', (S) *malk-*, Gad. *mel-* id., only the Southern dialect has vowel-lowering.

It appears from the above that a competing sound change is in process which has not yet developed a 'flip-flop' relation with Rule 1.[9]

4. The Vowel-raising Rule has relevance to the synchronic phonology of Parji as well as to certain types of dialect variation within it. In the earlier sections we have illustrated the application of the rule only morpheme-internally. It will be shown below that Rules 1 and 2 have a much longer history than is evident from the Parji data.

Burrow and Bhattacharya (1953: § 2, pp. 1–2) mentioned that the final *-a* of nominal stems alternates with *-e* before the plural suffix *-l* and the accusative-genitive

4 in Parji have a competing relation with Rule 1, because Rule 2 generates forms having environments to which Rule 1 could have applied if 2 preceded 1. Rule 4 has reversed the direction of the sound change in identical environments.

[9] It appears that when Parji was recorded (about 1950) the new sound change had just started, because the number of items involved is very small. We can see in *melk-*, *malk-* 'to lighten' that the Southern dialect shows *a*, while the North-west has *e*; even the interrogative *ār* could be a recent change from the more widely distributed *ēr* (see above). There is another doubtful etymology, Pa. *valip-* (*valit-*) 'to expel' from PD **veḷ-*V- (*DED* 4526), in which we notice deretroflexion of **ḷ* as well as vowel-lowering. As a sound change, the lowering of a high vowel before *r* is more commonly found than its reverse (see Bhat 1974: § 2.1.1.).

suffix *-n* in inflection. This can be formulated as a synchronic rule of vowel alternation within Parji as follows:

Rule 5.

$$V\ [+\text{low}, -\text{long}] \rightarrow [-\text{low}, -\text{high}, -\text{back}] / \_\_\_ + \left\{ \begin{array}{l} l\ [+\text{plural}] \\ n\ [+\text{acc.}, +\text{gen}] \end{array} \right\}_{\text{Noun}]}$$

A low short vowel *a* of noun stems changes to *-e* before *-l* (plural) and *-n* (accusative homophonous with genitive) in inflection.

Examples:

	Stem	Plural	Accusative-Genitive
'dog'	*netta*	*nette-l*	*nette-n*
'cloth'	*ganḍa*	*ganḍe-l*	*ganḍe-n*
'lemon'	*rimma*	*rimme-l*	*rimme-n*
'field'	*vāya*	*vāye-l*	*vaye-n*

This is a very productive process in Parji, and is regular and operative in both native and non-native words (Burrow and Bhattacharya 1953: §§19, 28, 38).

When we compare Parji stems with their cognates in Ollari, Gadaba, Kolami and Naiki, it is found that, corresponding to Parji stem-final *-a*, these languages have mostly *-e*, and in some cases doublets in *-a*/*-e*. In all these languages the plural is formed by a simple addition of the plural morph *-l*. Examine the data (the plural morph is *-l* uniformly in all):

	DED(S)	Parji	Ollari	Gadaba	Kolami	Naiki
'bullock; cow'	1837	*kōnda*	*kōnde*	*kōnde*	*kōnda*	*kōnda*
'vegetable'	1467	*kucca*	*kuse*	*kucce*	*kucce*	*kucce*
'goat'	4174	*mēya*	*mēge*	*mege*	*mēke*	*meke*
'dog'	3022	*netta*	*nēte*	*nette*	*(n)āte*	*āte*
'fly'	3430	*pinda*	*pinde*	—	—	*pinda, pinde*
'a caste'	2753	*tula*	*tule*	*tulle*	—	—
'egg'	1074	*kerba* (< **karba*)	*karbe*	—	—	—
'male call'	1497	*kurra*	*kurra*	—	*kurra*	*kurra*

There are also stems with final *-a* that does not alternate with *-e* in all languages except Parji, e.g. Kol. *kala* (*-l*) 'dream', *pāṭa* (*-l*) 'song', *goria* (*-l*) 'deer' (Emeneau 1955a: §4.48): Oll. *garnḍa* (*-l*), *baya* (*-l*) 'mad man' (Bhattacharya 1957: §13, p. 18). In Naiki of Chanda *-l* plural occurs after the *e-* stem only, even where there are doublets, e.g. sg. *pinda, pinde*, pl. *pinde-l* (Bhattacharya 1961–2: §3).[10] A comparison of these with the remaining Dravidian languages shows that *-a* is historically the older vowel in all cases and *-e* has resulted from change. It is therefore reasonable to conclude that

[10] This would have made a $a \rightarrow e / \_\_\_ l$ a synchronic rule in Nk. (Ch.), but, unfortunately, there is not sufficient data in Bhattacharya (1961) for us to make a clear statement about it.

Rule 6. *a* → *e* / ___ +*l* (plural)

started as a shared innovation in all these languages. But with the restructuring of the *a*-ending stems as *e*-ending, it was lost in all the sister languages before it covered the entire lexicon.[11] In Parji, however, it continues as a productive morphophonemic process.

4.1. One major difficulty in positing Rule 6 is that the plural morph *l* derives from Proto-Central Dravidian **ḷ*. We have noticed that in Parji, morpheme-internally deretroflexion (Rule 2) occurred after the Vowel-raising Rule ceased to operate. The assumption underlying Rule 6 requires that deretroflexion precede vowel-raising in nominal inflection. Insofar as the plural morph is concerned Parji, Ọllari, Gaḏaba show no trace of the original retroflex in their plural morphs *-l*, *-k V̆l* (< **ḷ*, **kV̆ḷ*); these three constitute a subgroup, the other subgroup being Kolami and Naiki (Chanda). Only Naikṛi (alleged to be a dialect of Kolami, cf. Bhattacharya 1961–2: §2; pp. 8, 9) preserves **ḷ* before non-front vowels and after apical consonants (Emeneau 1955a: §§10, 19). Following front vowels Naikṛi also has *l* only. It follows from the above discussion and examination of data comparatively that lateral deretroflexion started first in the plural morpheme (i.e. across the morph boundary) and then spread to the interior of morphemes by gradual lexical diffusion.

Vowel-raising before *-n* and *-r* in noun inflection is noticed sporadically in the other Central Dravidian languages also: Parji *-ed* (< *-eḏ* < **aḏ* < **-anḏ*) masc. sg. suffix; *-er*, masc. pl., e.g. *bert-ed* 'big man', *bert-er* 'big men'; *tend-er* 'fathers', *muttak-er* 'old men'; Kol. *-ar*/*-er* masc. pl., Nk (Ch.) *-en* masc. sg., e.g. *tol-en* 'brother', *kaym-an* 'wife's younger brother'; *-er*, *-ker*, *-ar* masc. pl., e.g. *tol-er* 'brother'; *rājaker* 'kings'; Oll. *-er*, *-or* masc. pl., e.g. *muttak-or* 'old men'; *il-er* 'bridegrooms' (Shanmugam 1971: §2.16.3). In all these languages (except Parji), the alternation of *a*/*e* is not phonologically conditioned.

Outside Parji, there is, then, evidence that *a* → *e* started before *l*, *r*, *n* in derivation and inflection, although only in Parji has it been generalized and developed into a productive sound change. Since *l*, *r*, *n* are alveolar sonorants in all these languages, we may say that before Parji split off Rule 6 tended to be gradually generalized in all of them in the following form, with 'sporadic' application:[12]

Rule 6'.
V [+low] → [–low, –high, –back] /+___C [+ anterior, + apical, + sonorant]

[11] Noun stems ending *a* or *e* in Kolami and Naiki (Naikṛi) are almost evenly distributed in the lexicon. Of cognates available in both languages, there are 34 stems in final *-a* and 35 in *-e*; only one item has *-e* in Kolami and *-a* in Naiki, viz. Kol. *tōke*, Nk. *tōka* (*DED* 2916). Wherever Parji has cognates for these it has mostly *a*. This is a case of rule loss in Kolami and Naiki, which continued synchronically in Parji.

[12] *a*→*e* before *n*, *r*, *l* as a sporadic change in bound forms is noticed to a lesser extent also in the other tribal languages of the area, viz. Kui, Kuvi, Koṇḍa, Pengo, etc., but it has not developed into a regular sound change in any of them (Shanmugam 1971: §§2.12–5; pp. 71–83).

5. Finite verbs and predicative nouns in Dravidian carry pronominal suffixes which agree with the subject noun or pronoun. They are generally of the shape -VC or VCC and may be tentatively reconstructed for Proto-Dravidian as follows:

		Singular	Plural
1		*-ē̆n*	*-ē̆m* (incl.)
2		*-i*(C)	*-ī̆r*
3	masc.	*-anṯ*	*-ar*
	neut.	*-at*	*-aw*

Since these occur as final syllables (of verbs or predicative nouns) carrying the weakest degree of prominence (or stress), their vowel nuclei tend to become neutralized and lose their qualitative distinction; this leads to the obscuring of the original vowel qualities. Contrasts tend to be maintained in the consonants, but when these drop out, the contrasts persist in the remaining vowels. By and large, the consonants of the pronominal suffixes can be reconstructed whereas the vocalic qualities cannot, even for some major subgroups. Consequently most of the languages have homophonous forms for the second plural and the third human plural.

The Parji personal suffixes reflect the operation of Rule 1 in the personal morpheme, wherever *a* is followed by a pre-Parji alveolar consonant. The vowel qualities differ from one paradigm to another and from one dialect to another. These variations result from different types of sound change with which the Vowel-raising Rule has interacted.

5.1. Burrow and Bhattacharya (1953) have supplied data for finite verb formation from the North-western and Southern dialects. They have given some information from the North-eastern dialect also. For predicative nouns, data are provided mainly from the North-western dialect, which 'forms the basis' of their grammatical treatment (ix). The following is the paradigm of a predicative noun formed from an adjective *pun-* 'new'.

		Singular	Plural
1		*pun-en* 'I am new'	*pun-om* 'we are new', etc.
2		*pun-ot*	*pun-or*
3	masc.	*pun-ed*	*pun-er*
	neut.	*pun-o(t)*	*pun-ov*

In the North-western dialect the personal morphemes are uniform for all verbs and nouns and have little variation except in the future tense. In the above, wherever there is an *e* it can be accounted for by the Vowel-raising Rule, *-en* (<*-an*), *-ed* (< *-eḏ* < **-aḏ*), *-er* (< *-ar*).[13] In the remaining cases, *o* is from an underlying *a* which

[13] We should expect *-er* in 2 pl., since it is also derived from underlying *-ar* (see § 5.6 of this article for future tense paradigm, where *-ar* is 2 pl. and 3 masc. pl.) : *a* → *o* here must be analogical to avoid homonymy.

developed as an unconditioned change, in unstressed position, perhaps under the influence of Oriya in which short /a/ is always phonetically a low back rounded vowel.[14] It is assumed here that the vowel quality of all the personal suffixes in their underlying form is *-a*. All the dialectal and paradigmatic variations can be derived from underlying forms with this vowel. As a matter of fact, they are still preserved in this form in the North-western and Southern dialects in the future tense paradigm (Burrow and Bhattacharya 1953: §79).

5.2. All finite verbs fit into the formula: stem + tense + person. One of the future tense morphs in the North-western dialect is *-r-*, corresponding to *-iy-* in the Southern. For a large number of verbs in both the dialects the future tense marker is *-t-*/*-d*.

(Example *cūṛ* 'to see'):

	North-west		South	
	Singular	Plural	Singular	Plural
1	*cūṛ-r-an*	*cūṛ-r-am*	*cūṛ -iy-an*	*cūṛ-iy-am*
2	*cūṛ-r-at*	*cūṛ-r-ar*	*cūṛ-iy-at*	*cūṛ-iy-ar*
3 masc.	*cūṛ-r-ad*	*cūṛ-r-ar*	*cūṛ-iy-ad*	*cūṛ-iy-ar*
neut.	*cūṛ-r-a*	*cūṛ-r-av*	*cūṛ-iy-a*	*cūṛ-iy-av*

When the stem has a long closed syllable, i.e. (C)V̄C- or (C)VCC- (where the final consonant is an obstruent), an 'auxiliary vowel' *u* is inserted between the stem and the tense suffix, e.g. *moṛk-* 'to salute', *moṛk-u-r-an* 'I will salute', etc. (Burrow and Bhattacharya 1953: §79).[15] The following rule accounts for the auxiliary vowel here:

	Singular	Plural
2	*ot*	**er > or*
3 masc.	*ed*	*er*

B & B point out that the future tense stems are identical with the past tense stems in the case of some high frequency verbs. In such cases the tense contrasts are signalled only by the different vowels in the personal suffixes, e.g. *cendan* 'I will go', *cenden* 'I went', etc. It is reasonable to think that it is because of this need to maintain distinction in tenses that $a \rightarrow e$ did not affect the vowels in the future tense.

[14] B & B (2) call attention to *a*/*o* alternation dialectically. They say that North-west has *o* corresponding to *a* in the South; NW *gurrol* 'horse', *kukonḍi* 'panther', *camoto* 'rotten' (3 sg. neut.): S *gurral, kukanḍi, camata*, etc. 'Sometimes, this variation appears in the form of an alternation between *o* and *e*, since in these cases *o* represents original *a*: NW *payot, poyov*, neut. sg. and pl. "green", *bayov* "elder sister", *poyor* "foam": S *payet, payev, bayev, poyer*, etc.' (2). We notice that all three dialects have *o* < *a* in verb inflection.

[15] Noun stems of the form (C)V_1CV_2C have either *u* or *i* as V_2 (*i* if the following consonant is a palatal, otherwise *u*). When any vowel follows across morph boundaries, V_2 is lost regularly, e.g.

merud	'medicine'	:	*merd-ul* (pl.)
polub	'village'	:	*polb-ul* (pl.), *polb-in* (acc.)
paḍic	'boy'	:	*paḍc-il* (pl.)

B & B (§3) describe these as anaptyctic vowels. The vowel is retained before word boundary or another consonant across the boundary. If the underlying forms of these are set up with final clusters, we need a rule of the type

Rule 7. Auxiliary (Epenthetic) Vowel Insertion

$$\emptyset \rightarrow u / \left\{ \begin{matrix} \bar{V}C \\ VCC \end{matrix} \right\} + \_\_ + C_{\text{Verb}]}$$

5.2.1. Present tense. The present tense morph is *-m-* in all dialects. The personal suffixes are:

		Singular	Plural
1		*-en*	*-om*
2		*-ot*	*-or*
3	masc.	*-ed*	*-er*
	neut.	*-o*	*-ov*

ver- 'to come', *ver-m-en* 'I will come', etc. Even here the Auxiliary Vowel Rule applies, but it is different in each dialect. In the South it is *a*, in the North-west *e* or *o* corresponding to the vowel of the termination, and in the North-east it is *u* (Burrow and Bhattacharya 1953: §74):

South

		Singular	Plural
1		*cūṛ-a-m-on*	*cūṛ-a-m-om*
2		*cūṛ-a-m-ot*	*cūṛ-a-m-or*
3	masc.	*cūṛ-a-m-od*	*cūṛ-a-m-or*
	neut.	*cūṛ-a-m-o*	*cūṛ-a-m-ov*

North-west		North-east	
Singular	Plural	Singular	Plural
cūṛ-e-m-en	*cūṛ-o-m-om*	*cūṛ-u-m-en*	*cūṛ-u-m-om*
cūṛ-o-m-ot	*cūṛ-o-m-or*	*cūṛ-u-m-ot*	*cūṛ-u-m-or*
cūṛ-e-m-ed	*cūṛ-e-m-er*	*cūṛ-u-m-ed*	*cūṛ-u-m-er*
cūṛ-o-m-o	*cūṛ-o-m-ov*	*cūṛ-u-m-o*	*cūṛ-u-m-ov*

Notice in the Southern dialect the auxiliary vowel is *a* which is identical with the vowel of the underlying personal morphemes as found in the future tense. Since the auxiliary vowel is a copy of the vowel of the following syllable, our proposal to take the personal morphs found in the future tense paradigm as underlying is reinforced here. After the auxiliary vowel is harmonized, the vowel in the personal morphemes unconditionally changes to *o*. In the North-west, we also start with underlying *a* in

---

$$\emptyset \rightarrow u / C\_\_C \left\{ \begin{matrix} +C \\ \# \end{matrix} \right\}$$

B & B report that in verb inflection, the epenthetic vowel follows the rule in the case of stems cited with final *p*/*t*, e.g. *culp- cult-* 'to rise', e.g. *culup-m-od* 'he is rising'; 'in the case of potential forms in *-tut, tum, -tur*', the epenthetic vowel comes after the stem final -CC, e.g. *culp-u-tut*, etc. (§3). Where the final consonant is not a stem alternant *p*/*t*, e.g. *moṛk-* 'to salute', the epenthetic vowel comes after the stem.

the personal morphemes and *u* as epenthetic vowel. The Vowel-raising Rule operates, first changing *a* to *e* before alveolars, followed by the Vowel-rounding Rule of remaining *a*'s. The Vowel Harmony Rule then copies whatever vowel there is in the personal morpheme. In the North-east, the two rules affecting the quality of the personal suffix vowel also operate, but the epenthetic vowel remains unchanged as *u*, as in the future tense paradigm. Both descriptively and historically it seems best to take *u* as the underlying auxiliary vowel in all dialects, and for all paradigms followed by vowel harmony in the Southern and North-western dialects.

The order in which the rules apply accounts for the existing dialect variation.

5.3. The relevant rules may be formulated as follows:

Rule 7. Epenthetic Vowel Insertion (revised). $\emptyset \rightarrow u / X \_\_ + C_{\text{verb}]}$

(X = a verb stem of (C)$\bar{V}$C or (C)VCC shape, and the C following the morpheme boundary represents tense. One of the two consonants between which the epenthetic vowel is inserted must be an obstruent.)

The epenthetic vowel *u*, inserted by Rule 7, is changed to harmonize with the vowel in the following syllable.

Rule 8. Vowel Harmony. $u \rightarrow V_i / X + \_\_ C + V_i\ (C)\ \#_{\text{verb}]}$

Rule 9. Vowel-raising (restricted form of Rule 1)

$$a \rightarrow e / \_\_ \begin{Bmatrix} \underline{d} \\ r \\ n \end{Bmatrix}$$

Rule 10. Low Vowel Rounding. $a \rightarrow o / + \_\_ (C)\ \#_{\text{verb}]}$

Rule 10 is in a 'bleeding relation' to Rule 9, i.e. Rule 10 applies to forms left out after Rule 9 has applied. In some cases the rules operate conjunctively and in others disjunctively.[16]

Rule 11. Alveolar Stop Neutralization (part of Rule 3 repeated). $\underline{d} \rightarrow d$

5.4. Let us examine how these rules interact in the derivation of the surface forms in different dialects in the case of the present tense:
cūṛ- 'to see', *-m-* present tense suffix.

[16] The application of Rule 10 blocks the application of Rule 9, because there will not remain any *a* segments to which 9 can apply. But it will be seen that whenever Rule 9 applies Rule 10 also applies conjunctively. For the definitions of 'conjunctive' and 'disjunctive' orderings, see Schane 1973: 89–90.

South

	1 sg.	1 pl.	3 masc. sg.	3 masc. pl.
Underlying forms	*cūṛ-m-an*	*cūṛ-m-am*	*cūṛ-m-aḏ*	*cūṛ-m-ar*
Rule 7	*cūṛ-u-m-an*	*cūṛ-u-m-am*	*cūṛ-u-m-aḏ*	*cūṛ-u-m-ar*
Rule 8	*cūṛ-a-m-an*	*cūṛ-a-m-am*	*cūṛ-a-m-aḏ*	*cūṛ-a-m-ar*
Rule 10	*cūṛ-a-m-on*	*cūṛ-a-m-om*	*cūṛ-a-m-oḏ*	*cūṛ-a-m-or*
Rule 11	—	—	*cūṛ-a-m-od*	—
Surface forms	*cūṛ-am-on*	*cūṛ-am-om*	*cūṛ-am-od*	*cūṛ-am-or*

Notice that the Vowel-raising Rule (Rule 9) does not operate in this paradigm; but Rule 11 which changes *ḏ* to *d* operates as the last rule.

North-western

	1 sg.	1 pl.	3 masc. sg.	3 masc. pl.
Underlying forms	*cūṛ-m-an*	*cūṛ-m-am*	*cūṛ-m-aḏ*	*cūṛ-m-ar*
Rule 7	*cūṛ-u-m-an*	*cūṛ-u-m-am*	*cūṛ-u-m-aḏ*	*cūṛ-u-m-ar*
Rule 9	*cūṛ-u-m-en*	—	*cūṛ-u-m-eḏ*	*cūṛ-u-m-er*
Rule 10	—	*cūṛ-u-m-om*	—	—
Rule 8	*cūṛ-e-m-en*	*cūṛ-o-m-om*	*cūṛ-e-m-eḏ*	*cūṛ-e-m-er*
Rule 11	—	—	*cūṛ-e-m-ed*	—
Surface forms	*cūṛ-em-en*	*cūṛ-om-om*	*cūṛ-em-ed*	*cūṛ-em-er*

The Southern dialect is characterized by the absence of Rule 9 and the North-eastern dialect by the absence of Rule 8 which harmonizes the epenthetic *u* to the vowel in the following syllable. However, all northern dialects share Rules 9 and 10 in that order. There is an interesting relationship between the South and the North-west. The Vowel Harmony Rule (Rule 8) precedes the Vowel-rounding Rule (Rule 10) in the South, whereas it follows 9 and 10 in the North-west. This is an excellent case of switch in rule ordering to achieve symmetry and a simplified grammar.

5.5. Preterite. There are two kinds of preterite formation. After one class of stems, the preterite marker is zero; a verb root like *cūṛ-* 'to see' is simply followed by personal morphemes (except in third neuter singular):

		Singular	Plural
1		*cūṛ-en*	*cūṛ-om*
2		*cūṛ-ot*	*cūṛ-or*
3	masc.	*cūr-ed*	*cūṛ-er*
	neut.	*cūṛ-ot-o*	*cūṛ-ov*

Here the third neuter singular should be **cūṛ-o*, but *cūṛ-ot-o*, which occurs in the extended form of preterite, has replaced it. Burrow and Bhattacharya (1953: §76) say that this conjugation is common to all three dialects, except for the third neuter singular which, in the Southern dialect, is *cūṛ-at-a*, a case of retention of the underlying form. The majority of stems form the preterite by the addition of *ñ* (from *ñj* < **nd* after a stem-final front vowel or *y*; e.g. *cay* 'to die', *ca-ñ-ed* 'he died' from underlying **cay-ñj-ad̠*),[17] *n*, *d*, *t* with sandhi variants which do not concern us here. No auxiliary vowel occurs in all such cases, because the roots are generally of (C)V̄ or (C)VC type. Burrow and Bhattacharya (1953: §78) report an extended form of preterite: 'it is much commoner in the South than in the North. Examples are recorded only from those verbs which do not change their stem in the past tense. It is quite likely that this form of the past tense is formed only from such verbs, but our evidence is not complete enough to be quite definite about this.' This tense is formed by the addition of *-t-* with a preceding auxiliary vowel. The auxiliary vowel is *a* in the Southern dialect, but it is identical with the vowel of the following syllable in the North-west. No material from the North-eastern dialect is available.

	North-west		South	
	Singular	Plural	Singular	Plural
1.	*cūṛ-e-t-en*	*cūṛ-o-t-om*	*cūṛ-a-t-en*	*cūṛ-a-t-om*
2.	*cūṛ-o-t-ot*	*cūṛ-o-t-or*	*cūṛ-a-t-ot*	*cūṛ-a-t-or*
3 masc.	*cūṛ-e-t-ed*	*cūṛ-e-t-er*	*cūṛ-a-t-ed*	*cūṛ-a-t-er*
neut.	*cūṛ-o-t-o*	*cūṛ-o-t-ov*	*cūṛ-a-ta*	*cūṛ-a-t-ov*

As in the case of the present tense conjugation, the North-western and Southern dialects are differentiated by the order of application of Rules 7–10. The Southern dialect forms are derivable by applying Rule 7 (insertion of *u* as epenthetic vowel after the stem), Rule 8 (hormonizing *u* to *a* of the following syllable), followed by Rule 9 (low vowel raising), and Rule 10 (low vowel rounding). Notice that there is a relic of this underlying representation in the Southern dialect in the third neuter singular where Rule 10 has not operated. This shows that the Southern dialect has a more highly complicated grammar in verb formation, which is simplified in the North-western dialect by reordering the Rules as 7, 9 + 10, 8. Examine the derivations:

	South				
	1 sg.	1 pl.	3 masc. sg.	3 neut. sg.	3 masc. pl.
Underlying forms	*cūṛ-t-an*	*cūṛ-t-am*	*cūṛ-t-ad̠*	*cūṛ-t-a*	*cūṛ-t-ar*
Rule 7	*-u-*	*-u-*	*-u-*	*u-*	*-u-*
Rule 8	*-a-*	*-a-*	*-a-*	*-a-*	*-a-*
Rule 9	*-en*	—	*-ed̠*	—	*-er*
Rule 10	—	*-om*	—	[–Rule 10] *-a*	*-er*
Rule 11	—	—	*-ed*	—	—
Surface forms	*cūṛ-at-en*	*cūṛ-at-om*	*cūṛ-at-ed*	*cūṛ-at-a*	*cūrat-er*

[17] The palatalization of the past tense *nd* to *ñj* (> *ñ*) also seems to be a recent development in Parji, because the past tense of *ver-* 'to come' is *ve-ñ-*; in this verb the front vowel *e* is from *a* before *r* by Rule 1, and only after Rule 1 had operated could palatalization take place. This gives us a relative chronology of vowel-raising and palatalization in Parji. The origin of *ñ* from **nd* is discussed in detail by Subrahmanyam (1964).

	North-west				
	1 sg.	1 pl.	3 masc. sg.	3 neut. sg.	3 masc. pl.
Underlying forms	*cūṛ-t-an*	*cūṛ-t-am*	*cūṛ-t-aḏ*	*cūṛ-t-a*	*cūṛ-t-ar*
Rule 7	*-u-*	*-u-*	*-u-*	*-u-*	*-u-*
Rule 9	*-en*	—	*-eḏ*	—	*-er*
Rule 10	*-e-*	*-om*		*-o*	—
Rule 8	—	*-o-*	*-e-*	*-o-*	*-e-*
Rule 11	—	—	*-ed*	—	—
Surface forms	*cūṛ-et-en*	*cūṛ-ot-om*	*cūṛ-et-ed*	*cūṛ-ot-o*	*cūṛ-et-er*

5.6. Extended Present. There is also an 'extended form of the present tense made by the addition of an extra suffix *-t-*... This is much commoner in the Southern dialect than in the North-western (material for the North-eastern is not available)' (Burrow and Bhattacharya 1953: §75, pp. 51–2). It may be recalled that the present tense is formed by adding *-m* to the verb stem. In stems of (C)V̄C type, the epenthetic vowel comes between the two tense markers *-m-* and *-t-*, e.g.:

	North-west		South	
	Singular	Plural	Singular	Plural
1	*ver-m-e-t-en*	*ver-m-o-t-om*	*ver-m-o-t-en*	*ver-m-o-t-om*
2	*ver-m-o-t-ot*	*ver-m-o-t-or*	*ver-m-o-t-ot*	*ver-m-o-t-or*
3 masc.	*ver-m-e-t-ed*	*ver-m-e-t-er*	*ver-m-o-t-ed*	*ver-m-o-t-er*
neut.	*ver-m-o-t-o*	*ver-m-o-t-ov*	*ver-m-o-t-a*	*ver-m-o-t-ov*

In these paradigms *ver-m-* is treated as a CVC-C- stem, although it already contains a tense morph- *m-*; the Southern dialect forms are derivable from the underlying *a-* vowel in the personal suffixes by applying Rule 7 (epenthetic *u* insertion), Rule 8 (vowel harmony changing *u* to *a*), Rule 9 (low vowel raising), and 10 (low vowel rounding converting all *a*'s to *o*'s in the ultimate and penultimate syllables). In the North-west, as usual, the rule ordering is changed—with the Vowel Harmony Rule (Rule 8) coming after Rules 7, 9 + 10. For the Southern dialect it appears that Rules 7 and 8 look unmotivated, but notice 3 neut. sg. *ver-m-o-t-a* (apparently a relic form) in which the personal suffix vowel *-a* has not undergone low vowel rounding, which should, therefore, be marked [–Rule 10].

When the verb root is of (C)V̄C or (C)VCC-type, we have two epenthetic vowels occurring: (C)V̄C + epenthetic V + *m* + epenthetic V + *t* + person. Such a paradigm is given only for the Southern dialect:

	South	
	Singular	Plural
1	*cūṛ-a-m-o-t-en*	*cūṛ-a-m-ot-om*
2	*cūṛ-a-m-o-t-ot*	*cūṛ-a-m-o-t-or*
3 masc.	*cūṛ-a-m-o-t-ed*	*cūṛ-a-m-o-t-er*
neut.	*cūṛ-a-m-o-t-a*	*cūṛ-a-m-o-t-ov*

These forms are derivable from **cūṛ-a-m-a-t-an*, *cūṛ-a-m-a-t-am*, etc. There are two epenthetic vowels here of which the post-stem vowel retains its underlying quality but the second one (occurring between two tense-suffixes in the penultimate syllable) undergoes the rounding rule.

The Southern dialect has apparently extended the domain of operation of Rule 10 to ultimate and penultimate syllables (except in the case of the third neuter singular suffix) in extended present. Rule 7, 8, and 10 have to be modified to provide for an extra epenthetic vowel as follows:

Rule 7'. $\emptyset \rightarrow u \,/\, X\,(+ \_\_ C)_{1}^{2}{}_{\text{verb}]}$

Thus *u* is inserted between a morpheme boundary and a tense marker. Such a sequence, i.e. + ___ C occurs at least once but never more than twice. This notation takes care of the double occurrence of the epenthetic vowel, one after the verb stem and the tense marker, the second between two tense markers. Other structural conditions stated in Rule 7 remain the same.

Rule 8'. $u \rightarrow V_i \,/\, X\,(+ \_\_ C)_{1}^{2}\, V_i\,(C)\,\#_{\text{verb}]}$

Rule 10'. $a \rightarrow o \,/\, + \_\_ C + \_\_ (C)\,\#_{\text{verb}]}$

5.7. The following chart shows the combination of rules applicable in the derivation of different tense forms in different dialects. (As already reported, data from the North-east are extremely limited.)

		South	North-west	North-east
1.	Future	—	7	—
2.	Present	7, 8, 10	7, 9 + 10, 8	7, 9 + 10
3.	Preterite (extended)	7, 8, 9 + 10	7, 9 + 10, 8	—
4.	Present (extended)	7', 8', 9 + 10'	7, 9 + 10, 8	—

This chart strikingly shows how dialect differences can be formally expressed. It is the presence or absence of a rule that distinguishes the three dialects in the present-tense formation. The Southern dialect lacks Rule 9 and the North-eastern Rule 8, whereas the North-western dialect has all the four rules 7–10. Secondly, the order in which rules apply also distinguishes the Northern dialects. Rule 8 must have preceded 9 and 10 historically, otherwise there is no way of accounting for *a* as an epenthetic vowel in the Southern dialect; since Rules 9, 10 followed the Vowel Harmony Rule (Rule 8), the effects of vowel harmony are overlaid by these later rules. The North-eastern dialect has reordered the rules, maximizing the utility of Rule 8 and making it 'transparent'.[18]

[18] Kiparsky (1971: §3) introduces the notion of transparency and opaqueness of rules, followed by further refinements in 1973a. Revising his earlier (1968) statement that 'feeding order tends to be maximized', he says: 'Rules tend to be ordered so as to become maximally transparent.' (1971: 623). 'A rule A → B/C__D is opaque to the extent that there are surface representations of the form (i) A in

In the extended present-tense conjugation, the Southern dialect tended to further complicate its grammar by revising the form of Rule 7, 8, 10 as 7', 8', 10'. Notice that no two conjugations are alike with respect to the epenthetic vowel and the personal suffix vowels in the Southern dialect, as compared to the North-west.

Surface forms of the non-stem vowels

	South	North-west
	S – T – P	S – T – P
Present	*a* *o*	$\left\{\begin{matrix} e \\ o \end{matrix}\right. \left\{\begin{matrix} e \\ o \end{matrix}\right.$
Extended past	*a* $\left\{\begin{matrix} e \\ o \end{matrix}\right.$	$\left\{\begin{matrix} e \\ o \end{matrix}\right. \left\{\begin{matrix} e \\ o \end{matrix}\right.$
	S – T – T – P	*S – T – T – P
Extended present	*a* *o* $\left\{\begin{matrix} e \\ o \end{matrix}\right.$	$\left\{\begin{matrix} e \\ o \end{matrix}\right. \left\{\begin{matrix} e \\ o \end{matrix}\right. \left\{\begin{matrix} e \\ o \end{matrix}\right.$

(S = stem; T = tense; P = person)

If data were available for the North-west for extended forms with two epenthetic vowels we could predict that the forms would be like *cūṛ-e-m-e-t-en*, etc.

It can also be argued that the North-western dialect has applied the vowel harmony rule twice, once before the application of Rules 9 and 10 as it happened in the South and a second time after their application;

	S – T – P	
	*Ø *a*	
	↓	
Rule 7	**u*	
	↓	
Rule 8	**a* *a*	
	↓	
	↓ $\left\{\begin{matrix} e \\ o \end{matrix}\right.$	Rule 9 / Rule 10
Rule 8	$\left\{\begin{matrix} e \\ o \end{matrix}\right.$	

What Kiparsky (1968) calls 'reordering' seems to be the consequence of one of a pair of rules recurring because of its versatility.[19] The first occurrence of Rule 8 in

environment C__D; or (ii) B in environment other than C__D. . . . Opacity as here defined is a matter of degree, although I have no suggestions as to how to quantify it formally'. 'Let us refer to the converse of opacity as "transparency."' (1971: 621–2). It is, however, not clear whether 'transparency' is a property of a rule or of ordering or both. In the Parji case, though Rule 8 remains unchanged, the ordering has made it 'transparent'.

[19] Rule reordering postulated by Kiparsky (1968: §§2, 8) seems to be the consequence of a linguistic process (or processes) rather than being a process itself. Every case of rule reordering cited by Kiparsky (177–9) can be accounted for by rule reapplication, e.g.

the North-west was at a time when both the North-west and the South were a single dialect area. The second occurrence of Rule 8 is part of the synchronic grammar of this dialect and was an innovation to achieve paradigmatic regularity.

6. **Summary**. The Vowel-raising Rule (*a* → *e*) seems to have started in Proto-Central Dravidian sporadically in nominal inflection, particularly before the plural morph *-l* (< **-ḷ*). From this it follows that deretroflexion of the plural morph preceded this rule in point of time: *a* → *e* is also noticed irregularly before *n* and *r* representing personal suffixes in the languages closely related to Parji. Only in Parji

Finnish:

Underlying forms		**vee**	**teɣe**
Rule a:	diphthongization	vie	—
Rule b:	loss of medial consonant	—	tee
Reordered (dialectal)			
Rule b:	loss of medial consonant	—	tee
Rube a:	diphthongization	vie	tie

German:

Underlying form		**bodə**
Rule a:	umlaut	bödə
Rule b:	lowering (before a coronal)	—
Recordered (Swiss German)		
Rule b:	lowering (before a coronal)	bɔ də
Rule a:	umlaut	bɔ də

The recordered rules thus optimize their application.

The two dialects, say, D_1 and D_2 in each case have a common stage and D_2 differs from D_1 by reapplying Rule a.

D_1	D_2
a }	a } }
b }	b } }
	a }

The result of such a process gives us a reordering relationship between rules, but it is not as though the same rules applied in a reverse order to start with. A similar case can be cited from Telugu.

In Classical Telugu, verb stems with three syllables have either *u* or *a* in the medial syllable, e.g. *aḍugu* 'to ask', *aṇagu* 'to hide' (intr.). When a suffix vowel follows, the stem-final vowel is lost and the medial *u* (not *a*) is harmonized to the following vowel, e.g.:

1	*aḍugu + i*	*aḍigi-i*	'having asked'
	aḍugu + an	*aḍag-an*	'to ask'
	aḍugu + cu	*aḍugu-cu*	'asking'
2	*aṇagu + i*	*aṇag-i*	'having hidden'
	aṇagu + an	*aṇag-an*	'to hide'
	aṇagu + cu	*aṇagu-cu*	'hiding'

Some time in Middle Telugu (AD 1300–1500) medial *a* merged with *u*, and Vowel Harmony Rule applies to this *u* also. Therefore, the historical ordering of the rules was: (a) vowel harmony, (b) *a* → *u*. But, in effect, the latter stage of Telugu can be described by reordering the rules: (b) *a* → *u*, (a) vowel harmony. What happened is that the Vowel Harmony Rule applies wherever its conditions are fulfilled. Therefore, it has reapplied to the output of Rule 2 by producing, in effect, a reversal in ordering. We have to look for a new phenomenon here. Certain rules have a generality of application and only such rules can be

does the Vowel-raising Rule remain as a synchronic morphophonemic process; in Ollari, Gadaba, Kolami, and Naiki, we find, through reanalysis of *a*-ending stems as *e*-ending, that the rule had been lost before it covered the entire lexicon in plural formation.

The Vowel-raising Rule then extended morpheme-internally in Parji in a more generalized form by allowing the process to take place before all alveolar consonants, including the obstruents. This change must have taken place : (a) before the dialects split up; and (b) before the deretroflexion rule spread to the interior of stem morphemes. Since *a* → *e* does not operate before *l*, *n* (< **ḷ* **ṇ*) within stems, it must be concluded that the Vowel-raising Rule is no longer operative. Otherwise, we would expect all such cases to be subject to vowel-raising, and this has not happened. The complete merger of pre-Parji **ṯ*, **ḏ* with *t*, *d* in the North-western and Southern dialects and with *ṭ*, *ḍ* in the North-eastern dialect has totally eliminated these alveolar segments from Parji phonology, providing no clue to their original existence except perhaps through comparative dialectology and reconstruction. What remains as a synchronic phonological process is what is now left in noun morphology, viz. Rule 5.

The Vowel-raising Rule has also historically covered the pronominal inflections in all conjugations except the future tense, where we have *a* before *n*, *r*, and **ḏ*. A trace of *a*/*e* alternation is synchronically left in the conjugation system—recoverable (a) by a comparison of the future-tense forms with the rest of the verb system; and (b) by the quality of the auxiliary (epenthetic) vowel, which has not undergone vowel harmony in the Southern dialect. A question, therefore, arises whether Rules 7–10 are historical or synchronic. In the North-western dialect, which has reordered (or reapplied) Rule 8 after 9 and 10 to simplify its grammar, the vowel in the penultimate syllable is descriptively a copy of the vowel in the final syllable. The conditions under which *a* split up into *e* and *o* are obscured by the subsequent neutralization of **ḏ*, exceptional retention of *a* in the future tense, the play of analogy, and the relic forms in the South.

It appears that the Vowel-raising Rule got 'frozen' before it covered the entire inflectional system of the verb, which leaves us relic forms in the future tense.

reapplied. The innovation could be in reapplying a general rule in order to obtain a simplified grammar rather than reordering rules—which, translated into speakers' performance operating in time and space, is hard to conceive. Kiparsky explains how it could happen in the wave theory fashion: 'If Rule A spreads from West to East and Rule B spreads from East to West across some dialect area, then, if the two rules are critically ordered with respect to each other, the Western area would end up with the order A, B and the Eastern area with the order B, A.' (1968: 189). This is a plausible hypothesis if it can be shown for all cases of reordering that this was what has happened. Such a dialect situation normally produces three isoglosses: an area covered only by Rule A, another area covered only by Rule B, and a third one where A and B overlap to produce reverse ordering of rules. The cases cited by Kiparsky do not fall into this type. Kiparsky replaced 'bleeding' and 'feeding' ordering by more generalized notions of 'opaqueness' and 'transparency' in his revisions of 1971 (612–34) and 1973 (79–84), but has not modified his stand with respect to rule reordering being a type of linguistic change. The arguments of Koutsoudas, Sanders, and Noll (1974) against extrinsic ordering among rules are ingenious, but counter-intuitive and unconvincing.

Whereas Rule 8 is reactivated in the North-western dialect, it has become 'opaque' in the Southern dialect, which has the most complex system of conjugation.

In establishing underlying representations in generative phonology on the basis of surface alternations, no distinction is made between different kinds of alternations. Proposals like rule 'transparency', 'opacity', 'unmarked rule ordering', etc., have been made with the aim of making abstract representations less abstract. This problem is intimately related to the question: Which is a synchronic rule in grammar and which is diachronic? The opacity–transparency scale proposed by Kiparsky (1971, 1973a) seems to correspond broadly to the traditional diachronic–synchronic differentiation which should be looked upon as a continuum and not as a dichotomy. Therefore, at any given point of time, linguistic structure reflects both diachronic and synchronic phenomena, and it is the degree of productive use of such phenomena by speakers that distinguishes one from the other. To the extent that an erstwhile transparent rule becomes opaque, it also becomes less productive in the synchronic grammar of the speakers. In the case of Parji Rule 1, which largely became historical (opaque), has left a more transparent remnant (Rule 5) in nominal inflection and a less transparent one (Rule 9) in the verb inflection. Rules 7 and 8 presumably are reformulated in the synchronic grammars of the Parji dialects to make them more transparent:

Rule 7" (North-west). $\emptyset \rightarrow u / X + \_\_ C$

Rule 8" (North-west). $\emptyset \rightarrow [e,o] / X + \_\_ C[e,o]+$

Rule 7" (South). $\emptyset \rightarrow a / X + \_\_ C$

In the synchronic grammar of the Southern dialect, Rule 8 is totally lost. Rules 9 (low vowel split) and 10 (low vowel rounding) have only marginal transparency in different dialects, because of the survival of the underlying *a* vowel in the future-tense paradigm and in some relic forms of the Southern dialect. Opaque (historically older) rules tend to be either lost or frozen (as exceptions and relics), or they are reformulated with increased transparency in the synchronic grammar of a language as illustrated by the Parji case in this paper.

12

A Vowel-Lowering Rule in Kui-Kuvi

1. The South-Central branch of the Dravidian family consists of seven languages whose genetic subgrouping can be represented by the following tree diagram:

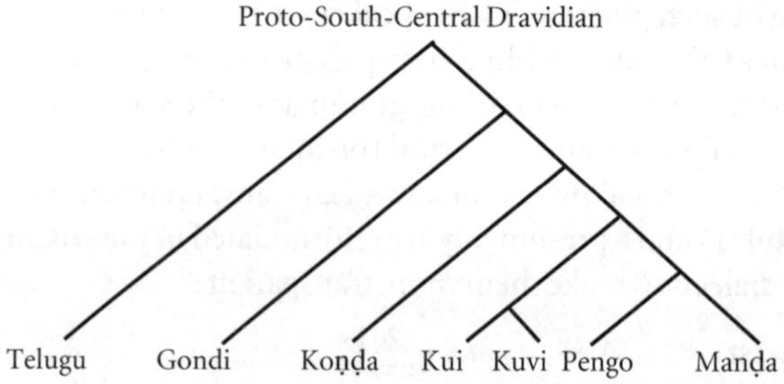

FIGURE 12.1. Family tree diagram of the South-Central Dravidian languages

Each of these languages has essentially a five-vowel system[1] /i e a o u/ with contrastive length /ī ē ā ō ū/. A comparative study of the vocabulary of Kui and Kuvi shows that, at some point in the history of the pre-Kui-Kuvi stage, long mid-vowels /ē ō/ merged with the long low vowel /ā/; i.e.

Rule C. {ē, ō} > ā/# (C)___ . . . (pre-Kui-Kuvi).

This is called Rule C, since it operates only on the output of two older rules, viz. the Vowel Contraction Rule (Rule A) and the Apical Displacement Rule (Rule B):

Professor Emeneau's publications have significantly contributed to comparative Dravidian phonology in addition to other areas, during the past three decades. If this short paper which is based on the data provided by the *Dravidian Etymological Dictionary* (1961) and its supplement (1968) can advance our knowledge of this area by another inch or so, I am sure my Guru will be happy to look at it as a small flower tucked in the bouquet of papers being presented to him by the Berkely Linguistic Society. I am grateful to the BLS for inviting me to join in their tribute to this great scholar and teacher.

The theme of this paper was conceived during my Fellowship year (1975–6) at the Center for Advanced Study in the Behavioral Sciences, Stanford, and a short mention of the underlying idea occurs in my review of Zvelebil's *Comparative Dravidian Phonology* (Krishnamurti 1976a: 144–5). However, this is a more detailed treatment of the problem with fuller data and a discussion of all the theoretical implications. Emeneau himself had encouraged me in 1976 to write it up into a full paper.

[1] Modern Telugu has developed /ǣ/ as a phoneme which arose from morphophonemic /iā/. [ǣ] can still be treated as a phonetic realization of underlying /iā/ in most of the native words.

Rule A. (C_1)[e, o]C_2-a- > (C_1) [ē, ō]- .
C_1 = any permissible Proto-Dravidian consonant in word-initial position: /p t c k m n ñ w/; for Proto-South-Central Dravidian we can set up /p b t d c j k g m n w/ as C_1.
(C_2) = any glide or glide-like continuant derived from PD **y*, **w*, **k* [ɣ].

Rule B. (C_1) [e, o]C_2-a- > $(C_1)C_2$[ē, ō]- (Proto-South-Central Dravidian).
C_1 = same as above; C_2 = an apical non-nasal consonant derived from PD **ṯ* [=ṟ], **l*, **r*, **ṭ*, **ḷ*, **ẓ*.

Rules A and B seem to share certain common features, viz. (a) the shape of the root as (C)VC; (b) the presence of a low vowel /a/ as the nucleus of the formative suffix; (c) contraction of root and formative vowels into a long vowel with the quality of the root vowel. However, the phonological processes yielding long vowels in the two rules are quite different and their relative chronology is also different. Rule A involves contraction of two syllabics across a weakly articulated glide into a long vowel, i.e. V_1C-*a* > $\bar{V}_1$. Rule B is an idiosyncratic development characterizing only the South-Central Dravidian subgroup. Whatever the underlying phonological process, the resultant sequences of this rule have either an apical as initial consonant if the underlying root begins with a vowel, or have an apical as C_2 in C_1C_2 if the underlying root begins with a consonant.

Rule A is found to operate at all stages and in all branches of Dravidian at different points of time, whereas Rule B is specifically a Proto-South-Central Dravidian rule (for details, see Krishnamurti 1978a: 18–19).

2. The following eighteen cases drawn from *DED(S)* show the operation of Rule C in Kui fully and in Kuvi partially.[2]

1. PSCD **ker-a-*, **ger-a-* / **krē-*, **grē-* 'to scoop up'. Kui *grāpa* (*grā-t-*): Koṇḍa *ker* (*ker-t-*) 'take handfuls, collect into a heap and pick up'; Kui *grēpa* (*grē-t-*), Kuvi *grec-* (*gre-t-*) Pe. *grē-*, Manḍa *grepa*, (BRR) *grē-* (S290).

2. PD **eḷ-a-*, PSCD **eḷ-a-*/**ḷē-* 'young, tender'. Kui *lāvenju* 'grown-up boy, young man', *lāa* 'grown-up girl'; Kuvi *rā'a*, *lā'a*, *ṛaˀa* 'young woman, virgin': Te. *ela*, *lē* adj. 'tender, young'; Go. *raiyōl* 'adult boy', *raiyā* 'adult girl', *layor*, *leyor* 'young male', *leyā* 'young female'; Kui *let* 'soft'; Koṇḍa *lēŋa* 'calf', *lēta* 'tender'; cf. Ta. Ma. *iḷa*, Ko. *eḷ*, To. *eḷ*, Ka. *eḷa*, Tu. *eḷe*, 'young, tender'; Pa. *iled* 'young man', *ile* 'young woman'; Gad. *ilenḍ* 'bridegroom', *iled* 'bride' (436).[3]

3. PD **il-a*/**el-a*, PSCD **el-a-* /**lē-* 'silk cotton tree'. Kuvi *ḍākāngi*: Go. *leke*, Koṇḍa *lēka maran*, Kuvi *lēko*; cf. Ta. *ela*, *ilavam*, *ilavu*, Ma. *ilavam*, *ilavu*, Ka. *elavu* (421).

4. PD **cup*, PSD **cup* : **cow-ar*, PSCD **sowar*/**sōr* 'salt'. Kui *sāru*, Kuvi *hāru*,

[2] My colleague at Osmania, B. Ramakrishna Reddy, recently did fieldwork on Manḍa and also reported about another related dialect/language (?) called 'Indi'. I am grateful to him for supplying me with cognates from his unpublished field data. Lexical items preceded by (BRR) are furnished by him.

[3] Burrow and Emeneau derive the Kui-Kuvi words with *ā* from PD **aḷ-a* 'strength' in 248, but in the light of the sound change discussed in this paper, Kui-Kuvi forms clearly go with 436.

Manḍa *jār*, Indi *jār*: Go. *sovar, hovar* (*savor, havor* by vocalic metathesis), Koṇḍa *sōru*, Pe. *hōr*, Indi *hūr* (2201).

5. PD **eṯ-a-*, **eṯ-ank*, PSCD **eṟ-a-*/ **ṟē-* 'to descend'. Kui *jāpa* (*jā-t-*), v.i./n., *jāppa* (*jāp-t-*) caus.: Go. *rey-*, *ray-*, Koṇḍa *ṟe-* v.i., *ṟep* caus., Kuvi *rec-*, *re'-* v.i., *reph-* caus., Manḍa, Indi *jē-*, *jēp-* (439).

6. PD **kil-a*, PSD **kel-a-*, PSCD **kel-a-*, pre-Kui-Kuvi **klē* 'to crow, lament'. Kui *klāp-* (*klā-t-*), 'to crow, coo, lament': OTe.*celāgu* 'to sound, cry loudly'; Go. *kilīt-* 'weep loudly'; Kui *klīri inba* 'to shriek' Kuvi *kileri kī* 'to shout', *klīri in* 'to yell'; cf. Ta. *cilai* 'to roar, sound', *cil* 'sound'; Ma. *cilekka* 'to chatter, chirp', Ko. *kilc* 'to utter shrill cry'; To. *kiṣ̱* 'to crow'; Ka. *kele* 'to cry', Tu. *kilepuni* 'to crow' (1311).

7. PD **kuẓ-a*, PSD **koẓ-a*, PSCD **koẓ-a*/**kẓō* 'pit, hollow'. Kui *kṛāu* (pl. *kṛānga*) 'pit, hole, cave'; Kuvi *graiyū, gṛāyu, glāyu*; Manḍa *kṛay*, (BRR) *kṛāy*: OTe. *krōlu, krōvi* 'tube', *groccu* 'to dig', *groyyi* 'pit'; Go. *koṛi* 'ditch, hole'; Koṇḍa *kuṛŋi-* 'to be hollowed out', *kuṛk-* 'to make pits'; Kui *krōḍu* (pl. *krōṭka*) 'tube, quiver'; Pe. *kṛoy* 'pit'; cf. Ta. *kuḻal* 'pipe', *kuḻi, kuḻumpu* 'pit'; Ma. *kuḻi* 'hollow', etc. (1511).

8. PD **kuṯ-a*, PSD **koṯ-a* [koṟ-a], PSCD **koṟ-a*/**kṟō* 'to cut'. Kui *krāpa* (*krā-t-*) 'to cut, saw', n. 'act of cutting': cf. Ta. *kuṟai-* 'to cut, reap'; *kuṟa* 'a piece'; Ma. *kuṟekka*, Ko. *korv-*, To. *kwaṟf-* v., Ka. *koṟe-* 'cut wood with a saw', Tu. *kudupuni* 'to cut, reap'; Pa. *kud-*/*kuḍ-* (*kutt-*/*kuṭṭ-*) 'to cut' (1544).

9. PD **keḷ-a*, PSD **keḷ-a-*, PSCD **keḷ-a-*/*kḷē-* 'family, kindred'. Kui *klāmbu* (pl. *klāpka*) 'family lineage, kin, tribe': cf. Ta. *kēḷ* 'kindred, friend'; *kiḷai* 'to ramify, multiply', n. 'kindred, relations, flock, herd, family'; Ko. *keḷ*; To. *keḷ*; Ka. *keḷe, geḷe, geṇe* 'friendship'; Tu. *geṇe* 'coupling' (1678).

10. PD **teṯ-a*, PSD **teṯ-a* [teṟ-a], PSCD **teṟa-*/**tṟē-* 'to open'; pre-Kui-Kuvi-Pengo-Manḍa **ṟe-* by loss of *t-* (see below). Kui *dāpa* (*dā-t-*) (< *jā-*) 'to open a door, clear a passage', n. 'act of opening'; OTe. *teṟacu*, Mdn. Te. *teruc-* 'to open'; Go. *tarīt-*, *teṟ-*, *terr-*, *reh-*; Koṇḍa *ṟe-*, *teṟe-*; Kuvi *de'-*, (*de-t-*); Pe. *je* (*-t-*); Manḍa *jē* (*-t-*), (BRR) *jēp ā* 'to be opened'; Indi *jē*; cf. Ta. *tiṟa-*; Ma. *tuṟakka*; Ko. *terv-*; To. *teṟ-*, v.; Ka. *teṟe-* v., *teṟa* n.; Koḍ. *tora*; Tu. *terapu* n. (2667).

11. PD **nil-a-*/**nel-a*, PSD **nel-a*, PSCD **nel-anj-*/**nlēnj-* 'moon'. (**nl-* > *l* in all South-Central Dravidian languages except Telugu in which *nl-* never occurred.) Kui *ḍānju* (pl. *ḍāska*) 'moon, month, season' (in Winfield 1928 Kui *l*/*ḍ* vary dialectally; here, *ḍ* < *l*): Te. nela; Go. *nalēnj, nelenj, lēnj*; Koṇḍa *nela* (pl. *neleŋ*), *lēnju*; Kuvi *lēnju* (pl. *lēska*); Pe.-Manḍa-Indi *lēnj*; cf. Ta. *nilavu, nilā*; Ma. *n(i)lāvu* 'moon'; To. *neṣ̱-of* 'moonlight'; Koḍ *nela* 'moon, moonlight' (South Dravidian has lost the meaning of 'month'; cf. **tinkaḷ* 'moon, month', *DED* 2626); Kol. Nk. *nela* 'moon'; Pa. *neliñ* (pl. *nelñil*) 'moon, month'; Oll. *neliŋ*, Gad. *nelling* 'moon', *nela* 'month' (3113).

12. PSCD **por-a-*/*prō-* 'to sell' (words meaning 'to sell' which occur only in South-Central Dravidian are mixed up with 'spread' words in this group, because of the '*a*' vowel in Kui. It appears reasonable to separate the two groups in this entry). Kui

prāpa (*prā-t*) 'to sell', n. 'selling'; Kuvi *prah-*, *pra-* (*pra-t-*): Koṇḍa *por-* (*por-t-*); Pe. *pro-* (*pro-t-*); Manḍa (BB) *pre-*, (BRR) *prē-* 'to sell' (3255).

13. PD **peṯ-a*, PSD *peṟ-v-*, PSCD *peṟ-a-*, *peṟ-u-* 'rice'. Kui *prāu* 'rice, husked paddy', *prāma* 'a grain of boiled rice'; Te. *prālu* 'rice': Go. *paṛēk*, *perek* 'husked paddy'; Koṇḍa *perku*; Pe. *preyi*; Manḍa *preyi* 'rice'; cf. Ta. *peṟukkal* rice; Nk. (Ch.) *perku* id. (3286).

14. PD **pic-ar*, PSD **pec-ar/*pey-ar/*pēr-*, PSCD **pēr* 'name'. Kui *pāru* 'name' : Te. *pēru*; Koṇḍa *pēr*; cf. Ta. Ma. Ko. *pēr*; Kol. Nk. *pēr* (3612).

15. PSCD **moẓ-al/*mẓōl* 'hare'. Kui *mṛāḍu*; Kuvi *mrālu*, *mṛālū*; Indi *mṇāl*: Pe. *mṛōl*; Indi *mṇōl*; cf. Go. *malōl*; Koṇḍa *morol* (4071).

16. PD **muṯ-a-/*moṯ-a*, PSD **moṯ-a-* [moṟ-a-], PSCD **mor-a-/*mṟō-* 'rope'. Kui *mrāsu* 'rope made of hide'; Kuvi *mārca* 'rope attaching bullock to plough': Go. *marōnj*, *maronj* 'bark', *moros*, *moṛos* 'rope made of fibre of *paur* tree'; cf. Ta. *muṟaṟci* 'a cord'; Ta. *muraje* 'rope made of straw' (4079).

17. PD **meẓ-a*, PSD **meẓ-a*, PSCD **meẓa-/*mẓē-* 'to plaster'. Kui *mrānḍa* 'to plaster, smear', n. 'plastering': Te. *mrēgu* 'to plaster'; Go. *maṛhutt-*; cf. Ta. *meẓuku* v./n. (4169).

18. PD **niṯ-yāṇṭu*, PSCD **niṟ-ēṇḍu/niṟ-ōṇḍu* 'last completed year'. Kui *ṛ-ānḍu* 'last year', *ṛ-ōnḍu*, Kui (dial.) *ōnḍu* 'year', *vāṛ-onḍi* 'next or coming year', Kuvi *r-ānḍu*, *ṛ-ānḍu* id.: Te. *nir-uḍu* 'last year', Koṇḍa *nīr-uṇḍ* 'last year', *iyōṇḍ* 'this year', Go. *iyēnḍ*, *iyānḍ* 'this year', *h-ēnḍ* 'the year before last', Pe Manḍa *ṛ-āṭihiŋ* 'last year', Manḍa *īyuṭ* 'this year', Pe. *iyonḍiŋ* 'this year' (4230, S567).[4]

3. Of the above eighteen items the operation of Rule C is found in the following language(s):

Kui only 1, 6, 8, 9, 10, 11, 13, 14, 17;
Kuvi only 3 (no cognate in Kui);
Kui and Kuvi 5, 7, 12, 15, 16, 18;
Kui, Kuvi, and Manḍa 2, 4.

Kui shows the operation of Rule C in 17 cases (94%); Kui alone shows the change in as many as 10 out of the 18 items (56%); Kui-Kuvi share the change in 8 items (45%); Manḍa shares the change with Kui-Kuvi in 2 cases (11%). It is clear that the sound change is commonly initiated at the Proto-Kui-Kuvi stage (in view of 8 shared items) and has spread more widely in Kui than in Kuvi through lexical diffusion. There is one exclusive case where Kuvi shows the change, but Kui has no known cognate. It is not clear if the Manḍa change is sporadic or if it carries a trace of the innovation shared presumably at the Proto-Kui-Manḍa stage. The difficulty in

[4] Because of their complicated phonology *DEDR* puts these items under two entries 5153, 3674. What is relevant here is that PD **yĀṇṭu* 'year' is represented by *ēṇḍ*, *ōṇḍ* in SCD; the change *ē* > *ō* must have been caused by the following retroflex sequence. It was these mid-vowels which became a low vowel *ā* in Kui-Kuvi. Unaccented *ō* in the compound word became *o* and *u* in different languages. Kui-Kui initial *ṛ* represents an older *r* from *ṟ* of **niṟ-* with *n*-loss; see 11 above.

holding this assumption is that Pengo, the nearest sister of Manḍa, has not a single case attesting the vowel-lowering rule.

The following analysis shows the sources of the mid-vowel /ē ō/ by the application of Rules A and B which constitute the input to Rule C.

	ē	ō
Rule A	14	4
Rule B	1, 2, 3, 5, 6, 9, 10, 11, 13, 17, 18	7, 8, 12, 15, 16

From the above distribution, there can be little doubt regarding the application of Rule C on the output of Rule B since there are sixteen etymologies testifying to apical displacement resulting in long mid-vowels. It is also clear that Rule B had operated in the entire subgroup, though less widely in Gondi and Koṇḍa than in the other languages. The word-initial consonant clusters formed by Rule B were subsequently simplified by the following rule, which I call Rule B':[5]

Rule B'. C_1C_2V > $C_1ØV/\#$___ (Te.)
> $ØC_2V/\#$___ (Go.-Koṇḍa-Kui-Kuvi-Pe.-Manḍa)

Out of the above cited eighteen cases, there are at least two which attest the operation of B' in South-Central Dravidian:

10. PD **teṯ-a-*, PSCD **teṟ-al*tṟē*: **tṟē* > *ṟē* (Gondi (dial.), Koṇḍa-Kui-Kuvi-Pengo-Manḍa) (2667).

11. PD **nil-al *nel-a*; PSCD **nel-anj/*nlēnj*: **nlēnj* > *lēnj* (Gondi-Koṇḍa-Kui-Kuvi-Pengo-Manḍa)[6] (3113).

C is also an older Rule which predates Rule B' since it involves many more languages than does Rule B'.

In our data, there are only two examples for Rule A which constitute input to Rule C. Item 4 is the clearest case showing vowel contraction: **sowar* > *sōr* as a shared innovation of Koṇḍa-Kui-Kuvi-Pengo-Manḍa. This is attributable to a common stage of these five languages rather than to Proto-South-Central Dravidian since Gondi dialects preserve the uncontracted form **sowar* (with metathesis of vowels **sawor* in some dialects). The Proto-Dravidian form is **cuwar* (< **cup* + *ar*) which becomes **cowar* in Proto-South Dravidian by the regular sound change **u* > **o* before C*a* in the next syllable. This change is shared by both South Dravidian and South-Central Dravidian. The descendants of Proto-South-Central Dravidian (except Telugu) have lost the derivatives of the root **cup* 'salt'. Item 14 is not a decisive case since only Kui has *pāru*, while Koṇḍa has *pēru*. The rest of the

[5] This rule provides a shared innovation in Gondi-Koṇḍa-Kui-Kuvi-Pengo-Manḍa as against Telugu. The full form of the rule is not stated here, for instance, Mdn. Telugu loses C_1 if it is /w/ and the following vowel is [+low], e.g. OTe. **wrāyu* > MTe. *rāyu* 'to write'.

[6] The Cluster formation Rule (Rule B) has died out in Gondi but it should have operated in pre-Gondi; otherwise, there is no way to explain forms resulting from the operation of Rule B' in Gondi. Note that Rule B' simplifies the consonant clusters created by Rule B.

languages have no cognates. There is another case where one would expect the Vowel-lowering Rule to operate in Kui-Kuvi but it does not, viz.

19. PSD **tokal/*tōl*, PSCD **tōl*, PCD **tōl*. Ta. Ma. Ko. Ka. Te. *tōl(u)* 'skin, hide'; also Ma. *tukal*, Ka. *togal*, *toval*, Tu. *tugalï*, Te. *togalu* id.; Go.-Koṇḍa-Kuvi *tōl(u)*; Kol. Nk. Pa. *tōl*. Here the contraction is found in all but the North Dravidian group which has no clear cognates.

From the above evidence, it appears that the output of Rule A is not subjected to vowel-lowering as widely as the output of Rule B. Secondly the Vowel Contraction Rule goes back to the Proto-Dravidian stage in 19 whereas in 4, Rule B belongs to South-Central Dravidian (pre-Koṇḍa-Kui-Kuvi-Pengo-Manḍa stage).

4. Contrasting with the above developments is the absence of vowel-lowering in cases where PSCD *ē ō* are traceable to PD **ē* **ō* or to contractions resulting from [e, o] C-V_2- where V_2 is a high vowel /i u/ and not a low vowel /a/ as in Rules A and B. Examine the following examples:

20. PD **ner-u-*; pre-Kui-Kuvi **nrē-* > Kui-Kuvi *drē-* 'fire'. Kui *drē* 'ignition', *drē inba* 'to be ignited': Ta. *neruppu*; Ma. *ñerippu* 'fire' (2389).

21. PD **yāṯ* 'river, water', PSCD **ēṟ*: Go. *ēr*; Koṇḍa. *ēṟu*; Kui *ēju*; Kuvi *ēyu*; Pe. *ēzuŋ*; Manḍa *ey* (4233).[7]

22. PD **ēr/*er/-V-*, PSCD **ēr/*er-V-* v. i. 'to burn, blaze': OTe. *eriyu*: v. i. 'to burn', *ērcu* v.t., *ēru* n. 'ache'; Go. *ērīt-* 'to hurt'; Koṇḍa *er-* 'to kindle fire'; Kui *ērpa* (*ēr-t-*) 'to light, ignite', n. 'lighting'; Kuvi *er-* v. (694).

23. PD **kōl*; PSCD **kōl* 'stick': Go. *kōla*; Koṇḍa *kōl*; Kui *kōḍ* (pl. *kōṭka*); Kuvi *kōlū* (pl. *kōlka*); Pe. *kōl*; Manḍa *kūl* (1852).

There are many more cases of the type where PSCD **ē* **ō* (< PD **ē* **ō*) do not merge with PSCD **ā* (< PD **ā*) in pre-Kui-Kuvi.

5. The question is how does one explain the different treatment given to *ē ō* derived from Rules A B from that given to continuing *ē ō* from the Proto-Dravidian stage? When PSCD /ē ō/ derived from Rules A B had merged with /ē ō/ (< PD **ē* **ō*), how was it possible that the former set underwent vowel-lowering and not the latter set? A solution to this should lie in one of the following assumptions: (a) The derived pair of long vowels from Rules A and B was not really /ē ō/ in quality, and therefore, there was no real merger of this pair with /ē ō/ (< PD **ē* **ō*) in South-Central Dravidian. Then, the derived set was phonetically mid-way between the mid-vowels /ē ō/ and the low vowel /ā/, somewhat like [ɛ̄ ɔ̄], leading to a subsequent merger with /ā/ rather than with the mid-vowels with which they had surface contrast. In other words, the derived vowels failed to produce new height contrasts in view of the small number of instances involved; subsequent changes

[7] PD **yā* develops to PSCD **ē* and is treated like PD **ē* (> PSCD **ē*).

were governed by the typological pressure exerted by the five-vowel system; (b) A rule can 'look back' at the derivational history of the forms to which it applies. Here Rule C could apply only to derived long mid-vowels but not to underlying long mid-vowels. This kind of rule, then, would be similar to what generative phonologists call 'a global rule' in synchronic phonology, which introduces derivational constraints on the application of certain rules (Kenstowicz and Kisseberth 1977: 197–229, Kiparsky 1973a).

I would rule out the second alternative because it does not make sense in historical linguistics. How would the speakers of South-Central Dravidian, at whatever stage, be endowed with the historical knowledge of the sources of the two sets of *ē and *ō so that they would give one type of treatment to one set (*ē *ō > ā) as opposed to the other (*ē *ō > ē ō). Secondly notice that Kui and Kuvi retain the qualities of *ē *ō even if they are derived from contraction rules (modified Rules A and B), provided that in the underlying environment there is no low vowel in the second syllable, i.e.

Rule A'. (C) [e, o] C-i/u > (C) [ē, ō]-

Rule B'. (C_1) [e, o] C_2-i/u > (C_1)C_2 [ē, ō]-

There are several examples for Rule B' (see item 20 above), e.g.

24. PD **koẓ-uw*, PSCD **koẓuw*/**kẓōw* 'fat'. Go. *koṛvinj*; Koṇḍa *koṛvu*; Kui *kṛōga*; Kuvi *koṛva, klōwa*; Pe. *kṛō* 'to be fat', *koṛva* 'fat'; Manḍa (?) *kṛūa* (1784).

The underlying environments of A and A' are complementary and they can be collapsed into a single rule; so too can B and B'. It is only /ē ō/ derived from Rules A, B that have undergone lowering and not those derived from Rules A' B'. Vowel-lowering in Kui-Kuvi etc. should then be related in some way to the lowering influence exerted by /a/ in Rules A and B.

6. Krishnamurti (1958a) has explained how PD **i*, **u* merged with **e*, **o* before C-*a* in Proto-South Dravidian. This is a clear case of vowel harmony or 'umlaut' which is one of the most widely discussed and recognized sound changes in Dravidian. It is now clear that the South-Central Dravidian group also shows the sound change (high vowel lowering). Therefore, both South Dravidian and South-Central Dravidian must have inherited this sound change from a common ancester. All South Dravidian languages retain PSD **e* **o* before C-*a* whereas Tamil and Malayāḷam shifted these to *i u* at an older stage, and again changed them later to *e o*. These developments, therefore, show neutralization of Proto-Dravidian vowels **i* **e* on the one hand, and **u* **o* on the other, in two of the major branches, South and South-Central Dravidian.

Bright (1966) has extensively examined the spread of the high vowel lowering phenomenon even outside the Dravidian linguistic area. Apart from a possible areal drift, we are dealing here with specific cases where the qualities attested by the South-Central Dravidian languages represent the merger stage, i.e. **e* **o* before C-*a* even where Proto-Dravidian has clearly **i* **u* (see particularly items 4, 6, 7, 14, and 18 above).

In most of the southern languages that have retained PSD **e*C-*a* and **o*C-*a*, the mid-vowels are pronounced opener in the environment C-*a*, than when they are followed by a closed vowel (Bright 1966: 316–19). The forms which constituted the input to Rules A B could therefore be expected to have had low mid-vowels allophonically before contraction took place, somewhat as follows:

(C) [e, o]C-a > (C) [ɛ, ɔ]C-a-

The resultant long vowels after contraction would be [ɛ̄] and [ɔ̄] or lowered /ē ō/, which would normally have become contrastive with /ē ō ā/, since the conditioning environment -*a* was obscured in the process of contraction. The process is similar to what has happened in standard Modern Telugu (Kelley 1963), e.g. *gōru+lu* [go:ru+lu] /gōḷḷu/ 'nails', *gōḍa+lu* [gɔ:ṛ^+lu] /gɔ: ḷḷu/ 'walls'. Telugu speakers do not cognitively perceive two phonemes /ō ɔ̄ / here; both are treated as variants of /ō/ with different phonetic realizations in different underlying phonetic environments. In coastal dialects the openness of the vowel in the environment C-*a* is much more than it is in Telangana and Rayalasima dialects.

It appears that the resulting lowered vowels [ɛ̄ ɔ̄] of Proto-South-Central Dravidian had merged in most of the descendant languages with *ē ō*. In Kui-Kuvi they were further lowered to merge with *ā* dialectally. The contraction cases are naturally too few to destabilize the five-vowel system. It appears that, when allophones become 'phonemic' through secondary split, the number of cases involved in such a split would be a potential factor in determining whether the resultant 'transient' phonemes will enlarge the phonemic system or will conform to the existing system by merging with the established phonemes. For instance, Emeneau (1970b: 146) shows how Proto-South Dravidian root vowel **e* merges with /a/ when followed by a retroflex consonant + *a* (derivative vowel) in Koḍagu.

As this change is found in Kui-Kuvi and Manḍa (also Indi), it is reasonable to assume that the underlying long vowels had lowered articulations in the entire subgroup that inherited the contracted forms. For instance, all languages (except Telugu and Gondi), viz. Koṇḍa-Kui-Kuvi-Pengo-Manḍa, might have inherited [*sɔ̄ru] (< *[sɔ̄ war]) 'salt' in which the [ɔ̄] vowel merged with *ō* in Koṇḍa, but remained as *[ɔ̄] at a common stage of Kui-Kuvi-Pengo-Manḍa. Then [ɔ̄] > /ā/ in pre-Kui-Kuvi, but proceeded as [ɔ̄] to the common stage of Pengo-Manḍa. In Pengo [ɔ̄] > *ō*, but in Manḍa [ɔ̄] > *ā*.

Notice that there are doublets in a few cases dialectally even in Kui and the other languages of the subgroup: Kui *grāpa/grēpa* 'to scoop up' (*S*290), Kuvi *ḍā kāngi/lēko* 'silk cotton tree' (421), Kui *kṛāu* 'pit', *krōḍu* 'tube' (1511), Indi *mṇā l/mṇōl* 'hare' (4071). In (1511) the two Kui lexical items have developed different meanings. This state of affairs suggests that the change is relatively recent and is an ongoing one.

7. There are a few counter-examples to Rule C, i.e. items which fulfil the structural conditions of Rule C for vowel-lowering still have not undergone it in any of the South-Central Dravidian languages.

24. PCD **cir-a*, PSCD **ser-a-*/**srē-* 'Chironji tree (*Buchanania latifolia*)'. Go. *sarēka, rēka*; Kui *srēko*; Kuvi *rēko*; Pe. *rēka maran*; Ma. *rēko* (2160).
25. PSCD **peẓan*/**pẓēn* 'bone'. Go. *peṛka, peṛeŋka, pen?ka, peṛeka, pareka*; Koṇḍa *peṛen, pṛēnu* (pl. *peṛek, pṛēku*); Kui *pṛēnu* (pl. *pṛēka*); Kuvi *prēnū, plēnu*; Pe. *pṛēnu, pṛēn* (*pṛēku*); Ma. *pṛēn* (pl. *pṛēke*) (3619).

Such apparent exceptions can be explained in one of the following ways: (a) All South-Central Dravidian languages merged the underlying (*ε̄ *ɔ̄ in these with ē ō; (b) The environments in the non-contracted forms had a high vowel and not a low vowel; (c) Since vowel-lowering in Kui-Kuvi is still an ongoing change, there are still residual forms which may undergo the change in the future. It would be interesting to see if any such residual forms have lower mid-vowels phonetically. The fact that a few exceptions exist will not disprove Rule C as formulated here.

8. Conclusion. The Vowel-lowering Rule which merged PD **i* **u* with **e* **o* in Proto-South Dravidian included not only the Southern group (Tamil, Malayāḷam, Toda, Kota, Kannaḍa, Koḍagu) but also the South-Central group (Telugu, Gondi, Koṇḍa, Kui, Kuvi, Pengo, Manḍa). By this observation, we can say that the two branches, South and South-Central Dravidian, had a common stage of development which can still be called Proto-South Dravidian. There are other types of evidence that would support the realignment of South-Central Dravidian as a branch of Proto-South Dravidian (Krishnamurti 1976a: §1.7). The mid-vowels *e, o* preceding C-*a* in almost all the languages had opener allophones, somewhat like ε and ɔ. Consequently, the vowels resulting from Rules A, B could be [ε̄] and [ɔ̄]. These subsequently merged with /ā/ in most instances in Kui and in quite a few cases in Kuvi, but to a much smaller extent in Manḍa (and Indi). This change is based on the following postulate: Surface phonetic contrasts which develop through merger or loss of conditioning factors (i.e. secondary split) will develop into new phonemes, if a sufficiently large number of lexical items is affected by the sound change; otherwise, they will merge with the phonemes already established in the system. Toda and Koḍagu have developed new vowel phonemes through such secondary splits because a large number of morphemes are affected by such splits.

13

Unchanged Cognates as a Criterion in Linguistic Subgrouping

With Lincoln Moses, *Stanford University*; Douglas G. Danforth, *Wang Laboratories*

0. If a sound change has lexically diffused without completing its course, one finds that among the lexical items qualified for the change, some have already changed (*c*), others have remained unchanged (*u*), and still others show variant forms (*u*/*c*). When such a change has affected a group of genetically related languages, the consequent comparative pattern *u*–*u*/*c*–*c* can be used to set up subrelations among languages. In this paper, we draw on data from six languages belonging to the South-Central subfamily of Dravidian, with reference to an atypical sound change called 'apical displacement'. There are 63 etymologies which qualify for the study. A total of 945 possible binary-labelled trees fall into six types for the six languages under study. In terms of our postulates, that tree is the best which scores the lowest *m*, i.e. the minimum number of independent instances of change needed to account for the *u*–*c*–*o* (*o* = no cognate) pattern of a given entry. Each of the 63 entries has been applied to the possible 945 trees, and the trees have been scored for the value *m* by computer. The one tree which scored the lowest (71 points) is identical with the traditionally established tree for these languages. This paper shows that: (a) one shared innovation is sufficient to give genetic subrelations among languages, within the framework of the theory of lexical diffusion; (b) unchanged cognates are as important as changed cognates in giving differential scores for possible trees; and (c) the notion of shared innovation can be further refined within the theory of lexical diffusion.

1. **Introduction**. In the standard theory of historical linguistics, subrelations among languages belonging to a family are established on the basis of 'shared innovations' (Dyen 1953: 580–2, Hoenigswald 1966: 7). Under ideal conditions, a family

When the central idea of this paper was conceived and developed, Krishnamurti and Moses were Resident Fellows at the Center for Advanced Study in the Behavioral Sciences, Stanford (1975–6). Danforth was a statistics advisor at the Center. We all gratefully acknowledge the facilities provided for our collaborative work at the Center. We are indebted to the following for their useful and encouraging comments on an earlier draft of this paper: M. B. Emeneau, G. B. Kelley, Hans H. Hock, George Cardona, Paul Kiparsky, Chin-Chuan Cheng, and R. M. W. Dixon. William S-Y. Wang gets a major share of gratitude for his numerous insightful comments, which helped us in the revision of this paper.

tree diagram can be constructed to reflect subrelationships among a group of genetically related languages: the more inclusive innovations account for branchings at higher nodes, while the more exclusive innovations correspond to branchings at lower nodes. A tree diagram also implies a relative chronology, with higher branchings representing older changes.[1] The shortcomings of both the comparative method and the tree diagram are all too well known to historical linguists. (For a lucid discussion, cf. Bloomfield 1933: §§18.9–13.) However, while their utility has not been rejected, no alternative procedure has yet been developed which captures subrelationships among the members of a language family in a more rigorous way.[2]

In linguistic subgrouping, it is the presence or absence of an innovation (say, a sound change resulting in a phonemic merger or split) that is taken into account, rather than the extent to which it has affected cognate morphs in the related languages. To quote Hoenigswald (1966: 8):

> Brugmannian innovations are not for counting—the question, in principle, is whether they are at all present or entirely absent in a given set of descendant languages. Of course, this amounts to saying that if languages A and B share an authentic 'innovation' as against language C, then there can be none linking C and B against A. Where this nevertheless happens, as it frequently does, it indicates the inadequacy of the family tree as a device to depict a language relationship.

Recent studies have conclusively shown that at least some sound changes are lexically gradual; i.e. lexical items which fulfil the structural conditions of a sound change are not all affected by it at once (Chen and Wang 1975). A commonly initiated sound change can spread across a set of related languages, engulfing more and more lexical items which qualify for the change; and the process may continue for several centuries. The number of innovative cognates (i.e. those affected by a given sound change) which any two languages share can then be taken as a measure of their relative distance. For instance, languages ABC may all show evidence of a shared innovation (a certain sound change), but AB may share more cognates-with-change; this would give us a subgrouping ((AB) C) as preferable to the possible subgroupings ((AC) B) and ((BC) A).[3]

[1] This is the point essentially implied by Hoenigswald (1960: §13.2.4) when he says: 'Each different reconstruction represents the proto-language of a subfamily. The component languages of those language pairs which yield identical reconstructions belong to one subfamily. If a language is thus found to belong to two subfamilies, that subfamily which is reconstructed from the smaller number of languages is, in turn, a subfamily within the subfamily reconstructed from the larger number of languages.'

[2] The method of lexicostatistics (also called glottochronology), proposed by Morris Swadesh, was much discussed in the 1950s as an alternative to traditional subgrouping. It is based on the hypothesis that, in any language, basic vocabulary is lost (or replaced) at a constant rate. The time-depth which separates any two languages of a family is calibrated by comparing the degree of loss in basic cognate vocabulary. In this theory, only the presence or absence of a 'true cognate' in a language matters, rather than how close a word is in form to cognates in the sister languages. Several aspects of this theory have been questioned, and it seems not to be as popular in historical studies now as it was two decades ago. For further details, see Gudschinsky 1956 (in Hymes 1964, with the latter's reference note).

[3] Here the assumption is that, after the ancestor of AB had separated from C, the two branches would have different lexical schedules in the implementation of the inherited sound change. Consequently, the

1.1. In a recent study of the areal and lexical diffusion of three sound changes in the South-Central group of Dravidian languages—viz. Gondi, Koṇḍa, Kui, Kuvi, Pengo, and Manḍa—Krishnamurti (1978a) shows that a tree structure reflecting the hierarchical relationships of these languages can be constructed, taking into account the number of cognates-with-change that each language has shared with the other five. The resulting tree diagram, shown here as Figure 13.1, perfectly matches the traditional diagram based on a number of phonological and morphological isoglosses (see Appendix I).

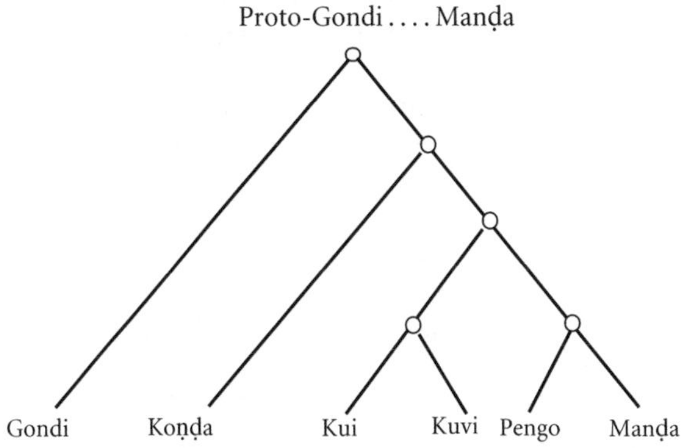

FIGURE 13.1. A tree diagram of the South-Central Dravidian languages

An exact replica of Fig. 13.1 has also been produced with the aid of a computer program developed by Roy D'Andrade of the University of California, San Diego,[4] using as input the numbers of cognates-with-change that each language has shared

shared innovative cognates between AB would be more numerous than between either one of them and C. Hsieh (1973: 71) introduces the notion of 'diffusion overlapping' to represent 'the sharing or overlapping of the phonological forms in cognate items across dialects', and he proposes to utilize 'the degrees of diffusion overlapping with respect to a commonly initiated sound change' to measure 'the relative genetic closeness' of three or more dialects. (A discussion of this concept is also given by Krishnamurti 1978a: 12.)

[4] It was through Matthew Y. Chen that Krishnamurti came to know in January 1977 about the 'U-statistic hierarchical clustering', a computer program developed by D'Andrade (cf. D'Andrade 1978). Chen used his good offices with D'Andrade to run the program, using as input the numbers given in Table 8 of Krishnamurti 1978a: the resulting tree diagram is identical with that given by Krishnamurti. In a personal communication (2 March, 1977), Chen wrote to Krishnamurti:

> The above tree (I'll refer to it as Diagram A) makes 40 predictions, 37 of which proved correct, and 3 wrong. The incorrect predictions have to do with the peripheral dialects, namely Gondi and Koṇḍa. Diagram A predicts that Kuvi should be closer to Koṇḍa than it is to Gondi. This turns out to be incorrect, since Kuvi shared 20 innovative items with Koṇḍa but 22 with Gondi. This is mistake 1. Diagram A also predicts that Koṇḍa should be closer to Manḍa than it is to Gondi. Again this is wrong, since Koṇḍa shares only 9 items with Manḍa but as many as 16 with Gondi. Finally, on the basis of Diagram A, Manḍa should be closer to Koṇḍa than it is to Gondi, an inference contradicted by the fact that whereas Manḍa shares 9 items with Koṇḍa (as noted before), it shares 10 with Gondi. Nevertheless, 37 correct predictions out of 40, that is 0.9250 correct, is an unusually high score of correct prediction, as Dr. D'Andrade commented.

with the other five; it is given as Table 13.1 (data taken from Krishnamurti 1978a, Table 8).

2. A new approach. The method of linguistic subgrouping proposed in the above studies mainly concerns itself with changed cognates, rather than with the cognates which remain unchanged in different languages. Within the framework of the theory of lexical gradualness of sound change, we find that consideration of unchanged cognates also has an important role to play in linguistic subgrouping. We introduce the postulate below, and we find that adherence to it implies that certain trees 'fit' more naturally with observed distributions of changed and unchanged forms of cognates. The key idea will be made clear from the examples.

TABLE 13.1. *Number of shared cognates-with-change*

	Gondi	Koṇḍa	Kui	Kuvi	Pengo
Koṇḍa	16				
Kui	18	18			
Kuvi	22	20	88		
Pengo	11	19	48	49	
Manḍa	10	9	40	42	57

POSTULATE I. A lexical item may change its form (phonemic content and/or arrangement) after it has undergone a sound change, but a changed item will not revert to its unchanged form through a subsequent sound change.

This is based on the famous principle of the irreversibility of the effects of sound change, particularly phonological merger (Hoenigswald 1960: §11.4). In the case of literary languages, it is possible that, after a sound change had completed its course, some of the changed lexical items might be replaced by corresponding unchanged ones borrowed from an earlier literary variety—preferred in certain formal styles, and used by certain individuals in speech and/or writing.[5] Such items must be identified and rejected by this postulate. Even in non-literary languages, comparativists

[5] Wang (personal communication) has drawn our attention to the fact that educated Swedish of Stockholm has recently revived, in formal styles, a word-final *-d* which had been lost earlier; this is a possible exception to Postulate 1. Janson 1977, who has discussed this change, says that, between the 14th and 18th centuries, there is evidence for loss of word-final /d/ ([d] after *l, n*, but [ð] elsewhere) 'in the dialects of Southern Sweden'. The loss of the dental fricative [ð] (spelled *-dh*) was very extensive, and spread to 'Svealand, the area where Stockholm is situated' (255–6). 'From the 18th century on, however, evidence in the written language for deletion of *-d* tapers off. Actually, the dentals must have been re-introduced in the endings *-ad* and *-at* in the language of the educated class' (256). Here, the revival or retention (the point is not clear from the paper) of word-final *-d* is apparently motivated by educated speakers of Stockholm on sociological and sociolinguistic grounds. A somewhat parallel case occurs in Mdn. Telugu. Late Old Telugu (*c.*12th century AD) had a sound change *Cr-* > C- (C = voiced or voiceless stop), e.g. *prā̃ta* > *pā̃ta* 'old', *krotta* > *kotta* 'new', etc. Mdn. Telugu has only the changed forms in both speech and writing. However, a few conservative writers prefer to use the *Cr-* forms in writing—and sometimes even in formal speeches, invoking ridicule. These are not illustrations of changed forms reverting to the unchanged stage by a later sound change.

can use several linguistic clues to detect borrowed unchanged items; these tend to be less systematically distributed than the changed forms, and also fewer in number. The co-occurrence of both changed and unchanged forms in synchronic usage is handled by Postulate II (see below, § **3.1**).

The effect of Postulate I is that, when a lexical item is definitely known as 'changed' for a given language, it cannot be treated as 'unchanged'. We represent this postulate schematically as follows ($>$ = becomes; $\not>$ = does not become): $u > c$, $c \not> u$. In the light of this postulate, we take an example and compare the possible trees that derive from the configuration of unchanged and changed lexical items in the six languages. (The reference numbers indicate entries in and *DED*(*S*); for detailed explanation, see Appendix I.)

2.1. The cognate group listed under entry 4524 has the following pattern of unchanged and changed cognates: Gondi, *u*; Koṇḍa, *o*; Kui, *c*; Kuvi, *c*; Pengo, *c*; Manḍa, *c*. Consider Fig. 13.2, which shows four possible trees for word 4524. In tree 1, the entire pattern could be explained by a single instance of change at the place marked II, followed by inheritance of that change in the four branches representing the four languages Kui, Kuvi, Pengo, and Manḍa. Since one instance of change will suffice to account for the *u–o–c* pattern, we score this tree with $m = 1$, where m = the minimum necessary number of instances of change for any proposed tree. But in Tree 2, this group implies a score of $m = 4$. This is because, from the presence of *u* in Gondi and *o* in Koṇḍa, it is not possible to posit a shared change for the four languages which show the change; thus each *c* must be an independent instance of change in each of the languages Manḍa, Pengo, Kuvi, and Kui which could be posited at the points marked II in the diagram. On grounds of parsimony of explanatory elements, we find Tree 1 preferable to Tree 2 to account for cognate group 4524. In Tree 3, $m = 2$, since a change at Kui, plus another below the second node representing common inheritance of change in Kuvi, Manḍa, and Pengo, will account for the pattern observed, with posited loss in Koṇḍa. For Tree 4, $m = 2$ again, since a change at Kuvi, plus another between the second and the third nodes, implying common inheritance, will account for all the observed changes.

From the example, it is clear that any etymological group can be used to provide a score m. Large values of m denote 'strained explanations', which require supposing many independent parallel changes. The idea of this paper is to allow all the cognate words appearing in two or more languages to be applied to every one of the logically possible trees—computing m in each subapplication. Then trees with low values of m are preferable to those with high values.

2.2. The further elaboration of this paper involves several tasks:

(1) We must establish that only those cognates which appear as *c* in at least two languages, and as *u* in at least one, are capable of discriminating among trees.

(2) We must establish that the problem can be narrowed, without loss, to those trees which always have just two branches at any node; and we must then exhibit the six types of such trees, and the 945 distinct possible trees that they generate.

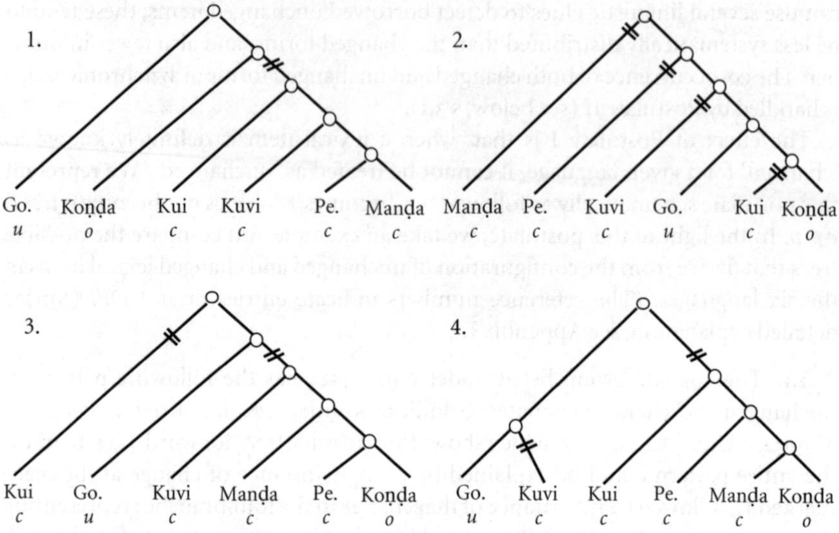

u = unchanged (cognate), *c* = changed (cognate), *o* = no cognate

FIGURE 13.2. Four possible trees for *DED(S)* 4524

(3) We must demonstrate the method of examining and scoring the 63 × 945 tree-word pairs.

(4) Data must be presented on the trees which emerged as the strongest candidates.

(5) Results must be discussed and interpreted.

3. Implementation. The tasks listed above correspond roughly to the sections which follow.

3.1. Identifying the discriminating items. The status of a cognate in a given language can be any of the following.[6]

(1) unchanged *u*
(2) changed *c*
(3) variant *u*/*c*
(4) non-occurrence *o*

For the moment, we ignore the third possibility, taking it up at the end of this section. The fourth possibility gives us no difficulty: where a cognate is absent, there is no information to consider; either a cognate has not been recorded, or it has simply

[6] In this paper, wherever we use the word 'changed' with respect to the members of a cognate group, we mean that they have undergone the same kind of change through the application of a specific phonological rule. Three phonological rules have produced different kinds of change in the 63 cognate groups considered here, of which Rules 1' and 1" are mutually exclusive (complementary); i.e. a set of cognates undergoes either 1' or 1", but not both. Rule 2 applies only to the output of Rule 1". The consequences of application of Rules 1' and 2 are not the same; e.g. if the cognates of languages ABC have undergone Rule 1", and within these the items of BC have undergone Rule 2, then the items of BC have undergone two changes each, as compared to the cognates in A. For further details, see Appendix I.

been lost. In either case, we cannot assign it the value of *u* or *c*; i.e. its value is undetermined.

We now turn to the *u*'s and *c*'s. A group which appears only in the *c* form (with or without *o*) fits all trees equally well: a single change followed by inheritance in some languages, and extinction in others, fits any tree. Similarly, a cognate group with only *u* members will also fit any tree. Such cognate groups have no power of discrimination. If cognates occur in only two languages, of which one is *c* and the other *u*, all possible trees give the same score (see §**3.2** below). Thus the discriminating cognates are just those which appear in at least one language as *u*, and in at least two others as *c*. The data studied by Krishnamurti 1978a contain 63 entries which meet this requirement. Table 13.2 gives the *u–o–c* distribution of these items, with their entry numbers from *DED(S)*.

TABLE 13.2. *Entries from* DED(S) *with* u–o–c *pattern for six languages.*

ENTRY	Gondi	Koṇḍa	Kui	Kuvi	Pengo	Manḍa
197	*c*	*u*	*o*	*o*	*c*	*c*
240	*u*	*u*	*c*	*c*	*u*	*c*
508	*u*	*o*	*c*	*c*	*o*	*c*
592	*u*	*c*	*c*	*c*	*c*	*o*
593	*u*	*c*	*c*	*c*	*c*	*o*
694	*u*	*u*	*c*	*c*	*o*	*o*
775	*o*	*c*	*u*	*u*	*c*	*o*
834a	*u*	*u*	*c*	*c*	*c*	*c*
S265	*u*	*u*	*c*	*o*	*c*	*o*
S290	*o*	*u*	*c*	*c*	*c*	*c*
S299	*o*	*u*	*o*	*c*	*c*	*o*
S407	*u*	*c*	*o*	*o*	*c*	*o*
S539	*o*	*u*	*c*	*o*	*c*	*c*
S642	*u*	*c*	*o*	*c*	*c*	*o*
S772	*u*	*o*	*c*	*c*	*o*	*o*
S787	*u*	*u*	*u*	*u*	*c*	*c*
S802	*u*	*o*	*c*	*o*	*c*	*o*
S877	*u*	*o*	*c*	*c*	*o*	*o*
S878	*u*	*o*	*o*	*o*	*c*	*c*
929	*u*	*u*	*c*	*c*	*o*	*c*
943	*u*	*c*	*c*	*c*	*o*	*o*
1090	*u*	*o*	*c*	*c*	*c*	*c*
1136	*u*	*o*	*c*	*o*	*c*	*o*
1142	*o*	*u*	*c*	*c*	*c*	*c*
1160	*u*	*u*	*c*	*c*	*o*	*u*
1311	*u*	*o*	*c*	*c*	*o*	*o*
1382	*u*	*o*	*c*	*c*	*o*	*o*
1485	*u*	*o*	*c*	*c*	*o*	*o*
1511	*u*	*u*	*c*	*c*	*c*	*c*

ENTRY	Gondi	Koṇḍa	Kui	Kuvi	Pengo	Manḍa
1538	*u*	*u*	*c*	*c*	*o*	*o*
1702	*u*	*o*	*c*	*c*	*u*	*o*
1782	*u*	*u*	*c*	*c*	*o*	*o*
1784	*u*	*u*	*c*	*c*	*c*	*c*
1787	*u*	*u*	*c*	*u*	*c*	*c*
1949	*u*	*c*	*c*	*c*	*c*	*c*
1986	*u*	*c*	*o*	*c*	*c*	*c*
2102	*u*	*u*	*c*	*c*	*c*	*c*
2529	*u*	*u*	*c*	*c*	*o*	*o*
2546	*u*	*u*	*c*	*c*	*c*	*c*
2655	*u*	*u*	*c*	*c*	*o*	*c*
3046	*u*	*u*	*c*	*c*	*c*	*c*
3255	*u*	*u*	*c*	*c*	*c*	*c*
3262	*u*	*u*	*u*	*c*	*c*	*o*
3286	*u*	*u*	*c*	*o*	*c*	*c*
3296	*u*	*u*	*c*	*c*	*c*	*c*
3446	*u*	*o*	*c*	*c*	*c*	*c*
3537	*u*	*u*	*c*	*c*	*c*	*o*
3613	*u*	*u*	*c*	*c*	*o*	*o*
3619	*u*	*u*	*c*	*c*	*c*	*c*
3856	*u*	*c*	*c*	*c*	*o*	*o*
3865	*u*	*u*	*c*	*c*	*o*	*o*
3897	*c*	*u*	*c*	*c*	*c*	*c*
3899	*u*	*o*	*c*	*c*	*o*	*o*
3901	*u*	*u*	*c*	*c*	*u*	*c*
3988	*u*	*u*	*c*	*c*	*o*	*o*
4071	*u*	*u*	*c*	*c*	*c*	*o*
4096	*u*	*o*	*c*	*c*	*o*	*o*
4169	*u*	*u*	*c*	*c*	*o*	*o*
4327	*o*	*u*	*o*	*u*	*c*	*c*
4347	*u*	*o*	*c*	*u*	*c*	*c*
4438	*u*	*u*	*c*	*c*	*u*	*u*
4459	*u*	*o*	*c*	*c*	*c*	*o*
4524	*u*	*o*	*c*	*c*	*c*	*c*

But what shall be done with those items which appear in variant forms in some language(s)? That is, how shall we treat the *u*/*c* cases? Here we can refer to Fig. 13.3, in which the three trees differ by having the upper branch marked with *c*, *u*/*c*, or *u*. We shall analyse them using a second postulate, as follows:

POSTULATE II: *u*/*c* should be counted as *c*.

The implication of this is that *u*/*c* is an intermediate stage in the process $u > c$. Thus $u > u/c > c$, or $u > u/c > \emptyset$; therefore, $u > u/c \not> u$.[7]

[7] Labov (1972a: 274–83) cites eight studies of speech communities which show evidence of sound change in progress. In all these, he shows that 'variability' of unchanged and changed segments

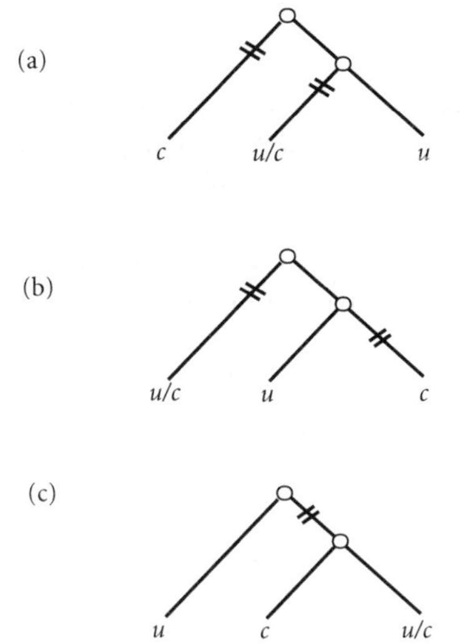

FIGURE 13.3. Status of *u/c* vs. *u* and *c*

Postulate II is needed to avoid triviality. If *u/c* could either revert to *u* by loss of *c*, or advance to *c* by loss of *u*, then every tree could be scored $m = 1$. This trivial result could be obtained as follows: label every non-terminal node as *u/c*, and then allow either *u* or *c* to be inherited—as convenient—at the terminal nodes. Postulate II prevents this, by barring the loss of *c* from *u/c*.[8]

Using both postulates now, we score the trees in Fig. 13.3 as follows:

Tree (a): The lower node must be *u* because of the *u* beneath it. Then the node above it must also be *u*. Therefore, both *c* and the *c* in *u/c* require the changes to operate independently, and $m = 2$.

Tree (b): The analysis is as above, and again $m = 2$.

Tree (c): The upper node must be *u*. The lower node should then be *u/c*, with *u/c* > *c* on the left. Thus one change at the lower node (*u* > *u/c*) will suffice, and $m = 1$.

(conditioned by sociolinguistic factors) is noticed before the categorical implementation of all sound change. Thus, in Swiss French, older-generation speakers (60–90 years) use *ł*, middle-generation speakers (30–60 years) use *ł* ~ *y*, and those under 30 use *y*. Also note the perceptive statements of Weinreich et al. (1968: 149–50):

> We argue that, while linguistic change is in progress, an archaic and an innovating form coexist within the grammar: this grammar differs from an earlier grammar by the addition of a rule, or perhaps by the conversion of an invariant rule to a variable rule. . . . We would expect social significance to be eventually attributed to the opposition of the two forms. At some point the social and linguistic issues are resolved together; when the opposition is no longer maintained, the receding variant disappears. This view of change fits the general observation that change is more regular in the outcome than in the process.

[8] Postulates I and II are intrinsically related; they can be collapsed into a single postulate which may be represented schematically as $u > (u/c) > c, (u)/c \not> u$. However, for the sake of clarity in discussion and application, we prefer to give separate postulates as above.

We observe that these three trees are scored exactly as if *u*/*c* were replaced by *c*, as a consequence of Postulate II.

3.2. Counting and listing the trees. We have restricted our consideration to those trees which, at every node, have only two branchings (binary trees); and this has simplified our task. If, in fact, some three-fold (or higher-order) branching occurs in a natural language family, then the fact is detectable, and such a tree is recoverable, from the binary tree analysis, as we show by the example in Fig. 13.4. From this it will follow that nothing is lost by restricting our study to binary trees.

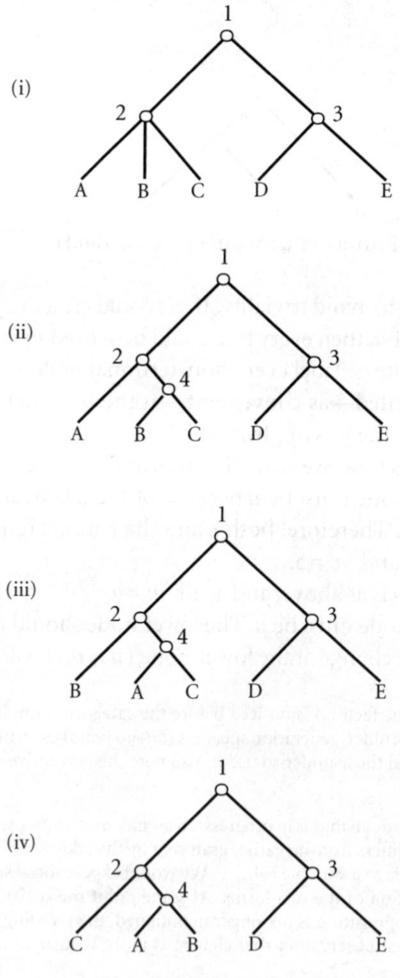

FIGURE 13.4. Ternary vs. binary trees

The tree depicted in (i) has a three-way split at node 2. The next three are all the possible binary trees that can result from 'breaking the tie'. It is obvious that either all three binary trees lead to a common value of *m*—in which case, any of them serves as well as Tree (i); or else some of the Trees (ii)–(iv) lead to different values of *m*—in which case, it is misleading to treat the three possibilities with the single form (i). It follows that the three binary trees represent a finer classification of Tree (i), and so we gain by restricting ourselves only to binary trees. The value of *m* can be seen as equal in Trees (ii)–(iv) for A B C all *u* or all *c*; but if A is *u*, and B and C are both *c*, then $m = 1$ for Tree (ii), and $m = 2$ for Trees (iii)–(iv).

3.2.1. Counting the binary trees with six branches is not difficult. Such a tree must have five nodes. The five nodes can be on five levels (yielding trees of Type I in Fig. 13.5), or on four levels (yielding trees of Types II, III, and IV), or on only three levels (yielding trees of Types V and VI).

Thus we have six types of trees, viewed as geometrical patterns. On each we have six terminal nodes to be labelled, in some order from left to right, with the letters A B C D E F. If we regard the order from left to right as representing increasing recency, we would have 6! = 720 time-sequences with each of our 6 tree types. But our method of counting 'necessary changes' leaves some of the 720 patterns indistinguishable in any tree type. Consider, for example, Type I in Fig. 13.5. If E and F are interchanged, the *m*-score for the tree will be unaffected—because, whatever the labels *u, c, o* are at those two terminal nodes, the resulting contribution to *m* (and the labelling of the node just above them) will be the same whether E is on the left or the right. For Type I trees, then, we have 360 pairs of distinguishable trees, rather than 720. Within each pair, the relative recency of the two right-hand elements is indeterminate. The number of distinguishable (sets of) trees is not the same for all the tree types. Different types have different numbers of left–right reflections, representing different indeterminacies with regard to relative recency:[9]

Type I: E and F may be interchanged without affecting the linguistic tree. Thus, divide 720 by 2 =	[360]
Type II: A and B may be interchanged, and so may E and F. Divide 720 by 2 × 2 =	[180]
Type III: B, C and E, F are both interchangeable. Divide 720 by 2 × 2 =	[180]
Type IV: C, D and E, F are interchangeable, and then these two pairs may also be interchanged. Divide 720 by 2 × 2 × 2 =	[90]
Type V: Languages in each of three pairs may be interchanged, and then the pair C, D may be interchanged with the pair E, F. Divide 720 by 2 × 2 × 2 × 2 =	[45]
Type VI: B, C and E, F may be interchanged, as well as the main branches forking from the top node. Divide 720 by 2 × 2 × 2 =	[90]
Total:	945

[9] We are indebted to William S-Y. Wang for drawing our attention to a National Science Foundation (USA) report by Meyers and Wang (1963: 94–5), which gives an algebraic formula to count binary-labelled trees for *n*-terminal nodes as $C_n = (2n - 3)C_{n-1}C_1 = 1$.

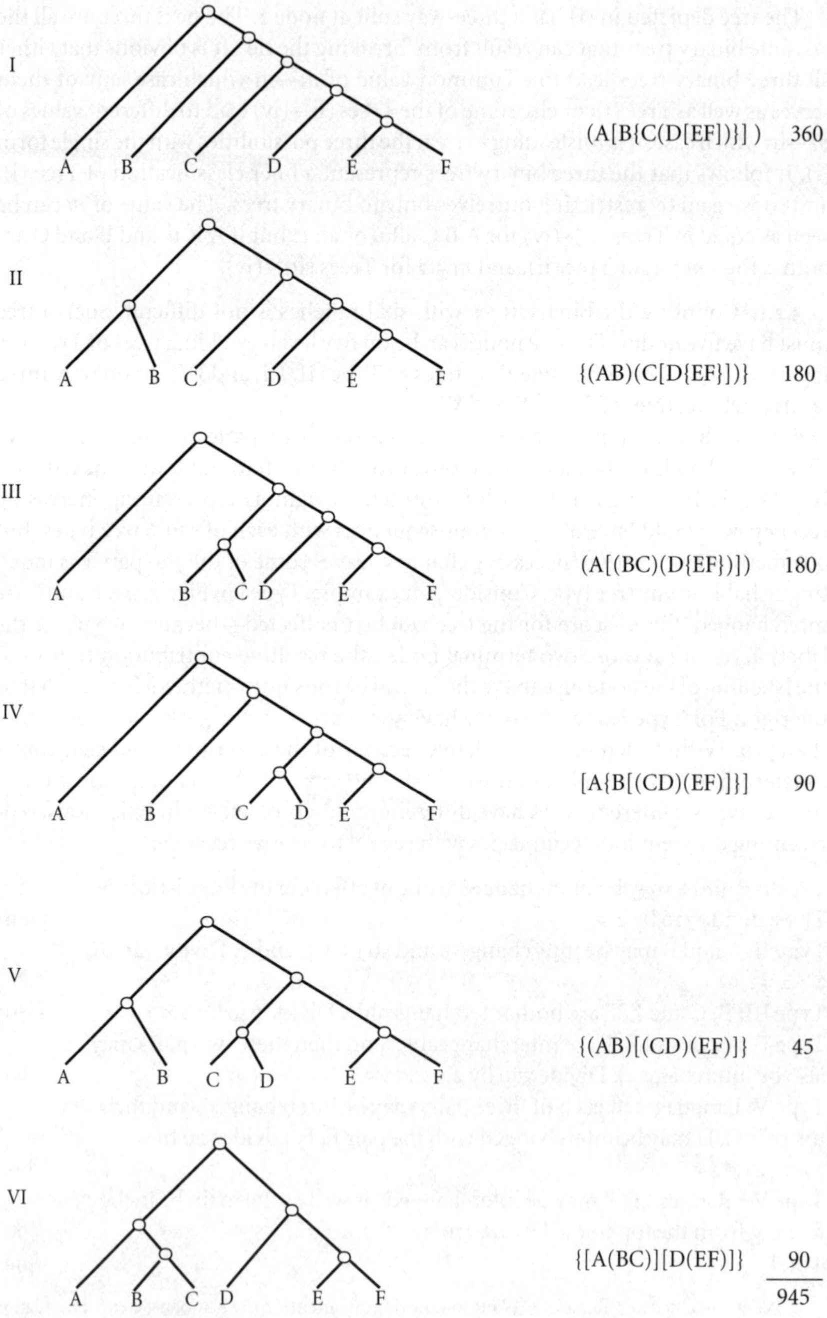

FIGURE 13.5. Six types of trees and their derivatives for six languages

3.3. Examining and scoring the 945 × 63 tree-word pairs. It is possible to write down the geometric pattern of a tree, with the letters attached to its branch terminals, as an algebraic expression involving those letters and suitably placed parentheses. The correspondence is shown in Fig. 13.5. The algebraic representation assists in the handling of the problem by computer.

The scoring procedure is as follows: Begin at a lowest node (an innermost parenthesis); here we find two elements. If they are both *u*'s, record the reconstruction at the node as a *u*, and treat it as a single branch for the next step; but if they are both *c*'s, reconstruct a *c* at the node, and treat it as a single branch for the next step; and if one terminal has a *u* and one has a *c*, record the reconstruction at the node as a *u*, treat it as a single branch at the next step, *and* record a contribution of one to the value of *m*.[10] Now repeat this process for any other node(s) which is/are as low as the one just handled. Then go to the next level. Whenever two branches dominated by a node carry a *u* and a *c*, increase *m* by one, and treat that node at the next level as a *u* branch; whenever two branches dominated by a node are alike (carrying two *c*'s or two *u*'s), record a reconstruction at the node marked *u* or *c*, as the case may be. The process takes five steps for a six-terminal binary tree. If there are at least two *c*'s, and at least one carries *u*, then the value of *m* will be one for some trees, and more than one for some others.

The reader can confirm that this computing method scores any tree the same as the method of counting proposed in § **2.1**. Appendix II gives a detailed exposition of the computer algorithm we have employed.

3.4. The data. Table 13.2 exhibits the information concerning the 63 words, showing the occurrence of changed and unchanged forms in the six languages. When one of our 63 cognate groups is applied to a tree, the minimum possible score is 1. Thus any tree's total score from 63 etymologies must be at least 63; that score for a tree would mean that, in every one of the 63 cognate groups, a single instance of change sufficed to explain (in accordance with our postulates) the occurrences of *u*'s and *c*'s which are observed in the data.

In fact, the trees' final scores ranged from a minimum of 71 to a maximum of 182.

[10] Since all trees are binary, only two branches are considered at a time. The following chart summarizes how the symbols are reconstructed at a node, from the symbols occurring at the terminals of branches, on the basis of the postulates proposed in this paper:

	Left branch terminal	Right branch terminal	Reconstructed symbol at node
(1)	*u*	*u*	*u*
(2)	*c*	*c*	*c*
(3)	$\begin{bmatrix} u/c \\ u \end{bmatrix}$	$\begin{bmatrix} u \\ u/c \end{bmatrix}$	*u*
(4)	$\begin{bmatrix} c \\ u/c \end{bmatrix}$	$\begin{bmatrix} u/c \\ c \end{bmatrix}$	*c*
(5)	$\begin{bmatrix} c \\ u \end{bmatrix}$	$\begin{bmatrix} u \\ c \end{bmatrix}$	*u*

It is better to think in terms of the excess above 63; the range is then from 8 to 119. Table 13.3 shows the distribution of scores, both as *m* and as excess.

TABLE 13.3 *Distribution of* m *and excess in 945 distinguishable trees based on 63 words*

m	Excess	Frequency	Cumulative Frequency
71	8	1	1
72	9	0	0
73	10	3	4
74	11	1	5
75	12	5	10
76	13	1	11
77	14	3	14
78	15	1	15
79	16	5	20
80	17	1	21
81	18	8	29
82	19	2	31
83	20	7	38
84	21	2	40
85	22	3	43
86	23	1	44
87	24	1	45
90–111	27–48	101	146
112–135	49–72	187	333
136–159	73–96	340	673
160–182	97–119	272	945

Table 13.3 has interesting features. Of the 945 trees, exactly 45 gave excesses of 24 or less, and the remaining 900 gave excesses ranging from 27 to 119—from about 3 to 15 times as great as the minimum observed excess. The gap between 24 and 27 encouraged the view that only the 45 trees with excess of 24 or less deserve serious consideration. In fact, we have restricted our consideration to the 11 lowest-scoring trees, those with excess of 13 or less; our reason is that the three trees with excess of 14 include one which disagrees with every lower-scoring tree by reversing the order of Gondi and Koṇḍa. We take this to indicate that a tree with an excess as large as 14 may well be unreasonable, and can be dropped from consideration. Thus Figs. 13.6, 13.7, and 13.8 show the eleven leading trees.

Tree 1 has the smallest excess of all; it is the tree proposed by Krishnamurti (see §**1.1** above), and here receives strong corroboration, for *it is assessed here by use of information not used at all in Krishnamurti's earlier analysis.* That analysis did not rest upon the occurrence of unchanged forms, nor upon the relation of those occurrences to the occurrences of changed forms. Thus this independent corroboration lends much weight to the earlier conclusion.

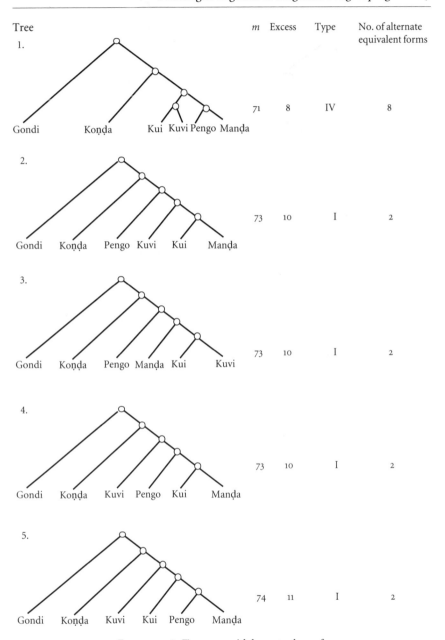

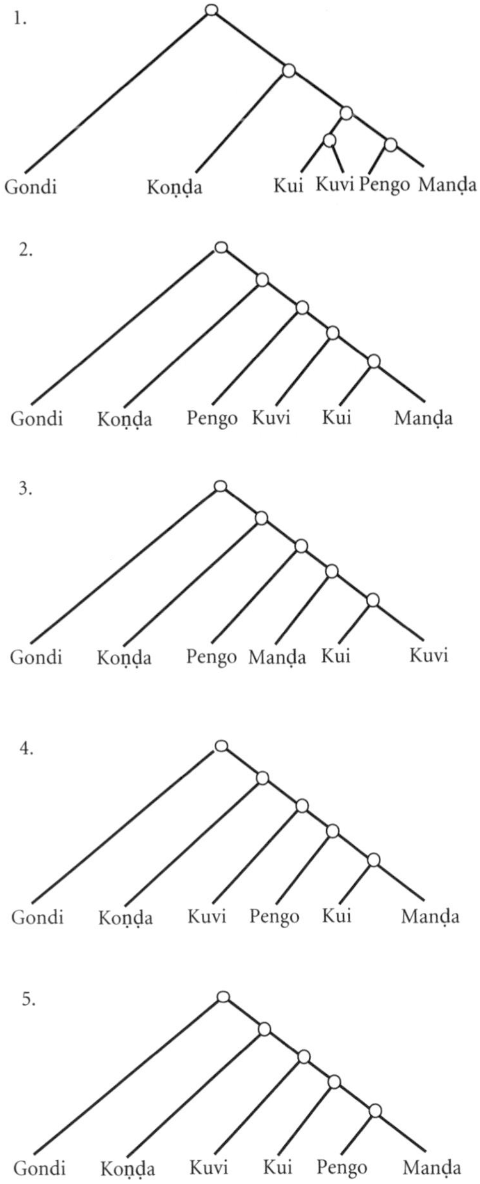

Tree	*m*	Excess	Type	No. of alternate equivalent forms
1.	71	8	IV	8
2.	73	10	I	2
3.	73	10	I	2
4.	73	10	I	2
5.	74	11	I	2

FIGURE 13.6. Trees 1–5, with lowest values of *m*

It is interesting to study these eleven trees with smallest excess scores. They comprise the most plausible of the 945 possibilities, and all rather resemble one another.

Tree	*m*	Excess	Type	No. of alternate equivalent forms
6.	75	12	IV	8
7.	75	12	I	2
8.	75	12	I	2
9.	75	12	I	2
10.	75	12	I	2

6.

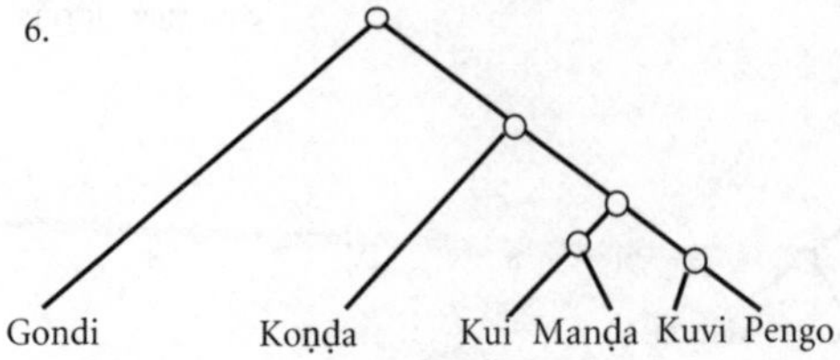

7.

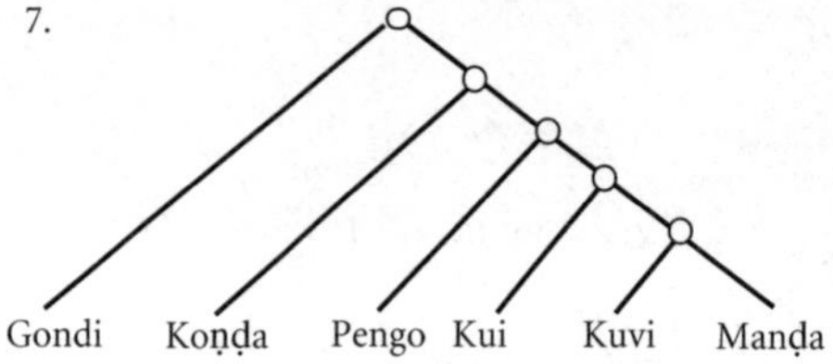

8.

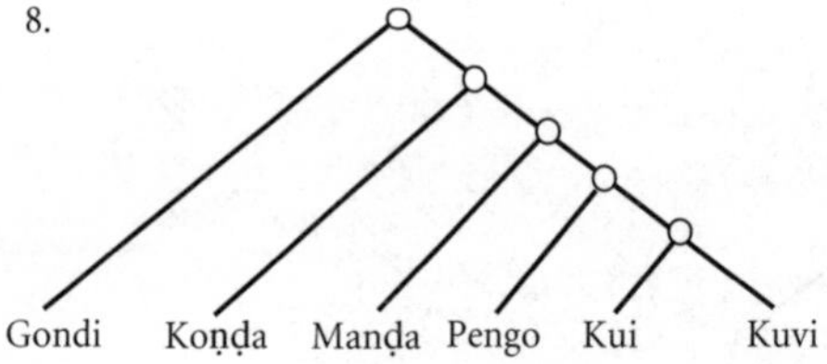

9.

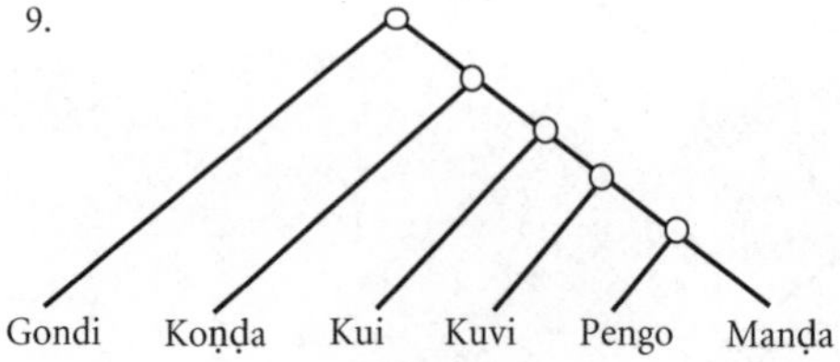

10.

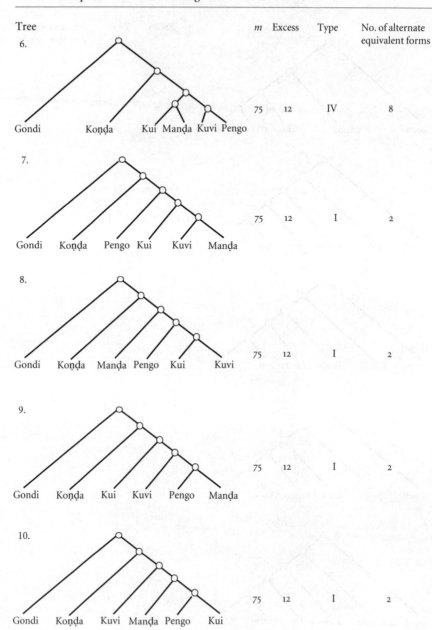

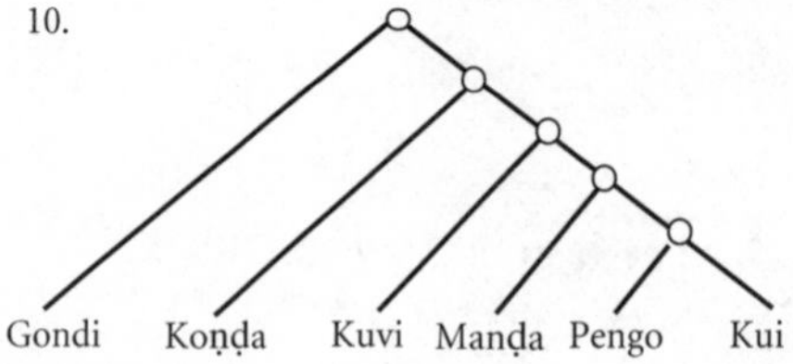

FIGURE 13.7. Trees 6–10, with low values of *m*

The leader, Tree 1, and two others, Trees 6 and 11, are of Type IV. These are all the only Type IV trees which begin with Gondi followed by Koṇḍa; of the three, the first has the sharply smallest excess, viz. 8 rather than 12 or 13. Type I Trees 2–5 and 7–10 can be seen upon examination to resemble Tree 1 rather closely. Consider Tree 3; it agrees with Tree 1 in that it first breaks off Gondi, then Koṇḍa, and maintains Kui and Kuvi as a closely related pair. It 'specializes' Tree 1 by first setting up the Pengo-Manḍa pair as an offshoot less recent than the Kui-Kuvi pair, and by then choosing Pengo as less recent than Manḍa. Each Type I tree shown is a 'specialization' of Tree 1, Tree 6, or Tree 11.

However, the tree with the smallest excess score—i.e. the one which demands the fewest independent changes among the 63 words—is Tree 1.

4. **A further analysis with two sound changes.** The foregoing treatment has regarded a cognate as either 'changed' or 'unchanged'. However, a further treatment considering more than one change under 'changed' is possible.

4.1. Define $c1'$ as the change VL > LV (V = vowel; L = apical consonant), and $c1''$ as the same change for a word beginning with a consonant, i.e. CVL > CLV. Now a word having reached the CLV stage by $c1''$ can undergo a second change ($c2$), the dropping of the initial consonant. We denote this compound change by *cc*, to represent the two-stage change of CVL > CLV > LV. (Appendix I gives fuller discussion of the multiple changes and their relations.) As before, we can determine whether or not a word is unchanged, and whether its changed form results from $c1'$ or $c1''$ (mutually exclusive possibilities, since a reconstructed word begins with either a vowel or a consonant) or from *cc* (i.e. $c1'' + c2$). The data for all 63 words appear in Table 13.4; these are the same items as those in Table 13.2, but a fuller description of the changes is now shown.

TABLE 13.4. *Entries from* DED(S) *with* u–o–c/cc *pattern for six languages.*

ENTRY	Gondi	Koṇḍa	Kui	Kuvi	Pengo	Manḍa
197	*c*	*u*	*o*	*o*	*c*	*c*
240	*u*	*u*	*c*	*c*	*u*	*c*
508	*u*	*o*	*c*	*c*	*o*	*c*
592	*u*	*c*	*c*	*c*	*c*	*o*
593	*u*	*c*	*c*	*c*	*c*	*o*
694	*u*	*u*	*c*	*c*	*o*	*o*
775	*o*	*c*	*u*	*u*	*c*	*o*
834a	*u*	*u*	*c*	*c*	*c*	*c*
S265	*u*	*u*	*c*	*o*	*c*	*o*
S290	*o*	*u*	*c*	*c*	*c*	*c*
S299	o	*u*	*o*	*c*	*c*	*o*
S407	u	*cc*	*o*	*o*	*cc*	*o*
S539	*o*	*u*	*c*	*o*	*c*	*c*
S642	*u*	*c*	*o*	*cc*	*cc*	*o*

Entry	Gondi	Koṇḍa	Kui	Kuvi	Pengo	Manḍa
*S*772	*u*	*o*	*c*	*c*	*o*	*o*
*S*787	*u*	*u*	*u*	*u*	*c*	*c*
*S*802	*u*	*o*	*c*	*o*	*c*	*o*
*S*877	*u*	*o*	*cc*	*cc*	*o*	*o*
*S*878	*u*	*o*	*o*	*o*	*cc*	*cc*
929	*u*	*u*	*c*	*c*	*o*	*c*
943	*u*	*c*	*c*	*cc*	*o*	*o*
1090	*u*	*o*	*c*	*cc*	*cc*	*cc*
1136	*u*	*o*	*c*	*o*	*c*	*o*
1142	*o*	*u*	*c*	*c*	*c*	*c*
1160	*u*	*u*	*c*	*c*	*o*	*u*
1311	*u*	*o*	*c*	*c*	*o*	*o*
1382	*u*	*o*	*c*	*c*	*o*	*o*
1485	*u*	*o*	*c*	*c*	*o*	*o*
1511	*u*	*u*	*c*	*c*	*c*	*c*
1538	*u*	*u*	*c*	*c*	*o*	*o*
1702	*u*	*o*	*c*	*c*	*u*	*o*
1782	*u*	*u*	*c*	*c*	*o*	*o*
1784	*u*	*u*	*c*	*c*	*c*	*c*
1787	*u*	*u*	*c*	*u*	*c*	*c*
1949	*u*	*c*	*c*	*cc*	*cc*	*cc*
1986	*u*	*cc*	*o*	*cc*	*cc*	*cc*
2102	*u*	*u*	*c*	*cc*	*cc*	*cc*
2529	*u*	*u*	*c*	*c*	*o*	*o*
2546	*u*	*u*	*c*	*c*	*c*	*c*
2655	*u*	*u*	*c*	*cc*	*o*	*c*
3046	*u*	*u*	*cc*	*cc*	*cc*	*cc*
3255	*u*	*u*	*c*	*c*	*c*	*c*
3262	*u*	*u*	*u*	*c*	*c*	*o*
3286	*u*	*u*	*c*	*o*	*c*	*c*
3296	*u*	*u*	*c*	*c*	*c*	*c*
3446	*u*	*o*	*c*	*c*	*c*	*c*
3537	*u*	*u*	*c*	*c*	*c*	*o*
3613	*u*	*u*	*c*	*c*	*o*	*o*
3619	*u*	*u*	*c*	*c*	*c*	*c*
3856	*u*	*c*	*c*	*c*	*o*	*o*
3865	*u*	*u*	*c*	*c*	*o*	*o*
3897	*cc*	*u*	*c*	*cc*	*cc*	*cc*
3899	*u*	*o*	*c*	*c*	*o*	*o*
3901	*u*	*u*	*c*	*c*	*u*	*c*
3988	*u*	*u*	*c*	*c*	*o*	*o*
4071	*u*	*u*	*c*	*c*	*c*	*o*
4096	*u*	*o*	*c*	*c*	*o*	*o*
4169	*u*	*u*	*c*	*c*	*o*	*o*

4327	*o*	*u*	*o*	*u*	*cc*	*cc*
4347	*u*	*o*	*c*	*u*	*cc*	*cc*
4438	*u*	*u*	*c*	*c*	*u*	*u*
4459	*u*	*o*	*c*	*cc*	*cc*	*o*
4524	*u*	*o*	*cc*	*cc*	*cc*	*cc*

m	Excess	Type	No. of alternate equivalent forms
76	13	IV	8

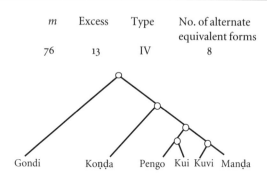

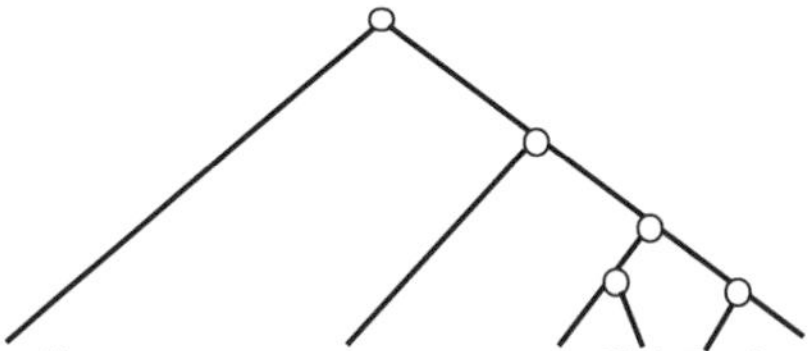

FIGURE 13.8. Tree 11, with low value of *m*

When a word occurs in more than one form in the same language, we treat it as if only the more changed form has occurred. Thus we score *u/c* as *c*, *c/cc* as *cc*, etc. The reasons are as before: we score candidate trees in terms of the minimum number of independent changes necessary to explain the presence of various forms of the word, as specified by the tree. The example in Fig. 13.9 illustrates the idea.

Let the given tree show *u*, *c*, or *cc* in accordance with which form occurs. Non-occurrence of the word is marked *o*. First we mark each non-terminal node as *u* if any terminal node descendant from it is marked *u*. Then we mark any remaining non-terminal node as *c* if any descendant terminal node is marked *c*. Finally, we mark any still remaining non-terminal node as *cc*. Then, throughout the tree, we replace each *cc* by the number 2, each *c* by the number 1, and each *u* by zero, and we enter no number for an *o*. Finally, we add up all the arithmetic differences between adjacent nodes in the tree. Fig. 13.9 has two instances of 0–1 and a single instance of 1–2. The sum of these is 1 + 1 + 1 = 3. That is the score for the tree. It represents the minimum number of independent linguistic changes demanded by this tree for the given incidence of changed and unchanged forms. Observe that 2 is the minimum possible score for any word-tree combination which contains both a *u* and a *cc*. The value of *m*–2 is thus the 'excess'. The distribution of *m* and excess, considering the fuller information on changes, appears in Table 13.5.

4.2. The minimum excess has now increased to 13 (from 8), and the maximum from 119 to 144. It is natural that these increases appear; they are the result of more complex body of data conditions existing to be satisfied. More notable is the rather sharp break between the two best-scoring trees and the remainder.

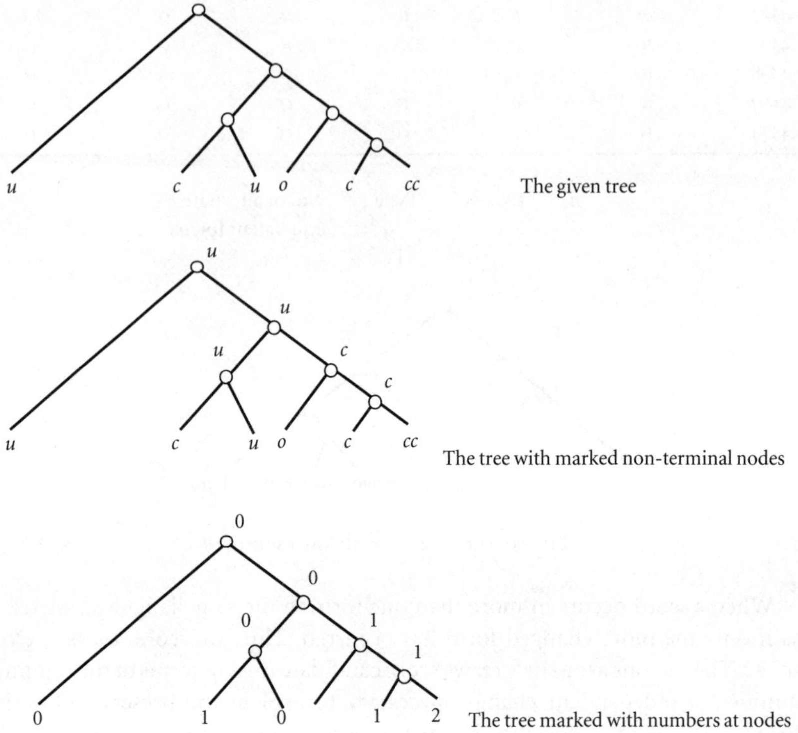

FIGURE 13.9. The given tree and two marked trees

TABLE 13.5. *Distribution of* m *and excess in 945 distinguishable trees, using 63 words, of which 16 have compound changes*

m	Excess	Frequency	Cumulative Frequency
92	13	1	1
93	14	1	2
94	15	0	2
95	16	0	2
96	17	2	4
97	18	0	4
98	19	2	6
99	20	1	7
100	21	3	10
101–140	22–61	122	132
141–180	62–101	339	471
181–223	102–144	474	945

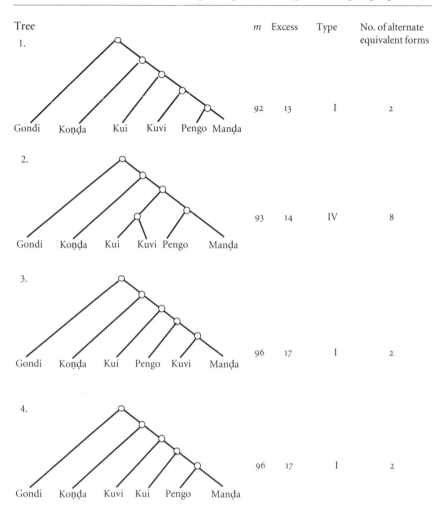

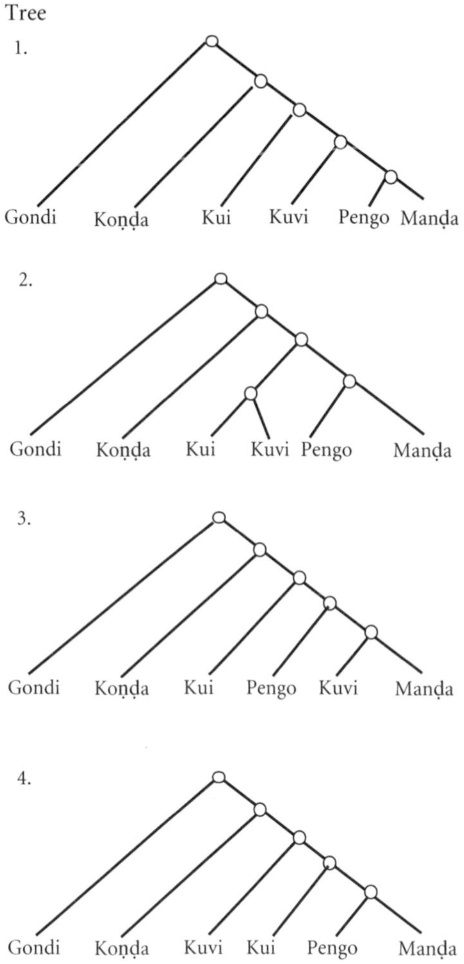

Tree	*m*	Excess	Type	No. of alternate equivalent forms
1.	92	13	I	2
2.	93	14	IV	8
3.	96	17	I	2
4.	96	17	I	2

FIGURE 13.10. Trees with lowest excess, counting two changes; best 4

Figs. 13.10 and 13.11 show the seven leading trees. Note once again that, after a certain marginal excess is surpassed, some trees invert Gondi and Koṇḍa; for these data, one of the three trees with excess of 21 exhibits this inversion. So we restrict our attention to the seven trees with excess of 20 or less. Here we find that the leading tree of the single-change analysis is in second place, one point behind Tree 9 of Fig. 13.7, which is now the leading tree in the two-change analysis. How is this inconsistency to be interpreted?

Our view is that 'inconsistency' is an inappropriate term. Note that Tree 1 of Fig. 13.6, which was at least two points better than all other 944 trees (judged on the

Tree	m	Excess	Type	No. of alternate equivalent forms
5.	98	19	I	2
6.	98	19	IV	8
7.	99	20	I	2

5.

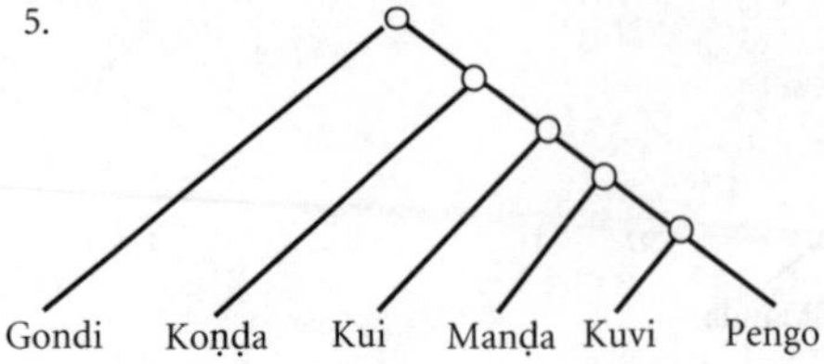

6.

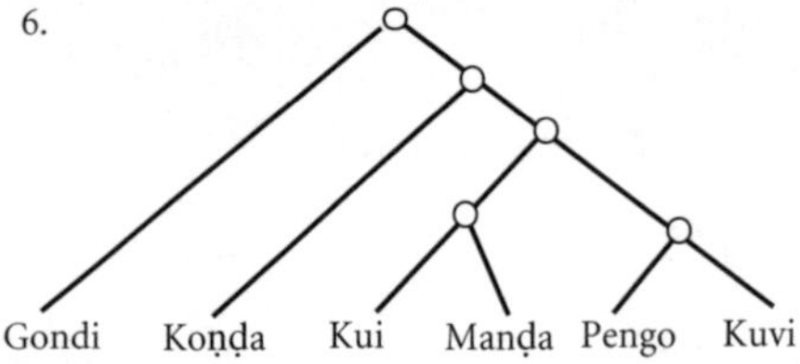

7.

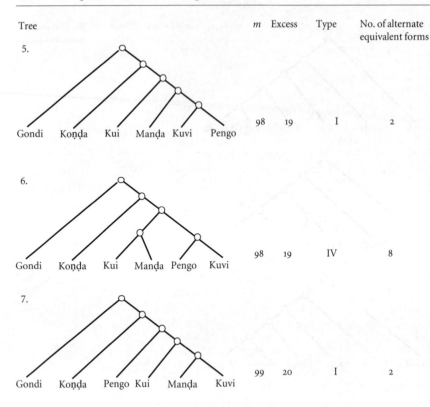

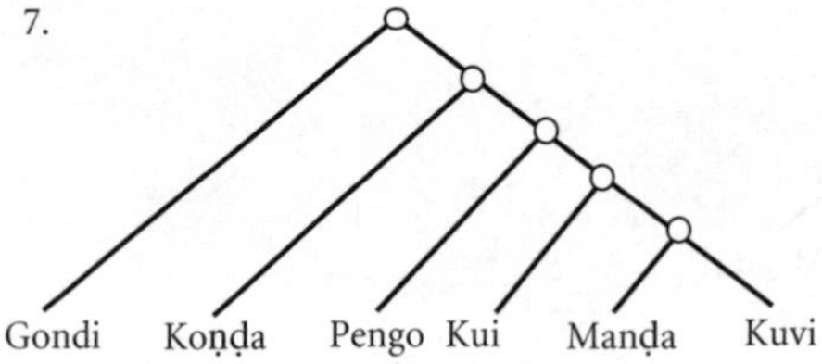

FIGURE 13.11. Trees with lowest excess, counting two changes; 5th, 6th, and 7th best

single-change study) is now better—again by at least two points—than all but one of the other 944 trees, when judged by the two-change standard; and that other tree is better by a single point. Tree 1' (or Tree 2') is indeed a plausible candidate for the best explanation.

But Tree 1' (or Tree 9) may be a superior candidate. Note that it is a 'specialization' of Tree 1 (Fig. 13.6); it preserves Gondi first, Koṇḍa second, and Pengo-Manḍa as a late pair; but then it chooses Kui and Kuvi to be less recent than the Pengo-Manḍa pair, and chooses Kui to be the least recent after Gondi and Koṇḍa. Is this 'specialized' version of Tree 1 actually the best interpretation of the data? Perhaps. It is not clear that the question can be resolved confidently.

To facilitate a closer view of the question, we examined the two trees by listing the entries for which they gave different *m* values. They gave identical values to 52 of the 63 words; in five of the remaining cases, Tree 2' had a smaller value of *m*, and in six cases Tree 1' had the smaller value. Table 13.6 lists those words. Note that, for eight of the words, one tree or the other had zero excess; but with three words, neither tree fitted perfectly. Does Table 13.6 illuminate a choice between Trees 1' and 2'?

TABLE 13.6. *Entries scored differently by Trees 1' and 2', using two-change analysis*

	Score		Minimum score for entry	Excess	
Entry	1'	2'		1'	'2'
240	3	2	1	2	1
1090	2	3	2	0	1
1160	2	1	1	1	0
1702	2	1	1	1	0
1949	2	3	2	0	1
2102	2	3	2	0	1
3262	1	2	1	0	1
3897	4	5	2	2	3
3901	3	2	1	2	1
4438	2	1	1	1	0
4459	2	3	2	0	1

4.3. We can search for an answer within the framework of sound change. First, consider the *u–o–c/cc* pattern in relation to the differential scores of Tree 1' and Tree 2'. Table 13.7a has five items which give lower scores for Tree 2', and Table 13.7b has six items which give higher scores for Tree 2'.

TABLE 13.7a. u–o–c *pattern with lower scores for Tree 2'*

							SCORES	
ENTRY	Gondi	Koṇḍa	Kui	Kuvi	Pengo	Manḍa	TREE 1'	TREE 2'
240	*u*	*u*	*c*	*c*	*u*	*c*	3	2
1160	*u*	*u*	*c*	*c*	*o*	*u*	2	1
1702	*u*	*u*	*c*	*c*	*u*	*o*	2	1
3901	*u*	*u*	*c*	*c*	*u*	*c*	3	2
4438	*u*	*u*	*c*	*c*	*u*	*u*	2	1

TABLE 13.7b. u–o–c/cc *pattern with higher scores for Tree 2'*

							SCORES	
ENTRY	Gondi	Koṇḍa	Kui	Kuvi	Pengo	Manḍa	TREE 1'	TREE 2'
1090	*u*	*o*	*c*	*cc*	*cc*	*cc*	2	3
1949	*u*	*c*	*c*	*cc*	*cc*	*cc*	2	3
2102	*u*	*u*	*c*	*cc*	*cc*	*cc*	2	3
3262	*u*	*u*	*u*	*c*	*c*	*o*	1	2
3897	*cc*	*u*	*c*	*cc*	*cc*	*cc*	4	5
4459	*u*	*o*	*c*	*cc*	*cc*	*o*	2	3

In each of the five items in Table 13.7a, both Kui and Kuvi show *c*, while either Pengo or Manḍa shows *u*. Naturally this pattern implies a shared change by Kui-Kuvi as against Pengo-Manḍa, which then become the branches of the final remaining node. These scores support the correct tree (Tree 2' of Fig. 13.10, or Tree 1 of Fig. 13.6). In Table 13.7b, note that Kuvi-Pengo-Manḍa share consonant simplification (*c*2), to the exclusion of Kui, in as many as five out of six entries. Consequently, Kuvi breaks away from its closest sister Kui—thereby providing a lower score for Tree 1' than Tree 2' for these items.

A plausible explanation for this discrepancy lies in the very nature of *c*2 (CL > L) as opposed to *c*1" ((C)VL > CLV) (see Krishnamurti 1978a, fn. 9). The Simplification Rule (*c*2), which was restricted in its structural conditions in the beginning, became generalized in Kuvi, Pengo, and Manḍa, thereby covering a large number of lexical items. It is possible that this generalization independently affected Kuvi, on the one hand (after its separation from Kui), and Pengo-Manḍa, on the other. *c*2 is not the kind of rule which necessarily requires a common stage of development for its implementation in a group of languages. However, the Apical Displacement Rules (VL > LV, CVL > CLV: see Appendix I) which account for the *u*–*o*–*c* pattern in Table 13.2 are atypical: we cannot expect them to be shared by two or more contiguous languages, accidentally and independently, in their innovative cognates. Computer scoring of *m* would naturally set up a single *c*, whenever Kuvi-Pengo-Manḍa show it by derivation from successive nodes labelled ((Kuvi) ((Pengo) (Manḍa))), leaving out Kui as an off-shoot of the higher node. Consequently, Tree 1' scores less than Tree 2' for the items in Table 13.7b.

Another limitation concerns the gaps in the lexical data of Pengo and Manḍa. Pengo has no cognate for 21 entries, and Manḍa for 31. They share this gap in as many as 16 entries. We do not know whether this represents shared and unshared loss of cognates in these two languages, or incomplete data collection—more likely, the latter. At least for Manḍa, the data are inadequate, based on a few days' field-study by Burrow and Bhattacharya. If fuller data were available for these two languages, Trees 1' and 2' would not appear as such close contenders. However, we hope that the method of subgrouping proposed in this paper is not invalidated by the inadequacy of data.

5. Conclusion. The postulates which we propose, as well as our assumption underlying the procedure of scoring *m* for all possible trees, are based on the standard theory of comparative method in historical linguistics. The contribution of this paper is in three areas:

(1) We have shown that a single atypical sound change shared by three or more languages is sufficient to give us subrelations among them—provided that unequivocal evidence exists that the sound change has lexically diffused, and has still left part of the eligible lexicon uncovered. Etymologies in which all cognates have or have not totally undergone change are not useful data for this study, i.e. all *c*'s or all *u*'s. Cognate groups in which at least two languages show change (*c*), and at

least one language lacks the change (*u*), are essential for such a study. Another constraint is that, if the change is not atypical—or if it is one that can commonly occur in contiguous languages independently—the results of the method may not be satisfactory. The method we have proposed here provides independent corroboration of the traditional method of establishing subgroups on the basis of shared innovations.

(2) Within the framework of the theory of lexical diffusion, a 'shared innovation' may be defined as the sharing of innovative cognates by genetically related languages, resulting from an identical sound change. The number of such shared cognates-with-change can then be used as an index of the degree of closeness between any two or more languages. Hsieh 1973 and Krishnamurti 1978a have successfully used this measure in linguistic subgrouping.[11]

(3) Within the model proposed in this paper, 'unchanged cognates' play as important a role as changed (innovative) cognates in scoring the binary trees in terms of the value *m*, i.e., the minimum number of independent instances of change posited by a given word group for a given tree. We believe that this proposal, making unchanged cognates a crucial criterion in linguistic subgrouping, is made for the first time here.

Our method can be applied to any family or subfamily of languages which fulfil the requirements of data, both to test the validity of the method and—if it works—to get a more systematic configuration of the family tree for such languages.

Appendix I

There are twenty-three Dravidian languages spoken in South Asia; the South-Central subgroup consists of seven languages: Telugu, Gondi, Koṇḍa, Kui, Kuvi, Pengo, and Manḍa. These languages are geographically contiguous, in the states of Andhra Pradesh, Madhya Pradesh, and Orissa.

[11] Hsieh proposes dialect subgrouping 'based on a corollary of the concept of lexical gradualness of sound change: that the more phonological forms two or more dialects share with respect to a commonly initiated but independently executed sound change, the longer they must have developed together, and hence the more closely related they are' (1973: 64, 88). Twenty dialects of the Jiang-su Province share an innovation, viz. the split of Middle Chinese Tone 1 into Tones 1a and 1b in complementary environments. Of the 533 items which qualify for the sound change, items which occur identically in all the dialects have been eliminated, leaving 43 items 'which show different degrees of diffusion overlapping' (see fn. 3 above) in the 20 dialects studied. Each of the dialects is then compared with the remaining 19, to see how many innovative cognates it shares with each one.

Hsieh operates with the notions of 'primary' and 'secondary' groups of dialects, setting up 'a certain number of shared items as a criterion of closeness' (81). The primary group is enlarged when the criterion of shared items is reduced, and has fewer members when the criterion of shared items is increased. The 'conclusive primary groups', set up with varying membership when the criterion ranged from 29 to 43 shared innovative cognates, broadly coincide with the traditional Mandarin and Wu groups of the twenty Jiang-su dialects. Hsieh's method is certainly pioneering and insightful, but it does not provide criteria to construct an unambiguous family tree diagram for all twenty dialects.

Consonant clusters, as well as apical consonants (here defined as including alveolars and retroflexes, but not dentals), did not occur word-initially in Proto-Dravidian. This situation is reflected in the native element of all Dravidian languages *except* those of the South-Central subgroup. The languages of this subgroup have many cognates with word-initial apicals, as well as consonant clusters having an apical as the second member. The phonological processes which underlie these changes can be represented by the generalized rules given below. We use the following symbols and abbreviations:

C_1 = [–syllabic]: all consonants admissible in word-initial position in Proto-South-Central Dravidian, viz. /p t c k b d j g m n w/.

V_1 = [V, –long]: any Proto-South-Central Dravidian short vowel which occurs in the root syllable, viz. /i e a o u/.

$\bar{V}_1 = V_1$ which is [+long].

L = [C, +apical, –nasal]: alveolar and retroflex non-nasal consonants, which occur only non-initially in Proto-Dravidian, viz. /ṯ r l ṭ ẓ ḷ/. In Proto-South-Central Dravidian, /ṯ/ = [ṟ]/[ḏ], i.e. the alveolar stop is realized either as a trill or as a voiced stop; so also the retroflex stop /ṭ/ is [ṛ]/[ḍ] (= voiced flap or stop).

V_2 = [V, –long, { +high, +low}]: non-mid short vowels /i u a/which are the only ones that occur in this position.

– = etymological boundary that separates the root from the formative suffix.

X = any consonant, obstruent or sonorant; or a nasal plus stop combination.

The phonological rules are as follows:

Rule 1' **a.** $V_1L\text{-}V_2X > L\bar{V}_1\text{-}X$
Conditions: $V_2 = V_1$; or V_2 is [+low] when V_1 is [–high, –low].
b. $V_1L\text{-}V_2X > LV_1\text{-}X(X)$
Conditions: V_2 is [+high], and $V_1 \neq V_2$; X is optionally geminated when it stands for a single consonant.

Note that a and b are complementary developments, and are therefore treated as a single rule.

Rule 1" is exactly the same as Rule 1', except that a C_1 precedes V_1. Rule 1' produces initial apicals, while Rule 1" produces a word-initial consonant clusters having apicals as second members. Rule 1' and 1" can be collapsed as follows:

Rule 1 **a.** $(C_1)V_1L\text{-}V_2X > (C_1)L\bar{V}_1\text{-}X$
b. $(C_1)V_1L\text{-}V_2X > (C_1)LV_1\text{-}X(X)$

Rules 1a–b occur in all seven languages of this subgroup, but not with the same degree of generality. Rule 1a has been called metathesis with vowel contraction (of V_1 and V_2 into $\bar{V}_1$), while Rule 1b has been called simple metathesis following loss of V_2 (*TVB*, §§1.121–1.159). Evidence also exists to show that Rule 1' operated first, and was subsequently generalized by involving syllables with initial consonants. Supporting evidence for this observation comes from the following facts: All languages have Rule 1' as formulated above. But Rule 1" does not occur in that form in all the languages. Thus, for Telugu and Koṇḍa in Rule 1", L = /ṯ r ẓ/ (only phonetic resonants and non-laterals), and C_1 excludes the anterior nasal /n/. In Telugu, /ṯ/ [ṟ] and /ẓ/ merge with the reflex of /r/ in CL clusters. In Gondi, Rule 1' occurs, but there are no instances of initial consonant clusters derived by Rule 1". However, in certain Gondi dialects, a few lexical items bear testimony to the operation of both Rule 1" and Rule 2 (see below). It appears that Rule 1' is the oldest, and Rule 1" a later extension, leading to the collapsing as Rule 1, which operates in its most generalized form in Kui-Kuvi-Pengo-Manḍa.

Rule 1" is diachronically followed by Rule 2, with which it has a feeding relationship:

Rule 2. CLV-X > **a.** CV-X (Telugu)
b. LV-X (all other languages)

The consonant clusters formed by Rule 1" are hereby simplified. In Telugu, the apical is lost; elsewhere, the simplification is by loss of the first member.

Telugu has not been included in this study, because it is unequally placed in relation to the other six members of the subgroup, as a result of its long literary history as well as its wealth of vocabulary. Rule 2 is a shared innovation in the other six languages, pointing to a common stage of development of these languages after Telugu had split off. Rules 1' and 1" produce apical displacement, while Rule 2 simplifies the consonant clusters formed by Rule 1".

Independent evidence is available to establish the hierarchical relations of these six languages as shown in Fig. 13.1, above. For instance, PSCD /ṯ ṯṯ nḏ/ develop differently in these languages, pointing to a stage of common development for Kui-Kuvi-Pengo-Manḍa (as shown in Table 13.8).

TABLE 13.8. *Shared phonological innovations among the South-Central Dravidian languages*

PSCD	Gondi	Koṇḍa	Kui	Kuvi	Pengo	Manḍa
*ṯ	r	ṟ	j	j	j	j
*ṯṯ	tt	R	s	c	c	c
*nḏ/*nṟ	nd	nṟ	nj	nj	nj	nj
*ḷ	l	l/ṛ	l	ṛ/l	ṛ	ṛ
*ẓ	ḍ/r	ṛ	ṛ	ṛ	ṛ	ṛ

Table 13.8 shows that all but Gondi share the innovation /ẓ/ > /ṛ/: all but Gondi and Koṇḍa share the innovations /ṯ/ > /j/, /ṯṯ/ > /c/. In Pengo and Manḍa, PSCD /ẓ ḷ/ merge into /ṛ/, whereas they are generally maintained in the other languages, at least dialectally. Kui and Kuvi shift long-mid vowels to low, which is a shared innovation (see Krishnamurti 1980). The conclusion we have reached thus corroborates the traditional subclassification of these languages, based on shared innovations in phonology and morphology.

The rules formulated above are illustrated by a few typical cognate groups below (*u* = unchanged; *c*1' = changed through Rule 1'; *c*1" = changed through Rule 1"; *c*2 = changed through Rule 2);

592. PSCD **ūẓ*/**uẓ*-V- 'to plough' (*VL > LV in Koṇḍa, Kui, Kuvi, Pengo).

[*u*] Gondi (Adilabad, Manḍla) *uṛ*-, (Adilabad) *ur*-. (Chanda) *uḍ*-, (Maṛia) *uṛd*-.
[*c*1'] Koṇḍa *ṛū* (*ṛū-t*-).
[*u*/*c*1'] Kui *ūṛ*- 'to dig with the snout, root up'; *ṛū* (*ṛūt*-) 'to plough: n. ploughing'.
[*c*1'] Kuvi (F) *ruiy*-, (Arku Valley) *ṛū*- id.: (S) *lū*- 'to nuzzle (of a pig)'.
[*c*1'] Pengo *ṛū* (*ṛūt*-) 'to till soil'.
[*o*] Manḍa.

834a. PSCD **ōr*/**or*-V- 'one', **oranṯ* 'one man' (*VL > LV in Kui, Kuvi, Pengo, Manḍa).

[*u*] Gondi (Yeotmal) *oror* 'one man', *orone* 'alone', (Manḍla) *oṛe* 'one man', (Maṛia) *orpan* 'at one place'.
[*u*] Koṇḍa *oren*(*ṟ*)- 'one man'; *or*- 'one'.
[*c*1'] Kui *ro* 'one', *roanju* 'one man', *ronḍe*, (Kuṭṭia) *ronḍe* 'one woman or thing'.
[*c*1'] Kuvi (F) *ro* 'one', *rō'osi*, (Arku Valley) *ro'esi* 'one man', *rondi* 'one woman or thing'.
[*c*1'] Pengo *ro* 'one', *ronje* 'one man', *ronjel* 'one woman'.
[*c*1'] Manḍa *ru*, *runḍi* 'one', *rukan* 'one man'.

*S*290. PSCD **ker-a*- 'scoop up with hand or ladle', 'to gather and scrape up' (*CVL > CLV in Kui, Kuvi, Pengo, Manḍa).

[*o*] Gondi.
[*u*] Koṇḍa *ker*-.
[*c*1"] Kui *grāp*- (*grāt*-), (Phalbani) *grēp*- (*grēt*-).
[*c*1"] Kuvi (F) *grec*- (*gret*-).
[*c*1"] Pengo *gre*- (*gret*-).
[*c*1"] Manḍa *grepa*.

*S*642. PSCD *paṟas* 'gourd' (*CVL > CLV in Koṇḍa, > LV in Kuvi, Pengo).

[*u*] Gondi *paras*, (Hill Maṛia) *paṛas*, (Manḍla) *parras*, *porrās*, (Betul, Manḍla) *parās*.
[*u*/*c*1"] Koṇḍa *paṟas*, *pṟāsu*.
[*o*] Kui.
[*c*1", *c*2] Kuvi (F, Arku Valley) *jācu* (pl. *jāska*).
[*c*1", *c*2] Pengo *jācka* 'gourd spoon'.
[*o*] Manḍa.

Note that Kuvi and Pengo *j*- is from **ṟ* (< **pṟ*-).

Appendix II

The tree search algorithm was written in the language SAIL running on a DEC PDP-10 computer owned by Stanford University's Institute for Mathematical Studies in the Social Sciences. The algorithm used SAIL records to represent the alternative linguistic subgroupings. Each node of one of the six possible tree shapes was implemented as a record composed of three words of computer storage. Two of the words represented the left and right sons of the node. If the node was a leaf of the tree, then both words were set to the null record. The third word was a pointer to the language currently associated with the node. If the node was not a leaf of the tree, then the value of the pointer was set to zero. Otherwise, it was set to an integer between 1 and 6 which was used to reference one of two arrays: of string names for each language, or of 'change types' for the current entry. Actually, the values 1–6 pointed to an index array which contained a permutation of the digits 1–6. The change types took the values *u*, *c*, or *o*: unchanged from the proto-form, changed from the proto-form, or 'no cognate in this language available for this entry'.

The six possible tree shapes were simply enumerated as case statements, rather than being generated algorithmically. For each shape, all possible permutations of the digits 1–6 were assigned to the leaf nodes successively (through permutations of the index array), and each resultant labelled tree was evaluated for each of the 63 words in the data. The evaluation process was easily accomplished with a recursive algorithm that assigned a score and a change type to each subtree in the following way. If the left and right sons of a node had been assigned a change type *u*, then the node was assigned the change type *u*, and was given a score equal to the sum of the scores of the two offspring. If one son was *u* and the other *c*, then the parent node was assigned the change type *u*, and was given a score one greater than the sum

TABLE 13.9.

	Change Type		
Left Son	Right Son	Node	Node Score
u	*o*	*u*	a
u	*u*	*u*	a+b
u	*c*	*u*	a+b+1
c	*o*	*c*	a
c	*c*	*c*	a+b
c	*u*	*u*	a+b+1
o	*o*	*o*	0
o	*u*	*u*	b
o	*c*	*c*	b

Here *a* and *b* represent the scores for the left and right sons respectively

of the two sons' scores. The parent node must have been unchanged from the proto-form in order to transmit to one of the sons an unchanged form (we are disallowing the possibility that a changed word will revert back to its old proto-form). Since the parent node has given birth to a changed child, this change must be counted in the total number of changes for the tree; hence the increase by one over the offspring's scores. In Table 13.9 we present the other possible parent–offspring relations.

The recursion starts at the top of the tree (the root), and defers scoring until the leaf nodes have been evaluated. The score is accumulated, and finally assigned as the value of the tree when the algorithm exists from the root node.

The output of the program states the frequency of the number of trees for a given score, identifies the trees with scores between 60 and 75, and gives the entry-by-entry scoring for the best tree.

No effort was made to apply only those permutations to the labels of the tree which would give unique labellings for a given tree shape. The resultant over-counting was corrected by decreasing the frequency of the number of trees with a given score by a symmetry factor for each tree. The symmetry factors for Trees 1–6 are 2, 4, 4, 8, 16, and 8, respectively.

14

An Overview of Comparative Dravidian Studies since *Current Trends in Linguistics* 5 (1969)

1. Introduction

1.1. Although the *Current Trends* vol. V which dealt with the South Asian Languages was published in 1969, contributions to the volume were submitted as early as 1966.[1] Emeneau (1971a: 34) deplored in 1968 that the *Current Trends* volume would become out of date even before it appeared. I wrote the chapter on comparative Dravidian studies in that volume—presenting a critical and comprehensive review of all available literature from the beginning up to 1966, with special reference to the post-independence period.[2] I would like to review the progress made since 1966 in the field of Comparative Dravidian. As I did in my *Current Trends* article, I would consider here only publications which explicitly deal with comparative Dravidian problems and not descriptive, typological, or other non-historical studies, even if they may indirectly aid comparative and historical research.

1.2. The enumeration of languages in the 1971 *Census of India* is much more disappointing than all the earlier Census reports. Languages with less than 10,000 speakers have not been listed in the mother tongue tables (cf. *Census of India* 1971, Series 1: Part II-C (i) Social and cultural tables). Consequently, we do not know the population figures of such important languages as Toda, Kota, Naiki, Ollari, Gadaba, Pengo, and Manḍa in the 1971 Census. We also do not know which languages and dialects with small populations are on the verge of extinction. For historical studies, there is a greater urgency for surveying and recording such languages. For instance, Pengo (returned by 1254 persons in the 1961 Census [recorded as 'Pengu']) and Manḍa (not listed so far) which were the recently discovered members of the South-Central Dravidian group will never find a place in the future Census reports. By this device, the Registrar General could reduce the total number of mother

[1] A version of the present paper was presented as the Presidential lecture to the 10th Annual Meeting of the Dravidian Linguistic Association on July 10, 1980, in New Delhi.

[2] Since I was editing the Emeneau Ṣaṣṭipūrti volume at that time, I could include in my survey some of the articles contributed to this volume, although it appeared in 1968.

tongues from 1652 (1961 Census) to a mere 210 (14 major languages of the VIII Schedule + 196 others) (ibid. 1). A few languages spoken by over 10,000 persons have also mysteriously disappeared in the 1971 Census. Malto, returned by nearly 89,000 people in the 1961 Census and a very important member of the North Dravidian subgroup, does not find a place in the 1971 enumeration. We could be sure that their population had not fallen below 10,000 from 90,000 in ten years, whatever the efficacy of our family planning programmes!

According to the 1971 Census, the Dravidian family of languages is spoken by 131 million people as opposed to 107 million of the 1961 Census—registering an increase of over 22%. Every fifth person in India speaks a Dravidian language. The population figures of the Dravidian languages are given in Table 14.1, listed in subgroups: justification for this subgrouping is given in §**6** below.

TABLE 14.1. *The number of speakers of the Dravidian languages*

	1961	1971
South Dravidian		
Tamil	30,562,698	37,690,106
Malayāḷam	17,015,782	21,938,760
Kannaḍa	17,415,827	21,710,609
Koḍagu	79,172	72,085
Toda	765	900[3]
Kota	956	1,300[3]
Iruḷa	4,124	5,200[3]
Tuḷu	935,108	1,158,419
	66,014,432	82,577,379
South-Central Dravidian or South Dravidian II		
Telugu	37,668,132	44,756,923
Gondi	1,501,431	1,688,284
Koya	140,776	211,877
Koṇḍa	12,298	33,720
Kui	512,161	351,017
Kuvi	c.190,000	196,316
Pengo	1,254	1,300
Manḍa	—	—
	40,026,052	47,239,437

[3] The 1971 figures for Toda, Kota, and Iruḷa are taken from the 'Classification of scheduled tribes by literates and illiterates' in Part II-C(i).

Central Dravidian[4]		
Kolami	51,055	66,868
Naiki	1,494	*c.*5,400
Parji	24,718	29,704
Ollari	*c.*800	9,100
Gadaba	8,401	11,200
	86,468	122,272
North Dravidian		
Kuṛux/Oraon	1,141,804	1,235,665
Malto	88,676	90,000[5]
Brahui	*c.*300,000	300,000[5]
	1,530,480	1,625,665
SUMMARY		
South Dravidian	66,014,432	82,577,379
South-Central Dravidian	40,026,052	47,239,437
Central Dravidian	86,468	122,272
North Dravidian	1,530,480	1,625,665
Total	107,657,432	131,564,753

1.3. A few new 'languages' have been reported during the past one and a half decades, although we cannot be sure if they should be called separate languages or dialects; e.g. Koraga (Bhat 1971), Iruḷa (Diffloth 1969, Zvelebil 1973), Kuruba (Upadhyaya 1972), Manḍa (Burrow 1976). Ramakrishna Reddy[6] reports two other 'languages' closely related to Pengo and Manḍa from Orissa, called Indi and Āwe. Koraga, Iruḷa, and Manḍa are definitely new members. We are not sure of the genetic positions of Iruḷa and Koraga in relation ṭo the other languages in the established subgroups.

[4] In the 1971 Census Parji is returned by 73,912; of these 39,563 are from Orissa and 29,704 from Madhya Pradesh. Since Parji is spoken only in Madhya Pradesh, the figures returned from Orissa are eliminated, because 'Poroja' is a common word for 'tribals' in Oriya (see Krishnamurti 1969b: 309, fn. 1). Similarly only those who returned Gadaba as their mother tongue from Andhra Pradesh are taken here to represent the Dravidian (Koṇḍēkōr) Gadaba. The figures for Naiki are taken from the *Census Centenary Monograph* 10 which listed in the Appendix all languages spoken by 5000 or less. When the main tables were presented in Part II-C(i), the policy was apparently changed.

[5] Malto is missing from the 1971 Census! The Brahui figures are old, taken from my *Current Trends* article (1969a), based on Emeneau's *Brahui and Dravidian Comparative Grammar* (1962d).

[6] Private communication.

2. Bibliographical Sources

2.1. During the period which is being reviewed, three bibliographies have appeared:

(1) *A Bibliography of Dravidian Linguistics* (4121 entries) (Agesthialingom and Sakthivel 1973), which in spite of inconsistencies and misprints is quite a comprehensive and painstaking collection.

(2) Acharya (1978) has prepared a classified list of articles published in *Indian Linguistics.*

(3) Ashok Kelkar's occasional bibliographical supplements to *Indian Linguistics.* Out of these and from my own knowledge of recent publications, there emerged a list of 110 entries which could be strictly labelled contributions to comparative Dravidian. During the past fifiteen years, research in Dravidian—both descriptive and historical—has made great strides. The establishment of the Dravidian Linguistics Association and its journal *International Journal of Dravidian Linguistics,* the proceedings of the World Tamil Conference, the several seminars on Dravidian held at Annamalai, the publication of *DED* and its supplements, liberal funds from the University Grants Commission for research support—all these factors are collectively responsible for this upsurge of research in Dravidian. The 110 titles may be classified as in Table 14.2. Significant contributions in each of the areas listed will be briefly discussed below.

TABLE 14.2. *Classified number of publications on comparative Dravidian, 1966–1980*

	Articles	Books
1. General surveys, collected works, proceedings	5	7
2. Bibliographies	—	3
3. Comparative phonology	34	4
4. Comparative morphology	10	3
5. Etymological studies	6	1
6. Subgrouping	5	1
7. Language contact		
(a) Dravidian *vs.* other families in India; India as a linguistic area	14	2
(b) Dravidian *vs.* families outside India	12	3
Total	86	24 = 110

3. Comparative Phonology

3.1. Emeneau leads the list of major contributors in this area followed alphabetically by Krishnamurti, Kumaraswami Raja, Sambasiva Rao, Subrahmanyam, and Zvelebil.

Emeneau's sketch of Dravidian comparative phonology (1970a) deals with straightforward correspondences of vowels and consonants of Dravidian languages and reconstructs the proto-phonemes. Since it was designed as a classroom course, originally in 1959 for the Coimbatore Summer School (further revised in Berkeley), Emeneau does not deal in this book with complex problems of Dravidian phonology. He gives the Toda, Kota, and Koḍagu developments of Proto-Dravidian phonemes for the first time in this short monograph.

'A Kota vowel shift' (1969a) reveals a set of chronologically ordered rules of the following kind:

Rule 1. *ay* > *e*/C___#

Rule 2. *ŏ* > *ĕ*/(C)___*Ce*#

Rule 3. *e* > Ø/___#

Derivative **ay* develops to **e* in pre-Kota; when preceded by this *-*e*, root vowel *ŏ* is fronted to its corresponding quality. Some time after this assimilation had taken place the conditioning vowel, i.e. **e* (< **ay*) was lost. Consequently, we have such forms as Ko. *keṛ* < **keṛe* < **koḍe* < **koṭay* (cf. Ta. *kuṭai*) 'umbrella' (*DED* 1386); **kuray* (-*w*-, -*tt*-) 'to bark' > PSD **koray* > Ko. *kerv*- (*kert*-). The Kota development is based on the Proto-South Dravidian vowel quality where o represents both PD **u* and **o* before *C-*a*. PD *ŭ* is fronted to *ĭ* before *CC-*e* (< *CC*ay*) (5–6). There are several exceptions to these rules many of which Emeneau explains as likely borrowings from Tamil and Baḍaga after the completion of the above changes. Such exceptions frequently 'denote objects of higher culture or of the context of the lower plains' (8). They can also be explained as the result of rule reordering in some of the dialects, i.e. if Rules 1 and 3 operate, Rule 2 is blocked. In the 'exceptional cases', Rules 2 and 3 could have applied in the reverse order (bleeding order):

Rule 1. *ay* > *e*/C___#

Rule 3. *e* > Ø/C___#

Rule 2. cannot apply

Therefore, **oṟay* > **ore* > *or* 'sheath' (*cf.* Ta. *uṟai*, Ka. *oṟe*; *DED* 621). There are doublets like *mel*, *mol* 'breast' (*DED* 4087), *keṛ*, *koṛ* 'umbrella' (*DED* 1386): the non-innovative (those which do not change *o* to *e*) forms either occur in proverbs or have developed contrastive meanings. It is difficult to go further without knowing the pattern of dialect variation in Kota.

Emeneau's 'Koḍagu vowels' (1970b) explains how *ë* and *ï* have developed out of pre-Koḍagu *e* and *i* under various statable phonological conditions which were subsequently lost or modified to give these vowels a contrastive status. After bilabial consonants *ĭ*, *ĕ* become *ŭ*, *ŏ* respectively—a change found in Tuḷu and to some extent in many other South Dravidian languages.

In another paper, Emeneau (1971b) discusses the developments of PD * *ẓ* (= **ṟ̤*) in Koḍagu and Brahui. This gives more precisely the conditions of the changes and represents an improvement on Krishnamurti's survey paper of 1958b. The developments are: *ẓ > *ḷ*/V___V, and *ẓ > Ø/V___C; *ẓ > *y*/___*i*. In the same paper Emeneau has discussed the Brahui developments of PD *ẓ, *ṭ, *r, *ṟ (*ṯ). As in most other Dravidian languages *ṯ [-ṟ-] merges with *r/rr* < **r*; *ṭ* and *ẓ* also develop to *r/rr*; in some cases *ẓ, *ṭ > *ṛ/ḍ* (190). In seven cases of metathesis in Brahui, all the three phonemes merge with **r* in producing consonant clusters of the type (C)*r*V- (192). In a more recent paper, Emeneau (1979) has comprehensively treated the developments of Proto-South Dravidian vowels in non-initial syllables in Toda.

3.2. In a sophisticated quantitative study, Krishnamurti (1976b, 1978a) has shown how the 'apical displacement' rules were inherited in the Telugu-Manḍa subgroup in a small segment of the lexicon and then lexically diffused to the other items in each subgroup and language. This has resulted in several languages attesting the change but not necessarily in shared cognates. He proposed that 'a shared innovation is a shared rule in shared cognates; lexical and areal diffusion result from a shared rule spreading through successive splits of a language subgroup into individual languages' (1976b: 209). In another paper (1978b), he discussed a vowel-raising rule in Parji resulting in synchronic variations which are dialectally stratified. Before pre-Parji (Proto-Dravidian) alveolar consonants—**r*, **l*, **n*, *ṯ*, *nṯ*, *ṯṯ*—a low vowel **ă* became *ĕ*; *e.g.* **kal* > *kel* 'stone'; after this change had completed, retroflex **ḷ*, *ṇ* became *l*, *n* in Parji. The vowel-raising rule does not operate before the *l*, *n* which resulted from the retroflexes; thus, **kaḷ*-V 'threshing floor' > Pa. *kali*. Generally counter-feeding orders are stable and essential in maintaining formal and semantic contrasts. Otherwise, homonymy would result causing confusion in communication. Contrary to the belief and claims of generative phonologists, counter-feeding orders are historically more stable and normal than feeding orders.

In a recent paper Krishnamurti (1980) discusses how in eighteen etymological groups drawn from *DED(S)*, Kui-Kuvi show the lowering of older long mid-vowels **ē* and **ō*. These vowels in turn resulted from *(C)*e/o* C-*a*- of Proto-South-Central Dravidian; *e.g.* PD **cup* + *ar* > PSD **cow-ar*: Koṇḍa *sōru*, Kui *sāru*, Kuvi *hāru*, Pengo *hōr*, Manḍa *jār* 'salt'. PD **ē* and *ō* which did not result from contraction or apical displacement in the above environment are not lowered. I used this additional evidence to consider the Telugu-Manḍa group as representing another branch of South Dravidian. Both South Dravidian I (Tamil-Kannaḍa) and South Dravidian II (Telugu-Manḍa) shared the vocalic umlaut of PD **i*, **u* > PSD **e*, **o* in the environment of *C-*a*; when these sequences contracted to produce long vowels, they might have been phonetically lower than *ē ō* < PD **ē* **ō*, i.e. somewhat like [ɛ] and [ɔ]. They were further lowered to *ā* in Kui-Kuvi and occasionally in the other languages, or developed to *ē ō*, in order to maintain the five-vowel system; otherwise, there would have resulted an asymmetrical system with five short vowels and seven long vowels in this subgroup.

3.3. One of the far-reaching discoveries of this period is Kumaraswami Raja's historical derivation of post-nasal voiceless stops in Telugu and Kannaḍa from old

*NPP (N = homorganic nasal, P = voiceless stop/affricate) (1969a, b). In his earlier formulation, Raja discussed this phenomenon with reference to only four languages, Tamil, Malayāḷam, Telugu, and Kannaḍa. He noticed contrasting correspondences as follows:

	Ta.-Ma.	Te.-Ka.	PD
(1)	V̄̆]PP	V̆]PP V̄]P	*V̄̆]PP
(2)	V̄̆]NP [NB]	V̆]NB V̄]B	*V̄̆]NP
(3)	V̄̆]PP	V̆]NP V̄]P	*V̄̆]NPP

Reconstruction of PD *NPP accounts for correspondence (3) best, although no extant language preserves it as such. He treated this phenomenon later (1969b) in a full-length monograph in which he examined the application of this rule with reference to various grammatical categories of the whole family.

3.4. In a monograph-length treatment, Pfeiffer (1972) has traced Kuṛux segments to their Proto-Dravidian sources. For his study, he systematically identified and eliminated all non-Dravidian lexical items. In Part II he compared Kuṛux phonemes with the other Dravidian languages and in Part III proceeded to derive the Kuṛux vowels and consonants from reconstructed phonemes. He has some interesting observations like Kuṛ. *k* does not become *x* before *u ū* (150). This makes sense because PD **k* then remains before high vowels *ī̆* and *ū̆* and becomes *x* before non-high vowels only (see Emeneau 1974a: 756). Appendix IV gives 195 Kuṛux entries with Dravidian cognates which are fairly certain.

3.5. Sambasiva Rao, in a stimulating paper (1973) which stirred up a needless controversy (see Subrahmanyam 1975, 1977c, Sambasiva Rao 1977) discovered the conditions under which exceptions to *(C)V̄C > *(C)VC-V-, or *(C)VCC- > *(C)VC-V- can be stated. He shows that where the underlying heavy syllable forms and the derived light syllable forms belong to the same form class (i.e. verb, noun, adjective, etc.), the rule operates; where the derived form belongs to a different form class from the underlying form, the rule does not operate; e.g. **nūṯ*: **nuṟ*-V-v. 'to grind' (*DED* 4330); **capp-*: **caw*-V- 'to chew' (*DED* 1927) (1973: 218–19); as opposed to these, cf. **kār* 'to be pungent': **kār-am* 'pungency' (236); **kaṭṭ-* 'to build': **kaṭṭ-ay* 'dam' (237). The fact that there are many apparently derived nouns which cannot be traced to extant verbs (Subrahmanyam 1975: 6) does not invalidate Sambasiva Rao's hypothesis, *e.g.* **kōẓ-i* 'fowl', **yān-ay* 'elephant'. Subrahmanyam observes that the rule is more regular in trisyllabic noun stems than in disyllabic ones (1975: 7–9). [Also study my critical review of the controversy in my postscript to Chapter 1.]

3.6. Subrahmanyam (1970a) discussed etymological groups to justify the reconstruction of long and short non-low root vowels before *y* in Proto-Dravidian. Only in Telugu is the length contrast lost before *y*. In a series of papers (1976b, 1977a, 1977b) Subrahmanyam explored the developments of PD **a*, **ā*, **l*, **ḷ*, and **r* in Toda. The Toda developments are numerous and complex, because in many cases the conditioning environments can only be seen in the reconstructed stages, having been eliminated during the historic period of Toda, e.g. **ā̆* > *ō̆*/*(C)___C-V_2, where V_2, is [–low]. There are many more conditioning factors in the case of rad-ical **a* than of **ā*. The suffix vowel (V_2) except where it is *i*, is lost in almost all cases (Subrahmanyam 1977b: 179). PD **l* > Toda *s̱* and *l*. All items with *l* are considered loanwords from Tamil, Kannaḍa, or Kota. Here, Subrahmanyam cannot think of any other reason than borrowing, because there are divergent correspondences. For instance, to consider To. *kōl* 'leg' a borrowing from Tamil is ridiculous. Could it not be that we have here an ongoing sound change which still has not run its full course? For instance, Toda has *pōs̱/pōl-* 'milk' < **pāl* (*DED* 3370), *pēs̱y/pēly* 'fence' < **wēli* (*DED* 4556), which clearly show that this is a sound change in progress. 'All the verb stems ending in *l* instead of the expected *s̱* must be loans' (1977b: 179). Why? A similar change of *ḷ* > *ḷ*/*ḷ* is noticed in Toda and the examples are 50: 50. Here again, Subrahmanyam applies the same 'rule of thumb' (1977b: 179–80). The developments of **r* (1977a) are quite interesting from the standpoint of the typology of sound change: *V_1*r*V_2 > $\bar{V}_1$; **r* > *š*/___V_2C (V_2 = [–back]); **r* > *ṣ*/___(V)C; **r* remains mostly finally (5).

3.7. Zvelebil's *Comparative Dravidian Phonology* (1970) is the first extensive synthesis of all published work in the area up to about 1968. Zvelebil has added his own data on Tamil dialects but he has neither observed nor formulated any significantly new correspondences or rules in phonology (see reviews by Emeneau 1973, Krishnamurti 1976a). With numerous new facts on comparative phonology, we hope Zvelebil will soon publish the second edition with revisions. An earlier paper of Zvelebil (1967) reprinted in his book of 1970 discusses three morphophonemic rules of Dravidian bases. All these deal with conditions inducing alternations of heavy and light syllables. I have commented on these rules extensively in my review (1976a: 146–8). In a statistical study of initial voiced stops in Dravidian based on *DED*, Zvelebil (1973) concludes that the ratio of voiced stops to voiceless in initial position is 1: 10 in Dravidian (220); for South Dravidian it is 1: 12, in Central Dravidian 1: 5, and in North Dravidian 1: 14. Telugu, Kolami, and Kannaḍa have the greatest number of lexical items with initial voiced stops, viz. 1: 4 (221). Kui, Kuvi, Koṇḍa, and Tuḷu have a voiced–voiceless ratio of 1: 5. These results reinforce the traditional reconstruction of only voiceless stops for Proto-Dravidian. The irregular ratios of different languages reflect their recent histories of contact with other languages and also of independent internal changes. In his 'Iruḷa vowels' (1971a: 116) Zvelebil discusses the sources of *ï*, *ë*, *ü*, *ö* central unrounded and rounded vowels in root syllables in Iruḷa; the conditions are similar to those that caused centralization of Koḍagu vowels, viz. retroflex consonants in the following position which are lost in some cases through subsequent sound changes: **kēḷkka-* > **kë̄ḷkka* > *kë̄kka-* (inf.) 'to hear' (PSD **kēḷ* 'to hear, ask') (117); if the retroflex is followed by a low vowel, centralization does not occur: *eḍa* 'waist' (< PSD **eṭay*) (117). The vowel system is much more symmetrical in Iruḷa than it is in Koḍagu. Zvelebil however is not clear about the phonetics of these vowels (116).

3.8. The accomplishments in comparative phonology are by far the most impressive during this period. Through various studies reviewed above, we now have a better view of the phonological developments in several subgroups and languages, particularly the Nilgiri languages—Toda, Kota, Koḍagu, and Iruḷa in South Dravidian; Kui-Kuvi in South-Central Dravidian; Parji in Central Dravidian; and Kuṛux-Malto and Brahui in North Dravidian. Descriptions dealing with the development of new vowel contrasts through secondary splits in the Nilgiri languages are extremely valuable for understanding the nature of sound change and the interaction between successive sound changes *vis-à-vis* the phonological structure of these languages.

4. Comparative Morphology

4.1. This period has seen some major contributions to comparative morphology, on which very little was done before 1966.

Andronov (1979) makes an attempt to compare and reconstruct the morphemes forming Proto-Dravidian non-finite verbs, viz. the relative participles, the infinitive, the perfective, the conditional, etc., as well as those of verbal nouns. In an earlier paper (1977a) he reconstructs Proto-Dravidian personal suffixes in finite verbs.

Emeneau's paper 'Dravidian verb stem formation' (1975) investigates four topics: (a) The medio-passive or intransitive suffix *-r-*, found in Kuṛux-Malto, has been set up as a voice-modifying morpheme which still remains at the synchronic level in these two languages, but was incorporated with the stems as a formative in the rest of the family. In this he has improved on the suggestion made by Krishnamurti in *TVB* (§2.38, 146–7). (b) In Kui and Pengo there is a well-developed system of forming plural action bases by adding **k(a)*, **p(a)* (~ **w(a)*, ~ *b(a)*) before tense-mode suffixes: Koṇḍa, Kuvi, and Maṇḍa also have a few stems of this kind. In the other languages too we notice that traces of these suffixes have become purely derivational and have been incorporated in simplex stems (12–16). Emeneau considers the Kui-Kuvi-Pengo-Maṇḍa system a retention of Proto-Dravidian plural action suffixes **kk*, **pp* (also **p* ~ **w*) which lost their original significance in synchronic grammars and became purely derivational in the rest of the languages (17). (c) Kui, Kuvi, and Pengo have a 'motion base', in *-ka-/-ga-*. Normally the 'motion' stem formative and the 'plural action' suffix are mutually exclusive; a stem can have one or the other, but not both. The stem means 'go and look', 'go and take', etc., incorporating 'motion' in the semantic structure of the root. Emeneau traces this to the Proto-Dravidian future suffix **-kk-/*-k-* which had undergone a syntactic-semantic reinterpretation in the Kui-Kuvi-Pengo-Maṇḍa subgroup like *I shall see > I am going to see > I shall go and see* (19). (d) A morpheme denoting the first and second person object (direct or indirect) incorporated in transitive stems in Kui-Kuvi-Pengo-Maṇḍa. In Kui the suffixes are *-ta-/-da-* (affirmative), *-tara-/-dara-* (negative). There are other phonologically conditioned variants of these. Pengo has *t(a)/d(a)* in affirmative and negative; Koṇḍa has a trace of this in *sida* 'give me' (you sg.), *sidaṭ* 'give me' (you pl.) as opposed to the regular imperatives *siʔa* (sg.), *sidu* (pl.) (20–1). Emeneau posits these suffixes for Proto-Dravidian related to the verb **tă/*tār*, 'give to first and second person' and agrees with Burrow and Bhattacharya that the use of this root as 'object marker' in verb stems is an innovation in Kui-Kuvi-Pengo-Maṇḍa (22–3). In this respect Old Telugu verbs with the auxiliary *-tencu* and *-tēr* should also be considered, e.g. *puttencu / puttēru* 'to send'; these 'morphemes' also occur with intransitive stems *aru(gu)dencu / aru(gu)dēru* 'to come', as opposed to *arugu* 'to go'. It appears to me that even the plural action suffix is an innovation in this subgroup. The mutual exclusiveness of 'plural action' and 'motion' suffixes points to underlying non-past morphemes—*p, mp* (intr.): *pp/mpp* (tr.), *k/nk* (intr.): *kk/nkk* (tr.)—being accorded new meanings when they lost their tense signification. The problem needs further research keeping the whole family in view with particular reference to the development of formative suffixes (see Krishnamurti 1978a: Appendix I; see also Ch. 17 of this volume).

4.2. In a recent article Krishnamurti (1975a) sought to resolve the question of the form and function of Proto-Dravidian number and gender categories. After an extensive comparison of all the existing subsystems (three major, comprising eight minor subsystems; 332), he argues in favour of 'male person' vs. 'non-male person' in singular and plural as the retention of the proto-system as represented by two subgroups, Gondi-Maṇḍa, and Parji-Kolami.[7] The split of the non-male person category in neuter plural into 'female human' vs. the rest (inanimate, non-human animate) is an expected innovation independently in Telugu, Kuṛux, and Malto, through possible syntactic and semantic changes. On the contrary, if PD **away* meant only 'non-human', as it does now in South Dravidian and Kuṛux-Malto-Telugu, there is no logical way one can innovate the inclusion of the female human category into it as it is now found in Central and South-Central Dravidian.

Krishnamurti also proposed a modification to his 1968 paper on personal pronouns, i.e. the innovation of **ñām* as the first person inclusive plural is not Proto-Dravidian but should be confined to Proto-South Dravidian, which split up into South Dravidian (Kannaḍa-Toda-Kota-Koḍagu-Tamil-Malayāḷam) and SCD (Telugu-Gondi-Koṇḍa-Kui-Kuvi-Pengo-Maṇḍa). The *n*-forms for the first person

[7] Sg. **awanṯu* 'he', **atu* 'she, it'; pl. **awar* 'they (men)', **awi/u* 'they (women, animals, and things)'.

singular occur only in these languages and it is exactly in the same languages that the inclusive–exclusive difference was originally disturbed and later revived. Those who proposed PD **nām* for inclusive plural could not explain *ñ-* in Ma. *ñān* 'I', *ñaŋŋaḷ* 'we' and the *nā-/nē-* alternation in Telugu, Kolami, and Naiki. The critics of this paper have also not answered why there is an alternation *mā-/mē-* as first plural oblique and why there arose a need to innovate forms for first plural inclusive in South and South-Central Dravidian. How does one also explain alternative forms *nēmu, mēmu* in Telugu, *ammoṭ, namoṭ, mammoṭ* in Gondi (199)? Subrahmanyam (1967–8) has no satisfactory explanation for PSCD **nā* (1st sg. obl.), **mā* (1st pl. obl.). The *ñ* consonant of PSD **ñām* is attested by Ma. 1st sg. *ñān* and pl. *ñaŋŋaḷ* (< *ñām* + *kaḷ*).

4.3. Shanmugam's *Dravidian Nouns: A Comparative Study* (1971) is the first book-length treatment of noun morphology. This book, though rich in data, is afflicted with too many misprints. Discussion of reconstructions follows a lengthy description of the grammatical categories from each of the languages. There are frequent statements of the following kind which lack scientific rigour.

> **-k* and **-kaḷ* are in complementation in the matter of geographical distribution. It is enough if we can reconstruct one of them to PD. Subrahmanyam decides in favour of **-kaḷ* because it is attested in Tamil even from the early period. (138)

> In Go.-Kui-Kuvi-Koṇḍa-Pengo group **k* has split into **k*. . . and **nk*. In Brahui **k* has split into *k* and *-a:k*. (139)

Notwithstanding such defects, the material of this book can be utilized for more systematic and scientific investigation of comparative noun morphology.

4.4. Subrahmanyam's *Dravidian Verb Morphology* (1971) can be taken as a major contribution to the comparative Dravidian grammar during the period under review. It discusses thoroughly the transitive-causative suffixes (1–101), past suffixes (102–238), non-past suffixes (239–330), followed by negative suffixes (331–96), and pronominal suffixes in finite verbs (397–422). The infinitive verb-stem formation is discussed in Chapter VI (423–52). There is an entire chapter on the imperative, optative, and prohibitive constructions (453–503). There is an Appendix (505–32) which discusses subgroups in Dravidian. In this scheme, a discussion of the South-Central Dravidian stem formatives comparatively treated by Emeneau (see §4.1 above) does not figure. The format and approach are similar to what Shanmugam uses (or has Shanmugam borrowed it from Subrahmanyam?). A complete review of this work is not possible, but it leaves many questions unanswered. For instance, the historical sources of formative suffixes constitute a major problem to be solved. I suggested (1978a: Appendix) that they can be shown to be Proto-Dravidian tense and transitivity morphemes, which have lost the meaning of tense in some languages and that of transitivity in others, and both in still others, thereby becoming formally separable formatives without carrying any definable meaning. The (N)P/(N)PP suffixes related as intransitive–transitive can all be interpreted this way. This book lays a firm foundation for a more detailed and sophisticated study of comparative verb morphology.

4.5. Part 1 of Zvelebil's sketch of *Comparative Dravidian Morphology* (1977) was published seven years after the copy was submitted to press. Dedicated to Emeneau, this short monograph (76 ff.) deals with nouns, pronouns, numerals, and adjectives. Parts 2 and 3 which deal with the verb, indeclinables, and derivation are promised, but none of these has appeared yet. This monograph presents basic descriptive information for each grammatical category and attempts reconstruction. Much of this work was anticipated in Shanmugam's book (see §4.3), but Zvelebil noticed that work only after he had completed the manuscript in 1971 (72). Zvelebil follows Kandappa Chetty (1969) in reconstructing PD **nām* for first plural inclusive (40). It is surprising that he says 'There is in fact no conclusive evidence for any form beginning with **ñ* in PD'. How does he explain *ñ-* in Ma. *ñān* 'I' and *ñaṅṅaḷ* 'we', Te. *nẽnu/nā-*, *nẽmu*: Kol. Nk. *nēm/nēnḍ*, etc.? There should be some basis for saying that 'the Kolami and Naiki forms with *ē* seem to be later innovations' (40).

In the reconstruction of oblique (genitive) stem formatives (i.e. inflectional increments) of nouns, both Zvelebil (1977: 23–5), and Shanmugam (1971: 196–249) miss the point. The multiplicity of these morphs can only be explained by setting up for PD **tt*, **n*, **i*, and **a* as discrete and autonomous morphemes, since each of them is reconstructable independently on comparative evidence. Almost all possible combinations of these also have come to serve as oblique formatives, as laid out in the following chart:

	*tt	*n	*n+tt→*nṯṯ	*tt+i/a+n
*i	**itt*/**tti*	**in/ni*	**inṯṯ*	**tt-i-n*
*a	**att*/**tta*	**an*/**na*	**anṯṯ*	**tt-a-n*

This sketch, like Zvelebil's *Phonology*, represents a readable summary of all known facts about Dravidian noun morphology, but it is presented in a very sketchy manner.

5. Etymological Studies

5.1. The great spurt of research activity in Comparative Dravidian during the past two decades is, to a large extent, due to the publication of A *Dravidian Etymological Dictionary* by Burrow and Emeneau in 1961. Since then, they have updated the book by adding two supplements (1968, 1972). [A revised version of *DED*, *DEDR*, incorporating the earlier supplements and further revisions was published in 1984.] In *DEDS*, there are 890 new entries *S*1 to *S*889 in addition to corrections and additions to numbered *DED* entries. *DEDS* is enriched with fresh and heretofore unnoticed data from many new and old languages of the South-Central group, viz. Gondi-Koṇḍa-Kui-Kuvi-Pengo-Maṇḍa. Cognates from the last two appear for the first time in the *Supplement* (1968). Further revisions appeared as two lengthy articles (1972) in *JAOS* (92.397–418, 475–91) under the title *Dravidian Etymological Notes (DEN)*. The same format as in *DED* has been followed in these two supplements. Besides additions and corrections to *DED* and *DEDS*, *DEN* has 77 new entries listed as S^{2}1 to S^{2}77 (475–6). The authors deserve congratulations from all Dravidian scholars for their continuing contribution to this monumental effort (also see Zvelebil's review (1971b)).

5.2. There are a few other short etymological studies in the form of papers.

Burrow (1972) examines the Dravidian words for 'horse'. He suggests that Skt. *ghoṭa* is derived from a Pkt. verb *ghoḍa-* 'sway, oscillate'. He derives Te. *guṟṟam(u)* also from Pkt. *ghoḍ-* by positing *ḍ* > *ḏ* between vowels. Here the difficulty is how to account for Pkt. *o* > Te. *u*. There are cases of PD *-ṭ- > PSCD *-ṯ-, but this would be the solitary case of Pkt. *ḍ* > SCD *ḏ*. He finally concludes that the true Proto-Dravidian word for horse has to be reconstructed out of Ta. *ivuḷi* and Brahui *hullī* 'horse'. The article, though very speculative, is quite enlightening.

5.3. Andronov's (1972) derivation of *brăʼūī* (Brahui) from PD **waṭa* + *kū* + *ī* 'a northern hill man' is ingenious, but it is more a matter of faith than an establishable etymology.

In his etymological study of Dravidian numerals, Andronov (1976) seeks to derive PD **on-ṯu* and **ōr/or*-V from **ol*. This is again a matter of faith but not a comparative reconstruction. It would be more logical to consider **o* to be the underlying pre-Dravidian root with *-*n*, *-*r*, *-*kk* as suffixes (cf. OTa. **o* 'to unite'). He goes on to derive some of the numerals from verbs **īr* 'to split', **mun* 'point', etc., but this approach is methodologically unsound. Could not numerals be primary (non-derived) words in languages? Andronov connects PD **cay-* with **kay* 'hand' (9). Though semantically attractive, formally it is impossible to posit palatalization from pre-Dravidian to Proto-Dravidian, simply because it is not based on comparative method. Except for these *ad hoc* derivations, the paper is good. Andronov does not consider Te. *wēyi* 'thousand' which is not apparently borrowed from any other language.

6. Subgrouping

6.1. During this period, the only significant proposal which departs from the traditional subgrouping of the family is the alignment of the Telugu-Maṇḍa subgroup (which I now call South-Central Dravidian) to South Dravidian. This leaves the Parji-Kolami group as the only branch of Central Dravidian. There has emerged clearer evidence that the Tamil-Kannaḍa subgroup (South Dravidian) and the Telugu-Maṇḍa subgroup (South-Central Dravidian) had a common ancestor (stage of development), Proto-South Dravidian. Among the most important pieces of evidence are (a) the sharing of the vocalic umlaut PD **i *u* to **e *o* before C-*a*; (b) The development of PD *c* > [*s*] > *h* > Ø; (c) Sharing of the innovated first person singular **ñān-* backformed from the first person plural inclusive **ñām* (see Krishnamurti 1975a, 1976a, 1980).

Subrahmanyam (1971: 505–30) deals with the isoglosses binding each of the traditional subgroups and major branches. He asserts that Tuḷu is a branch of South Dravidian (1968b). The matter is still not clear because its plural morphemes, **ḷ*, **kVḷ* are shared only by the Parji-Kolami subgroup. No other South Dravidian language has **ḷ* for common plural; secondly its oblique-genitive stem formative **(n) Vḍ* looks similar to those of Parji. The development of intervocalic *ṯ* to an affricate (between vowels) in Tuḷu is unlike the developments in any other South Dravidian language. Tuḷu is heavily influenced by contact with the South Dravidian languages—particularly Kannaḍa. Most of the features that Subrahmanyam lists for South Dravidian (1971: 509–14) are retentions of Proto-Dravidian traits which do not count in subgrouping. For his Central Dravidian also (i.e. South-Central and Central Dravidian), Subrahmanyam takes 'retentions' as 'innovations', e.g. the gender distinction as obtaining in the South-Central and Central Dravidian subgroups (1971: 519–26). Similarly the morphological representation of the past negative as found in Koṇḍa-Kui-Kuvi-Pengo-Maṇḍa (520) is a retention which the Southern group had lost. There is no reason why such a grammatical morpheme would be innovated and embedded into the verb in these languages. The other languages have lost this construction and innovated other devices to express past negative. Here, Telugu behaves like the other South Dravidian languages.

6.2. Southworth (1976) says 'There is no single innovation providing valid evidence for the existence of SD-Tuḷu as a distinct subgroup of Dravidian' (119). Subrahmanyam's criteria for Central Dravidian are also vulnerable (Southworth 120–3). Southworth maps the innovations of overlapping isoglosses (127–9), which, in a dynamic way, present a picture of language relationships within Dravidian in terms of genetic distance. He speaks of seven closely knit groups in which Tuḷu, Kannaḍa, Toda-Kota stand isolated (131). Suggestions made in this paper need careful consideration. For a general survey of all the proposals on subgrouping in Dravidian, see Shapiro and Schiffman (1975: 117–30).

6.3. Kameswari (1969) and Namboodiri (1976) applied glottochronological techniques to Dravidian and came up independently with the time depth separating the major literary languages. According to Kameswari Tamil–Malayāḷam separated around AD 1100–1500 (272), whereas Namboodiri's calculations put the divergence around 7th century AD (52); Tamil and Kannaḍa separated around 400 BC to AD 100 (Kameswari), 2nd century AD (Namboodiri); Tamil and Telugu diverged around 400 BC to AD 400 (Kameswari), 11th century BC (Namboodiri). The difference of opinion between these two scholars should tell us something about the reliability of the method or its implementation! There is also a lot of flexibility in the interpretation of true vs. false cognates which can give different time depths. Since Kameswari does not give her data, it is difficult to compare the two.

7. Language Contact

(a) *Other language families in India* vs. *Dravidian*

7.1. The question of contact between Dravidian and Indo-Aryan is as fascinating as it is speculative. This question has been reviewed again from the standpoint of most probable Rigvedic loanwords from Dravidian by Emeneau (1971a). He recapitulates the structural features in which Indo-Aryan and Dravidian show convergence with Dravidian as the source of such features, viz. the use of gerunds, the use of Skt. *iti* as a quotative, the morphological causatives, etc. During the period under review, Emeneau has published several studies (1969b, 1974b) in support of the 'linguistic area hypothesis' that he formulated in 1956. All these articles have been collected in the most recent publication of Stanford University Press (1980c) under the title *Language and Linguistic Area* (selected and introduced by Anwar S. Dil). Part I of this volume has four essays of Emeneau's on the theory of diffusion and structural borrowing (1–84); Part II (85–319) has essays 5–11, all focusing on 'India as a linguistic area'; Part III has four essays dealing with Brahui.

7.2. One of the most original and impressive contributions on the linguistic area hypothesis with special reference to India is Masica's *Defining a Linguistic Area* (1976), based on a study of scores of grammars of the South Asian languages. Masica takes a total of thirty-seven linguistic features (phonological, morphological, and syntactic) and goes on to determine how many of these define India as a linguistic area. He discovered four definite ones—retroflex consonants, the enclitic particle Skt. *api*, Drav. *um* 'even/also/indefinite/and', dative-subject construction, and echo words. He has a qualified 'Yes' for nine features which have been considered pan-Indic earlier; e.g. morphological causatives, the conjunctive particle; etc. (187–90). Masica looked at the features from the standpoint of universal language typology and was able to isolate traits which are definitely area-bound.

7.3. Kuiper's article (1967) makes a profound study of prehistoric influences of non-Aryan linguistic features in Old Indo-Aryan texts. He discusses the retroflex consonants and the use of Vedic *iti* 'thus' which corresponds syntactically to the usage of the past participle of Proto-Dravidian verb **an*/**en* 'say'. Evidence of the use of *iti* as a complementizer of onomatopoeic expressions corresponding to Ta. *eṉṟu* and Te. *ani* clinches its Dravidian origin. Thus Kuiper shows definite traces of the beginnings of Dravidian influence on Indo-Aryan.

7.4. Southworth's survey article (1979) brings together all published evidence on Dravidian loanwords in Indo-Aryan classified semantically (194–5). He sets up a category of lexical items which is found both in Dravidian and Indo-Aryan but the direction of borrowing cannot be determined (196–8). These include Skt. *carati* (D **cal* 'to go'), *paṭhati* (D **pāṭu* 'to sing'), *vaśi* 'knife, axe' (Ta. *vay*: SD **wac-*), *śava* (D *cā̆(y)* 'die'), etc. On the basis of the vocabulary study, Southworth makes certain assumptions regarding the nature of Aryan and Dravidian contact which led to structural and lexical borrowing in both directions. He thinks that there was a period of social adjustment and 'village co-existence' between the Aryan land owners and the Dravidian tenants and labour (207–8).

(b) *Dravidian* vs. *other language families outside India*

7.5. There have been numerous studies relating Dravidian with the other language families. The most widely discussed have dealt with the relationship between Dravidian and Uralic-Altaic (See Krishnamurti 1969a: 328).

From the English-speaking world Tylor has a convincing paper (1968) showing lexical comparisons between Dravidian and Uralian based on 153 etymologies. He has also given a convincing set of correspondences between Proto-Uralic and Proto-Dravidian. Nearly half of these are items originally suggested by Burrow (1944). Where Dravidian has more than one reflex corresponding to one in Uralian (like Ur. *ä*: D *a*, *ā*, *e*, *ē*, *ay*, *i*, 801), Tylor does not give the conditioning environments indicating split or merger of the proto-segment in these two branches. The phonetic-semantic similarities are striking, although one does not know how to interpret these data genetically.

7.6. The most publicized proposal during the recent years is the relationship between Dravidian and Elamite advanced by McAlpin (1974). He compares 57 lexical items drawn from an Achaemenid Elamite (640 BC) corpus of 'about 5000 words' (90) with possible Dravidian parallels, taken from *DED(S)*, and constructs phonological correspondences and a theory of relationship between Dravidian and Elamite. He even reconstructs Proto-Elamo-Dravidian (PED). There are 47 correspondences or phonological rules which account for 57 etymological groups. It appears that McAlpin was carried away on a flight of his imagination. Given two unrelated languages or language families it is possible for any shrewd scholar to notice 50 or 60 lexical items which accidentally match; it is also possible to set up correspondences for these and write rules. Notice, for instance, Ananda Vasudevan (1973) shows 71 'shared cognates' between Dravidian and Greek. With a little effort, he could have set up decent correspondences also like Greek *t* = D *t*, e.g. Greek *trepō*: Ta. *tiruppu* 'to turn' etc. (183). The following are my comments on McAlpin's work:

(1) Many of the rules formulated by McAlpin lack intrinsic phonetic/phonological motivation and appear *ad hoc*, invented to fit the proposed correspondences; e.g. PED **i*, *e* > Ø (Elamite) when followed by *t*, *n*, which are again followed by *a*: but these remain undisturbed in Dravidian (93). How does a language develop that kind of sound change? This rule was dropped a few years later, because the etymologies were abandoned (see 1979: 184).

(2) He set up retroflexes as an innovation in Dravidian resulting from PED *rt (94). Later he abandoned this rule and set up retroflexes and dentals for PED and said that Elamite merged the retroflexes with dentals (McAlpin 1979; see chart on 184–5). But the following statement in the body of the article, referring to his updated version of correspondences, is puzzling: 'The major additions have been . . . the splitting of the Proto-Elamo-Dravidian dental series into dental and post-dental series reflecting the dental–retroflex contrast in Dravidian' (176). But the chart shows merger in Elamite and no split of PED dentals into dental and retroflex in Dravidian! The correspondences between 1974 and 1979 have undergone total change which meant that earlier 'etymologies' were abandoned and new ones commissioned. The 1979 correspondences sound more plausible, but the etymologies are weak; e.g. PD *īn* 'to bear young (of animal), to wean' is said to be cognate with Elamite *šinni* 'approach, arrive' by positing loss of PED *š in Proto-Dravidian. This semantic connection is perhaps dictated by the author's English language background in which people refer to 'the arrival of a baby'. But it is extremely odd to attribute this *ad hoc* semantic connection to Proto-Dravidian. For those who know Dravidian, this meaning shift is extremely spurious and *ad hoc.*

(3) McAlpin's adventure into comparative morphology is even more disastrous. A full review of this literature has to await the publication in 1981 of his full monograph, *Proto-Elamo-Dravidian: The Evidence and Implications*, by the American Philosophical Society.

7.7. The most exciting but yet the least understood has been the decipherment of the Indus script as Proto-Dravidian. Even an attempt at a bibliography of recent literature on this theme would be formidable. Mahadevan's concordance and tables of the texts of the Indus script (1977) is a monumental work and a basic tool for all scholars who can spend the rest of their lives trying to break the code. Both the Russian and Finnish scholars' efforts in this regard during the past one and a half decades are both exciting and laudable but they have not produced any concrete proof that can be tested by the linguist's more reliable tool, viz. the comparative method (Zide and Zvelebil 1970, 1976). There is a whole issue of the *Journal of Tamil Studies* (1970) devoted to recent researches in the decipherment of the Indus script which has many stimulating ideas, particularly from Zide, Knorozov, Gurov, Parpola, and Mahadevan.

7.8. A scholarly address to an enlightened audience in Madras in 1974 by President Senghor of Senegal (1975) shows his linguistic sophistication, his knowledge of pre-history and anthropology. He shows many word parallels between Dravidian and Wolof and refers to many scholarly works describing this relationship during the recent years. Upadhyaya (1976) gives substantial lexical evidence which is much more impressive (57–8) than that between Dravidian and Elamite. He simply has not attempted correspondences and rules on the same scale as McAlpin. Some definite ones are illustrated (48). Professor Greenberg told me, in a personal conversation in 1976, that Dravidian seems to be very closely related to the Nilo-Saharan languages of North Africa.

7.9. I have just seen a manuscript by Susumu Shiba (1980) of Kyoto University, connecting Dravidian with Japanese. Since Japanese and Korean are 'said to be combinations of Altaic and Austronesian' (4), there is a reasonable basis for Dravidian which is 'related to Altaic' to have some kind of genetic relationship with Japanese! This article produces a lot of grammatical and lexical evidence in support of Japanese-Dravidian relationship. The bibliography attached to this article gives some more recent works on this theme.

8. I have only sketched the recent major writings in the field of comparative Dravidian. Although the breadth and the depth of these studies is indeed impressive, several basic tasks still remain to be undertaken and accomplished. There is no reliable description of any of the Gondi dialects (some perhaps are distinct languages). The new Dravidian languages viz. Iruḷa, Kuṟumba, Koraga, and Manḍa should be fully described and published with texts and lexicons. The time has come for a new comparative grammar of the Dravidian languages to be written, and I have been working in my own modest way toward this end for some years.

15

A Problem of Reconstruction in Gondi: Interaction between Phonological and Morphological Processes

With Garapati U. Rao (*Osmania University*)

1.0. Introduction. Proto-Dravidian has the following reconstructions for demonstrative pronouns of human (masculine) category: **awanṯ(u)* [*awanḏu/awanṟu*] 'he (that man)', **awar* 'they (those men (and women))'; **iwanṯ(u)* [*iwanḏu/iwanṟu*] 'he (this man)', and **iwar* 'they (these men (and women))'. The oblique stems of the singular forms are **awan-* and **iwan-* respectively; in the plural there does not seem to be any difference between the nominative and oblique bases. The languages of South Dravidian (i.e. Tamil, Malayāḷam, Toda, Kota, Koḍagu, and Kannaḍa) have a shared innovation in the loss of final *-*ṯu* (< **-*tu*) of the PD nom. sg. **awanṯu*/**iwanṯu* (Krishnamurti 1961: §4.44, 1975: 340–1, Burrow and Bhattacharya 1970: 35–6). Consequently the nominative and oblique stems become identical in the singular as they are in the plural, viz. sg. **awan* (nom.): **awan-* (obl.).

1.1 In the group of languages called South-Central Dravidian (i.e. Telugu, Gondi, Koṇḍa, Kui, Kuvi, Pengo, and Manḍa) as well as in the Central Dravidian languages, we find systematic reflexes for the final sequences of the reconstructed singular forms *-*nṯ(u)* and *-*n* (for nominative and oblique) which apparently represent the retention of the Proto-Dravidian distinction between nominative and oblique case forms.

Study the forms from the languages of South-Central Dravidian and Central Dravidian given in Table 15.1.

This paper was to be submitted to a volume edited by George Cardona and Norman Zide to felicitate Prof. H. M. Hoenigswald, on his seventieth birthday in 1986. However, we could not submit it in time for inclusion in the Festschrift. Krishnamurti was Hoenigswald's student at Pennsylvania in the early fifties. Rao is a student of Krishnamurti. Both of them had gained their insights in historical linguistics from the scholarly contributions of H. M. Hoenigswald. To this great teacher and scholar, we humbly dedicate this paper.

TABLE 15.1. *Forms derived from PD* *awanṯu [awanḏu/awanṟu] *'he (that man)' in South-Central and Central Dravidian languages*

LANGUAGE/DIALECT	Singular		Plural	
	Nom.	Obl.	Nom.	Obl.
SCD	**awanṯu* [awanḏu]/[awanṟu]	**awan-*	**awar*	**awar-*
Telugu (inscr.)	wānṟu	wāni-	wāru	wāri-
OTe.	wāṇḍu			
M Te.	wā̃ḍu			
Mdn. Te.	wāḍu	wāni- / wāḍi- (dial.)	wāḷḷu	wāḷḷa-
Gondi (dial.)	ōl	ōn-	ōṛ	ōṛ-
	ōr		ōrk	ōr(k)-
	ōʀ		ōṛ	ōṛ-
	ōṇḍ		ōr-	ōr-
Koṇḍa	wānṟu	wani-	wār	wari-
Kui	aanju	aani-	aaru	aari-
Kuṭṭia dial.	eyanja	eyani-	eyara	eyari-
Kuvi	evasi	evana-	evar	evara-
Pengo	avan	avan-	avar	avar(i)
Manḍa	evan	evan-	evar	evar-
CD	**awanṯu*	**awan-*	**awar*	**awar-*
Kolami	am/amd	am-/amn-	avr	avr-
Naiki	avnd	avn-	avr	avr-
Parji	ōd/ōḍ	ōn-	ōr	ōr-
Gadaba	ōṇḍ/ōṇ	ōṇ(ḍ)-un-	ōr	ōr-un-

1.2. The comparative (dialectal) data from Gondi present the following problems: (a) It has no trace of the preconsonantal nasal of the original *-nḏ/-nṟ* sequence in the nominative singular form. Gondi nominative singular forms given in *DEDR*, drawn from different dialects, are *ōl*, *ōr*, *ōʀ*, and *ōṇḍ(u)* (the last possibly borrowed from Old Telugu); the oblique stem is uniformly *ōn-* preserving the underlying nasal corresponding to **awan-*. (b) The alternation of *l-r-ʀ* in nominative singular (particularly *l* in *ōl*) cannot be traced to the proto-form and explained in terms of normal sound change. (c) The addition of *-k* to the plural stems in some dialects as in *ōr*: *ōrk*, *ōṛ*: *ōṛk*, etc. (d) The apparent lack of distinction in some dialects between the nominative singular and plural (see Sets 3a and 3b given in Table 15.2).

Regarding the origin of the *-l* form in Gondi (dialects), Emeneau (1955a: 147) says:

The Gondi forms must be given separate treatment because of their uncertainty. They are in Trench *ōl*, *ēl*, *bōl*; he records, however (*Grammar*, p. 4), that 'we hear' also *ōr*, and presumably also *ēr* and *bōr*. All other reporters of Go. give only forms with *r*, to which Lind adds a form with *g̣* (equivalent, he says, to Arabic *g̠h̠ain*) . . .

In the pronominals the masc. pl. *ōṛ* is from PD **avar*. The masc. sg. *ōr* is in all probability from, or somehow connected with, the form that we have reconstructed as **avanṟu*. Both have gone through stages with loss of the second *a* and replacement of **ava-* by *ō*. The unsolved problem for *ōr* is the loss of *-n-*; **nṟ* normally > Go. *nd* (§10.25). Trench (loc. cit.) assumes that *ōl* and *ōr* are interchangeable forms, giving a parallel instance and referring to interchange of *l* and *r* as 'frequent'. He may be right; 'for the moment no better explanation is at hand.

Subrahmanyam (1968a: 178) says, 'The demonstrative pronouns *vōr* and *vēr* (3.25) are ultimately related to **avan* and **ivan* though at present nothing is known about the origin of the final *r* (*l* in Chanda and Betul, see *CVGD* 441)'.

A comparative study of the Gondi dialect data found in Burrow and Bhattacharya (1960) included in *DEDR* (1984) as well as the field-notes on Gondi dialects by Rao (1987) now seem to provide a plausible solution to all the problems enumerated above.

2.0. Gondi is spoken by about 2,197,227 persons according to the 1981 Census. There are apparently many regional dialects of Gondi spread over large stretches of hills and forests in the four adjacent states of Madhya Pradesh, Maharashtra, Andhra Pradesh, and Orissa. The Gonds are a tribal population with a very low rate of literacy and they are fond of maintaining their traditional ways of life. Although we have not studied the pattern of intercommunication among the speakers of different dialects, it appears that the speakers of different dialects are slowly drifting apart and there may not be much mutual intelligibility between the speakers from two distant ends of the Gondi-speaking area.

There are a number of ongoing sound changes in Gondi and a systematic survey of these dialects should yield rich data for the historical linguist interested in a theoretical study of a sound change in progress.[1] Unfortunately, there have been few reliable and comprehensive descriptions of any of the dialects, and we are also not certain about the true dialect profile of Gondi.

2.1. The data collected from different Gondi dialects for Proto-Dravidian demonstrative pronouns can be presented in ten major sets (see Table 15.2), each set differing from the other in at least one item.

[1] Gondi dialects exhibit a number of ongoing sound changes like *s* → *h* → Ø, *e/o* → *a*, *e/o* → *i/u*, *ṛ*, *r* → *r*, *ṟ* → *r*, etc. Instead of using the 'Brugmannian innovations' in which case a historical linguist is concerned only with the presence or absence of a rule, the *extent of the operation* of a particular sound change could be exploited usefully in subgrouping various Gondi dialects.

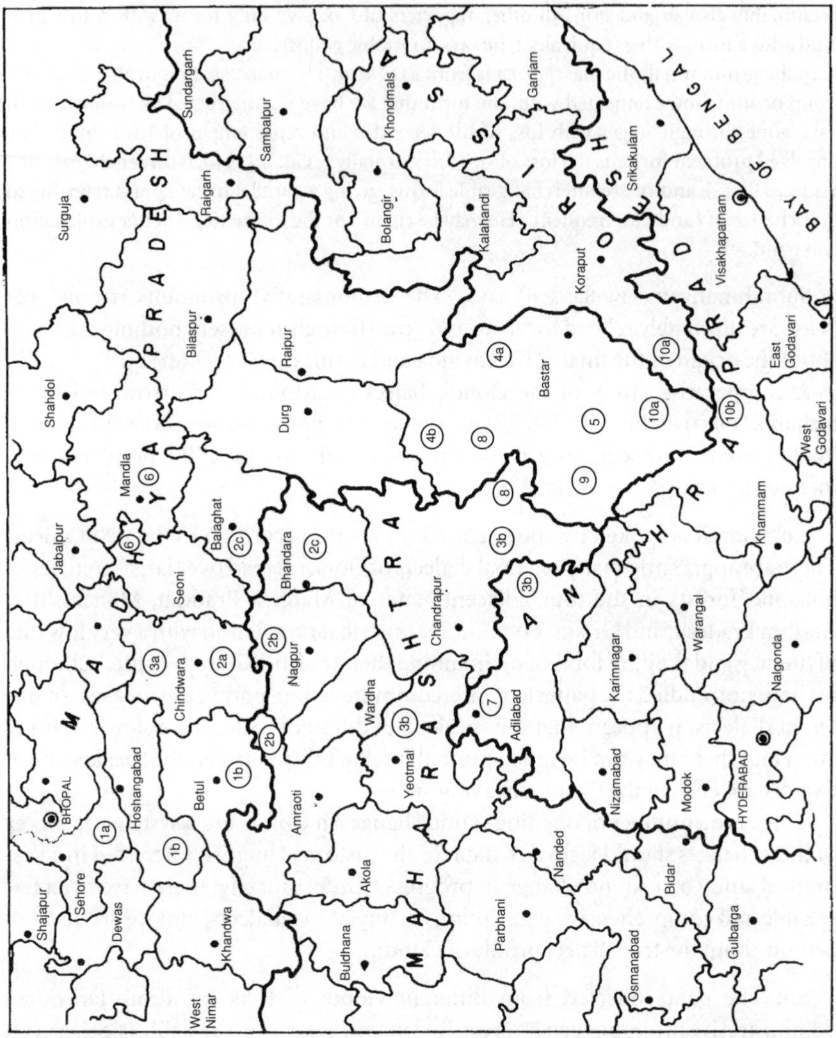

MAP 15.1. The distribution of masculine demonstrative pronominal sets in Gondi dialects (see Table 15.2)

TABLE 15.2. *Demonstrative pronouns 'he' and 'they' (proximal and distal) in Gondi dialects*

	Contrast	Singular				Plural				Region
		Distal		Proximal		Distal		Proximal		
Set No.	Sg./Pl. (Nom.)	Nom.	Obl.	Nom.	Obl.	Nom.	Obl.	Nom.	Obl.	
1a.	l/r	ōl	ōn-	ēl	ēn-	ōr	ōr-	ēr	ēr-	Sehore
1b.	l/ṛ	ōl	ōn-	ēl	ēn-	ōṛ	ōṛ-	ēṛ	ēṛ-	Hoshangabad, Betul
2a.	r/rk	ōr	ōn-	ēr	ēn-	ōrk	ōr(k)-	ērk	ēr(k)-	Chindwara
2b.	r/rk	hōr	hōn-	hēr-	hēn-	hōrk	hōr(k)-	hērk	hēr(k)-	Nagpur, Wardha
2c.	r/ṛk	ōr	ōn-	ēr	ēn-	ōṛk	ōṛ(k)-	ēṛk	ēṛ(k)-	Balaghat, Bhandara
3a.	r/r	ōr	ōn-	ēr	ēn-	ōr	ōr-	ēr	ēr-	Chindwara (west)
3b.	r/r	ōr	ōn-	wēr	wēn-	ōr	ōr-	wēr	wēr-	Yeotmal, Chandrapur, Adilabad (east)
4a.	ṛ/ṛ+loṛ	ōṛ	ōn-	ēṛ	ēn-	ōṛlor	ōṛ-	ēṛlor	ēṛ-	North-east Bastar
4b.	r/r+lor	ōr	ōn-	wēr	wēn-	ōrlor	ōr-	wērlor	wēr-	North-west Bastar
5.	r/ṛ	ōr	ōn-	wēr	wēn-	ōṛ	ōṛ-	wēṛ	wēṛ-	South Bastar
6.	ō/ū, ē/ ī	ōr	ōn-	ēr	ēn-	ūr	ūr-	īr	īr-	North-west Mandla North-east Seoni
7.	ō/ū, wē/wī	ōr	ōn-	wēr	wēn-	ūr	ūr-	wīr	wīr-	Adilabad (west)
8.	R/r	ōR	ōn-	wēR	wēn-	ōr	ōr-	wēr	wēr-	Abujhmar region of Bastar, Garhchiroli
9.	n/r	ōn	ōn-	wīn	wīn-	ōr	ōr-	wīr	wīr-	South-east Bastar
10a.	ṇḍ/r	ōṇḍ	ōn-	wēṇḍ	wēn-	ōr	ōr-	wēr	wēr-	Malkangiri Koya
10b.	ṇḍ/r	ōṇḍ	ōn-	wīṇḍ	wīn-	ōr	ōr-	wīr	wīr-	Khammam

The area of usage of each numbered set is keyed to the same number in the map.

2.2. The Proto-Dravidian reconstructions remain unchanged for Proto-South-Central Dravidian. However, it appears that PD **-nṯ* [*nḏ*] was phonetically represented in the proto-stage of South-Central Dravidian both as [*nḏ*] and as [*nṟ*]; Telugu normally develops **-nṯ* to *-ṇḍ*; in Early Old Telugu (inscriptional) *-nṟ* was preserved orthographically. In one case, it developed to *-ṇḍr*, i.e. *taṇḍri* (< **tanṟi*) 'father', reflecting the affricate pronunciation of **-nḏ* as [*nḏr*].[2] Koṇḍa preserves the PSCD *nḏ*/*nṟ* as *-nṟ*, e.g. *wānṟu* 'he', *mūnṟi* 'three', and *panṟi* 'pig'. The fact that **nḏ* is generally represented as *-nj* in Kui, Kuvi, Pengo, and Manḍa suggests that at the proto-stage of Koṇḍa, Kui, Kuvi, Pengo, and Manḍa, the pronunciation of *nḏ* was

[2] The masculine singular suffix *-ṉṟu-* changed into *-ṇḍu-* by the 7th century, although it was preserved orthographically up to the 10th century (Radhakrishna 1971: lxxxvi).

somewhat like an affricated **nṟ* in a few lexical items. We are, therefore, justified in writing the reconstructed form as **awanṟu* for South-Central Dravidian.

2.3. At least three successive sound changes have to be posited for the pre-Gondi stage as follows:

Rule 1. Nasal Loss: **awanṟ(u)* > **awaṟ(u)*

Rule 2. Contraction: **awaṟ* > **wāṟ*

Rule 3. Vowel-rounding: **wāṟ* > *wōṟ*

Since Gondi dialects do not show the loss of *-n-* in *-nṟ(-)* after an initial long vowel[3] we are suggesting that pre-Gondi **-nṟ* became **-ṟ* in the unaccented syllable before the contraction of **awa-* to **wā-* took place. A similar loss of *-n-* of the masculine singular ending *-nḏ* [nṟ] occurs in the etymological group (*DEDR* 3085) listed in Table 15.3.

TABLE 15.3. *An example of loss of* n *in* *nṟ *in Telugu-Gondi-Koṇḍa-Kui*

	Nominative	Oblique
PSCD	**tamb*-V-*nṟ(u)*	**tamb*-V-*n-*
Inscr. Te.	tambunṟu	
Early Te.	tambuṇḍu	
OTe.	tammuṇḍu	tammuni-
M Te.	tammũḍu	
Mdn. Te.	tammuḍu	tammuni-/ tammuḍi- (dial.)
Gondi	tammur, tammoR (< *tammuṟ)	tammun-
Koṇḍa	tamberi	tamberi-
Kui	tambesa	tambesai-

Notice that Koṇḍa also shows the loss of *n* in this position. It seems that *n* loss took place in these two languages independently.

[3] Proto-Dravidian **-nṟ-* > *nd/nḍ* in Gondi. e.g. *DEDR* 2920 Ta. *ñānṟu* 'time, day', Ma. *ñānnu*, Te. *nẽḍu* 'today', Koṇḍa *nēnṟu*, Pe. *nēnje*, Kui *nēnju*, Kuvi *nīnju* (Israel 1979), *nēnju* (Burrow and Bhattacharya field-notes), Go. *nēnḍu*. *DEDR* 5052 Ta. *mūnṟu* 'three', Ma. *mūnnu*, Ko. *mūnḍ*, Koḍ. *mūndi*, Tu. *mūji*, Te. *mūnṟu* (inscr.) *mū̃ḍu*, Koṇḍa *mūnṟi*, Kui *mūnji*, Nk. *mūndi*, Gad. *mūnd*, Kuṛ. *mūnd*, Go. *mūnd* (north-western dialects), *mūnḍ* (south-eastern dialects). Hence, we may have to explain the following reconstructions in which the *-nṟ* is not apparently simplified to *-r* but has developed to *-nd/-nḍ*: *DEDR* 2819 **sēṟunṟu*: Go. *sernḍu* 'brother-in-law'; *DEDR* 4762 **maṟunṟu*: Go. *marnḍu* 'father's sister's son or mother's brother's son'. It appears that in the above two cases the morpheme *-unṟu* was added to free forms (secondary derivation), viz. *sēṟ(i)* and *maṟi*, whereas *-nṟu* in **awanṟu* and **tambunṟu* is a bound gender-number suffix (i.e. primary derivation). A parallel to this would be Te. *manci(w)āḍu* 'good person' vs. *alluḍu* 'son-in-law' where-*(w)āḍu* and *-ḍu* fulfil the same function but have different structures as derivative morphemes.

3.0. The entire Gondi region is divided into two areas, in terms of the development of the PD *ḷ. Word initially, through apical displacement PD *-ḷ- > Proto-Gondi *ḷ- > ṛ- > r- in Area I, and l- in Area II (see Map 15.1). In both the areas the Proto-South-Central Dravidian post-vocalic *ḷ is still retained as ṛ (in some dialects it is represented by /ḍ/). This two-way development (i.e. *l-/ṛ-*) in different dialects requires us to reconstruct *ḷ word-initially in Proto-Gondi in the following items: PD *ḷ- > *l/r~ṛ*: *DEDR* 513 *ḷey-/ṛey-/ṛiy-* 'tender, young'; *DEDR* 510 *lēŋ-/rēŋ-* 'to loosen, untie': *DEDR* 698b *lōn/rōn* 'house'; *DEDR* 698a *lopo/ropo* 'in, inside'; *CVGD* 3075 *lōh-/rōh-* 'to send'; *DEDR* 3791 *lōp-/rōp-* 'to swallow, gulp down'; *DEDR* 3790 *losk-/locc-/rosk-* 'to bale out (as water)'. It is clear from the above that in word-initial position *ṛ-* has developed to *r-*, because *ṛ- > r-* was almost complete in all subdialects in this position.[4]

Proto-South-Central Dravidian *ẓ has developed to ṛ in all Gondi dialects. The change PD * ẓ > ṛ must have been the earliest since it is also shared by the other South-Central Dravidian languages, except Telugu. The following examples show that Proto-Gondi *ḷ merged with ṛ (< PD *ẓ) in all non-initial positions (cf. *DEDR* 857 *eṛj* (< **eḷj*), *DEDR* 1376 *kaṛa* 'threshing floor' (< **kaḷa*), *DEDR* 5312 *waṛi* 'wind' (< **waḷi*), *DEDR* 3656 *nāṛi* 'tomorrow' (< **nāḷi*), *DEDR* 400 *āṛ* 'woman, wife' (< **āḷ*) etc.). Only in initial position did Proto-Gondi *ḷ maintain its distinction from *ṛ (< *ẓ). In two cases only Proto-Gondi *ẓ developed to *ḍ word-initially (e.g. *DEDR* 692 *ḍuwwal* 'tiger'; *DEDR* 694 *ḍuppal* 'deer').[5]

3.1. Proto-Dravidian *-ṭ- [ḍ] which occurred only in non-initial position had merged with PD *ṯ [ṟ] in Proto-South-Central Dravidian (cf. *DEDR* 4065 **pāṟ-* 'to sing' (< **pāṭ-*), *DEDR* 442 **iṟ-* 'to keep' (< **iṭ-*), etc.). This change is evidenced in Telugu to some extent (cf. *DEDR* 1942 *ceḍu* 'to perish', *ceṟucu* 'to kill' (< **keṯu*)), but has spread extensively after Telugu had split off from the subgroup consisting of Gondi-Koṇḍa-Kui-Kuvi-Pengo-Manḍa. Eventually we get only one set of reflexes for both PD *-ṭ- and *-ṯ- as *ṟ. For all practical purposes, so far as Gondi is concerned, we can take ṟ [ḏ] as the pool of Proto-Dravidian *ṭ [ḍ] and *ṯ [ḏ]. Proto-Gondi-Manḍa *ṟ [ḏ] must have been preserved in all Gondi dialects until recently as a separate phoneme; it is still retained in Hill Māṛia Gondi (a dialect of Gondi spoken to the north-west of the Indravati river) as /ʀ/ (post-velar uvular fricative): cf. *DEDR* 3693 *nīʀ* 'ash' (< **nīṟ*), *DEDR* 5159 *ēʀ* 'water' (< **ēṟ*), *DEDR* 3638 *nāʀ* 'village, country' (< **naṟ* < **nāṭu*), etc. In the rest of the dialects *ṟ has merged with *r*. Notice that, before the plural suffix *-k*, Go *-ṟ* alternates with *h* only when it is preceded by a long vowel, traceable to a Proto-Gondi alternation *ṟ~ *h. The latter is still retained in Modern Koṇḍa as *R*, a voiceless trill (cf. Krishnamurti 1969c).

[4] *ṛ-* initial forms occur only in Adilabad dialect of Gondi. Even in this dialect *ṛ-* occurs only in one cognate group *ṛiyor* 'young man', *ṛiyya* 'young lady', *DEDR* 513 **eḷ-ay-* 'tender, young'.

[5] The forms *lup(pi)* 'deer' and *ḍig-* 'to descend' occurring only in South Bastar Gondi dialect need to be explained. An initial *l-* corresponding to PD *ẓ is not attested in any other similar correspondence, and may therefore be considered a stray correspondence. The latter form with an initial *ḍ-* is considered a loan from Telugu.

3.2. One may suggest that Proto-South-Central Dravidian **awa-* developed to *wō-* in pre-Gondi, which is quite possible. In that case the *w-* in *wōr* found in some of the dialects could be treated as a glide on the word-initial rounded vowel as is common in South Dravidian. The difficulty in accepting this development is the fact that proximal demonstrative forms for masculine are **wēr̲*/**wēn-* (sg.), **wēr*/**wēr-* (pl.) traceable to **ewar̲*/**ewan-* (sg.), **ewar-*/ **ewar-* (pl.), where the addition of an automatic glide *w-* on an unrounded initial vowel cannot be justified. These latter forms also correspond to Koṇḍa *wēnr̲(u)/weni-* (sg.), *wēr/weri-* (pl.), and Telugu *wīḍu* (OTe. *wī̃ḍu,* < inscr. Te. *wīnr̲u*[6]) (sg.), and *wīru* (pl.). In order to maintain parallel developments in proximal and distal forms we must assume the following steps between Proto-South-Central Dravidian and pre-Gondi.

		PSCD			Pre-Gondi			Proto-Gondi		
		nom.	:	obl.	nom.	:	obl.	nom.	:	obl.
Sg.	Dist.	*awanr̲u*	:	*awan*	*awar̲*	:	*awan*			
					> *wār̲*	:	*wān*	*wōr̲*	:	*wōn*
	Prox.	*ewanr̲u*	:	*ewan*	*ewar̲*	:	*ewan*			
					> *wēr̲*	:	*wēn*	*wēr̲*	:	*wēn*
Pl.	Dist.	*awar*	:	*awar*	*wār*	:	*wār*	*wōr*	:	*wōr*
	Prox.	*ewar*	:	*ewar*	*wēr*	:	*wēr*	*wēr*	:	*wēr*

Note that PD *i, u* > *e, o* before C*a* in the next syllable at a common stage of South Dravidian and South-Central Dravidian (Krishnamurti 1975a: 347, 1981).

The Proto-Dravidian pattern is still preserved clearly in the distinction between singular and plural forms of demonstrative pronouns (masculine) despite the loss of *-n-* in *-nr̲*. The contrast was then restricted minimally to *r̲* in singular and *r* in plural. Apparently this distinction remained undisturbed until recently as attested by the Hill Māṛia dialect in *-ʀ* (sg.) vs. *-r* (pl.).

4.0. We can now explain the different changes that have affected the above inherited Proto-Gondi pattern in various dialects. The sound changes leading to the split (acting on the output of Rules 1 to 3, see §§ 2, 3 above) of different Gondi dialects should be chronologically ordered as:

Rule 4. *r* > *ṛ* / V ___ (V)

Proto-Gondi non-initial *r* became *ṛ*, e.g. *(v)ōr* > *(v)ōṛ* 'they (dist.)', *mara* > *maṛa* 'tree', *taras* > *taṛas* 'snake'. This change is found in the dialects of Hoshangabad, Betul, Amraoti, Bhandara, Balaghat, North-east of Bastar, and South-east of Bastar.

Rule 5. *r̲* > *r* / V ___ (V) #

[6] The OldTelugu form *wī̃ḍu* (< *wīṇḍu* < *wīnr̲u*) was derived from the pre-Telugu *wēnr̲u* (< **iwanr̲u*) on the analogy that *i/ī* indicate proximal contrasting with *a/ā* which indicate distal relation.

Proto-Gondi *ṟ* became *r* in most of the dialects. As a phoneme, **ṟ* is retained in Hill Māṛia Gondi (phonetically a post-velar or uvular fricative [ʀ]). Rule 4 should precede Rule 5 in time, because *r* which results from Rule 5 does not become *ṛ*; consequently the Proto-Gondi contrast of *ṟ* : *r* was maintained as *r*:*ṛ* (see the sets 1b, 2c, and 5, Table 15.2).

Rule 4'. *r* > *ṛ* / V___(V)>#

This looks like Rule 4 recurring after Rule 5. But it could also be said that in some dialects of Gondi (see set 4a, Table 15.2) Rules 4 and 5 were reordered as Rule 5 followed by Rule 4', though this led to no simplification of the grammar (Kiparsky 1982: 37).

4.1. In set 5 of Table 15.2 we see the singular versus plural contrast as *ōr*: *ōṛ* which indicates that after *r* > *ṛ* in the plural, *ṟ* of the singular became *r*, for the latter is not affected by the earlier rule (also see sets 1b and 2c). There are dialects in which Rule 4 did not take place, but only Rule 5 occurred. In such dialects the contrast between PGo. sg. **wōṟ* and pl. **wōr* would be lost (see sets 1a, 2a, 2b, 3, 4b, 6, 7, and 9).

The change *ṟ* > *r* seems to have taken place independently in different Gondi dialects with the exception of Hill Māṛia Gondi where **ṟ* phonetically changed its point of articulation from alveolar to uvular and is thus phonemically maintained as distinct from *r* of the plural form.

The PGo. **r* has remained *r* in all dialects in the initial position. But in the non-initial position it tends to vary freely with *ṛ* in a number of subdialects of dialect area I (Hoshangabad, Betul, Amraoti, Balaghat, and Bhandara), i.e. the *ṛ*-area, e.g. *taṛas* 'snake', *maṛa* 'tree', *aṛmi* 'buffalo', *iṛup* '*Bassia longifolia*' etc. This sound change (*r* > *ṛ*) has spread into dialect area II (*l*-area), i.e. north-east and south-east of Bastar, to some extent, in non-initial positions. PGo. **ṟ* which developed to *r* in almost all the dialects in all the three positions i.e. #___, V___V and ___# does not further change to *ṛ*, as do the reflexes of PGo. **r*. This distinction seems to reflect the historic fact that the proto **ṟ* and **r* retained their contrast in all the three positions until recently. The independence of *r* (< **ṟ*) is also reflected in its alternation with *h* in plural formation deriving from the underlying /*ṟ*/.

5.0. The multiple mergers from **ẓ*, **ḷ*, **ṭ* [ḍ], **ṯ* [ṟ], and **r* which can be seen in Table 15.4 have complicated the morphological distinctions in most of the dialects. The resulting homophony has led to innovations in various dialects to maintain the morphological distinctions between singular and plural masculine demonstrative pronouns. The interaction between the phonological and morphological processes and the consequent pattern that has emerged from these are explained below.

TABLE 15.4 *The reflexes of PD* *ẓ, *ḷ, *ṭ, *ṟ, *r *in various Gondi dialects*

1	2	3	4	5	6	7	8	9	10	11	12	13	14	15	16	17	18
	#___	r	r	r	r	r	r	r	r	r	r	r	r	r	r	r	r
*r	V___	r	r/ṛ	ṛ	r/<ṛ>	r	r	r/ṛ	r	r/ṛ	r	r/<ṛ>	r	r/ṛ	r	r	r
	___#	r	r/ṛ	r/ṛ	r/ṛ	r	r	r	r	r	r	r/ṛ	r	r/ṛ	r	r	r
	#___	r	r	r	r	r	r	r	r	r	r	r	r	r	r	r	r
*ṟ	V___	r	r	r	r	r	r	r	r	r	ʀ	r	r	r	r	r	r
	___#	r	r	r	r	r	r	r	r	r	ʀ	r	r	r	r	r	r
	V___	rr	rr	rr	rr	rr	rr	rr	r	r	ʀ	rr	rr	rr	rr	rr	r
*ṭ	V̄___	r	r	r	r	r	r	r	r	r	ʀ	r	r	r	r	r	r
	___#	ḍ	ḍ	ḍ	ḍ	ḍ	ḍ	ḍ	ḍ	ḍ	ḍ	ḍ	ḍ	ḍ	ḍ	ḍ	ḍ
	#___	r	r	r	r	r	r/ṛ	r	l	l	l	l	l	l	l	l	l
*ḷ	V___	r	ṛ/r	ṛ	ṛ/r	r	ṛ	ṛ	ṛ	ṛ	ṛ	ṛ	ḍ	ṛ	ḍ	ḍ	ḍ
	___#	ṛ/r	ṛ	ṛ	ṛ	ṛ/r	ṛ	ṛ	ṛ	ṛ	ṛ	ṛ	ḍ	ṛ	ḍ	ḍ	ḍ
	#__	ḍ	ḍ	ḍ	–	–	ḍ	ḍ	–	ḍ	ḍ	ḍ	ḍ	ḍ	ḍ	ḍ	ḍ
*ẓ	V___	r/ṛ	ṛ	r	r/ṛ	ṛ	ṛ	ṛ	ṛ	ṛ	ṛ	ṛ	ḍ	ṛ	ḍ	ḍ	ḍ
	___#	r/ṛ	ṛ	ṛ	r	r/ṛ	ṛ	ṛ	ṛ	ṛ	ṛ	ṛ	ḍ	ṛ	ḍ	ḍ	ḍ/ṛ

1 Proto-Dravidian phoneme
2 Environment
3 Sehore
4 Hoshangabad
5 Betul, Amraoti
6 Chindwara, Nagapur
7 N. Seoni, Mandla
8 Adilabad
9 Balaghat, Bhandara
10 NW Bastar, Narainpur
11 NE Bastar, Keskal
12 Abujhmarh, Garhchiroli
13 South Bastar
14 Sironcha
15 SE Bastar, Sukma tl.
16 Dorla of S-W Bastar
17 South Bastar, Konta Tl. Malkangiri ti.
18 Bhadrachalam (Koya)

5.1. The developments of **awa-* > **wā-* and **ewa-* > *wē-* are also found in Telugu, Gondi, and Koṇḍa (cf. Te. *wānṟu, wāṇḍu, wā̃ḍu, wāḍu*; Koṇḍa *wānṟu*). At this point it is difficult to say whether this is an independent isogloss or a shared innovation at a common stage of the three languages; for the latter assumption there is not enough evidence. After the metathesis and vowel contraction rules have applied to these forms, the pre-Gondi **wā-* must have changed to *wō* (vowel-rounding) because the latter change is inherited by all the Gondi dialects. Subsequently the singular distal and proximal forms *wōṟ* and *wēṟ* became *wōr* and *wēr* in practically all the dialects (except for Hill Māṛia Gondi). This change *ṟ* > *r* appears to be typological rather than historical, and attributable to a more recent time (i.e. after *r* > *ṛ* in certain dialects).

5.2. Following the loss of contrast between the singular and the plural, each dialect has innovated a different method of reintroducing the contrast; this suggests that the loss of the distinction between singular and plural was a recent phenomenon. Notice how the innovations proceeded (see Table 15.2).

(1) set 1a. *ōl* (sg.) : *ōr* (pl.)
set 1b. *ōl* (sg.) : *ōṛ* (pl.)

The form *ōl* as the nominative singular has an *-l* taken from the singular masculine derivative suffix *-(a)l* which occurs in the language (e.g. *muriyal* 'father-in-law', *wartal* 'guest', *pēṛal* 'boy' etc). It is, therefore, not a sound change of *r* > *l* but a substitution of *l* for *r* in order to reintroduce the contrast between homophonous sg. *ōr* and pl. *ōr*. There is, however, no problem between the oblique forms of singular and plural which contrast by *-n* vs. *-r*.

(2) The second type of innovation, reflected in sets 2a, 2b, and 2c, is by the addition of a plural morpheme *-k* to the plural stem in nominative and optionally in oblique; *-k* is a non-masculine plural suffix which occurs in typical nouns like *marsk* 'axes', *kālk* 'legs', and *kayk* 'hands'.

(3) The third type of innovation as seen in the sets 4a and 4b is by the addition of the masculine plural suffix or the suffix sequence *-lor* {*-l* + *-or*} in the nominative only. Note that the oblique does not take the suffix since the contrast is not disturbed. The suffix *-lor* is wrongly analysed from a composite form in which it is a sequence of *-l* (masc. sg. derivative suffix) plus *-ōr* (masc. pl. ending). In 4a *-lor* must have been added more recently after *-r* > *-ṛ* was completed because *-lor* did not change to *-loṛ*.

(4) The fourth type of innovation is by changing the quality of the vowel in the plural stems from mid to high: *ōr* is changed to *ūr* and *wēr* to *wīr*. This is found in sets 6 and 7. The proximate forms with original *ē* which replaced it by *ī* in the plurals of sets 9 and 10b look as if they were formed under the influence of the neighbouring Telugu where the corresponding forms are *wīru/wīri-*.[7]

(5) In set 9 the nominative singular *ōr* is replaced by the corresponding oblique *ōn* so that the contrast between singular and plural is maintained as *ōn*: *ōr*, although the nominative and oblique contrast in the plural *ōr*/*ōr* is lost.

(6) In sets 10a and 10b the singular forms are restructured as *ōṇḍ* and *wēṇḍ* which correspond to MTe. *wāṇḍu* and **wēṇḍu*. They were apparently borrowings from Middle Telugu.

(7) There still remain some islands where the nominative forms of masculine demonstrative pronouns do not seem to exhibit any distinction between the singular and plural (see sets 3a (Chindwara west) and 3b (Yeotmal, Adilabad east, and Chandrapur)). Consequently, the singular *ōr* and plural *ōr* have remained homophonous. It would be interesting to see if any effort is being made to introduce a distinction between the singular and the plural by making a more extensive survey of this area.

[7] Sets 9 and 10b are attested by South Bastar Gondi and South-eastern Gondi which show strong influence of Telugu in their phonology and morphology.

6.0. Conclusion. The foregoing study enables us to make the following observations:

(1) A sound change may lead to homonymy in a devastating manner even in basic vocabulary as has happened in the Gondi dialects where *ṟ merged with *r* thereby removing the distinction between masculine singular and plural.

(2) Such a sound change is immediately followed by processes both phonological and morphological which reintroduce the lost contrasts. The addition of plural suffixes *-k* and *-l + or* to plural, and the extension of the oblique to the nominative in set 9, and the change of *ōr* to *ōl* in 1a and 1b are all morphological processes; whereas the replacement of mid-vowels by high vowels in sets 6 and 7 is a phonological innovation.

(3) The traditional notion that a sound change is deterred by threatened homonymy does not seem to have much to suggest in its favour from these data.

(4) The fact that there are as many as six or seven different innovations in different dialects indicates that the merger of *ṟ with *r* which led to the collapse of the singular and plural contrast was a recent change, which is not a shared innovation by these dialects from Proto-Gondi. In the literary languages, viz. Tamil, Kannaḍa, and Telugu *ṟ gradually merged with *r* independently in each language under different historical conditions and with different results.[8]

This paper, while throwing light on some important theoretical issues, solves the problem of reconstruction of Proto-Gondi forms of the third person masculine singular and plural, and interprets a wide range of variation in different dialects.

[8] There is inscriptional evidence to show that Telugu (4th–5th century AD), Kannaḍa (12th century AD), and Tamil (10th century AD) lost PD *ṯ recently. It is preserved only in Malayāḷam and certain dialects of Tamil, and in Toda and Koṇḍa (cf. *TVB* 44–46).

16

The Emergence of the Syllable Types of Stems (C)VCC(V) and (C)V̄C(V) in Indo-Aryan and Dravidian: A Case of Convergence?

1. **Introduction.** M. B. Emeneau, the proponent as early as 1956 of an Indian 'Sprachbund,' made the following observation in his paper 'The Indian linguistic area' ([1971a], 1980c: 175):

> Other traits have been suggested as belonging to the Indian linguistic area but have not been investigated, usually because data and analysis are not yet under control. Examples are the phonological development of syllabic structure and phoneme distributions that is seen in proceeding from OIA to MIA, with an end result that is suspiciously close to the structure of PD, as represented fairly closely by old or literary Tamil.

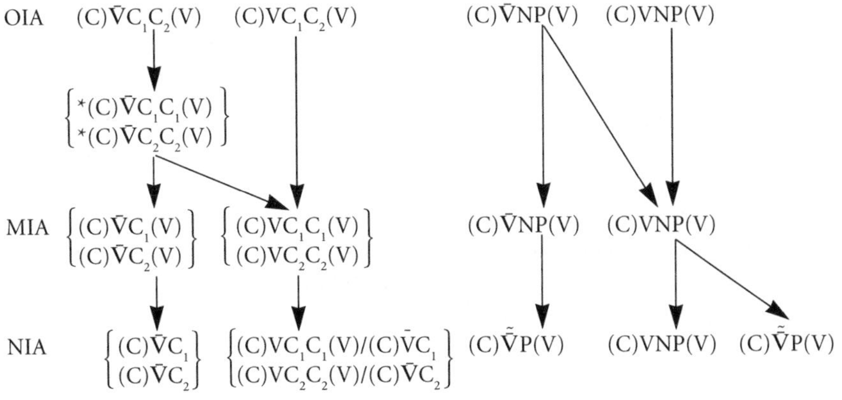

*C_1C_2 are heterogeneous consonants but not nasal + stop; N = homorganic nasal; P = stop/obstruent, voiced or voiceless

FIGURE 16.1. Historical adjustments in the syllable structure of Indo-Aryan

Earlier versions of this paper were presented at a National Seminar on 'The Syllable in Phonetics and Phonology' held at Osmania University. Hyderabad, on January 17–18, 1986, as well as presented before the Departments of Linguistics at the State University of New York at Stony Brook and Cornell University.

In making these remarks Emeneau was evidently referring to processes which are the subject matter of this paper as well as to other phonological changes between Old and Middle Indo-Aryan (e.g. simplification of consonant clusters word-initially, the weakening or lenition of intervocalic stops). It is my intention here to discuss in detail these phonological phenomena alluded to by Emeneau. In so doing I will deal specifically with those phonological processes which favoured the emergence of the syllable types with a long vowel followed by a single consonant or a short vowel followed by two consonants in Dravidian and Indo-Aryan, approximately within the same time frame.

The developments may be represented graphically for Indo-Aryan in Figure 16.1.

2. Indo-Aryan. It is well established that consonant clusters of Literary Old Indo-Aryan (*c.*1500–500 BC) developed into geminates through assimilation in Middle Indo-Aryan (*c.*600 BC–AD 600) and were then degeminated following a long vowel. The preceding long vowel sometimes remained in Pāḷī but became short in Early and Middle Prakrits (Turner [1967] 1975: 405–15, 421–9; Mehendale 1948: xxxii–xxxiii, 21–7). Examples of these phenomena are as follows (entry numbers in *CDIAL* are given in parentheses):

OIA *dīrghá* (6368)	'long'	>	**dīggha*	>	Pāḷī *dīgha*, Pkt. *diggha*
OIA *kāṣṭhá* (3120)	'wood'	>	**kāṭṭha*	>	Pāḷī, Pkt. *kaṭṭha*
OIA *śīrṣa* (12497)	'head'	>	**sīssa*	>	Pāḷī. *sīsa(ka)*, Pkt. *sissa/sīsa*
OIA *kárman* (2892)	'act'	>			Pāḷī, Pkt. *kamma*
OIA *aṣṭá*, *aṣṭáu* (941)	'eight'	>			Pāḷī, Pkt. *aṭṭha*
OIA *aṇḍa* (1111)	'egg, testicles'	>			Pāḷī *aṇḍa*, Pkt. *aṃḍā*

The shortening of the long vowel is mainly found in the Central, Southern, and Eastern dialects. The North-western languages, viz. Sindhi, Lahnda, Western Panjabi, and Kashmiri, preserve the long vowels. The long vowels and geminates are attested in north-western and western Aśokan inscriptions (e.g. Girnar).

A further development which started about the second century AD (as evidenced from Sinhala) was the simplification of the geminates with compensatory lengthening of the preceding vowel in all New Indo-Aryan languages with the exception of Sindhi, Lahnda, and Panjabi (Beames 1872–9, I: 73–85; Bloch 1965: 92; Turner [1967] 1975: 405, fn. 8; Arun 1961: 93–121). The change was well under way by the ninth or tenth century AD:

1. Pāḷī, Pkt. *kamma* 'work' > (a) K. *kam*, S. *kamu*, L., P. *kamm*, WPah. *kamm*; (b) Ku., Nep., A., B., Mth., Bhoj., H., Marw., Mar. *kām*, Or. *kāma*, G. *kam/kāmū*, Kon. *kāma*, Sinh. *kama*.

2. Pāḷī, Pkt. *aṭṭha* 'eight' > (a) S. *aṭha*, L. *aṭṭh*, P., WPah. *aṭṭh*; (b) Ku., Nep., A., Mth., Bhoj., Aw., H., Marw. *āṭh*, G., Mar. *āṭh*, B. *āṭ*, Or., *āṭha*, Sinh. *aṭa*.

3. Pāḷī, Pkt. *kaṭṭha* 'wood' > (a) S. *kāṭhu*, L., P. *kāṭh*, *kāṭṭhī* (b) Ku., Nep., A., B., Mth., Bhoj., Aw., H., G. *kāṭh*, Mar. *kāṭhī*, Or. *kāṭha*, *kāṭhi*; Sinh. *kaṭa*.

Both Bloch and Turner remark that assimilation and compensatory lengthening can be observed in isolated words even from a pre-Sanskritic or Early Old Indic stage: e.g. Skt. *majjati* 'dive' < * *madj-* (cf. *madgu*); *uccá* 'upwards' from *ut-* (cf. Av. *usča*) (Bloch 1965: 80); pre-Vedic **niẓ-d* > RV *nīḍa* 'nest' (Turner [1967] 1975: 422); RV *vrīhi* (< **vriṃhi*; cf. Persian *birinj*). Turner ([1967] 1975: 429) observes that 'the process of simplifying a consonant group or shortening a long consonant with accompanying lengthening of the preceding vowel, which had begun in the pre-Sanskritic stage, was continued throughout the history of Indo-Aryan'.

Beames (1872–9, Bk I, Ch. IV) presents a very useful typology of assimilative changes, progressive and regressive, in terms of the relative strength of the segments involved in consonant groups. With a few exceptions, his theory works and anticipates recent studies in the dimension of strength/weakness of segments in phonological processes (e.g. Hyman 1975: 161–9).

According to Beames, if the cluster has a nasal + stop, it is not assimilated in Pāḷī and Prakrit. In New Indo-Aryan the preceding vowel is lengthened and nasalized in languages which apply the degemination rule. The cluster also remains in the North-western languages. One exception is the cluster *mb*, which becomes *mm*, followed by degemination and lengthening of the preceding vowel (295). Indo-Aryan data drawn from *CDIAL* that illustrate the phenomena pointed to by Beames are the following:

4. *kaṇṭa*, *káṇṭaka* 'thorn' (2668): Pāḷī *kaṇṭa*, *kaṇṭaka*, Pkt. *kaṃṭaya* > (a) S. *kaṇḍo*, L., P. *kaṇḍā*, WPah. *kaṇṭā*: (b) Ku. *kāno*, Nep. *kā̃ro*, B. *kā̃ṭā*, Or. *kaṇṭā*, Aw., H. *kā̃ṭā*, G. *kā̃ṭ.*, Mar. *kā̃ṭā*, *kāṭā*, Kon. *kāṇṭo*; Sinh. *kaṭuwa*.

5. *jambú*, *jambū́* (5131) 'rose apple tree (*Eugenia jambolana*)' > Pāḷī *jambu*, Pkt. *jaṃbū* > (a) S. *jamū̃*, L. *jamū̃*, P. *jammū*, WPah. *jEmmu*; (b) Nep. *jāmu*, A. *zāmū*, B. *jām*, Or. *jāmba*, *jāma*, *jāmū*, H. *jām*, G. *jām*, *jā̃bu*, *jā̃buṛī*, Mar. *jā̃b(h)*, Kon. *jā̃mba*, Sinh. *daṁba*; S. *jāmu*, Or. *jāmbu*/*jāma* 'the guava'.

3. **Dravidian.** There are parallels to the above phonological processes in Dravidian from an early time. Attention to the alternation between a long vowel + C and a short vowel + CC was drawn in *TVB* (125), in explaining the alternation between **kāṇ* and **kaṇ*(*ṇ*) 'to see' in Dravidian. For Proto-Dravidian we can set up the following types of stem morphemes (CC = geminate or nasal + stop):

(1) (a) (C)VC(V) (b) (C)V̄C(V)
(2) (a) (C)VCC(V) (b) (C)V̄CC(V)

In (2a) and (2b), CC may represent a Proto-Dravidian obstruent geminate or a sequence of N (homorganic nasal) + P (voiceless stop, phonetically voiced).

Where the final vowel is the non-morphemic *u*, it is difficult to establish contrast between C and CC following a short vowel; thus, **cupp*/**cup* 'salt': when followed by a vowel, the form is **cuw-a-*. The type (C)V̄CCV/(C)V̄CV with grammatical alternation (**māṯṯu* 'to change' (v.t.): **māṯu* 'to change' (v.i.)) involves a morph boundary, i.e. **māṯ* + *tt-* > **māṯ-ṯṯ-* > *māṯṯ-*. It is also possible to set up a type *(C)VCCC for Proto-Dravidian, where CCC = NPP, but there is definitely a morph boundary here, descriptively + NP-P (transitive) as opposed to + NP (intransitive); e.g., **kānku* 'to boil' (v.i.): **kānkku* 'to boil' (v.t.).

The following syllable changes are established as part of the morphophonemics of Proto-Dravidian: (Krishnamurti 1961, Zvelebil 1970b, Subrahmanyam 1983):

$$\left\{\begin{matrix}\text{(C)}\bar{\text{V}}\text{C} \\ \text{(C)VCC}\end{matrix}\right\} \rightarrow \text{(C)VC/\_\_\_+V}$$

The next question that arises is the extent of the occurrence of the alternation (C)VCC(V)/(C)V̄C in Dravidian. Zvelebil (1970b: 185) has discussed this problem, providing two pertinent examples from Tamil, namely the contrast between *meṭṭu* 'mound' and *mēṭu* 'height, hillock', as well as between *yāṉ* 'I' and *eṉṉ-ai* 'me' (acc.). Zvelebil also notes the existence of the alternations of Ta. *pāṭu* 'sing' with *pāṭṭu* 'song' and Ta. *āṟu* 'river' with *āṟṟu* 'of river'. He observes (187) that these phenomena occur in place of the expected proto-forms **paṭṭu* and **aṟṟu*. He cautions, however, that these phenomena require further investigation.

The following data, drawn from *DEDR*, demonstrate the existence in Dravidian of the patterns V̄C/VCC, although they are irregularly distributed:

6. *DEDR* 765. Ta. *ekku* 'to pull cotton with fingers', Ma. *ekkuka*, Ka. *ekku* 'to separate cotton', Tu. *ekkuni* 'to gin': Te. *ēku*, Kui *ēspa* 'to unravel', Pa. *ēk* 'to pick and throw away woods.'

7. *DEDR* 2715. Ta. *cuṟṟu* 'to revolve, spin', Ma. *cuṟṟuka*, Ka. *suttu*, Koḍ. *cutt*, Tu. *suttuni*, Te. *cuṭṭu*, Go. *cuṭṭ*, Kui *huce*, Nk. *sutt*, Gad. *cuṭṭ*: Ta. *cūṟai* 'whirlwind', Kuvi *sūt* 'to roll up', *hūc* 'to put on clothes'.

8. *DEDR* 3323. Ta., Ma. *tuppu* 'to spit; spittle', Koḍ. *tuppu-*, Te. *tuppuna* (imitative adverb), Pe. *cup*, Kuṛ. *tupp* (v.), *tuppalxō* 'saliva', Malto *tup* 'to spit', *tupglo* 'spittle': Ka. *tūpu*, Kui *sūpa* (v. and n.), Kuvi *hūp* (v.), *hūpka* (n. pl.).

9. *DEDR* 3570. Ta. *nakku* 'to lick, lap', Ma. *nakkuka*, Ka. *nakku*, *nekku*, Koḍ. *nakk-*, Tu. *nakkuni*, *nekkuni*: Te. *nāku*, Go. *nāk-*, Koṇḍa *nāk*, Pe. *nāk*, *nāng-*, Manḍa *nēk*, Kui, Kuvi *nāk*, Kol., Nk. *nāk-*, Pa. *nēk*, Gad. *nāk*, (? related to PD **nā* 'tongue' [*DEDR* 3633]; cf. Gad. *nāŋ* (< **nālnk-*/**nālnkk-* 'tongue'), Te. *nā(lu)ka*).

10. *DEDR* 4167. Te. *pittu* 'break wind', Go. *pitt/pihk*: *pīt* (n.) 'fart', Koṇḍa *pīt-*, Kui, Kuvi *pīt-*, Pe., Manḍa *pīt-*, Kuṛ. *pītna* (*pittyas* v.), Malto *pīto* (cf. PD **pī* 'excrement' [*DEDR* 4210]).

11. *DEDR* 5401, Ta. *vittu*, *viccu* 'to sow seed', (n.) 'seed', Ma. *vittu* (n.), Ka. *bittu* (v. and n.), Koḍ. *bitt* (v.), *bittï* (n.), Tu. *bittuni* (v.), *bittu* (n.), Te. *vittu* (v. and n.), Go. *wit*, Koṇḍa *vit* (v.), *vitu* (n.), Kui *vitka* (n.), Nk. *vit*, Pa. *vit* (v.), *vittid* (n.), Ga. *vit* (v.): Oll. *vīti*, Go. *wīt* 'seed', Kuvi *vīcana* 'semen', Malto *bīc* (Kuvi, Malto < IA *bīja*).

12. *DEDR* 5117. Ta. *mottu* 'strike, beat' (n.), *mōtu* id., Ma. *mōtuka*, Ka. *mōdu*, Te. *mottu* 'to strike', also *mōdu*.

The above cases indicate two points: (a) the alternation (C)VCC/(C)V̄C is not reconstructable to Proto-Dravidian; and (b) the forms with compensatory lengthening appear, by and large, in South-Central, Central, and North Dravidian, where they are in contact with Indo-Aryan. Less regularly distributed, the alternation is found in different languages. Subrahmanyam (1983: 169–71) cites thirty-two cases, which he states constitute more or less a complete list of such instances for the operation of this process. Of these, thirteen are restricted to Tamil alone, one occurs only in Malayāḷam, three only in Kannaḍa, and one only in Telugu. In eight instances a language of South-Central or Central Dravidian shows compensatory lengthening corresponding to the structural pattern (C)VCC of South Dravidian.

During the historic period of each of the Dravidian languages certain phonological changes led to the emergence of two patterns, (C)VCCV and (C)V̄CV, at the expense of (C)V̄CCV. This is not a case of compensatory lengthening, but rather of the creation of two complementary patterns, whereby two syllabic types have come to be favoured.

In Kannaḍa and Telugu (C)V̄CCV became (C)V̄CV; in other words, geminate stops (always voiceless) became degeminated following a long vowel. This change goes back to the prehistoric period of these two languages. The same development is also seen in all the other languages except Tamil and Malayāḷam. Examples of this phenomenon are given below:

13. *DEDR* 347. PD **āṭu* (v.) 'move, dance, play', **āṭṭu*, **āṭṭam* (n.) 'play' (< *āṭ* + *ttu*, *āṭ* + *ttam*):

	Verb	Noun
Ta., Ma.	*āṭu*	*āṭṭam. āṭṭai*
Ko.	*āṛ*	*āṭ*
To.	*āṛc*	*āṭ*
	ōḍ	*ōṭ*
Ka.	*āḍu*	*āṭa*
Koḍ.	*āḍ*	—
Tu.	*āḍuni*	*āṭa*
Te.	*āḍu*	*āṭa*
Go.	—	*āṭa*
Kol.	*āḍ*	—
Nk.	*āṛ*	—

14. *DEDR* 4834. PD **māṯu* 'change' (v.i.), *māṯṯu* (v.t.), *māṯṯam* (n.) 'diversity, exchange, word, reply':

	Verb intr.	Verb tr.	Noun
Ta., Ma.	*māṟu*	*māṟṟu*	*māṟṟam*
Ko.	*mār*	*māt*	*mānt*
To.	*mōr*	—	*mōt*
Ka.	*māru*	—	*mātu*

Te.	*māṟu, māru*	—	*māṭa*
Go.	*māri*	—	*māndi, māṭa* (lw. < Te.)
Koṇḍa	*mār*	—	*māṭa* (lw. < Te.)
Kui	*māsk*	—	
Kuvi	*māsk*	—	

15. *DEDR* 2019. PD **kēṟ* 'to winnow', **kēṟṟam* 'winnowing basket':

Ma.	*cēṟuka* (v.)	—
Ko.	*kēṟ*	—
To.	*kōṟ*	—
Ka.	*kēṟu*	—
Te.	*cerugu*	*cēṭa* (< **cēṭṭa* < **kēṟṟa*)
Go.	*hēc, hēh, ēc*	*sēti, hēti, ēti*
Koṇḍa	—	*sēRi*
Pe.	*jēc*	*hēci*
Manḍa	—	*hēci*
Kui	—	*sēsi*
Kuvi	—	*hēci*
Kol.	*kēd*	*kēt*
Nk.	*kēd*	*kēt*
Pa.	*kēd, kēḍ*	*kēti, kēṭi*
Gad., Oll.	*kēy*	*kēṭin, kēṭen*
Kuṛ.	*kẽs (kisyas)*	*kēter*
Malto	*kēs*	*kētnu*

In Toda, Kota, and all languages of South-Central, Central, and North Dravidian even geminates after short vowels became degeminated, and the contrast between -C- and -CC- of identical consonants seems to have been lost in South-Central and Central Dravidian:

16. *DEDR* 1147. PD **kaṭṭ* (v.), *kaṭṭay* (n.) 'knot, dam, bank'. All languages show double consonants, except Ko. *kaṭ* (v. and n.), To. *kaṭ* (v. and n.), Go. *kaṭ* (n.), Koṇḍa *kaṭ* (v.), *kaṭa, gaṭu* (n.), Pe. *kaṭa* (n.), Kui *kāṭ* (v.), Kuvi *gaṭu* (n.), Kol. *kaṭ* (v.), *kaṭṭa* (n.), Nk. (Ch.) *kaṭ/kaṭṭ* (v.), Oll. *kaṭ* (v.), Malto *gaṭa*.

It is significant that the contrast in Proto-Dravidian of C vs. CC (single vs. double) has come to be maintained as a contrast of voiced vs. voiceless following a long or short vowel (i.e. **āṭ(u)* [āḍ(u)]: **āṭṭa* [āṭṭa] > *āḍ(u): āṭa)* in most of the languages; so also **kaṭṭa* > *kaṭa* in South-Central Dravidian languages.

The only other consonant group allowed within a stem is N (= homorganic nasal) + P (= stop) in the following sequences:

(1) (C)VNP(V) phonetically [(C)VNB]
(2) (C)V̄NP(V) phonetically [(C)V̄NB]
(3) (C)VNPP(V)
(4) (C)V̄NPP(V)

Pattern (1) is, by and large, preserved in all languages. Toda loses the nasal before P, which appears as B. In Malayāḷam, NP > NN through progressive assimilation in the velar, palatal, dental, and alveolar series. In the labial series in all languages except Ta. and Ma. **mp* > *mm*:

17. *DEDR* 4469. PD **poṅku* 'to boil'. Ta. *poṅku* 'to boil, bubble up', Ma. *poṅṅuka*, Ko. *poŋg*, To. *pïg* (with loss of *n*), Ka. *poṅgu*, Koḍ. *poŋŋ*, Tu. *bonguni*, Te. *pongu*, Go. *pōŋ*, Koṇḍa *poŋi*, Kuvi *poŋg*, Kol. *pong*, Nk. *poŋk*, Malto *pongje*.

Type (2) is preserved only in Tamil, Malayāḷam, and Central Dravidian. Many languages simplify V̄NB by the loss of N with or without nasalization of the preceding long vowel. This is very systematic in Telugu (datable to Early Telugu, 7th or 8th century AD) and Kannaḍa; cf. **mūṉṯu* 'three' > Te. *mūṉṟu* > *mūṇḍu* > *mū̃ḍu* > *mūḍu*; Ka. *mūṟu* (already in Pampa Bhārata of the 10th century (Ramachandra Rao 1972: 27, 28, 514)); *tōḍu* (< **tōṇṭu*) 'to burrow, dig' (Ramachandra Rao, 1972: 382). *NPP following V or V̄ is simplified as NP or PP in different languages (Kumaraswami Raja 1969b). Consider the following examples:

18. PD **tūnku* (v.i.) 'to hang, swing'; **tūnkku* (v.t.) 'to suspend, swing': **tūnkk-am* (n.) 'balance, sleep'

	Verb intr.	Verb tr.	Noun
Ta.	*tūṅku*	*tūkku* (v.t.)	*tūkkam*
Ma.	*tūṅṅuka*	*tūkkuka*	*tūkkam*
Ko.	*tūg*	*tūk*	—
To.	*tūx*	*tūk*	—
Ka.	*tūgu*	*tūnku*	*tūka*
Koḍ.	*tūng*	*tūk*	—
Tu.	*tūnguni* (v.i./t.)	*tūnkuni* (v.i.)	*tūnki, tūnka, tūku*
Te.	*tūgu*	—	*tūkam*
Koṇḍa	*dūŋ*	*dūk*	—
Pe.	*tūŋ(g)*	*tūk*	—
Kui	*dūŋg*	—	—
Kuvi	*tūŋg*	*tūk*	—
Kuṛ.	—	—	*tūngul*
Malto	—	—	*tūngḷe*
Br.	—	—	*tūg̱ẖ*

From the above data we notice that most Dravidian languages have evolved toward the pattern (C)VCC/(C)/V̄C, where CC/C is historically traceable to geminates following a short and long vowel; where the older sequences were *NP (following a V̄), and *NPP (following a V̆/V̄) there was a regular loss of the N of the *NP sequence and loss of *P of the *NPP sequence in Telugu and Kannada. Assimilation of NP to a single segment, as illustrated by the changes *ng* > *ŋ* and *mb* > *m*, occurs in many Central and South-Central Dravidian languages.

There is, however, no case where, as in the case of Indo-Aryan, assimilation is followed by compensatory lengthening in the preceding vowel:

19. *DEDR* 3178. Ka. *taggu* 'to be lowered, to diminish' (< **taẓunku*) can never become **tāgu*.

20. *DEDR* 690. Ta. *uẓuntu* 'black gram', Ma. *uẓunnu*, Ka. *urdu*, *uddu*, Tu. *urdu*, To. *uddulu*, Kol. *urunde*, Nk. *urndal* (< **uẓuntu*).

For the most part Kannaḍa and Telugu show reduction of trisyllabic bases through the loss of the unstressed vowel followed by consonantal assimilation (*c.* 10th century AD). In the Central and South-Central Dravidian languages assimilation does not take place in sequences of liquid + stop:

DEDR 485. PD **iruppay* 'mahua tree (*Bassia longifolia*)': Ta. *iruppai*, Ma. *irruppa*: Ka. *ippe*, Tu. *ippe*, *irippe*, Te. *ippa*, Koṇḍa *ipa* (< Te.), Go. *irup*, *irp(i)*, Kui *irpi*, *ripi*, Kuvi *irpi*, Kol. *ippa* (< Te.), Nk. (Ch.) *irpu*, Pa. *irpa*, Gad. *irpa*.

4. **Discussion.** The most important question raised by the facts presented above is whether the occurrence in Indo-Aryan of a process whereby consonantal assimilation led to the emergence in Middle Indo-Aryan of geminates can be ascribed to Dravidian influence.

Caldwell (1875: 53) supports the hypothesis that 'the North Indian vernaculars had been derived from Sanskrit, not so much by the natural process of corruption and disintegration, as through the overmastering, remoulding power of the non-Sanskritic element contained in them'. While dealing with assimilation, Beames (1872–9: 282–3) rejects Dravidian influence, saying that similar cases of assimilation are also found in Italian.[1] Chatterji (1926, vol. I: 171) takes the position that simplification of consonant clusters was a parallel development in Indo-Aryan and Dravidian. He states that

> in the matter of simplification of OIA consonant groups by assimilation which gave rise to MIA it was probably internal, as it took place also in Italic among other IE languages, but here, IA reached that stage at least a thousand years before Italic; contact with Dravidian, as well as the adoption of the Aryan speech by Dravidians early in the history of IA has probably something to do with it.

[1] The following defensive remarks made by Beames (Bk. I: 282–3) in this connection are amusing:

> It is, however, held by some writers, who are never easy unless they can drag in some kind of non-Aryan influence to account for changes which require no such explanation, that the weakness of Dravidian enunciation, which forbids the use of any complex accumulation of consonants, is parallel to the weakness which led the Prakrits to assimilate kt into tt. As, however, the Italians do precisely the same, it is not evident why non-Aryan intervention should be suggested. There is a process in Prakrit, carried on into the moderns, which certainly does resemble Dravidian customs, namely, that of splitting up a nexus by the insertion of a vowel; when the custom is discussed it will be seen how far this supposition is true; at any rate it has become of late years quite a nuisance, this perpetual suggestion of non-Aryans here, there, and everywhere; one will soon have to believe that the Aryans did not know how to speak at all till the Dravidian taught them the use of their tongue, and that the Vedas are a mangled copy of some ancient Tamil liturgy!

The reduction of geminates following a long vowel is a change in pre-Telugu and pre-Kannaḍa, going back to the pre-Christian era, about the time that a similar change was developing in Pāḷi and early Middle Indo-Aryan (Bloch 1965: 89), e.g. *śīrṣa* > **sīssa* > Pāḷī *sīsa*; *pārśva* > * *pāssa* > Pkt. *pāsa*; *siṃha* > *sīha*. Bloch observes (92) that 'the Middle Indian word contains strong consonants only when initial or geminate and has none in final position and in which hiatuses occur frequently'.

There is, therefore, a clear case of phonological convergence in the emergence of (C)VCC(V) and (C)V̄C(V) as the favoured types of nominal and verbal stems in Indo-Aryan and Dravidian. Even in modern spoken Tamil and Malayāḷam, V̄CC can be interpreted as V̄C., i.e. there is a quantitative reduction of long consonants after long vowels, e.g. Ta. *mūṇï* 'three' < *mūṇṇï* < * *mūṉṟu*; *pāṭï* 'song' < *pāṭṭu*. Both Dravidian and Indo-Aryan also agree in progressive assimilation and gemination of *ng* > *ŋŋ* > *ŋ* and *mb* > *mm* > *m*.

5. **General Observations.** The shortening of a long vowel before a consonant cluster or when more than two syllables follow is observed in several languages of the world. Kiparsky (1968: 179–81) formulates a rule for such changes occurring in Old and Middle English:

$$V \rightarrow [-\text{long}] / \_\_\_ \begin{array}{l} CC \\ \ldots V \ldots V \end{array}$$

The Modern English alternations of *keep* and *kept*, *severe* and *severity*, as well as that of Old English *gōdspel* with Modern English *gospel* and Early Middle English *hūsband* with Modern English *husband* are accounted for by this rule.

Stampe (1973: 47–9) questions both the form of the rule as well as the arguments given in favour of its psychological reality for speakers of English, and asserts that the reduction of vowel length here is a 'process' within the framework of Natural Phonology. This rule is stated by Stampe as follows:

$$V \rightarrow [-\text{long}] / \_\_\_ CC\$ \qquad \text{(for Old English)}$$
$$V \rightarrow [-\text{long}] / \_\_\_ C\$ \qquad \text{(for Middle English)}$$

In the Indian linguistic area these developments seem to be based on the placement of stress on the initial syllable of a word and the balancing of length between the stressed vowel and the following consonant. In both Dravidian and Indo-Aryan it appears that it is the vowel which wins out in this balancing game. Compensatory lengthening occurs in languages that lose the final vowel.

These developments also suggest the syllable division for forms like Te. *nakku* 'to hide' and *nāku* 'to lick' as shown in Fig. 16.2.

Mohanan (1986: Ch. 4), following the theory of the syllable outlined in Halle and Vergnaud (1980), proposes for Malayāḷam and Dravidian in general a so-called 'no coda hypothesis' according to which he advocates a syllable division of the form *na-kku* (instead of *nak-ku*). Mohanan's arguments are not convincing. Although I will not present a detailed refutation of Mohanan's views here, I can state that my analysis simplifies the definition of a metrical long syllable. I claim that it is possible to describe a long syllable as simply a syllable that has a branching rime.

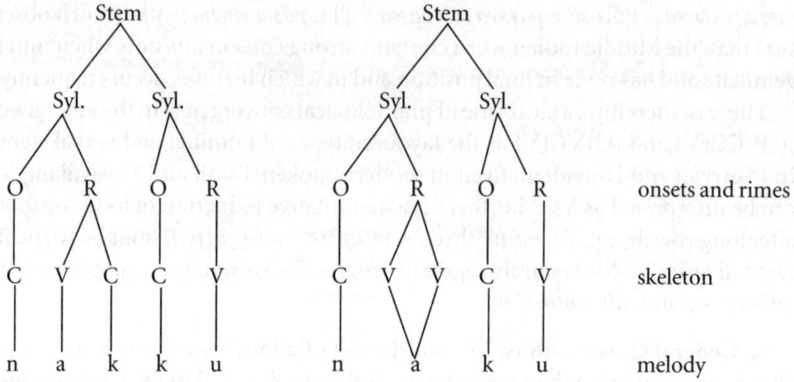

FIGURE 16.2. Configuration of the syllable structure of Te. *nakku* 'hide' and *nāku* 'lick'

Then the change of *nakku* to *nāku* can be stated as a change affecting the constituents of the rime of a syllable instead of the rime of one syllable and the onset of the next. The change is therefore confined to lower levels of structure, viz. the skeleton and melody. The reduction of (C)V̄CCV to (C)V̄$CV in Dravidian and to (C)VC$CV in Indo-Aryan also supports the division of the former as (C)V̄C$CV, because the extra long syllable V̄C (i.e. V̆ + V̆ + C) has dropped a V̆ or C to bring about parity of syllable weight between (C)V̄$CV and (C)VC$CV. Hock (1986) explains compensatory lengthening as a result of adjustment of morae representing the segments of successive syllables.

6. Conclusion. The reduction of extra-long syllables to long (i.e., V̄C$CV to V̄$CV) took place in Old Indo-Aryan and Dravidian at about the same time, viz. in the centuries immediately before the beginning of the Christian era. In early Middle Indo-Aryan this development was preceded by assimilation of heterogenous consonants into geminates, irrespective of the quantity of the preceding vowel. This appears to be quite similar to constraints of Proto-Dravidian phonotactics, which allowed only geminates and NP(P) sequences within stems. The development of Old Indo-Aryan V̄C-CV to VC-CV was an early Middle Indic development which probably spread throughout the Indo-Aryan area. This was followed by the loss of the final vowel, leading to degemination and compensatory lengthening of the preceding vowel in South, East, and Western New Indo-Aryan languages. Kashmiri, Sindhi, Punjabi, Lahnda, and West Pahari, which preserve the geminates, also preserve the final vowel or vowel release.

The alternation of VCC(V)/V̄C(V) is found in Dravidian only sporadically, and is not traceable to Proto-Dravidian. However the types VCC(V) and V̄C(V) emerged as the favoured syllable types in Dravidian to the exclusion of V̄CCV and V̄̆NPPV.

Turner traces the two 'tendencies', i.e. assimilation of heterogenous consonants and compensatory lengthening of the preceding vowel, to Early Old Indic, suggesting a gradual areal and lexical diffusion of these changes into Middle and New Indo-Aryan stages. The development of these 'tendencies' into general rules in Middle Indo-Aryan (particularly assimilation) must have been triggered by intimate contact with the Dravidian languages spoken in the Indo-Gangetic plains.

Vowel nasalization eliminating a pre-consonantal nasal in Indo-Aryan (i.e. V̄NP > V̄̃P; VNP > V̄̃P [where P = voiceless/voiced obstruent]) compares favourably with nasal loss in Dravidian (i.e. V̄NP > V̄̃B > V̄B; V̄NPP > V̄̃NP > V̄̃P > V̄P; VNPP > VNP/VPP [where P is a voiceless obstruent and B its voiced counterpart]) to produce the favourite stem types V̄C/VCC. To the Dravidian examples of this phenomenon, given above in § **2**, may be added the following from Indo-Aryan:

21. OIA *kā́ṇḍa* (*CDIAL* 3023) 'single joint of a plant' > MIA: Pāḷī *kaṇḍa*, Pkt. *kaṃḍa* > NIA: B. *kā̃ṛ* 'arrow', H. *kā̃ṛī* 'yolk', Mar. *kā̃ḍ* 'trunk', etc.

22. OIA *pañca* (*CDIAL* 7655) 'five' > MIA:Pa., Pkt. *pañca* > NIA: S. *pañja*, L. *panj*; B. *pā̃c*, H. *pā̃c*, Mar. *pā̃ts*, etc.

It is true that changes resulting in the balancing of weight between vowels and consonants in successive syllables are well attested in languages other than those of South Asia. However, we have noted that successive changes in Middle Indo-Aryan and Dravidian have produced the same end-result of shaping within the same time frame V̄C(V)/VCC(V) patterns into favourite stem types. This does not seem to be the result of an accident of phonological conspiracy. Judged from the other evidence supporting structural convergence in morphology and syntax, etc., the emergence of these syllable types points to a phonological phenomenon which must have resulted from a very intimate contact between speakers of Dravidian and Indo-Aryan for over a millennium prior to the emergence of Middle Indo-Aryan.

17

The Origin and Evolution of Primary Derivative Suffixes in Dravidian

1. Introduction

1.0. In the 1950s, when he was still in Czechoslovakia, Ladislav Zgusta wrote several reviews of works on comparative Dravidian linguistics, in collaboration with Kamil Zvelebil. This paper is a tribute to his profound contributions to the comparative method in general and to his early interest in Dravidian linguistics.

1.1. The monumental work of this century in comparative Dravidian linguistics, the *Dravidian Etymological Dictionary* of 1961, extensively revised in 1984, has scores of entries which lead us to reconstruct primary roots as well as extended stems for Proto-Dravidian (mainly of verbs but also of nouns), in which it is possible to assign some meaning to the monosyllabic roots, but no tangible meaning to the derivative suffixes. Consider for instance the data in 1.

1 (a) **tir-a-y* v.i. 'to roll'; v.t. 'to roll up'; n. 'wave, screen', **tir-a-nku* v.i. 'be curled up', **tir-a-nkku* v.t. 'to shrivel' [*DEDR* 3244]
(b) **tir-a-ḷ* v.i. 'to become round' [*DEDR* 3245]
(c) **tir-i-(-v-, -nt-)* v.i. 'to turn'; *(-pp, -tt-)* v. t. 'to turn'; **tir-uku* v.i., **tir-u-kku* v.t. 'to twist'; **tir-u-mpu* v.i., **tir-u-mppu* v.t. 'to twist, turn' [*DEDR* 3246]
(d) **tir-u-ntu* v.i. 'to be corrected, be repaired'; **tir-u-nttu* v.t. 'to correct, rectify' [*DEDR* 3251]

The Proto-Dravidian root obviously must be **tir-*, meaning 'turn, roll, twist, change shape → correct', etc. The purpose of this paper is to examine the origin of

I am indebted to M. B. Emeneau whose papers of 1967 and 1975 triggered my interest in exploring the subject matter of this paper—the obscure origins of the primary derivatives of Dravidian extended verbal stems. An earlier outline of my ideas is found in Krishnamurti 1978a, Appendix [see Ch. 10 of this volume].

I express my gratitude to Hans Henrich Hock for reworking some parts of the first version of this paper so as to make its arguments easier to understand for scholars trained in Indo-European linguistics. One of the changes that he has made in this regard is to use the symbols R for sonorant, T for voiceless stop, and D for voiced stops, where Dravidianists would use L, P, and B, respectively. I refer to four subgroups in Dravidian: I. South Dravidian; II. South-Central Dravidian; III. Central Dravidian; IV. North Dravidian. Tuḷu shares many features of CD as well as of SD.

the stem extensions or *primary derivative suffixes* in forms of the type 1, in two or more layers of extended stems. The first layer is V = *i, a, u*; and the second layer either sonorant (R) as in *y, l*; or (± homorganic nasal)+ simple or geminated stop: T as in **ku*; TT as in **kku*; NT as in **nku*, **ntu*, **mpu*; NTT as in **nkku*, **nttu*, **mppu*.

It is well known that the pairs of suffixes **k*: **kk*, **nk* **nkk*, **nt*: **ntt*, **mp*: **mpp* synchronically encode an intransitive : transitive distinction in both South Dravidian and South-Central Dravidian. But why should there be so many series of suffixes fulfilling the same function? And how do sets of related forms such as those in 1 above arise? These are the problems that I want to address in this paper.

1.2. Morphological reconstruction in Dravidian, unlike phonological reconstruction, is fraught with many pitfalls and uncertainties because of (a) the interplay between sound change and analogy, (b) semantic change and loss, (c) lack of data for earlier stages of the non-literary languages (some 22) as compared with the four literary languages, and (d) the non-availability, or at least dearth, of diagnostic environments or illustrations regarding (a) and (b). Added to these are the temporal and spatial gaps between the different members of North and Central Dravidian, which suggest the possible disappearance of many smaller members of the family.

We can try to steer clear of some of these pitfalls by extending the comparative method to the reconstructed stages of Proto-Dravidian and by supplementing it with textual materials from the literary languages, coupled with certain assumptions about the nature of language change.

2. Background Information

2.1. Proto-Dravidian roots are monosyllabic with the shape (C)V, (C)V̄, (C)VC, (C)VCC, or (C)V̄C. When (C)V̄C and (C)VCC were followed by a short vowel *i, u*, or *a* (*e, o* do not occur here), they merged with the (C)VC type as (C)VC-V (Krishnamurti 1955, 1961: 121–5; Emeneau 1975: 1–2). No particular meaning can be assigned to the vowel derivatives in *i, u*, or *a*. The open-syllable roots (C)V, (C)V̄, (C)VC-V- can be followed by two series of suffixes: the sonorant series (R) and the (±nasal+) stop series (T, TT, NT, NTT); cf. 2. and 3.

2. Sonorant series (R): *l ḷ r ẓ*[1] *w y*

3. Stop series:

	T	TT	NT	NTT
Labial	*p*	*pp*	*mp*	*mpp*
Dental	*t*	*tt*	*nt*	*ntt*
Alveolar	*ṯ*	*ṯṯ*	*nṯ*	*nṯṯ*
Retroflex	*ṭ*	*ṭṭ*	*ṇṭ*	*ṇṭṭ*
Palatal	*c*	*cc*	*ñc*	*ñcc*
Velar	*k*	*kk*	*nk*	*nkk*

1 Alternative transcription, adopted e.g. in *DEDR*: r̤.

The alveolar and retroflex series in 3. are derivable through certain Proto-Dravidian sandhi changes involving root-final and suffix-initial consonants as in 4. (Root-final ***l* and ***n* are alveolars; *n* in *nt* is dental.)

4. (a) *l+t* → *t̲*
   ḷ+t → *ṭ*
   (b) *l+tt* → *t̲t̲*
   ḷ+tt → *ṭṭ*
   (c) *l+nt* → *nt̲*
   ḷ+nt → *ṇṭ*
   n+t → *nt̲*
   ṇ+t → *ṇṭ*
   (d) *l+nt-t / n+tt* → *nt̲t̲*
   ḷ+nt-t / ṇ+tt → *ṇṭṭ*

The changes in c and d presuppose the change of dental [n] to alveolar [n̲] and retroflex [ṇ] following alveolar [l] and retroflex [ḷ], respectively. Note that dental [n] and alveolar [n̲] are allophones of /n/ in Proto-Dravidian, just as in Old Tamil.

The members of the palatal series likewise can in most cases be derived by sandhi rules of the proto-language, as in 5.

5. *y/i+tt* → *y/i+cc*
   y/i+nt(t) → *y/i+ñc(c)*

The above sandhi rules can be simplified through the use of distinctive features, but no attempt to do so is made here.[2]

2.2. Through comparison of the cognates of (C)V̄C(C)-type stems involving suffixes in R or T within reconstructed Proto-Dravidian, it is possible, in some cases, to identify an underlying root of the type *(C)V̄-. For instance, the stems **kā-y*/**kā-*, **kā-nku* : **kā-nkku*, **kā-ntu* : **kā-nttu*, **kā-mpu* : *kā-mppu* 'be(come) hot, burn, be dried up, etc.' [*DEDR* 1458], and **kā-ḷ* 'burn, flame' [*DEDR* 1500] could possibly be related to words meaning 'black, burnt, etc.', such as **kār* : **kar-V-* 'be scorched, burnt, black, black' [*DEDR* 1278], with the semantic development 'burn' → 'burn black' → 'black colour' → 'coal', etc. (see *TVB* 183–6).

2.3. No Dravidian language preserves Proto-Dravidian *NTT as such, but Kumaraswami Raja (1969) has conclusively shown that such a reconstruction is warranted by the correspondence NT : TT in different Dravidian languages, such as Ka. *eṇṭu* 'eight' : Ta., Ma. *eṭṭu* (< **eṇ-ṭṭu*), Ko. *eṭ*, To. *öṭ*, Koḍ. *ëṭṭï* [*DEDR* 784]. The NT sequences are generally attested in Telugu and Kannaḍa and occasionally in North Dravidian, where voiced and voiceless stops contrast after homorganic nasals; ef. e.g. Ka. *tirumpu* 'to cause to go round' : Ta., Ma. *tiruppu* id. (< **tir-umpp-*);

2 In an earlier publication I proposed a distinctive feature matrix for Proto-Dravidian consonants [see Ch. 10, fn. 2].

Te. *peṇṭi* 'female of animal' : Ta. *peṭṭai*, Ma. *peṭṭa* (< **peṇ-ṭṭ-ay*). The solution provided by Kumaraswami Raja has a far-reaching effect on our understanding of a number of problems of comparative Dravidian morphology.

3. Primary Derivative Suffixes as Earlier Inflectional Suffixes: The Hypothesis

3.0. Based on a critical study of many etymologies of type 1 above, I venture to propose that primary derivative suffixes arose through the incorporation of inflectional suffixes into the stem, and that this development took place in several stages, largely within Proto-Dravidian.

3.1. At a very early stage within Proto-Dravidian, sonorant suffixes of the R type were added to (C)V̄- or (C)VC-V-stems to form extended intransitive/middle-voice stems. This assumption is based on the observation that verb stems ending in sonorant suffixes tend to be intransitive in the descendant languages. Forms with these suffixes are preserved intact in the literary languages of the south, viz. Tamil, Malayāḷam, Kannaḍa, and Telugu.

At a later period, -R, -V-R lost their identity as grammatical elements and became incorporated into the preceding stems, as in 1ab above (*TVB* 146–7; Emeneau 1975: 2–3).[3]

3.2. Proto-Dravidian also had a very early stage in which T suffixes were added to primary roots, and later to extended stems with -R and -V-R. Only a subgroup of South Dravidian consisting of Tamil, Malayāḷam, Koḍagu, Toda, Kota, and Baḍaga preserves this stage of development in verb conjugation.[4] The new T-suffixes signal both tense and voice. Dental vs. non-dental indicates past vs. non-past; simple (N)T signals intransitive, and geminate (N)TT, transitive:

6.

	Non-past		Past
Intransitive	**p*	**k*	**t*
	**mp*	**nk*	**nt*
Transitive	**pp*	**kk*	**tt*
	**mpp*	**nkk*	**ntt*

3 I made this observation by comparing -(V)R-suffixes of Telugu verbal bases with those of the other Dravidian languages. I pointed out that the use of *-r-* as an intransitive reflexive marker occurs synchronically in Kuṛux (*kam-* 'to make' : *kam-r-* 'to be made') reflecting the Proto-South Dravidian situation. Since such a construction also occurs in Malto, Emeneau proposed the reconstruction of *-r-* as intransitive marker in Proto-Dravidian and suggested that it was incorporated into verb stems in all Dravidian languages except Kuṛux and Malto (1975: 2–3; for Malto see also Mahapatra 1979: 144–52). I have not gone beyond this point in investigating the *V-R-suffixes of Proto-Dravidian.

4 Emeneau (1967a: 366, 388–90) and Subrahmanyam (1971: 95–9) consider the system an innovation within South Dravidian.

The non-past paradigms include present, future, aorist (habitual), infinitive, imperative, negative, etc. Within the non-past, there must have been a morphological contrast between the labial and velar series, but the contrast tended to be blurred later.

3.3. The next stage consists of the incorporation of tense/voice suffixes into the preceding stems, with loss of tense meaning but preservation of the voice distinction. The latter is preserved mostly in disyllabic and trisyllabic roots, with NT : (N)TT indicating an intransitive : transitive alternation in most of South Dravidian. Traces of this alternation are found in Kannaḍa and Tuḷu;[5] South-Central Dravidian also preserves this stage, with the exception of Telugu and Gondi; and some traces exist in all other subgroups and languages (Subrahmanyam 1971: 52–4). As a consequence of this change, the contrast *NT : *NTT (or its reflexes NT : TT, (N)D : (N)T, etc.) has come to signal only an intransitive : transitive distinction.

Now, when an intransitive of one series wound up being matched up with the transitive of another series (e.g. Te. *tiru-gu* v.i. 'to turn' : *t(r)i-ppu* v.t. (< **tir-pp-*), Te. *jaru-gu* v.i. 'to slide' : *jaru-pu* v.t. 'to move') the alternation broke down as a symmetrical system and led to the next stage, of isolating certain markers as transitivizers.

3.4. It is through this development that *-pp*, *-tt* (and its palatalized derivative *-cc*) became transitivizers, added to intransitive bases to form transitive stems. Some of the intransitive base stems reflect simple Proto-Dravidian roots such as **mēy-* 'to graze', **kāy-* 'to burn', others are originally extended stems with incorporated intransitive suffixes as in the Telugu examples just cited.

3.5. A final, analytic, stage is found in all South Dravidian literary languages: new transitive stems are derived by the addition of different explicator or operator verbs to non-finite forms of the main verb, as in Te. *wirugu* v.i. 'to break'; *wiraga goṭṭ-* v.t. 'to break or snap' (< *wirag-an-* (inf.) + *koṭṭ* 'to beat'). In some cases, the older suffixal structures coexist with the final analytic stage, but with semantic differences; cf. Mdn. Te. *kāl-cu* 'to light (a cigarette), to burn' beside *kāla beṭṭ-* 'to burn something down'.

3.6. I assume that the first three developments took place at various stages within Proto-Dravidian, with each successive stage having a wider spread—lexical and areal—than the earlier one, but with all the three stages still synchronically

5 *DEDR* 169: Ta. *amuṅku* v.i. 'to sink, be pressed down, crushed', *amukku* (< **amuṅkk*) v.t. 'to crush', Ka. *amugu*, *avugu* v.i. 'to yield to pressure', *avuṅku* (beside *amuku*, etc.) v.t. 'to press or hold firmly', Tu. *avuṅkuni*, *avumpuni* 'to press down'. (Notice that Tuḷu here offers evidence for **nkk* and **mpp* of Proto-Dravidian with loss of the tense contrast.) *DEDR* 240: Ta. *alaṅku* v.i. 'to be shaken, etc.', *alakku* v.t. 'to cause to move, shake', Tu. *alaṅkuni* v.t. 'to agitate, wave'; *alaṅguni* has both intransitive and transitive meanings. *DEDR* 524: Ta. *iṟuku* v.i. 'to become tight', *iṟukku* v.t. 'to tighten', Ka. *iṟuṅku* v.t. 'to compress' (also *iṟanku, iṟinku*, presupposing PSD *iṟunkku* v.i.). So also *DEDR* 3246: Ka. *tirumpu* v.t. 'to cause to go round' (<* *tirumppu*).

coexisting. Typologically we notice a progression from synthetic to analytic in this scenario. Note also that extended stems of three or four syllables are more numerous than monosyllabic roots in the later stages of Proto-Dravidian.

The next question is to find empirical support for the above proposal and to find missing links in the morphological development of extended stems.

4. Corollaries of the Hypothesis and Background Assumptions

Before producing and discussing such supporting evidence, let me briefly note some corollaries that flow from the above proposal, as well as some other, background assumptions about linguistic change.

(1) Just as in any modern language, linguistic forms reflecting different chronological strata should have coexisted in Proto-Dravidian, before it broke up into subgroups.

(2) Evidence for the loss of the original function of a grammatical element in an extended stem may be found in the fact that a new element with the same or similar function can be added. Sometimes, in a synchronic stage both kinds of stems co-occur as free variants, particularly in literary texts.

(3) When a grammatically significant affix has lost its original function and remains as a dummy formative, one or more languages may innovate by assigning a new grammatical function to it.

(4) When underlying markers of intransitive and transitive have lost their structure and function, voice neutralization can lead to some original intransitive stems acquiring transitive form and meaning and, conversely, some transitive stems acquiring intransitive form and meaning.

(5) Since all Dravidian verbal formatives generally also function as nominal derivatives without change of structure, the intransitive : transitive contrast may also be reflected in a large number of derived nominals. Moreover, some languages may preserve only derived nouns and lose their verbal counterparts, and vice versa.

(6) Analogy can operate in unpredictable ways. It is therefore not possible to determine all the conditions under which levelling or other analogical processes took place when we are dealing with reconstructed strata within Proto-Dravidian.

Against the background of these metaconditions and corollaries, let us provide evidence and arguments in favour of our proposal.

5. Case Studies

5.1. Let us begin by looking at the etymology of PD **ā*- 'to be, happen, become' [*DEDR* 333].[6]

6. Unless otherwise indicated, the suffixes in parentheses after a verb root stand for non-past and past stem suffixes.

7. (a) **ā-*: Ta. *ā* (past stem *ān-*, *āyi-*) 'to be, happen', *ā* (*-pp*, *-tt-*) v.t. 'to cause, bring about'; *ā* (n.) 'becoming', *ā-m* (< **ā+um*) 'yes'; Tu. *ā-pini* (2nd sg. neut. past *āṇḍu*); OTe. *ā* (in *āyen/ayyen* 3rd past suffix *-en* with inserted glide *y*) id.; Go. *ay-* (irreg. 3rd sg. impf. *ānd*; some forms from *ā*), most dialects have *ā* 'to be'; Koṇḍa, Kui, Kuvi, Pengo, Manḍa *ā* (*ā-t-*) id.
   (b) **āku* v.i.: **ākku* v.t.: Ta. *āku* (*āku-v-*, *āk-i*) v.i., *ākku* (*ākk-i-*) 'to make', *ākk-am* n. 'creation' (tr. noun), *āk-a* inf. 'completely'; Ma. *āku-ka* v.i., *ākku-ka* v.t., *ākk-i-kka* (< **ākku-wi-kka-* caus. inf. of tr. with loss of *-w-*) 'to cause to make'; Ko. *āg* v.i. (*āy-/ān-*; some forms from *ā*); *āk-* v.t.; To. *ōx* (*ōy-*, *ōn-*, *ō-*) v.i., *ōk-*(*ōky-*) v.t.; Ka. *āgu* (*ān-*, *āy*, etc.); Koḍ. *āg-* (irr. *āy-*, *ān-*, *ā-*) v.i., *āk* (*āk-i*) v.t.; Te. *agu*, *awu* (*ay-i* ppl., *ay-na* adj.); Nk. *akk-* 'to make'.
   (c) **ā-p-* v.i. 'to become': **ā-pp-* v.t. 'to make, etc.': Kui *āva-* (*ā-t-*) 'to become', *āp-ka* (*āp-ki*) pl. action stem; Kol. *āp-* (*āp-t-*) 'to keep in a place': Nk. *āp-* 'to keep'. Cf. Ta. *ā-*(*pp-*) 'to cause, bring about'.
   (d) **ān-/an-* v.i.: Tu. (2nd sg. neut. past *āṇḍu*); Kol. *an-* (irreg., past *anḍ-*, imper. *ān*) 'to be in place'; Nk. *anḍ* 'to be'; Br. *anning* (St. *an-*, *as-*, *a-*) 'to be'.

Note that both *ā-* and *āku-* are used as inflectional bases in Old Tamil (Puṟanāṉūṟu), as in *āk-iṉ-* 'if' beside *ā-(y)iṉ* id., *ākum* '(subject) will become': *ā-m* id. (Subramoniam 1962). The last two forms are also given by Tolkāppiyam (1st century AD or BC). It can therefore be concluded that *ā-* is not simply a contraction of *āku-* (Israel 1973: 235).[7]

As for the putative suffixes in 7 (b–d), note that the Old Tamil classics use *-k-* beside *-t-* in aorist, i.e. non-past, constructions (Israel 1973: 145, 192 ff.), as in *uṇ-k-um* 'we drink', *kaṇ-ṭ-um* 'we see', *varu-t-um* 'we come' from the roots *uṇ-* 'to drink', *kāṇ-* 'to see', and *varu-* 'to come'. (The suffix *-um* of these structures, when not following *-k-* or *-t-*, appears simultaneously to mark habitual tense and person. In Malayāḷam, the suffixes *um* : *kkum* similarly occur as non-past, aorist markers.) Further, **-p-* [-w-] occurs as a future-tense marker added to *āku* in OTa. *āku-pa/-va* 'they will become' (Israel 1973: 235). That is, it too marks a non-past structure. Finally, the base form in 7 (d) corresponds to the past stem of the South Dravidian languages.

Given this evidence, we can interpret the data in 7 as follows: Set (a) naturally contains the original, unmodified root. Set (b) is based on an extended stem *ā-k-* of set (a), which incorporates an old non-past suffix *-k-* (intransitive): *-kk-* (transitive). This set shows variation between **ā* and **āk* in inflection. Set (c) is based on another non-past stem of (a), viz. *ā-p-* [ā-w-] : *ā-pp-*. Set (d) is based on the past stem of set (a), viz. *ān-*. All the four sets can be derived from the following reconstructed system of early Proto-Dravidian.

7 The infinitive *āka* is ambiguous, since it can be analysed either as *ā-ka* or as *āk-a*. Classical Tamil also has the simple infinitive *ā* < *ā-a* with loss of the short *a* (Agesthialingom 1979: 94).

8.

	Non-past		Past
Intransitive	**ā-k-*	**ā-p-*	**ā-(i)n-*
Transitive	**ā-kk-*	**ā-pp-*	**ā-tt-*

As we have seen, the formations in *-k(k)-* and *-p(p)-*, as well as the one in *-(i)n-*, have become generalized verb stems, losing their tense distinctions. In set (c), however, **-pp-* (> *-p-*) has retained traces of its voice distinction by serving as a transitive marker in some of the languages. Only the suffix *-tt-* is retained as an inflectional morpheme in South-Central Dravidian.

Further support for the reconstructed formations in 8 comes from the distribution of forms in the various subgroups of Dravidian; cf. 9. None of the extended forms is limited to just one subgroup, a fact which precludes the assumption that they originated in the various descendant subgroups. The geographical distribution, combined with the data in 8, further suggests that the incorporation of suffixes into the stem began within Proto-Dravidian, for, again, the use of extended forms with loss of their original tense and/or voice distinctions cuts across the different descendant subgroups.

9.	(a)	**ā*	SD, SCD
	(b)	**āk-* : *ākk-*	SD; Nk. of CD
	(c)	**āp-* : *āpp-*	Ta. of SD; Te., Kui of SCD; Kol., Nk. of CD
	(d)	**ān*	Tu. of SD; Go. of SCD; Kol., Nk. of CD; Br. of ND

5.2. A structural parallel in Proto-Dravidian is found in **pō* beside **pōku* 'to go' attested only in South Dravidian and South-Central Dravidian (cf. *DEDR* 4572):

10. (a) **pō-*: Ta. *pō-* (non-past: *pōv-/pōkuv-/pōtuv-*, past: *pōn-/pōyin-*; neg. *pōk-*); Ma. *pōka*; Koḍ. *pō* (*pōp-*, *pōk-*, *pōc-*, *pōy-*); Ka. *pō*, *pō-li*, *pō-lu* 'state of going, ruin'; Te. *pō* (*pō-yi*).
    (b) **pō-k-*: **pō-kk-*: Ta. *pōku* (future: *pōku-v-*, neg. *pōk-*), *pōk-ai* n. (intr.) 'departure'; *pōkku* (*pōkk-i-*) 'to cause to go, send'; *pōkk-am* n. (tr.) 'causing to go; exit, way'; Ma. *pōka* (inf., interpreted as *-ka*, but historically *-k+a*), *pōk-al* n. 'going', *pōkkuka* v.t. 'to make to go, remove', *pōkk-al* n. 'removing'; Ko. *ōg* (*ōy-/ōn-*, also *ō* based on **pō*), *ōk-c* 'to cause to go', *pōk-* (*pōk-y-*) 'to spend time'; To. *pïx* (*pï-*); Ka. *pōgu*, *hōgu*; Koḍ. *pōk-*; Te. *pōwu* (*-w-* < *-g-*), non-past neg. *pō-*, *pōw-* (intr.), *pōka* n. 'going, departure'; Koṇḍa, Pe. *pōk* (*-t-*) 'to send; Manḍa *pūk-* (*-t-*) id.

These forms illustrate the way the stems of set (b) were remade from the root of (a) by incorporating the non-past suffixes *k* : *kk* into the stem in the intransitive and transitive respectively. Interestingly, there is a greater regularity in the inflection of the extended stem than that of the original root **pō-*. Also notice the occurrence of *pōku* in the *non-past* intransitive paradigm of Old Tamil as *pōku-v-*, neg. *pōk-* as opposed to *pō* in *past pō-y-iṉ*, *pō-ṉ*. This distribution preserves a trace of *-ku-* as a non-past (aorist, optative) marker, even though the suffix generally has lost its meaning. Koṇḍa, Kui, and Pengo of South-Central Dravidian retain only the transitive forms of the derived stem. Telugu shows both South Dravidian and South-Central Dravidian features.

5.3. As noted in the preceding two sections, original tense/voice suffixes such as **-k(u) :-kk(u)* became incorporated into the preceding stems and lost their tense meaning, while preserving traces of their voice distinctions. Another valuable etymology, where a tense morpheme has become a formative, is illustrated by **uḷ* 'to be, have' : **uṇṭu* 'is, are' [*DEDR* 697]. The form **uḷ* is attested in Ta. Ma. *uḷ*; Ko. *oḷ*; Ka. *uḷ*, *oḷ* 'to be; to have'; Koḍ. *uḷḷ-*; Kui *lopha* (*loh-t-*) 'to remain'; the form **uṇṭu* is reflected in Ta. *uṇṭu* 'is, are' (existence), *uṇmai* 'truth'; Ma. *uṇṭu* 'there is, exists'; Ko. *oḍo* (3rd pers. neut. of **oḷ*); To. *wïḷd-* 'to exist' (3rd pers. *wïḍ-i*); Ka. *uṇṭu* 3rd pers. 'that is, that exists', n. 'existence'; Koḍ. *uṇḍï* (3rd pers. of *uḷḷ-*); Tu. *uṇḍu* (3rd sg. neut. of *uḷḷ-*, pres. tense); Te. *uṇḍu* 'to exist, live, dwell', *uṇḍu(nu)* finite verb 'he, she, it, they (neut.) are', *uṇ-ḍ-r-u* 'they are' (hum.), where *-ḍ-* is a sandhi variant of the aorist suffix *-d-* (an alternative form occurs later as *uṇḍu-du-ru* where *uṇḍu* is entirely treated as a root); Br. *uṭ* (pres. 1st sg.), *us* (pres. 2nd sg.), *un* (1st pl.), *ure* (2nd pl.), *ur* (3rd pl.) related irregularly to the root *anning* 'to be'.

Since both South Dravidian, South-Central Dravidian, and Brahui of North Dravidian inherit reflexes of **uṇṭu*, the form must be reconstructed for Proto-Dravidian, as an inflected form of the root **uḷ*. Now, Tolkāppiyam analyses **uṇṭu* (< **uḷ-ntu*) as containing *-tu-*, a non-past marker. But in terms of Proto-Dravidian morphophonemics the morph should have the form **-ntu* 'to yield' *uṇ-ṭu* < **uḷ+ntu*; and this **-ntu-* is clearly different from the past-tense marker *-tu-* (Ka. *uṇṭu* is derivable from **uṇ-ṭṭu*) in which case the underlying sequence is interpretable as *t* (non-past) + *tu* (singular neuter). In old Kannaḍa the form is used in the neuter singular and plural; cf. Ramachandra Rao 1972: 257.[8]

Moreover, the form *uṇ-ṭu* is nowhere used in the past tense. The incorporated suffix **-ntu-* must therefore be the same aorist marker as that retained in Old Tamil (*-t-*) and also in Literary Telugu (*-d-*). In Old Tamil it occurs with only a limited number of verbs in the first plural and the second singular and plural (Glazov 1968: 106). It expresses an indefinite present-future meaning, as in *varu-t-i* (KT 91.14) 'you come', *āṭu-t-um* (Cilap.9.63) 'we will bathe ourselves'.

The use of **uṇṭu* differs from these other structures with **-ntu-* in two significant ways: (a) It is used in the third person in almost all the Dravidian languages, and (b) it is not limited to Old Tamil and Literary Telugu but is found in all the subgroups of Dravidian. The latter fact permits us to consider it an inheritance from Proto-Dravidian. Now, its third-person use is in complementary distribution with the first- and second-person use of non-past **-tu-* in Old Tamil and Literary Telugu. It therefore provides the 'missing link' that permits us to reconstruct a

8 Another etymology similar to **uṇṭu* is **wēṇṭu* [*DEDR* 5528] from **wēḷ-ntu/*wēṇ-ṭu* which has cognates for the composite form in most of the languages of South-Dravidian and Central Dravidian, and Telugu of South Central Dravidian. Here **(n)tu* is a non-past morpheme of Proto-Dravidian.

complete Proto-Dravidian paradigm for forms containing the suffix **-ntu-* and thus permits us to show that the Old Tamil and Literary Telugu forms are not just regional innovations.[9]

Notice finally that the Telugu verb *uṇḍu* occurs in both past and non-past paradigms (*uṇḍ-i-ri* 'they (3rd hum.) were', *uṇḍu-du-ru* 'they are/will be'), thereby losing the original signification of *ḍ* < **nt* as a non-past marker. (The only exception is the third person human plural *uṇ-ḍ-ru* 'they are' of Classical Telugu, which is now archaic.) Here, then, we find the same phenomenon of 'tense loss' as with incorporated markers such as **-k(k)-* discussed in §§ **5.1–2.**

5.4. In all the South Dravidian languages, except Kannaḍa, there is a verbal conjugation (*Tamil Lexicon* Class IV) in which tense and voice are combined in the same morphs. Roots which generally end in *i*, *u*, *y* (including *ay*), *r*, and *ẓ* belong to this class. The conjugation is characterized by the following original suffixes.

11.

	Non-past		Past	
	Intransitive	Transitive	Intransitive	Transitive
Aorist	*(k)-um*	*kk-um*	*nt*	*tt*
Future	*p [-w-]*	*pp*		

In the following discussion we will see how these tense-voice suffixes were incorporated to form extended stems in different South Dravidian and South-Central Dravidian languages. Let us begin with an examination of reflexes of the verb **iẓi* 'to descend' [*DEDR* 502].

12.

	Non-past		Past	
	Intransitive	Transitive	Intransitive	Transitive
Tamil	*iẓi-v-*	*iẓi-pp-*	*iẓi-nt-*	*iẓi-tt-* (> *iẓi-cc-*)
Malayāḷam	*iẓi-v-*	*iẓi-pp-*	*iẓi-ññ-*	*iẓi-cc-*
Koḍagu	*ïḷi-v-*	*ïḷï-p-* (dial. *ï p-*)	*ïḷi-nj-*	(*ïḷïp-i-*)
Toda	*īx-* (< **iẓ-g-*)	*īk-* (< **iẓ-kk-*)	(*īx-y-*)	(*īk-y-*)
Kannaḍa	*iḷi-v-*	*iḷi-p*	*iḷi-d-*	*iḷi-s-i*
Telugu	*ḍiggu/ḍigu* (< **iẓ-g*)	*ḍi-mp-*	[*ḍindu*] (arch.)	*ḍi-nc-*
Koṇḍa	*ḍig-*	*ḍip-*	(*ḍig-it-*)	*ḍi-p-t-*
Kui	*dī v-*	*dīp-*	*dī-t-*	*dī -p-t-*
Parji	*iṛv-* (< **iṛ-g*)	*iṛk-ip-*		*iṛk-it-*
Gadaba, Ollari	*iṛg-*	*iṛig-p-*		*iṛig-t*
Proto-Dravidian	**iẓi(m)p-*	**iẓi-mpp-*	**iẓi-nt-*	**iẓi-ntt-*

9 An alternative analysis of *uṇ-tu* as containing the third singular neuter suffix *-tu* must be rejected, since it would not permit us to account for its tense meaning (present-future) and since the attested forms are not confined to the neuter singular.

Note that in the non-past there is evidence for both a labial and a velar suffix as seen in Toda, Kannaḍa (*iẓaku* v.t.), Parji, Gadaba, Telugu, and Koṇḍa. The Toda stem is remade in the intransitive and transitive by incorporating the erstwhile non-past morphs **k*: **kk* (or **nk*: **nkk*). So also in Parji and Ollari *iṛv-/iṛg-* have become the basic stems without any tense meaning attached to their *v/g*. In Parji the intransitive : transitive alternation is retained as *g* : *k*, whereas it is only signalled by suffixation in Ollari. In Kui, too the *-v-* : *-p-* alternation signifies intransitive and transitive in the non-past (infinitive).

The Telugu forms are diagnostic for the reconstruction of the proto-suffixes. A new verbal base *ḍindu* (< **iẓ-nd-*; cf. Ta. *iẓi-nt-*) v.i. 'to sink, fall, droop, die' is created incorporating the Proto-Dravidian intransitive past tense morph *-nt-* (*TVB* 52). The intransitive form *ḍiggu/ḍigu* is from **ẓi-gg-* < **iẓ-g-* (see *TVB* § 1.124; 52, 53) through metathesis, gemination of the voiced stop after (C)V-, and subsequent degemination. The comparison with Parji, Ollari, and Toda shows an underlying velar *g* (< *-k-*) which was apparently a non-past marker. There are two transitive forms in Telugu: *ḍi-nc-* which occurs as a base before past tense suffixes and *ḍi-mp-* which occurs before non-past suffixes in Classical Telugu. Owing to the retention of the nasal, these forms are traceable to PD **iẓ(i)-ncc-* (< **iẓi-ntt-*) for the past tense base and **iẓ(i)-mpp-* for the non-past base.

Tamil, Malayāḷam, and Koḍagu attest the past-tense form *iẓi-cc-* from *iẓi-tt-*. The nasal of **ntt* (tr. past, corresponding to **nt* intr. past) is lost here in accordance with normal sound change (see § **2.3** above). The Telugu suffix retains the original alternation of **nt* : **ntt*. Again, *ḍi-mp* (< **iẓi-mpp*) presupposes an intransitive **-mp* as opposed to transitive **-mpp* in the non-past. This piece of evidence allows us to reconstruct **mp* beside **p* as non-past intransitive marker within Proto-Dravidian; however, while we have evidence for **k* there is none for **nk* in the intransitive non-past.

I propose that **nk* and **mp* were incorporated into stems as (derivative) voice suffixes carrying intransitive meaning in a deeper chronological stratum of Proto-Dravidian. The morphs **p* and **k* must have replaced **mp* and **nk* respectively in all non-past environments. Note that Old Kannaḍa (Pampa Bhārata; cf. Ramachandra Rao 1972: Index) has *iḷi-s-* and *iḷi-p-* as past and non-past bases requiring underlying *iẓi-cc-*, *iẓi-pp-* as found in the Tamil-Koḍagu subgroup (with *-cc-* > *-c-* > *-s-*; *-pp-* > *-p-* in Kannaḍa).

This illustration shows that the tense/voice conjugation, which is still retained intact in the Tamil-Koḍagu subgroup of South Dravidian, is reconstructable for Proto-Dravidian. In the other members of South Dravidian, Central Dravidian, and South-Central Dravidian, these morphemes have lost their tense meaning, becoming derivative suffixes. The erstwhile tense marking can, however, be reconstructed from the distribution of these morphemes in verb paradigms as illustrated above.

The past suffix *-ttu* and the non-past suffix *-ppu*, when delinked from their unlikely-looking relatives *-nt* (past intr.) and *-p*, *-mp-* (non-past intr.), have come to be segmented as pure transitive markers which have become additive morphemes in a later chronological stratum of Proto-Dravidian. Cf. Ta. *iẓi-ttu* (*iẓi-tt-i*), *iẓi-ccu* 'to lower'; *iẓi-vu*, *iẓi-pu* n, 'inferiority' (intr.), *iẓi-ppu* n, 'contemptuous treatment' (tr.).

The above discussion leads us to set up the following reconstructions within Proto-Dravidian.

13.

Non-past		Past	
Intransitive	Transitive	Intransitive	Transitive
**iẓi-p- : *iẓi-mp-*	**iẓi-pp- : *iẓi-mpp-*	**iẓi-nt-*	**iẓi-ntt-*
**iẓi-k- : *iẓi-nk-*	**iẓi-kk- : *iẓi-nkk-*		

In this particular example evidence is lacking for the suffix *nk*: *nkk*, but such evidence is found in various other etymologies where the suffix is seen to have been completely incorporated into the base in early Proto-Dravidian. Consider for instance **wir-i* 'to extend, open, split, crack, burst' [*DEDR* 5411]. The data in 14 (a) present a similar picture to 12; but as 14 (b) shows, for this stem, some languages presuppose a velar non-past suffix, instead of a labial.

14.

		Non-past		Past	
		Intransitive	Transitive	Intransitive	Transitive
(a)	Tamil	*viri-v-*	*viri-pp-*	*viri-nt-*	*viri-tt-*
	Malayāḷam	*viri-v-*	*viri-pp*	*viri-ññ*	*viri-cc-*
	Koḍagu	*biri-v-*	*biri-p-*	*biri-ñj-*	*biri-c-*
	Toda			*pir-s-* (<*piry*+*θ*)	*pir-c-* (<*piry*+*t*)
	Kannaḍa	*biri-v-*		*biri-d-*	
(b)	Telugu	*viru-gu*			
	Kui	*vringa*	*vripka* (< **vrik-pa*)	*vring-i*	*vrik-t-*
		vrī-va		*vrī-t-*	

The Kui forms presuppose the non-past forms **wiri-nk* : **wiri-nkk* beside the original root **wiri-* (with non-past *-w-*) in *vrī-va*. However, as shown by *vring-i* (past intr.), the velar suffix has been incorporated into the stem. The nominal suffixes also exhibit variation, e.g. Te. *virivi* 'abundance'; Ta. *virivu* n. 'expansion', *virippu* n. 'opening out'; Ma. *viriccal* (< **viri-tt-al*) n. 'split'. Such nominals are based on underlying tense/voice suffixes.

On the basis of the above discussion, we can also provide a morphological account for the Proto-Dravidian reconstruction of extended stems derived from the root **tir-* 'to turn, twist', etc. (§ **1.1** above); cf. (15).

15. Proto-Dravidian root: **tir-*:
   (a) With vowel suffixes: **tir-i-* [*DEDR* 3246], *tir-a-*, *tir-u-*.
   (b) With R suffixes: **tir-a-ḷ*, **tir-a-y* [*DEDR* 3245, 3244]

(c) With stop suffixes:

Non-past			Past		
Intransitive		Transitive	Intransitive		Transitive
**tir-u-ku*	:	**tir-u-kku* [3246]	**tir-u-ntu*	:	**tir-u-nttu* [3251]
**tir-a-nku*	:	**tir-a-nkku* [3244]			
**tir-u-mpu*	:	**tir-u-mppu* [3246, 3258]			

5.5. There are in addition several examples of fresh verbal bases in different Dravidian languages, formed by incorporating the proto-Dravidian past tense morph **nt*. Subrahmanyam (1971: 204–6) cites the following examples:

16. (a) PD **iru-* (**iru-nt-* past intr.) 'to exist, be' [*DEDR* 480]: Kui *rı̄nd-* 'to be stable, steady' (earlier: Emeneau 1967a:391).
    (b) PD **nōy* (*nōy-nt-*) 'to pain' [*DEDR* 3793]: Kuṛ. Malto *nunj-* 'to pain'.
    (c) PSD **pāy* (**pāy-nt-*) 'to spring, leap' [*DEDR* 4087]: Kui *pānj-* 'to fly, leap'.
    (d) PD **piẓi* (**piẓi-nt-*) 'to squeeze, press' [*DEDR* 4183]: Ka. *piṇḍu, hiṇḍu*; Koḍ. *puṇḍ-*; Tu. *puṇḍiyuni*; Te. *piṇḍu*: Kol. Nk. *piṇḍ-* 'to squeeze, wring': Ta. Ma. Ka. *piẓi*, Kui, Koṇḍa, and North Dravidian also have forms from **piẓi*. Tu. *purñcuni, pureñcuni* 'to squeeze' are from **piẓ(i)-ntt-* and **pi-ẓ-ay-ntt-*, respectively. Note a restricted Proto-Dravidian sandhi rule **ẓ+nt* → **ṇṭ-*.
    (e) PSD **kuṟay* (**kuṟay-nt-* : **kuṟay-ntt-*) 'to be reduced in size' [*DEDR* 1851]: Ko. *kornj* v.i., *korc* v.t.; PSD **piri* (**piri+nt* : **piri-ntt*) 'to separate' [*DEDR* 4176]: Ko. *pirnj* v.i., *pirc-* v.t.
    (f) **paẓ-V-* (*paẓ-V-nt-*) 'to ripen' [*DEDR* 4004, not included in Subrahmanyam's list]: Te. *paṇḍu* 'to ripen, mature', n. *fruit*; Kol. Nk. *paṇḍ-* 'to become ripe'; Pa. *paṇḍ* 'a plant matures'; Go. *paṇḍ-*, Koṇḍa *paṇḍ-* 'to ripen'; Kuvi *paṇḍu* 'ripe fruit' (< **paẓ(u)-nt-*, past intr. stem); Tu. *parnduni* 'to ripen', *parndï* 'ripe fruit'; Pa. *paṛñ-* 'to ripen'; Oll. *paṛng-* 'to become grey (of hair)'. Tamil, Malayāḷam, etc. have *paẓu*; cf. Malto *pān-*, Kuṛ. *pān* (*pañjā*) 'to ripen', *pañjka* 'fruits', PD **paẓ-i-/-u-* with non-past **-nk-*, past **-nt-* would explain all the items in this etymology.

5.6. Let us at this point take stock of our findings so far, amplifying them with a few additional comments.

(1) The verb conjugation with inflectional morphemes signalling both tense and voice is an ancient one, still preserved in the Tamil-Koḍagu subgroup of South Dravidian.

(2) The non-past intransitive morphs **-nk*, **-mp* lost their inflectional value and were incorporated as mere voice markers in early Proto-Dravidian.

(3) In the Tamil-Koḍagu subgroup the loss of N in NTT led to its merger with TT in the non-past; cf. 17.

17.

Proto-Dravidian Non-past		Tamil-Koḍagu subgroup Non-past	
Intransitive	Transitive	Intransitive	Transitive
**p*	**pp*	*p*	*pp*
**mp*	**mpp*	—	*pp*
**k*	**kk*	*k*	*kk*
**nk*	**nkk*	—	*kk*

The merger of **mpp* with *pp* and of **nkk* with *kk* must have led to the analogical replacement of the intransitive suffixes **mp* and **nk* by *p* and *k* respectively in South Dravidian (Tamil-Koḍagu subgroup). This did not happen in the case of **nt* because the past suffix **t* had a very low functional yield (only nine Old Tamil verbs take it in their past tense), whereas **nt* had a much higher frequency, and transitive formation by geminating the final consonant of the tense marker affected the past allomorph *-*nt*- in many more cases than **t* in the Tamil-Koḍagu subgroup.

(4) Palatalization of a dental stop (single or double) after **y/i* is witnessed in many languages, requiring its reconstruction for the Tamil-Koḍagu subgroup, for pre-Parji, and for Proto-South-Central Dravidian (see the next section), and also perhaps for Kuṛux-Malto. Apparently, the sound change was developing dialectally within Proto-Dravidian itself.

5.7. The Proto-Dravidian causative suffix is *-*pi*- (allomorphs *-*wi*-, *-*pi*-, and *-*ppi*-) which is generally added to transitive stems requiring a second agent subject in the sentence (Meenakshisundaram 1965: 111); cf. e.g. *amma kēṭ-pi-kk-um* 'Amma will make someone else listen' (Tolk. 761). The causative morpheme in Old Telugu has two alternants, -*inc*- before past suffixes and -*imp*- in the non-past paradigm; cf. e.g. 18.

18. Past participle — *cēy-inc-i* 'having caused (something) to be done'
Past finite — *cēy-inc-en(u)* (3rd sg. subject) 'caused (it) to be done'
Past adjective — *cēy-inc-ina* 'that which was caused to be done'
Negative — *cēy-imp-a-* (+ personal affixes) 'someone will not cause it to be done'
Infinitive — *cēy-imp-aN* 'to cause (it) to be done' (N here = /n/ ~ Ø sentence finally, but /n/ before a vowel)
Imperative — *cēy-imp-umu* (2nd sg.) '(you sg.) cause it to be done'
cēy-imp-ūḍu (2nd pl.) '(you pl.) cause it to be done'

Comparison of the Telugu causative stems with Old Tamil inflectional stems permits reconstruction of Proto-Dravidian causative stems as follows:

19. PD **key* 'to do' : Ta. *cey*, Te. *cēyu*.

	Tamil	Telugu	Proto-Dravidian
Past	*cey-vi-tt*	*cēy-i-nc*	**key-pi-ntt-*
Non-past	*cey-vi-pp-*	*cēy-i-mp-*	**key-pi-mpp-*
Aorist	*cey-vi-kk*	—	**key-pi-(n)kk* (?)

The following rules account for the Tamil and Telugu causative stems:

20. (a) *_p_	> _w_ / {Semivowel, Vowel}___ + V(PSD)	
(b) *_k_	> _c_ / #___[V, –back]	[C, –retr.] (Ta., Te.; ignoring details)
(c) *N	> Ø/___TT	(Ta.-Koḍ. subgroup)
(d) *_w_	> Ø/___i + (causal morph)	(Ma., Ka.; SCD, incl. Te.)
(e) *_ntt_	> (i) _ncc_ > _nc_/ V___V	(Te.)
	(ii) _cc_ > _c_ > _s_/ V___(V)	(Ka., Gondi, Koṇḍa, etc.)
(f) *(C)V_y_	> V̄_y_	(OTe., Mdn. Te. V̄_y_/V̆_y_)

As noted by Subrahmanyam (1971: §1.27, 90–95), Telugu agrees with Tamil in several cases in its selection of causative allomorph, such as the allomorph _*-pp-_ in 21.

21.	Tamil	Telugu	Proto-Dravidian
Past	_naṭa-ppi-tt-_	_naḍa-pi-inc-_	_*naṭa-ppi-ntt-_
Non-past	_naṭa-ppi-pp-_	_naḍa-pi-mp-_	_*naṭa-ppi-mpp-_
	naṭa-ppi-kk-	—	_*naṭa-ppi-nkk-_

However, he fails to explain the origin of Telugu causative _-inc-/-imp-_ in Te. _naḍapinc-/-pimp-_ 'to cause someone to walk.' He says (1971: 92):

> It is to be noticed that although _i_ in Telugu _-incu_ is from _*-vi-_, the remaining part _-ncu_ cannot be the development of the Tamil-Malayāḷam strong verb formative _kk_ as supposed by Ramaswami Aiyar. It will be more plausible to connect it to the transitive suffix _*-cc-_ and _-incu_ will be a combination of two original suffixes _-i-_ (< _*vi_) and _-ncu_ (< _*cc_).

But it is difficult to understand how _-ncu_ can be derived from _-cc_. Moreover, the alternation of _-inc/-imp_ also remains unexplained.

The Telugu morpheme _-inc/-imp_ must instead be explained as follows: _-inc_ is a reanalysed causative morpheme incorporating the proto-past-tense suffix with palatalization of _*-intt_ to _*-incc_; the alternating _*-impp_ is the original non-past suffix. In both cases, TT is simplified to T, but the nasal (N) of the proto-sequence *NTT is retained. Although the tense meanings were lost, the distribution of the allomorphs between past and non-past are reminiscent of their original distribution. Kannaḍa of South Dravidian and a number of South-Central Dravidian languages use the derivatives of _*icc/*ipp_ and _*picc/*pipp_ as transitive-causative suffixes.

Old Kannaḍa has _-isu_ as a transitive-causative suffix alternating with _-ipu_. The suffix _-isu_ occurs in past-tense formations like _kiḍ-is-i_ 'having made to ruin'; it is also used in infinitive _kiḍ-is-al_ 'to destroy', _kiḍ-is-e_ 'to spoil', while _-ipu_ occurs in future paradigms (Ramachandra Rao 1977: 147, 317). Compare 22 (_-isu_ is causative).

22. _kiḍu_	'to be spoiled'	_kiḍ-isu_	:	_kiḍ-ip-ar_ 'they will spoil'
karagu	'to be melted'	_karag-isu_	:	_karag-ip-en_ 'I will melt'
_āḷ_	'to rule'	_āḷ-isu_	:	_āḷ-ip-avu_ 'we will cause to rule'
gel	'to win'	_gel-isu_	:	_gel-ip-am_ 'we will cause to win'

The evidence of Old Kannaḍa supports the origin of *-isu*/*-ipu* from underlying tense-based causative morphs, although *-isu* was generalized, replacing *-ipu* in later Kannaḍa. Similarly, in Middle and Modern Telugu *-inc* has been analogically extended to all environments. The morphs Te. *-incu* and Ka. *-isu*, besides being causative markers, are also added productively to intransitive bases to form transitives.

Derivatives of **-i(n)cc* (< **in-tt*) and **i(m)pp* are found in several languages of South-Central Dravidian, Central Dravidian, and North Dravidian. In South-Central Dravidian, the distribution has come to be phonologically conditioned.

In Adilabad Gondi, *-us*, *-pūs* are frequently used as transitive-causative morphs, as in *kar-ūs-* 'to teach', *muṛ-ūs-* 'to immerse', *aṭṭ-ūs* 'to cause to cook' (Subrahmanyam 1968a: 5). Koya has *-is* as causative marker in such forms as *ūḍ-* 'to see' : *ūḍ-is* 'to make see', *niṇḍ-* 'to fill' : *niṇḍ-is* 'to make full' (Tyler 1969: 80). The use of *-is/-pis/-bis* is quite productive in Koṇḍa, e.g. *kaṭ-* 'to bite' : *kaṭ-is-/kaṭ-pis* 'to cause to bite'; *uRk-* 'to run' : *uRk-is* 'to make run'; *ki-* 'to do' : *ki-b-is* 'to cause to do' (Krishnamurti 1969c: 274-6).

As Subrahmanyam observers, 'Malto has a special causative *-t-it-* added to a base with a transitive marker. Parji *-ip/-it* (present vs. past and future), Kol. *-ip*, and Br. *-if* added to a transitive with *-f-* to form a causative (e.g. *kas-f-if-* 'to cause to kill') can also be traced to the same source' (1971: 93).

The above evidence points to the palatalization of **(n)tt* to **(n)cc* following a front vowel in a large number of South and South-Central Dravidian languages. The development of this morpheme actually provides us an isogloss separating these languages from Central Dravidian (Parji, Kolami, Naiki, Ollari, and Gadaba) and North Dravidian.

6. Some Additional Case Studies

6.1. In Kota there are two stems, S_1, the basic form which in some items corresponds to the future stem of Old Tamil, and S_2, which corresponds to the past stem of Old Tamil.

23. *DEDR*	Proto-Dravidian	Old Tamil	Kota base	past stem
3630	**nān* : *nan*-V-	*naṉai* (-v-, -nt-) v.i. 'to become wet' (*-pp-*, *-tt-*) v.t. 'to make wet'	*nanv-*	*nan-d-* *nan-t*
4760	**maṯ*-V-	*maṟai* (*-v-*, *-nt-*) v.i. 'to be hidden' (*-pp-*, *-tt-*) v.t. 'to hide'	*marv-*	*mar-d-* *mar-c-* 'to keep secret, in mind'

The past stem becomes a restructured base to which new past suffixes are added, as in *vad-t* 'having come' (cf. Ta. *vant-* past stem). The past tense suffixes that are added to the historically derived past stem (S_2) are *-v-* and *-p-* which look more like the non-past morphs of Proto-Dravidian. Another type of past (irrealis) is formed by adding *-c-* to S_2, as in *vad-c-* (Subrahmanyam 1971: 120; see Emeneau 1967: 374–8 for a full description of S_1 and S_2 in Kota and Toda).

6.2. Many Old Telugu verbs ending in *-cu* do not have corresponding palatal formatives in other language groups, e.g. *ēḍ-cu* 'to weep', *naḍa-cu* 'to walk', *nil-ucu* 'to stand', *maṟa-cu* 'to forget'. In the conjugation of these verbs, the formative *-cu* occurs in the past inflection (also in the durative) alternating with *w* in the non-past, as in *nil(i)-ci* 'having stood', *nil(a)-w-an* (inf.) 'to stand'.

I have shown elsewhere (*TVB* §§ 2.84–87, 162–163; §§ 2.43–42, 45, 14–15.2) that the *c* is incorporated into the base from an old past suffix **-cci* which occurs as past participle morph in the other South-Central Dravidian languages. Similarly *cēyu* 'to do' : *cē-si* 'having done' has a **si* traceable to **-ci*. Because of the wider occurrence of *-i* as past participle suffix in verbs like *win-i* 'having heard', *kaṭṭ-i* 'having built', etc. which goes back to PD **-i*, **-c-* and **-cc-* have been reanalysed as parts of the stems; hence **cē-si* → *cēs-i*, **nil-ci* → *nilc-i*. The *-w-* variant is a reflex of PD non-past **-p-* [-w-]. I have also demonstrated that even Gondi, which synchronically preserves *-sī*, *-cī*, *-jī* (< **-ci*, **-cci*) as past participle suffixes, also incorporated the palatal/sibilant into some of its bases, just like Telugu, although to a more restricted extent (164). I further have shown that a similar incorporation of the *c* of **ci* into the verb bases can be suspected in many other languages of South-Central and North Dravidian (165). Note that Kuṛux-Malto and Brahui retain a Proto-Dravidian suffix **cc* as past tense marker whose **cc* does not result from palatalization of **tt* (165); cf. 24.

24. Te. *pāṟu*, *paṟ-acu* 'to flee': Malto *par-ce* 'to run away'
[*DEDR* 4020; cf. 3963]

6.3. Where Telugu *-cu*/*-ncu* are used as transitive markers (alternating with *-pu*/*-mpu*) they can be traced back to the palatalized past suffix **-tt*/**-ntt* following a front vowel or *y* as in *ḍinc-*/*ḍimp-* 'to lower', *kā̃cu*/*kā̃pu* (< **kāy-ntt*/**kāy-mpp*) 'boil'. Later on, *-cu* was generalized as a transitive marker and extended to stems of different underlying structure, e.g. *kālu* intr. 'to burn' : *kāl-cu* tr. 'to burn'.

6.4. The past and non-past transitive markers of *Tamil Lexicon* Class IV, reconstructable as **-(n)tt-* and **-(m)pp-*, must have occurred in syntactic contexts where they could be interpreted as mere transitive markers added to the corresponding intransitive stems. Thus R. Kothandaraman (n.d.) identifies three types of Old Tamil stems derived from the conjugation in **nt*: **ntt*, and these stems reflect three pre-Tamil stages of change in their syntactic functions; cf. 25. In Type 1 both sets of forms are used as past participles, in their original intransitive : transitive function. In Type II the first form functions as a past participle, while the second one has become a new verbal base in which *-ttu* occurs only as a transitive marker, having lost its tense meaning. A new past participle is formed from this form, as in *vāẓ-tt-i* (cf. Ta. *vāẓ-ttu* 'to felicitate, bless'). This development helps explain how **tt* and **pp* came to develop into transitive suffixes within Proto-Dravidian. In Type III, pre-Tamil or Proto-South Dravidian totally lost the inflectional meaning of **nt*: *(n)tt*, and the stem was remade retaining only the voice difference. This last type is apparently the latest of the three.

25.	DEDR		Past intransitive	Past transitive
Type I	5093	**mēy* 'graze'	*mēy-ntu*	*mēy-ttu*
Type II	5372	**wāẓ* 'live, flourish'	*vāẓ-ntu*	*vāẓ-ttu* 'felicitate, bless'
Type III	3251	**tir-* 'be correct'	*tiruntu* (*tirunt-i*) 'be changed'	*tiruttu* (*tirutt-i-*) 'rectify'
	368	**ar* : *ar*-V- 'be full'	*aruntu* (*arunt-i*) 'eat, drink' (tr.)	*aruttu* (*arutt-i*) 'feed' (caus.)

6.5. Extended stems with **nk* : **nkk*, **mp* : **mpp* must, then, go back to a much deeper chronological stratum within Proto-Dravidian, since none of the descendant languages preserves **nk* : **nkk* in the non-past. Telugu provides indirect evidence for **mpp* (non-past tr.) presupposing a corresponding **mp* (non-past intr.). Therefore, wherever these suffixes are found in extended stems their history is to be traced by extending the logic or parallel developments of the dental series.

Alveolar and retroflex outcomes, wherever they occur (cf. Ta. *curuḷ* 'to curl up', past *curuṇṭ* (v.i.) : *curuṭṭ* (v.t.) < **curuḷ-nt-* : **curuḷ-ntt*), are to be taken as sandhi variants of the dental suffix. Note that *curuṭṭu* belongs to Type II above; it acts as remade stem only in the transitive.

There is no evidence to set up an independent palatal series of *(c)* : *nc* : *ncc* for Proto-Dravidian since the series is derivable through palatalization of dentals following front vowels—a widely inherited dialectal change within Proto-Dravidian.

We have noticed that, when the tense signification is lost, **tt* and **pp* came to be interpreted as mere transitive suffixes within Proto-Dravidian. Tamil generally has *pp* after roots of Class IV ending in *i* and *y*, and *tt* after others. Other languages have generalized one or the other through a combination of phonological and morphological criteria. What is interesting is that **tt*, **pp*, **kk* in derived nouns carry transitive meanings, while **t/nt*, **k/nk*, and **p/mp* carry intransitive meanings. Consider the following examples:

26. DEDR	Verb and Noun	Verbal noun
277	Ta. *aẓi* (*-v-*, *-nt-*) 'to perish'	tr. *aẓippu* 'loss'
	(*-pp-*, *-tt-*) 'to destroy'	intr. *aẓimpu* 'evil deed'
		intr. *aẓivu* 'destruction'
	Ma. *aẓiyuka* 'to be sold, etc.'	intr. *aẓivu* 'expense'
		tr. *aẓicc-al* (< *aẓi-tt-al) 'expense'
	Te.	tr. *ḍappi* 'destruction'

314	Ta. *aṟi* (*-v-*, *-nt-*) 'to know'	intr. *aṟivi* 'knowledge'
		aṟivai 'wisdom'
		tr. *aṟi-kkai* 'notice'
	Ma.	intr. *aṟi-vi* 'knowledge'
	Ko.	intr. *aru* 'sense'
		intr. *aṟkym* 'information given'

7. Earlier Studies on Primary Derivatives

7.1. Following Gundert, Caldwell states that Dravidian roots are monosyllabic and of two types—vowel-final and consonant-final (1956: 197). Caldwell calls the extension elements following the roots 'formative suffixes':

> These particles seem originally to have been the formatives of verbal nouns, and the verbs to which they are affixed seem originally to have had the force of secondary verbs, but whatever may have been the origin of these particles, they now serve to distinguish transitive verbs from intransitives and the adjectival form of nouns from that which stands in an isolated position and is used as nominative. (198)

Caldwell further states, 'it seems to have been euphony only that determined which of the consonants *g*, *ś*, *ḍ*, *d*, or *b* should be affixed as a formative to any particular verb or noun'. As regards VR-suffixes (V+*r*, *l*, *ḷ*, *w*, *ẓ*, etc.), Caldwell tries to derive some of these from two independent roots **il* 'house', **uḷ* 'to be' (1956: 208–9), but this remains a mere guess in the absence of clinching comparative evidence.

7.2. Kui-Kuvi-Pengo-Manḍa have 'special forms' of the verb which add the derivative suffixes *-k-*, *-p-/-v-/-b-* to express what Winfield calls 'modes of plural action,' viz. 'one person doing a number of things, one person doing one thing many times, more than one person doing a number of things, more than one person doing one thing many times' (Winfield 1928: 142–3). In Kuvi, the plural action stem is formed by adding *-k-* or *-p-* to a verb stem 'to express an action done . . . repeatedly, thoroughly, intensively, etc.' (Israel 1979: 147–51). In Pengo the corresponding constructions are called 'intensive-frequentative' (Burrow and Bhattacharya 1970: 82–5). Koṇḍa also has traces of such stems which were wrongly interpreted as 'reflexive' (Krishnamurti 1969: 278–9). Examples are: Kui *kat-a-* 'to cut down' : plural action/intensive *kat-ka*, Kuvi *kaṭ*: *kat-k*, Pe. *kat-* : *kat-ka*, Koṇḍa *kat-k-* : *kat-ki* [*DEDR* 1208]; Kui-Pe.-Manḍa *kā* (*kā-t-*) 'to wait, watch': plural action/intensive, Kui-Pe. *kā-pa* (cf. Ta. *kā-pp-*, *kā-tt-* 'to watch, guard', *DEDR* 1416).

After conducting a comprehensive comparative study of such constructions, Emeneau concludes:

> PD had a system of plural action stem derivation with a set of allomorphs including **-kk-*, **-pp-* and **-p-/-v-*; the distribution of these allomorphs is still a problem. This system appears as a retention in the closely related subgroup made up of Pengo-Manḍa and

Kui-Kuwi. All the other languages lost the system but retained some of the derived stems, either paired with the basic simplex or some other derivative therefrom, or in isolation (plurale tantum). (1975: 17)

7.3. In terms of the hypothesis of this paper, 'plural action/intensive-frequentative' is considered an innovative meaning given to the morphs **-p-*[w/b]/**-pp-* and **-kk-* which came to represent non-past tense and voice (intr./tr.), after they had lost their original grammatical function. This conclusion is supported by the following arguments:

(1) The 'plural action/intensive' markers are strikingly similar to the older tense-voice markers, cf. Ta. *aḻu* (*aḻu-v-*, *aḻu-t-*) 'cry, weep, lament', Te. *ēḍ-* (*ēḍ-w-*, *ēḍ-c-*): Koṇḍa *aṛ-ba-* (without corresponding simplex **aṛ-*) 'to weep', Kui *ṛīva* (*ṛī-t-*) id. : *ṛī-va* also plural action; Pe. *aṛ-* (*aṛ-t-*) 'to weep' : intensive *aṛ-ba-* (PD **yāḻ-/yaḻ-V-*, *DEDR* 282). Similarly, Kui-Pe. *in-ba* 'to say' corresponds to the Tamil non-past stem *eṉ-p-* [en-b] 'to say' (PD **yan*, *DEDR* 868). Note that Kui-Pe. *kā-pa* (plural action) 'to wait, watch' looks unmistakably like the Tamil future *kā-pp-* (< **kā-pp-*); see above.

(2) In Kui, there are four conjugation classes whose infinitives end in *-a*, *-pa*, *-va*, and *-ba*, respectively. Compare the past forms of the four classes as opposed to the infinitive and present participle in the following paradigms:

Class	Infinitive	Past	Present participle
I	*aḍ-a* v.i. 'to joint'	*aḍ-it-*	*aṭ-ki*
II	*aṭ-pa* v.t. 'to join together'	*aṭ-t-*	*aṭ-pi*
III	*ā-va* v.i. 'to become'	*ā-t-*	*ā-i* (with sandhi loss of *-v-*)
	gi-va v.t. 'to do'	*gi-t*	*gip-ki*
IV	*ēṇ-ba* v.t. 'to receive'	*ēṭ*	*ēṇ-bi*

The plural action base is formed by adding *-ka-* to Class I. For the other classes, the same augments *-pa-*, *-va*, and *-ba*, that are found in the infinitive and present participle of the corresponding simplex verbs also serve as plural action stem formatives. The resulting stems then are inflected like Class I stems; i.e. in contrast to the simplex verbs, the augments are not dropped in the past tense; cf. *lep-ka* (< *lek-pa-* by metathesis) 'to break' (conjugation 2), past *lek-te* 'I broke' vs. plural action stem past *lepk-ite* (< *lek-p(a)-ite*) 'I broke up (a number of times)' (Winfield 1928: 143). The double function of the same augments as markers of non-past (infinitive, present participle) and of plural action reflects their older historical meanings, as well as their later innovated ones.

(3) Burrow and Bhattacharya (1970: 83) note that in Pengo 'a fair number of intensive forms in *-pa-* and *-ba-* occur without any corresponding simple forms', e.g. *ī-ba* v.i. 'to bathe', *īt-pa* v.t. 'to bathe'. This is also true of Kuvi and Koṇḍa; cf. Israel (1979: 150), Krishnamurti (1969c: 278, 279). Burrow and Bhattacharya further state

> the intensive *-pa* is commonly added to causatives, without apparently adding much to the sense, and in some cases it is more commonly used than the simple causative, e.g. *ācpa-* 'feed'

which is more frequently used than the simple *cā̆c-*. In some cases only the form of the causative occurs, e.g. *hātpa-* 'to extinguish'. (84)

The causative of **tin* 'to eat' in South-Central Dravidian is **tī̆ṯṯ-* 'to feed' (where **ṯṯ* > Koṇḍa *R*, Kui *s*, Pengo *c*). Koṇḍa *tīR-pis*, whose *-pis* is a causative suffix, corresponds to Kui *tī̆s-pa* and Pe. *cā̆c-pa* (plural action). It thus appears that the Kui-Pengo plural action suffix *-pa* is structurally parallel to the Proto-Dravidian causative morph **-ppi*. Kui-Manḍa, which have lost the causative suffix **-pi/*-ppi*, must have reinterpreted its reflex *p* as both a causative and an intensive/frequentative (or 'plural action') morph.

The above arguments show that the Proto-Dravidian non-past transitive morphs **-kk-* and **-p-/-pp-* (as well as caus. **-pi/-ppi*) have developed a new meaning in the Kui-Manḍa subgroup as the result of a shared innovation.

8. Conclusions and Outlook

8.1. The findings of this paper can be summarized as follows:

Proto-Dravidian monosyllabic verb roots became disyllabic and trisyllabic by the incorporation of what have come to be called 'formative suffixes' or 'primary derivatives'.

Such derivative suffixes evolved in several stages within Proto-Dravidian:

In the first stage they were inflectional suffixes signalling both tense and voice. The intransitive suffixes became transitive by the doubling of their final stop. The non-past suffixes are intr. **p, *mp, *k, *nk* : tr. **pp, *mpp, *kk, *nkk*; the past suffixes, intr. **t, *nt* : tr. **tt, *ntt*. This system is preserved in a subgroup of South Dravidian: Tamil, Malayāḷam, Toda, Kota, and Koḍagu. (In Tamil, such verbs belong to Class IV of the *Tamil Lexicon* or Class II of Arden 1976: 148.)

Because of the sound change *NTT > TT affecting most languages (except Telugu and Kannaḍa in some cases), TT came to replace both T and NT as the corresponding transitivizer. This led to the obsolescence of NT in the case of non-past **nk, *mp* which became incorporated as mere formatives of monosyllabic and disyllabic Proto-Dravidian bases. While losing their tense meaning, the elements still retained a trace of their original voice function by rendering intransitive the stems into which they were incorporated, cf. e.g. **kā-nku* 'to boil', **ala-nku* 'be agitated', **tir-umpu* 'to turn'.

In some languages the pairing of related intransitive : transitive stems in terms of the NT : (N)TT alternation was disrupted. This is true of Kannaḍa and Tuḷu of South Dravidian, Telugu of South-Central Dravidian, and all the Central and North Dravidian languages. Where the suffixes *NT (> D) and *NTT (> NT/T) have lost their derivational matching, they have also lost their derivational meaning as voice markers.

The elements **(n)tt* and **(m)pp* isolated from the transitive past and non-past of the earliest derivational stage of Dravidian became mere transitive suffixes within Proto-Dravidian and were inherited by the descendant languages of different subgroups.

The Proto-Dravidian causative suffix **ppi* followed by the markers **ntt* (past) and **mpp* (non-past) gave rise to OTe. *-incu/-impu*, Ka. *is(u)/ip(u)* incorporating the older tense signs with loss of meaning. Some languages of South-Central Dravidian (Gondi, Koṇḍa) use *-is/-pis/-bis* very productively in forming transitive-causative stems.

Evidence for the incorporation of tense suffixes into verb stems as formatives is available in all the Dravidian languages, when inflected stems from different Dravidian languages are compared. The South Dravidian languages preserve both primary roots and extended forms in a large number of cases.

Some of these 'formatives' have innovated, new derivational meanings in Kui-Kuvi-Pengo-Manḍa as 'plural action' or 'frequentative' morphs.

Proto-Dravidian verbal roots as well as extended stems in most cases also occur in nominal function. Such nominals are derived from verbs and therefore originally convey the intransitive : transitive contrast, as attested by many of the south Dravidian languages. There are also nouns which are not related to verbal roots but whose stems are not formally different from the verb-derived ones, such as **mar-u-ntu* 'medicine' possibly related to **mar-am* 'tree'. Members of the suffix series V, R, T, NT, TT, NTT may occur in languages in different combinations in producing extended stems:

27. *DEDR* 240:

Root+V	+ Suffix	
al-a	CC-(V)-	*al-a-nk-u* (v.i.) 'to shake'
	V-CC-VR	*al-a-nk-a-l* (n.) 'commotion'
	R-CC-V-R	*al-a-y-tt-a-l* (n.) 'wandering'

8.2. A parallel for the developments postulated in this paper can be found in Indo-Aryan. In the evolution of the Modern Indo-Aryan languages from Middle and Old Indo-Aryan there are many established cases of older tense morphs losing their meaning and becoming parts of the remade verbal bases (Beames 1966: 32–98):

28.		OIA		MIA		NIA
	Skt.	*upa-viṣṭa* 'seated'	Pkt.	*uvaviṭṭho* *uvaiṭṭho* *vaiṭṭho*	H.	*baiṭh-* 'to be seated'
	Skt.	*pakva-* 'cooked'	Pālī, Pkt.	*pakko*	H.	*pak-* 'to be cooked'
					P.	*pakka*
					B. G.	*pak*
					Mar.	*pīk*

Similarly, Hindi *sun* 'to hear' incorporates the nasal infix of Skt. *śṛṇoti* 'he, she, it hears'.

The historical developments in Indo-Aryan are clear, transparent, and well understood. They provide excellent support for this paper's account of the much less straightforward situation in Dravidian.

18

Patterns of Sound Change in Dravidian

The major sound changes in Dravidian are classified into Historical and Typological. The historical changes are classified into (a) those internal to Proto-Dravidian, and (b) innovations confined to major branches, sub-branches, and individual languages, e.g. palatalization of velars, *c* > *s* > *h* > Ø, umlaut, apical displacement, etc. Some of these are common in human languages and others peculiar to Dravidian. Typological changes include the unconditional merger of PD **ñ*- and **y*- with *n*- and Ø-, the gradual merger and elimination of PD **ṯ* yielding a five-point stop system, the emergence of two syllable types CV̄C and CVCC, and single–double stop contrast becoming voiced–voiceless contrast. These changes have led to convergence between Dravidian and Indo-Aryan phonological systems within the Indian linguistic area. Criteria for distinguishing the historical from the typological have been stated. It is proposed that typologically motivated changes in phonology tend to be more regular than the products of historical change.

1. Introduction

The twentieth century has seen remarkable progress in comparative Dravidian studies, mainly in the area of phonology. The major contributors to this development are K. V. Subbiah, L. V. Ramaswami Aiyar; T. Burrow, M. B. Emeneau, Bh. Krishnamurti, P. S. Subrahmanyam, K. Zvelebil, and N. Kumaraswami Raja. The publication of *A Dravidian Etymological Dictionary* by Burrow and Emeneau (1961, revised edition 1984) has both inspired and facilitated much of the research on comparative phonology during the past three decades. Although some problems still

I am grateful to M. B. Emeneau and H. H. Hock for their valuable comments on this paper when it was first presented at a symposium on Language and Prehistory in South and South-east Asia organized by the Center for South Asian Studies at the University of Hawaii at Manoa in March, 1995. I express my gratitude to the Director of the Center for South Asian Studies, Professor Cromwell Crawford, the Executive Committee of the Center and the Dean of SHAPS for selecting me for a Watumull Fellowship which made it possible for me to spend the spring of 1995 at the University of Hawaii in the stimulating company of many eminent linguists. I must express my thanks to Ms Karina Bingham, for her help in converting, editing, and laser-printing this paper in time for the Symposium. Thanks are due to Brett Benham of the University of Texas at Arlington for incorporating the final corrections and revisions.

remain unsolved, we now have a reliable knowledge of the phonological system of Proto-Dravidian and the processes of sound change which have shaped the modern Dravidian languages. These have not been presented in a systematic manner in any one place, and therefore have not attracted the attention of historical and comparative linguists at large.

The Dravidian phonological changes (in the form of rules) are organized in this paper in two categories—historical and typological. The historical ones are subclassified as: (a) changes internal to Proto-Dravidian, (b) phonological innovations shared by one or more subgroups, (c) innovations shared by more than one language within a subgroup, and (d) innovations peculiar to individual languages. The typological changes are classified as follows: (a) unshared common changes which cut across different subgroups with a common direction and output, e.g. **ḷ*, **ṇ* to *l*, *n* in South-Central, Central, and North Dravidian, (b) universal changes, i.e. processes found in several language families in the world, e.g. *s* > *h*, palatilization of velars, vowel harmony, etc., (c) changes predominantly found in the South Asian area, e.g. assimilative retroflexion, (d) changes peculiar to the Dravidian family, e.g. apical displacement, or to certain subgroups within Dravidian.

The twenty-four or so Dravidian languages are divided into four geographic-cum-genetic subgroups, i.e. South Dravidian: Tamil, Malayāḷam, Koḍagu, Toda, Kota, Iruḷa, Kannaḍa, Tuḷu; South-Central Dravidian: Telugu, Gondi, Koṇḍa (Kūbi), Kui, Kuvi, Pengo, Manḍa; Central Dravidian: Parji, Kolami, Naiki, Ollari and Gadaba; North Dravidian: Kuṛux, Malto, Brahui. The South (SD I) and South-Central (SD II) have developed from an original major branch, which I call Proto-South Dravidian [see Fig. 21.1].

2. Historical Changes

2.1. *Proto-Dravidian*

Proto-Dravidian had ten vowels, *i e a o u* plus their long counterparts, and sixteen consonants, as shown in Table 18.1. In addition, a laryngeal **H* is needed for some reconstructions.

TABLE 18.1. *Proto-Dravidian consonants*

Obstruents	p	t	ṯ	ṭ	c	k	
Nasals	m	n		ṇ	ñ		
Laterals			l	ḷ			
Flap/Tremulant			r				
Frictionless continuant				ẓ			
Semivowels	w				y		(H)

Proto-Dravidian roots have the shape (C)V_1(C), i.e. V_1, CV_1, V_1C, CV_1C (V_1 = long or short). There are some bases of (C)V_1CC-type contrasting with (C)V_1C. There are no prefixes in Dravidian. Alveolar and retroflex consonants do not begin a word. Any consonant can occur as C_2 root-finally, other than **ñ*. Word-initial **y* and **ñ* occur only before **ā̆*/**ē̆* which is an archiphoneme. Word-initially **w* is not followed by rounded vowels. All consonants except *r* and *ẓ* can be geminated post-vocalically. The vowel-final roots may take formative suffixes of the shape C, CV, CCV, CCCV. Roots ending in C take formative suffixes of the above types preceded by V_2 = *a, i, u*. A base-final stop is followed by an enunciative *u*. There are no consonant clusters word-initially. Post-vocalic clusters are either geminates or sequences of nasal (N) + stop (P) (+ stop (P)). The obstruents had lenis allophones when intervocalic [w d ḏ/ṟ ḍ s g]; after a nasal, they were voiced stops, and geminates were always voiceless. Except for Tamil and Malayāḷam and to some extent Toda, the descendant languages have maintained this pattern, but have also developed word-initial voicing and aspiration through sound changes and borrowing from Indo-Aryan.

A study of etymologies from languages cutting across genetic subgroups shows stem alternations which recur in derivation and inflection requiring their reconstruction in Proto-Dravidian. On the basis of verb-inflection which is preserved intact in Old Tamil with reflexes in other subgroups, the following sandhi processes can be reconstructed within Proto-Dravidian.

Rule 1. Apical Obstruent Formation

a. l + t → ṯ
l + tt → ṯṯ
l + nt → nṯ
l + ntt → nṯṯ

b. n + t → nṯ
n + tt → nṯṯ

c. ḷ + t → ṭ
ḷ + tt → ṭṭ
ḷ + nt → ṇṭ
ḷ + ntt → ṇṭṭ

d. ṇ + t → ṇṭ
ṇ + tt → ṇṭṭ

These are all apparently cases of reciprocal assimilation producing alveolar and retroflex consonants secondarily. There are, however, many more lexical items in which alveolar and retroflex obstruents are primary. The following alternations are attested and distributed widely in different subgroups:

Rule 2a. Alternations **l*: **ṯ*: **ṯṯ*: **nṯ*

1. PD **nil* (past *ninṯ-*) 'to stand': SD: Ta. *nil* (*ninṟ-*), Ma. *nil* (*ninn-*), Ko. *nil-*/*nin-* (*ninḏ-*), To. *nil-* (*niḏ-*), Ka. *nil* (*nind-*), Koḍ. *nil-* (*nind-*). PD **nil* (past *niṯṯ*): SCD:

Go. *nil* (*nitt-*), Koṇḍa *nil-* (*niR-*). PD *nil (past *nil-tt-*): Ka. *nil* (*nilt-*); CD: Pa. Oll. Gad. *nil-* (*nilt-*), Kol. Nk. *nil-* (*nilt-*); SCD: Pe. *nil* (*nilt-*), Manḍa *li-* (*lit-*); ND *il-* (*il-c-*). PD *niṯ- (< *nil-t-): SD: Ta. Ma. *niṟu* 'to put, place'. PD *niṯṯ-: SCD: Go. *nitt-/nit-* 'to stand', Kui *nisa* (*nist*); CD: Pa. *nit-* (*nit-it-*) [*DEDR* 3675].

Another such case is *kal (*kaṯṯ-*) beside *kaṯ- 'to learn', the former in South Dravidian and the latter in South-Central and Central Dravidian. Note that in the above cases, *niṯ, *niṯṯ, and *kaṯ are represented as bases within Proto-Dravidian, perhaps restructured with the past suffix incorporated as a derivative at a later stage, still within Proto-Dravidian. Such alternations are also noticed in non-verbs, e.g. PD *kil/*kiṯ-V 'small' with cognates in South and South-Central Dravidian [*DEDR* 1577, 1594].

2. PSD *kil- (*kiṉṯ-*) 'to be able'. Tamil and Malayāḷam have cognates. The Tamil present-tense suffix *-kiṟ-/-kiṉṟ-* is traced to this root (Steever 1993: 172–8) [*DEDR* 1570].

3. PD *el, *eṉṯu 'sunshine, sun': SD, SCD, and CD [*DEDR* 829, 869].

4. PD *niṯ-V- 'to be full': SD: Ta. Ma. Ko. To. Ka. Tu.

PD *niṉṯ- v.i. 'to be full', *niṉṯṯ-* v.t. 'to fill': SCD: Te. Go. Koṇḍa, Kui, Kuvi, Pe., Manḍa; ND: Kuṛ. Malto [*DEDR* 3682].

Rule 2b. Alternations *ḷ: *ṭ: *ṭṭ: *ṇṭ

5. PD *koḷ (*koṇṭ-*) 'to receive, seize, buy': SD: Ta. Ma. *koḷ* (*koṇṭ-*), Ko. *koḷ-/koṇ-* (*koḍ-*), To. *kwïḷ-* (*kwïḍ-*), Koḍ. *koḷḷ-* (*koṇḍ-*), Ka. *koḷ-* (*koṇḍ-*), Tu. *koṇ-* (*koṇḍ-*); SCD (past *koḷ-ntt-): Te. *kon-* (*koṇṭ-*), tr. *kolupu*, Koṇḍa *koṛ-/kol-* (*koṇ-*, *koṭ-*), Kui *koḍa* (*koḍi*), Kuvi *koḍ-* (*koḍ-it-*), Pe. *koṛ- koṛ-t-*, Manḍa *kṛag-* (*kṛakt-*); CD: Kol. Nk. *kor-/ko-* (*kott-*) [*DEDR* 2151].

Similarly, PD *kaḷ- (*kaṭṭ-*) 'to steal', *kēḷ- (*kēṭṭ, kēṇṭṭ-*) 'to hear, ask', *wēḷ (*wēṇṭ-, wēṇṭṭ*) 'to desire, want', *kāṇ- (*kaṇṭ-*) 'to see' are widely represented in different subgroups.

Contraction of two syllables into one, i.e. $(C_1)V_1C_2\text{-}V_2\text{-}$ to $(C_1)\bar{V}_1\text{-}$ (where C_2 is *y, *w, or *k) is reconstructable to PD, e.g.

Rule 3. Syllable Contraction

$$(C_1)V_1\left\{\begin{matrix} y\\ w\\ k\end{matrix}\right\}\text{-}V_2\text{-} > (C_1)V_1[+\text{long}]$$

6. PD *tiy-am > *tē-m/*tī-m 'honey'. PSD *tey-am > *tē-m*: Ta. Ma. *tēṉ*, Ko. *tēn*, To. *tȫn*, Koḍ. *tēnï*, Ka. *tēnu*, *jēn*. Tu. *tīya*; SCD: Te. *tēne*, Go. Koṇḍa *tēne*; CD *tiy-am > *tī-m:* Pa. Oll. Gad. *tīn* (Kol. Nk. borrowed *tēne* from Telugu); ND *tiyam > *tīn:* Kuṛ. *tīn-ī* 'bee', Malto *tēni* 'honey, bee' [*DEDR* 3268b].

Other such cases are *tok-al > *tō-l 'skin, peel' [*DEDR* 3559], *mical/*miy-al >

**mē-l* 'above, high' [*DEDR* 5086], **kic-ampu* > **kiy-ampu* > **kē-mpu/kī-mpu* [*DEDR* 2004]. Note that the last case has *ī* and not *ē* as expected in Central and North Dravidian.

All Dravidian languages carry evidence of alternation between heavy and light root syllables, when a 'formative' vowel follows as V_2, or when a monosyllabic root becomes disyllabic:

$$(C)\bar{V}_1C : (C)V_1C\text{-}V_2\text{-}$$
$$(C)V_1CC : (C)V_1C\text{-}V_2$$

Contrasting with the above, there are non-alternating pairs like:

$$(C)V_1C : (C)V_1C\text{-}V_2\text{-}$$

Therefore, in the neutralizing environment, i.e. -V_2, a heavy syllable is said to have merged with a light syllable, by internal reconstruction within Proto-Dravidian.

Rule 4. Quantitative Variation

$$(C)\bar{V}_1C\text{-}/(C)V_1CC\text{-} > (C)V_1C\text{-}/\#\_\_\_+V_2\text{-}$$

7. PD **pāṯ-*: **paṯ-*V- 'to run, flee': SD: Ta. Ma. *pāṟu*, *pāṟ-a*, Ko. *parn-*, To. *pöṟ*, Ka. *pāṟu*, *paṟi*, Koḍ. *pār*, Tu. *pāruni*; SCD: Go. *parī-*, Te. *pāṟu*, *paṟacu*, Kui *pāsk-*, Kuvi *prāḍ-* [*DEDR* 4020].

8. PD **cupp*: **cuw-ar* (< **cup-ar*) 'salt': SD: Ta. Ma. Ka. Tu. Te. *uppu*, Ko. To. *up*, Koḍ. *uppï*, also Ta. *uvar* 'to taste saltish, brackish', n. 'brackishness, saltishness', Ma. *uvar*, n., Ka. *ogar*, Te. *ogaru* 'astringent taste', Tu. *ubarï*, *ogarï* 'brackishness'; PSCD **cow-ar*: Go. *sovar*, *sawwor*, *hovar*, *ovar* (dial.), Koṇḍa *sōru*, Kui *sāru*, Kuvi *hāru*, Pe. *hōr*, Manḍa *jār*; CD: Kol. Nk. *sup*, Pa. *cup*, Oll. *sup*, Gad. *cuppu* [*DEDR* 2674].

The isogloss of *c*-loss also includes Telugu, but not the other languages of South-Central Dravidian (see Rule 6).

G. Sambasiva Rao suggested that Rule 4 operates systematically if the underlying and derived forms belong to the same grammatical class, e.g. both verbs, or both nouns, etc. (for further details, see Postscript to Chapter 1).

3. Sound Changes in Subgroups

3.1. *South and South-Central Dravidian*

Rule 5. Umlaut

$$\text{PD} \quad {}^{*}\begin{bmatrix} i \\ u \end{bmatrix} > \begin{bmatrix} e \\ o \end{bmatrix} /\#(C)\_\_\_C+a \text{ (Proto-South Dravidian)}$$

When Proto-Dravidian *-V_2 is [+low], the preceding root vowels which are

[+high] become mid [–high, –low] in Proto-South Dravidian (i.e. SD or SD I and SCD or SD II), e.g.

9. PD **tur-a-* 'to push, drive away': SD: Ta. Ma. *tura, turattu* v.t., n. *turappu*, Ka. Tu. *dobbu* (< *tor-pp-*); SCD: Te. *trōcu, drobbu*, Go. *ro-, ropp-* (< *tro-*), Kui, Kuvi *trō-* (*trō-t-*); CD: Pa. *turkip-* (*turkit-*), Gad. *tu-rus key-, turuyp-* [*DEDR* 3340].

10. PD **wil* 'to sell', **wil-ay* n. 'price': SD: Ta, *vil* v., *vil-ai* n., Ma. *vil* v., *vilai* n., Ko. *vel* n., To. *pïl* n., Ka. *bil* v., *bele* n., Koḍ. *bele* 'cost', Tu. *bilè, belè* n.; SCD: Te. *wil(u)cu* v., *wela* n. [*DEDR* 5421].

Old Tamil and Malayāḷam had changed these mid-vowels to high vowels and again to mid-vowels in modern times. In the above examples Ta. Ma. *i, u* are derived from PSD **e, *o*, respectively (see below under South Dravidian, Rules 8a and 8b).

Rule 6. Deaffrication and Sibilant Reduction

- **a.** PD **c* > **s*/#___V (Proto-South Dravidian, Proto-Central Dravidian, irregular)
- **b.** SD **s* > **h* > Ø/#___V (*h*-stage is prehistoric)
- **c.** SCD **s* > *h*/#___V (Gondi-Kui-Kuvi-Pengo-Manḍa dial.)
- **d.** *h* > Ø/#___V (Hill Maṛia and Koya dial. of Gondi)

In South Dravidian **c* is phonetically represented as [ś] in spoken Tamil, [s] in Kannaḍa, Tuḷu, and non-standard Telugu; in Central Dravidian it is [c] in Parji, [c/s] in Gadaba, and [s] in Kolami, Naiki and Ollari. In South-Central Dravidian all languages except Telugu have [s]. It is assumed here that those lexical items which had *s*-variants at the reconstructed stage in South Dravidian changed [s] to [h] which tended to become Ø. This rule was shared by South and South-Central Dravidian, although Telugu, because of the areal influence, goes with South Dravidian in losing **c* in cognate items. In Middle Indo-Aryan *s* becomes *h* in Sinhala (non-finally), e.g. *satta* > *hatta* 'seven'; palatal *c* becomes *s* regularly, e.g. *chā(y)ā* > Sinh. *seya* 'shade' (Masica 1991: 205–7). This is certainly an areal trend involving Dravidian and Indo-Aryan.

11. PD **ciy-*/**cī-* 'to give': SD: Ta. Ka. *ī*; SCD: Te. *icc-/iy-/ī-*, Go. *sī-, hī, ī-*, Koṇḍa *sī-, si-*, Kui *sī-, jī, hī-*, Kuvi *hī-*, Pe. *sī-*, Manḍa *hī-*; CD: Kol. *sī-*, Nk. *s'ī-*, Pa. *cī-*, Oll. Gad. *sī*, ND: Kuṛ. *ciʔ-* (*cicc-*), Malto *ciy-* (*cic-*) [*DEDR* 2598]. Also cf. 8 above.

3.1.1. South Dravidian (SD I)

Rule 7. Palatalization

PD **k* > *c*/#___V [–back]C [–retr.] (Tamil, Malayāḷam)

12. PD **key* 'to do, make': SD: Ta. Ma. *cey*, Ko. *key, gey*, To. *kïy*, Koḍ, *key*, Ka. *key, gey*, Tu. *gey*; SCD: Te. *cēyu*, Go. *kī-*, Koṇḍa *ki-*, Kui *ki-/gi-*, Kuvi *kī*, Pe. Manḍa *ki-*; ND: Br. (*kann-*), pres. tense *kē-* [*DEDR* 1957].

Rule 8. Dissimilation and Umlaut

a. $\begin{bmatrix} {}^{*}e \\ {}^{*}o \end{bmatrix} > \begin{bmatrix} i \\ u \end{bmatrix}$ /#(C)___(C)+*a*- (Old Tamil, Malayāḷam)

b. $\begin{bmatrix} i \\ u \end{bmatrix} > \begin{bmatrix} e \\ o \end{bmatrix}$ /#(C)___(C)+*a*- (spoken Tamil, Malayāḷam)

The output of Proto-South Dravidian Rule 5 is input to Rule 8a; the output of 8a is input to 8b. In 8–10, 13 and 14 PD **e*, **o*[C-*a* > PSD **e*, **o*[C-*a* > pre-Tamil *i*, *u* [C-*a* (see Ch. 2).

13. PD **weḷ*-V-, PSD **weḷ-a*-, PSD I: **weḷ-a* 'to shine': Ta. *veḷi* adj. 'white', *viḷ-aṅku* v.i., Ma. *veḷi* 'light', *viḷ-aṅṅuka* v.i., Ko. *veḷ*, To. *pöḷ* adj., Ka. *beḷagu* v. and n., Te. *welūgu* v. and n.; all other subgroups point to **weḷ* [*DEDR* 5496].

14. PD **col*-V-, PSD **col-ay*, PSD I: **col-a*/**ol-a* 'fireplace, furnace': Ta. *ulai*, Ma. *ula*, Ka. *ole*, Koḍ. *ole*, Tu. *ule*; SCD: Koṇḍa *solu*, Kui *soḍu*, Pe. *hol*; CD: Pa. *colŋgel* (*kel* 'stone') 'fireplace' [*DEDR* 2857].

3.1.1.1. Changes in individual languages

A. Consonants

Rule 9. Nasal Assimilation

NP [NB] > NN/#(C)V___V, (C)VCV___V (Middle Malayāḷam, mainly in velar, palatal, dental, and alveolar series; also in Koḍagu in a few cases. For details, see Subrahmanyam 1983: 309–12.)

15. PD **ponku* 'to boil': SD: Ta. *ponku* [poŋgu], Ma. *poṅṅu*, Ka. *pongu*, Koḍ. *poŋŋ*-, Te. *pongu* [*DEDR* 4469].

Rule 10. Deaffrication

PSD I **c* > *t*/#___V (Toda regularly; Tuḷu dialectally)

16. PD **cuṭu* 'to be hot': SD: Ta. Ma. *cuṭu* (*cuṭṭ*-) 'to be hot', Ka. *suḍu* (*suṭṭ*), Koḍ. *cuḍ* (*cuṭṭ*), Tu. *suḍu*, *tuḍu*: To. *tuṛ* (*tuṭṭ*) [*DEDR* 2654].

Rule 11. Labial Spirantization

p > *h*/#___V (Old Kannaḍa within historical period)

17. PD **pāl* 'milk': Ka. *pāl*, *hāl* [*DEDR* 4096].

Rule 12. Labial Glide to Stop

w > *b*/#___V (Old Kannaḍa within historical period; ? extended to Koḍagu and Tuḷu through diffusion). See 10.

There are numerous changes of consonants in Toda and Kota, both synchronically and diachronically, which have not been treated here owing to constraints of space; also several changes of Tuḷu and Koḍagu are skipped.

B. Vowels

Rule 13. Vowel Assimilation (assimilation of a vowel to an adjacent vowel and/or consonant)

i. *Umlaut*

a. $\begin{bmatrix} e \\ o \end{bmatrix} > \begin{bmatrix} i \\ u \end{bmatrix}$ /#(C)___C-*i*/*u* (Kannaḍa)

18. PSD **keṭ-u* (*keṭṭ-*) 'to perish': Ka. *kiḍu* (*keṭṭ-*) [*DEDR* 1942].

19. PSD **koṭ-u* 'to give to 3rd person': Ka. *kuḍu* (*koṭṭ-*) [*DEDR* 2053]. The underlying mid-vowels in Kannaḍa can be recovered through internal reconstruction.

b. $\begin{bmatrix} o \\ \bar{o} \end{bmatrix} > \begin{bmatrix} e \\ \bar{e} \end{bmatrix}$ /#(C)___C-*e* (*-*e* > *-*ay*; pre-Kota). The final vowel -*e* is lost after the sound change. Exceptions abound. See Emeneau (1994).

20. PSD **koṭ-ay* 'umbrella': Ta. *kuṭai*, Ma. *kuṭa*, Ka. *koḍe*: Ko. *keṛ*, *koṛ* [*DEDR* 1663].

c. $\begin{bmatrix} u \\ \bar{u} \end{bmatrix} > \begin{bmatrix} i \\ \bar{i} \end{bmatrix}$ /#(C)___C(C)-*e* (pre-Kota).

21. PSD **kupp-ay* 'heap': Ta. *kuppai*, Ma. *kuppa*, Ka. *kuppa*: Ko. *kip* (< **kipp-e* < **kupp-e*) [*DEDR* 1731a].

d. $\begin{bmatrix} a \\ \bar{a} \end{bmatrix} > \begin{bmatrix} o \\ \bar{o} \end{bmatrix}$ /#(C)___C_2-V_2 (V_2 is not *-*a*/*-*ay*; for the short vowel C_2 is [–alveolar, –nasal]; pre-Toda).

22. PD **kaṇ* 'eye': To. *koṇ* [*DEDR* 1159(a)]; here there is no **ay* in the second syllable.

23. PSD **pakal* 'day': To. *poxol* (C_2 is non-alveolar) [*DEDR* 3805]; elsewhere PD **a*, *ā* remain (see Subrahmanyam 1983: 54–60).

ii. *Labialization*

e. $\begin{bmatrix} i \\ \bar{i} \\ e \\ \bar{e} \end{bmatrix} > \begin{bmatrix} u \\ \bar{u} \\ o \\ \bar{o} \end{bmatrix}$ /#(C_1)___C_2-V_2 (C_1 = labial stop, C_2 = retroflex or alveolar **ṯ*; V_2 = [–low]; pre- Koḍagu, Tuḷu)

24. PSD **piṭ-i* 'catch'; n. 'handle': Koḍ. *puḍi*, Tu. *puḍi*,

iii. *Vowel-lowering*

f. *e* > *a*/#C_1___C_2-*a*/*ay* (C_1 = **k*, **c*, **p*; C_2 = retroflex; pre-Koḍagu)

25. PSD I **piḷ-ay* 'child': Koḍ. *paḷḷe* [*DEDR* 4194].

iv. *Vowel centralization*

g. $\begin{bmatrix} i \\ \bar{i} \\ e \\ \bar{e} \end{bmatrix} > \begin{bmatrix} \ddot{i} \\ \bar{\ddot{i}} \\ \ddot{e} \\ \bar{\ddot{e}} \end{bmatrix}$ /#C_1___C_2-V (C_1 is not labial or palatal, C_2 = retroflex or **ṯ*; pre-Koḍagu)

26. PSD **kiḷi* ~ **kiṇi* 'parrot': Ta. *kiḷi*, *kiḷḷai*, Ma. *kiḷi*, Ka. *giḷi*, *giṇi*: Koḍ. *gïṇi*.

h. [*e*] > [*ö*]/#C_1___C_2 (C_2 = [–alveolar]; pre-Toda)

27. PSD I **etir* 'opposite': To. *öθïr* [*DEDR* 795]; SD **eṇṭṭ* 'eight': Ta. *eṭṭu*, Ka. *eṇṭu*: To. *öṭ* [*DEDR* 784].

i. $\breve{\bar{e}} > \breve{\bar{ö}}$ /#C_1___C_2- (C_2- is not (C)y); pre-Toda)

28. PSD **cēr (cēr-nt-)* 'to reach': To. *sȫr* (*sȫd-*).

j. *i* > *ï*/# C_1___C_2 (C_1 or C_2 is not a palatal or sibilant)

29. PSD **iru* 'to be': Ta. *iru* (*iru-nt-*), To. *ïr* (*ïθ-*) 'to sit, live'.

v. *Back vowel fronting and rounding*
k. *u* > *ü*/#C_1___C_2-V_2 (C_2=**y*, or V_2 = [–back, +high]; pre-Toda)

30. PSD **puli* 'tiger': Ta. Ma. Ka. *puli*; To. *püsy* [*DEDR* 430].

vi. *Glide formation*

l. $\begin{bmatrix} o \\ \bar{o} \end{bmatrix} > \begin{bmatrix} wạ \\ w\bar{ä} \end{bmatrix}$ /#(C_1)___C_2-*ay* ($C_1 \neq p$; pre-Toda)

m. $\begin{bmatrix} o \\ \bar{o} \end{bmatrix} > \begin{bmatrix} wï \\ w\bar{ï} \end{bmatrix}$ /#(C_1)___C_2-*i*/*u*/ (pre-Toda)

31. PSD **oṭ-ay* 'to break': Ta. *uṭai*; To. *waṛ* (*waṛ-θ*) [*DEDR* 946].

32. PD **onṭu* 'one'; Ta. *onṟu*; To. *wïḏ* [*DEDR* 990(d)].
vii. *Dissimilation*
n. *u* > *ï*/#C_1___C_2-V_2 (C_1 or C_2 is [+labial] and V_2 = [+low]; pre-Toda)

33. PD **puẓ-ay*, PSD **poẓ-ay* 'hole': Ta. *puẓai*, Ma. *puẓa*, Ka. *poẓe*; To. *pïṭ* 'drainage hole in wall' [*DEDR* 4317].

The above changes show how vowels are influenced in their quality by adjacent vowels or consonants or both, creating variation between features such as front–back, high–low, and rounded–unrounded. Since Toda and Kota have lost the conditioning factors (most of the non-initial vowels and sometimes the original consonants), changes have to be recovered (only) from earlier historical stages by applying the comparative method. (For a detailed discussion of these changes, see Subrahmanyam 1983, Emeneau 1994.)

3.1.2. South-Central Dravidian (SD II)

Rule 14. Apical Displacement

a. $(C_1) \begin{bmatrix} a \\ e \\ o \end{bmatrix} C_2\text{-}a\text{-} > (C_1)C_2 \begin{bmatrix} \bar{a} \\ \bar{e} \\ \bar{o} \end{bmatrix}\text{-}$

$$\textbf{b.}\ (C_1)\left[\begin{matrix} i \\ e \\ o \\ u \end{matrix}\right] C_2 + \left\{\begin{matrix} i \\ u \end{matrix}\right\} > (C_1)\, C_2 \left[\begin{matrix} \bar{i} \\ \bar{e} \\ \bar{o} \\ \bar{u} \end{matrix}\right] \text{-}$$

$$\textbf{c.}\ (C_1)\left[\begin{matrix} i \\ e \\ a \\ o \\ u \end{matrix}\right] C_2 \left\{\begin{matrix} i \\ u \end{matrix}\right\} C_3\text{-} > (C_1)\, C_2 \left[\begin{matrix} i \\ e \\ a \\ o \\ u \end{matrix}\right] \text{-Ø-}C_3C_3\text{-}$$

(Conditions: 1. C_1 = Ø; C_2 = [+apical, –nasal], i.e. *_ṭ_, *_r_, *_l_; *_ṭ_, *_ḷ_, *_ẓ_: All languages of South-Central Dravidian; 2. C_1 = *_p_, *_t_, *_c_[s], *_m_, *_w_; C_2 = *_ṯ_, *_r_, *_ẓ_: Telugu and Koṇḍa; 3. C_1 = *_p_, *_t_, *_c_[s], *_k_, *_m_, *_n_, *_w_ or Ø; C_2 = [+apical, –nasal]: Kui, Kuvi, Pengo, Manḍa)

Rules 14a–c represent an atypical sound change or complex of changes innovated by the members of the South-Central (SD II) branch of Proto-South Dravidian—Telugu, Gondi, Koṇḍa, Kui, Kuvi, Pengo, and Manḍa. This is an areally and lexically diffused sound change which shifted intervocalic apical consonants of Proto-Dravidian to the word-initial position (not allowed in Proto-Dravidian) and also created word-initial consonantal clusters with apicals as second members (also not allowed in Proto-Dravidian). As we proceed from south to north and east (Kui, Kuvi, Pengo, Manḍa), the structural conditions widen and more and more lexical items become involved in the change. Gondi and Koṇḍa are much less affected by these changes than the others. A subsequent series of sound changes simplified the clusters by dropping either C_1 or C_2 in different languages (for details, see Krishnamurti 1978a; Ch. 10 of this volume). In 14a–b, the root vowel V_1 and suffix vowel V_2 are contracted to lengthen V_1. In 14c, the unaccented suffix vowel V_2 is lost in heavy syllables.

34. PSD *_ūẓ_/*_uẓ-u_ 'to plough'. SCD (SD II): OTe. _ḍukki_ 'ploughing' (> Mdn. _dukki_), Go. _uṛ-_, Koṇḍa, Kui, Kuvi _ṛū_, _rū_, _lū-_, Pe. Manḍa _ṛū_ (PD *_ūẓ_/*_uẓ-u_) [_DEDR_ 688].

35. PSD *_carac_/*_tarac_ 'snake'. SCD (SD II): OTe. _trācu_ (> Mdn. _tācu_) 'cobra', Go. _tarāsh_, _taras_, Koṇḍa _saras_ (dial. _srāsu_), Kui _srās_, _srācu_, Kuvi _rācu_, Pe. _rāc_, Manḍa _trehe_ (cf. Ta. Ma. _aravu_ 'serpent') [_DEDR_ 2359].

Rule 15. Retroflex-Alveolar Merger

PD *_ṭ_ > *_ṯ_/#(C)V̆___ ; [–anterior, +apical] > [+anterior] (South-Central Dravidian). Even post-nasal *_nṯ_ is involved in this change.

36. PSD *_nāṭu_ 'country, village, location, cultivated land'. SD I: Ta. Ma. _nāṭu_, To. _nōṛ_, Ko. _nāṛ_, Ka. _nāḍu_; SCD *_nāṯu_ [nāṟu] (Te. _nāḍu_), Go. _nār_ (pl. _nāhku_), Koṇḍa _nāṟu_ (pl. _nāRku_), Kui _nāju_ (pl. _nāska_), Kuvi _nāyu_, Pe. _nāz_, _nās_, Manḍa _nāy_ (obl. _nāṭ-_) [_DEDR_ 3638].
In Telugu, only a few lexical items are affected by this change.

Rule 16. Retroflex Mergers and Deretroflexion

a. $\left\{ \begin{matrix} ẓ \\ ḍ \end{matrix} \right\}$ > *ṛ*/#C_1___ (All South-Central Dravidian languages except Telugu; Kui has *ḍ*-, if C_1- is Ø).

b. *ḷ* > *l*/#C___(Kui dial.)
> *ṛ*/#C___(All South-Central Dravidian except Telugu and Koṇḍa)
> *ṇ*/#C___(Kuvi dial; where C = *m*)

c. *l* > *r*/#C___(Pengo, Manḍa, sometimes Kui-Kuvi; all retain *l* if C=Ø)

37. PD **puẓ*-V- 'worm, insect': OTe. *pruwwu, purwu*, MTe. *purugu*, Go. *puṛi*, Koṇḍa *piṛvu* (pl. *piṛku*), Kui *pṛiu* (pl. *pṛīka*), Kuvi *prī*- (*prīka*) [*DEDR* 4312].

38. PD **kaḷ-am* 'threshing floor': Go. *kaṛā*, Koṇḍa *kaṛan, kalan*, Kui *klai*, Kuvi *kṛānu*, Manḍa *kāṛa* [*DEDR* 1376].

Rule 17. Cluster Simplification

C_1 > Ø /#___C_2 . . . Three developments:

a. where C_1 = *n* and C_2 =**l* or **ẓ*, C_1 is lost in pre-Gondi-Koṇḍa-Kui-Kuvi-Pengo and Manḍa;
b. where C_1 = *s* (< **c*-) or **w*-, and C_2 = **r*, pre-Gondi-Kuvi-Pengo-Manḍa lose C_1 (irregular sound change);
c. where C_1 = an obstruent /p t k/ and C_2 = **ṟ* (< *-*ṯ*-), pre-Gondi, pre-Koṇḍa, and Kuvi-Pengo-Manḍa lose the initial consonant (irregular sound change; **ṟ*- > *j*-/*d*- in Kuvi-Pengo-Manḍa).

(For examples, see Ch. 10, item 4; Ch. 12, items 10, 11; Ch. 18, item 35 above. Telugu loses C_1 in two cases where C_1 = **w*, e.g pre-Telugu **war-a*- (inf. of *war*- 'to come') > **wrā*- > *rā*- in Old and later Telugu; OTe. *wrāyu* 'to write' > Middle and Mdn. Te. *rāyu*. Elsewhere, Telugu loses C_2 (not C_1), when C_2 = **r*, **ṟ*, **ẓ* all of which became *r* (< **r*) even by the pre-literary period, e.g. Ote. *prā̃ta* 'old' > *pāta*; for further examples, see §§ **9.1** and **9.2** of Ch. 1. Also see Rule 19 below.)

Rule 18. Mid-vowel-lowering in Kui-Kuvi

$\left\{ \begin{matrix} \bar{e} \\ \bar{o} \end{matrix} \right\}$ > *ā*/#(C)(C)___ (The mid-vowels must have resulted from vowel contraction with a low vowel -*a*- as -V_2 in the original form, e.g. PSCD **sow-ar* 'salt' > *sōru* in Koṇḍa, but *sāru* in Kui and *hāru* in Kuvi; see Rules 3 and 14).

3.1.2.1. Changes in individual languages

Rule 19. Apical Mergers

a. SCD $\left\{ \begin{matrix} ẓ \\ ṯ[r] \end{matrix} \right\}$ > *r*/#C___ (Early Old Telugu)

b. SCD **ẓ* > *ḍ*/#___ (Old Telugu)

c. OTe. *ṯ*[*ṟ*] > *r*/#___(Middle and Modern Telugu)
d. OTe. *ḍ* > *d*/#___ (Middle and Modern Telugu)
e. OTe. *r* > Ø/#C_1___ (Middle and Modern Telugu)

Sub-rules 19c–e operate on apicals resulting from displacement rules 14a–c and 19a–b.

Rule 20. Palatalization

a. PD **ay* > *ē*/#(C)___ (pre-Telugu)
b. PD **k* > *c*/#___[+V, –back] (pre-Telugu). This rule is independent of a similar rule (Rule 7 above) in Tamil and Malayāḷam. The palatalizing environment includes *ē* resulting from 20a; the following retroflexes do not inhibit palatalization as in Tamil-Malayāḷam.

Rule 21. Sonorant Deretroflexion

$\begin{bmatrix} ḷ \\ ṇ \end{bmatrix} > \begin{bmatrix} l \\ n \end{bmatrix}$ /#CV___(Old Telugu). Even geminated ones are affected by this change. It appears to be an areal change in South-Central, Central, and North Dravidian (see below).

3.2. *Central Dravidian*

There are no significant shared sound changes in Central Dravidian. The ones which need mention refer to C_2-obstruents which are treated separately. A single PD **ṯ*[*ḏ*] is represented as a stop, i.e. *d*/*ḍ* in Kolami, Naiki, and Parji, further softened to *y* in Ollari and Gadaba. PD **ẓ* develops to *ṛ* in the Parji-Ollari-Gadaba subgroup, to *r* in Kolami and to *l*, *ṛ*, *y* in Naiki (Chanda). Word-initial **n*- is generally lost in Kolami-Naiki as a shared innovation.

3.2.1.1. *Changes in individual languages*

Rule 22

a. Low Vowel Raising

PCD $\begin{bmatrix} {}^*a \\ {}^*\bar{a} \end{bmatrix} > \begin{bmatrix} e \\ \bar{e} \end{bmatrix}$ /#(C)___[+C, +alveolar] (pre-Parji)

b. Sonorant Deretroflexion

PCD $\begin{bmatrix} {}^*ḷ \\ {}^*ṇ \end{bmatrix} > \begin{bmatrix} l \\ n \end{bmatrix}$ /#(C)V___(pre-Parji)

c. Alveolar Merger with Dental or Retroflex Reduction

PCD $\begin{bmatrix} {}^*\underline{tt} \\ {}^*n\underline{t} \end{bmatrix} > \begin{bmatrix} tt/ṭṭ \\ nd/nḍ \end{bmatrix}$ /#CV___ (Parji in different dialects).

The above three are chronologically ordered rules. The vowel-raising Rule 22a took place before 22c; 22a will not apply to the output of 22b; e.g. PCD **kal* > Pa. *kel* 'stone', PCD **man* > Pa. *men* 'to be', but PCD **kaḷam* > Pa. *kali* 'threshing floor', PCD **kaṇ* > Pa. *kan* 'eye', PCD **waṯ* > Pa. *ved-p* (*ved-t-*) 'to dry'.

3.3. *North Dravidian*

Rule 23.

a. Velar Spirantization
PD **k* > *x*/#___V[–high] (Kuṛux, Malto, Brahui)

39. PD **kaṇ* 'eye': Kuṛ. Malto Br. *xan* [*DEDR* 1159(a)].

b. Velarization of Palatal
PD **c* > *k*/#___ V [+back, +high] (North Dravidian, irregular)

40. PD **cuṭu* 'be hot': Kuṛ. *kuṛ* (*kuṭṭ-*), Malto *kuṛe* 'embers' [*DEDR* 2654].

3.3.1.1. *Changes in individual languages*

Rule 24. Denasalization

$$\text{PND} \quad \begin{bmatrix} {}^{*}n \\ {}^{*}m \end{bmatrix} > \begin{bmatrix} d \\ b \end{bmatrix} /\#\_\_\_\text{V}[-\text{back}] \text{ (pre-Brahui)}$$

Rule 25. Mid-vowel Loss

$$\text{PND} \quad \begin{bmatrix} {}^{*}e \\ {}^{*}o \end{bmatrix} > \begin{bmatrix} i/a/\bar{e}/ \\ i/a/\bar{o} \end{bmatrix} /\#(\text{C})\_\_\_\text{(pre-Brahui)}$$

Brahui lost the short mid-vowels under the areal influence of Baluchi, etc.

41. PD **ne(y)tt*-V- 'blood': Br. *ditar* [*DEDR* 3748].
42. PD **mēy* 'to graze': Br. *bei* 'grass fit for grazing' [*DEDR* 5093].

3.4. *Patterns of Change of Intervocalic Obstruents*

It is not possible to find consistently shared innovations in the case of intervocalic consonants, particularly the obstruents. Therefore, they are depicted as patterns in Fig. 18.1 with an indication where they appear to be shared ones. The most common reflex is shown in bold.

4. Typological Classification

4.1. *Unshared but widespread changes*

A number of sound changes have occurred or are occurring in contiguous languages at different times, producing a final result, which, if we looked back after many years, would give the impression that they were shared innovations. These are different from the sound changes discussed so far in two respects: (a) they do not have a fixed definable time frame, except that they are all post-Proto-Dravidian; (b)

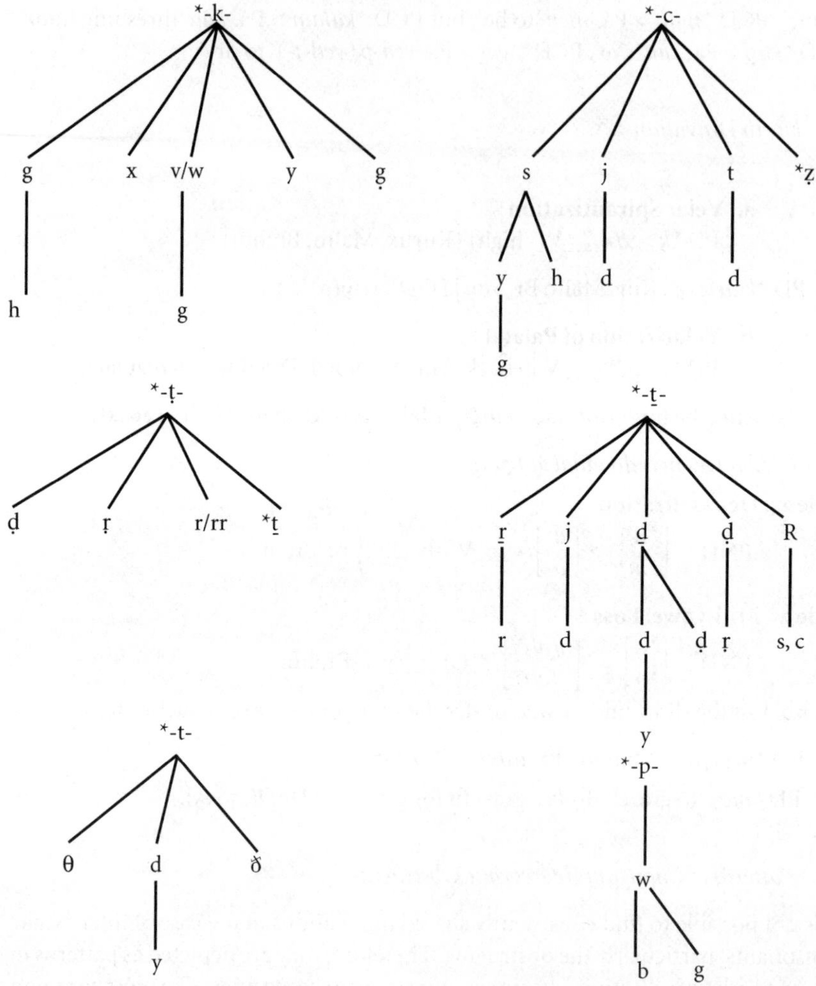

FIGURE 18.1. Developments of Proto-Dravidian intervocalic obstruents

there is evidence that they have been occurring in different languages at different times; some are ongoing; (c) they cut across the subgroups set up on the basis of shared innovations; (d) it seems possible that their spread can be defined in terms of broad geographical regions. For these reasons, they are not formulated as rules below, although it is possible to do so.

(1) PD root final *-ay* develops to *ĕ* and *ĭ* in almost all South-Central, Central, and North Dravidian languages (see etymologies 11 and 12 above).

(2) PD **y-* is lost in all languages except Old Tamil; Modern Tamil and Malayāḷam also do not have it. The vowel following **y-* was *Ă, which is represented

as *e*/*ā* in South Dravidian, as *ē*/*ā* in South-Central Dravidian, as *a*/*ā* in Central Dravidian, and as *e*/*ē* in North Dravidian. Similarly PD **ñ* merged with *n* in all languages except in Malayāḷam which retains some items with **ñ* but not all.

(3) PD **ẓ* is lost in all languages consequent on splits and mergers during historic times, except in Standard Tamil and Malayāḷam. In Parji of Central Dravidian, it develops to *ṛ* distinctively. It merges in different languages with *ḍ ṛ l ḷ r y š ṣ θ*. No clear isoglosses seem possible.

(4) PD **ṇ *ḷ* became deretroflexed as dental/alveolar *n l* in South-Central, Central, and North Dravidian. They are internally reconstructable in certain languages of South Central and Central Dravidian. All South Dravidian languages preserve them. The change, however, is a sweeping one.

(5) PD **ṯ*, **ṯṯ*, **nṯ* are preserved only in Toda and Kota and, to some extent, as *ṯṯ* in Malayāḷam in South Dravidian and in Koṇḍa in South-Central Dravidian. In the rest of the languages, *ṟ* merged with the flap *r* and *ṯṯ*, *nṯ* with dental *tt*, *nd* or retroflex *ṭṭ*, *ṇḍ*. Some of these changes are datable within the literary languages; no common historical stage can be postulated.

(6) Two syllable types have become normalized in all languages except Tamil and Malayāḷam, viz. (C)VCCV or (C)V̄CV. A number of phonological changes have occurred leading to this typological goal. Such a shift is also evidenced in Indo-Aryan (Krishnamurti 1991a, Masica 1991: 187–8, 198). PP > P, NP > B/#(C)V̄___ is part of this strategy. Loss of a high vowel *i u* in the medial (unaccented) syllable has led to the creation of disyllabic forms from underlying trisyllabic ones, e.g. **mar-untu* 'medicine': Te. *mandu*, Ka. *maddu*, *mardu*, Pa. *merd-* (< **mar-nt-*). Consequent on changes in canonical shapes, obstruent voicing became phonemic in almost all the languages except Tamil, Malayāḷam, and Toda, as follows:

PD	*P-	*-P-	*-PP-	*-NP-	*-NPP-
post-PD	?	-B-	-P-	-NB-	-NP-

The initial position is filled by secondary voicing and through borrowings from Indo-Aryan. The older single vs. double contrast became voiced vs. voiceless.

(7) PD **w-* > *b-* in Kannaḍa, Koḍagu, and Tuḷu in South Dravidian and in Kuṛux and Malto of North Dravidian. A similar sound change is found in Indo-Aryan in the Northern and Eastern languages, viz. Hindi, Rajasthani, Nepali, Bihari, Bengali (Masica 1991: 202).

4.2. *Some suggestions on areal types*

The elimination of the alveolar in all its occurrences has led to the emergence of a five-point obstruent system in most of the languages, which has then produced a common Indo-Aryan–Dravidian type in phonology. Secondary retroflexion of dentals in word-initial position though assimilative changes in South-Central, Central, and North Dravidian is another type which looks suspiciously Indo-Aryan. The opposite tendency is noticed in the case of retroflex sonorants, word-initial or non-initial retroflexes—*ḷ ṇ ẓ*; they merged with alveolars in Central, South-Central, and North Dravidian. Apical displacement (Rule 14) seems to be the only atypical Dravidian development.

4.3. *Observations and questions to be addressed*

(1) Most of the historically identifiable shared innovations have exceptions. The typologically motivated ones are extremely regular (those in §4.1 as opposed to the changes proposed as rules).

(2) It is likely that shared innovations generally spread through lexical diffusion. Typologically triggered sound changes spread without exception but are spatially gradual.

(3) Is it necessary or possible to make a distinction between these two types of changes? What are the implications of such a distinction to the comparative method?

Questions of this kind have not been seriously addressed by language typologists and historical linguists. It is claimed that typology imposes certain constraints on reconstructed states of a language or a family in order to make it conform to what is plausible in human languages (Fox 1995: 250–60).

What is claimed here is that certain changes (mainly sound changes) are motivated or caused by system-internal pressures and such changes tend to be much more regular than the changes caused by sporadic shifts in the speech habits of speakers. For instance, in Dravidian, the palatalization of a velar before front vowels (Rules 7, 20) is a change of this latter kind. There is nothing system-internal to this change, although it may have brought about changes in the distribution of certain phonemes. But the replacement of PD **ṯ* either by a dental **t* or retroflex **ṭ* is typologically motivated; hence its spread is sweeping and there are hardly any exceptions after its operation.

In Austronesian languages, Proto-Oceanic had word-final consonants as well as vowels, while some of the derived subfamilies and languages became totally vowel-ending in two ways: (a) either the final consonants are lost, or (b) an 'echo vowel' which harmonizes with the preceding vowel is added, e.g. (a) Proto-Oceanic **manuk* 'bird' > (South-east Solomonic languages) *manu*; similarly, **ikan* 'fish' > *iγa, iʔa*, **niuR* 'coconut' > *niu*; (b) > (North-west Solomonic languages) *manuyu*; *viyana, iana*; *niunu*, respectively. Final vowels of Proto-Oceanic remain in the derived languages, **bebe* 'butterfly' > South-west and North-west Solomonic languages *bebe*, **kutu* 'louse' > *γutu, utu* (communication from Robert Blust and Malcom Ross, the latter mainly for the examples). What is important to note is that the vowel-ending descendant languages have no items being retained as consonant-ending. This is a case of a regular typological change. These could have been shared innovations (I have not checked!), but still they were clearly typologically motivated or triggered.

19

Evidence for a Laryngeal *_H_ in Proto-Dravidian

0. Old Tamil records of the early Christian era (3rd century BC to 3rd century AD) noted the occurrence of a phoneme called _āytam_ with some kind of _h_- colouring in about a dozen lexical items. _Tamil Lexicon_ transliterates it as _ḵ_, transcribed here as _ḥ_. Its distributional properties include the following: (a) _ḥ_ generally occurs after a short vowel; (b) it lengthens the preceding vowel compensatorily; (c) it is assimilated to the following voiceless stop; (d) it is lost before voiced consonants; (e) it alternates with the semivowels *_y_ and *_w_ under certain statable conditions. After examining the developments of the roots involved in definite cases like Old Tamil _aḥtu_ 'that one', _iḥtu_, 'this one', and _paḥtu/pattu_ 'ten', _ḥ_ was traced to a Proto-Dravidian laryngeal *_H_. By examining a number of cases in Dravidian with similar phonological behaviour, I have attempted to show that a Proto-Dravidian laryngeal *_H_ would explain the developments of several lexical and grammatical items with aberrant phonology, better than heretofore. These include: (a) the root for the numeral 'three' (_*muH-_); (b) eight irregular and high frequency verbs like _*caH-_ 'die', _*taH-_ 'bring', _*waH-_ 'come', etc.; (c) eight pairs of nouns and verbs alternating in vowel length, e.g. _*kōḷ_ 'seizure': _*koḷ_ 'to hold', both from _*koHḷ_; (d) seven sets of personal pronouns _*yaH-n_: _*yaH-m_, etc. in which the length variation between the nominative and the oblique stems can be explained; and finally, (e) the Early Proto-Dravidian or pre-Dravidian negative morpheme in verb inflection was reconstructed as _*aHa(H)_ which remained _*aHa(H)_ in Proto-South Dravidian, Proto-Central Dravidian, and Proto-North Dravidian, but became _*Ha(H)_ in Proto-South-Central Dravidian. Tentative rules of sound change involving a laryngeal have been framed for Early Proto-Dravidian. A PD *_H_ thus solves several difficult problems in comparative Dravidian phonology.

A laryngeal is a _h_-type of sound (presumably a fricative or more likely a frictionless continuant) like the semivowels _y_ and _w_ which are characterized by the feature complex [–syllabic, –consonantal][1]. In Proto-Indo-European, 'most scholars

I am grateful to M. B. Emeneau, George Cardona, Hans Hock, Henry Hoenigswald, Kamil Zvelebil, Sanford Steever, and F. B. J. Kuiper for their valuable opinions and comments on the earlier version of this paper. Not all of them agree with all that is said in the paper. The purpose of this paper is to invite discussion and constructive criticism from Dravidian scholars and historical linguists.

[1] Regarding the subgrouping of the Dravidian languages adopted in this paper and for further supporting evidence on PD *_H_ since 1963, see Krishnamurti 1969a, 1976a, 1985, and 1991a.

now agree that the parent language had one or more additional stop or spirant consonants for which the label laryngeal is used. These consonants, however, have mostly disappeared or have become identical with other sounds in the recorded Indo-European languages, so that their former existence had to be deduced mainly from their effects on the neighbouring sounds . . . Probably, there were three or four, which can be written H_1, H_2, H_3 (and H_4), and probably some or all of them are palatal or (labio-)velar spirants. The principal traces they left outside Anatolian are in the quality and length of neighbouring vowels . . . All laryngeals lengthened a preceding vowel.' (*The New Encyclopaedia Britannica* 1977, 'Languages of the world: Indo-European languages', vol. 9: 434–5). H_2 (and H_4) changed a neighbouring *e* to *a* and H_3 changed it to *o*. In Anatolian H_2 and H_3 remained *h* in some positions. Some laryngeals disappeared between consonants leaving a vowel instead, e.g. PIE **st*H_2*tis* > Skt. *sthitis*, Greek *stasis*. Ablaut (vowel gradation) is also explainable in terms of laryngeals, e.g. **ste*H_2-: Greek *stā*- 'stand', *H_3*ek*^{w}-: Greek *op*- 'see', **g*^{w}*i*H_3*wós*: Latin *vīvus* 'alive'. Though the laryngeal theory has not been accepted by Indo-Europeanists in its entirety, the need to reconstruct some laryngeals is no longer disputed.

1. Ancient Tamil *āytam*. Krishnamurti proposed a laryngeal **H* for Proto-Dravidian as early as 1963 while reviewing in *Language* (39, 556–64) the first edition of Burrow and Emeneau's *A Dravidian Etymological Dictionary* (1961). He proposed that PD **H* had a relic reflex in the peculiar sound called *āytam* [āydam] in Early Tamil, traditionally written with three small circles $\overset{\circ}{\circ\circ}$ bearing similarity to Sanskrit *visarga* $\overset{\circ}{\circ}$. This sound is transliterated as k̲ by *Tamil Lexicon*. I prefer to transliterate *āytam* as *ḥ*. Even by the time of Tolkāppiyam (early Christian era), the earliest Tamil grammar, this sound was becoming archaic because of its restricted distribution in Tamil phonology and also because of the controversies surrounding its phonetic and phonological status. The description of its characteristics by Tolkāppiyam and its commentators can be summarized as follows (Subrahmanya Sastri 1934: 64–70, Swaminatha Aiyar 1975: 282–4):

1.1. It was not included in the thirty sounds (from *a* to *ṉ*) of the Tamil alphabet. The sound called *āytam* was included among the so-called 'secondary sounds', short *u*, short *i* and *āytam*. Unlike short *u* (high back unrounded vowel) and short *i* (high central unrounded vowel), *āytam* contrasts with other consonants and its absence, e.g. *iḥtu* 'this one, *itti* 'a plant', *itaẓ* 'a petal', etc. Consonants were referred to as *puḷḷi* in Tolkāppiyam and Tolkāppiyanār referred to *āytam* as a *puḷḷi* three times (Balasubramanian 1976: 577–8).

1.2. 'It appears after a short vowel and before a voiceless consonant followed by a vowel, and its place of production is determined by that of the consonant in whose company it is' (Subrahmanya Sastri 1934: 66). In other words *āytam* is assimilated to the following voiceless stop, e.g. *eḥku*/*ekku* 'to rise, climb', *paḥtu*/*pattu* 'ten', although such assimilation is recorded only for certain items in Ancient Tamil.

1.3. It was classed neither as a vowel nor as a consonant. Subrahmanya Sastri thinks that Tolkāppiyanār must have been influenced by the behaviour of *visarga* in Sanskrit which was pronounced as a voiceless glottal fricative [x/ḥ] (*jihvāmūlīya*) before *k*, *kh* and as a voiceless bilabial fricative [ɸ] (*upadhmānīya*) before *p*, *ph*.

1.4. It also occurred in certain external sandhi situations as an alternant of *l* or *ḷ*, e.g. *kal # tūtu → kaḥṯītu/kaṯṯītu* 'the stone is bad', *muḷ # tītu → muḥṭītu/muṭṭītu* 'the thorn is bad' (non-case sandhi), *al # tiṇai → aḥṯiṇai/aṯṯiṇai* 'low class' (adjective + noun). Here gemination was the normal development and *ḥṯ* and *ḥṭ* represent a spelling convention, presumably to keep the identity of the conjoined words distinct (also Kuiper 1974: 206). According to Tolkāppiyam the point of articulation of *āytam* is the same as the following voiceless stop. Therefore, the same phonemic sequence is represented in two spellings.

1.5. The medieval and modern mode of reading an *āytam* is rather arbitrary and does not represent a continuous oral tradition, e.g. OTa. *eḥku* 'steel' is pronounced [ehɣï]; the late T. P. Meenakshisundaran wrote it as [exxï] but pronounced it as [eḥgï]. Early Tamil *aḥtu* 'that one', *iḥtu* 'this one' are now read by some as [ahïdï] and [ihïdï].

1.6. Most of the writers on *āytam* concentrated on how to interpret its role within the ancient Tamil phonological system and did not give a serious thought to Krishnamurti's interpretation of this phenomenon historically and comparatively. A. Chandrasekhar (1973, 1975) considered *āytam* as a stress accent in early Tamil. I could not understand his rationale on how such 'stress accent' could be integrated into the phonological system of Old Tamil. F. B. J. Kuiper (1958, 1974) considered *āytam* + voiceless stop as a variant spelling of a geminate, resulting from sandhi, viz. *l* + *t* → *ḥṯ*/ *ṯṯ*, *ḷ* + *t* → *ḥṭ*/*ṭṭ*. He also noted that not all geminate stops can be replaced by sequences of *ḥ* + voiceless stop, e.g. Ta. *ciṟṟ-eli* 'mouse', *neṭṭ-eḻuttu* 'long vowel', *putt-ōṭu* 'new pot' (Kuiper 1958: 200).

2. Tamil *āytam* traced to Proto-Dravidian laryngeal **H*. Arguments are advanced below for setting up a Proto-Dravidian laryngeal **H* not only to account for *āytam* in Ancient Tamil but also to explain many other developments which have remained obscure until now both in comparative phonology and morphology of Dravidian.

2.1. Old Tamil *aḥtu* 'that one', *iḥtu* 'this one', *paḥtu*/*pattu* 'ten' are clear cases of the retention of PD **H* as /*ḥ*/ in early Tamil. Note that *āytam* /*ḥ*/ occurs only in the root-final position before a morph or word boundary. In early Tamil it occurred only before voiceless stops within a word, but this was not true of Proto-Dravidian, e.g. the demonstrative bases (adjectival) were **iH*, **aH*, **uH*, and the interrogative **yaH*. The short vowels were lengthened compensatorily when **H* was dropped, i.e. alternations **aH* ~ **ā*, **iH* ~ *ī*, etc. were present within Proto-Dravidian itself as evidenced by long vowels *ā* and *ī* in most of the descendant languages, e.g. Ta. Ma.

Ko. Ka. Tu., Te. Go. Kui-Kuvi-Pe. Kol. Nk. Pa. Oll. Gad., Kuṛ. Malto *ā* (adj.) 'that', *ī* 'this', in addition to Ta. *ap-poẓutu* 'that time', Te. *ap-puḍu* 'then', etc. in which *a*C-/*ā*-, *i*C-/*ī* reflect PD **aH*/*ā*, *iH*/*ī*. Similarly, **paH*-~**pā*- was attested in Old Tamil, e.g. *oṉ- pā-ṉ* 'nine'. In all such cases with two spellings in early Tamil *ḥt*/ *tt*, the *ḥt* spelling must be considered more archaic, representing an older pronunciation and spelling. Kuiper was not right in considering the geminate forms as original here (see Balasubramanian 1976: 573). Some scholars considered *av*-, *uv*-, *iv*- to be the underlying demonstrative roots in Old Tamil, e.g. *av yāṉai* 'that elephant', in which *av*- allomorph occurred before vowels and semivowels. They consider that *aḥtu* is through sandhi of *av*+*tu* which is patently incorrect (Meenakshisundaran 1965: 70–1, Balasubramanian 1976: 574), because there is no phonetic motivation for **w* (= Ta. *v*) to become *ḥ* before a voiceless stop. In the Caṅkam classics, *aht'* and *iht'* (followed by vowels) occurred with the highest frequency, eighty-nine times, and they were not represented as *attu* and *ittu*, anywhere. The latter spellings occurred in medieval Tamil (Kuiper 1958: 201). There were only seventeen instances of *ḥ*+ stop in external sandhi, e.g. *paḥ-ṟolai, paḥ-ṟalai*, etc. (Kuiper 1958: 205–6).

2.2. In the case of forms resulting from external sandhi, *kaḥ-ṯītu* and *muḥ-ṭītu*, there is no phonological justification for *l*, *ḷ* to become *ḥ* before an alveolar *ṯ* or a retroflex *ṭ*; also the fact that *ṯ* and *ṭ* occurred as second members presupposed the first members also to be the same *ṯ* and *ṭ* in assimilative sandhi. That was why Tolkāppiyam said that *ḥ* had the same point of articulation as the following voiceless stop. These are, therefore, a case of reverse or hyperstandard spellings of *ṯṯ* and *ṭṭ* to keep the morphological identity of the conjoined words. In this case Kuiper (1974: 206) is correct in interpreting the geminates as original and that the sequences *ḥṯ* and *ḥṭ* reflected a writing convention in Old Tamil; but his guess that this was true of all cases where an *āytam* was followed by a stop is not correct. Primary *ḥ* in Tamil is a reflex of PD **H*; secondary (sandhi derived) *ḥ* is a hyperstandard spelling and is, therefore, spurious.

2.3. Laryngeal **H* behaves like the other semivowels **y* and **w* and intervocalic **k* [ɣ] in producing compensatory lengthening of the preceding vowel in Proto-Dravidian, e.g. **tok-al* [toɣ-al] > **tōl* 'skin' [*DEDR* 3559], **tiyam*/**teyam* > **tīn*/**tēn* [*DEDR* 3268a and b] 'honey'. This criterion indicates the phonetic nature of the laryngeal that it was not a stop or spirant but a kind of semivowel, perhaps glottal in origin. It also explains the alternation of **H* with **y* and **w* in Proto-Dravidian and also in some of the descendant languages, although we are not sure of the conditioning factors.

2.4. PD **H* → **w*/___+*a*. This was a Proto-Dravidian rule which says that within a word when followed by -*a* across a morph boundary, the laryngeal alternated with a bilabial semivowel. This rule gave rise to the forms **aw-anṯu* 'that man', **aw-aḷ* 'that woman', **aw-ar* 'they (masc./hum.)', **aw-ay* 'they (non-masc./non-hum.)', and Old Tamil *av-aṇ* 'that place', but **a-tu* 'she/it', etc. In some of the languages, in the place of a long vowel like *ā*, *ī*, etc., there is evidence of an older segment surfacing as *h* or as a semivowel, e.g. Ta. *av-*, *iv-*, To. *ay-*[V, *a-*[C, Ma. *ay-*, Ka. *ah-a(n)ge/hā(n)ge* 'that manner', *ih-a(n)ge/hī(n)ge* 'this manner', *eh-a(n)ge/hē(n)ge* 'which manner' (medieval Kannaḍa from the 12th century; no satisfactory explanation is available for the *h*-element), Koṇḍa *aya-* 'that', *iya/yā* 'this'. In non-standard speech of Telangānā Telugu, the deictic bases are *ga-/gā*, *gi-/gī* (*gā* 'that', *gappuḍu* 'then', *ganta* 'that much' for standard *ā*, *appuḍu*, *anta*). The intrusive *g-* can only be related to some consonant (velar or glottal) that must have undergone metathesis as in Kannaḍa, possibly **ag(a)- puḍu* >*gappuḍu*, where *g* < **h* or **w*. In inscriptional Tamil of the 9th century *iht-eẓuti* was transcribed as *iyd-eẓudi* (Subrahmanya Sastri 1934: 68).

In South-Central Dravidian some dialects of Gondi show a *h-* in deictic bases freely alternating with a zero, *id/hid*, *iv/hiv*, *ad/had*, *av/hav* (Yeotmal, Adilabad). In Kuvi the deictic series from proximate to remote is *i e he hu*; Israel's (1979: 82–3) Kuvi dialect has *i e u he hu*. Kuṛux also has *isan/hisan* 'here', *iyyā/hiyyā* 'in this place', *asan/hasan* 'there', *ayyā/hayyā* 'in that place'; Pengo *he-* and *ha-* freely alternate with *e a* in the series *i e a* (Emeneau 1994: 307–9). Emeneau has shown that the Indo-Aryan languages of East India also have initial *h-* in demonstratives. In Munda *h-* is added before demonstratives to indicate 'farther distance'. In view of sharp distributional and meaning differences between Dravidian and these other languages, Emeneau has ruled out borrowing by Dravidian from them (311–12). Since, according to Emeneau, 'no reconstruction of PD *h* is possible for the demonstratives nor is *h* one of the PD phonemes', he considers the South-Central and North Dravidian instances of *h* as involving an 'expressive *h*'. Now with the reconstruction of a laryngeal **H* for Proto-Dravidian, which is anyway needed to explain *āytam* in Early Tamil, *h* in the deictics of South-Central and North Dravidian can be traced to the same source. Another plausible explanation is that several of the Dravidian languages which were in contact with Pāḷī and early Prakrits might still have *h-* in a fuller set of deictics, and thus influenced the Indo-Aryan demonstratives in some of the Prakrits of Eastern India, the Aśokan inscriptions and Sindhi (Emeneau 1994: 310)[2].

2.5. A third development of **H* (> OTa. *ḫ*) was its loss before consonants (perhaps the voiced sounds), e.g. OTa. *aḫt-/at-u* [ad-u], *iḫt-/it-u* [id-u], etc. The forms representing **H* > Ø can be reconstructed for Proto-Dravidian. As already mentioned, *aḫt(u)*, *iḫt(u)*, etc. were relic forms, only preserved in Early Tamil records; *at-u*, *it-u* occurred more frequently than the *-ḫt-* forms in Tolkāppiyam and early classics. Alternatively, we can apply the Proto-Dravidian rule

[2] Interestingly, citing my reconstruction of a laryngeal for PD deictics, McAlpin reconstructed **ah* 'that (not far)', **(h)ih-* 'this', **huh-* 'that (remote)' for Proto-Elamo-Dravidian to account for Middle Elamite *ahar* 'there', *hi*, *i* 'here', and *huh* 'thus' corresponding to PD **aH*, **iH*, and **uH* (1981: 81–2, A3–A6; also 26, § 221. 31 (5)). I am not, however, convinced of the connection between Dravidian and Elamite because the data base for comparison is highly limited.

VḥP/VPP → VP/___+V, (*ḥ* assimilates to the following P and, in effect, the sequence behaves like a voiceless geminate) where the added V was a formative and not a non-morphemic or enunciative *u*; in other words, *aḥt*-#V bears the same relation to *at*-V#C as *putt*-#V to *put*-V #C 'new' (see §§**1.6** and **3**).

2.6. The numeral 'ten' is the other lexical item noted with an original *āytam* in Old Tamil, viz. *paḥ-tu/pat-tu*. The Proto-Dravidian root was apparently **paH*- followed by the neuter suffix *-*tu*. The geminate form *pattu*, the lengthened form *pā-n* and the zero form *pa-tu, pa-n, -pa* were all fairly ancient, attested in South Dravidian. Tolkāppiyam records *iru-paḥtu* 'twenty', *eẓu-patu* 'seventy', *o<u>ṉ</u>-patu, o<u>ṉ</u>-pā<u>ṉ</u>* 'nine', *pa<u>ṉṉ</u>-iraṇṭu* 'twelve', *pat-i<u>ṉ</u>-o<u>ṉṟ</u>u* 'eleven' (Israel 1973: 64); there was another numeral compound *paḥ-pattu* 'ten tens = hundred', in which the root *paḥ*- occurred as a word [*DEDR* 3918]. Kannaḍa (medieval and modern) in addition to *pattu (-battu, -vattu)* has also an aspirated stop in the word for 'ten', *ombhattu* 'nine', *tombhattu* 'ninety' (AD 869; *SII* xi, Part 1, No.13, Gadag: *nū<u>r</u>atombhattu* 'one hundred and ninety') *eṇbhattu* 'eighty' (AD 1051; *Epigraphia Indica*, vol. 15, No. 60)[3]. An early literary work, Pampa Bhārata (10th century AD), uses *pay-in-chāsirvar* 'ten thousand persons', in which *pay*- is traceable to pre-Kannaḍa or PSD **paH*- with **H* becoming *y* (Ramachandra Rao 1972: 422). Kota has *pan*- 'ten' (for eleven to eighteen), Toda has *pon*- for numbers eleven to thirteen, Tuḷu has *patti, padun-, -pa, -va* for 'ten'. Telugu has several allomorphs *padi, -wadi* (Classical), *-phadi/ -bhadi, -bhayi* (inscriptional from the 7th century onwards: *ēmbhadi* 'fifty': Radhakrishna 1971: 249), *-phadi, -phay, -way, -bhay* (*mu-pphay* 'thirty', *nala-bhay* 'forty', *ē-bhay* 'fifty', *ḍe-bbhay* 'seventy', *ena-bhay* 'eighty', *tom-bhay* 'ninety', *ira-way* 'twenty', *ara-way* 'sixty'), *pan-neṇḍu* (< *pan-reṇḍu*) 'twelve' (modern standard). How can one interpret the aspirated *ph, bh* in Kannaḍa and Telugu unless one evokes an older *h*-element shift? This is the only native word which has an aspirated stop; elsewhere, aspirated consonants occur only in words borrowed from Indo-Aryan. Modern Telugu has other compounds (for fourteen to nineteen) in some of which -*h*- occurs as a hiatus preventer when the numeral 'ten' is followed by a vowel, e.g. *padh-nālugu* 'fourteen', *padi-h-ēnu* 'fifteen', *pada-h-āru* 'sixteen', *padi-h-ēḍu* 'seventeen', **padh-y-enimidi* [pajj(h)-enimidi, padd(h)-enimidi] 'eighteen', *pan-dhommidi* 'nineteen'. We see in these the shifting of *h* to the second or the third syllable, for which it is not possible to frame rules since these are idiosyncratic. However, the 'hopping' aspirate and alternation between long and short vowels in different languages can only be explained in terms of a *h*-like sound in the reconstructed root.

2.7. The frequency of use of the demonstratives and the numeral 'ten' in ancient Tamil classics is a tell-tale sign of the different degrees of the archaic nature of these forms, which were kept alive by tradition. The frequency of occurrence of the following items in ancient Tamil is based on *Index de mots de la litérature tamoule*

[3] I am indebted to Professor B. Ramachandra Rao for these two citations.

ancienne: *aḥtu* 128,? *attu* 23, *atu* 316; *iḥtu* 40, *itu* 173; *uḥtu* nil, *utu* 9; *paḥtu* 1, *oṉ-paḥtu* 4, *pattu* 35, *pat-iṉ-* 26, *-patu* in *oṉ-patu* 15, *oṉ-pāṉ* 11. These show clearly that *aḥtu* and *iḥtu* were the oldest spellings preserved; *uḥtu* does not occur at all, although it could have; in the case of 'ten' *pattu* is more frequent than the underlying *paḥtu*. In the case of the interrogative, there is no trace of the *āytam* being recorded, although the root behaved as though it derived from an older **yaH/*yāH*, e.g. *yāvaṉ* (< ? *yaH-/yāH-an*) 2, *yāvar* 55, *yātu* 75 (in early classics), *yār* 200+, *yāvatu* 18, *yāvat-um* 24, *evaṉ* 181; there are also forms in which *ḥ* was assimilated to the following voiceless stop, e.g. *ep-peyar* 'which name?', *ep-poruḷ*, *ev-vayiṉ* (Israel 1973: 48–53). Israel lists *uḥtu* but it is not found in the French concordance cited above.

2.8. The other lexical items which are recorded in Tolkāppiyam and Caṅkam anthologies with an *āytam*, recorded in *DEDR*, are as follows:

1. *DEDR* 252. Ta. *aḥku* 'to be reduced, Ka. *akkuḍ-isu* 'to become small' (suspected to be related to Ta. *alku* 'to shrink'); no other cognates are available; therefore, its reconstruction for Proto-Dravidian is not possible.

2. *DEDR* 765. Ta. *eḥku*, Ma. Ka. *ekku*, Te. *ēku* 'to card cotton', Pe. *ec-* 'id.', Kui *ēs-* 'to unravel', Pa. *ēk* 'to pick and throw away weeds'; it appears reasonable to reconstruct PD **eH-k-* because of **eH-* > *ē*, **Hk* > *kk*. It is also possible that PD **c* might have developed to **h*.

3. *DEDR* 766. Ta. *eḥku*, *ekku* 'to rise', Ma. Ka. Te. *ekku* 'to ascend, climb', Go. Koṇḍa *ek-*, Kui-Kuvi *eŋg-* 'id.', cf. *DEDR* 870 *ē* 'increase, abundance', Ta. Ma. *ē-ntu* 'to rise high', Te. *ē-cu* 'to increase' (< PD **eH-* 'to rise, increase').

4. *DEDR* 5528. Ta. *veḥ-ku* 'to desire ardently', *vēḷ* 'to desire' (<**weH-ḷ*), *vēṇ* n. 'desire', *vēṇṭu* 'to want', Ma. *vēḷ* 'lust', *vēṇṭum* 'it is desired', Ka. *bēḷ*, *bēḷku bēku* (< *bēkku*) 'it is wanted'; Te. *wẽḍu* (< **wēṇḍu*) 'to ask, want', *wẽḍ(u)ka* 'desire, pleasure, festivity', Go. *veṛkā* 'pleasure', Koṇḍa *vēṟika* 'festivity'; Kol.-Nk. *vēl* 'to ask', Pa. *veṛka* 'pleasure' (PD **weH-kk-*, **weH-ḷ*, **wēḷ*, **wē-ṇṭu* [< ***wēḷ* + *nt*]).

2.9. No other item with Tamil *āytam* has been included in the *DEDR* carrying cognates from other languages. This shows that the above are the only retentions still persisting in the writing tradition of Early Tamil. Several other items have been quoted with an *āytam* for early Tamil, but they do not have clear cognates from the other languages, e.g. *paḥṟi* 'boat' (Patiṟ. 39) (Balasubramanian 1976: 578). Meenakshisundaran (1965: 68–72) sets up either *v*-ending roots or *l*-ending roots for all *ḥ* + stop sequences in Early Tamil, *av*, *iv*, *uv* (demonstrative), *ev* ~ *ey* ~ *e* 'to pierce' (*eḥ-ku* 'javeline'), *kav* (*kaḥpu*, *kappu* 'branch'; *DEDR* does not give the *āytam* form; *kap* → *kaw*/___+V is a Proto-Dravidian rule which derives **w* from **p* in the intervocalic position, hence *DEDR* 1325 has no *āytam* form), *pav* for *paḥtu* 'ten' (from **pav* 'to spread'), *pal* 'many' for *paḥṟi* 'boat' ('made with many planks'!), etc. Most of these are decidedly speculative. I propose that **H* is original in the demonstrative bases and the semivowel is secondary and rule-derived. This is true also of the numeral 'ten'. It does not follow that these were the only ones that had a Proto-Dravidian laryngeal. I have already explained that, in external sandhi, *ḥ* + stop for a geminate stop was a case of reverse spelling because of hypercorrection.

3. **Quantitative variation in Proto-Dravidian.** At the Proto-Dravidian stage itself, we know that two rules (actually two parts of one rule) operated accounting for alternations between a long syllable and a short syllable:

Rule A. (C)V̄C → (C)VC-/#___+V

Rule B. (C)VCC- → (C)VC-/#___+V

When a derivative suffix beginning with a vowel follows in the second syllable, an underlying V̄C of the root syllable becomes VC-, and an underlying VCC- also becomes VC-, e.g. PD **pēr* > **per*-V 'big' [*DEDR* 4411], **cup(p) + ar* → **cuw-ar* 'salt' [*DEDR* 2674 a and b] (Krishnamurti 1955, *TVB* §§ 1.191–202, 1.288–94, Subrahmanyam 1983: 158–200). The above conclusion was based on internal reconstruction within Proto-Dravidian, because V̄C and VCC contrasted with VC in the root syllables in Proto-Dravidian, when a derivative vowel did not follow; but when a derivative vowel followed, only VC occurred. This means that V̄C and VCC merged with VC when a formative suffix with a vowel followed. There are some exceptions which have been explained in different ways.

4. **New data for Proto-Dravidian laryngeal** ****H*.** Now we have to look at cases where there is alternation between (C)V̄C and (C)VC(C) in etymologically related sets when no derivative vowel followed, and examine if these can be explained in terms of a Proto-Dravidian laryngeal **H* causing the alternation. The following are the candidates for reconstructing a laryngeal **H* for Proto-Dravidian:

4.1. PD **mūnṯu* 'three' [*DEDR* 5052] consists of a root **mū* and a neuter suffix **-nṯu*. The reconstructed root must be **muH-* because when a consonant followed, **H* was assimilated to it, e.g. Early Ta. *mup-paḥtu* 'thirty', *mup-patt-iru* 'thirty-two', *muk-kalam*, 'three ships', *mun-nūṟu* 'three hundred', Ta. Ma. *mup-patu* 'thirty', Ka. *muk-kaṇṇam* 'three-eyed god, Śiva', Tu. *mup-pa* 'thirty', OTe. *mup-padi*, Mdn. Te. *mup-phay* 'thirty', OTe. *muk-kaṇṭi* 'three-eyed god, Śiva'. Tamil-Malayāḷam, Kannaḍa, Tuḷu, Koḍagu, and Telugu geminated the other consonants also, e.g. Ta. Ka. Te. *mun-nūṟu*, Tu. *mun-nūdu*, Koḍ *mun-nūrï* 'three hundred'. The alternation of *mū-* and *mu*C- can only be explained in terms of PD **muH-* which can be inferred from the effects that the laryngeal had on the neighbouring segments. These developments belonged to Proto-South Dravidian; hence, they were not retained in early Tamil writings. In Central Dravidian, Kolami, Naiki, Parji, Ollari, and Gadaba require **muy-aḷ* 'three women' in which the root is *muy-* (< **muH-*). SCD : Koṇḍa *muʔ-*, (< **muw-*), ND: Br. *mus-* adj. 'three' probably carry a reflex of PD **H*.

4.2. A few verbs have puzzling length variation in different languages which has baffled satisfactory explanation. In some of these the vowel qualities are also unstable. I propose a laryngeal at the reconstructed stage to account for several of these seeming aberrations:

(1) PD **caH-* 'to die': PSD **caH-/*cā-*: Ta. *cā* (non-past *cā-v-*, past *ce-tt-* < **ca-tt*), Ma. *cā-* (*catt-*); with **H > y*, To. *soy-* (*sot-*) (borrowing from Baḍaga), Ka. *sāy-* (*satt-*), Tu. *sai-* 'to die'; all the South Dravidian languages also have a noun in **cāw* (< **caH-w-*) 'death'; PSCD: **caH-/ *cā-*: Te. *cacc-* (past *cacc-* < **caH-cci*, non-past (imper./inf.) *cā-/cāw-*, by contraction of **aH* to *ā*) 'to die', *ca-mpu (< *caH-mpp-)* v.t. 'to kill', *cāwu* n. 'death', Go. *sai-*, *sāy-*, *sā-*, *hā-*, Koṇḍa *sā-*(*sā-t-*), Kui *sā-* (*sā-t-*), Kuvi *hai-*, *hā-*(*hā-t-*), Pe.-Manḍa *hā-* (*hā-t-*); PCD: **cay-/*cāy-*: Pa. *cay-* (*ca-ñ-* < *cay-nj-* < **cay-nd-*), Oll. *say-*, Gad. *cay-* 'to die'; ND **keH-*, **key-*: Kuṛ. *xē-* ~ **kē* (*ke-cc-*), Malto *key-* (*kec-*) 'to die', *keype* n. 'death', Br. *kah-* (*kask-*, neg. *kas-*) 'to die', *kas-if-* 'to kill' [*DEDR* 2425].

I proposed the reconstruction **caH* in 1963 (557, fn. 4). Emeneau discussed at length (1961b) the relationship between ND *k-* forms and *c-/s-* forms elsewhere, by positing a rule PD **c* > PND **k/#___{e ē, i ī, u ū}*. While there is little doubt about the velarization of PD **c* in North Dravidian before back high vowels, the phonological basis for front vowels causing the change was not considered convincing. In his 1988 paper he considered the velarization of *c* forms before front vowels in North Dravidian sporadic (1994: 365–9). Pfeiffer (1972: 88–9), while half-heartedly endorsing the above etymology, says, 'Maybe this is also an example of PD alternation **k-/ *c-*'. The problem is not solved by saying that the alternation was in Proto-Dravidian itself (Emeneau 1994: 13). Surprisingly, McAlpin (1981: 99) reconstructs **cah* for Proto-Elamo-Dravidian to account for the Dravidian developments and those of Middle Elamite, viz. *sa-* 'life to be cut off', *sahri* 'death, destruction' with a query. He derives PD laryngeal **H* from PED **h*. Zvelebil (1990a: 12) endorsed the reconstruction of Proto-Dravidian laryngeal **H* in the deictic-interrogative system and in irregular verbs like 'die'. The alternation *cā-/cay-/ce-* in most of the subgroups cannot suggest PD **cay/*cey*, because PD *C*ay* develops to C*ey* and to C*ē*/C*ī* (C = consonant) as in the case of words derived from PD **kay* 'hand' [*DEDR* 2023]. Also **ay* does not contract to **ā*. Therefore, the consonant must have been **H* which could develop into a semivowel later in subgroups. In Kuṛux-Malto the change **H > y* could have caused the shift *a > e*. Brahui seems to have retained the laryngeal as *h*; it appears that PND **a* is retained in *kah-* in Brahui. There is a possibility that the laryngeal with its 'back quality' could have triggered the change of **c* to **k* in North Dravidian. For more than one reason we need to posit a Proto-Dravidian laryngeal in the root **caH-* 'to die'.

(2) Two verbs are traditionally reconstructed with a variable quantity in Proto-Dravidian itself: (a) **tā*, **tār*, **tar*-V 'to give to 1st or 2nd person', 'to bring' [*DEDR* 3098], (b) **wā*, **wār*, **war*-V- 'to come' [*DEDR* 5270]. Their morphological behaviour is parallel in most of the languages. I reconstruct these with a laryngeal **H* as **taH-r* and **waH-r*. With compensatory lengthening we get alternative roots *tā* and *wā* in the imperative. Proto-Dravidian had an allomorph in each of these with a long grade by the addition of a grammatical suffix *-r* (whose meaning and function

have to be investigated), as *tār* and *wār*; when these were followed by a derivative vowel *-u, tar-u* and *war-u* would result. Proto-South Dravidian past stems **ta-nt-* and **wa-nt-* are instances of loss of the laryngeal **H*.

(a) South-Central Dravidian had a past **taH-tt-* which accounts for Go. *ta-tt-*, Koṇḍa-Kui-Kuvi-Pe.-Manḍa *ta-t-* with the loss or assimilation of **H* to the following past allomorph. Te. *te-cc-* (past) is derived from **tey-cc-* (< **tay-cc-* < **taH-cc-*), the infinitive and negative allomorphs *tē-*, *tēr-* are again from **tey-r-* by vocalic change and contraction. Gondi has *tar-* in the imperative. Kui-Kuvi-Pengo-Manḍa have developed **-ta*, **-tara* as transition suffixes in tensed transitive verbs to signal a first or second person object (Steever 1993: 35–68).[4] Koṇḍa *si-d-a* 'give me/us' (imper. 2nd sg.), *si-da-ṭ* (imper. 2nd pl.), Old Telugu *in-da-mu*, Mdn. Te. *in-da* 'you take this' (2nd imper.) from PD **ciy-/cī-* 'give' are the only survivals of this construction in these two languages. In Kolami there is *ko-tar* 'to bring'. In North Dravidian Brahui *tin-*, *tir-*, *ti-ss-* (past), *tē-* 'give', *ha-tin-/ha-tir-*, *ha-ta-/ha-tar-*, *ha-tit-* 'bring' are allomorphs traceable to this verb (Emeneau explains the *n/r* alternation as well as vocalic changes, etc. 1994: 49–70). Kuṛ. *tai- (tai-yy-), tēy- (tēyy-)* 'to send', Malto *tey-* 'send' [*DEDR* 3418] do certainly belong to this etymology (Pfeiffer also asserts the same, see p. 18). The North Dravidian developments are parallel to **caH* > **cay* /**cey* with the vocalic change resulting from **H* > *y* (also see the discussion of the developments by Emeneau in his 1962 article, reprinted 1994: 58, §3.21).

(b) PSD **wā* imp., neg. **wār-*, other inflections **war-*V-, and past **wa-nt-* presuppose *wa-* (< **waH-*). SCD: Te. *wa-cc-* (past st. < **waH-cc-*), imper.-inf.-neg. stem *rā-*(< **wrā-* < **war-a*); Gondi has *wai-*, *vāy-* as the root in most of the dialects (also Kuvi *waiy-* in one dialect) suggesting the development of Proto-Dravidian laryngeal **H to y*; the Gondi imperative preserves the *r-* form, *varā*. Koṇḍa imperative *raʔ-/ra-*, negative *reʔ-* indicate a shared innovation with Telugu. Go.-Koṇḍa-Kui-Kuvi-Pe.-Manḍa *wā-t-* (past); CD: Kol.-Nk. *var-(vat-)*, *va-*, *vā-* imper.; Pa. *ver-* (< *var-*; *veñ* past < *ve-nj* < *ve-nd*; cf. South Dravidian), Oll. Gad. *var-(vad-)*. ND: Kuṛ.-Malto *bar-*, Br. *bann-* (*bar-*, *ba-*; imper. *ba*, past *bass-*). There are contrastive developments of this verb outside South Dravidian. It does not have any special usage as found in the case of **taH-r-* in South-Central Dravidian. The parallel phonology of (a) and (b) suggests that both these verbs involved a Proto-Dravidian laryngeal **H* leading to similar developments. Otherwise, there is no satisfactory explanation for *ā* alternating with *a* in the root syllable, the occurrence of a semivowel *y* in some languages and subgroups, etc.

[4] Steever has argued convincingly that the use of **-ta~*-tar-*V- as object agreement markers in Kui-Kuvi-Pengo-Manḍa is derived from PD **tā-/*tar-*V- 'give to 1st or 2nd person' by a compound contraction rule which operated in other cases also in South-Central Dravidian. I would only like to point out that traces of this are found restricted to one verb in Telugu and Koṇḍa also taking this change to Proto-South-Central Dravidian. The literary languages of South Dravidian and Telugu in their older records have evidence of the use of the derivatives of PD **taH-r-* as an auxiliary with a different connotation.

(3) Five other verbs of high frequency have irregular vocalism:

(a) For Proto-Dravidian 'say, utter', the traditional reconstruction was **ān- ~ *an-/*en-/*in-* or **yan ~ yen* (*TVB* 282, item 24; listed under **e-* in *DEDR* 868). The reconstruction **yan* explains Ta. Ma. *en-*, Ka. *en-/an-*, Koḍ. *en-*, Tu. *en-/an-*, Te. *an-*, Kol.-Nk.-Pa. **en-*. The vowel *i* in Ko. *in-*, To. *ïn-*, Tu. (dial.) *in-*, and PSCD **in-* (past **in-ṯṯ-*) representing Gondi-Koṇḍa-Kui-Kuvi-Pengo-Manḍa has no satisfactory answer. Kuṛux and Malto *ān-* has a long vowel which is difficult to explain. A reconstruction **aHn-* at a deeper time level of Proto-Dravidian (or presumably in pre-Dravidian) would explain the irregularities better than **yan-* and multiple reconstructions for Proto-Dravidian, viz. **aHn-* > *ān* in Kuṛ.-Malto is straightforward; **H* > *y* within Proto-Dravidian itself with subsequent changes in the vowel qualities would account for the rest of the changes in all other subgroups, for instance, like **ayn-* > **eyn-* / ** iyn* > *an-*, *en-*/ *in-*. The reason for setting up this reconstruction at a deeper chronological layer is that **H* occurred here within a root syllable and not at the morph boundary, a condition which had remained into a later stage of Proto-Dravidian, illustrated in all the earlier cases. Zvelebil (1970b: 58, §1.14.1.1.) says, 'In a few roots there is an alternation of *e*/*a*/*i* which is so widespread (yet the factors conditioning it have so far remained hidden) that it may be PD in origin'. Subrahmanyam (1983: 389) reconstructs **yān-/*yan-* for Proto-Dravidian without going into the details of *e*/*i* alternation.

(b) PD **tiHn-* 'eat' in the place of the traditional reconstruction **tin-/*tīn-* [*DEDR* 3263 a and b]. The short vowel form **tin-* occurs as the basic verb meaning 'eat' in all subgroups; however, the long vowel form **tīn-* which occurs as the base of a derived causative and nouns is not explainable. SD: Ta. Ma. *tīṟṟu* (< **tīn-ṯṯ-* < ***tīn* + *tt-* transitivizer) 'feed', *tīn*, *tīni* 'food', Ma. *tinni*, *tīni* 'eater', *tīn* 'food', Ko. *tīṭ-* 'feed by hand', *tīn* 'food', To. *tīny* 'food', Ka. *tīṟ* 'take mouthfuls', *tīni* 'food, eating', Tu. *tīni*, *tīnï* 'food'; SCD: Go. *tih-*, *tiht-*, Koṇḍa *tīR-pis-*, Kui *tīs-* (*tīs-t-*), Kuvi *tīh-* (*tīs-t-*), Pe. *tīc-* (< **tīṯṯ-*) caus. 'feed'. PD **tiHn* accounts for the long vowel form **tīn* by contraction **iH* to *ī*, and **tin* is derived by the loss of **H*. Like the verb in (c) the laryngeal **H* occurs in the interior of the root and therefore belongs to a deeper chronological layer of Proto-Dravidian. A PD **i* in closed syllables is a stable vowel without qualitative changes in the descendant languages (*TVB* 102, §1.244).

(c) Another verb with variable vowel length in a closed syllable is PD **uṇ/*ūṇ* [*DEDR* 600] which can now be represented as PD **uHṇ-*: SD: Ta. Ma. *uṇ* (*uṇ-ṭ-*) 'eat, drink', *ūṭṭ-* (< *ūṇ-ṭṭ-* < ***ūṇ-tt-*) 'feed', *ūṇ* 'rice, food', Ta. *ūṭṭam* 'food eating'; Ko.-To. *uṇ-* (*uḍ-*) 'suck', *ūṇ* 'food', Ka. *uṇ-* (*uṇ-ḍ-*) 'eat, drink mother's milk', *ūḍisu* 'feed', *ūṭa* 'meal', Koḍ. *uṇṇ-* (*uṇ-ḍ-*) 'eat a meal', Tu. *uṇ-* 'eat rice', *ūṭa* 'meal'; SCD: Te. *ūṭu* '(cattle) to drink water', Go. *uṇḍ-*, *ūṇḍ-* 'drink', *uht-*, *ūht-* 'cause to drink', Koṇḍa *uṇ-* (*uṭ-*) 'drink', *ūṭpis-* 'cause to drink', Kui-Kuvi-Pengo *uṇ-* (some dialects of Kuvi *un-*) (*uṭ-*) 'drink', *ūṭ-* 'give to drink', Manḍa *un-* (*uc-*) 'drink', *ūṭ-* 'cause to drink'; CD: Kol. *un-* (*un-d-*) 'drink', Kol.-Nk. *ūr-t-* 'cause to drink', Nk.-Pa.-Oll.-Gad. *un-* (*un-ḍ-*) 'drink'; no long vowel form is attested in Parji-Ollari-Gadaba; ND: Kuṛ.-Malto *ōn-* (*on-ḍ-*) 'drink', Kuṛux also 'eat rice', *ōn-kā* 'thirst', Br. *kun-* 'eat, drink'. As in the case of 'eat' words in (3b) the long grade form occurs in derived causatives and in the noun formation; the short grade vowel with loss of **H* occurs as the basic verb in all subgroups. Kuṛux and Malto have a long grade vowel in the basic verb also in the case of (3a). A laryngeal **H* following the vowel in early Proto-Dravidian explains all these parallel irregularities in the root vowel quantity and quality.

(d) With similar justification, we can reconstruct PD **weHn-* 'hear' [*DEDR* 5516] to account for *i/e* alternation in the root syllable *(< *weyn-/*wiyn-)* and for the long grade in Te. *wīnu* n. 'ear'. Telugu, Kolami-Naiki (perhaps borrowed from Telugu) have **i*; Ta. Ma. *vin-avu* resulted from a shared rule *i*C-*a*- < **e*C-*a*-. The *e*-vowel occurs in Kota *vent-* (*vey-nt-*); South-Central Dravidian Koṇḍa-Kui-Kuvi-Pengo-Manḍa require **wen-* (past **we-ṯṯ-* < **wen-ṯṯ-*), the Central Dravidian languages other than Kolami-Naiki need **wen-*, and Kuṛux-Malto of North Dravidian **men-*. Brahui *bin-* can be explained through **e* > *i* since a short mid-vowel cannot occur in that language.

(e) One more candidate for positing a laryngeal **H* is suggested by comparing PD **kaṇ* 'eye' [*DEDR* 1159] with PD **kāṇ* (past **kaṇ-ṭ-*) 'see, consider, appear' [*DEDR* 1443]. That both these are phonologically related is beyond question, although *DEDR* has different entries. PD **kaṇ* has derived forms in almost all the subgroups as a noun. PD **kāṇ* is represented in all the languages of South Dravidian with variable length, but only with a short vowel in all Central and North Dravidian languages. The long grade occurs in nouns, in causative stems, and in non-past inflection and the short in the past inflection consistently in South Dravidian. Old Telugu *kanu, kān-cu* 'see' show both long and short vowels. Central Dravidian and North Dravidian have only a short vowel in the verb forms as in the case of nouns. PD **kāṇ* also accounts for derived nouns and transitive-causative stem in South Dravidian and Telugu. An early Proto-Dravidian reconstruction **kaHṇ* would explain both the noun and verb forms with variable length. The only peculiarity compared to the earlier cases is that the long vowel form became specialized as a verb and the short vowel form as a noun mainly in Proto-South Dravidian. Note that, even in the case of the verb, the root shows a short vowel in the past stem. Earlier, the variable length was explained by positing **ūṇ-*/**uṇṇ-* and **kāṇ*/**kaṇṇ-* in Proto-Dravidian in which *ṇṇ* was said to have fallen together with *ṇ* before a vowel or a consonant (*TVB* 125, §1.300). This solution is less elegant than the one involving a laryngeal **H* which has many parallels elsewhere, as already illustrated.

4.3. There are some twenty-one cases where the verbs have a short grade and the etymologically related nouns have the long grade (Subrahmanyam 1983: 185–7). Eight such cases are confined only to Tamil and Malayāḷam, e.g. *aṭu* 'cook': *āṭu* 'cooking' [*DEDR* 76], *iṟu* 'die': *īṟu* 'termination'. Two etymologies are doubtful. Of the remaining eleven, if we drop the items meaning 'eat, drink, hear' discussed above, there are some eight cases in which the alternation between long and short vowels need to be explained. Only the long vowel form occurs as the noun, while in verb inflection the short vowel is more widespread than the long vowel stem, e.g. Ta. Ma. Ka. *kōḷ*, Te. *-kōlu* 'taking, seizure', **koḷ-/*koṇ-* 'receive, buy, take' [*DEDR* 2151]. In the case of **tiHn-* and **uHṇ-* and **weHn-* it was shown that the long vowel occurred in related nouns; in the first two, the long vowel stem was also the basis of transitive-causative forms. This gradation difference can be interpreted by stating a condition that the laryngeal **H* lengthens the preceding vowel when the output is a free form (noun) and is generally lost where the output is a bound form, i.e. a verb stem. Of course, **kāṇ/*kaṇ* is an exception to this and we need to examine further to define the conditions more precisely.

The pairs of nouns and verbs illustrated below follow the rule as stated above.

5. *DEDR* 1942. (a) PD **keṭ-u* v. 'be spoiled, perish', n. 'peril' > PSD I **keṭ-u*: Ta. Ma. *keṭu*, Ko. *keṛ-*, To. *köṛ*, Ka. *keḍu*, Koḍ. *köḍ-*, Tu. *keḍag-* v.t.; PSCD **keṭ-u*: Te. *ceḍu*, Kuvi *hēḍ-*; PCD **kiṭṭ-*: Kol. *kiṭ-* 'to be extinguished', Nk. *kiṭ-*, Nk. (Ch.) *kiṛ*, Oll. *siṭ-*, Gad. *ciṭṭ-*. (b) PD **kēṭu* n. 'damage, evil' > PSD I **kēṭu*: Ta. Ma. *kēṭu*, Ko. *kēṛ*, To. *kȫḍ* 'dead person, funeral', Ka. *kēḍu* Koḍ. *kēḍï*, Tu. *kēḍu/ï*; PSCD **kēṭ* as a verb base underlies the Telugu noun *cēṭu* (< **cēṭ-ṭ-* < **kēṭ-t-*) 'evil, damage'. There is an alternative nominal base **keṭ-ṭ-* (< **keṭ-t-*) in almost all the languages represented above.

6. *DEDR* 2151. (a) PD **koḷ* 'seize, take, buy' > PSD I **koḷ*: Ta. *koḷ* (past *koṇ-ṭ-* < **koḷ-nt-*), Ma. *koḷ* (*koṇṭ-*), Ko. *koḷ-/koṇ-*, To. *kwïḷ-*, Ka. *koḷ*, Koḍ *koḷḷ-*, Tu *koṇ-*; PSCD **koḷ/*koṇ*: Te. *kon-*, Koṇḍa *koṛ-/kol-*, Kui *koḍ-*, Kuvi *koḍ-*, Pe. *koṛ-*, Manḍa *kṛag-*; PCD **koḷ*: Kol. *kor-*, Nk.? *koy-* (*kor-*). (b) PSD I **kōḷ* n. 'seizure': Ta. Ma. Ka. Koḍ. *kōḷ* 'taking, seizure'; SCD: Te. *-kōlu* noun formative from refl. verbs with *-kon* as auxiliary. Kuvi *kōd* (F) is doubtful.

7. *DEDR* 2654. (a) PD **cuṭu* v.i./t. (past *cuṭṭ-*) 'to burn, roast' > PSD I **cuṭ-*V- (*cuṭṭ-*) 'burn, roast': Ta.-Ma. *cuṭu* (*cuṭṭ-*) v.i./t., Ko. *tuṛ* 'to roast', To. *tuṛ* 'to burn' tr., Koḍ. *cuḍ-* v.t. (*cuṭṭ-*) 'to burn', Ka. *suḍu* v.i./t. (*suṭṭ-*), n. 'burning', Tu. *suḍ(u)*, *tuḍ-*. (b) PSD I **cūḍu* v.t. and n. 'to burn; burning, heat': Ta. Ma. *cūṭu* 'to brand, cauterize', *cūṭṭu* 'torch', Ko. *cūṛ*, Ka. *sūḍu* 'burning', *sūṭe* 'torch', Koḍ *tūḍï* 'torch', Tu. *cūḍu* 'heat', *sūṭè/tūṭè* 'torch'. In South-Central Dravidian the long vowel occurs in OTe. *cūḍu* 'to burn, brand with a hot iron', n. 'burning' and Kuvi (dial.) *hūḍ-* v.t. 'to burn'.

8. *DEDR* 3852. (a) PD **paṭ-u* 'to fall, lie down' > PSD I **paṭu*: Ta. Ma. *paṭu*, Ko. *paṛ*, To. *poṛ*, Ka. *paḍu*, Koḍ *paḍ*. (b) PSD I **pāṭ*: Ta. Ma. *pāṭu* 'fall'; PSCD **paṭ-/*paṯ*, also **pāṭ* 'to fall, lie down': Te. *paḍu*, v.t. *paṟacu; pāṭu* n. 'fall' from **pāṭṭ-* (< **pāṭ-t-*); cf. Kol. (SR) *pāṛ* 'fall'.

9. *DEDR* 3853. (a) PD **paṭu* 'to occur, suffer' > PSD I **paṭu* 'to suffer, experience, occur': Ta. Ma. *paṭu*, Ko. *paṛ-*, To. *poṛ-*, Ka. *paḍu*, Koḍ *paḍ-*, Tu. *paḍe-*; PSCD **paṭ-/*paṯ-*: Te. *paḍu* 'experience'. (b) PSD I **pāṭu* n. 'experience, suffering': Ta. Ma. *pāṭu*, Ko. *pāṛ* 'work, concern', To. *pōḍ* 'suffering', Ka. *pāḍu* 'suffering';

cf. *pāṭu(< *pāṭ-ṭ-)* 'suffering' presupposes a verb base **pāṭ*, Tu. *pāḍu* 'likeness'; in South-Central Dravidian only Telugu has the long vowel from *pāṭu* 'suffering', presupposing an underlying verb stem **pāṭ*.

The other cases are *DEDR* 4422 Ta. Ma. *peṟu* 'to be born': *pēṟu* 'birth', Tu. *ped-* 'to bear young': *pēti* 'childbed' (< PSD I **peṯ-: *pēṯ); DEDR* 4876 PSD **min* 'glitter': **mīn* 'star, fish'. Cognates occur in Tamil, Malayāḷam, Kota, Toda, Kannaḍa of South Dravidian and Telugu of South-Central Dravidian. Kuṛux has a long vowel in *bīnkō* 'star'; *DEDR* 5393 PD **wiṭ-u* 'to leave': **wīṭu* 'liberty'. South Dravidian has cognates in Tamil, Malayāḷam, Kota, Kannaḍa, Tuḷu. In South-Central Dravidian only Telugu has cognates, *wiḍucu, wīḍu* v.i. 'to leave', *wīṭi* adj. 'wasteful'.

4.4. A study of the above cases leads us to conclude that (a) vowel-gradation relating verbs and nouns is mainly a characteristic of South Dravidian; by its contiguity to the literary languages of the South, Telugu also shares this feature; (b) since vocalic ablaut (e.g. English *sing–song*) is not expected in an agglutinative family like Dravidian, the best explanation for the alternation is by positing a laryngeal **H* in the underlying basic stems in early Proto-Dravidian. The different phonological developments, by and large, in later Proto-Dravidian led to certain grammatical differences, viz. **H* lengthens the preceding vowel in the formation of nouns and causative stems; elsewhere it is lost; (c) all cases of vocalic ablaut involve a laryngeal **H* preceding a coronal consonant, **ṯ, *ṭ, *n, *ṇ, *ḷ* and not velar, palatal, and labial stops. It appears that the voicing environment on both sides of a laryngeal (*V*HS*, where S is a sonorant) would promote lengthening of the preceding vowel as well as its loss before a voiced consonant. The phonetic bases of these changes need further research.

5. *H in personal pronouns. Another set of forms which justify a laryngeal are the personal pronouns, for which the traditional reconstructions have been (nominative/oblique): **yān/*yan-* 'I', **yām/*yam-* 'we (exclusive)', **ñām/*ñam-* 'we (inclusive)', **nīn/*nin-* 'you (sg.)', **nīm/*nim-* 'you (pl.)' (Krishnamurti 1968b), **tān/*tan-* 'self', **tām/*tam-* '-selves'. The long grade forms occur in the nominative and the short grade ones in oblique (non-nominative) cases. The oblique stems have a short vowel whether they are followed by a vowel or a consonant. Emeneau has demonstrated that the oblique stems of personal pronouns occur as bound first members of certain morphological complexes denoting kinship terms, e.g. Ta. *taṅkai* 'younger sister', Ma. *taṅga*, Ka. *taṅgi*, Koḍ. *taŋge*, Tu. *taṅgi, taṅgaḍi*, Kui-Kuvi *tangi* 'younger sister' require a reconstruction for Proto-South Dravidian as **tam-kay* (Emeneau 1953b: 339–53, particularly Etymologies A, item 6, p. 350). Clearly, the reduction of vowel length is not caused by a following derivative or inflectional vowel. In view of what we have noticed, the easiest solution is to set up a laryngeal **H* root finally in all cases **yaH-n: *yaH-m, *ñaH-n: ñaH-m, *niH-n: *niH-m, *taH-n: *taH-m*. Note that *-n: -m* represent singular: plural. The nominatives can be derived by *V*H*>V̄, and the oblique stem by the loss of *H*. The loss of **H* was induced by extended constructions with bound obliques, whereas the long grade occurred in the independent (nominative) forms.

6. **H* in negative verb inflection. The negative allomorphs used in inflected verbs have been of uncertain origin in the Dravidian languages.

6.1. South Dravidian I. All languages have markers in the third neuter in negative finite verbs (tenseless) and in adjectival and adverbial forms. In other persons the negative is signalled by a zero suffix. In Ta. Ma. *-ā-*, adj. *-ā*, *-āda*, Ko. *-āy-*, adj. *-ā(d)-*, Koḍ. *-a*, adj. *-at-*, Ka. *-a-*, Tu. *-ay-* in all persons, *-a-* in 3rd neut. sg. PD **-aH-* (? **āH-*) explains different developments *-ā-*, *-āy-*, *-ay-*, *-a-*, and *-Ø-*. Study the following examples (finite verbs involving first singular, third neuter singular, non-finite adjective (Subrahmanyam 1971: 331–96)):

10. Ta. *kāṇ-Ø-ēṉ* 'I do not see', *var-ā-tu* 'it does not come', *ceyy-ā*/*ceyy-āt-a* adj. 'that does not do', *tīṟ-ā*/*tīṟ-ātu* adv. 'without ending'.

11. Ma. (Old) *oẓiy-Ø-ēn* 'I will not exclude myself', cf. *var-āy-um* '(subject) will not come' (*y* is not a glide here), *kāṇ-ā-ññ-a* past adj. 'that did not see' (< **kāṇ-āy-ñj-a* < **kāṇ-āy- nd-a*; the final *-y* of the negative allomorph must have been lost), *kāṇ-āte* adv. 'without seeing', *kāṇ-āy-ka* neg. verbal noun 'not seeing'.

12. Ko. *tin-Ø-ēn* 'I will not eat', *tin-Ø-kō* 'it/they will not eat', *vār-āy-p-ē (n)* 'I was not coming' (lit. come-neg.-past-1st pers.), *koṛ-ā(d)* neg. adj. 'that does not give', *gey-ād* neg. adv. 'without doing'.

13. To. *kïy-Ø-ini* 'I do/did not do', *tïn-oθ* neg. adv. 'without eating'. Koḍ. *keyy-a-Ø* '(subject) will not do', *cuḍ-at-ë* 'that . . . not burn' (all tenses), *keyy-ate* adv. 'without working'.

14. Ka. *nōḍ-Ø-e (nu)* 'I do not see', *nōḍ-a-du* 'it does not see', *nōḍ-ad-a* adj. 'that . . . not see' (all tenses), *nōḍ-ade* adv. 'without seeing'.

15. Tu. *kēṇ-ay-ɛ* 'I do not hear', *kēṇ-a-ndï*/ *-nï* 'it will not hear', *bar-ay-aḷï* 'she does not come'. The negative adjective and adverb are compound constructions.

The above data show that in South Dravidian the negative suffix occurring in finite verb inflection had at least four allomorphs *āy*/*ay*~*ā*~*a*~Ø. The verbal adjective and adverb have presumably incorporated erstwhile past allomorphs **t*~**tt* with neutralized tense meaning. In *āy*/*ay* the *y* element is not a hiatus filler (contrary to Subrahmanyam's suggestion in 1971: 348, fn.), because its occurrence is not predictable in terms of the preceding and following segments, vowels, or consonants. To account for *ā*/*a* and also the *y* element, we need to set up for Proto-South Dravidian **aH* (or more legitimately **āH*) as the negative marker.

6.2. The South-Central Dravidian (South Dravidian II) data may be examined below:

16. Te. *cepp-a-nu* 'I do not tell', *cepp-a-ni* 'that . . . not told' (all tenses), *cepp-aka* adv. 'without telling'.

17. Go. *tinn-Ø-ōn* (< **tin-v-ōn* with loss of *-v-* before a labial vowel), 'I do not eat', cf. *tin-v-ī* 'you do not eat', *sūṛ-vāk* adv. 'without seeing'.

18. Koṇḍa *ki-ʔ-e* 'I will not do' (dial. *ki-v-e*), *ki-ʔ-i* (non-past neg. adj.), *ki-ʔi-t-i* (past neg. adj.), *ki-ʔ-eṇḍa* (adv.) 'without doing'.

19. Kui *tin-ʔ-enu* (non-past) 'I do not eat', *tin-ʔa-t-enu* (past: root-neg. past personal suffix) 'I did not eat', *tin-ʔa-n-i* (non-past neg. adj.), *tin-ʔa-t-i* (past neg. adj.).

20. Kuvi *pāy-ʔo-di* 'you do not beat', *pāy-ʔa-t-i* 'you did not beat'. *pāy-ʔa* (non-past neg. adj.), *pāy-ʔa-t-i* (past neg. adj.).

21. Pe. *huṛ-u-ŋ* (non-past neg.) 'I do not see', *huṛ-va-t-aŋ* (past neg.) 'I did not see', *huṛ-v-i* (non-past neg. adj.), *huṛ-vi-t-i* (past neg. adj.).

For South-Central Dravidian it appears that we need to reconstruct *-*wa-* as the basic negative morpheme. In Koṇḍa-Kui-Kuvi *-*w-* became a glottal stop -ʔ-, and the following vowel vanished in Koṇḍa but was preserved in different shapes in Gondi, Kuvi, and Pengo. It appears that we can reconstruct *-*Ha-* as the negative morpheme for Proto-South-Central Dravidian with **H* developing into *-*w-* in pre-vocalic position.

6.3. The data from Central Dravidian and North Dravidian:

22. Kol. *sī-e-n* 'I do not give', *sī-e-t-an* 'I did not give', *tin-e* (neg. adj. in all tenses).

23. Pa. *cūṛ-a-n-a* 'I do not see' (the final *-a-* is idiosyncratically a copy of the neg. -*a-* repeated after the personal suffix), *cūṛ-ay-Ø-a* (neut. sg.) 'it does not see' (note-*ay-* instead of *-a-*), *cūṛ-a* (non-past neg. adj.), *cūṛ-aka* (adv.) 'without seeing'.

Oll. *sūṛ-a-n* 'I will not see', *sūṛ-a* 'that . . . not see' (all tenses), *sūṛ-a kerin* (adv.) 'without seeing'.

The Central Dravidian languages uniformly require PCD **a* as the negative marker. There is a suspicious alternation between *a* and *ay* in Parji. In any case **aH* explains this aberration as in the case of South-Central Dravidian. Among the North Dravidian languages Kuṛux and Malto have no negative inflectional suffix. Brahui has *a*/Ø in negative verbs, preceded by a tense-marking consonant.

24. Br. *tix-p-a-r* 'I do not place', *tix-t-avaṭ* 'I did not place' (past stem followed by the negative present form of the substantive verb *affaṭ* → *avaṭ* 'I am not').

6.4. Subrahmanyam (1971: § 4.22–24) reconstructs *-*ā-* for Proto-Dravidian. He says it was preserved only in the third neuter in South Dravidian and in the other persons it became a zero; its shortened form *-a-* occurred in Telugu, Tuḷu, Central Dravidian, and Brahui. He does not explain the widely distributed allomorphs *-āy-*/ *-ay-* and also how *-ā-* could be totally lost in most of the inflectional forms. For South-Central Dravidian, he reconstructs *-*vā-* (because some Gondi dialects have a long vowel) and says, 'at present it is difficult to explain the additional *v* in the suffix' (387). Alfred Master (1947: 146) cites Bloch (1935), in which Bloch suggested that the negative suffix-_a_- 'was preceded prehistorically by an ill-determined consonantal element, possibly guttural, laryngeal or glottal'. It is not clear why Bloch suggested this 'element' to have preceded rather than followed *_-a-_. He must have thought so because of the developments in South-Central Dravidian and Brahui. He guessed correctly that Kui 'glottal stop should be the remnant of an old consonantal articulation'. (Bloch 1954: 67)

6.5. Taking the total scenario into account, we can reconstruct *_-aHa-_ (or *_-aHaH-_ > _-āy-/-ay-_) for Early Proto-Dravidian or pre-Dravidian which developed into a long grade _-ā-_ (by contraction), and a short grade *_-a-_ by a process of reduction of this vowel in unaccented syllables; the short vowel *_-a-_ further developed to zero grade *-Ø- in South Dravidian paradigms by loss before personal suffixes beginning with vowels. In some of the languages (Malayāḷam, Kota, Tuḷu, Parji) the morpheme-final *_H_ was further softened into a semivowel _-y_. These developments explain the entire data of South Dravidian, Tuḷu, and Central Dravidian, Ṭelugu of South-Central Dravidian and Brahui of North Dravidian. Telugu, being geographically close to the South Dravidian literary languages, had followed the southern pattern by selecting _-a-_ in negative inflection.

How can we relate the Proto-South-Central Dravidian reconstruction *_-wa-_ to PD *_-aHa(H)-_? Three possibilities are suggested: (a) The SCD *_-wa-_ was an independent innovation not related to PD *_-aHa(H)-_. (b) Early PD *_-aHa(H)-_ split into *_-āH-_ in Proto-South Dravidian I and to *_-Ha(H)-_ in Proto-South-Central Dravidian, as an innovation that separated these two branches, by a process of contraction and truncation (reducing the morpheme size with loss of _-a-_ in unaccented positions). Then, the other subgroups (Central and North Dravidian) require minimally a proto-form *_-aH-_ which must have developed on the same lines as SD _-a(y)-_ > *_-a-_ > -Ø-. (c) The Proto-Dravidian suffix remained *_aHa(H)-_ in all subgroups except Proto-South-Central Dravidian, either in its full form as *_-aHa(H)-_ or its contracted form as *_-āH-_, because both these could lead to *_-āy-_/ *_-ay-_>_-ā-_/ _-a-_>-Ø-. In that case, only South-Central Dravidian innovated *_-Ha(H)-_ by a rule of truncation; *_-H-_ developed to *_-w-_ originally in intervocalic or prevocalic position, later generalized to all positions; a further change of *_-wa-_ > _-ˀa-_ occurred in Koṇḍa-Kui-Kuvi as a shared isogloss. Koṇḍa-Kui further reduced it to -ˀ- in non-past paradigms, but the trace of the vowel is preserved in the past negative, e.g. Koṇḍa _ki-ˀ-en_ 'he does/will not do', _ki-ˀe-t-an_ 'he did not do', _ki-ˀi-t-i_ 'you (sg.) did not do'. Alternative (a) is ruled out because of the widespread phonetic, semantic, and grammatical similarity of the relevant allomorphs in different subgroups. Alternative (b) is less likely, because the developments of the reconstructed morpheme have to be replicated in different subgroups independently. Therefore, alternative (c) seems closer to the truth. I believe that the process of contraction *_-aHa(H)-_ > -*_āH-_ is not as atypical a sound change as truncation *_-aHa(H)-_ to *_-Ha(H)-_. Therefore, only Proto-South-Central Dravidian could have innovated the latter type of change. In any case, the involvement of a laryngeal *_H_ in negative verb inflection, as already guessed by Jules Bloch over sixty years ago, would account for the data better than any of the earlier explanations.

7. Conclusion.

7.1. Summary of observations. The foregoing case studies point to one conclusion. In addition to the sixteen consonants and ten vowels reconstructed for Proto-Dravidian so far, we need at least one more phoneme to account for the peculiar sound-letter (phoneme) called *āytam* in Ancient Tamil, which was recorded in the neuter (non-masculine) demonstrative pronouns (*aḥ-tu*, *iḥ-tu*), the numeral 'ten' (*paḥ-tu*), and a few other lexical items (§1)[5]. I analysed the phonological behaviour of the *āytam* (a) in lengthening the preceding vowel, (b) in geminating the following stop, (c) in its loss before certain voiced consonants (which Tolkāppiyam did not register), and (d) in its alternation with semivowels (which Tolkāppiyam could not have recorded because it was based on comparative evidence) (§2). I have looked for similar phenomena in other parts of the reconstructed Proto-Dravidian grammar and lexicon. A number of cases have emerged which have baffled explanation in the present state of our knowledge of comparative Dravidian phonology. I have examined each one of these (there could be others too), if they carry the properties similar to those involving an *āytam*. I have come to the conclusion that a number of cases come under the *āytam* phenomenon in some or all of its properties, in addition to the deictic and interrogative bases and the numeral 'ten', viz. (a) the numeral root for 'three', (b) certain high frequency verbs meaning 'die', 'give/bring', 'come', 'say', 'eat', 'drink', 'hear', 'see', and (c) pairs of forms in which the nouns and verbs are etymologically related with alternation in vowel-length (§4). In all these cases, the alternation between long vowels and short vowels cannot be traced to the established rules which require the addition of a vowel derivative -V to cause such alternation, as in (C)VC-V (§3).

The existence of some 'new' phoneme which had caused vowel length in all such cases cannot be denied. That phoneme cannot be identified either as *y* or as *w*, because there are different correspondences for Proto-Dravidian reconstructions involving a vowel + a semivowel. PD *V + *y* > V̄ is an established rule with all but the low vowel **a*. PD **a* + *y* in the root syllable would not alternate with *ā*; it merged with *ey*/*ē*, *iy*/*ī* in Central, South-Central, and North Dravidian languages. In most of the cases discussed in (§§2,4), there is alternation between *ā* and *a*, along with clear evidence of a secondary *y* which arose from this new phoneme. PD **y* following a non-low vowel (**i* **u* **e* **o*) is also attested, and is preserved in several languages. But the cases I have examined here involving non-low vowels are the ones in which there is only length variation but the presence of a primary **y* is not

[5] PD had ten vowels *i e a o u* and their long counterparts and sixteen consonants as shown in Table 18.1 (a laryngeal **H* is now added in the glottal column of the semivowel series).

attested (§§4.2 (2)(b)–(d), 4.3). These two peculiar phenomena attending the variation of long and short vowels led me to reconstruct this mysterious 'new' phoneme as a laryngeal **H* in Proto-Dravidian. I have extended its occurrence to the personal pronouns with unexplained length variation between nominative and oblique stems (§5) and to the reconstruction of the negative morpheme PD **-aHa(H)-* (§6); the last one, I think provides decisive evidence for the reconstruction of the laryngeal. It appears that **H* lengthens the preceding vowel compensatorily in free forms, but tends to be lost in bound stems (see the deictics *ā*, *ī*, interrogative *ē*, imperatives of the verbs *cā*, *tā*, *wā*, noun forms *tīn*, *ūṇ*, *wīn*, derived nouns in §4.3 and the nominatives of pronominal forms in §5). There are, however, a few exceptions to this statement. I have also drawn attention to the peculiar qualitative changes in vowels where a laryngeal **H* is involved in Proto-Dravidian reconstructions. One could call the new phoneme by some other name but the phonetics of Old Tamil *āytam* and its recording with three small circles ஃ similar to the Sanskrit *visarga* ः primarily dictated my choice to call it a laryngeal. Additionally, it seems to have properties similar to those attributed to Proto-Indo-European laryngeals, viz. all of them compensatorily lengthen a preceding vowel (W. P. Lehmann 1955: §§2, 12; 22–35, 85–97).

7.2. **Relative chronology.** Even before the split of Proto-Dravidian into different subgroups, the developments attributed to PD **H* (contraction, loss, semivowel replacement, etc.) must have been taking place dialectally within the parent language. However, there must have been a dialect of South Dravidian which became part of ancient high Tamil (? *c.* 3rd century BC) that preserved the distinct pronunciation of **H* (as *āytam*) in a few relic forms, beside those in which the changes had taken place beyond recognition, e.g. **aw-an̲ṯu* 'that man', **iw-an̲ṯu* 'this man', **a-tu* 'that one' (neut. sg.), **i-tu* 'this one' (neut. sg.), **pat-tu*/ **pat-in-* 'ten', **mū-n̲ṯu* 'three', **cā-*/ **ca-* 'die', **wā-*/ **wa-* 'come', **tā-*/ **ta-* 'give to 1st or 2nd person' (beside **tay-* in some other dialects), **yān*/ **yan-* 'I' etc. The contraction and reduction of the negative morpheme as *ā* > *a* > Ø must have been completed in Proto-South Dravidian. But note the occurrence of **āy*/**ay* as a negative marker in Malayāḷam, Kota, and Tuḷu bearing witness to the change of an erstwhile **H* to *y* in some regional varieties within South Dravidian. The laryngeal or glottal phoneme must have been lost or become archaic in the speech of the high class, by the time PD **c-* (> **s-* > **h-*) > Ø started operating in the South Dravidian languages (? post-3rd century BC). This competing change, which probably spread in common speech, must have accelerated the sound changes which led to the total loss of **H* in South Dravidian.

7.3. **New evidence.** Early Tamil attests the loss of Sanskrit and Prakrit sibilants *ś*, *ṣ*, *s* in loanwords (Burrow 1943: 132–5) more than any other southern language. It is reasonable to assume that, even in loanwords, *s* first became *h* as it happened in Sinhala, an Indo-Aryan language, at about the same time (non-initial *-s* > *-h* in the second century BCE), before becoming Ø. There is crucial evidence in Tamil lexical phonology which supports this assumption. Only Tamil, and no other member of South Dravidian I, has *-ā* as V_2 in stems of the type (C)V_1C-V_2. In several lexical items where Tamil has *-ā*, the other languages point to an older *-ac*V[-asu] which perhaps became *-ah*(V) that resulted in *-ā* through contraction. Examine:

25. PD **car-ac-* [sar-asu] > SD I: Ta. *ar-ā* 'snake' (also *ara, aravu*), Ma. *aravu*; SD II: Te. *trācu* (<**tar-a-ncc-*) 'cobra', Go. *taras, taranj*, Koṇḍa *saras, srāsu*, Kui *srāsu, srācu*, Kuvi *rācu*, Pe. *rāc*, Manḍa *trehe.* Pkt. *sarāhaya-* (DNM) [*DEDR* 2359]. The Proto-Dravidian reconstruction would be **car-a-ncc-* > ** car-a-cc-* > **car-a-c-* [car-as-V]. *-as* > *-ah* > *-ā* accounts for the long *-ā* in Tamil. The *-h* element is reflected in Deśīnāmamālā's borrowing and also in Manḍa *trehe.* Note that Tamil adds a further formative suffix *-vu* whenever it ends in a long vowel in V_2 position and the long vowel in the unaccented position is shortened.

26. PD **kal-ac-* 'to quarrel' > SD I: Ta. *kal-ā-vu* 'to be angry', *kal-ā-y* 'to quarrel', *kal-ā-m* 'war, battle' (< **kal-ah-* < **kal-ac-*), Ma. *kalacuka* 'be disturbed', *kalacal* 'quarrel'; SD II: Kui *glahpa* (*glah-t-*) 'to confuse'; || > Skt. *kal-aha-* 'quarrel, fight' [*DEDR* 1303; also see Burrow 1948: 371]. Cognates occur in all subgroups, but the diagnostic ones are given; the occurrence of the *-s* form in Malayāḷam, the *h-* form in Kui, and *-h* in the Sanskrit borrowing point to *-as* > *-ah* > *-ā*.

27. PD **kan-ac*V 'dream, to dream' > SD I: Ta. *kaṉ-ā* (< **kan-ah-* < **kan-ac-*), *ka-avu* 'dream', v.i. 'to dream', Ma. *kan-āvu, kin-āvu, kan-avu* n., *kan-avu* v.i., Ko. *kancn* 'dream', Koḍ. *kenaci*, Ka. *kanasu, kanasa* n.; SD II: Go. *kansk, kansk-, kanjk-* v.i. [*DEDR* 1407].

28. PD **tuẓ-ac*V 'sacred basil' > SD I: Ta. *tuẓ-āy, tuḷ-aci, tuḷ-avu*, Ma. *tuḷ-asi*, Koḍ. *toḷ-asi*, Ka *toḷ-aci, toḷ-asi*, Tu. *tuḷ-asi, tul-asi*; SD II: Te. *tul-asi*; CD: Pa. *tul-ca*; || > Skt. *tulasī*; some of the Modern Dravidian forms could have been reborrowed from Sanskrit [*DEDR* 3357].

29. PD **nel-a-nc/*nel-a-ncc-* 'moon, moonlight' > SD I: Ta. *nil-ā* (< **nel-ah-* < **nel-ac-* < **nel-acc-*), *nil-avu*, Ma. *nil-ā*, Koḍ. *nel-aci*; SD II: Go. *nelanj*, Kui, Kuvi, Pe. Manḍa *lēnj-* (< **nlēnj* < *ənelanj-*), Kui *ḍānju* (< **lānj- lēnj-*); CD: Pa. *neliñ*[nelinj-], Ga. *neliŋ*. This compares well with **car-a-ncc-* in (25) above [*DEDR* 3754].

30. PD **pal-ac*V/**pan-ac-*V 'jack fruit tree' > SD I: Ta. *pal-ā, pil-ā, pal-avu*, Ma. *pal-āvu, plāvu*, Koḍ. *palaci*, Ka. *panasa, palasa, palasu*; SD II: Te. *panasa*, Kuvi *panha, paṇha*; CD: Pa. *penac*, Gad. *panis*; || > Skt. *panasa-, palasa-, phanasa-, phalasa-* [*DEDR* 3988].

31. PD **kaṭ-aca-* [kaṭ-asV- ~ kaḍ-as] 'male of cattle, heifer' > SD I: Ta. *kaṭ-ā, kaṭ-āy, kaṭ-avu, kiṭ-ā, kiṭ-āy*, Ma. *kaṭ-ā, kiṭ-ā(vu), kaṭ-acci* 'young cow', Ko. *kaṛc nāg/kurl* 'calf of buffalo/cow', Koḍ. *kaḍ-ïci*, Tu. *gaḍ-asu*, Ka. *kaḍ-asu*; SD II: Go. *kāṛ-ā*, Koṇda *gṛālu*, Kui *grāḍu, kṛai*, Kuvi *ḍālu*; ND: Kuṛ. *kaṛ-ā* 'young male buffalo', *kaṛ-ī* 'young female buffalo' (final vowels are gender markers borrowed from Indo-Aryan), Br. *xarās* 'bull'; || > Skt. *kaṭāha-* 'young female buffalo' [*DEDR* 1123;

also Burrow 1948: 368]. Note the occurrence of *-cV*/*-sV* in South Dravidian and Brahui and the Sanskrit loanword with *-ha*.

In all these cases and similar ones, the unique Old Tamil formative *-ā* can be interpreted as having developed from the contraction of an older **-ah* < **-as*. These examples provide the missing phonetic links otherwise shrouded in history, because *-h* was sub-phonemic. The laryngeal **H* had already disappeared from Tamil speech except in some relic forms with restricted distribution. All this evidence supports the view that the change *s* > *h* > Ø which occurred in South Dravidian I had spread to Gondi dialects in South Dravidian II from Telugu. The sound change is still running its course dialectally in South Dravidian II. Also notice that *s* > *h* occurs dialectally in the other members of South Dravidian II also, viz. Kui, Kuvi, Pengo, and Maṇḍa. Burrow (1947a: 133) cited items 28 and 30 as instances of Sanskrit words losing *-s* > -Ø in Early Tamil. In *DEDR* these are included as native groups indicating Sanskrit as the borrower with cross references to *CDIAL* entries. Furthermore Burrow (134) explicitly mentioned the loss of Sanskrit sibilants, but only with reference to a few items with Sanskrit affricate *c-*. The examples given by Burrow showed the loss of sibilants irrespective of their position in a word. Another point which receives indirect support from these examples is the possible merger of the Proto-Dravidian laryngeal **H* with **h* < **s*, leading to parallel phonetic developments.[6]

7.4. **Rules involving **H*.** The sound changes involving a laryngeal **H* within Proto-Dravidian may be summarized in the following rules, based on internal reconstruction within Proto-Dravidian and comparative method:

Rule 1. Semivowel Formation

a. ***H* → **w*/ #(C)V___ + [+ vocalic, +low] ... #
b. ***H* > **y*/# (C)V___[+segment] ...#

a. A laryngeal became a bilabial semivowel *w* within a word across a morpheme boundary before a low vowel **a* within Proto-Dravidian, e.g. ***aH-an̠ṯu* > **aw-an̠ṯu* 'he, that man', ***iH-an̠ṯu* > **iw-an̠ṯu* 'he, this man', ***yaH-an̠ṯu* > **yaw-an̠ṯu* 'who? which man?'; similarly, PD **aw-ar*/ **iw-ar* 'they (men/persons)', **aw-ay*/ **iw-ay* 'these (non-men/non-persons)', etc. (§ **2.4**); in Ancient Tamil this rule was extended to non-back semivowel *y* also, *aw yān̠ai* 'that elephant'. **b.** **H* historically became **y* sporadically in the later stages of Proto-Dravidian (§ 4).

Rule 2. Stop Assimilation.

**V[–long]*H* → *V[–long] P/#(C)___ +P

A laryngeal **H* following a short vowel and preceding a voiceless stop (P) became the same voiceless stop across a morph boundary, e.g. ***aH-pōẓ* > **ap-pōẓ* 'that time, then', *paH-tu* > *pat-tu* 'ten' (for further cases, see § **2.8**).

[6] Section 7.3 has been added since the original publication.

Rule 3. Compensatory Lengthening of Vowel.

**V[–long]*H* → V[+long]Ø/# (C_1)___C_2~Ø# (C_2 = a voiced coronal stop or sonorant, viz. **t* [d], **ṯ* [ṟ], **ṭ* [ḍ], **n*, **ṇ*, **r*, **l*, **ḷ*, **ẓ* or zero).

A short vowel followed by a laryngeal is lengthened generally when it is followed by zero or a coronal sonorant (within the same word). The resultant form is in most cases a free form (adjective, noun, or pronoun in nominative, imperative of a verb), e.g. ***aH* > **ā* 'that', ***iH* > **ī* (demonstrative adj.), **cā* 'die', **cā-w* 'death', **tā* 'bring', **wā* 'come' (imper.), ***koHḷ* > **kōḷ* 'seizure', ***yaH-n-* > **yān* 'I' etc.

Rule 4. Loss

The same as Rule 3 except that **H* occurs only in a closed syllable and the resultant form is bound and not free (in most cases), e.g. ***aH-t* > ***att-* > **at*-V- 'it', ***paH-t-* > **patt-* > **pat-in-* 'ten', ***waH-nt-* > **wa-nt-* (past stem of ***waH-* 'come'), ***aHn* > **an-*/**en-*/**in-* (with an intermediate stage in which ***H* > ***y*), ***koHḷ* > **koḷ* 'take', ***yaH-n* > **yan*(*n*)-'I' (oblique), etc.

20

Regularity of Sound Change through Lexical Diffusion: A Study of *s* > *h* > Ø in Gondi Dialects

0. Gondi is a Dravidian language spoken by 2.2 million speakers (Census of India, 1981) in the mountains and forests of four adjacent states in central India. Gondi is a chain of several dialects, some of which, at distant points, are perhaps not mutually intelligible. A major dialect division is provided by a two-step sound change: *s*- > *h*- in the west, north, and north-west and *h*- > Ø- in the south and south-east. The present article studies this two-step sound change, which is still in progress, and establishes two facts. First, contrary to the normal expectation that this sound change would be phonetically gradual and lexically abrupt (neogrammarian type), there is evidence that it has been lexically gradual and perhaps also phonetically gradual (lexical diffusion). Second, phonetic gradualness and regularity in implementation of sound change are properties not incompatible with the mechanism of lexical diffusion. Labov's observation that *s* > *h* > Ø has not been reported as a lexically diffused change in many quantitative studies of Portuguese and Spanish (1981) finds a clear exception in Gondi. Under the lexical diffusion model, the regularity of a sound change is defined as the final outcome in a three-stage change of the relevant lexicon: unchanged (*u*), variant (*u* ~ *c*), and changed (*c*). If the entire eligible lexicon passed from *u* to *c* through *u* ~ *c*, the change would become regular. If all *u* ~ *c* became *c* and for some reason no item under *u* became *u* ~ *c*, the sound change would die prematurely, since the variant stage which provided the rule for the innovation would be absent. Since a regular sound change can result from either the neogrammarian model or the lexical diffusion model, Labov's (1994: 542–3) theoretical proposal of complementarity between the kinds of changes resulting from the two mechanisms calls for more studies of sound change in progress to decide the issue.

I am grateful to William Labov, who read this article thoroughly and made some very positive comments. I am indebted to David Karl Beine for lending me a copy of his Master's thesis and to G.U. Rao for his useful comments. An earlier version of this article was presented at a Roundtable on Lexical Diffusion at the 16th International Congress of Linguists in Paris (July 20–25, 1997). I thank the Organizers of the Congress for granting me financial assistance to attend the Congress. I am indebted to Robert Nicolai for including this article in the panel and the discutants at the Roundtable on July 21st, 1997.

1. The Problem

1.1. Regularity of sound change is the cornerstone of the comparative method and reconstruction. The celebrated hypothesis of the neogrammarians has three components: (a) sound change (phonetic change) is gradual and progresses by imperceptible steps; (b) sound change is regular in the sense that all lexical items containing a given sound in the defined environment undergo the change simultaneously; (c) sound change is mechanical and does not admit exceptions. Most of the exceptions to the principle of regularity are attributed to non-mechanical (non-phonetic/non-phonological) factors, such as borrowing and analogy. Subsequent research has added taboo, avoidance of homonymy, onomatopoeia, sound symbolism, and social and grammatical factors to the possible causes of exceptions to the principle of the mechanical regularity of sound change (Campbell 1996). The neogrammarian position on regularity has been challenged by many dialectologists, philologists, and linguists (see Labov 1994: Ch. 15–17). However, historical linguists have not abandoned the doctrine of regularity of sound change.

1.2. During the last three decades, the neogrammarian controversy has been brought to the fore by a group of historical linguists called lexical diffusionists. Wang and a team of Chinese linguists in several publications have questioned the neogrammarian position. Wang (1969) summarized the issue as follows: sound change is thought to be either phonetically gradual and lexically abrupt (neogrammarians' claim) or phonetically abrupt and lexically gradual (lexical diffusionists' claim). A number of scholars have given incontrovertible evidence in favour of lexical diffusion. Wang and his collaborators published evidence from Swiss German, Classical Tibetan, Old Welsh, Swedish, Middle and Modern English, in addition to studies in language acquisition by children of English and Chinese (see Wang 1969, 1977, 1979). Krishnamurti (1976b, 1978a) showed that the shift of apical consonants from word medial to word initial syllable ('apical displacement') in a subgroup of South-Central Dravidian languages is a definite case of a sound change spreading from one word to another. Wang claimed that lexical diffusion is the basic mechanism of the actuation and implementation of a sound change, contrary to the neogrammarian position.

1.3. The crucial question of whether a given sound change is conditioned by the phonological unit or by the word was thoroughly addressed in Labov (1981, 1994); chapters 15 to 18 of the latter were devoted to the neogrammarian controversy and its 'resolution.' Only future studies will be able to determine if Labov has truly resolved the controversy. Some of his observations are extracted here (from Labov 1994: 542–3).

> *Regular sound change* is the result of a gradual transformation of a single phonetic feature of a phoneme in a continuous phonetic space. It is characteristic of the initial stages of a change that develops within a linguistic system without lexical or grammatical conditioning or any degree of social awareness ('change from below').

Lexical diffusion is the result of the abrupt substitution of one phoneme for another. The older and newer forms of the word will usually differ by several phonetic features. This process is most characteristic of the late stages of an internal change that has been differentiated by lexical and grammatical conditioning, or has developed a high degree of social awareness or of borrowings from other systems ('change from above').

Given this range of properties, we would predict that the realms of regular sound change and lexical diffusion would display complementary distribution:

Regular sound change	*Lexical diffusion*
Vowel shifts in place of articulation	Shortening and lengthening of segments
Diphthongization of high vowels	Diphthongization of mid and low vowels
Consonant changes in manner of articulation	Consonant changes in place of articulation
Vocalization of liquids	Metathesis of liquids and stops
Deletions of glides	Deletion of obstruents

The changes listed under lexical diffusion are, according to Labov, not real phonetic changes but 'changes of membership in higher-order classes' (1994: 531). Still some questions remain regarding the underlying linguistic logic of this partitioning. For instance, why should diphthongization of high vowels be a regular sound change while that of mid and low vowels follows the path of lexical diffusion? Is one change always and inherently from below and the other from above? The loss of Modern English /k/ before /n/ is a totally regular sound change, but it should have taken the path of lexical diffusion since it is deletion of an obstruent. Is there evidence that the loss was in fact phonetically gradual?

Labov (1994: Ch. 16, 17) gave persuasive arguments to show that most changes, including some claimed to be cases of lexical diffusion, still follow the neogrammarian regularity, by applying acoustic and statistical refinements. He also adduced evidence for clear cases of lexical diffusion (1994: Ch. 15). While questioning the stand taken by Wang and his team that lexical diffusion is the basic mechanism in the implementation of sound change, Labov (1994: 438) stated:

> To the best of my knowledge, no partisan of lexical diffusion has presented evidence of regular sound change. In each case examined, the fundamental mechanism of change argued for is that words migrate, one at a time, from one class to another.

Labov wondered why lexical diffusionists close their eyes to the innumerable sound changes that follow the neogrammarian protocol (i.e. being phonetically gradual and lexically abrupt). He pitted regular sound change against lexical diffusion as though they were opposite poles. The implication is that lexical diffusion is not compatible with the regularity of sound change since such a change is not phonetically motivated. My stand is not anti-neogrammarian, and I go along with Labov that sound changes can be divided into those that take the neogrammarian path (the phoneme as a unit of change) and those that take the path of lexical diffusion (the word as a unit of change), and that these are not conflicting but complementary mechanisms. I cannot, however, agree with the implication that the path of lexical diffusion does not lead to regular sound change. Is the change of the sound *s* to *h* to Ø a change in manner of articulation or place of articulation? Labov (1981: 302) considered it as a change in manner (in view of his bipartite division cited earlier): 'The sizable literature on the aspiration and deletion of /s/ shows no evidence of lexical conditioning in the many detailed quantitative investigations of Spanish . . . and Portuguese.' Labov (1994: 543) claimed no finality for the complementary distribution that he proposed, calling instead for 'a broader and deeper set of inquiries that will display the value and the limitations of their [neogrammarians'] initial results'. It is in this spirit that I present my analysis of Gondi data.

1.4. The purpose of this article is twofold. First, I intend to show that lexical diffusion can lead to (or is not incompatible with the final outcome of) regular sound change, when all relevant lexical items are affected by the sound change. The change of *s* > *h* > Ø, which is thoroughly implemented in the south-eastern and southern dialects of Gondi, is one such change. Second, the fact that it is a two-step change, *s* > *h* and *h* > Ø, would give the impression that it was not a discrete jump from *s* to Ø (as evidenced in Spanish and Portuguese) but apparently a phonetically gradual one that should have followed the neogrammarian path of covering the entire target lexicon at one stretch but did not. The data clearly show that the mechanism has been one of proceeding from one word (or one class of words) to another. The Gondi change, then, may be characterized as phonetically gradual as well as lexically gradual. This combination was pointed out by Wang (1969: 15) as one of the aspects of the mechanism of lexical diffusion, although most subsequent studies focused on changes that were phonetically abrupt and lexically gradual.

2. Gondi Data: A Case of Regular Sound Change through Lexical Diffusion

2.1. Gondi [gōṇḍī] is a non-literary Dravidian language spoken by 2.2 million people (Census of India 1981), mostly in the hills and forests of four contiguous states in Central India: Maharashtra, Madhya Pradesh, Andhra Pradesh, and Orissa (see Maps 20.1 and 2). It is a group of several regional varieties representing a dialect chain with greater mutual intelligibility at nearer points but low mutual intelligibility at distant points. According to Beine (1994: 89), 'Based on these intelligibility testing results, it has been determined that there are seven mutually unintelligible dialects of the Gondi language.' On the basis of shared phonological innovations, Smith (1991) identified eight regional dialects of Gondi, and Rao (1991) set up ten, taking into account both phonological and morphological isoglosses. The major dialect division in both the studies is between southern and south-eastern (sharing *s* > *h* > Ø and **ḻ*- > *l*-) as opposed to western, northern, and central (sharing **s* > *s*, with some items showing *s* > *h*, and *ḻ*- > *r*-).

The Gonds are listed as scheduled tribes, and most of them live in the hills and forests. A considerable number also live on the plains in and around urban centres,

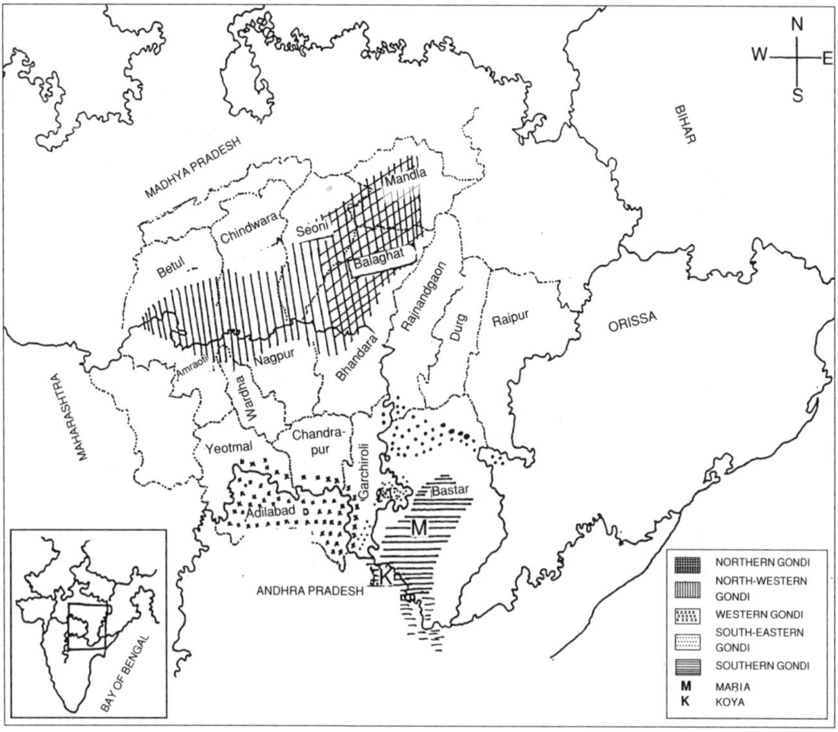

MAP 20.1. The Gondi language area

where they have become bilinguals in the neighbouring dominant regional languages (Marathi, Hindi, Telugu, and Oriya). There has been a decline in the number of speakers of Gondi from 4.6 million in the 1931 census to 2.2 million in the 1981 census, suggesting that over 50% have assimilated into the general population of the neighbouring states by slowly abandoning their native language (Rao 1987: 6–7).

There are several ongoing sound changes in Gondi, of which the most diagnostic is the two-step sound change *s* > *h* and *h* > Ø. According to Burrow and Bhattacharya (1960: 77),

> The most obvious feature dividing the Gondi dialects into two main groups is the treatment of *s*-. This is preserved with a few exceptions in the northern Gondi and western Gondi. Further to the south and east, in Chanda, Bastar and Kanker it has been changed to *h*-, while in the Hill-Maria dialect and Koya (Malkanagiri, South Bastar, and south of Godavari) this *h*- has been completely elided.

2.2. Nearly a century ago, Grierson (1906) recorded the sound change in the sample texts of Gondi from different districts of Maharashtra and Madhya Pradesh. (The Nizam's Dominions and the Madras Presidency were not covered by the survey.) Even then we can see the profile of the sound change in six or seven items in

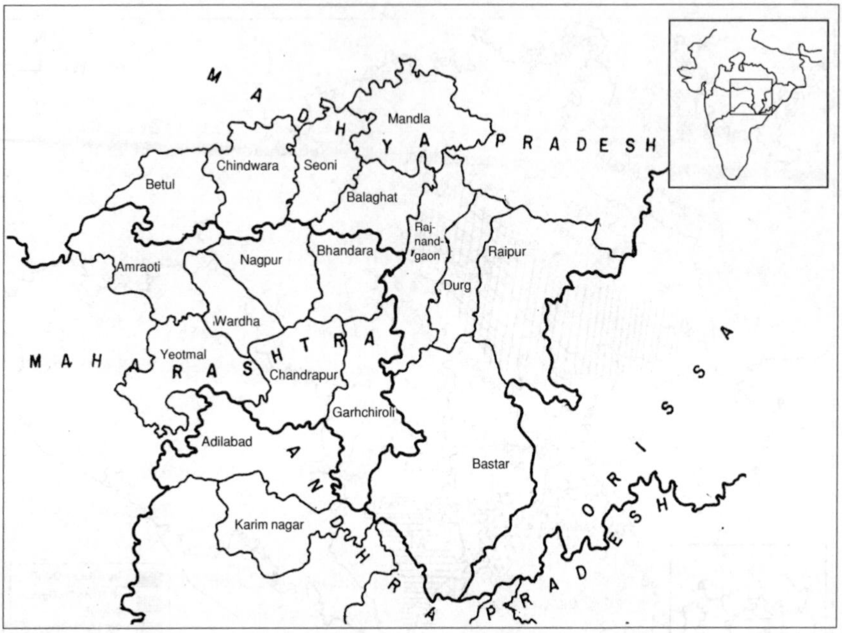

Map 20.2. Districts in which Gondi is spoken, partly or fully

the texts (see Appendix I). These texts do not tell us the age or gender of the informants or whether such texts were elicited from one or more than one informant. The ordering of centres is from north to north-east to south to south-east. In the northern dialects, three verbs, **sūṛ*- 'to see', **son*- (past **sot*-) 'to go', and **sille* 'is/was not' (from **sil*- 'not to be'), already show *h*- forms, while *s*- forms occur unchanged in four items. As we proceed to the south, the verbs **sā*- 'to die' and **sī*-/*siy*- 'to give' develop *h*-. In Bastar, both *h*- and Ø- forms co-occur. Finally, in the southern part of Bastar and further south (Godavari district of older Madras; Grierson cited a text from the Bible translation), only the Ø- forms occur.

2.3. My second source is the comparative vocabulary of the Gondi dialects by Burrow and Bhattacharya (1960). I have taken fifity-eight native lexical items that are given in *DEDR*. These represent over a score of published sources spread over ninety years as well as items collected at different places by the authors (see in particular the bibliography in Burrow and Bhattacharya 1960). No information on social factors correlating with language variation is available. The transcription is not precise but broadly quasi-phonemic and quasi-phonetic. Appendix II shows the Proto-Gondi reconstructions and the correspondences of Proto-Gondi **s*- from different sources are arranged geographically, west to north-west to north-east to south-east and south. Fig 20.1 shows the number of items in each of the selected locations (districts) and the number of instances with *s*, *s*/*h*, *h*, *h*/Ø, and Ø.

Sound(s)	Adilabad	Yeotmal	Betul	Chindwara	Mandla	Chanda	Muria	Sironcha	Maria-A	Maria-B	Koi/Koya
c	3	3	0	0	0	0	0	0	0	0	0
s	48	25	45	36	38	1	1	0	0	0	0
s/h	0	0	1	1	1	2	0	0	0	0	0
h	0	0	1	0	2	25	46	22	21	0	0
h/zero	0	0	0	0	0	0	2	10	1	0	0
zero	0	0	0	0	0	0	1	1	8	54	33
N	51	28	47	37	41	28	50	33	30	54	33

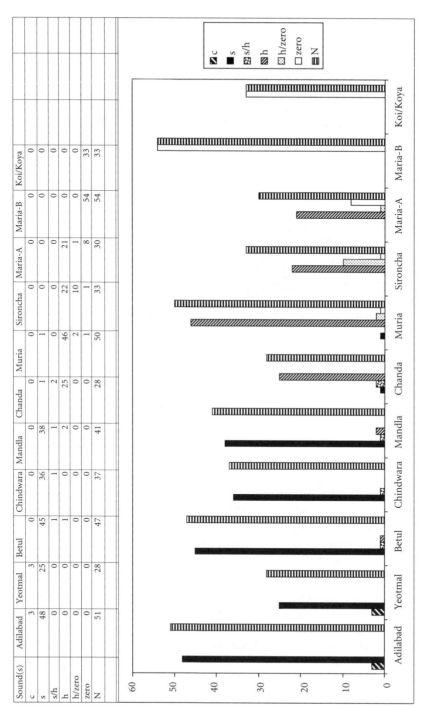

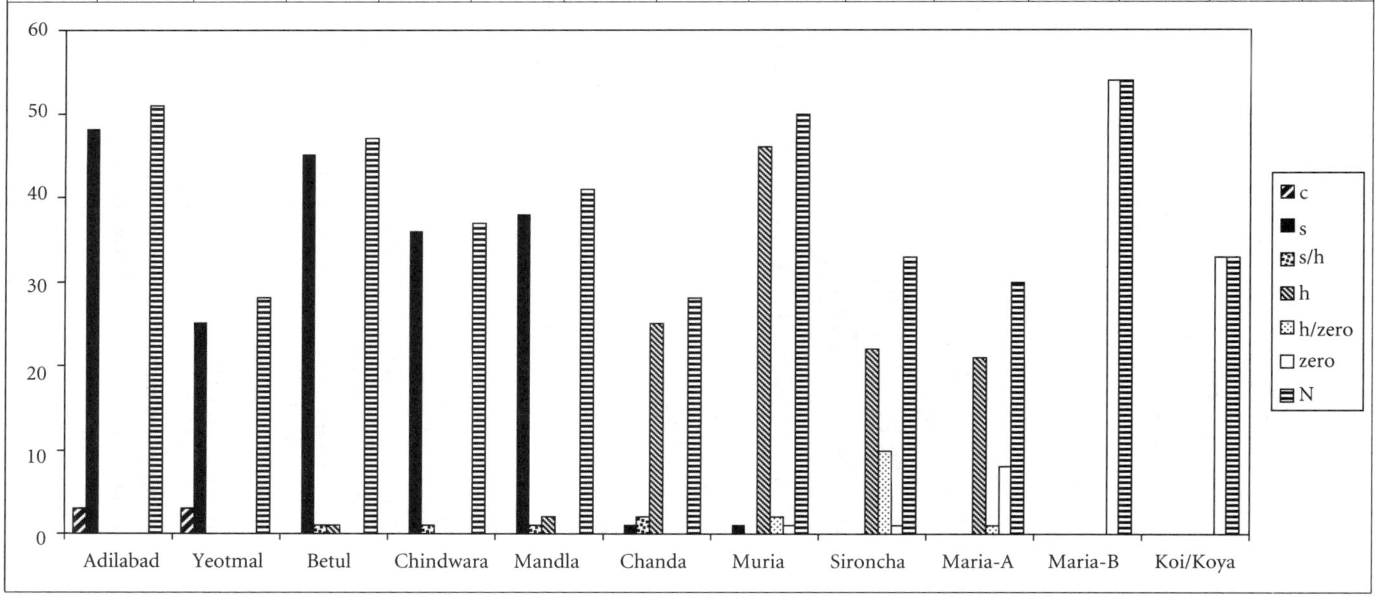

FIGURE 20.1. Number of items with *s-*, *s-/h-*, *h-*, *h-/Ø-*, and Ø in different Gondi subregions, based on *DEDR* (for *c* items, see Appendix II)

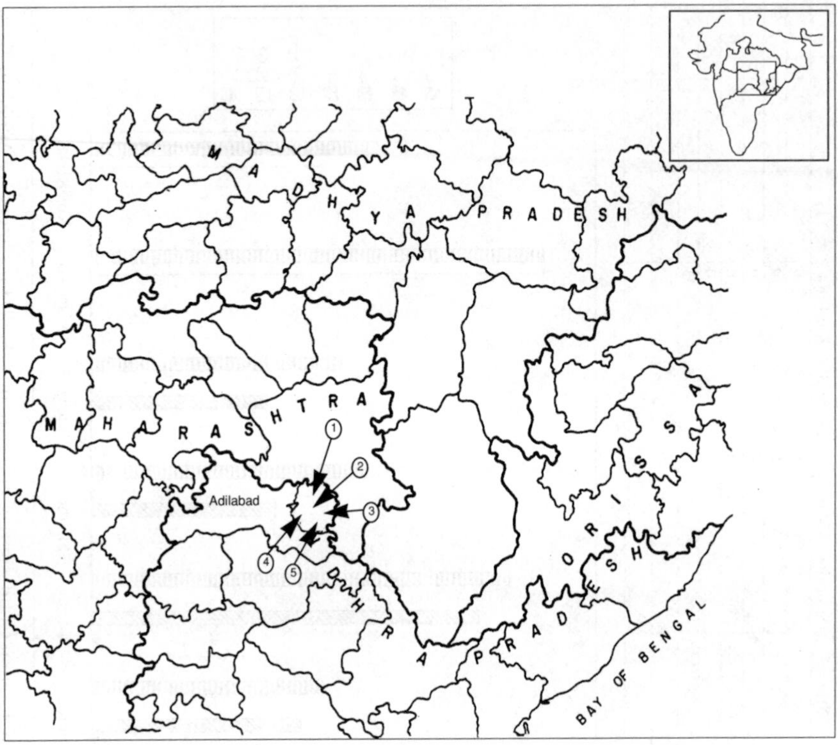

MAP 20.3. Fieldwork sites visited by Rao in Sirpur Taluq of Adilabad district

Variation in this study must have been caused by different authors collecting data from different sites and informants (dialectal) or from different periods (diachronic). Therefore, it should not be mistaken as synchronic variation in different tokens of the same lexical item by the same informant. However, the variant representations of a given lexical item clearly indicate the direction of change, their geographical location, and their participation in the process of diffusion. The graph in Fig 20.1 depicts the progression of the sound change strikingly, showing how the sound change has spread lexically from unchanged *s-* in the west and north to *h-* in the south-east to Ø- in the south-east and south (Muria of Chanda and Sironcha and Koi of South Bastar and Koya of the East Godavari district of Andhra Pradesh).

2.4. My third source is Rao (1982), who addressed the question of lexical diffusion of *s-*/*h-*/Ø- in Gondi dialects based on his fieldwork. He selected five villages in the Sirpur Taluq of Adilabad district from the point where the sound change *s* > *h* began and travelled east and south towards its change to *h* and Ø, covering a distance of sixty kilometres (see Map 20.3). He selected 40 commonly used lexical items from Burrow and Bhattacharya (1960) and Burrow and Emeneau (1961, 1968): 10 verbs, 1 adverb, and 29 nouns. The items denote 'kinship relations, agricultural and domestic tools, food and vegetables, numerals, etc.' (Rao 1982: 13). The initial segment (*s*/*h*/Ø) occurs before all possible vowels. He interviewed 48 informants in 4 villages, selecting 12 from each village, distributed equally among three age groups (over 47, 25 to 46, under 25). In Village 1, only 5 informants (all men) were selected. Some 40% of the total respondents were women. He elicited the desired words as answers to simple questions such as 'How many fingers are there in an open palm?' [shows an open palm]. A notebook and a pencil were used, and occasionally the material was tape-recorded. Only one token was available for each lexical item for a given speaker. Because of this constraint, we do not know, in the case of variations such as *s*/*h* or *h*/Ø which of the alternants occurred more than once and under what social and stylistic conditions. However, Rao computed indexed values for each speaker's utterance of segments ($s = 1$ and $h = 2$ for the first change and $h = 1$ and $Ø = 2$ for the second), following Labov's quantitative technique. These tables are not cited here for reasons of space.

Table 20.1 gives the number of lexical items with *s*, *s*/*h*, *h*, *h*/Ø, and Ø in each of the villages in terms of the averages for the male and female informants in each of the three age groups. Figs. 20.2–6 refer to the sound changes $s > h$ and $h > Ø$ in progress with identifiable areal and lexical diffusion of the changes. In Village 1, which is close to the border of Maharashtra, *h*- (see Map 20.3) occurs in 3 items and *s*/*h* in 1. The former items are the same as those that Grierson (1906) found with *h*-, namely *hon*- 'go', *hūṛ*- 'see', and *hille* 'no'. Innovation is limited to 10% of the data. In Village 2, situated to the south of Village 1, *s*/*h* has spread to 4 items, and *h* occurs in 4 items in the older and middle-aged men (20% innovation). In middle-aged women, *s*/*h* occurs in 7 items and *h* in 6, accounting for 33% of spread of the innovation. In the youngest age group, *s*/*h* occurs in 8 items and *h* in 11 (averaged), accounting for a 50% spread in innovative forms. Women are more innovative than men, and Rao (1982: 44–5) provided a sociological explanation for this. However, this social variable does not clearly emerge from the data, and it needs further study. In Village 3, the first part of the change is complete without exception. That is, no *s* or *s*/*h* forms were encountered: *h* occurs in 37 lexical items (averaged for all informants); *h*/Ø occurs in 2 items and Ø in 1 (the word for 'yoke' *ēr* < *hēr* < *sēr*) in the older and middle-aged groups; 2 Ø-forms occur in the youngest age group. In Village 4, only the younger generation shows more innovative forms: *h*/Ø in 6 forms and Ø in 1 (17.5%). Village 5 is apparently the transition zone between *h*/Ø and Ø, and the lexical spread of change acquires greater momentum. Both age and gender seem to be critical factors in the propagation of the change. Among older men, 28 items have *h* (70%), 10 have *h*/Ø (25%), and 2 (5%) have Ø. In the middle-aged group, 14 items (35%) have *h*, 16 (40%) have *h*/Ø, and 10 (25%) have Ø. In the youngest age group, 6 items (15%) have *h*, 14 (35%) have *h*/Ø, and 20 (50%) have Ø. The sound change has spread to 85% of the eligible lexicon. If Rao had selected another village in the Koya area, one further south, he would have registered the completion of $h > Ø$. This study is still important for registering the completion of the first leg of the sound change, $s > h$.

TABLE 20.1. *Retention or innovation of* s/h/Ø *among 53 informants, classified by age and gender*

	Village 1: Irdandi						Village 2: Mogaddhagad					
	Over 47		26 to 46		Under 25		Over 47		26 to 46		Under 25	
	Male	Female	Male	Female	Male	Female	Male	Female	Male	Female	Male	Female
s	37		35		35		31	32	32	27	21	18
s/h	1		1		1		5	4	4	7	8	8
h	2		4		4		4	4	4	6	11	14
h/Ø	0		0		0		0	0	0	0	0	0
Ø	0		0		0		0	0	0	0	0	0
	Village 3: Kukuda						**Village 4: Sulugupalli**					
	Over 47		26 to 46		Under 25		Over 47		26 to 46		Under 25	
	Male	Female	Male	Female	Male	Female	Male	Female	Male	Female	Male	Female
s	0	0	0	0	0	0	0	0	0		0	0
s/h	0	0	0	0	0	0	0	0	0		0	0
h	39	39	38	37	33	37	38	38	38		32	34
h/Ø	1	1	1	3	6	2	2	2	2		7	6
Ø	0	0	1	0	1	1	0	0	0		1	0
	Village 5: Yellur											
	Over 47		26 to 46		Under 25							
	Male	Female	Male	Female	Male	Female						
s	0		0	0	0	0						
s/h	0		0	0	0	0						
h	28		11	16	3	9						
h/Ø	10		22	10	13	16						
Ø	2		7	14	24	15						

What sort of lexical items become the targets of change in its initial and later stages? What is the lexical profile of the propagation of sound change? In Village 1, only 3 lexical items have *h* in all the respondents (one has *s*/*h* in *son*/*hon*), while 3 items show *s*/*h*, one each in a different individual. These include *hon-* 'go', *hūṛ-* 'see', and *hille* 'no', exactly the same items that occurred with *h* at the beginning of the century. Variation between *s* and *h* occurs in *sen*/*hen* 'ear of corn', *sarri*/*harri* 'way', and *sukk-*/*hukk-* 'to wash'. In Village 2, the *s*/*h* variation progressively spreads to the commonly used words for salt, ear of corn, sickle, oven, meat, way, headpad, and three kinship terms. Only *h-* forms occur in some items, such as salt, thorn, root, to rot, sickle, and in three kinship terms, while continuing the established *h-* items of Village 1. In Village 3, all forms have only *h-*, and the change of *s* > *h* is completed; a few forms start alternating with Ø. The rest of the profile of the sound changes is obvious from Table 20.1 and the graphs in Figs. 20.2–6. This description provides conclusive evidence for the lexical diffusion of sound change. What should be noted is that not all speakers in a community or age group show identical profiles in the implementation of the change.

2.5. The fourth source is Beine (1994), who visited 47 places covering the whole of the Gondi-speaking area except the Koya dialect (southern) of Andhra Pradesh (see Map 20.4).[1] Out of the word list of 210 items that he collected and transcribed (included as Appendix A to his thesis), 11 lexical items require Proto-Gondi **s*. I selected six items (**son-*/*sot-* 'go', **sūṛ-* 'see', **sowar* 'salt', **sā-* 'die', **sī-*/**siy-* 'give', **sāru-* 'six') and plotted the developments of their initials in six Gondi area maps at the 47 points given by Beine (see Maps 20.5–10). These show clearly that *s-* is still retained in the west, *h*/Ø occurs in the Garhchiroli district (part of older Chanda), and only Ø- forms occur in Maṛia of South Bastar. No item with variation of *s*/*h* is cited in any of the northern or western dialects. There are also some leaders and some laggers in the implementation of the sound change. The dialects in the north and west show *s-* in most cases (*sowar* 'salt') but *h-* in the case of the high frequency verbs (*sūṛ-* 'see', *son-* 'go', and *sille* 'not to be'). In Maṛia Gondi (Koi), only Ø occurs without exception, which is the same further south in places not visited by Beine.

3. Discussion

3.1. Data from the four studies undoubtedly show that lexical diffusion can lead to a chain of regular sound changes. None of the neighbouring Indo-Aryan languages shows *s* > *h*. Telugu shared with its southern neighbours a prehistoric change of Proto-Dravidian **c-* > Ø-, but the intermediate stage of *h-* was not

[1] Since Beine's survey does not include Andhra Pradesh, I have added to his data cognates from three places from the Koya dialect of Gondi spoken in the West Godavari District along the Andhra Pradesh–Madhya Pradesh border based on Tyler (1969) and Subrahmanyam (1968a). Koya has no surviving items with *h-* <*s-*.

Village	1	Irdandi						
Age group	>47		26–46		<25			
Gender	Male	Female	Male	Female	Male	Female		
No. Items	40		40		40			
s	37		35		35			
s/h	1		1		1			
h	2		4		4			
h/zero	0		0		0			
zero	0		0		0			

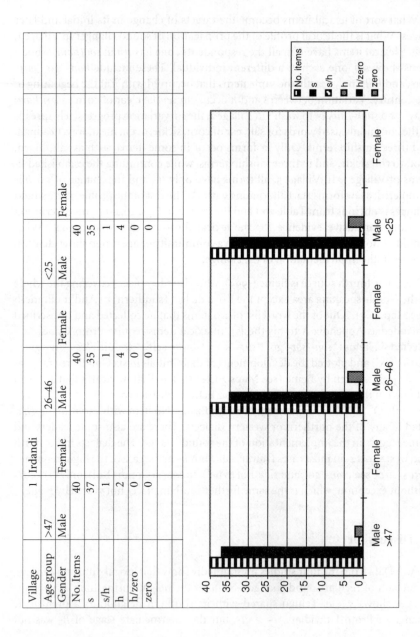

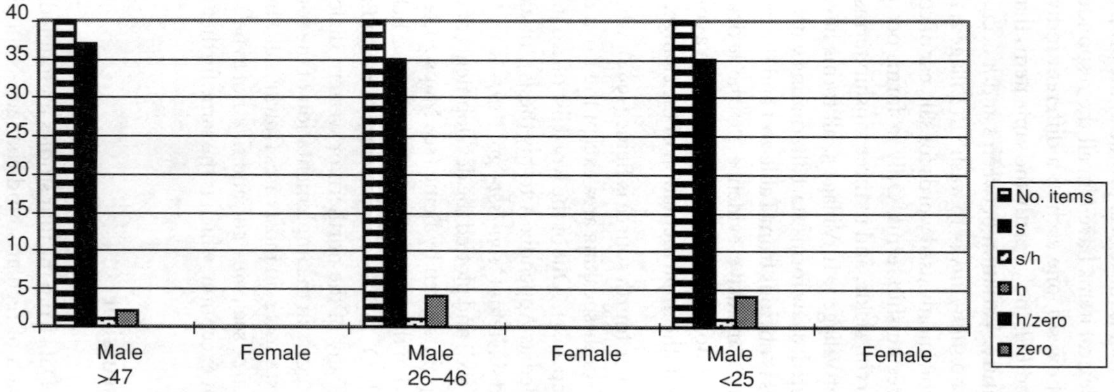

FIGURE 20.2. Profile of sound change $s > h > Ø$ in Village 1 (Irdandi)

attested [see ch. 19 §73]. This change has been extensively discussed in comparative Dravidian literature (see Emeneau 1994: 350–6), but the change was arrested mid-way after covering 12% of the eligible lexical items. In my opinion, the prehistoric change of South Dravidian and what is happening in South-Central Dravidian (and in Kui-Kuvi-Pengo-Manḍa, which shares the innovation *s* > *h* in different degrees but not *h* > Ø) are one and the same. The change must have operated in South Dravidian in certain lexical items in which **c* became **s* (presumably co-varying with certain social factors which cannot be retrieved) and then **h* (not recorded because it was subphonemic) and finally Ø. This is one of the isoglosses that binds South and South-Central Dravidian into a major branch (see Krishnamurti 1976a).

In the case of Gondi dialects, the sound change must have started in the southern dialects (Koya and Maṛia bordering on Telugu in which Proto-Dravidian **c* > [**s* > **h*] > Ø occurred in its early history) and spread to the north and north-west, leaving the western dialects mostly untouched beyond a few lexical items. The high frequency verbs *son* 'go' and *sūṛ* 'see' and the negative verb *sille* were the first to undergo *s*- > *h*- in the north, north-west, and north-east over ninety years ago. At some later point in time, the sound change was arrested. In the south, in the Muria dialect of Garhchiroli and in the northern Maṛia of Bastar *h* > Ø is still ongoing

Village 2						
Age group	>47		26–46		<25	
Gender	Male	Female	Male	Female	Male	Female
No. Items	40	40	40	40	40	40
s	31	32	32	27	18	18
s/h	5	4	4	7	8	8
h	4	4	4	6	11	14
h/zero	0	0	0	0	0	0
zero	0	0	0	0	0	0

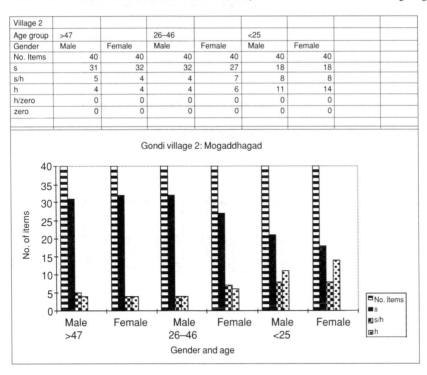

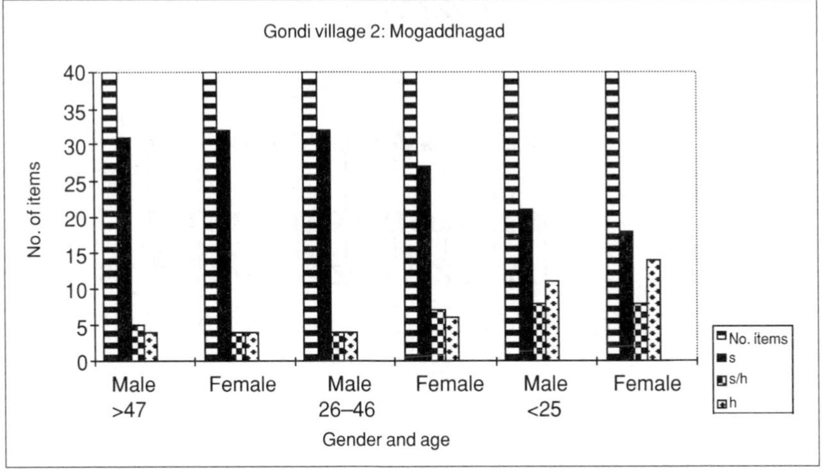

FIGURE 20.3. Profile of sound change *s* > *h* > Ø in Village 2 (Mogaddhagad)

Village						
Age group	>47		26–46		<25	
Gender	Male	Female	Male	Female	Male	Female
s	0	0	0	0	0	0
s/h	0	0	0	0	0	0
h	39	39	38	37	33	37
h/zero	1	1	1	3	6	2
zero	0	0	1	0	1	1
N	40	40	40	40	40	40

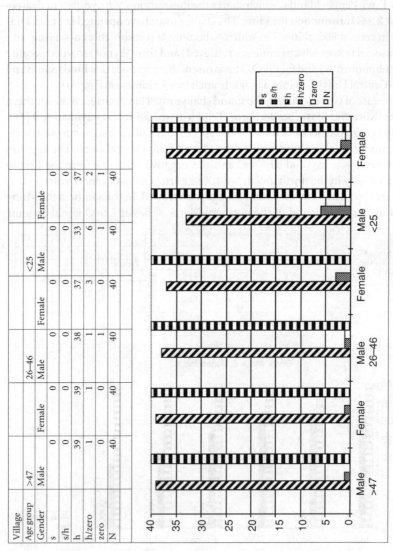

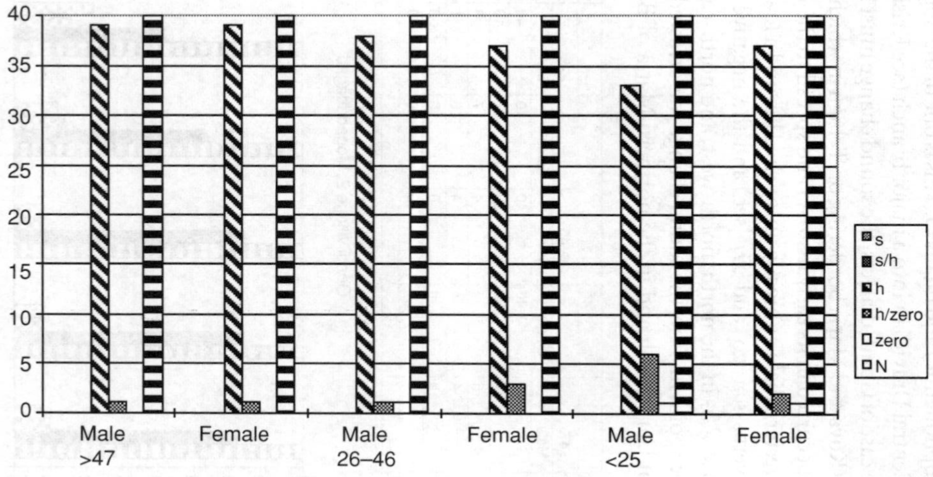

FIGURE 20.4. Profile of sound change $s > h > \emptyset$ in Village 3 (Kukuda)

Village	4	Sulugupalli					5	Yellur				
Age group	>47		26–46		<25		>47		26–46		<25	
Gender	Male	Female	Male	Female	Male	Female	Male	Female	Male	Female	Male	Female
N=	40	40	40	40	40	40	40	40	40	40	40	40
s	0	0	0		0	0	0		0	0	0	0
s/h	0	0	0		0	0	0		0	0	0	0
h	38	38	38		32	34	28		11	16	3	9
h/zero	2	2	2		7	6	10		22	10	13	16
zero	0	0	0		1	0	2		7	14	24	15

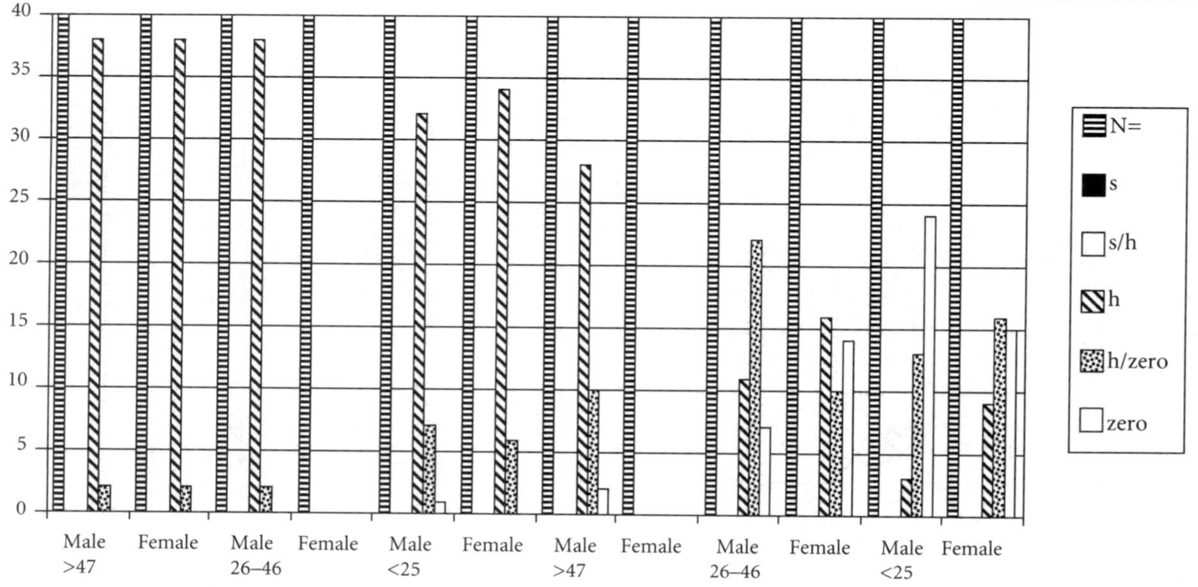

FIGURE 20.5. Profile of sound change $s > h > Ø$ in Village 4 (Sulugupalli)
FIGURE 20.6. Profile of sound change $s > h > Ø$ in Village 5 (Yellur)

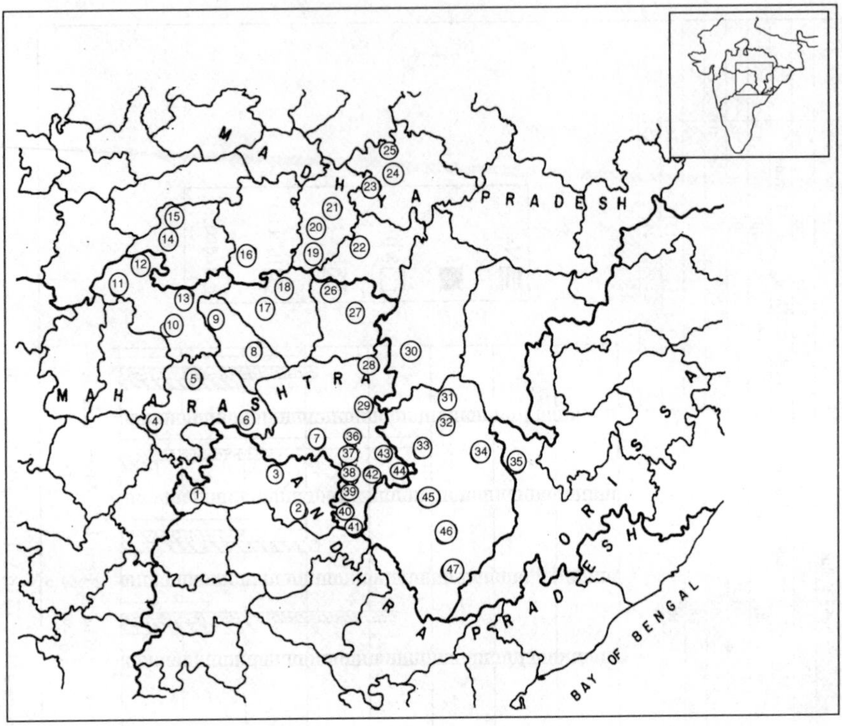

MAP 20.4. Places visited by Beine (1–47) for fieldwork

because the synchronic variation of *h*/Ø is also ongoing. In Southern Maṛia and in Koya to the south of the River Godavari only Ø-forms occur, attesting to the completed regular sound change [see Ch. 19 §7.3].

3.2. The following questions need to be addressed. Within the framework of lexical diffusion, what is the mechanism by which a sound change dies midway? What circumstances would lead it to a complete regularity in implementation?

When a sound change spreads from word to word, there are three phases attested: unchanged (*u*), variable (*v*), and changed (*c*). Table 20.2 shows a model of progression of a sound change along this dimension.

At T^0 in a given speech community, there were 10 lexical items beginning with *h*. At T^1, items 1 and 2 developed variants with Ø, while items 3 to 10 remained unchanged. At T^2, the variable forms developed Ø in place of *h*, while items 3 to 5 developed variation *h* ~ Ø. At T^3, the same steps were repeated with only 2 items unchanged (9, 10), 3 items in the variable phase (6–8), and 5 items (1–5) in the changed phase. If the same steps were repeated at T^4 and T^5, the result would be a regular sound change. Alternatively, at any stage (say T^4), all variable forms could move into the changed phase, while the unchanged items (for some reason) would

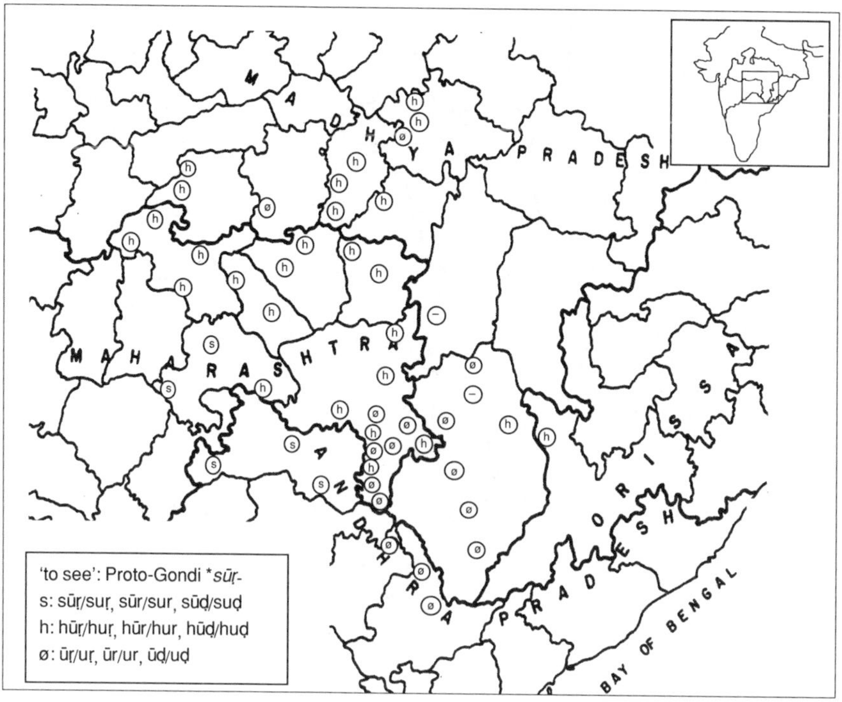

MAP 20.5. *s* > *h* > Ø for Proto-Gondi **sūṛ-* 'to see' (Beine's data)

fail to develop *h* ~ Ø variants. The sound change would then be arrested, since the rule (the generalization of younger speakers to correlate an innovative Ø- with the *h*- of older people in different lexical items) governing the synchronic variation of *h*/Ø would have died out. Now *h*- and Ø- would contrast in the language of the speakers if this had happened extensively. Therefore, the most important phase in lexical diffusion is the availability of a synchronic rule accounting for lexical variation. Something similar to this must have happened in many of the northern dialects of Gondi where *s* > *h* occurs in a few high frequency items like *son-/hon-* 'go', *sūṛ-/hūṛ-* 'see', and *sille/hille* 'not to be'. But it appears that this change is frozen, and that no new items are changing *s* to *h*, because there is no synchronic variation of *s/h*. Therefore, *s*- persists in otherwise frequent items like *sowar* 'salt', *sāy* 'die', and *sī/siy* 'give'. Beine (personal communication, September 30, 1997) confirmed that he had not come across any *s/h* or *h*/Ø variation in the lexical items that he collected in the northern and western dialects.

This is, of course, an idealized model, and it can be taken to represent one or more individuals in a particular speech community, possibly with some accompanying significant social variables. But essentially the model explains both the regularity of sound change and how exceptions arise when a sound change is arrested midway. In my study of apical displacement as a lexically diffused sound change in

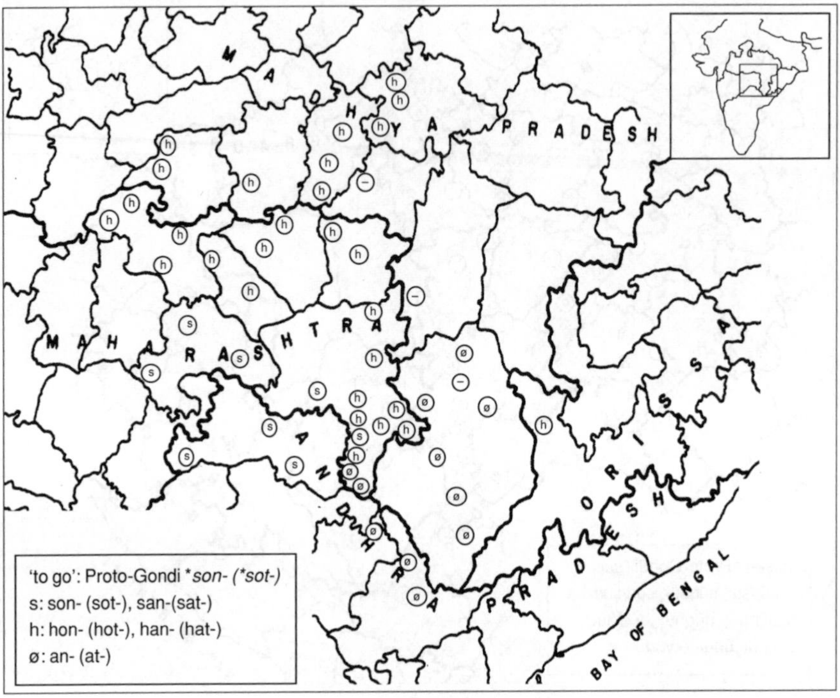

MAP 20.6. $s > h > \emptyset$ for Proto-Gondi **son-* (**sot-*) 'to go' (Beine's data)

a group of South-Central Dravidian languages, I showed that the sound change died midway in Gondi after it had affected only 16% of the eligible items (Krishnamurti, 1978a: 9–10). It is still in progress in the sister languages, Kui-Kuvi-Pengo-Manḍa. No dialect of Gondi now shows any instance of variation in any dialect, which would have kept the rule underlying the change alive.

TABLE 20.2. *A model of lexical diffusion leading to either completely regular or partially regular sound change (as an example,* h > Ø *is taken in a possible lexicon of ten words)*

Time		Unchanged: *h*	Variable: *h* ~ Ø	Changed: Ø
T^0		Words 1–10	—	—
T^1		Words 3–10	Words 1–2	—
T^2		Words 6–10	Words 3–5	Words 1–2
T^3		Words 9–10	Words 6–8	Words 1–5
T^4	Alternative 1	—	Words 9–10	Words 1–8
T^5		—	—	Words 1–10
T^4	Alternative 2	Words 9–10	—	Words 1–8
T^5		Words 9–10	—	Words 1–8

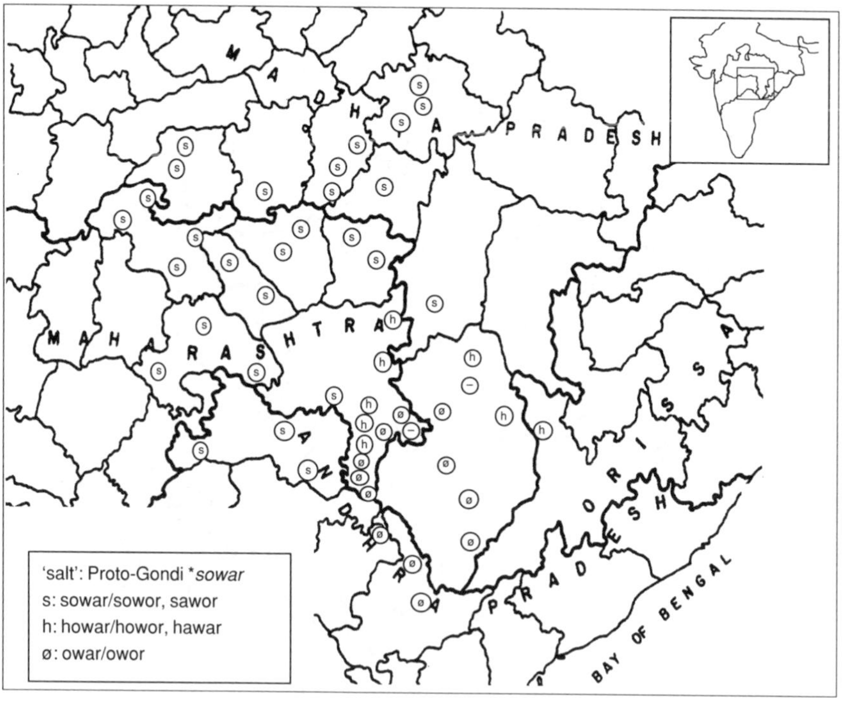

MAP 20.7. $s > h > \emptyset$ for Proto-Gondi **sowar* 'salt' (Beine's data)

3.3. The second question to examine is whether Gondi $s > h$ is the result of an abrupt substitution of *h* for *s* as a change from above. There is no evidence for this assumption. Incidentally, *h* develops from more than one source in Gondi within the native system, and *s* and *h* still contrast in all dialects. Recent borrowings from Indo-Aryan show *s* in many forms, even in the *h*- or Ø-dialects. The change of *s* to *h* is a natural phonetic change found in many languages of the world like Greek, Iranian, Indic (Sinhala and Assamese), and Iberian (Spanish and Portuguese). Such a phonetic change might have occurred among some speakers but not in the whole speech community. This could have led to variation between *s* forms and *h* forms, and the variation could have then spread lexically and geographically from that point. But all this is speculation. The truth is that the availability of variation has led to a regular sound change in two stages. Therefore, phonetic gradualness and regularity in outcome are properties not incompatible with the mechanism of lexical diffusion.

Consonantal changes not conditioned phonetically (unlike umlaut, vowel harmony, or lenition of intervocalic stops) represent a change in the speech habits of the speakers, like $s > h$. Here, there is nothing in the environment which would change the pronunciation of all speakers simultaneously. Could such changes have operated in a small segment of the speech community in such a way that they were

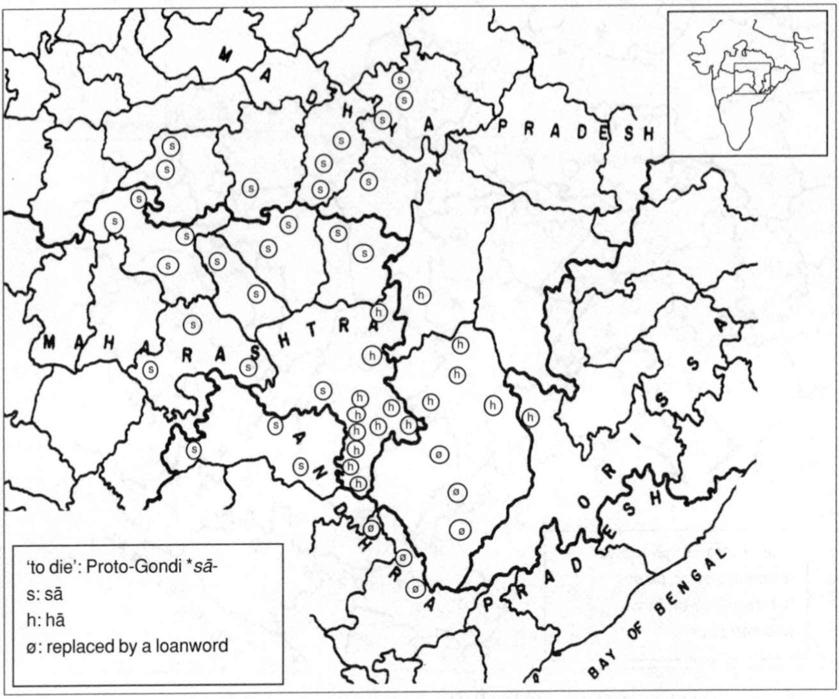

MAP 20.8. *s* > *h* > Ø > loanword for Proto-Gondi **sā*- 'to die' (Beine's data)

phonetically gradual in a few words of high frequency and then spread to other words which affected the target segment? Labov's suggestion that lexical diffusion begins after a regular phonetic change (at the allophonic level) has operated has some supporting evidence from Dravidian. In modern standard Telugu /m /is [w̃] (nasalized *w*) intervocalically, finally, and before /*w s h*/. This is a thoroughgoing, subphonemic change. Now only four lexical items with intervocalic [w̃] have replaced this segment by /w/: /māmayya/ → /māwayya/ 'maternal uncle', /māmiḍi/ → /māwiḍi/ 'mango', /manamaḍu/ → / manawaḍu/ 'grandson', and /manamarālu/ → / manawarālu/ 'granddaughter' in the younger generation of standard speakers. These represent a clear case of lexical diffusion following a phonetic change which provided the ground for a phonological jump through lexical selection. Underlying /w/ also becomes /m/ in two items: /cewuḍu/ → /cemuḍu/ [cew̃uṛu] 'deafness' and /dēwuḍu/ → /dēmuḍu/ 'god' (on the analogy of /rāmuḍu/ 'Lord Rama'), a case of hyperstandardization. There are not too many in both the classes. Lexical diffusion thus seems to operate in such a way that the subphonemic output of a phoneme may be affected by a subsequent sound change as, for instance, by the loss of nasalization of [w̃] in the Telugu examples, causing the allophone to become phonemic.

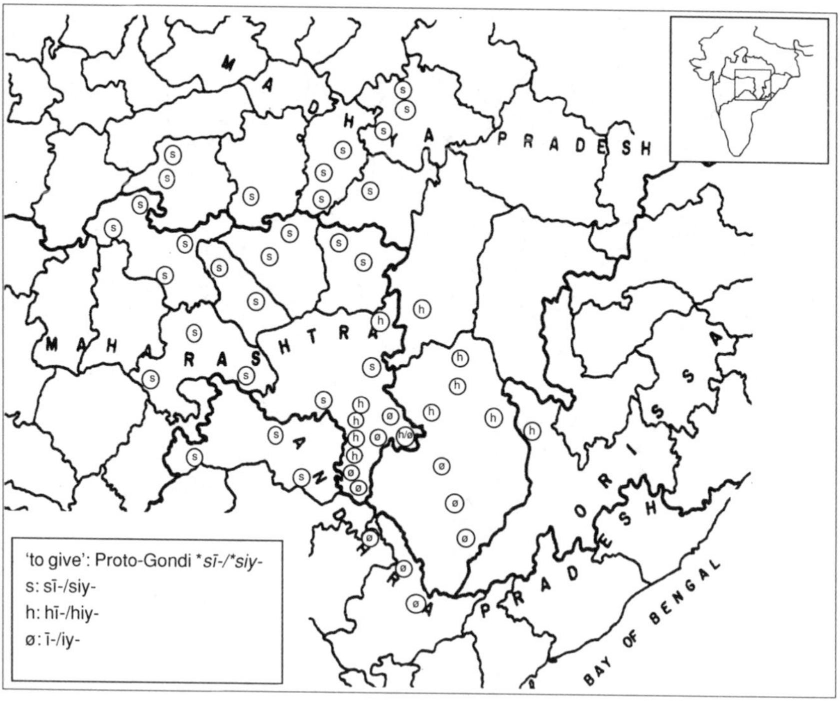

MAP 20.9. $s > h > \emptyset$ for Proto-Gondi **sī-*/**siy-* 'to give' (Beine's data)

One other dimension of regularity of sound change is a distinction between typologically motivated changes and other kinds of changes. A change which is motivated by some kind of asymmetry in the phonological system or some need to balance certain parts of the system tends to be regular, as opposed to non-typological ones. Considerable evidence can be given in favour of this from consonantal changes in Dravidian. A diagnostic feature of a typologically motivated sound change is that it is replicated in different languages and at different times, producing the same output (see Krishnamurti 1998a).

4. Conclusion

The two-step sound change in the Gondi dialects is a conclusive case of lexical diffusion leading to a regular sound change. More studies are needed to define precisely the terms of the working hypothesis of Labov that both the neogrammarian model and lexical diffusion tend to be complementary and not overlapping. The present study calls for further empirical research on sound change in progress in literate and non-literate societies.

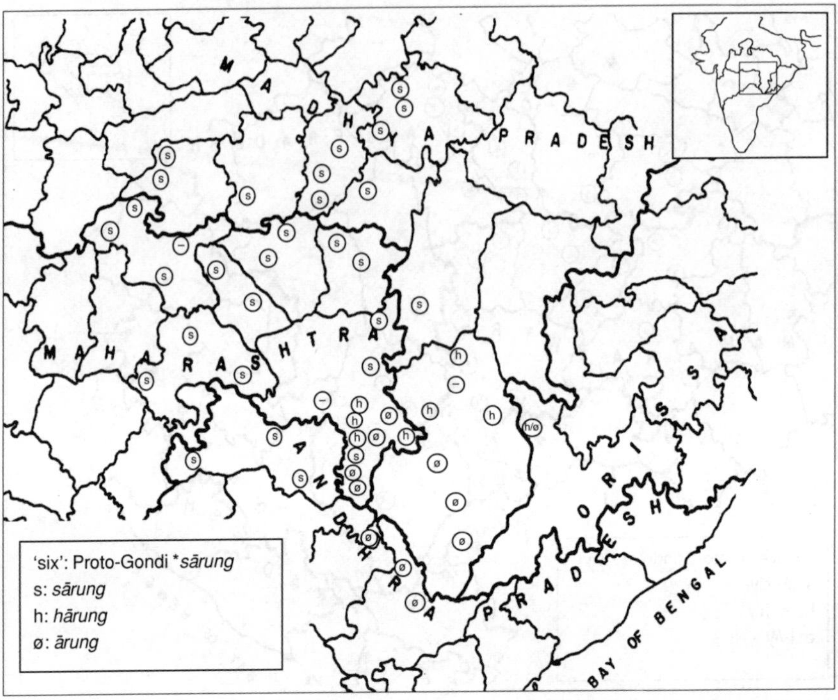

MAP 20.10. *s* > *h* > Ø for Proto-Gondi **sārung* 'six' (Beine's data)

Appendix I

Evidence for the sound change s → *h* → Ø *in Gondi texts given in the* Linguistic Survey of India, *Vol. IV: 472–560 (1906)*

Region	'bread'	'sandal'	'die'	'give'	'see'	'go'	'no/not'
Proto-Gondi	*sāri	*serpu-	*sāy	*sī-/*siy	*sūṛ-	*son-, *sot-	*sil(l)e
Mandla	—	sarpuk	say-^{4}	sī-^{3}	hūṛ-^{2}	han-, hat-^{3}	hille^{6}
Bilaspur	—	—	—	sī-/siy-	—	han-^{2}	hile
Jabalpur	—	—	—	sī-^{3}	—	hat-^{3}	hill-^{2}
Narsingpur	—	—	sāy^{2}	sī-^{2}	hūr-	han-, hat-^{3}	hill-^{2}
Chindwara	sārī	—	sai-	sī	—	han, hat-^{5}	halle^{5}
Hoshangabad	—	—	—	—	huṛ-^{2}	han-, hat-^{8}	haile^{3}
Betul	—	—	—	sī-^{4}	—	hat-^{3}	halle^{2}
Akola	—	—	—	sī-^{2}	—	hat-^{2}	hille
Basim	—	—	sā-	sī-	huṛ-	hat-^{3}	hil(l)e^{2}
Wun-	—	—	sā-^{3}	sī-^{5}	suṛ-, huṛ-^{2}	sot-^{2}, hot-^{2}	sila^{6}

Nagpur	—	—	sā-^{2}	sī-/siy-^{7}	hūṛ-^{5}	han, hat-^{7}	ḥalle^{2}
Bhandara	—	—	—	sī-^{3}	huṛ-^{4}	han,- hat-^{2}	hile^{5}
Balaghat	—	—	sā-	sē-/sī-^{4}	—	han-^{2}	hille^{3}
Seoni	—	sarpum	sā-^{3}	sī-^{6}	huṛ-^{2}	han-^{4}	hille^{7}
Kairaghar	—	—	—	sī	—	han-, hat-^{2}	—
Nandgaon	—	—	—	sē-^{2}	—	han-, hat-^{3}	hille^{2}
Raipur	sāṛī	—	sā	sē-	—	han-, hat-^{5}	hille^{2}
Saranghar	—	—	—	sī-^{4}	huṛ-	—	—
Patna	—	—	—	sē-^{2}	hur	—	hile/hale^{2}
Kanker-	—	—	—	sī/hī-^{2}	—	—	—
Bastar (Go.)	—	—	hā-	hī-/hē-^{2}	—	hat-	—
Bastar (Ma.)	—	erpuŋ	—	hī-^{2}/ī-	hūṛ-^{2} /ūṛ-	hat-^{4}, at^{2}	—
Chanda (Go.)	sārī	—	sā-^{2}	sī-/ī-^{2}	huṛ-^{2}	hon, hot-^{5}	hi(l)le^{5}
Chanda (Ma.)	—	—	—	hī-^{4}	huṛ-^{2}	hon-	hille
Chanda (Go.)	—	helpuk	hā-^{2}	iyy-/ī-^{4}	ūṛ-	hon-, hot^{7}	hille^{2}/ille
Chanda (Ko.)	—	—	—	hī-^{3}/ī-^{4}	ūṛ-	hon-, hot^{2}	il(l)e^{3}
						ot-	
Bastar (Ko.)	—	—	—	it-	ūṛ-	an-	ille
Godavari (Ko.)	—	erpuk	—	ī-, itt-^{2}	ūṛ-	an-	ille^{2}

The item in column 3 is a pre-Gondi borrowing from Proto-Telugu **cerpu*- 'sandal' (< **kerppu*). Note that *h* > Ø broadly corresponds with another change, viz. Proto-Gondi **e*, **o* > *a* in many dialects of the north and west. Frequency of occurrence within the texts is indicated by a raised number.

Appendix II

s→h→Ø *in Gondi Dialects*

The chart is based on Burrow and Bhattacharya (1960). Most of the relevant items were included in *DEDR*. Exceptions are marked 'G'. The District (State) is indicated by: 1. Adilabad (Andhra Pradesh), 2. Yeotmal (Maharashtra), 3. Betul (Madhya Pradesh), 4. Chindwara (MP), 5. Mandla (MP), 6. Chanda (Mah), 7. Muria of Bastar (MP), 8. Sironch Tehsil of Chanda (to the west of Muria of Bastar) (Mah), 9. Dandami Maṛias of Bastar (MP), 10. Hill Maṛias in the north of Bastar, to the east of Chanda (MP), 11. Koi or Koya of south Bastar (MP), Koya of East Godavari, Khammam, Warangal, and Karimnagar (AP).

DEDR	Proto-Gondi	1	2	3	4	5	6	7	8	9	10	11
2303	*saṭṭa 'shoulder'	s	—	s	s	s	h	h	h	Ø	Ø	Ø
2410	*saṇai 'son-in-law'	s	s	s	s	s	h	h	h	—	Ø	—
5155	*sēm VI 'tortoise'	—	—	—	—	—	s/h	h	—	h	Ø	Ø
2426	*sāy-'die'	s	—	s	s	s	—	h	h	h	—	—
2416	*saṟ- 'tear'	s	—	s	s	s	h	h	h/Ø	—	Ø	—
2417	*saṟi 'way'	s	s	s	s	s	h	h/Ø	—	h	Ø	Ø
3340G	*sari-'open mouth'	—	—	—	s	s	—	—	h	—	—	—

DEDR	·Proto-Gondi	1	2	3	4	5	6	7	8	9	10	11
3341G	*sarus 'weave'	s	—	—	—	—	—	—	h	—	Ø	Ø
3351G	*sar- 'drip'	s	—	s	s	—	—	h	—	—	Ø	—
2402b	*saṛapi 'dung'	s	s	s	s	s	s/h	h	h/Ø	h	Ø	Ø
3354G	*saliya 'red ant'	—	—	—	s	—	—	h	—	h	Ø	—
2341	*savi 'go bad'	s	—	s	s	s	—	h	—	—	Ø	—
2074	*sovar 'salt'	s	s	s	s	s	—	h	h	—	Ø	Ø
2860	*sovta 'sour'	s	—	s	—	s	—	h	—	—	Ø	—
2391	*sahki 'mortar'	c	c	s	s	s	h	h	—	—	Ø	Ø
2433	*sāŋg- 'spread'	s	—	s	s	s	—	h/Ø	—	—	Ø	Ø
2468	*sāp 'thorn'	s	c	s	—	—	h	h	h	—	Ø	—
3370G	*sāpa 'egg plant'	s	s	—	s	—	h	h	—	h	Ø	Ø
2485	*sārung 'six'	s	s	s	s	s	s	h	—	h	Ø	Ø
2604	*sīkaṭi 'darkness'	s	—	s	s	s	—	h	h	Ø	Ø	Ø
2529	*sitta 'tamarind'	s	s	s	s	s	h	h	h	Ø	Ø	Ø
2617	*sīnd 'wild date palm'	ś	s	—	—	s	—	h	h	h	Ø	Ø
2515	*sirna 'bell'	ś	—	—	—	—	—	h	—	—	—	—
2584	*sir 'below'	—	—	s	—	s	—	—	h/Ø	h	Ø	—
2465	*sāṛi 'pancake'	s	s	s	s	s	—	h	—	—	Ø	—
2569	*silka 'rivulet'	s	—	—	—	—	h	h	—	h	Ø	Ø
2559	*sille 'no, not'	s	s	—	—	h	—	—	h/Ø	—	Ø	Ø
2598	*sī 'give'	s	—	s	s	s	h	h	h	h	Ø	Ø
2615	*sīr 'nits'	—	—	s	s	s	—	h	h/Ø	—	Ø	—
2626	*sīr 'root'	ś	s	s	s	s	h	h	h/Ø	—	Ø	—
2667	*sukk- 'wash'	s	s	s	s	s	h	h	h	h	Ø	Ø
2646	*sukkVm 'star'	s	s	s	—	s	h	h	h	—	Ø	Ø
3433	*sukkur 'ladle'	s	—	s	s	s	—	h	—	h	Ø	—
2677	*summā 'headpad'	c	—	—	s	s	—	h	Ø	—	Ø	Ø
2654	*suṟ- 'cook'	s	—	s	s	s	—	h	h	—	Ø	Ø
2689	*surve 'beehive'	s	—	s	s	—	—	—	—	h	Ø	Ø
2621	*suhk- 'suck'	—	—	s	—	s	—	—	—	—	Ø	—
2730	*sūre 'a tree'	s	—	—	—	—	—	—	—	h	Ø	—
2735	*sūṛ 'see'	s	s	s/h	s/h	s/h	h	h	h	Ø	Ø	—
2756	*seṭer 'sickle'	s	—	s	—	s	h	h	h/Ø	h/Ø	Ø	—
2798	*sen 'ear of corn'	ś	—	s	—	—	—	h	h	—	Ø	Ø
2599	*sai- 'sweep'	s	s	s	—	s	h	h	h/Ø	h	Ø	Ø
2819	*seṟanṟ- 'spouse's brother'	s	s	s	s	s	—	h	h/Ø	—	Ø	Ø
1963	*serpum 'sandals'	s	—	s	—	s	h	h	h	h	Ø	Ø
2488	*sever 'gum'	ś	s	s	—	—	—	h	—	h	Ø	Ø
2019	*sētti 'winnower'	s	s	s	—	s	h	h	h/Ø	—	Ø	Ø
2815	*sēr 'plough'	s	s	s	s	—	h	—	—	—	Ø	—
2816	*seṟi 'snake'	s	—	s	s	—	—	h	—	—	Ø	—
2783	*sēlāḷ 'sister'	s	ś	s	s	s	h	h	—	Ø	Ø	Ø
2826	*saiyung 'five'	s	s	s	s	s	h	h	—	Ø	Ø	Ø
2857	*sodel 'fire place'	s	s	s	s	s	h	h	h	Ø	Ø	—

2781	*son- (sot-) 'go'	s	s	h	—	h	—	h	h	h	Ø	—
2776	*soy 'porcupine'	s	s	s	s	—	h	h	h	—	Ø	Ø
2876	*soṛi 'enter'	—	—	s	s	s	—	h	h	Ø	Ø	—
2865	*soh- 'itch'	c	c	s	s	—	h	h	—	—	Ø	Ø
2872	*sōk 'apply oil'	s	—	s	—	s	h	h	h	—	—	Ø
3504G	*sōŋ 'anger'	s	s	s	—	s	—	s	—	h	Ø	Ø
3511G	*sōṛ 'be sharp'	s	—	s	s	—	—	—	—	h	Ø	—

Total items 58; out of these, those with word-initial

c	03	03	—	—	—	—	—	—	—	—	—
s	48	25	45	36	38	01	01	—	—	—	—
s/h	—	—	01	01	01	02	—	—	—	—	—
h	—	—	01	—	02	25	46	22	21	—	—
h/Ø	—	—	—	—	—	—	02	10	01	—	—
Ø	—	—	—	—	—	—	01	01	08	54	33
Total number of cognates	51	28	47	37	41	28	50	33	30	54	33

Note: Only two dialects of Gondi show *c* instead of *s* in three lexical items. This is perhaps due to the influence of the neighbouring Marathi. It is not a case of retention of Proto-Dravidian **c*.

21

Landmarks in Comparative Dravidian Studies in the Twentieth Century

Introduction:

The Dravidian languages (around 25) are spoken by 191 million in India (Census 1991; for details see Appendix I) mainly in India; immigrant speakers of the major Dravidian languages in other countries such as Sri Lanka, Maldives, Mauritius, Singapore, Malaysia, Indonesia, etc. would be at least 10 million. The four literary languages, Tamil, Malayāḷam, Kannaḍa, and Telugu account for 95% (182 million) of the total population speaking the Dravidian languages. They possess written documents (literature and/or inscriptions) going back to the early Christian era in the case of Tamil, to the 5th century CE in Kannaḍa, 6th century CE in Telugu, and 9th century CE in Malayāḷam. Traditional grammars and lexicons in verse form are available in the literary languages from an early period (see Krishnamurti 1991b). The name Dravidian is derived from Sanskrit *draviḍa/drāviḍa* of doubtful etymology, which presumably meant 'Tamil' originally. Caldwell (1856) adopted it as a name of the whole family. Racially, 'Dravidians' are said to be a 'Proto-Mediterranean branch of Caucasoid race with some admixture of proto-Australoid traits' (see Sjoberg 1971a: 13; also Basham 1979: 2). Rig Vedic Sanskrit (1500 BCE) already had some words borrowed from Dravidian (see Emeneau 1980c: 93–9). There have been several theories relating Dravidian to Altaic, Mongolian, Korean, Japanese, Elamite, etc. but proof is still lacking. 'All this is still in the nature of speculation' (Zvelebil 1990a: 123).

In this brief end of century assessment, I will only consider major works (books and/or papers) which have had a significant impact on Dravidian studies during this century. I will deal with only two areas: (1) historical-comparative studies; (2a) descriptive grammars and lexicons/vocabularies of the non-literary languages; (2b) reference grammars and dictionaries in the four literary languages. Earlier I wrote two survey articles (Krishnamurti 1969a, 1985: Ch. 5 and 14 in this volume) in which I critically examined the contribution of different scholars to comparative Dravidian studies from the beginning up to 1980. I will not repeat what I have said there, but will only make cross-references to those articles. Landmark writings are indicated by setting their authors' names in bold type.

Presented to the National Seminar on Dravidian Linguistics: Diachronic, Synchronic and Applied Perspectives. February 19–20, 1999. Centre of Advanced Study in Linguistics, Osmania University.

Francis Whyte Ellis of the Indian Civil Service (1816) noticed the resemblance in vocabulary and some aspects of grammar among the four major South Indian languages, Tamil, Telugu, Kannaḍa, Malayāḷam (and Tuḷu) and said that they constituted 'the family of languages which may appropriately be called the dialects of Southern India'. He also noticed the affinity of Koḍagu and Malto with this group. He said that his purpose was to show that the four literary languages 'form a distinct family of languages' with which 'the Sanscrit has, in later times, especially intermixed, but with which it has no radical connexion' (Krishnamurti 1969a: 311–12). **Rev. Robert Caldwell's** *Comparative Grammar of the Dravidian or South Indian Family of Languages*, published in 1856 (second edition revised by the author in 1875), was a real breakthrough, although comparative linguistics was still in its infancy. He extended the usage of the term *drāviḍa-* (originally 'Tamil') to designate the whole family. He knew of only twelve Dravidian languages; besides the four literary ones, he listed Tuḷu, Kudagu or Coorg (Koḍagu), Tuda (Toda), Kota, Goṇḍ (Gondi), Khond or Ku (Kui-Kuvi), Orāon (Kuṛux or Orāon), Rajmahāl (Malto). In the 1875 edition he added a note on Brahui as an appendix (633–5). **Charles Philip Brown's** *A Dictionary, Telugu and English* was published in 1852. **Rev. Winslow's** *Comprehensive Tamil and English Dictionary* was published in 1862. **Rev. H. Gundert** published *A Malayalam and English Dictionary* in 1872 and **Rev. F. Kittel** his *Kannaḍa-English Dictionary* in 1894. The last two are still considered standard dictionaries in their respective languages. **A. Männer's** *Tuḷu-English Dictionary* was published in 1886, which until recently was the main source for cognate search in this language. Not much work was done on comparative Dravidian during the second half of the 19th century. Both Kittel and Caldwell identified a number of words of Dravidian origin in Sanskrit.

1. 1900–1950

In the twentieth century the first landmark publication was the *Linguistic Survey of India*, vol. IV, edited by **Sir George Grierson** (with the help of Sten Konow), dealing with the Dravidian and Munda languages. But it excluded from the survey the Madras Presidency, the southern princely states, and the Nizam's dominions. Despite mistakes like considering Parji as a dialect of Gondi, it listed a number of immigrant dialects of the literary languages outside their major area. **L. V. Ramaswami Aiyar** stands out as the most prolific contributor to Dravidian studies with about a hundred papers published during 1925–50 (Krishnamurti 1969a: 314–15). **Jules Bloch's** *Structure grammaticale des langues dravidiennes* was published soon after the Second World War and was a clear landmark in comparative Dravidian grammar after Caldwell, with a focus on the non-literary languages, mainly Kui, Gondi, Kuṛux, Malto, and Brahui. S. K. Chatterji and Bloch also wrote about the possible Dravidian substratum of Indo-Aryan (Krishnamurti 1969a: 315). **Thomas Burrow's** series of articles ('Dravidian Studies' I to VII, published in

BSO(A)S vols. 9–12) during the period 1938 to 1948 marked the beginning of true comparative Dravidian phonology with reconstructions. He made insightful remarks on the developments of Proto-Dravidian (which he called Primitive Dravidian) **k*, **c*, **y*, **ñ*, and initial voiced stops, besides treating the alternations *i/e* and *u/o* in root syllables in the literary languages. He also wrote extensively on the Dravidian loanwords in Sanskrit (Krishnamurti 1969a: 315–16). **M. B. Emeneau,** an anthropological linguist and the latter-day collaborator of Burrow, studied Kolami of Central India and the Nilgiri languages Toda, Kota, and Koḍagu during 1935–8. His *Kota Texts* (vols. 1–3) were published during 1944–6. A number of standard dictionaries/vocabularies and grammars were published during this period for Tamil, Telugu, Gondi, Kui, Kuvi, Kuṛux, and Brahui (see Bibliography in *DEDR* xxii–xxxiv). Several dialects of Gondi were described, but none too well. Similarly the two descriptions of Kuvi by Schultze (1911) and Fitzgerald (1913) are equally unsatisfactory.

2. 1947–1980

The latter half of the century was the most productive period for Dravidian studies, both historical-comparative and descriptive. The number of both Indian and foreign scholars drawn into the Dravidian field considerably increased. Liberal funding for promoting linguistics in Indian universities was available, thanks to the vision of the late S. M. Katre (Director, Deccan College Postgraduate and Research Institute, Poona) and C. D. Deshmukh (Chairman, University Grants Commission, Government of India, New Delhi). The Deccan College project of holding summer and winter schools in India, beside the exchange of senior and junior scholars between India and the USA funded by the Rockefeller Foundation (1955–9) helped to create a qualified cadre of committed scholars in different branches of linguistics. Studies in long-range genetic relationships and the hunch that the language of the Indus seals could be Dravidian contributed to this world-wide interest in Dravidian studies.

2.1. **Burrow** concentrated during this period on fieldwork in Central India in order to analyse new Dravidian languages in collaboration with the anthropologist **Sudhibhushan Bhattacharya.** They published two grammars with texts and lexicon on Parji (1953) and Pengo (1970) and papers on Kui (1961), Kuvi (1963), Gondi (1960), Ollari, Naiki (Bhattacharya 1957, 1961), and Manḍa (Burrow 1976). They offered a general discussion of the historical developments of Proto-Dravidian phonemes, particularly those of **c*, **ẓ*, **ṭ*, and **ḷ* in their descriptive accounts (Krishnamurti 1969a: 317). The monumental *A Dravidian Etymological Dictionary* by **T. Burrow** and **M. B. Emeneau** was published in 1961 followed by Supplements in 1968 and 1972 (Krishnamurti 1969a: 321–2). Research in comparative phonology received a great impetus from the availability of this dictionary. Burrow published a paper on the developments of Proto-Dravidian *r̤* in Kuṛux and Malto in 1968. He asserted that *r̤* became Ø in Kuṛux and Malto, and not a palatal *c* or a sibilant *s* as proposed by Krishnamurti (1958b).

2.2. M. B. Emeneau started working in different areas simultaneously. In comparative phonology, he published: 'Proto Dravidian **c-*: Toda *t-*' (1953a), 'North-Dravidian velar stops' (1961), 'A Kota vowel shift' (1969a), 'Koḍagu vowels' (1970b), 'Koḍagu and Brahui developments of Proto-Dravidian *-r̤-*' (1971b), 'Toda vowels in non-initial syllables' (1979), 'Brahui laterals from Proto-Dravidian *r̤*' (1980b). He has written several papers bearing on comparative morphology: 'The Dravidian verbs "come" and "give"' (1945), 'The Dravidian kinship terms' (1953b), 'Numerals in comparative linguistics' (1957), 'Brahui demonstrative pronouns' (1961a, c), 'Some South Dravidian noun formatives' (1966). *Brahui and Dravidian Comparative Grammar* (Emeneau 1962d) tackles many issues of phonology and morphology of Brahui from a comparative standpoint. His 'Studies in Dravidian verb-stem formation' (1975) is the most significant of this period. Emeneau published a number of etymological studies (1948, 1958a, 1962c, 1968). (For a review of these, see Krishnamurti 1969a: 317–20, 1985: 215–16, 219) Many of these have been reprinted in his collected papers (Emeneau 1994). A brief review of Emeneau's papers on phonology, morphology, and etymological studies was carried out by Krishnamurti in his 'Introduction' to that volume. Another significant contribution of Emeneau's has been his theoretical formulation of 'India as a linguistic area' in a paper in 1956. This was followed by a number of publications in 1962, 1964, 1965, 1969, 1971, 1974, culminating in the publication of his collected papers on this theme as a volume in 1980c (see for a review of these Krishnamurti 1969a: 323; 1985: 224). Earlier, Emeneau published *Kolami, a Dravidian Language* (1955a). He also published a short monograph on comparative phonology of Dravidian in 1970a.

2.3. Bh. Krishnamurti's first paper in a professional journal was published in 1955 (Ch. 1 in this volume) on the question of quantitative variations in root syllables with special reference to Telugu verbal bases. This has been cited and discussed widely in later literature. His magnum opus (revised Ph.D. dissertation with two additional chapters) *Telugu Verbal Bases: A Comparative and Descriptive Study* was published in 1961 by the University of California Press as UCPL 24. It dealt with many topics in comparative Dravidian for the first time: a systematic analysis of Proto-Dravidian root structure and that of formatives, a comparative phonology of Dravidian with Telugu as the main focus, an original discussion and resolution of many phonological problems, such as (C)V̄C-/(C)VCC-becoming (C)VC- in the environment of [V in the formative syllable, alternations *i/u* and *e/o* in South Dravidian in the environment [C-*a*, rules for the formation of initial apicals as well as consonant clusters initially and non-initially, the incorporation of tense suffixes in stem morphemes, etc. He made pioneering observations on the formation of subgroups within Dravidian. An etymological index of 1236 primary verbal bases is given in the Appendix with reconstructions. He published several papers on phonological problems: Alternations *i/e* and *u/o* in South Dravidian (1958a, Ch. 2 in this volume), Proto-Dravidian **ẓ* (1958b, Ch. 3 in this volume), *d/b* developing word-initially from *n/m* in Brahui before front vowels (1969b, Ch. 6 in this volume), raising of *ă* to *ĕ* before pre-Parji alveolars (1978b, Ch. 11 in this volume), a quantitative study of 'apical displacement' in South-Central Dravidian (1978a, Ch. 10 in this volume), and a peculiar vowel-lowering rule in Kui-Kuvi (1980, Ch. 12 in this volume) (see Krishnamurti 1969a: 318, 1985: 216). In comparative morphology, Krishnamurti published a paper on 'Dravidian personal pronouns' (1968b, Ch. 4 in this volume) and one on 'Gender and number in Proto-Dravidian' (1975a, Ch. 8 in this volume) (see Krishnamurti 1969a: 320–1, 1985: 220). Krishnamurti published *Koṇḍa or Kūbi: A Dravidian Language* (grammar, texts, and lexicon) in 1969. During this period Krishnamurti suggested a revision of the subgrouping that he proposed earlier in *TVB*. The subgroup Telugu-Gondi-Kui-Kuvi-Pengo-Manḍa is now attached to Proto-South Dravidian as South Dravidian II, while Tamil-Malayāḷam-Kannaḍa-Tuḷu-Koḍagu-Toda-Kota-Iruḷa are taken as South Dravidian I. South Dravidian II is optionally called South-Central Dravidian. He gave supporting evidence for this regrouping in his papers since 1970 (1975a, b, 1976a, 1980; see 1985: 220, 223). A number of scholars have accepted this regrouping since then (see Fig. 21.1).

2.4. N. Kumaraswami Raja's paper and a monograph-length treatment of reconstructing *NPP to account for voiceless stops in post-nasal position in Kannaḍa-Telugu and several other languages has resolved a long-standing problem in comparative phonology (see Krishnamurti 1985: 216–17).

2.5. P. S. Subrahmanyam (1964) deals with two problems of Parji tense formation, past and non-past, comparatively. In another paper (1965) he compares Kui intransitive and transitive stems with corresponding ones in Tamil (see Krishnamurti 1969: 321). In three papers (1976b, 1977a, b) he treats Toda developments of PD **a*, **ā*, **l*, **ḷ*, and **r* (see Krishnamurti 1985: 217–18). Subrahmanyam's criticism of the personal pronouns (1970b) and gender-number categories (1976a) set up by Krishnamurti (1968, 1975a) is answered in Krishnamurti 1985: 220. Subrahmanyam published his Ph.D. thesis *Dravidian Verb Morphology* (1971) which is useful as a basic work for further research and reinterpretation in comparative verb morphology. His questioning the revision in subgrouping (1976a) has not attracted any attention in the Dravidian scholarly world. He published *A Descriptive Grammar of Gondi* in 1968 (based on fieldwork in Adilabad).

2.6. S. V. Shanmugam's *Dravidian Nouns: A Comparative Study* (1971) is another basic work during this period, which provides extensive comparative data for scholars to make further improvements in interpretation (Krishnamurti 1985: 220).

2.7. K. V. Zvelebil is a prolific writer on Dravidian linguistic and literary aspects, with special reference to Tamil. His book on comparative Dravidian phonology (1970b) was reviewed by me in (1976a) (also see Krishnamurti 1985: 218). He has put together whatever was available and known on comparative Dravidian up to that point. Zvelebil has not come up with any new concepts or ideas in comparative Dravidian himself. He published two short volumes describing a Nilgiri language, Iruḷa (1973, 1979). He has also published a sketch of comparative Dravidian morphology (1977; see my brief review of this, Krishnamurti 1985: 221).

2.8. In the foregoing brief review of landmarks, I have not written about contributors of one or two articles, which have not influenced the field significantly. I have left out of consideration studies relating to long-range relationship between Dravidian and other families or languages outside India, e.g. Ural-Altaic, Elamite, Japanese, etc. I have also not gone into the validity of the language of the Indus seals being a form of Proto-Dravidian. Zvelebil (1990a) discusses these topics in some detail. Most of these studies are speculative and nothing has emerged as solid knowledge. However, I briefly reviewed these in my two survey articles (Krishnamurti 1969: 323–4, 1985: 225–6). **M. S. Andronov** of Moscow has written many papers on various aspects of Dravidian. His short monograph on the Dravidian languages (1970) is descriptive and typological. He published a comparative grammar of the Dravidian languages in Russian in 1978, which I could not read. I have also not seen any reference to it in the writings of other Dravidian scholars. I hope it will be translated into English. I have reviewed some of his papers in my two surveys (Krishnamurti 1969: 321, 1985: 322). I have treated him as a significant author because of his prolific productivity.

3. 1980–1998

I have not previously reviewed the works of the two last decades of this century. Since I cannot write an extensive survey as I did earlier, I will only take those authors and works that either have or are expected to have a lasting impact on historical and comparative Dravidian studies. Again, I arrange the authors alphabetically.

3.1. **T. Burrow** and **M. B. Emeneau** have brought out the second edition of *A Dravidian Etymological Dictionary* in 1984 incorporating all supplements and new data from old and new languages. It has 5557 entries, *a* to *v*. It has an Appendix of 61 entries which constitute a supplement to an earlier volume, *Dravidian Borrowing from Indo-Aryan* (Emeneau and Burrow 1962), followed by indexes of words of individual languages (515–820). Cross-reference to entries of the first edition (*DED*) and supplements (*DEDS, DEN*) occur at the end of the volume. Following the practice of the first edition, reconstructions are not given. Following the Devanagari alphabetical order (as adopted by the literary Dravidian languages), citation of comparative vocabulary starts with Tamil or any other language that has a cognate available, followed by the other languages. The languages are arranged in a fixed order, from south to north, Tamil to Brahui. This volume is an indispensable tool of research for any student of historical-comparative Dravidian.

Emeneau's selected papers were brought out in a volume in 1994. A number of his papers (pre-1980 and post-1980) were reprinted in that volume. In phonology: 'Brahui laterals from Proto-Dravidian **ṟ*' (1980b), 'Proto-Dravidian **c*- and its developments' (1988); in comparative morphology: 'Indian pronominal demonstrative bases—a revision' (1980a); in word-studies: 'Kannaḍa *Kampa*, Tamil *Kampaṉ*: Two proper names' (1985), 'Some notes on Dravidian intensives' (1987a), 'The right hand is the "eating hand": An Indian areal linguistic inquiry' (1987b) have been reprinted in this volume. Krishnamurti reviewed these briefly in his 'Introduction' to the volume, xv–xxvii. Emeneau published a long-awaited grammar of Toda with texts (1984). Emeneau's papers in the nineties have clarified some crucial problems of phonetics and phonology, such as the additional conditions blocking the palatalization rule in Telugu and Tamil-Malayāḷam (1995), initial voiced stops in expressives in Tamil (1993) and the phonetics of Brahui mid vowels (1997a) with newly identified etymologies. An etymological and botanical study of the names of fourteen species of plants found in the Nilgiri tribal languages (1997b) is a pioneering exercise in a new branch of ethnolinguistics.

3.2. Bh. Krishnamurti (1991a, Ch. 16 in this volume) shows that PD (C)V̄CCV changed to (C)V̄C(V) thereby making this pattern complementary to (C)VCCV; a similar change in syllable structure also happened in Indo-Aryan approximately at the same time. In a paper on Proto-Dravidian laryngeal **H* (1997c, Ch. 19 in this volume), he developed an idea that he expressed in a footnote in an article as early as 1963. He observed that Tamil *āytam* was a relic reflex of this Proto-Dravidian phoneme. It has the properties of lengthening the preceding vowel in free forms, geminating a voiceless stop in the following position, and dropping when followed by a voiced apical stop or sonorant. It was retained in Early Tamil in the deictic roots *aḥ-tu, iḥ-tu* and the numeral 'ten' *paḥ-tu/pat-tu*. These properties are also found in other parts of the grammar and vocabulary whose aberrant phonology is explained more systematically in terms of a laryngeal. In another paper (1998a, Ch. 18 in this volume) he summarized the major sound changes in Dravidian and noticed that typologically motivated sound changes tend to be more regular than simple historical changes. In yet another paper (1998b, Ch. 20 in this volume) he showed how Gondi $s > h > Ø$ is a totally regular sound change in some of the regional dialects through lexical diffusion. This is a theoretical paper showing that lexical diffusion is not incompatible with regular sound change. In comparative morphology, Krishnamurti (1989 with G. U. Rao, Ch. 15 in this volume) discusses the reconstruction of the third person pronouns in different Gondi dialects with focus on the interaction between phonological and morphological rules in language change. In another paper (1997b, Ch. 17 in this volume) he has traced the origin and evolution of formative suffixes in Dravidian with copious illustrations. It was established that the so-called formative suffixes, which currently signal intransitive vs. transitive in some of the languages of South and South-Central Dravidian, were originally tense and voice morphemes. Some languages lost tense but not voice; others have lost both the grammatical functions, thereby converting them into mere formatives. He published three papers in

Encyclopedias, one on the 'Dravidian languages' (1992), one on 'Dravidian lexico-graphy' (1991b), and the other on 'Indian names: Dravidian' (1994b).

3.3. **S. B. Steever** who submitted his Ph.D. on Tamil Linguistics in Chicago in 1983 has published several studies on Tamil and Comparative Dravidian. His research into the formation of serial verbs in Kui, Koṇḍa, and Pengo published as papers, and later as a book (1988), led to the publication of a major collection *Analysis to Synthesis* (1993) in which he included five of his earlier papers with appropriate revisions. He was able to show how two verbs, of which the second was an auxiliary 'be, give, etc.', became fused into a single finite verb through contraction. This explained clearly the formation of object incorporation in Kui, past negatives in South, South-Central, and Central Dravidian languages, and that of the past perfect in different subgroups. His publications mark the beginning of research in the interface of comparative morphology and syntax in Dravidian. He edited a volume on the Dravidian languages, published by Routledge in 1998. It includes descriptive accounts of ten Dravidian languages. Since several authors could not write chapters assigned to them, Steever had to write these by consulting original sources.

3.4. **P. S. Subrahmanyam** published his book *Dravidian Comparative Phonology* (1983) which brought together all that was available on the developments of Proto-Dravidian phonemes in different Dravidian languages up to that point. It certainly made progress over Zvelebil's book (1970) or Emeneau's phonological sketch (1970a), but in many places he took a subjective stand. He has not included the subgrouping, which became standard by 1983, viz. four subgroups instead of three (see Fig. 21.1.). Since *DEDR* was published a year later (1984), his reference to etymologies still depended on *DED* of 1961 and its Supplements. He published a short survey article in 1988, in which he has not said a word about the remarkable contribution of Sanford B. Steever to comparative Dravidian studies. He also questions the revised subgrouping without giving any substantive arguments. The reflexes of the innovation **ñān* 'I' occurs only in South Dravidian I and South Dravidian II languages. Central and North Dravidian have no doublets in *n-* for 'I' beside those derived from **yān*/**yan-*. I answered his objection in 1985: 220. Without answering my arguments, he simply says, 'To maintain that Ma. 1st person singular *ñān* and plural *ñāŋŋaḷ* vouch for **ñ* in the inclusive plural is indeed a very strange way of argument' (1988: 64). What is strange must be spelt out. In my latest reconstruction I have a laryngeal in those personal pronouns which have unexplained length between nominative (free form) and oblique (bound form), i.e. *yaHn*/*yan-* (see § **3.2** above).

3.5. **K. V. Zvelebil** has published several papers and books on Dravidian during the past two decades. The significant ones are Parts II and III of his work on Iruḷa (1979, 1982b) and two articles on Kuṟumba (1982a, 1988) and one on Shōlega (1990b). The Pondicherry Institute of Linguistics and Culture published his book *Dravidian Linguistics: An Introduction* in 1990. It is a textbook covering a brief history of research in comparative studies. Half of the book is devoted to speculative topics such as Dravidian-Uralic, Dravidian and Mohanjodaro, etc.

During recent years there have been several intensive studies on the languages and ethnography of the Nilgiri tribes, particularly the different Kuṟumba tribes and Baḍagas (**Hockings** 1989, 1997). **Kapp** (1984) gives a thorough description of Ālu Kuṟumba with grammar, texts, and vocabulary. Kapp (1987) discusses the origin of centralized vowels /ï ë/ (short and long) in Ālu Kuṟumba from /i ī e ē/ before retroflex consonants and *ṯ, quite close to a similar phenomenon in Koḍagu (Emeneau 1970b). Furthermore, Kapp indicates that Pālu Kuṟumba, like Literary Tamil, shows *i*, *u* [C-*a* (Kapp 1978: 513) and not *e*, *o* [C-*a* like the other South Dravidian languages. This gives us a clue to the date of migration of this tribe from the speech area of Early Tamil or pre-Tamil, i.e. sometime in the early centuries BCE. **Pilot-Raichoor** (1997) argues for the status of independent language for Baḍaga, which was earlier considered a dialect of Middle Kannaḍa after the completion of the sound change *p- > h-. The retroflex vowels reported by Emeneau in Baḍaga (1939; also his reference in 1992) were not in evidence in the dialects studied by Hockings and Pilot-Raichoor in the preparation of their enormous *A Badaga-English Diction-ary* (1992). Zvelebil's proposal (1980) to consider the Nilgiris as a language area in terms of shared centralized vowels and the three-way distinction of apicals /t ṯ ṭ/ of pre-Tamil would have been acceptable but for two problems. Kota has three apicals but no centralized vowels and Baḍaga has neither the three apical consonants nor the centralized vowels (in the majority of dialects).

3.6. Grammars, dictionaries, doctoral dissertations, etc. There have been a number of publications and several unpublished dissertations, some of which are comparative and descriptive, particularly relating to the non-literary languages: Andres (1978), Mahapatra (1979), Sumati (1982), Natarajan (1985), Rao (1987), and Suvarchala (1992). Reference grammars of the literary languages are now available: Krishnamurti and Gwynn (1985) and T. Lehmann (1989, 1991). Revised dictionaries of Tamil, Kannaḍa, and Malayāḷam have been brought out by the Universities of Madras and Kerala (see Krishnamurti on 'Dravidian lexicography', 1991b). A six-volume dictionary of Tuḷu has been published recently (Hardasa Bhat and Upadh-yaya 1987–97). Standard dictionaries for Modern Telugu (Gwynn 1991) and Tamil (Subramanian 1992) are now available. Asher (1982) and Schiffman (1999) are systematic descriptions of spoken Tamil, almost an untrodden area of traditional Tamil scholarship. Sridhar's *Kannada* (1990) and Asher and Kumari's *Malayalam* (1997) are excellent reference grammars of modern standard usage following the pattern of Routledge series.

3.7. Conclusion. Descriptions of the remaining Gondi dialects, some of which are mutually unintelligible, are a desideratum. The long-awaited volume on Manḍa (grammar, texts, and lexicon) has become a tantalizing mirage. It appears that there are still some unrecognized languages which need to be identified and described in Madhya Pradesh and Orissa. B. Ramakrishna Reddy said that he came across two other speech communities, called 'Indi' and 'Āwe', near the Manḍa-speaking area. The relative position of Koraga and Kuṟumba among the South Dravidian languages is yet to be determined. The position of Tuḷu continues to be doubtful. It is time that Dravidian scholars started working on comparative syntax, particularly the evolution of complex predicates in Dravidian. There has been much descriptive work in this area, especially in the case of the literary languages. The time is ripe for a new comparative grammar of the Dravidian languages, and I am currently engaged in this effort.

Appendix I

Dravidian languages, number of speakers, and their geographical distribution (1991 Census)[1]. *The main literary languages are indicated in bold type.*

Subgroup and Language	Population	Where spoken (Indian State, unless stated otherwise)
SOUTH DRAVIDIAN I (SD I)		
1. **Tamil** [tamiẓ]	53,006,368	Tamil Nadu
2. **Malayāḷam** [malayāḷam]	30,377,166	Kerala
3. Toda [toda]*[2]	1,600	Tamil Nadu
4. Kota [kōta]*	1,400	Tamil Nadu
5. Iruḷa [iruḷa]*	5,200	Tamil Nadu
6. Kuṟumba [kuṟumba]*	4,874	Tamil Nadu
7. Koḍagu [koḍagï]	92,698	Karnataka
8. Baḍaga [baḍaga]	125,000	Tamil Nadu
9. **Kannaḍa** [kannaḍa]	32,753,676	Karnataka
10. Tuḷu [tuḷu]	1,552,259	Karnataka, Kerala
Total	**117,920,241**	
SOUTH DRAVIDIAN II (SD II, ALSO KNOWN AS SOUTH-CENTRAL DRAVIDIAN)		
11. **Telugu** [telugu]	66,017,615	Andhra Pradesh
12. Gondi [gōṇḍi] (several dialects, incl. Koya)*	2,395,507	Madhya Pradesh, Andhra Pradesh, Maharashtra, Orissa
13. Koṇḍa [koṇḍa, kūbi]*	17,864	Andhra Pradesh, Orissa
14. Kui [kūʔi]*	641,662	Orissa
15. Kuvi [kūvi]*	246,513	Orissa, Andhra Pradesh
16. Pengo [peŋgo]*	1,300	Orissa
17. Manḍa [manḍa]*	—	Orissa
Total	**69,320,461**	

[1] Languages marked with an asterisk * are spoken by scheduled tribes in India. The census reports since 1971 have dropped listing languages spoken by less than 10,000 persons. Therefore, the figures for Toda, Kota, Iruḷa, Kuṟumba of SD I, Pengo of SD II (SCD), and Ollari and Gadaba of CD are based on recently published sources or the census of 1961 or estimates for 1971 or 1981. There are two varieties of Gadaba, Koṇḍēkōr Gadaba (Dravidian) and Gutob Gadaba (Austro-Asiatic). The 1991 Census treated Gadaba as an Austro-Asiatic or Munda language with 24,158 speakers. I have, therefore, taken only the Gadabas listed for Andhra Pradesh, i.e. 9,197, as a nearer figure for Konḍēkōr Gadaba which is mainly spoken in the Salur district of Andhra Pradesh; both the languages are spoken in Andhra Pradesh as well as

Central Dravidian (CD)			
18.	Kolami [kōlāmī]*	99,281	Maharashtra, Andhra Pradesh
19a.	Naikṛi [nāykṛi]*[3]	1,494	Andhra Pradesh, Maharashtra
b.	Naiki [nāyki]*	5,400	Madhya Pradesh
20.	Parji [poroja, dhurwa]*	44,001	Orissa, Madhya Pradesh
21.	Ollari [ollāri]*[4]	9,100	Orissa
22.	Gadaba [koṇḍēkōr gadaba]*	9,197	Andhra Pradesh, Orissa
	Total	**168,473**	
North Dravidian (ND)			
23.	Kuṛux [kuṛux]*	1,426,618	Bihar, West Bengal, Madhya Pradesh, Orissa
24.	Malto [mālto]*	108,148	Bihar, West Bengal
25.	Brahui [brāʔūʔī][5]	1,710,000	Pakistan, Afghanistan
	Total	**3,244,766**	
	Total for the family:	**190,653,941**	

With immigrant speakers in other parts of the world the total number would be well over 200 million.

in Orissa. Numerically, those outside the major languages do not make much difference for the census figures when computing the population figures in millions.

2 The population figures of the Nilgiri tribes, Toda, Kota, Iruḷa, Kuṟumba, and Baḍaga are based on figures given as estimates for 1981 by D. G. Mandelbaum's article 'The Kotas in their social setting' in Hockings (ed.) 1989: 145–6.

3 Burrow and Emeneau treat Naikṛi as a dialect of Kolami while Naiki of Chanda is considered a separate language. However, in the absence of supporting data and evidence, I am taking both Naikṛi and Naiki as separate languages. Only the 1961 Census gives the figure of Naikṛis (spelt Naikadi) as 1494, and Naikpodi 46. Thomasaiah (1986), who took his doctorate on Naikṛi at Annamalai University, has a chapter on a comparative study of Kolami, Naikṛi, and Naiki to show that they are closer together, but he has not established that Naikṛi is closer to Kolami than to Naiki (Chanda). At least one feature distinguishes both Naikṛi and Naiki from Kolami, viz. a number of native words with initial voiced stops, like Naikṛi *ghāḷi*, Nk. *ghāy* 'wind' [*DEDR* 1499]. The feature of aspiration in such items is not shared by any other language of the family including the other closer sisters within Central Dravidian. Thomasaiah does not discuss this.

4 Burrow and Emeneau in *DEDR* treat Ollari and Koṇḍēkōr Gadaba as dialects of the same language. They call these Gadaba (O) and Gadaba (S) in *DEDR*; S stands for Sālūr, where some lexical items from Koṇḍēkōr Gabada were collected by Burrow and Bhattacharya. Again, no comparison of the phonology and morphology of these two varieties has been made to support this hypothesis. In the fifties I did fieldwork on Koṇḍēkōr Gadaba. I have decided to treat these as languages until they are proved to be dialects of the same language.

5 Brahui is spoken in Pakistan and Afghanistan. The Brahui figure is taken from the *Encyclopedia of Languages and Linguistics* (Pergamon, 1994). Elfenbein's article on Brahui (1998) says that out of '700,000 Brahui tribesmen, 100,000 are primary speakers of Brahui, mainly in Pakistan; perhaps 300,000 are secondary speakers of Brahui in Pakistan and Afghanistan'. In view of this statement the Brahui population figures given in the above encyclopedia look suspicious.

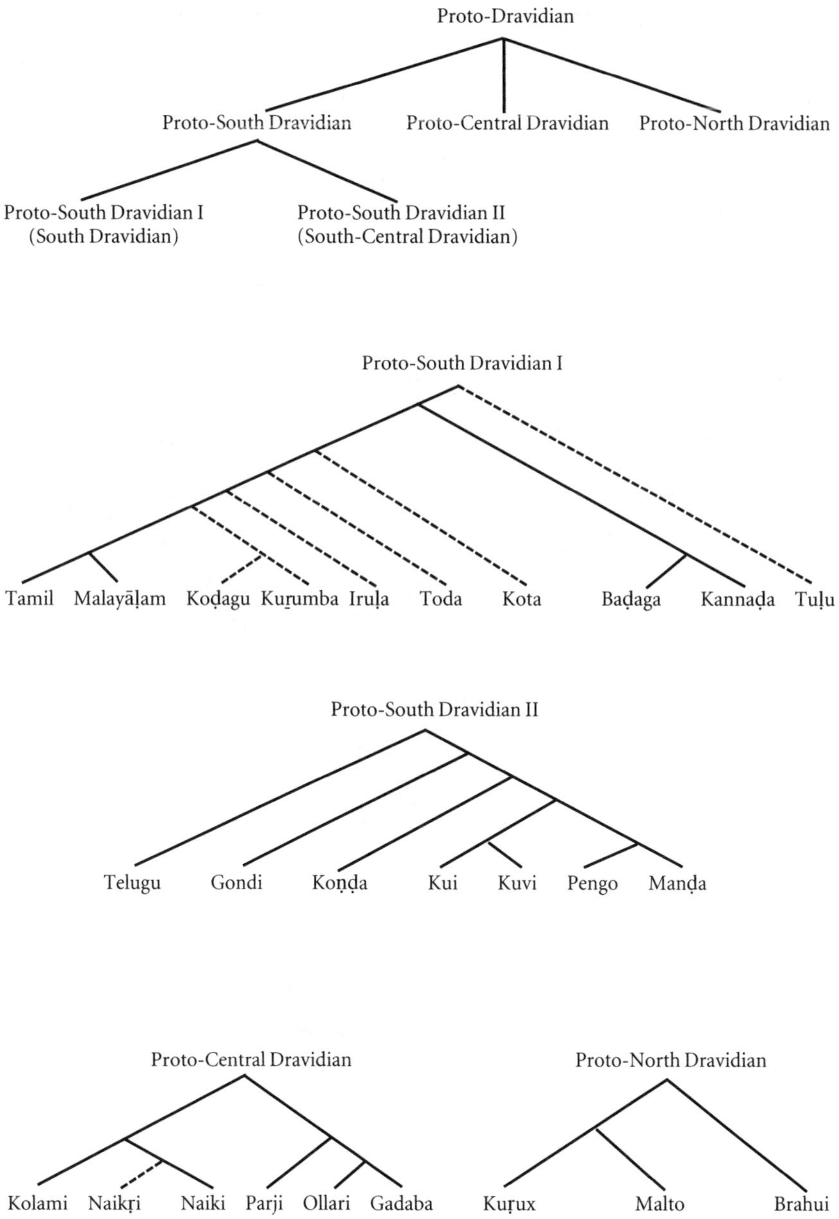

Broken lines reflect uncertainty as to a language's position within the group.

FIGURE 21.1. Family tree of the Dravidian languages (revised)

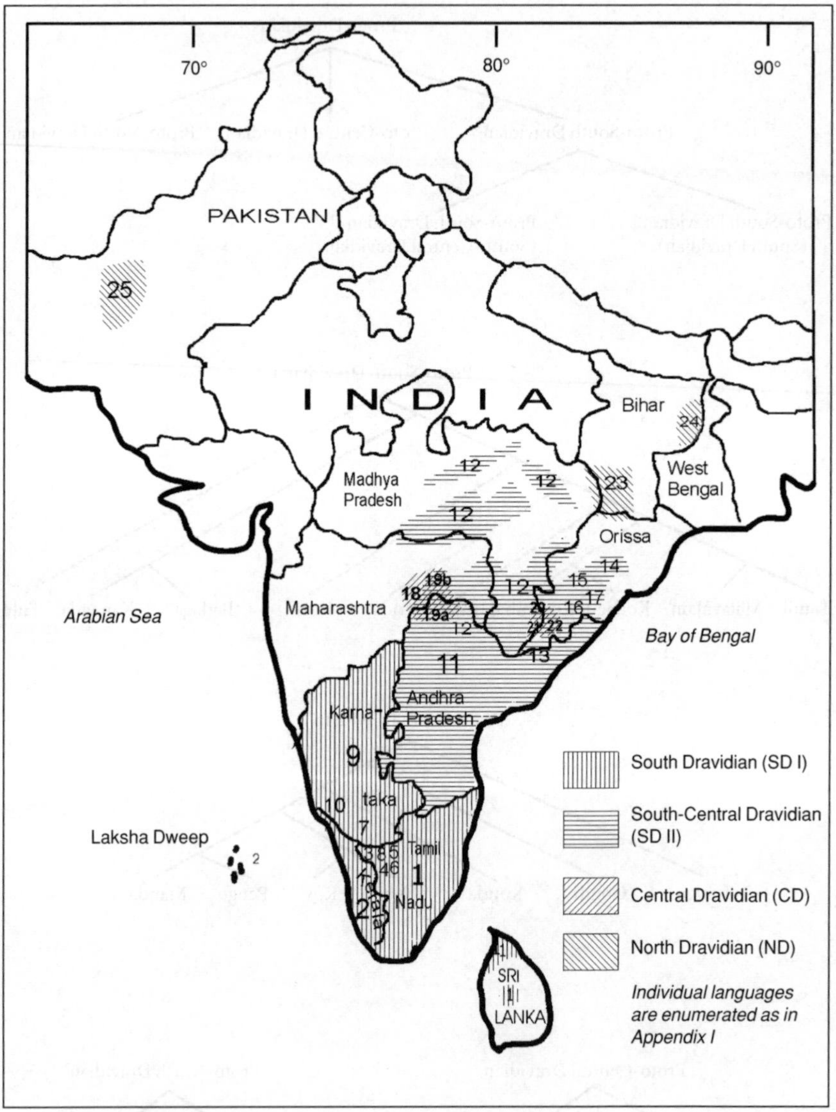

MAP 21.1 Geographical distribution of the Dravidian languages in South Asia

Bibliography

Abbreviations

AJP	*American Journal of Philology*
AO	*Archiv Orientální*
BDCRI	*Bulletin of the Deccan College Research Institute*
BSO(A)S	*Bulletin of the School of Oriental (and African) Studies*
DLA	Dravidian Linguistics Association
IA	*Indian Antiquary*
IIJ	*Indo-Iranian Journal*
IFDL	*International Journal of Dravidian Linguistics*
IL	*Indian Linguistics*
JA	*Journal Asiatique*
JAOS	*Journal of the American Oriental Society*
JASB	*Journal of the Asiatic Society, Bengal*
JTS	*Journal of Tamil Studies*
P1ICSTS	*Proceedings of the First International Conference-Seminar of Tamil Studies.* Kuala Lumpur
P2ICSTS	*Proceedings of the Second International Conference-Seminar of Tamil Studies.* Madras: International Association of Tamil Research
PAICDL	*Proceedings of the All-India Conference of Dravidian Linguists*
PAPS	*Proceedings of the American Philosophical Society*
PSDL	*Proceedings of the Seminar in Dravidian Linguistics. Annamalainagar: Annamalai University*
QJMS	*Quarterly Journal of the Mythic Society*
TC	*Tamil Culture*
TPS	*Transactions of the Philological Society*
UCPL	University of California Publications in Linguistics. Berkeley and Los Angeles: University of California Press

Acharya, K. P. (1978). *Classified Bibliography of Articles in* Indian Linguistics. Mysore: Central Institute of Indian Languages.

Agesthialingom, S. (1979). *A Grammar of Old Tamil, with Special Reference to Patiṟṟuppattu.* Annamalainagar: Annamalai University.

———, and Kumaraswami Raja, N. (eds.) (1969). *Seminar Papers on Dravidian Linguistics.* Annamalainagar: Annamalai University.

———, and Sakthivel, S. (eds.) (1973). *A Bibliography of Dravidian Linguistics.* Annamalainagar: Annamalai University.

———, and Shanmugam, S. V. (eds.) (1972). *Proceedings of the Seminar on Dravidian Linguistics III.* Annamalainagar: Annamalai University.

———, and Subrahmanyam, P. S. (eds.) (1976). *Proceedings of the Seminar on Dravidian Linguistics V.* Annamalainagar: Annamalai University.

Aiyappan. A. (1971). 'Aryanization and sanskritization of Dravidian speaking tribal groups in central and eastern India', *P2ICSTS*, **2**: 289–94.

Ananda Vasudevan, C. P. (1973). 'Dravidian-Greek connections', *IJDL*, **2**: 180–6.

Ananthanarayana, H. S. (1970). 'Prakrits and Dravidian languages', *Proceedings of the Seminar on Prakrit Studies*, 65–75. Baroda.

Anavaratavinayakam Pillai, S. (1923). *Dravidic Studies III. The Sanskritic Element in the Vocabularies of the Dravidian Languages.* Madras: Superintendent, Government Press.

Andres, S. (1978). '*A Description of Muria Gondi Phonology and Morphology*'. Ph.D. dissertation. Poona: Department of Linguistics, Deccan College.

Andronov, M. S. (1961). 'New evidence of possible linguistic ties between the Deccan and the Urals', *Dr. R. P. Sethu Pillai Silver Jubliee Commemoration Volume*, 137–140. Madras.

——— (1963). 'Dravidian languages', *AO*, **31**: 177–97.

——— (1964a). 'Materials for a bibliography of Dravidian linguistics', *TC*, **11**: 3–50.

——— (1964b). 'On the typological similarity of New Indo-Aryan and Dravidian', *IL*, **25**: 119–25.

——— (1964c). 'Lexicostatistic analysis of the chronology of disintegration of Proto-Dravidian', *IIJ*, **8**: 170–86.

——— (1965). *The Tamil Language.* Moscow: Nauka Publishing House.

——— (1970). *Dravidian Languages.* Moscow: Nauka Publishing House.

——— (1971). 'Comparative studies on the nature of Dravido-Uralian parallels: A peep into the prehistory of language families', *P1ICSTS*, **2:1**: 267–77.

——— (1972). 'Notes on Brahui', *JTS*, **1:1**: 1–6.

——— (1975a). 'Dravidian pronouns: A comparative study', *JTS*, **7**: 14–18, **8**: 18–32.

——— (1975b). 'Observations on accent in Tamil', in Schiffman and Eastman (eds.) 1975: 3–10.

——— (1976). 'Dravidian numerals: an etymological study', *IJDL*, **5**: 5–15.

——— (1977a). 'Pronominal suffixes in Dravidian: A comparative study', *IJDL*, **6:1**: 97–114.

——— (1977b). 'Hypercorrection in Dravidian', *IL*, **38:4**: 221–6.

——— (1978). *Sravnitelnaya grammatika Dravidiskikh yazykov* [A Comparative Grammar of the Dravidian Languages]. Moscow: Institute of Oriental Studies, Academy of Sciences, USSR.

——— (1979). 'Verbals in Dravidian: A comparative study', *IJDL*, **8**: 52–70.

Annamalai, E. (1968). 'Onomatopoeic resistance to sound change in Dravidian', in Krishnamurti (ed.) 1968a: 15–19.

Arden, A. H. (1976). (5th print). *A Progressive Grammar of the Tamil Language.* Madras: The Christian Literature Society.

Ārudra, *Samagr(a)-āṃdhra-sāhityaṃ* (1965). Machilipatnam: M. N. Seshachalam & Co.

Arun, V. Bh. (1961). *A Comparative Phonology of Hindi and Punjabi.* Ludhiana: Punjabi Sahitya Akademi.

Asher, R. E. (1982). *Tamil.* Lingua Descriptive Studies, vol. 7. Amsterdam: North-Holland Publishing Company.

—— and Kumari, T. C. (1997). *Malayalam.* London & New York: Routledge.

Austerlitz, R. (1971). 'Long range comparisons of Tamil and Dravidian with other language families in Eurasia', *P2ICSTS*, **2:1**: 254–61.

Balasubramanian, K. (1976). 'Historical development of *āytam*', in Agesthialingom and Subrahmanyam (eds.), 561–82.

BANERJEE, MURALYDHAR (1931). *The Deśīnāmamālā of Hemachandra, Part 1: Text with Readings, Introduction and Index of Words.* Calcutta: University of Calcutta.

BASHAM, A. L. (1979). 'Aryan and non-Aryan in South Asia', in Deshpande and Hook (eds.), 1–6.

BEAMES, J. (1872–9, repr. 1966). *A Comparative Grammar of the Modern Aryan Languages of India: Hindi, Panjabi, Sindhi, Gujarati, Marathi, Oriya, and Bengali.* Delhi: Munshiram Manoharlal.

BEINE, D. K. (1994). '*A Sociolinguistic Survey of the Gondi-speaking Communities of Central India*'. MA dissertation in Anthropology. California: San Diego State University.

BHASKARARAO, P. (1980). *Koṇekor Gadaba: A Dravidian Language.* Poona: Deccan College Postgraduate and Research Institute.

BHAT, D. N. S. (1970). 'Velar consonants in Kurux', *IL*, **31**: 177–81.

——— (1971). *The Koraga Language.* Poona: Deccan College Postgraduate and Research Institute.

——— (1974). 'The phonology of liquid consonants', *Working Papers on Language Universals*, **16**: 73–104. Stanford: Department of Linguistics, Stanford University.

——— (1978). *Pronominalization.* Poona: Deccan College.

BHATTACHARYA, S. (1957). *Ollari, a Dravidian Speech.* New Delhi: Department of Anthropology (Memoir No. 3), Government of India.

——— (1961). 'Naiki of Chanda', *IIJ*, 5: 85–117.

——— (1969). 'New Dravidian languages', in Agesthialingom and Kumaraswami Raja (eds.), 139–61.

——— (1972). 'Dravidian and Munda', in Agesthialingom and Shanmugam (eds.), 241–56.

Bibliography of South Asian Linguistics 71, 72, 73, 74, 1973–78. Poona: Linguistic Society of India.

BLOCH, J. (1934). *L'Indo-Aryen du veda aux temps modernes.* Paris: Adrien Maisonneuve.

——— (1946). *Structure grammaticale des langues dravidiennes.* Paris: Adrien Maisonneuve.

——— (1952). 'Le dravidien', in A. Meillet and M. Cohen (eds.), *Les langues du monde* (2nd edn.), 485–503. Paris: Centre National de la Recherche Scientifique. (1st edn 1924: 345–9).

——— (1954). *The Grammatical Structure of the Dravidian Languages* (trans. R. G. Harshe). Poona: Deccan College Postgraduate and Research Institute.

——— (1965). *Indo-Aryan from the Vedas to Modern Times* (trans. A. Master). Paris: Adrien Maisonneuve.

BLOOMFIELD, L. (1933). *Language.* New York: Holt.

BOUDA, K. (1953). 'Dravidisch and Uralaltaisch', *Ural-Altaische Jahrbücher*, **25**: 161–73.

——— (1956). 'Dravidisch and Uralaltaisch', *Lingua*, 5: 129–44.

BRAY, D. (1909). *The Brahui Language*, Part I. Calcutta: Superintendent, Government Printing, India.

——— (1934). *The Brahui Language*, Part II: *The Brahui Problem.* Part III: *Etymological Vocabulary.* Delhi: Manager of Publications.

BRIGHT, W. (1966). 'Dravidian metaphony', *Language*, **42**: 311–22.

BROWN, C. P. (1852). *A Dictionary, Telugu and English.* Madras. (1905: 2nd edn. revised and enlarged by M. Venkata Ratnam, W. H. Campbell, and K. Veeresalingam. Madras: The Christian Literature Society. 1966: 1st edn. reprinted by A. P. Sahitya Akademi, Hyderabad.)

Burrow, T. (1938). 'Dravidian studies I: Initial voiced stops', *BSOS*, 9: 711–22.
——— (1940). 'Dravidian studies II: Notes on the interchange of short *e* and *o* with *i* and *u* in South Dravidian', *BSOS*, 10: 239–97.
——— (1943). 'Dravidian studies III: Two developments of initial *k*- in Dravidian', *BSOAS*, 11:1: 122–39.
——— (1944). 'Dravidian studies IV: The body in Dravidian and Uralian', *BSOAS*, 11:2: 328–56.
——— (1946a). 'Dravidian studies V: Initial *y*- and *ñ*- in Dravidian', *BSOAS*, 11:3: 595–616.
——— (1946b). 'Some Dravidian words in Sanskrit', *TPS*, *1945*: 79–120.
——— (1947a). 'Dravidian studies VI: The loss of initial *c*-/*s*- in South Dravidian', *BSOAS*, 12: 132–47.
——— (1947b). 'Loan words in Sanskrit', *TPS*, *1946*: 1–30.
——— (1948). 'Dravidian studies VII: Further Dravidian words in Sanskrit', *BSOAS*, 12:2: 365–96.
——— (1955). *The Sanskrit Language*. London: Faber and Faber.
——— (1968a). 'The treatment of primitive Dravidian *-ṛ- in Kurux and Malto', in Krishnamurti (ed.) 1968a: 62–9.
——— (1968b). *Collected Papers on Dravidian Linguistics*. Annamalainagar: Annamalai University.
——— (1972). 'The primitive Dravidian word for the horse', *IJDL*, 1: 18–25.
——— (1976). 'A sketch of Maṇḍa grammar in comparison with Pengo', in Agesthialingom and Subrahmanyam (eds.), 39–56.
———, and Bhattacharya S. (1953). *The Parji Language*. England: Hertford & Sons.
——— ——— (1960). 'A comparative vocabulary of the Gondi dialects', *Journal of the Asiatic Society*, 2: 73–251.
——— ——— (1961). 'Some notes on the Kui dialect as spoken by the Kuṭṭia Kandhs of north-east Koraput', *IIJ*, 5: 118–35.
——— ——— (1962). 'Gadaba supplement', *IIJ*, 6:1: 45–51.
——— ——— (1963). 'Notes on Kuvi with a short vocabulary', *IIJ*, 6: 231–89.
——— ——— (1970). *The Pengo Language*. Oxford: Oxford University Press.
———, and Emeneau, M. B. (1961). *A Dravidian Etymological Dictionary*. Oxford: Clarendon Press.
——— ——— (1968). *A Dravidian Etymological Dictionary—Supplement*. Oxford: Clarendon Press.
——— ——— (1972). 'Dravidian etymological notes', *JAOS*, 92: 397–418, 475–91.
——— ——— (1984). *A Dravidian Etymological Dictionary* (rev. 2nd edn). Oxford: Clarendon Press.
Caldwell, R. (1913). *A Comparative Grammar of the Dravidian or South Indian Family of Languages*. 3rd edn. London: Kegan Paul, Trench, Trubner.
——— (1956, 1961; 1856 1st. edn, 1875 2nd edn, 1913 rev. 3rd edn) *A Comparative Grammar of the Dravidian or South Indian Family of Languages* (rev. 3rd edn, repr.). Madras: University of Madras.
Campbell, L. (1996). 'On sound changes and challenges to regularity', in M. Durie and M. Ross (eds.), *The Comparative Method Reviewed*, 77–89. Oxford: Oxford University Press.
Census of India 1961, Vol. I, Part II C (ii), 'Language tables'. Calcutta: Registrar General of India.

Census of India 1971. 'Handbook of mother tongues in Census'. New Delhi: Registrar General of India.

Census of India 1981. (1987). 'Households and household population by language mainly spoken in the household'. New Delhi: Registrar General of India.

Census of India 1991. (1997). Series 1-India, Paper 1 of 1997 'Language: India and States (Table C-7)'. New Delhi: Registrar General and Census Commissioner, India.

CHANDRASEKHAR, A. (1953). *Evolution of Malayalam*. Poona: Deccan College Research Institute.

——— (1971). 'The names of Dravidian languages', *Proceedings of the All-India Conference of Linguists*, **1**: 102–13. Poona.

——— (1973). 'The *āytam* problem re-examined', *IL*, **34:3**: 211–15.

——— (1975). 'Kuiper's note on *āytam* problem'. *IL*, **36:1**: 37–40.

CHATTERJI, S. K. (1926). *The Origin and Development of the Bengali Language*. 3 vols. Calcutta: University Press. [Repr. 1970. London: George Allen & Unwin.]

——— (1954). 'Old Tamil, ancient Tamil, and primitive Dravidian', *IL*, **14**: 1–19. (1956. Rev. repr., *TC*, **5**: 1–28.)

——— (1957). 'Dravidian philology', *TC*, **6**: 195–225.

——— (1971). 'Observations on linguistic and cultural studies of Tamil and Dravidian', *P2ICSTS*, **2:1**: 243–8.

CHEN, M. (1972). 'The time dimension: Contribution toward a theory of sound change', *Foundations of Language*, **8**: 475–98.

———, and Hsieh, Hsin-I. (1971). 'The time variable in phonological change', *Journal of Linguistics*, **7**: 1–13.

———, and Wang, W. S.-Y. (1975). 'Sound change: Actuation and implementation', *Language*, **51**: 255–81.

CHOMSKY, N. and HALLE, M. (1968). *The Sound Pattern of English*. New York: Harper and Row.

COLE, R. A. (1867). *An Elementary Grammar of the Coorg Language*. Bangalore: Wesleyan Mission Press.

CORNELIUS, J. T. (1972). 'Key to the problem of Dravidian origins', *PAICDL*, **1**: 354–62.

D'ANDRADE, R. G. (1978). 'U-statistic hierarchical clustering', *Psychometrika*, **43**: 59–67.

DESHPANDE, M. M. and HOOK, P. E. (1979). *Aryan and Non-Aryan in India*. Ann Arbor: University of Michigan, Center for South and Southeast Asian Studies.

DIFFLOTH, G. P. (1969). 'The Iruḷa dialect of Tamil—some phonological remarks', *P1ICSTS*, **2**: 559–62.

——— (1976). 'The South Dravidian obstruent system in Iruḷa', in Schiffman and Eastman (eds.), 47–56.

DROESE, E. (1884). *Introduction to the Malto Language*. Agra: Secundra Orphanage Press.

DYEN, I. (1953). 'Review of *Malgache et maanjan: Une comparaison linguistique*, by Otto Chr. Dahl', *Language*, **29**: 577–90.

EKKA, F. C. (1972). 'Remarks on the treatment of PDr. **o* in Kurux and Malto', *IJDL*, **1**: 19–28.

ELFENBEIN, J. (1998). 'Brahui', in Steever (ed.) 1998: 388–414.

ELLIS, F. W. (1816). 'Note to the Introduction of A. D. Campbell's *A Grammar of the Teloogoo Language*', 154–5. Madras. [Repr. with an editorial note by N. Venkata Rao in *Annals of Oriental Research of the University of Madras*, **12**: 1–35. Madras: University of Madras.]

EMENEAU, M. B. (1939). 'The vowels of the Badaga language', *Language*, **15**: 43–7.

Emeneau, M. B. (1945). 'The Dravidian verbs "come" and "give"', *Language*, **21**: 184–213.
——(1948). 'Notes on Dravidian etymologies (Taboos on animal names)', *Language*, **24**: 180–1.
——(1953a). 'Proto-Dravidian **c*-: Toda *t*-', *BSOAS*, **15**: 98–112.
——(1953b). 'The Dravidian kinship terms', *Language*, **29**: 339–53.
——(1954). 'Linguistic prehistory of India', *PAPS*, **98**: 282–92. [Repr. in *TC*, 5 (1956), 30–55.]
——(1955a). *Kolami, a Dravidian Language.* UCPL, 12.
——(1955b). 'India and linguistics', *JAOS*, **75**: 145–53.
——(1956). 'India as a linguistic area', *Language*, **32**: 3–16. [Repr. in Hymes (ed.) 1964: 642–53.]
——(1957). 'Numerals in comparative linguistics (with special reference to Dravidian)', *Bulletin of the Institute of History and Philology*, Academia Sinica, **29**: 1–10.
——(1958a). 'Some Indian etymologies', *IL*, **19**: 71–4.
——(1958b). 'Toda, a Dravidian language', *TPS*, *1957*: 15–66.
——(1960). [Hindi translation of 1961b] 'Brahui demonstrative pronouns'. *Hindī Anuśīlan (Dhīrendrā Varmā Viśeṣānk)*, 140–6. Prayaga. [Also in Emeneau 1961b; 1994, 17–22.]
——(1961a). 'North Dravidian velar stops', *Te. Po. Mī. Maṇiviẓāmalar* (Festschrift for T. P. Meenakshisundaran), 371–88. Coimbatore. [Repr. in Emeneau 1994: 1–16.]
——(1961b). 'Brahui demonstrative pronouns', *JASB*, **3**: 1–5. [Repr. in Emeneau 1994: 17–22.]
——(1962a). 'Bilingualism and structural borrowing', *PAPS*, **106**: 430–42. [Repr. in Emeneau 1980c, 38–65.]
——(1962b). 'Brahui *n/r* verbs', in Emeneau 1962d: 21–46. [Repr. in Emeneau 1994: 49–70.]
——(1962c). 'New Brahui etymologies', in *Indological Studies in Honor of W. Norman Brown*, 59–70. American Oriental Series 47. New Haven: American Oriental Society. [Repr. in Emeneau 1994: 23–34.]
——(1962d). *Brahui and Dravidian Comparative Grammar.* UCPL, 27. [Ch. 2 repr. in Emeneau 1994: 35–48.]
——(1964a). 'Linguistic desiderata in Baluchistan', *Indo-Iranica (Mélanges présentés à Georg Morgenstierne à l'occasion de son soixante-dixième anniversaire)*, 73–7. Wiesbaden: Otto Harrassowitz.
——(1964b). 'Review of T. Burrow and S. Bhattacharya, *A comparative vocabulary of the Gondi dialects*', *Language*, **40**: 503–4.
——(1965a). *India and Historical Grammar.* Annamalainagar: Annamalai University.
——(1965b). 'The South Dravidian languages'. Unpublished MS. read at the International Seminar on Tamil Studies held in Kuala Lumpur in April, 1966, 1–113. [See 1967a.]
——(1966). 'Some South Dravidian noun formatives', *IL*, **27**: 21–30.
——(1967a). 'The South Dravidian languages', *JAOS*, **87**: 365–413.
——(1967b). *Dravidian Linguistics, Ethnology and Folktales* (Collected Papers). Annamalainagar: Annamalai University.
——(1968). 'Brahui *sal/salī*- "to stand": An etymology', *Pratidānam*, 339–41. [Repr. in Emeneau 1994, 171–4.]

EMENEAU, M. B. (1969a). 'A Kota vowel shift', *JTS*, 1: 21–34. [Repr. in Emeneau 1994: 175–82.]
——— (1969b). 'Onomatopoetics in the Indian linguistic area', *Language*, **45**: 274–99.
——— (1969c). 'The non-literary Dravidian languages', in T. A. Sebeok (ed.), *Current Trends in Linguistics*, vol. 5: 334–42.
——— (1970a). *Dravidian Comparative Phonology: A Sketch.* Annamalainagar: Annamalai University.
——— (1970b). 'Koḍagu vowels', *JAOS*, **90**: 145–58. [Repr. in Emeneau 1994: 183–201.]
——— (1971a). 'Dravidian and Indo-Aryan—the Indian linguistic area', in Sjoberg (ed.) 1971a: 33–68.
——— (1971b). 'Koḍagu and Brahui developments of ProtoDravidian *-ṟ-, *IIJ*, **13:3**: 176–98. [Repr. in Emeneau 1994: 203–22.]
——— (1973). 'Review of K. V. Zvelebil, *Comparative Dravidian Phonology* (1970)', *Linguistics*, **107**: 77–82.
——— (1974a). 'Review of M. Pfeiffer, *Elements of Kuṛux Historical Phonology* (1972)', *Language*, **50**: 755–8.
——— (1974b). 'The Indian linguistic area revisited', *IJDL*, **3**: 92–134.
——— (1975). 'Studies in Dravidian verb stem formation', *JAOS*, **95**: 1–24. [Repr. in Emeneau 1994: 223–63.]
——— (1979). 'Toda vowels in non-initial syllables', *BSOAS*, **42**: 225–34. [Repr. in Emeneau 1994: 275–86.]
——— (1980a). 'Indian pronominal demonstrative bases—a revision', *Proceedings of the Berkeley Linguistic Society*, 20–7. [Repr. in Emeneau 1994: 307–16.]
——— (1980b). 'Brahui laterals from Proto-Dravidian *ṟ', *JAOS*, **100**: 311–12. [Repr. in Emeneau 1994: 303–6.]
——— (1980c). *Language and Linguistic Area.* Essays by Murray B. Emeneau, selected and introduced by Anwar S. Dil. Stanford: Stanford University Press.
——— (1984). *Toda Grammar and Texts.* Philadelphia: American Philosophical Society.
——— (1985). 'Kannaḍa *Kampa*, Tamil *Kampaṉ*: Two proper names', *JAOS*, **105**: 401–4. [Repr. in Emeneau 1994: 317–22.]
——— (1987a). 'Some notes on Dravidian intensives', in *Festschrift for Henry Hoenigswald on the Occasion of his Seventieth Birthday*, ed. G. Cardona and N. H. Zide, 109–13. Tübingen: Gunter Narr Verlag. [Repr. in Emeneau 1994: 323–8.]
——— (1987b). 'The right hand is the "eating hand": An Indian areal linguistic inquiry', in *Dimensions of Social Life: Essays in Honor of David Mandelbaum*, ed. P. Hockings, 263–73. Berlin: Mouton de Gruyter. [Repr. in Emeneau 1994: 329–38.]
——— (1988). 'Proto-Dravidian **c*- and its developments', *JAOS*, **108**: 29–68. [Repr. in Emeneau 1994: 339–86.]
——— (1989). 'The languages of the Nilgiris', in Hockings (ed.) 1989: 133–42.
——— (1991). 'Brahui personal pronouns: 1st singular and reflexive', in Lakshmi Bai and Ramakrishna Reddy (eds.), 1–12.
——— (1992). 'Foreword' to Hockings and Pilot-Raichoor (eds.), vii–x.
——— (1993). 'Tamil expressives with initial voiced stops', *BSOAS*, **56**: 75–86.
——— (1994). *Dravidian Studies: Selected Papers.* Delhi: Motilal Banarsidass.
——— (1995). 'The palatalizing rule in Tamil-Malayalam and Telugu', *JAOS*, 115: 3.401–9.
——— (1997a). 'Brahui etymologies and phonetic developments', *BSOAS*, **60**: 440–7.

EMENEAU, M. B. (1997b). 'Linguistics and botany in the Nilgiris', in Paul Hockings (ed.), 74–105.

——— and BURROW, T. (1962). *Dravidian Borrowings from Indo-Aryan.* UCPL, 26.

Epigraphia Indica, 42 vols. (1892–1978). Delhi: Manager of Publications, Government of India.

FIRTH, J. R. (1934). 'Appendix to A. H. Arden, *Progressive Grammar of Common Tamil*'. Madras: The Christian Literature Society.

FITZGERALD, A. G. (1913). *Kuviṅg Baṣ̌a. The Kondha Language as Spoken by the Parjas of the Madras Presidency.* Calcutta.

FOX, A. (1995). *Linguistic Reconstruction: An Introduction to Theory and Method.* Oxford: Oxford University Press.

FÜRER-HAIMENDORF, C. VON (1979). *Gonds of Andhra Pradesh: Tradition and Change in an Indian Tribe.* New Delhi: Vikas.

GAI, G. S. (1946). *Historical Grammar of Old Kannada (based entirely on the Kannaḍa inscriptions of the 8th, 9th and 10th centuries AD).* Poona: Deccan College.

GEORGE, K. M. (1956). *Rāmacaritam and the Study of Early Malayāḷam.* Kottayam: The National Book Stall.

GLAZOV, YU. (1968). 'Non-past tense morphemes in ancient Tamil', in Krishnamurti (ed.) 1968a: 103–9.

GODA VARMA, K. (1941–2). 'A study of personal pronouns in the South Dravidian languages', *New Indian Antiquary*, 4: 201–17.

——— (1949). 'Nasal assimilation in Dravidian', *Proceedings of the All-India Oriental Conference*, 318–19.

GOPINATHAN NAIR, B. (1979). 'On quantitative alternations in Dravidian', *IJDL*, 8: 32–45.

GREENBERG, J. H. (ed.) (1963). *Universals of Language.* Massachusetts: MIT Press.

GRIERSON, G. A. (1906). *Linguistic Survey of India*, vol. IV, *Muṇḍā and Dravidian Languages.* Calcutta: Government of India.

GUDSCHINSKY, S. C. (1956). 'The ABC's of lexicostatistics (glottochronology)', *Word*, 12: 175–210. [Repr. in Hymes (ed.) 1964: 612–23.]

GUNDERT, H. (1869). 'Die dravidischen Elemente in Sanskrit', *Zeitschrift der Deutschen Morgenländischen Gesellschaft*, 23: 517–30.

——— (1872). *A Malayalam–English Dictionary.* Mangalore: Basel Mission Press.

GUROV, N. (1991). 'Some remarks on the basic structures of Proto-Dravidian', in Lakshmi Bai and Ramakrishna Reddy (eds.), 13–26.

GWYNN, J. P. L. (assisted by J. V. Sastry) (1991). *A Telugu-English Dictionary.* Delhi: Oxford University Press.

HALLE, M., VERGNAUD, J. R. (1980). 'Three dimensional phonology', *Journal of Linguistic Research*, 1:1: 83–105.

HARIDAS BHAT, K. S., UPADHYAYA, U. P. (1988–97). *Tuḷu Lexicon* (in six volumes). Udupi: Rashtrakavi Gonda Pai Samshodhan Kendra.

HEESTERMAN, J. C., SCHOKKER, G. H., and SUBRAMONIAM, V. I. (eds.) (1968). *Pratidānam: Indian, Iranian, and Indo-European Studies Presented to Franciscus Bernardus Jacobus Kuiper on his Sixtieth Birthday.* (Janua Linguarum Series Major 34.) The Hague, Paris: Mouton.

HESTON, W. L. (1980). 'Some areal features: Indian or Irano-Indian?' *IJDL*, 9: 141–57.

HOCK, H. H. (1986). 'Compensatory lengthening in defence of the concept "mora"', *Folia Linguistica*, 20: 432–60.

HOCKINGS, P. (ed.) (1989). *Blue Mountains (The Ethnography and Biogeography of a South Indian Region on the Nilgiri Hills)*. Delhi: Oxford University Press.

——— (ed.) (1997). *Blue Mountains Revisited (Cultural Studies on the Nilgiri Hills)*. Delhi: Oxford University Press.

———, and PILOT-RAICHOOR, C. (1992). *A Badaga-English Dictionary*. Trends in Linguistics, Documentation 8. Berlin and New York: Mouton de Gruyter.

HOENIGSWALD, H. M. (1946). 'Sound change and linguistic structure', *Language*, **22**: 38–43.

——— (1960). *Language Change and Linguistic Reconstruction*. Chicago: The University of Chicago.

——— (1966). 'Criteria for subgrouping of languages', in H. Birnbaum and J. Puhvel (eds.), *Ancient Indo-European Dialects*, 1–12. Berkeley and Los Angeles: University of California Press.

HOMBURGER, L. (1955). 'L'Inde et Egypte', *JA*, **243**: 129–30.

——— (1957). 'De quelques éléments communs à l'egyptien et aux langues dravidiennes', *Kêmi*, **14**: 26–33.

——— (1958). 'Les dravidiens et l'Afrique', *Proceedings of the Eighth International Congress of Linguists*, 617. Oslo.

HSIEH, HSIN-I. (1973). 'A new method of dialect subgrouping', *Journal of Chinese Linguistics*, **1**: 64–92.

HYMAN, L. M. (1975). *Phonology: Theory and Analysis*. New York: Holt, Rinehart and Winston.

HYMES, D. (ed.) (1964). *Language in Culture and Society*. New York: Harper and Row.

Index des mots de la littérature tamoule ancienne. (1967: vol. I), (1968: vol. II), (1970: vol. III). Pondicherry : Institut Francais d'Indologie.

ISRAEL, M. (1966). 'Additional materials for a bibliography of Dravidian languages', *TC*, **12**: 69–74.

——— (1973). *The Treatment of Morphology in Tolkāppiyam*. Madurai : Madurai University.

——— (1979). *A Grammar of the Kuvi Language* (with texts and vocabulary). Trivandrum: Dravidian Linguistics Association.

JANSON, T. (1977). 'Reversed lexical diffusion and lexical split: Loss of *-d* in Stockholm', in Wang (ed.), 252–65.

Journal of Tamil Studies (1970). Special number on the decipherment of the Mohenjodaro script. Vol. 2, No. 1. Madras: International Association of Tamil Research.

KAMATCHINATHAN, A. (1972). 'More on Dravidian umlaut', *PSDL*, **3**: 155–66.

KAMESWARI, T. M. (1969). 'The chronology of Dravidian languages—a lexico-statistic analysis', in Agesthialingom and Kumaraswami Raja (eds.), 269–74.

KANDAPPA CHETTY. M. (1969). 'Personal and reflexive pronouns in Dravidian', *PSDL*, 2.

KAPP, D. B. (1978). 'Pālu Kuṟumba riddles', *BSOAS*, **41:3**: 512–22. (Linguistic notes and vocabulary list appended.)

——— (1984). *Ālu Kuṟumbaru Nāya^{n} (Die Sprache der Ālu-Kuṟumbas: Grammatik, Texte, Wörterbuch)*. Wiesbaden: Otto Harrassowitz.

——— (1987). 'Centralized vowels in *Ālu Kuṟumba*', *JAOS*, **107:3**: 409–26.

KEDILAYE, A. S. (1969). 'Gender in Dravidian', in Agesthialingom and Kumaraswami Raja (eds.), 169–76.

KEKUNNAYA, PADMANABHA (1994). *A Comparative Study of Tulu Dialects*. Udupi: Rāshtakavi Govind Pai Research Centre.

KELLEY, G. B. (1963). 'Vowel phonemes and external vocalic sandhi in Telugu', *JAOS*, 83: 67–73.

KENSTOWICZ, M., KISSEBERTH, C. (1977). *Topics in Phonological Theory*. New York: Academic Press.

KIPARSKY, P. (1968). 'Linguistic universals and linguistic change', in E. Bach and R. T. Harms (eds.), *Universals in Linguistic Theory*, 170–202. New York: Holt, Rinehart and Winston.

——— (1971). 'Historical linguistics', in W. O. Dingwall (ed.), *A Survey of Linguistic Science*. College Park (Maryland): Author, University of Maryland.

——— (1973a). 'Abstractness, opacity and global rules', in Osamu Fujimura (ed.), *Three Dimensions of Linguistic Theory*, 57–85. Tokyo: Institute of Advanced Studies of Language.

——— (1973b). 'Phonological representations (a collection of three papers)', in Osamu Fujimura (ed.), *Three Dimensions of Linguistic Theory*, 1–26. Tokyo: Institute of Advanced Studies of Language.

——— (1982). *Explanation in Phonology*. Dodrecht: Foris.

KITTEL, F. (1872). 'On the Dravidian element in Sanskrit dictionaries', *IA*, 1: 235–9.

——— (1873). 'Notes concerning numerals in the ancient Dravidian', *IA*, 2: 24–5, 124–5.

——— (1894). *A Kannaḍa-English Dictionary*. Mangalore: Basel Mission Press and Tract Depository. [1968–71. Revised and enlarged by M. Mariappa Bhatt. Madras: Madras University.]

——— (1903). *A Grammar of Kannada Language in English Comprising the Three Dialects of the Language (Ancient, Mediaeval and Modern)*. Mangalore: Basel Mission Press and Tract Depository.

——— (1920). *Kēśirāja's Jewel Mirror of Grammar*, re-edited by P. Mangesh Rau. Mangalore: Kanarese Mission Book and Tract Depository.

KOTHANDARAMAN, P. (1969). 'Koḍagu vowels', in Agesthialingom and Kumaraswami Raja (eds.), 232–47.

——— (1976). 'Alternation *i*/*u* in Dravidian', in Agesthialingom and Subrahmanyam (eds.) 187–92.

KOTHANDARAMAN, R. (n.d.). 'Functional shift in finite constructions in Tamil', Ten page MS from the author.

KOUTSOUDAS, A., SANDERS, G., NOLL, C. (1974). 'The application of phonological rules', *Language*, 50: 1–28.

KRISHNAMURTI, BH. (1955). 'The history of vowel-length in Telugu verbal bases', *JAOS*, 75: 237–52. [In this volume, Ch. 1.]

——— (1958a). 'Alternations *i*/*e* and *u*/*o* in South Dravidian', *Language*, 34: 458–68. [In this volume, Ch. 2.]

——— (1958b). 'Proto-Dravidian **ẓ*', *IL*, 19: 259–93. [In this volume, Ch. 3.]

——— (1961). *Telugu Verbal Bases: A Comparative and Descriptive Study*. UCPL, 24.

——— (1963). 'Review of *A Dravidian Etymological Dictionary*, by T. Burrow and M. B. Emeneau (1961)', *Language*, 39: 556–64.

——— (1967). 'Gender systems: A typological sketch'. (Mimeo. summary of a paper presented to the IX International Congress of Linguists, Aug.-Sept., 1967, Bucharest.)

——— (ed.). (1968a). *Studies in Indian Linguistics: Professor M.B.Emeneau Ṣaṣṭipūrti Volume*. Poona and Annamalainagar: Centers of Advanced Study.

——— (1968b). 'Dravidian personal pronouns', in Krishnamurti (ed.), 1968a: 189–205. [In this volume, Ch. 4.]

Krishnamurti, Bh. (1969a). 'Comparative Dravidian studies', in T. A. Sebeok (ed.), *Current Trends in Linguistics*, vol. 5: 309–33. [In this volume, Ch. 5.]
——(1969b). 'Dravidian nasals in Brahui', in Agesthialingom and Kumaraswami Raja (eds.), 65–74. [In this volume, Ch. 6.]
——(1969c). *Koṇḍa or Kūbi, a Dravidian Language*. Hyderabad: Tribal Cultural Research and Training Institute.
——(1971). 'Some observations on the Tamil phonology of the 12th and 13th centuries', in R. E. Asher (ed.), *P2ICSTS*, 356–61. [In this volume, Ch. 7.]
——(1975a). 'Gender and number in Proto-Dravidian', *IJDL*, **4**: 328–50. [In this volume, Ch. 8.]
——(1975b). 'Review of M. B. Emeneau (1970a)', *JAOS*, **95**: 312–13.
——(1976a). 'Review of K. V. Zvelebil (1970)', *Lingua*, **39**: 139–53.
——(1976b). 'Sound change: shared innovation vs. diffusion', *Phonologica, 1976*: 205–11. [In this volume, Ch. 9.]
——(1978a). 'Areal and lexical diffusion of sound change: Evidence from Dravidian', *Language*, **54**: 1–20. [In this volume, Ch. 10.]
——(1978b). 'On diachronic and synchronic rules in phonology: A case from Parji', *IL*, **39**: 252–76. [In this volume, Ch. 11.]
——(1980). 'A vowel-lowering rule in Kui-Kuvi', in B. R. Caron et al. (eds.), *Proceedings of the Sixth Annual Meeting of the Berkeley Linguistic Society*, 495–506. Berkeley: University of California. [In this volume, Ch. 12.]
——(1983). (with L. Moses and D. Danforth) 'Unchanged cognates as a criterion in linguistic subgrouping', *Language*, **59**: 541–68. [In this volume, Ch. 13.]
——(1985). 'An overview of comparative Dravidian studies since *Current Trends in Linguistics*, vol. 5 (1969)', in V. Z. Acson and R. L. Leed (eds.), *For Gordon Fairbanks*, 212–31. Honolulu: University of Hawaii Press. [In this volume, Ch. 14.]
——(1989). (with G. U. Rao) 'A problem of reconstruction in Gondi: Interaction between phonological and morphological processes', *Osmania Papers in Linguistics*, **13**: 1–21 (1987 volume). [In this volume, Ch. 15.]
——(1991a). 'The emergence of the syllable types of stems (C)VCC(V) and (C)V̄C(V) in Indo-Aryan and Dravidian: Conspiracy or convergence?', in W. G. Boltz and M. C. Shapiro (eds.), *Studies in the Historical Phonology of Asian Languages*, 160–75. Current Issues in Linguistic Theory, 77. Amsterdam: John Benjamins B.V. [In this volume, Ch. 16.]
——(1991b). 'Dravidian lexicography', *Wörterbucher, Dictionaries, Dictionnaires (An International Encyclopedia of Lexicography)*, 2521–34. Berlin: Walter de Gruyter.
——(1992). 'Dravidian languages', *International Encyclopedia of Linguistics*, ed. W. Bright, 1: 373–6. Oxford: Oxford University Press.
——(1994a). 'Introduction' to M. B. Emeneau, *Dravidian Studies: Selected Papers*, xv–xxvii. Delhi: Motilal Banarsidass.
——(1994b). 'Indian Names: Dravidian', in L. Zgusta (ed.), *Namen Forschung, Proper Name Studies, Les noms propres*, 665–71. Berlin: Walter de Gruyter.
——(1997a). 'Le genre et le nombre en dravidien', in *Fait de langues*, 71–6. Revue de Linguistique, 10 (Les langues d'Asie du sud). Paris: Ophrys.
——(1997b). 'The origin and evolution of primary derivative suffixes in Dravidian', in H. H. Hock (ed.), *Historical, Indo-European and Lexicographical Studies (A Festschrift for Ladislav Zgusta on the Occasion of his 70th Birthday)*, 87–116. Berlin: Mouton de Gruyter. [In this volume, Ch. 17.]

Krishnamurti, Bh. (1997c). 'Proto-Dravidian laryngeal *H revisited', *PILC Journal of Dravidic Studies*, 7:2: 145–65. Pondicherry: Pondicherry Institute of Linguistics and Culture. [In this volume, Ch. 19.]

——— (1998a). 'Patterns of sound change in Dravidian', in R. Singh (ed.), *The Yearbook of South Asian Languages and Linguistics 1998*, 63–79. New Delhi: Sage Publications India Pvt. Ltd. [In this volume, Ch. 18.]

——— (1998b). 'Regularity of sound change through lexical diffusion', *Language Variation and Change*, 10: 193–220. [In this volume, Ch. 20.]

——— and Gwynn, J. P. L. (1985). *A Grammar of Modern Telugu*. Delhi: Oxford University Press.

Kuiper, F. B. J. (1958). 'Two problems of Old Tamil phonology', *IIJ*, 2: 197–207.

——— (1967). 'The genesis of the linguistic area', *IIJ*, 10: 81–125.

——— (1974). 'The *āytam* problem', *IL*, 35:3: 205–17.

Kumaraswami Raja, N. (1969a). 'Post-nasal plosives in Telugu: A comparative study', in Agesthialingom and Kumaraswami Raja (eds.), 75–84.

——— (1969b). *Post-nasal Voiceless Plosives in Dravidian*. Annamalainagar: Annamalai University.

——— (1975). 'A note on *kuiṟṟiyal ukaram*', *JTS*, 8: 1–7.

Kushalappa Gowda, K. (1968). 'Gender distinction in Gowda Kannada', in Krishnamurti (ed.) 1968a: 210–20.

Labov, W. (1972a). *Sociolinguistic Patterns*. Philadelphia: University of Pennsylvania Press.

——— (1972b). 'The internal evolution of linguistic rules', in Stockwell and Macaulay (eds.), 172–98.

——— (1981). 'Resolving the neogrammarian controversy', *Language*, 57: 267–308.

——— (1994). *Principles of Linguistic Change*, vol. 1: *Internal Factors*. Oxford: Basil Blackwell.

Lahovary, N. (1948). 'Aperç us nouveaux sur des rapports insoupç onnes du basque et des langues dravidiennes', *Boletin de la Real Academia de Buenas Letras de Barcelona*, 21.

——— (1954). 'Substrat linguistique méditerranéen, basque et dravidien', in *Substrat en langues classiques*. Florence.

——— (1957). *La diffusion des langues anciennes du Proche-Orient: Leurs relations avec le basque, le dravidien et les parlers indo-européens primitifs*. Berne: Francke.

——— (1963). *Dravidian Origins and the West*. Bombay: Orient Longmans. (Trans. of Lahovary 1957)

Lakoff, R. (1972). 'Another look at drift', in Stockwell and Macaulay (eds.), 172–98.

Lakshmi Bai, B., Ramakrishna Reddy, B. (eds.) (1991). *Studies in Dravidian and General Linguistics: A Festschrift for Bh. Krishnamurti*. Osmania University Publications in Linguistics, 6. Hyderabad: Osmania University.

Lehmann, T. (1989). *A Grammar of Modern Tamil*. Pondicherry: Pondicherry Institute of Language and Culture.

——— (1991). *Grammatik des Alttamil: Morphologische und Syntaktische Analyse der Cankam-Tamil des Dichters Kāpilar*. Ph.D. dissertation, University of Heidelberg.

Lehmann, W. P. (1955). *Proto-Indo-European Phonology*. (Fourth printing). Texas: The University of Texas Press.

Männer, A. (1886). *Tuḷu-English Dictionary*. Mangalore: Basel Mission Press and Tract Depository.
Mahadevan, I. (1977). *Indus Script (Texts, Concordance and Tables)*. Memoirs of the Archaeological Survey of India, 77. New Delhi: The Director General, Archaeological Survey of India.
Mahapatra, B. P. (1979). *Malto, an Ethnosemantic Study*. Mysore: Central Institute of Indian Languages.
Marshall, W. E. (1873). *A Phrenologist among the Todas* (with 'A brief outline of the grammar of the Toda language' by the Rev. G. U. Pope . . . from a collection of Toda words and sentences presented by the Rev. Friedrich Metz, pp. 239–69). London: Longmans, Green.
Masica, C. P. (1991). *The Indo-Aryan Languages*. Cambridge: Cambridge University Press.
——— (1976). *Defining a Linguistic Area—South Asia*. Chicago: Chicago University Press.
Master, A. (1947). 'The zero negative in Dravidian', *TPS* [1946], 137–55.
——— (1948). 'Indo-Aryan and Dravidian III', *BSOAS*, **12:2**: 340–64.
Mayrhofer, M. (1956). *Kurzgefaßtes etymologisches Wörterbuch des Altindischen*. Heidelberg: Carl Winter Universitätverlag.
McAlpin, D. W. (1974). 'Toward proto-Elamo-Dravidian languages', *Language*, **50**: 89–101.
——— (1975). 'Elamite and Dravidian: Further evidence of relationship', *Current Anthropology*, **16**: 105–15.
——— (1979). 'Linguistic prehistory: The Dravidian situation', in Deshpande and Hook (eds.), 175–89.
——— (1981). *Proto-Elamo-Dravidian*. Philadelphia: The American Philosophical Society.
Meenakshisundaran, T. P. (1965). *A History of Tamil Language*. Poona: Deccan College Postgraduate and Research Institute.
——— (1968). 'The phoneme *y* in Ancient Tamil', in Krishnamurti (ed.) 1968a: 226–30.
Mehandale, M. A. (1948). *Historical Grammar of Inscriptional Prakrits*. Poona: Deccan College Postgraduate and Research Institute.
Meile, P. (1943–5). 'Sur la sifflante en dravidien', *JA*, **234**: 73–89.
——— (1948). 'Observation sur quelques caractères communs des langues dravidiennes et des langues altaiques', *Actes du XXIe congres international des orientalistes*. Paris.
Menges, K. H. (1964). 'Altajisch und Dravidisch', *Orbis*, **13**: 66–103.
Meyers, L. F. and Wang, W. S.-Y. (1963). 'Tree representations in linguistics', *POLA Reports*, Series I, **3**: 55–139. Columbus: Ohio State University.
Mohanan, K. P. (1986). *The Theory of Lexical Phonology*. Dodrecht: D. Reidel.
Montgomery, Jr. S. E. (1968). 'Supplemental materials for a bibliography of Dravidian linguistics', in Krishnamurti (ed.) 1968a: 234–46.
Nagaraja Chetty, T. (1984). 'Kuṭṭia Dialect of Kui (Phonology, Morphology, Texts and Vocabulary)'. M.Phil. dissertation, Department of Linguistics. Hyderabad: Osmania University.
Namboodiri, E. V. N. (1976). *Glottochronology (as applied to four Dravidian languages)*. Trivandrum: Sangama.
Nara, Tsuyoshi. (1979). *Avahaṭṭa and Comparative Vocabulary of New Indo-Aryan Languages*. Tokyo: Institute for the Study of Languages and Cultures of Asia and Africa.
Narasimhia, A. N. (1941). *A Grammar of the Oldest Kanarese Inscriptions*. Mysore: The University of Mysore.
Narayana Rao, C. (ed.) (1939). *Paṇḍitārādhyacaritra* by Pālkuriki Sōmanātha. Madras: Andhra Patrika Press.

NATARAJAN, G. V. (1985). *Abujhmaria Grammar.* Mysore: Central Institute of Indian Languages.

The New Encyclopaedia Britannica (1977). Macropaedia, vol. 9. Chicago: Encyclopaedia Britannica, Inc.

OHALA, J. J. (1974). 'Phonetic explanations in phonology', *Papers from the Parasession on Natural Phonology*, 251–74. Chicago: Chicago Linguistic Society.

PADMANABHAN NAIR, R. K. (1972). 'Efatese: a language of Dravidian origin', *PAICDL*, 1: 546–9.

PFEIFFER, M. (1972). *Elements of Kuṛux Historical Phonology.* Leiden. 1974. [Review by Emeneau 1974a].

PILOT-RAICHOOR, C. (1997). 'Badaga and its relations with neighbouring languages', in Hockings (ed.) 1997: 136–47.

Pratidānam. Indian, Iranian and Indo-European Studies Presented to Franciscus Bernardus Jacobus Kuiper on his Sixtieth Birthday (1968). The Hague: Mouton.

RADHAKRISHNA SARMA, CH. (1964). 'Tamil Elements in Telugu'. M.Litt. thesis. Madras: Madras University.

RADHAKRISHNA, B. (1971). *Early Telugu Inscriptions (up to 1100 AD).* Hyderabad: Andhra Pradesh Sahitya Akademi.

RAMACHANDRA RAO, B. (1964). 'A Descriptive Grammar of Pampa Bhārata'. Ph.D. dissertation of the Department of Kannaḍa. Hyderabad: Osmania University.

——— (1972). *A Descriptive Grammar of Pampa Bhārata.* Mysore: The University of Mysore.

RAMAKRISHNAIYA, K. (1951). *Studies in Dravidian Philology.* Madras: The University of Madras.

RAMAKRISHNA RAU, A., VENKATAVADHANI, D. (1960). *Nannaya-pada-prayōga-kōs'am* [A Concordance of Nannaya's *Mahābhārata*]. Hyderabad: A. P. Sahitya Akademi.

RAMASWAMI AIYAR, L. V. (1931–2). 'Aphaeresis and sound displacement in Dravidian', *QJMS*, 22: 448–80.

——— (1934–8). 'Dravidic sandhi', *QJMS*, 25–28: 91–112.

——— (1935). 'Tamil *ḻ*', *Journal of Oriental Research*, 9: 140–7, 195–210.

——— (1947). 'Indigenous grammars on the verbs "come" and "give"', *JAOS*, 67: 215–16.

——— (1950). 'Dravidic word-studies: (1) Dravidic "fish", "star", "sky"; (2) Dravidic forms for the "moon"', *IL*, 11: 1–16.

RANGANATHACHARYULU, K. K. (1987). *A Historical Grammar of Inscriptional Telugu (1401 AD to 1900 AD).* Hyderabad: Department of Linguistics, Osmania University.

RAO, G. UMA MAHESHWAR (1982). '*Lexical diffusion and sound change in progress*'. M.Phil. dissertation. Hyderabad: Department of Linguistics, Osmania University.

——— (1987). '*A Comparative Study of the Dialects of Gondi with Special Reference to Phonology and Morphology*'. Ph.D. dissertation. Hyderabad: Osmania University.

——— (1991). 'Subgrouping the Gondi dialects', in Lakshmi Bai and Ramkrishna Reddy (eds.), 73–90.

SAMBASIVA RAO, G. (1973). 'On Proto-Dravidian morphophonemics', *IJDL*, 2:2: 217–42.

——— (1977). 'Dravidian Alternations', *IL*, 38:2: 86–94.

——— (1991). *A Comparative Study of Noun Derivation.* New Delhi: Bahri Publications.

SAPIR, E. (1949). *Language* (2nd edn). New York: Harcourt, Brace and World, Inc. [1921: 1st edn.]

SCHANE, S. A. (1972). 'Natural rules in phonology', in Stockwell and Macaulay (eds.), 198–229.

SCHANE, S. A. (1973). *Generative Phonology*. Englewood Cliffs, N.J.: Prentice Hall.

SCHIFFMAN, H. F. (1976). 'On the ternary contrast in Dravidian coronal stops', in Schiffman and Eastman (eds.), 69–85.

——— (1999). *A Reference Grammar of Spoken Tamil*. Cambridge: Cambridge University Press.

———, and EASTMAN, C. (eds.) (1975). *Dravidian Phonological Systems*. Seattle: Institute for Comparative and Foreign Area Studies, University of Washington.

SCHULTZE, F. V. P. (1911). *A Grammar of the Kuvi Language*. Madras: Graves, Cookson & Co.

——— (1913). *Vocabulary of Kuvi-Kond Language*. Madras.

SENGHOR, L. S. (1975). 'Why create a Department of Indo-African studies at Dakar University?', *IJDL*, 4: 1–13.

SESHAGIRI SASTRI, M. (1884). *Notes on Aryan and Dravidian Phililogy*. Madras.

SETHU PILLAI, R. P. (1937–8). 'Tamil—literary and colloquial', *Journal of Oriental Research*, 2:2: 1–60.

——— et al. (ed.) (1959). *Dravidian Comparative Vocabulary*, vol. I. Madras: The University of Madras.

SETUMADHAVA RAO, P. (1950). *A Grammar of the Kolami Language*. Hyderabad.

SHAFEEV, D. A. (1964). *A Short Grammatical Outline of Pashto*. Bloomington: University of Indiana Press.

SHANMUGAM, S. V. (1971). *Dravidian Nouns: A Comparative Study*. Annamalainagar: Annamalai University.

——— (1972a). 'Gender-number sub-categorization in Dravidian', in Agesthialingom and Shanmugam (eds.), 383–97.

——— (1972b). 'Dental and alveolar nasals in Dravidian', *BSOAS*, 35: 74–84.

SHAPIRO, M. C., and SCHIFFMAN, H. F. (1975). *Language and Society in South Asia* (Final report). Department of Asian Languages, and Literatures. Seattle: University of Washington.

SHEPARD, R. N. (1962). *The Analysis of Proximities*. Bell Telephone System Technical Publications, Monograph 4380. Murray Hill, NJ.

SHIBA, SUSUMU. (1980). 'Dravidian and Japannese-Connection of Altaic and South Asian'. Mimeo., 41 pages. Kyoto.

SJOBERG, A. F. (1971a). 'Who are the Dravidians? The present state of knowledge', in Sjoberg (ed.), 1971b: 1–31.

——— (ed.) (1971b). *Symposium on Dravidian Civilization*. Austin and New York: Jenkins Publishing Company, The Pemberton Press.

SMITH, I. (1991). 'Interpreting conflicting isoglosses: Historical relationships among the Gondi dialects', in Lakshmi Bai and Ramkrishna Reddy (eds.), 27–38. Hyderabad: Department of Linguistics, Osmania University.

SOMAYAJI, G. J. (1947). *Āndhrabhāṣāwikāsamu* [Evolution of the Telugu Language]. Visakhapatnam: The author, Maharanipeta.

SONNENSCHEIN, E. A. (1925). *What is Rhythm?* (An essay by E. A. Sonnenschein accompanied by an appendix on experimental syllable-measurement in which Stephen Jones and Eileen Macleod have cooperated). Oxford: Basil Blackwell.

South Indian Inscriptions. (1892–1983). Madras: Archeological Survey of India; (currently available with) New Delhi: Navrang.

SOUTHWORTH, F. C. (1976). 'On subgroups in Dravidian', *IJDL*, 5: 114–37.

Southworth, F. C. (1979). 'Lexical evidence for early contacts between Indo-Aryan and Dravidian', in Deshpande and Hook (eds.), 191–233.

Sreekanthaiya, T. N. (1935). 'The mutation of *i, u, e* and *o* in Kannaḍa', *Proceedings and Transactions of the Eighth All India Oriental Conference*, 769–800.

Sridhar, S. N. (1990). *Kannada.* London & New York: Routledge.

Stampe, D. (1973). 'A Dissertation on Natural Phonology'. Ph.D. dissertation. Chicago: University of Chicago.

Steever, S. B. (1980). 'The genesis of poly-personal verbs in South Central Dravidian', *IJDL*, **9:2**: 337–73.

———(1981). *Selected Papers on Tamil and Dravidian Linguistics.* Maturai: Muttu Patipakkam.

———(1987a). 'Remarks on Dravidian complementation', *Studies in Linguistic Sciences*, **17:1**: 103–19.

———(1987b). 'The roots of the plural action verb in the Dravidian languages', *JAOS*, **107:4**: 581–604.

———(1988). *The Serial Verb Formation in the Dravidian Languages.* Delhi: Motilal Banarsidass.

———(1993). *Analysis to Synthesis.* Oxford: Oxford University Press. 1997.

———(ed.) (1998). *The Dravidian Languages.* London and New York: Routledge.

Stockwell, R. P., and Macaulay, R. K. S. (eds.) (1972). *Linguistic Change and Generative Theory.* Bloomington: Indiana University Press.

Subbaiya, K. V. (1909). 'A primer of Dravidian phonology', *IA*, **38**: 159–70, 188–221.

———(1910–11). 'A comparative grammar of Dravidian (nouns—gender, nouns and cases)', *IA*, **39**: 145–58; **40**: 184–9, 241–6.

———(1923). 'The pronouns and pronominal terminations in the first person in Dravidian', *Dravidic Studies II*, 17–79. Madras: Superintendent, Government Press.

Subrahmanya Sastri, P. S. (1930). *Tolkāppiyam: Eẕutt-atikāram.* Madras: The Journal of Oriental Research, Madras University.

———(1934). *History of Grammatical Theories in Tamil.* Madras: The Journal of Oriental Research, Madras University.

———(1947). *A Comparative Grammar of the Tamil Language.* Tiruvadi, Tanjore Dist.

Subrahmanyam, P. S. (1964). 'Two problems in Parji verb forms', *IL*, **25**: 47–55

———(1965). 'The intransitive and transitive suffixes of Kui', *JAOS*, **85**: 551–65.

———(1968a). *A Descriptive Grammar of Gondi.* Annamalainagar: Annamalai University.

———(1968b). 'The Position of Tulu in Dravidian', *IL*, **29**: 47–66.

———(1969a–i). 'The Central Dravidian languages', in Agesthialingom and Kumaraswami Raja (eds.), 107–34.

———(1969a–ii). 'The Central Dravidian languages', *JAOS*, **89**: 739–50.

———(1969b). 'The gender and number categories in Dravidian', *Journal of Annamalai University*, **26**: 79–100.

———(1970a). 'Long vowels before *y* in Telugu bases', *IL*, **31**: 69–73.

———(1970b). 'The personal pronouns in Dravidian', *BDCRI* [1967–68], **28**: 3–4: 1–16.

———(1971). *Dravidian Verb Morphology: A Comparative Study.* Annamalainagar: Annamalai University.

———(1973). 'Notes on Dravidian etymological notes', *IL*, **34**: 138–46.

———(1975). 'Quantitative variation in Dravidian', *IL*, **36**: 11–15.

SUBRAHMANYAM, P. S. (1976a). 'Review of Krishnamurti (1975a)', *IJDL*, 5: 138–43.

——— (1976b). 'The Toda developments of Proto-Dravidian **a *ā*, **l* and **ḷ*', in Agesthialingom and Subrahmanyam (eds.), 87–120.

——— (1977a). 'Proto-Dravidian **ṛ* in Toda', *IL*, 38: 1–5.

——— (1977b). 'The Toda reflexes of PDr. **l* and **ḷ*', *JAOS*, 97: 178–81.

——— (1977c). 'Dravidian alternations: A critique', *IL*, 38: 227–33.

——— (1981). '*I/e* and *u/o* alternation in South Dravidian and Telugu', in M. S. Sunkapur and Jayavant S. Kulli (eds.), *Papers in Linguistics*, 165–9. Mysore: Sharat Prakashan.

——— (1983). *Dravidian Comparative Phonology*. Annamalainagar: Annamalai University.

——— (1988). 'Comparative Dravidian studies from 1980', *IJDL*, 17:1: 59–91.

——— (1991). 'Tense formation in Kota-Toda: A comparative study', in Lakshmi Bai and Ramakrishna Reddy (eds.), 49–72.

SUBRAMANIAN, P. R. (ed.) (1992). *Dictionary of Contemporary Tamil (Tamil-Tamil-English)*. Chennai: Cre-A.

SUBRAMONIAM, V. I. (1962). *Index of Puṟanāṉūṟu*. Trivandrum: University of Kerala.

——— (1968). 'A problem in the reconstruction of the Proto-Dravidian nasal phonemes', *Pratidānam*, 344–7. The Hague.

SUMATI, S. (1982). 'Comparative Phonology of the South-Central Dravidian Languages'. M.Phil. dissertation. Hyderabad: Department of Linguistics, Osmania University.

SUVARCHALA, B. (1992). *Central Dravidian Comparative Morphology*. New Delhi: Navrang.

SWAMINATHA AIYAR, R. (1975). *Dravidian Theories*. Madras: Madras Law Journal Office.

Tamil Lexicon. 6 vols. (1924–39). Madras: Madras University.

THIAGARAJU, A. F. (1933). 'Developments of Dravidian *ḻ*', in *Vyāsangrahamu: Miscellany of Essays Presented to G. V. Ramamurthi*, ed. T. Venkataratnam, 75–88. Guntur.

THOMASAIAH, K . (1986). 'Naikṛi Dialect of Kolami: Descriptive and Comparative Study'. Unpublished Ph.D. thesis in linguistics of Annamalai University, Annamalainagar.

Tolkāppiyam: see Subrahmanya Sastri 1930.

TRENCH, C. G. C. (1919). *Grammar of Gondi*, vol. I. Madras: Superintendent, Government Press.

——— (1923). *Grammar of Gondi*, vol. II. *Gondi Vocabulary and Texts*. Madras: Superintendent, Government Press.

TURNER, R. L. (1966). *A Comparative Dictionary of the Indo-Aryan Languages*. 3 vols. London: Oxford University Press.

——— (1967). 'Geminates after long vowels in Indo-Aryan', *BSOAS*, 30:1: 73–82. [Repr. in *Collected Papers 1912–73*, 405–15. (1975). London: Oxford University Press.]

TUTTLE, E. H. (1930). *Dravidian Developments*. Language Monographs, 5. Philadelphia: Linguistic Society of America.

TYLER, S. A. (1968). 'Dravidian and Uralian: The lexical evidence', *Language*, 44: 798–812.

——— (1969). *Koya: An Outline Grammar, Gommu Dialect*. UCPL 54. Berkeley and Los Angeles: University of California Press.

UPADHYAYA, U. P. (1972). 'Kuruba: A Dravidian language', *Proceedings of Seminar on Dravidian Languages*, 3: 307–28. Annamalainagar: Annamalai University.

——— (1976). 'Dravidian and Negro-African', *IJDL*, 5: 32–64.

WANG, W. S.-Y. (1969). 'Competing changes as a cause of residue', *Language*, 45: 9–25.

——— (1974). 'How do we study the sounds of speech?' in J. L. Mitchell (ed.), *Computers in Humanities*, 39–53. Edinburgh: Edinburgh University Press.

WANG, W. S.-Y. (ed.) (1977). *The Lexicon in Phonological Change.* The Hague: Mouton.

——— (1979). 'Language change: A lexical perspective', *Annual Review of Anthropology,* 8: 353–71.

WEINREICH, U., LABOV, W., and HERZOG, M. (1968). 'Empirical foundations for a theory of language change', in W. P. Lehmann and Y. Malkiel (eds.), *Directions in Historical Linguistics,* 97–195. Austin: University of Texas Press.

WIJERATNE, P. B. F. (1945). 'Phonology of the Singhalese inscriptions up to the end of tenth century AD', *BSOAS,* 11: 592–3.

WILLIAMSON, H. D. (n.d.). *Gondi Grammar and Vocabulary.* London.

WINFIELD, W. W. (1928). *A Grammar of the Kui language.* Calcutta: The Asiatic Society of Bengal.

WINSLOW, MIRON, (1862). *A Comprehensive Tamil and English Dictionary of High and Low Tamil.* Madras. Repr. Asian Educational Services, New Delhi, 1987.

ZIDE ARLENE, R. K. and ZVELEBIL, K. V. (1970). 'Review of *Decipherment of the Proto-Dravidian inscriptions of the Indus civilization* and *Progress in the decipherment of Proto-Dravidian Indus Script*, by Asko Parpola et al.', *IIJ,* **12**: 126–34.

——— (eds.) (1976). *The Soviet Decipherment of the Indus Valley Script (Translation and Critique).* The Hague: Mouton.

ZVELEBIL, K. V. (1955). 'The present state of Dravidian philology', *TC,* **4**: 53–7.

——— (1956). 'One hundred years of Dravidian comparative philology', *AO,* **24**: 599–609.

——— (1961). 'Dravidian philology, general linguistics and early history of India', in *Dr. R. P. Sethu Pillai Silver jubilee Commemoration Volume,* 127–34. Madras.

——— (1962). 'Personal pronouns in Tamil and Dravidian', *IIJ,* **6**: 65–9.

——— (1964). *Tamil in 550 AD: An Interpretation of Early Inscriptional Tamil.* Dissertationes Orientales, 3. Prague: Publishing House of the Czechoslovak Academy of Sciences.

——— (1967). 'On morphophonemic rules of Dravidian bases', *Linguistics,* **32**: 87–95.

——— (1970a). 'From Proto-South Dravidian to Old Tamil and Malayalam', *AO,* **38**: 45–67. (1971: repr. in *P2ICSTS,* **1**: 54–72.)

——— (1970b). *Comparative Dravidian Phonology.* The Hague: Mouton.

——— (1971a). 'Iruḷa vowels', *IIJ,* **13**: 113–22.

——— (1971b). 'Review of T. Burrow and M. B. Emeneau, *A Dravidian Etymological Dictionary (Supplement)*', *IIJ,* **13**:2: 152–4.

——— (1972a). 'Initial plosives in Dravidian', *Lingua,* **30**: 216–26.

——— (1972b). 'The descent of the Dravidians', *IJDL,* **1**: 57–63.

——— (1973). *The Irula (Ëṟla) language,* [Part I]. Wiesbaden: Otto Harrassowitz.

——— (1977). *A Sketch of Comparative Dravidian Morphology* (Part I). Mouton: The Hague.

——— (1979). *The Irula (Ëṟla) Language,* Part II. Wiesbaden: Otto Harrassowitz.

——— (1980). 'A plea for Nilgiri areal studies', *IJDL,* **9**: 1–22.

——— (1982a). 'Beṭṭa Kuṟumba: First report on a tribal language', *JAOS,* **102**: 523–27.

——— (1982b). *The Irula (Ëṟla) Language,* Part III. *Irula Lore, Texts and Translations.* Wiesbaden: Otto Harrassowitz.

——— (1988). 'Jēnu Kuṟumba. Brief report on a "tribal" language of the Nilgiri area', *JAOS,* **108**: 197–301.

——— (1990a). *Dravidian Linguistics: An Introduction.* Pondicherry: Pondicherry Institute of Linguistics and Culture.

——— (1990b). 'The language of the Shōlegas, Nilgiri area, South India', *JAOS,* **110**:2: 417–33.

———, and ZGUSTA, L. (1961). 'Review of four works by N. Lahovary', *AO,* **29**: 127–30.

Index

Note: *Language names (abbreviated or unabbreviated) occurring in numbered etymologies are not included in the index. Only those occurring in the text are included.*